W9-CZU-186

A DOCUMENTARY HISTORY OF

The Negro People in the United States

A DOCUMENTARY HISTORY

OF

The Negro People in the United States

1945–1951

Volume 5

From the End of World War II
to the Korean War

Edited by

HERBERT APTHEKER

Preface by

HENRY LOUIS GATES, JR.

CABRINI COLLEGE LIBRARY
610 King of Prussia Road
Radnor, PA 19087

A Citadel Press Book
Published by Carol Publishing Group

E
185
.D623
1990
v.5

#2966249

Copyright © 1993 by Herbert Aptheker

All rights reserved. No part of this book may be reproduced in any form, except by a newspaper or magazine reviewer who wishes to quote brief passages in connection with a review.

A Citadel Press Book
Published by Carol Publishing Group
Citadel Press is a registered trademark of Carol Communications, Inc.

Editorial Offices: 600 Madison Avenue, New York, N.Y. 10022
Sales & Distribution Offices: 120 Enterprise Avenue, Secaucus, N.J. 07094
In Canada: Canadian Manda Group, P.O. Box 920, Station U, Toronto, Ontario M8Z 5P9
Queries regarding rights and permissions should be addressed to Carol Publishing Group, 600 Madison Avenue, New York, N.Y. 10022

Carol Publishing Group books are available at special discounts for bulk purchases, for sales promotions, fund-raising, or educational purposes. Special editions can be created to specifications. For details contact: Special Sales Department, Carol Publishing Group, 120 Enterprise Avenue, Secaucus, N.J. 07094

Manufactured in the United States of America

10 9 8 7 6 5 4 3 2 1

Library of Congress Cataloging-in-Publication Data

(Revised for vol. 5-6)

Aptheker, Herbert, 1915–
   A documentary history of the Negro people
in the United States.

   Vols.   have imprint : Secaucus, NJ : Carol
Pub. Group; also have statement : A Citadel
Press book.
    Contents : [1. 1661-1910]—[etc.]—v. 5
From the end of the Second World War to the
Korean War.—v. 6. From the Korean War to
the emergence of Martin Luther King, Jr.
    1. Afro-Americans—History—Sources.
I. Title.
E185.A58   973'.0496073   51–14828
ISBN 0-8065-1421-3

*To the memory of Carter G. Woodson,
founder of modern African-American History*

Contents

Preface

Herbert Aptheker was born in Brooklyn, New York, July 31, 1915. He received three degrees from Columbia University: a B.S. in 1936, an A.M. in 1937, and a Ph.D. in 1953. He has been awarded honorary degrees by Martin Luther King University and the University of Halle. He served in the U.S. Army from 1942 till 1946 and was discharged with the rank of major.

Dr. Aptheker has received awards from the Guggenheim Foundation, the Social Science Research Council, the Rabinowitz Foundation, and the American Council of Learned Societies. He has been editor of *Masses and Mainstream* and *Political Affairs*. He has been a visiting lecturer at University of California at Berkeley Law School, Bryn Mawr, Yale, and the University of Massachusetts. He served for many years as the director of the American Institute of Marxist Studies. He was one of W. E. B. Du Bois's closest friends and was chosen by Dr. Du Bois to be his literary executor.

Aptheker's published books and pamphlets include:

1938	*The Negro in the Civil War*
1939	*American Negro Slave Revolts*
1940	*The Negro in the American Revolution*
1941	*The Negro in the Abolitionist Movement*
1945	*Essays in the History of the American Negro*
1948	*To Be Free: Studies in American Negro History*
1951–1974	*Documentary History of the Negro People in the United States* (3 vols.)
1954	*Lauriats of Imperialism*
1955	*History and Reality*
1955	*Era of McCarthyism*
1956	*Toward Negro Freedom*
1957	*The Truth About Hungary*
1959–1960	*History of the American People* (2 vols.)

1959 *The German Question: Toward War and Peace*
1960 *The World of C. Wright Mills*
1960 *Disarmament and the American Economy*
1960 *John Brown, American Martyr*
1961 *The American Civil War*
1961 *And Why Not Every Man?*
1961 *Dare We Be Free?*
1962 *The Negro Today*
1962 *The Fraud of Soviet Anti-Semitism*
1962 *American Foreign Policy in the Cold War*
1963 *Communism: Menace or Promise?*
1964 *Marxism and Democracy*
1964 *Soul of the Republic: The Negro Today*
1965 *One Continual Cry: David Walker's "Appeal"*
1965 *Marxism and Alienation*
1966 *Nat Turner's Slave Rebellion*
1966 *Mission to Hanoi*
1967 *The Nature of Democracy, Freedom, and Revolution*
1967 *Dr. Martin Luther King, Vietnam, and Civil Rights*
1967 *Marxism and Christianity*
1970 *Urgency of the Marxist-Christian Dialogue*
1971 *Afro-American History: The Modern Era*
1973 *W. E. B. Du Bois Bibliography*
1973–1986 *The Published Writings of W. E. B. Du Bois*, ed. (40 vols.)
1976–1978 *Correspondence of W. E. B. Du Bois*
1976 *Early Years of the Republic, 1783–1793*
1977 *The Negro People in America: A Critique of Myrdal*
1977 *American Foreign Policy and the Cold War*
1979 *The Unfolding Drama: Studies in U.S. History*
1980 *Prayers for Dark People*, ed.
1983 *W. E. B. Du Bois and the Struggle Against Racism in the World*

1985	*Against Racism*, ed.
1987	*Racism, Imperialism, Peace*
1989	*The Literary Legacy of W. E. B. Du Bois*, ed.
1989	*Abolitionism, a Revolutionary Movement*
1992	*Antiracism in U.S. History*

I first encountered Herbert Aptheker's name in an undergraduate survey course in Afro-American history taught at Yale in the 1969–1970 academic year by William McFeely. I was a sophomore. We read Professor Aptheker's *American Negro Slave Revolts*. I was astonished to learn both that the slaves had resisted slavery, so consistently and so nobly, and that most other historians had completely ignored these acts of resistance.

As I matured as a student, I read more and more of Dr. Aptheker's considerable list of works, relying upon him increasingly as one of the principal commentators on the African experience in America. When his monumental complete edition of Du Bois's works was published, I managed to find the savings to purchase it, and I read it straight through.

Had he published these volumes alone, his reputation as a judicious scholar and as a meticulous editor would have been secure.

Shortly after the Du Bois editions appeared, Dr. Aptheker was the victim of a pernicious attempt by certain members of the History Department at Yale to block him from teaching a "college seminar" course there. Because they were unable to state publicly any sound reason for refusing to authorize the course, many of my fellow faculty members at Yale felt that Dr. Aptheker was being censored for ideological reasons. So we noisily protested the actions of the History Department and found an alternate sponsor, and the course was offered. When I became the chairman of the Department of Afro-American Studies at Harvard, one of the first scholars I invited to lecture here was Dr. Aptheker.

The Documentary History of the Negro People in the United States brings together most of the germinal pieces of writing created by Afro-Americans reflecting on their condition as Afro-Americans in a racist state. These volumes, now grown to six with the publication of *A Documentary History of the Negro People in the United States, 1945–1951, volume 5, From the End of World War II to the Korean War* and *A Documentary History of the Negro People in the United States, 1951–1959, volume 6, From the Korean War to the Emergence of Martin*

Luther King, Jr., are indispensable to a full understanding of African-American history. Dr. Aptheker's editorial apparatus is superb. These volumes are essential reading for all students and scholars of Afro-American Studies.

Henry Louis Gates, Jr.

Introduction

THE FIRST VOLUME of this *Documentary History* appeared in 1951. That ended with the founding of the National Association for the Advancement of Colored People (NAACP) in 1910. Other volumes brought the drama to the closing year of the Second World War (1945).

The present volume begins with that year. (One hopes that will be the last world war.) Its structure, like the predecessors, is chronological, but the first five documents cover several years prior to and after this volume. This is done in an effort to convey a sense of the sweep of the period.

As in previous volumes, the words come from African-American people themselves, with rare exceptions, whose need will appear to the reader. The only changes made were corrections in typographical errors.

The fifteen years preceding the explosion of the 1960s tend to be neglected in the available literature. They were, however, momentous, and the reader will see how they prepared the foundation for the 1960s.

In the preparation of this book, the aid offered by David Fathi and Katharine Gelles has been invaluable. As has been true for over fifty years, the assistance of my wife, Fay, has been crucial.

A DOCUMENTARY HISTORY OF

The Negro People in the United States

1

CHAIN GANG DOCUMENT

Joseph Brock was arrested in Los Angeles in December 1948 for extradition to the South. His union, Local 26 of the International Longshore and Warehouse Workers Union (ILWU), and other groups and individuals, including the Civil Rights Congress, came to his aid. In February 1949, that fight was lost, and Joseph Brock returned. Eight years later, he finished his term. Here he tells the story of his life as of 1957.

I was born in Vicksburg, Mississippi. Jefferson Davis was born in nearby Natchez—about a hundred years before me—but his spirit was still alive. Education, jobs, medical care, housing for Negroes were primitive. By the time I was eight, my mother, only 27 years old, was dead because we never had the money to pay for the medical care she needed. My brother, 3 and I, were taken in by my Aunt Lizzie, who brought us up.

My aunt sent us both to Catholic School. She was "working out," doing housework, to pay for school. When she took sick, there was no more money, and she had to go on relief.

I tried to help by working at whatever I could get—cleaning up, mowing lawns. It wasn't enough to feed us. When I was 15, she suggested that I join the Civilian Conservation Corps. Maybe there, she thought, I could learn a little something that would help me get along. And the CCC paid $30 a month. So I put my age up to 18—the lowest they would take—and joined.

It was an all-colored camp. They taught us a little about agriculture and forestry. The athletic program included boxing and wrestling. I stand six feet, with broad shoulders, and was pretty good at athletics. The way things worked out later, it was a good thing I had the training.

Altogether, because it was so tough to get a job on the outside, I stayed in the camp about two and a half years. When I left, I found a job doing construction work. It lasted about two years and then things began to change around.

3

I took the little money I'd managed to save up and bought a small truck to haul wood and coal. I had a little wood and coal yard and bought stuff for resale from a couple of boys. They brought me all kinds of things. I didn't know it was stolen merchandise. The police caught me with the stuff and I was sentenced to four years in prison, to run concurrently.

After I got to prison, they had me booked eight years running consecutively. I knew the judge gave me four years, and I wasn't intending to make it eight. So I ran away to another aunt in Mobile, Alabama. I hoped she would be able to lend me a little money so I could get out of the South and get to California. But she had lots of children and no money, so after a month, I began to ride the freights to get away.

I was on the Alabama-Florida state line when a sheriff picked me up on suspicion. He took me to a justice of the peace, in an old house. The justice was an old man. He asked,

"Boy, what you doing here? What they bring you here for?"

"They just picked me up in the yard," I explained.

"If you've got $50, I'll let you go."

I answered, "If I had $50, I wouldn't be riding on the freights."

The justice looked me over, saw that I was big and husky. "If you've got $25, I'll let you go," he said.

I gave him the same reply and was told, "Then I'll have to send you to the county jail in Pensacola."

He bound me over to the county seat in Pensacola, where they put me in jail without charge. I was there for two months. The deputy sheriff (white) always cussed out the prisoners and hollered at them like we were all dogs. A couple of the guys decided to do something about it, and asked me if I'd be with them. I knew I was already wanted in Mississippi and had nothing to lose in breaking out, so I decided to go with them.

We plotted to take the key away from the deputy sheriff when he came in. He suspected that something was up and began to back out of the door, hollering for help. They grabbed him and put something around his mouth, but he kept hollering.

I knew we had to shut him up, so I hit him in the jaw—just once—and knocked him out. His keys flew all over the floor. I tried to find the one that would let us out, but before I could get the right key, the police and forest police came running. We fought for our freedom for half an hour before they conquered us and carried us downstairs to the sheriff's office for questioning.

They questioned us one at a time to find out who was the leader. Because I was the biggest and the one who slugged the sheriff, the whole blame was laid at my door.

The sheriff told me, "I should throw you off in the bay and get rid of you!" But the other prisoners lived there, so I guess he figured they would get somebody to protest if he did throw me in the bay. He ended by telling the deputy sheriff to take me back upstairs and give me a good whipping.

He had one of those big old straps, about eight feet long and about nine inches wide. Every time he raised it to use it on me, I would grab it. They got hot with me for that and three or four of them jumped me. While we were tussling, one of them used a little penknife and got me around the right eye. The blood began to pour out and they stopped. Somebody said, "You better lock this guy up before you kill him!"

They locked me in solitary confinement, took out the mattress, blankets and stuff and turned the hose on me. I stayed in there—a cell about twelve by eight feet—for eighteen days, on bread and water. When I took sick, they took me out and brought me to see the judge.

The judge set my trial date, along with the two guys who tried to break out with me. The judge gave one two years, one three years and me five.

After four or five days in the county jail, they carried me to the state penitentiary in Raiford, Florida. The medical examiners said I was fit for the road gang, so I was sent to work throwing dirt on the shoulders of the road. After two months, I saw my chance and broke away. They caught me fast, carried me back and put me in solitary for fifteen days. When I got out, they put chains around my legs.

After about 18 months, the white driver on the road gang told me he'd take the chains off if I'd promise not to run. I wouldn't make any such promise, but he took the chains off.

I ran again. They put the dogs behind me, with a colored convict to run them. I tried every trick I knew—turning over logs, running in streams of water, pepper in my shoes, all the methods I had learned—to get rid of the dogs. But they finally caught up with me.

I got behind a tree to get away from the "big boy." We ran each other and I knew I had to jump him to keep him from catching me. He was a pretty big fellow, almost as big as I, and I knew I'd have to hurt him in order to get away. So I jumped him and pinned him to the ground. Holding him down, I said,

"I could break your neck if I want to, but I don't believe in that kind of life. I believe in live and let live. We're both colored. Let me go on my way and don't turn me in, and I'll let you go."

He could see it my way, so I let him go. He went back with the dogs, and I don't believe he told them anything about it. I kept going—and this time the white guards came after me with the bloodhounds. They were harder to get away from. I swam the river and they lost me.

Traveling day and night, swimming, riding the freights, I found myself back in Alabama and stopped again in Mobile to rest at my aunt's home.

My uncle gave me a few dollars—all he could spare—to help me get away. I was being very careful, because now I was on the run from two states. A young man about my own age offered to sell me a bike. I thought the bike would help me get to where I could catch a train for California, and paid him $10 for it. A sheriff stopped me, said the bike was stolen, and put me in jail on a charge of stealing. A colored family was brought to the jail, where they identified the bike. I told them how I came to buy it, and what I had paid for it, and they said that since they had their property back, they didn't want anything done to me.

No charges were pressed—but the judge sentenced me to ten years.

When he asked me if I had any statement to make, I said I wasn't guilty—that I had never stolen anything. But he replied, "Well, regardless of that, I have it here in black and white that you signed a confession. I'm going to give you ten years in the state penitentiary, and if you want, you can give it back to me."

"Judge, I'm going to do my best," I said.

"Take him out!" said the judge.

In another week I was in another road camp, with ten years there ahead of me. But I knew I hadn't signed a confession. I knew I was innocent. So I did what I told that judge I would do. I ran away again—and this time the freights got me to California and freedom.

I had an aunt and uncle living in Los Angeles and went straight to them, believing that at last I was free of the land of prison and jim crow. I changed my name, found a job, joined the ILWU, Local 26—and thought that now I could make the kind of life for myself that I'd always wanted.

For five years it looked as though I would be successful. All the nationalities were among the workers in my shop, and they voted me in for chief steward. Not many of the shop workers were in the union at first—only about fifty percent. I felt that the union could help us and we needed the union, so I went to the workers who were not in it and tried to get them to understand. After a while, it was 97 per cent of the shop in the union. I missed two or three of them. I wanted to get them all in, but I guess I didn't try hard enough.

I'd been in Los Angeles for about three and a half years when I met a young, pretty girl and married her. We found a little apartment and fixed it up nice, and for a year and a half we were happy.

Then one day, the Los Angeles police stopped me. They had pictures of me from the South, and said I was wanted by three southern states.

There I was, back in jail again. The news came as a blow to my wife. She was only 23, and I had never told her about my past. When she came to see me in jail for the first time, I told her why I was there, and that it was true I was wanted. She was so shocked, she fainted.

The next day she went to the union and told them my story—and the union went to the Civil Rights Congress. The firm I worked for told my wife I was a good worker and they thought I was honest. They turned my case over to their company lawyer and gave my wife a hundred dollars toward my defense. The lawyer got me out on bond, and the CRC put up my bail.

Marguerite Robinson, a very active little Negro woman, was head of the CRC. She took my wife and me around to parties and meetings to tell people about my case so they'd help me fight against extradition. Margie told me that before it was over, she'd fight my case to the Supreme Court.

I never saw folks like those before. They were all nationalities—and they wrote thousands of letters to the government. They came to meet me at San Francisco and a lot of them went to the governor with me to ask him not to extradite me to the South.

The only one who got in to see the governor was my lawyer. But I felt that all these people were on my side and were trying to help me in every way they could.

I did get a stay for two months. The CRC carried my case to the Circuit Court of California, and when they turned it down, Mrs. Robinson brought it to the California District of the Supreme Court.

The District Attorney walked into that courtroom carrying a stack of books. My attorney told the Court that if I were sent back to the South, it would mean sure death for me after the way I'd been treated before.

The District Justice leaned down from the bench and told my lawyer that he mustn't talk that way or the Court would fine him. I knew then, I didn't stand a chance.

I walked out of the Court with Los Angeles detectives who turned me over to the waiting officer from Alabama. "You better take this guy back to Alabama right away because if you don't, they'll have something else cooked up around here to keep him out," they told the officer.

That day, I kissed my crying wife good-bye and went back to Alabama. As soon as the train crossed the Mason-Dixon line, I could feel that I was in the South again. The officer who had me in charge made that clear.

I was sent right to solitary confinement. They didn't have a cell for solitary, but they put me in the "condemned cell" where men wait to be electrocuted. I spent six months in that cell.

During that time, I had my first heart attack. When I could write, I managed to get a letter smuggled out to Margie Robinson. The CRC sent me a wire asking whether I was getting proper medical care. The prison authorities held it for two days, finally brought it to me so crumpled up, I could see they didn't want to give it to me.

After they got the prison fixed up, they transferred me to a solitary cell called "little Alcatraz." I was allowed no books except a Bible, and given only one meal a day. I was kept there three months, and during that time, I read the Bible all the way through.

Then the director came to see me. He said I was getting a lot of mail from different places—New York, Los Angeles and others—and it looked like I was getting a lot of publicity. So he was going to keep me in solitary until he got ready to turn me out. I knew I'd have to take some step to get myself out of solitary, and wrote to Margie Robinson about what was happening.

But before my letter got to Margie, the warden had me turned out of solitary. Not long afterward a white woman from CRC came to Montgomery, got a colored woman lawyer, and together they came to visit me. When I was allowed to talk with them, I told them about my nine months in solitary. They demanded an explanation from the warden, who just brushed them off. But when he told them I had to make good to get out on parole, I knew my friends' support was helping me.

I specially understood the value of my friends now, because from my cell in solitary, I could see many men walk their last mile to the electric chair for crimes that did not deserve the death penalty.

For myself, I had one real disappointment. The thought that I faced 23 years in prison was too much for my wife. While all the others were helping me, she had stopped writing to me after the first month.

I had ten years to serve in the Alabama Prison—but they released me on parole at the end of three years and seven months. Part of that, I think was due to the pressure of my friends on the outside and part to my good behavior.

I tried to put my time to good use. At first, I had worked in the warehouse, but the cotton lint was hard on my health and I asked for another job. They transferred me to a job in the library. There, I got a chance to read and study for myself, and to teach other prisoners to read and write.

When I was released on parole, I knew I was headed for Mississippi, which would be, if anything, worse. I asked a white prisoner to write a recommendation for me, and the warden, the chaplain and the deputy-warden all signed it. I took that recommendation with me to the prison at Parchman, Mississippi, and gave it to the superintendent there.

For the first two or three months it wasn't too bad, in spite of the fact that I worked at the road camp. But I was writing to my friends in Los Angeles, and they were sending me books, letters and packages of canned food. The sergeant didn't like that and started to make it tough for me. I only got one of all the books they sent, and then he told me to write and "tell those people not to send any more packages."

The sergeant assigned a white driver to keep after me. We were hoeing cotton and corn—and the driver said everything I did was wrong. I could see that he wasn't picking on any of the others the way he did on me, and asked him why he was picking on me. He told me the truth: the sergeant had told him to drive me.

The day came when I was caught between the sergeant's orders and the driver's. No matter what I did was wrong. So I wrote to my friends in Los Angeles and they sent a lawyer.

I was not allowed to talk to the lawyer without the sergeant listening to every word, so I played it cool and didn't say too much. The lawyer didn't seem to understand. When he left, the sergeant called me in and said,

"Remember that cow we buried out in back? I could kill you and put you down beside that cow and they wouldn't know nothin' about it." He added he had "something set up for me" for sending the lawyer.

The "something" was a whipping. When they whip prisoners, the sergeant, director, chaplain, and educational director come down and have a feast as if it was a ceremony. Then, one by one, they order the prisoners to strip and stretch out on the concrete floor. They use a strap about nine feet long and what seemed like more than a foot wide. The "recommendation" for each prisoner tells how many lashes to give him.

They saved me for the last of five, and I had to stand by and watch the other prisoners whipped and listen to them holler and beg. I made up my mind they weren't going to do that to me.

When I refused to strip, they came at me. I hit at the trusties, beat up a couple of them, and the sergeant said, "If you can't get him down, I'll shoot him down."

They all came in at me and we wrestled for about an hour. The sergeant used the whip, but he was catching more of the trusties than me with it. In the end, I was ordered back to the cells.

The sergeant told me I was trying to be hard-boiled because I had a lot of friends back in California, but he "had something cooked up for me." That was solitary—again, a place called "Alcatraz."

But I wasn't sent there because I had made friends with one of the other prisoners who was a "houseboy" in the sergeant's house. The sergeant's wife read my mail and discussed me with this "houseboy," who told her that I was a good guy who was only trying to be free again. She must have talked to her husband about me—and he evidently went along with her, because after that it was easier.

While he let up on me, he turned to making it harder for the other colored prisoners. Saturday was supposed to be the day of slacking off a little, taking it a little easier. Instead, he drove them harder than ever on Saturday, so they never got any rest.

At the end of two years and eight months, the sergeant gave me a choice of surrendering myself to Florida or fighting my Florida case. I knew my lawyer had been fighting my Florida case all along—and my friends in Los Angeles wrote that they had paid the lawyer $500 to fight it. So the sergeant's offer sounded like a trick. I signed the paper to go to Florida, hoping that I'd get there to find myself free.

But the lawyer had only succeeded in getting my state "good time" back. I had a year and nine months ahead of me in the prison at Raiford. During that time, they did everything imaginable to keep me there.

Because the doctor had said I had a weak heart, they sent me to a farm camp instead of a road camp. When the backwater from the river runs up on the cornfields, the snakes come with it. We'd be out there pulling corn in the midst of the rattlesnakes. I refused to work there, with the rattlesnakes and sandy spurs—little brown stickers that grow neckhigh and jab into a man's flesh and can't be pulled out.

To punish me for refusing, they put me in "the box." This is an iron and cement cell about five by three feet, constructed so that the prisoner can't sit up or stand upright. Food in this cell is two biscuits and some water for the day.

I was kept in "the box" nine days, but I still wouldn't give in and agree to work among the snakes. So they put me on the construction gang building a hospital.

Things were going along bearably until about a month before I was supposed to get out. Then I caught a heavy cold. I asked the assistant captain to let me see the doctor, and was told the doctor only came on Monday and Friday. This was Thursday. The next day, as the assistant captain had told me to do, I stayed in my cell to see the doctor.

When I didn't report for work, the assistant captain called me out and said it was a lie—that he had never told me to wait for the doctor. He was going to send me to "the box" instead.

We had a little row and he went for his gun. Some of the trusties advised me that I didn't have much more time to go and it was better to go to "the box" quietly than get shot down.

It was February and freezing cold. They put me in that iron and cement box without a blanket. The cold came in the crack at the door and the opening at the top until I thought I would freeze to death. And I still had that heavy cold.

Finally they gave me half a blanket. Between the intense cold, the two-biscuits-and-water diet, plus my own cold, I didn't know if I'd get out of there alive.

They had me in there for ten days. On the last day, I knew the doctor was coming by, and if I moved fast to get a little warmer, it would start my heart pumping real fast. I jumped up and down just before the doctor got there, and when he examined me, he could hear that pumping in his stethoscope. I told him I didn't think I could make it—and he ordered them to let me out.

I was due to go free—but they had to find one more dirty trick to hold me. Because I had resisted the box—they added another week to my time!

Finally, they turned me over to my lawyer. In order to get me out of that Florida prison, he had to tell them that he was taking me back to the prison in Birmingham, Alabama.

We did go to Birmingham. There, he wired my friends in Los Angeles—and put me on a plane.

The people who had stood by me and fought for me all those years were waiting to greet me. And thanks to my union, I'm back in my old job, too. Now I want to start life all over again.

Mainstream (N.Y.) (August 1957) X, no. 8 8–16.

2

THE LIFE OF MORANDA SMITH

Moranda Smith was a figure of legendary proportions in African-American and labor history in the 1940s. She expired, exhausted, with health care neglected, prior to her thirty-fifth birthday. The editor of this *Documentary*, in North Carolina in the 1940s, remembers her tall figure, commanding voice, and tireless efforts. She was beloved. Here is a brief account of her life written by fellow black workers.

On June 3, 1951, thousands of workers, Negro and white together, paused to pay tribute to the memory of Sister Moranda Smith.

Moranda Smith was a young Negro woman who had moved as a child with her family from their sharecropper's farm in South Carolina to the tobacco center of Winston-Salem, North Carolina. She was a striking spark of the union spirit that set thousands of workers into militant motion for labor's cause.

She died on April 13, 1950, a casualty of the southern workers' fierce struggle, though she was still in the very prime of life and in the midst of her great work. Born June 3, 1915, she died at the age of 34. Her work as International Representative for FTA took her into contact with many thousands of workers throughout the South Atlantic States.

She was the first woman to serve as Regional Director for an International Union in the South.

In 1943, when an elderly Negro worker fell dead from overwork in a Reynolds plant in Winston-Salem, N.C., after the foreman had refused to let him go home, thousands of Negro women in the plant staged a spontaneous sit-down.

Ten thousand walked. This soon spread into a walkout covering some 100,000 workers which forced all the Reynolds Camels-Prince Albert plants to shut down for several days until the company agreed to meet with a workers' committee.

Thousands of workers joined the union to form Local 22, later winning elections and bargaining rights, with contracts won from 1944 through 1947.

In the course of the long union struggle with the R. J. Reynolds Tobacco Company, the workers, led in the main by Negro women workers like Sister Smith, helped to end what amounted to almost slave working conditions and low pay. Many of the workers who joined up were not acquainted with labor unions; but, once members, they were its best supporters.

Memories of Misery. Others could remember 1919 and 1929, when the Reynolds Company ruthlessly crushed attempts by the workers to organize in hopes of gaining a fairer share of the tremendous wealth they were creating by their long hours of drudgery in the tobacco plants.

With the advent of Local 22, these workers won $1,250,000 retroactive pay in the leafhouses and stemmeries. Though before the union they received as little as 40–53 cents an hour, today—because of the Local's fight—they receive a minimum of 93 cents. This was made possible because of many great workers who became union leaders—such as Moranda Smith.

Working to build and to keep unity among the workers in the R. J. Reynolds plants, Sister Smith would visit workers at night, and even at lunchtime she would devote the few minutes to persuading workers to join or to become more active in the Local.

Demanded Respect. Because Sister Smith was determined and militant, she was chosen to serve on the union's negotiation committee. The white bossmen who had heaped abuse and poor wages on Negro women now had to deal with them in a respectful manner.

At first, they tried to ignore her presence on the negotiating committee, but she would stand up and forcefully present her arguments. When the bossmen would speak only to the men leaders of the union, the men rejected this attempt to snub her and said: "Address your remarks to Sister Moranda Smith, she is a member of this committee."

And then, much against their wishes, the bosses would have to recognize her. This was a new day and a new way, and Moranda Smith was one of those greatly responsible for making it come about.

Before Local 22 was organized, there were only 163 Negro voters registered in Winston-Salem. After the Union's campaign to register more voters, more than 8,000 new names were placed on the books. The first Negro Alderman to be elected in the South since the turn of the century was elected on the strength of these newly won rights.

Sister Smith held many classes to give instructions on the "know how" of registration and led many workers groups to the courthouse to demand the right to vote.

While Sister Smith was in Apopka, Florida, Klan members seized a Negro worker and tried to force him to tell her whereabouts. He refused to tell. They beat him, threatened to kill him, ground his face into the Florida soil. Still he refused to tell. They gave up and left him lying there, still keeping the secret of her whereabouts.

Defying the Klan. When Sister Smith heard of the Klan attack, she walked, as a friend relates, "down the middle of the street just to show the bosses that union members would not be intimidated."

Meanwhile, the white and Negro workers saw to it that Sister Smith was protected and could leave town after her visit, with no harm.

To Moranda Smith, the union was one of the most important things in her life. She read and studied so she could pass the information on to her fellow-workers. She would travel all night by bus, and the next day— without any sleep—would participate in a meeting or picket line.

It was the terrible strain of [working and organizing]...which finally proved too great for this working class heroine. But when she died, she left an inspiring example for all workers to follow.

Today, many Negro women in the South are carrying on the spirit of Moranda Smith.

From the *Union Voice* (Winston-Salem, N.C.) June 3, 1951; in Gerder Lerner, ed., *Black Women In White America* (N.Y.: Pantheon 1972), pp. 11–13.

3

PAULI MURRAY'S CAREER

Pauli Murray, African-American feminist, lawyer, priest and poet, wrote an autobiography, *Song in a Weary Throat*, that was published in 1987, two years before her death. In that book will be found cogent remarks on the beginning of the modern civil rights movement in the 1940s. Here, too, she wrote on Adlai Stevenson's campaigns of the 1950s and their relation to black people and described Eleanor Roosevelt's limitations on the antiracism front. Important, too, are her comments on the early nationalist and Black Power movements toward the close of Martin Luther King's role.

After a description of pioneering sit-in efforts by some Howard University students during World War II, she continued:

It remained for historians to place our wartime effort in proper perspective. Eleanor Holmes (Norton), a student activist of the early 1960s, who graduated from the Yale Law School in 1964 with a simultaneously awarded graduate degree in American Studies (and who later chaired the EEOC in the Carter administration), chose for her history honors paper the topic "World War II and the Beginnings of Non-Violent Action in Civil Rights." I was working on my doctorate at the Yale Law School at the time and gave her access to my files. After analyzing the records of the 1943–44 Howard University sit-ins, she wrote: "They had achieved a nearly perfect demonstration based on Gandhi's methods.... After the coordination and mastery their effort revealed, non-violent resistance awaited only a mass following." Her conclusion affirmed my own feeling about the continuity of social movements, even when interrupted for a period of time:

Non-violent resistance to gain civil rights did not begin with the bus boycott in Montgomery, Alabama in 1956. It began with bus incidents in 1940 and was perfected as a technique before 1945. The Negro movement for integration today [1963], like mass movements before it, had its dedicated *avant-garde*.

Economic distress, armed forces segregation, and war slogans denouncing racism produced bitterness that ran through all classes of Negroes in the early forties. Out of their anger came interracial conflict in countless incidents. But out of it also came the search for a new, dignified, and more direct way to protest....

Perhaps the greatest gain from the war years is that they inspired the use of a tactic that would be consistent with militancy and peaceful protest. The non-violent experiments reduced tension and encouraged hope among Negroes. And they pointed the way toward a movement for integration that would for the first time reach the Negro masses and bring daring campaigns to the very heart of racism.

A more immediate consequence of our 1944 campaign was the discovery that ultimate victory over Jim Crow in the city of Washington did not require the enactment of civil rights legislation by Congress. Professor A. Mercer Daniel, our law librarian and the oldest member of the law school faculty, recalled talk among older Washingtonians of an earlier civil rights law in the District of Columbia. If such a law had existed, no one seemed to know what happened to it.

"Poppa" Daniel, as we students affectionately called him behind his back, did not pretend to be a brilliant legal theoretician, but he possessed a plodding patience necessary to sustained legal research. He conscientiously rummaged through forgotten dusty volumes in the library stacks and, one day toward the end of the school term, gleefully showed me what he had unearthed in a book entitled *Compiled Statutes in force in the District of Columbia in 1894.*

The volume included an act passed in 1872 by the Second Legislative Assembly of the District of Columbia (a local body to which Congress had delegated legislative authority during the years 1870–74), which made it a misdemeanor, punishable by a fine of $100 and forfeiture of license for a period of one year, for proprietors of restaurants, ice cream saloons, soda fountains, hotels, barbershops, and bathing houses to refuse to serve "any respectable, well-behaved person without regard to race, color or previous condition of servitude...in the same room, and at the same prices as other well-behaved and respectable persons are served." (An act of 1873, discovered later, strengthened and extended the coverage in the 1872 law.)

With the galling Thompson's cafeteria fiasco fresh in my mind, I could hardly contain myself when I read those words, and I set out to discover why this law had fallen into disuse. Preliminary research showed that it did not appear in any code of laws for the District of Columbia after 1894; yet I could not find an express repeal of the statute. Nor could I find any citation that it had been declared invalid by judicial decision.

The D.C. Code of 1901 omitted the civil rights ordinance but contained an enabling clause which declared that all laws herein before enacted but not expressly repealed were held to be in full force and effect. I concluded that the omission was deliberate on the part of the compilers of the 1901 code. The law had fallen victim to the general disregard of civil rights following the Supreme Court's invalidation of the federal Civil Rights Act of 1875 in the *Civil Rights Cases* decision of 1883. By the early 1900s, and particularly during the administration of President Woodrow Wilson, a rigid pattern of segregation by custom had been imposed, which escaped legal challenge by a later generation of lawyers who were unaware of the existence of the earlier local law.

Elated over these preliminary findings, I went around the law school waving the statute and arguing that the old civil rights legislation was still in force. We should bring a test case to get the issue of segregation in the District of Columbia before the courts, I maintained. Although our direct action campaign had been stifled, a successful court test would vindicate our initial efforts. I have wondered since then whether my theory would have been acted upon more promptly if discovery of the statute had come earlier in the school year, giving me time to incorporate my proposal into a formal legal memorandum. And I have also wondered whether it would have made any difference if the suggestion had come not from a woman but from a man, whether a residue of skepticism remained about a woman's capacity to advance bold new ideas. Perhaps costly experimental litigation was too risky at the time or perhaps law professors' agendas were overburdened with more pressing matters. Whatever the reasons, my suggestion was not taken seriously in 1944, although after graduation, and far from the Washington scene, I continued to peddle it in civil rights circles. Five years later, seven other lawyers, including the NAACP's Charles H. Houston, presented the same theory in a written opinion, and the idea of a test case became a reality.

One determined individual had not forgotten the existence of the old District of Columbia civil rights law. Mary Church Terrell, militant civil rights activist and longtime feminist who had fought for woman suffrage, completed the struggle we Howard University students had begun. A patrician born in the year of the Emancipation Proclamation, and the essence of Victorian respectability, Mrs. Terrell led picket lines against downtown eating places and ultimately chaired the Coordinating Committee for the Enforcement of the D.C. Anti-Discrimination Laws.

Appropriately, when a test case finally materialized in 1950, our old adversary, Thompson's cafeteria, was the defendant in a prosecution under the 1872 and 1873 laws. The management's refusal to serve Mrs. Terrell and her interracial parties on several occasions culminated in a bitterly fought contest in the local municipal and federal courts. The case of *District of Columbia v. John R. Thompson Co., Inc.* reached the Supreme Court of the United States in the spring of 1953, and in June of that year the high court ruled that the acts of 1872 and 1873 had not been repealed by subsequent legislation and that failure to enforce a law does not operate to repeal it. The decision came down nine years after our sit-in at Thompson's cafeteria and three months before Mrs. Terrell's ninetieth birthday, and it spelled the end of racial segregation in public places in the nation's capital. Mrs. Terrell died the following year.

By a coincidence, Adlai Stevenson's two unsuccessful campaigns to win the presidency bracketed my four-year effort to write *Proud Shoes* and marked both the beginning of the manuscript and the publication of the book. In 1952 I was so impressed by Stevenson's integrity, eloquence, wit, and liberal civil rights record as governor of Illinois that I took time off from the manuscript long enough to work for his election. As a Volunteer for Stevenson, I was part of a team headed by Lloyd K. Garrison to bring out the Negro vote in New York City. The Stevenson magic was contagious, the campaign exciting, and in the 1952 election he captured an estimated 79 percent of the nationwide black vote. Our efforts in Harlem, where Stevenson appeared at a rally, produced 83 percent in his favor.

Except for final revisions, I had finished my work on *Proud Shoes* by the time Stevenson began making his second bid for the Democratic nomination. He had the strong backing of Eleanor Roosevelt, and I enthusiastically accepted an invitation to join the Stevenson for President Committee. From the beginning, however, and notwithstanding my preference for Stevenson over the other early contenders, Averell Harriman and Estes Kefauver, I was disturbed by his approach to the explosive civil rights crisis, which then dominated the front pages of the *New York Times*. The racial climate had changed drastically since 1952. In the wake of the 1954 Supreme Court decision on school desegregation, Negroes were making a determined assault on the Jim Crow system in the South. In the Montgomery Boycott, which began in December 1955, nonviolent direct action was being used successfully to combat segregation on local buses—the campaign that brought Dr. Martin Luther King, Jr., to national prominence. At the same time, southern Democratic politicians were leading campaigns of "Massive Resistance" to the Court's ruling, maintaining that states could interpose their sovereignty between the people and the federal government to nullify actions the states held to be in violation of the federal Constitution. This instigation to defy federal authority encouraged increasing acts of intimidation and violence intended to suppress civil rights activities in the South. As historian-journalist Thomas R. Brooks summed up that period: "Blacks, particularly in the South, were caught in a cruel dilemma. On the one hand, there were the decisions of the Supreme Court against segregation and the encouraging—indeed exhilarating—victory of the Montgomery bus boycott; on the other hand, there was a growing—and partially successful—white reaction and repression, especially against school desegregation."

Stevenson, in his preoccupation with mending fences in a party badly split on the question of compliance, seemed bent upon placating southern Democrats at the expense of reaffirming the moral principles at stake in the gravest issue facing the nation in 1956. As one of his earliest supporters, I wrote him in January of my concern that he had not publicly expressed his views on two critical issues: (1) continued economic reprisals and silence against Negro citizens in southern states who had evidenced leadership in the NAACP, and (2) the recent vote in Virginia to call a constitutional convention for the express purpose of evading the Supreme Court mandate on integration of the public schools. "I am acutely aware of your silence and the news stories surrounding your silence," I wrote, adding: "I strongly urge you to clarify your position on the issues posed in this letter. Unless and until you do, it will be difficult for independents and liberal Democrats in New York to withstand the pressures that will take advantage of your silence to swing opinion in favor of some other candidate." Knowing her desire to maintain support among Negroes for Stevenson's candidacy, I sent a copy of my letter to Mrs. Roosevelt.

The burning question to Negroes was what firm measures the federal government, when confronted with southern defiance, would take to enforce the Supreme Court's decision outlawing segregation in public schools. Forced to address himself to this question in early February when speaking to a group of Negroes in Los Angeles, Stevenson angered the embattled civil rights leadership by dismissing Congressman Adam Clayton Powell's proposed amendment to a federal construction bill. Of the Powell proposal, which would bar funds to segregated schools, Stevenson declared: "I hardly think such an amendment is necessary." When asked whether, as President, he would use the army or navy, if necessary, to enforce school desegregation, he replied, according to *New York Times* reporter W. H. Lawrence: "I think that would be a great mistake. That is exactly what brought on the Civil War. It can't be done by troops, or bayonets. We must proceed gradually, not upsetting habits or traditions that are older than the Republic." Several days later Stevenson urged that all candidates ban the integration issue from the presidential campaign, as if a conflict people openly spoke of as impending civil war could be resolved by silence on the part of anyone aspiring to become President of the United States.

The questions put to Stevenson were realistic ones for Negroes, who knew that ultimately only the superior authority of the federal government would prevent the violent suppression of rights so painfully won and finally reaffirmed under the Constitution. They anticipated the 1957 crisis in Little Rock, Arkansas, some eighteen months later, when President Eisenhower (who also thought the use of armed force inconceivable) had to send in federal troops to carry out a federal court order to desegregate the schools.

Stevenson's rejection of specific measures without offering alternatives, together with his emphasis upon gradualism, touched off a bruising controversy within liberal ranks. A mark of the deepening crisis was the intense Negro reaction against white liberal supporters who called for moderation and conciliation in the struggle while passing over in silence the recalcitrance of southern segregationists. To victims of the Jim Crow system, this posture was a retreat from principle, abandoning Negroes to the unrestrained violence of white racism. My own strong reaction to Mr. Stevenson's various statements boiled over in correspondence with syndicated columnist Doris Fleeson, a Stevenson enthusiast who saw him as a leader steeped in the lore of Abraham Lincoln, someone who reflected the moderation and conciliation of Lincoln in his determination to avert a second Civil War. On February 11, I wrote to her that I believed "as of *now* Mr. Stevenson has lost the Negro vote." I also said:

It is all very well for Mr. Stevenson to be preoccupied with conciliation and with the dangers involved in upsetting the "traditions of centuries," but unless he understands how passionately determined the Negro is that once and for *all* we will be brought up to par, or die in the attempt, he will underestimate the new situation we are facing in the United States today.... Civil rights cannot be dealt with with moderate feelings. It involves a passion for justice and for human decency, and if Mr. Stevenson has not felt this passion, then he does not belong in the White House.

To me, the most distressing aspect of this phase of the campaign was that not even Mrs. Roosevelt seemed to appreciate fully the depth of our feeling that the subordination of the moral imperatives of our struggle to political expediencies was little short of betrayal by our friends, hence our outrage. Although she sat on the NAACP board and was abreast of developments, she angrily defended Stevenson from NAACP executive director Roy Wilkins' sharp criticism of his emphasis upon gradualism. In dismay, I wrote her that the apparent cleavage between her point of view and that of the Negro leaders she had known and worked with over many years "may be more fundamental than you realize. If so, it would be tragic for all of us." Because she had spoken of her perplexity over the confusion and misunderstanding Mr. Stevenson's statement caused, and because I feared further misunderstandings, I urged her "to counsel informally with leaders in this field whose opinions you respect and in whom you have trust and confidence." After suggesting a meeting with Ralph Bunche and several others, I added: "I think such an informal exchange of views might clarify the issues and help all of us to formulate a sound approach to the present crisis."

It may have been one of those times when Mrs. Roosevelt wanted no qualms of conscience to interfere with her course of political action, but she was sufficiently affected by my disturbed view to have a long talk with Ralph Bunche, which she reported on in her reply. Although affectionate as always, her letter possessed a tone of defensiveness. She did not think there was any "fundamental cleavage" between the point of view she shared with Stevenson and that "of the really wise Negro leaders."

I did not like Roy Wilkins' hot-headed statement which I thought poorly thought out, nor did I like the garbled reporting of what Mr. Stevenson said in Los Angeles. Unwittingly Mr. Stevenson used the word "gradual" and this means one thing to the Negroes but to him it is entirely different.

Mrs. Roosevelt did not attempt to explain what Mr. Stevenson really meant, but declared that his "record remains remarkably good and he certainly was courageous in the statements he made in the last campaign." She considered it "a mistake for the Negro leaders to be tearing down Stevenson who is after all the only real hope they have," since President Eisenhower had indicated "that he would make no statement on whether the Executive would refrain from allocating funds where schools were segregated. Yet the papers and the Negro leaders have not attacked the President. Why this discrimination?"

Unhappily, Mrs. Roosevelt and I were separated by differences in our perception of the racial experience as well as by the intensity of feeling I shared with other Negroes against segregationist efforts to snatch away a hard-won victory almost within our grasp. She perceived the civil rights issue as secondary to winning the White House for Adlai Stevenson. At the Democratic convention in August, her concern for party unity led her to support a civil rights plank that omitted endorsement of the Supreme Court decision on desegregation of the public schools. "You can't move so fast that you try to change the mores faster than people can accept it," she advised Negro and other civil rights leaders who fought for a stronger statement. "That doesn't mean that you do nothing, but it means that you do the things that need to be done according to priority." Her pragmatism, directed toward holding southern Democrats within the party, ignored another reality—the increasing momentum of the civil rights movement and the growing militancy of Negroes who found that with each advance toward the goal of equality, remaining barriers to its fulfillment became all the more intolerable. Cautioning us against moving too fast while watering down the civil rights plank of the Democratic party platform blunted the moral force of the Supreme Court decision. It had the same jarring impact as reminding us "how far you have come" when our privations were so many that our primary focus was on "how far we still have to go."

For all the affection and esteem Mrs. Roosevelt enjoyed among Negroes, she was unable to bridge this gap in perception and feeling. At best, Negroes looked upon the 1956 campaign as an uneasy alliance, and Stevenson could not recapture the high enthusiasm they had felt for his candidacy four years earlier. In spite of my own reservations, Lloyd K. Garrison persuaded me to work with him again that fall, along with Sylvia Ravitch and Frank Horne, to mobilize the Negro vote in New York City. It was a disheartening effort, the sparkle was gone, and days before the election we felt the gloom of Stevenson's impending defeat. When the returns were in, they showed not only that Stevenson had lost to Eisenhower by a wider margin than in 1952, but also that Negroes had defected in large numbers, their percentage of votes for Stevenson dropping from 79 percent to 61 percent. Negroes in southern cities, who voted overwhelmingly for Stevenson in 1952, rolled up substantial majorities for Eisenhower, and Stevenson lost strength in the black districts of urban centers in the North and West as well. His equivocation on civil rights, rather than aiding his cause, had increased the black vote for the Republican party for the first time in twenty years...

At another level, most Negroes remained in impoverished circumstances, isolated in ghettos and unable to take advantage of the substantial benefits to be gained from the new legislation. A massive, sustained national effort comparable to a domestic Marshall Plan was essential to removing the blight of centuries of oppression—an effort that necessarily entailed painful dislocations and sacrifices on the part of the dominant and heretofore privileged white population. Yet, once the anti-bias laws were passed, the growing indifference of white Americans to the continuing plight of Negroes walled into the decaying inner cities, mired in poverty and unemployment or in the most menial jobs, jobs that were fast disappearing under the impact of new technology, had turned the bright hopes of millions of black people into disillusionment and despair. For younger, impatient civil rights activists who threw themselves passionately into the movement for Freedom Now in the late 1950s and early 1960s, their efforts had seemed to bring only a harvest of bitterness. After all the jailings, the bombings, the burnings, the killings, the battered bodies and shattered careers, the supreme sacrifices of their youth, the dream was as distant as ever.

The earlier consensus, which had unified church groups, labor and liberal groups, and the major civil rights organizations around the goal of integration, was shattered in the mid-1960s, and interracial coalitions fell apart. Older leaders whose patient toil had made possible civil rights victories up to that time were being discredited and shunted aside by younger, embittered black nationalistic radicals. With the assassination of Martin Luther King, Jr., advocacy of the moral principle of nonviolent resistance to injustice coupled with the promise of racial reconciliation was quickly overtaken by the idea of black liberation by any means necessary and a mood of violent response to racial subjugation, real or imagined. Ghettos in the North and West exploded into the self-inflicted destructiveness of despair. President Johnson's National Advisory Commission on Disorders, appointed in 1967 to review the riots, reported: "This is our basic conclusion: Our nation is moving toward two societies, one black, one white, separate and unequal."

A new phase of the struggle emerged, variously called Black Power, Black Liberation, and, in its most extreme form, Revolutionary Black Nationalism, profoundly affecting the outlook of thousands upon thousands of people of color who embraced the new movement as a means of survival and self-respect. Emphasis shifted from interracial cooperation to self-determination and a strong identification with the rising African nations and other nonwhite third world peoples. "Black and white together, we shall overcome"—the song that had rallied the old civil rights movement—was discarded by many, who now shouted "Black is beautiful," "Black Consciousness," or "Black Nationhood."

A generation of Negro students, in their infancy when the historic 1954 desegregation decision was handed down by the Supreme Court and whose entire lives were shaped by continuous, overt racial strife, were now entering college, bringing with them a legacy of nearly two decades of unrelieved turbulence. Although fully aware of this unsettling trend, which confused and distorted earlier goals to which I had given my allegiance, I had not had to grapple with it in face-to-face, student-teacher relationships.

The convulsions of my own youth had been more universal, emphasizing the international solidarity of the working classes, the racial component of which had been a fire burning underground with only an occasional spurt of smoke and flame becoming visible. I had fortified my longing to belong with the words of great poets: Walt Whitman, who said, "We shall not convince them by our words, we shall convince them by our presence"; or that poignant line of Langston Hughes, "I, too, sing America"; or the heroic declaration of Claude McKay, the Caribbean poet who wrote in his "America":

> Although she feeds me bread of bitterness,
> And sinks into my throat her tiger's tooth,
> Stealing my breath of life, I will confess
> I love this cultured hell that tests my youth!
> Her vigor flows like tides into my blood,
> Giving me strength erect against her hate...

And there was Georgia Douglas Johnson's "Interracial," which ended: "Oh, let's build bridges everywhere/And span the gulf of challenge there."

Then, too, as a veteran of the earlier civil rights movement, I saw no contradiction between racial consciousness and the pursuit of excellence in making my way into the cultural mainstream of life in the United States. Being part of the mainstream had meant to me not the blind imitation of dominant values but a choice of those verities, handed down through centuries of human experience, that enriched the quality of life. Chief among these was the sacredness of the individual, who, in Biblical tradition, is created in the image of God, and from that vision followed my obligation to work with others to transform the planet Earth into a place where each individual would have an opportunity to fulfill his or her highest creative potential.

Cast in this mold, I found it grated upon my sensibilities to hear from young people—beneficiaries of the ongoing effort to create a more open society—that integration was "irrelevant to the problems of the masses of black people," that it was merely the "acceptance of a few token Negroes into white institutions on the white man's terms," resulting in "the loss of black identity and pride in blackness."

"Pride in blackness" ranged from adoption of African dress to flirtation with extreme black nationalism, accompanied by a strong tendency toward separatism and antiwhite feelings expressed in epithets like "Honkie" and "Whitey," and a generally uncivil manner toward white individuals. (Having lived in West Africa and been on the receiving end of arrogance directed at American Negroes, I thought much of this newfound cultural nationalism was misplaced.) For a time, I was living in a world turned upside down; in a complete reversal of goals that had fired my own student activism, some of the young militants were now demanding separate dormitories and cultural centers, from which whites were to be excluded, as well as Afro-American/Black Studies departments controlled by blacks, taught by black professors, and attended exclusively by black students.

As a teacher observing variations of this theme on a predominantly white campus, it seemed to me that such withdrawal into a self-imposed segregation was a symptom of a deep-seated fear of failure in an open, competitive society, a drawing back from the stringent demands of equality at a high academic level, a self-deception that would lead ultimately to isolation and abandonment to the mediocrity of a second-class citizenship which was now partially self-induced. Of the many crosses I had had to bear labeled "the race problem," this was to be the most painful during that ghastly period of readjustment.

Pauli Murray, *The Autobiography of a Black Activist, Feminist, Lawyer, Priest and Poet* (Knoxville: University of Tennessee Press, 1989); reprint of *Song in a Weary Throat* (New York: Harper, 1987), pp. 229–31, 306–310, 394–96.

4

ELLA BAKER IS INTERVIEWED

A decisive figure in the Civil Rights movement through the 1950s to the present has been Ella Baker. Ella Baker was pivotal in the creation and early functioning of the Southern Christian Leadership Conference (SCLC); she was a founder and participant in the Student Non-Violent Coordinating Committee (SNCC) and, in 1964, helped found the Mississippi Freedom Democratic party (MFDP). An interview with Gerda Lerner in December 1970 illuminates her self-effacing mode of work and its decisive character.

In my organizational work, I have never thought in terms of my "making a contribution." I just thought of myself as functioning where there was a need. And if I have made a contribution I think it may be that I had some influence on a large number of people.

As assistant field secretary of the branches of the NAACP, much of my work was in the South. At that time the NAACP was the leader on the cutting edge of social change. I remember when NAACP membership in the South was the basis for getting beaten up or even killed.

I used to leave New York about the 15th of February and travel through the South for four to five months. I would go to, say, Birmingham, Alabama and help to organize membership campaigns. And in the process of helping to organize membership campaigns, there was opportunity for developing community reaction. You would go into areas where people were not yet organized in the NAACP and try to get them more involved. Maybe you would start with some simple thing like the fact that they had no street lights, or the fact that in the given area somebody had been arrested or had been jailed in a manner that was considered illegal and unfair, and the like. You would deal with whatever the local problem was, and on the basis of the needs of the people you would try to organize them in the NAACP.

Black people who were living in the South were constantly living with violence. Part of the job was to help them to understand what that violence was and how they in an organized fashion could help to stem it. The major job was getting people to understand that they had something within their power that they could use, and it could only be used if they understood what was happening and how group action could counter violence even when it was perpetrated by the police or, in some instances, the state. My basic sense of it has always been to get people to understand that in the long run they themselves are the only protection they have against violence or injustice. If they only had ten members in the NAACP at a given point, those ten members could be in touch with twenty-five members in the next little town, with fifty in the next and throughout the state as a result of the organization of state conferences, and they, of course, could be linked up with the national. People have to be made to understand that they cannot look for salvation anywhere but to themselves.

I left the NAACP and then worked at fund-raising with the National Urban League Service Fund and with several national health organizations. However, I continued my work with the NAACP on the local level. I became the advisor for the Youth Council. Then I served as President of the New York branch at a point where it had sunk to a low level in membership and otherwise. And in the process of serving as President we tried to bring the NAACP back, as I called it, to the people. We moved the branch out of an office building and located it where it would be more visible to the Harlem community. We started developing an active branch. It became one of the largest branches. I was President for a couple of years. It was strictly volunteer work which lasted until four o'clock in the morning, sometimes.

When the 1954 Supreme Court decision on school desegregation came, I was serving as chairman of the Educational Committee of the New York branch. We began to deal with the problems of *de facto* segregation, and the results of the *de facto* segregation which were evidenced largely in the achievement levels of black children, going down instead of going up after they entered public school. We had called the first committee meeting and Kenneth Clark became the chairman of that committee. During that period, I served on the Mayor's Commission on School Integration, with the subdivision on zoning. In the summer of 1957, I gave time to organizing what we called Parents in Action for Quality Education.

I've never believed that the people who control things really were willing and able to pay the price of integration. From a practical standpoint, anyone who looked at the Harlem area knew that the potential for integration *per se* was basically impossible unless there were some radically innovative things done. And those innovative things would not be acceptable to those who ran the school system, nor to communities, nor even to the people who call themselves supporters of integration. I did a good deal of speaking, and I went to Queens, I went to the upper West side, and the people very eagerly said they wanted school integration. But when you raised the question of whether they would permit or would welcome Blacks to live in the same houses with them, which was the only practical way at that stage to achieve integration, they squirmed. Integration certainly had to be pushed concurrently with changing the quality of education that the black children were getting, and changing the attitudes of the educational establishment toward the black community.

I don't think we achieved too much with the committee except to pinpoint certain issues and to have survived some very sharp confrontations with the Superintendent and others on the Board of Education. But out of it came increased fervor on the part of the black communities to make some changes. One of the gratifying things to me is the fact that even as late as this year I have met people who were in that group and who have been continuously active in the struggle for quality education in the black communities ever since.

There certainly has been progress in the direction of the capacity of people to face this issue. And to me, when people themselves know what they are looking for and recognize that they can exercise some influence by action, that's progress.

Come 1957, I went down South a couple of times in connection with the formation of the Southern Christian Leadership Conference. At the end of '57 there was the need for someone to go down to set up the office of SCLC in Atlanta and to coordinate what it considered its first South-wide project, which was the holding of simultaneous meetings on February 12th in twenty different cities. I went down with the idea of not spending more than six weeks there, giving myself a month to get the thing going, and then two weeks to clean it up. I stayed with SCLC for two and a half years, because they didn't have anybody. My official capacity was varied. When I first went down, I didn't insist on a title, which is nothing new or unusual for me; it didn't bother me. I was just there in person. And then they were looking for a minister, a man, and I helped to find a minister and a man, and he stayed a while, and when he came I decided that since I was doing what I was doing, he was the director and I became, I think, co-director. And then there was nobody, and of course there was no money in those days, so I kept on until the summer of 1960. And prior to that, of course, the sit-ins had started, and I was able to get the SCLC to at least sponsor the conference in Raleigh. We had hoped to call together about 100 or 125 of the young leaders who had emerged in the sit-ins in the South. But of course the sit-ins had been so dynamic in the field that when we got to the meeting we had two hundred and some people, including some from the North. And out of that conference of the Easter weekend of 1960, which I coordinated and organized, we had a committee that came out of it, and out of that committee SNCC was born.

And after SNCC came into existence, of course, it opened up a new era of struggle. I felt the urge to stay close by. Because if I had done anything anywhere, it had been largely in the role of supporting things, and in the background of things that needed to be done for the organizations that were supposedly out front. So I felt if I had done it for the elders, I could do it for young people.

I had no difficulty relating to the young people. I spoke their language in terms of the meaning of what they had to say. I didn't change my speech pattern and they didn't have to change their speech pattern. But we were able to communicate.

I never had any income or paid relationship with SNCC. In order to be available to do things with SNCC, I first found a two-year project with the Southern Region of the National Student YWCA in a special Human Relations Program. Then I took up a relationship with the Southern Conference Educational Fund (SCEF). I still am on their staff in a consultative role, and I stayed in Atlanta until the summer of '64, spring and summer of '64. I was asked to come up and help organize the challenge of the Mississippi Freedom Democratic Party at the Democratic Convention. So offices were set up in Washington and I functioned there until after the convention, closed up the office, and then moved back to New York from Atlanta.

There are those, some of the young people especially, who have said to me that if I had not been a woman I would have been well known in certain places, and perhaps held certain kinds of positions.

I have always felt it was a handicap for oppressed peoples to depend so largely upon a leader, because unfortunately in our culture, the charismatic leader usually becomes a leader because he has found a spot in the public limelight. It usually means he has been touted through the public media, which means that the media made him, and the media may undo him. There is also the danger in our culture that, because a person is called upon to give public statements and is acclaimed by the establishment, such a person gets to the point of believing that he *is* the movement. Such people get so involved with playing the game of being important that they exhaust themselves and their time, and they don't do the work of actually organizing people.

For myself, circumstances frequently dictated what had to be done as I saw it. For example, I had no plans to go down and set up the office of SCLC. But it seemed unless something were done whatever impetus had been gained would be lost, and nobody else was available who was willing or able to do it. So I went because to me it was more important to see what was a potential for all of us than it was to do what I might have done for myself. I knew from the beginning that as a woman, an older woman, in a group of ministers who are accustomed to having women largely as supporters, there was no place for me to have come into a leadership role. The competition wasn't worth it.

The movement of the '50's and '60's was carried largely by women, since it came out of church groups. It was sort of second nature to women to play a supportive role. How many made a conscious decision on the basis of the larger goals, how many on the basis of habit pattern, I don't know. But it's true that the number of women who carried the movement is much larger than that of men. Black women have had to carry this role, and I think the younger women are insisting on an equal footing.

I don't advocate anybody following the pattern I followed, unless they find themselves in a situation where they think that the larger goals will be shortchanged if they don't. From the standpoint of the historical pattern of the society, which seems to assume that this is the best role for women, I think that certainly the young people who are challenging this ought to be challenging it, and it ought to be changed. But I also think you have to have a certain sense of your own value, and a sense of security on your part, to be able to forgo the glamor of what the leadership role offers. From the standpoint of my work and my own self-concepts, I don't think I have thought of myself largely as a woman. I thought of myself as an individual with a certain amount of sense of the need of people to participate in the movement. I have always thought what is needed is the development of people who are interested not in being leaders as much as in developing leadership among other people. Every time I see a young person who has come through the system to a stage where he could profit from the system and identify with it, but who identifies more with the struggle of black people who have not had his chance, every time I find such a person I take new hope. I feel a new life as a result of it.

Gerda Lerner, ed., *Black Women in White America* (New York: Pantheon, 1972), pp. 346–52.

5

WE CHARGE GENOCIDE (1945)

by William L. Patterson

On December 1, 1951, William L. Patterson, executive director of the Civil Rights Congress, presented to the UN Secretariat in Paris, a 225-page printed petition entitled *We Charge Genocide*. He left copies with Trygve Lie, general secretary of the United Nations and Luis Padillo Nervo, chairman of its General Assembly. He tried to leave a copy at the offices of the U.S. delegation, but Mrs. Eleanor Roosevelt refused to see him. A copy, therefore, was left with her secretary.

The petition was widely discussed in the African-American press and in European newspapers; Patterson also spoke on the French radio system. But the petition was ignored in the United States by the dominant media of communication.

Under the UN definition, not only systematized killing of members of a defined population was labeled genocide; the concept included systematized deprivation and insult and brutalization of a given population.

The genocide petition was signed by almost one hundred U.S. citizens, including Mary Church Terrell, Stetson Kennedy, Paul Robeson, and Howard Fast.

Important in the staff producing the petition, under Patterson's direction, were Richard O. Boyer, Oakley C. Johnson, Yvonne Gregory, and Elizabeth Lawson. Article II(a), "Killing Members of a Group," follows, in full.

It cannot be emphasized too often that those killings of members of the group which are recorded are a distinct minority of those actually killed. This is historically true. Thus former Confederate General Reynolds, of Texas, testifying before the Congressional Joint Committee on Insurrectionary Affairs, said during Reconstruction, "The murder of Negroes is so common as to render it impossible to keep accurate account of them." And as recently as 1940, a Congressional report quotes, "a native Southerner who must remain anonymous" to the effect that "countless Negroes are lynched yearly, but their disappearance is shrouded in mystery, for they are dispatched quietly and without general knowledge."

We call attention to the number of cases in which the Government of the United States of America is directly involved, such as the slayings of Willie McGee, Edward Honeycutt and the Martinsville Seven, when the Supreme Court of the United States refused to permit them life despite its legal power and duty to do so under the Fourteenth Amendment guaranteeing the due process of law and equality before the law which those executed never in fact received.

We emphasize, too, the several cases enumerated below in which the Department of Justice, of the executive branch of the Federal Government, was asked to intervene under the Fourteenth and Fifteenth Amendments but refused. If these two amendments were enforced, few of the slayings on the basis of race listed below would have occurred.

We call attention, too, to the spreading pattern of murder and violence in the North as well as the South, similarly protected and participated in by police officials.

1945

June 6.—DENICE HARRIS, 22-year old war veteran, was shot to death in *Atlanta, Georgia,* by police and a civilian as he drove a white man to meet a white woman at a rendezvous the pair had made by telephone. The telephone conversation was overheard by the woman's husband. Harris was killed by bullets from a police pistol. He had driven the car at the request of the white man. The Fulton County coroner's jury called the killing a "justifiable homicide."

August 15.—LILA BELLA CARTER, 16 years old, was raped and murdered at *Pine Island, South Carolina*, under circumstances which pointed suspiciously to a white insurance agent. When the young woman's father went to authorities to demand an investigation, he was jailed. Miss Carter's neck and jaw were broken and she had been placed face down in a pool of water in order to give the impression that she had met her death by drowning. No action was taken against the alleged rapist.

August 21.—ERVIN JONES was fatally wounded in his home in *Portland, Oregon*, when three police officers came to the house to search the premises. They had no warrant and failed to identify themselves as officers. The Jones family believed them to be burglars. Jones defended his home against their entry. One of the officers went to the rear of the house, entered, and shot Jones in the back with a sawed-off shot gun, killing him. The coroner's jury exonerated the police and a grand jury subsequently refused to indict them.

September 9.—MOSES GREEN, veteran of World War I, was shot to death by two Aiken County law officers near *Elenton, South Carolina*. The Officers were deputy sheriffs who were identified. Green was returning from town in his truck and as he stepped out into his own yard he was shot without warning.

October 10.—JESSE PAYNE was taken from the jail at *Madison, Florida*, and shot to death by a lynch mob. Payne had been removed from the lynch-proof state prison and taken to an unguarded one-story shack jail at Madison and left there unguarded. On the date of his arrest, July 4, he was attacked and wounded by a posse. Attorney General J. Tom Watson of Florida recommended the suspension of the sheriff in charge of the jail, stating that the evidence indicated that the jail had not been broken into but that Payne had been delivered up to the lynchers by law officers. Nevertheless, the two Madison County grand juries refused to indict the sheriff and Governor Millard Caldwell refused to suspend him.

October 29.—Police emptied their guns into an unidentified Negro man at 8th Avenue and 144th Street, in *New York City*. Eyewitnesses stated that the man, with his hands raised in surrender after having been pursued by a police patrol car, was alighting from a Buick sedan when he was shot. When a crowd gathered to protest, police reinforcements arrived and clubbed the protesters. Several witnesses went to Harlem Hospital where the man lay bleeding. This and subsequent delegations were unable to find out the man's name.

October 29.—The body of SAM MCFADDEN, veteran, was found floating in the Suwanee River, near *Live Oak, Florida*. Governor Millard Caldwell's own investigator and twenty witnesses gave evidence that McFadden had been lynched. Evidence was also given that the Brandford, Fla., police chief, a wealthy turpentine operator reputed to use peon labor, and another man were the lynchers. According to the evidence, McFadden, who had left his home to buy groceries, was put into a car and driven in the direction of the river. His body was discovered by two fishermen, and the date of the lynching was fixed by the authorities as approximately September 21. The Suwanee grand jury refused to indict any of the three. Later, the ex-marshal of Brandford was tried for allegedly subjecting McFadden, who was 60 years old, to a "trial by ordeal" and then forcing him to drown himself. He was charged with arresting McFadden, beating him with a whip and pistol and making him jump in the river. The ex-marshal was convicted, sentenced to one year in prison and a $1,000 fine.

November.—Seventy-year-old MRS. NICEY BROWN of *Selma, Alabama,* was beaten to death by a drunken policeman who was off duty. He beat her over the head with a bottle. The officer was acquitted in November, 1945, by an all-white jury which deliberated a few minutes. The attorney for the policeman stated at the trial: "If we convict this brave man who is upholding the banner of white supremacy by his actions, then we may as well give all our guns to the n——s and let them run the black belt."

November.—A new trial which had been ordered by the U.S. Supreme Court freed a Baker County, Ga., sheriff and two former white police officers for the death by beating of ROBERT HALL in October, 1943. Hall had been arrested at his home near *Newton, Georgia,* on January 29, 1943. The next day the sheriff and two other whites beat him about the head with a blackjack until he fell unconscious. His death occurred soon afterwards.

November 1.—Fourteen-year-old WILBERT COHEN was killed when two bullets from a policeman's gun were fired at him as he was leaving a friend's house. No action was taken against the policeman either by the grand jury or by the police department.

November 17.—ST. CLAIRE PRESSLEY, war veteran, was killed in *Johnsonville, South Carolina.* As he stepped off the train in Johnsonville on his way to Hemingway, S.C., Pressley was arrested on suspicion of implication in a minor disturbance which had occurred several days before. Pressley offered no resistance to arrest, but as he was being marched down the street, the policeman suddenly pulled the trigger of his gun and killed the Negro veteran.

December.—Charges were made that PVT. ERIC L. BOLTON of *Chicago* died en route to France of an inter-cerebral hemorrhage "possibly caused by his head being rammed against a cement wall." The words are those of Capt. Earl J. Carroll of San Francisco. General Eisenhower ordered an investigation into the death.

December.—PHINIZEE SUMMEROUR was shot and killed by a white man on an *Atlanta, Georgia,* bus, following an argument over smoking. A grand jury in December, 1945, freed the white man.

December.—Two persons were killed when a reign of terror swept over the Negro community of *Union Springs, Alabama.* A third Negro was wounded and a fourth was hounded out of town. The white policeman who was the murderer was known. EDGAR THOMAS was murdered when the white policeman heard him discuss the Negro question with a friend in Thomas' own store. JESSE HIGHTOWER was also murdered. ED DAY GARY, a veteran, had one eye shot out.

REV. J. L. PINCKNEY was ordered to leave town because he had been a witness to Thomas' murder.

December 16.—WALTER CAMPBELL, union organizer of the Food, Tobacco, Agricultural and Allied Workers of America, CIO, was stabbed to death at *Little Rock, Arkansas.* He was organizing workers, particularly Negroes, against a 12 hour working day and 50¢ per hour pay. The confessed slayer was set free.

December 23.—MR. AND MRS. H. O'DAY SHORT and their two small daughters were burned to death two days before Christmas, 1945, in a fire of incendiary origin set by persons who did not want them to move into a "white neighborhood" in *Fontana, California.* The family had received threatening notes and the police had told the family they were "out of bounds." There was no electricity in the Short's home and neighbors knew that the family was temporarily using lamps. While the Shorts were away, people broke into their home, sprayed the interior with an inflammable chemical, and left. When the Shorts returned, the father struck a match, and the lamp fuel, believed to be kerosene, exploded. All four were fatally burned.

1946

February.—FRANK ALLEN, taxi driver, was killed by police of *Memphis, Tennessee.* A field report of the American Council on Race Relations characterized the killing as "suspicious." The two white officers said that Allen shot at them. However, another version stated that Allen was unarmed; that the officers dragged Allen from his cab and shot him in a vacant lot.

February.—JAMES MANGUM, 17 years old, was sentenced to death for alleged "rape." He charged that his "confession" had been forced from him by brutality. Nevertheless, the U.S. Supreme Court twice denied his appeals, and the state parole board refused to pardon him or commute his sentence.

February 5.—A policeman of *Freeport, L.I., New York,* shot and killed PFC. CHARLES FERGUSON and his brother, ALFONSO FERGUSON. A third brother, SEAMAN THIRD CLASS JOSEPH FERGUSON was wounded in the shoulder and thrown into the brig, while a fourth brother, RICHARD FERGUSON was arrested and sentenced to 100 days in jail. The brothers had protested jim crow at a local cafe, where the proprietor had refused them service because they were Negroes. After the killings, Freeport police threw a cordon around the bus terminal and stationed men with tommyguns and tear gas there, saying that they wanted to "prevent a possible uprising of local Negroes." Investigation proved that none of the brothers was armed, and that they were peaceably on their way from the cafe to the bus station when they were attacked by the policeman. Witnesses, including two white women, made affidavits that the brothers were not disorderly. The killer-policeman was exonerated by the Chief of Police and by the Nassau Grand Jury. An investigation ordered by Governor Dewey after five months of organized protest, whitewashed the police, the grand jury which refused to indict the policeman, and the District Attorney of

Nassau County. The investigation also denied the lawyer for the slain brothers' families the right to cross-examination and the right to put specific questions to witnesses.

February 9.—Pvt. NATHANIEL JACKSON was shot to death by a guard with a tommygun at the U.S. Disciplinary Barracks at *Granville, Wisconsin,* after a group of prisoners complained that meat had been omitted from their lunch. Two other Negroes not named in newspaper accounts, were injured in the ensuing attack by guards.

February 11.—Accused of a robbery and murder that had occurred on February 11, 1946, EDWARD PATTON was sentenced to die by the criminal court of *Lauderdale County, Mississippi.* Attorneys for Patton showed that his "confession" had been forced from him, he had been grilled for three consecutive days, and had been twice taken to the woods to be shown the scene of the crime. The U.S. Supreme Court set aside the decision but Patton was again convicted at *Meridian, Mississippi,* in Sept., 1948.

February 17.—TIMOTHY HOOD, veteran, was shot to death in *Bessemer, Alabama,* by a police chief. Previously, a street car conductor had fired five shots into Hood's body because Hood had attempted to pull down a jim crow sign. Hearing that Hood was in a nearby house, wounded, the police chief entered the home and fired into Hood's brain. The Bessemer coroner called the acts "justifiable homicide."

February 25.—Five hundred National Guardsmen swarmed into the Negro section of *Columbia, Tennessee,* firing riot guns and other firearms. Police opened up with machine guns on the Negroes barricaded in their homes. Every Negro business establishment in the two black business areas was completely wrecked.

The terror against the Negro community (Mink Slide) began officially the day before when MRS. GLADYS STEPHENSON and her son JAMES, a veteran, had an argument with a radio repair man. The repair man kicked and slapped Mrs. Stephenson and tore the sleeves out of her coat. Her son, James Stephenson, came to her defense and was arrested immediately and beaten by the police. As a lynch mob formed on Court Square, friends spirited James Stephenson and his mother out of the state and the Negro community prepared to defend itself from attack and prevent any lynchings from occurring. A large number of Negroes were arrested and jailed.

WILLIAM GORDON and JAMES JOHNSON were shot and killed on February 28 by police while they were being held in jail. Napoleon Stewart was also shot and wounded while in jail. The three were shot by five policemen at three-yard range. Gordon and Johnson might have been saved after the shooting had they been taken at once to the City Hospital. But this hospital was for "whites only" and they were driven over rough roads 43 miles to Nashville instead.

JOHN BLACKWELL was nearly killed by police beatings. An all-white Maury County Grand Jury began to hand down indictments against members of the Negro community on March 23. Subsequent legal events took place over a period of many months.

The trial itself was characterized by Vincent Sheean, special writer for the

New York Herald Tribune, as a "travesty of justice." It was proved by the defense that the Negroes in the area had good reason to fear a lynching since the area had a record of many. It was further proved by the defense that James Stephenson had been removed from the jail and sent out of the state only a short time before a lynch mob collected at the jail demanding his life; that the mob gathered at Court Square spoke openly of lynch plans. The defense also presented more than 200 witnesses, Negro and white, to prove that Negroes are systematically excluded from the grand and petit juries of that county. The trial judge refused to eliminate prospective jurors who admitted past or present membership of the Klan; those who said they approved of the Klan's activities, or those who said they would give less credence to a Negro than to a white witness.

February 25.—KENNY LONG, veteran, was shot to death by a highway patrolman in *El Campo, Texas.* Together with his brother, MERON LONG, also a veteran, and a cousin, COSBY CLAY. Kenny Long was at a filling station drinking soda pop. A white lounger began to order Clay about, then called a police car. A deputy sheriff in the car stated: "Don't you know I hate a goddam n——r?" The three white officers began slapping and punching the three Negroes, and one of them shot Kenny Long dead. Meron Long and Cosby Clay were handcuffed, beaten and arrested.

March 12.—JAMES LEWIS, 14, and CHARLES TRUDELL, 15, condemned to death at *Meadville, Mississippi.* They were charged with a pistol slaying, and indicted, tried and convicted—all in one day. The case was appealed to the Mississippi Supreme Court, which overruled a suggestion of error in the trial. They were refused a pardon by Governor Fielding Wright, and were executed.

Spring.—A Veteran's Justice Committee met April 9, 1946, to press an investigation into the killing of two members of the 1310th Engineer Regiment on May 22, 1945 in Camp Lucky Strike, St. Valerie, France. The two were PFC. ALLEN LEFTRIDGE and T/5 FRANK GLENN. They were shot dead while unarmed by two white guards posted at a Red Cross tent with orders to keep Negroes from talking to French girls employed there. Court-martial proceedings had absolved the killers. At a subsequent hearing before the Veteran's Administration, Alfred A. Duckett, formerly of the 1310th cavalry, testified that there had been prejudice against Negro soldiers at the camp. He also stated that a French civilian employee on the post had told him that the guards had orders to prevent Negro GIs from talking with French women.

April.—GEORGE COLLINS, a Negro shore patrolman, was killed early in April, 1946 at the Navy Marine base at *McAlester, Oklahoma,* by a local police officer. Collins had been stationed at the naval ammunition depot. Negroes in the community stated that Collins' death was the third such incident since the establishment of the Navy Marine Base a few years previously. They declared that the city police carried on a veritable reign of terror against the Negro shore patrolmen; that on numerous occasions they swooped down on the Negro section, making searches and seizures without warrants.

May 1.—At a secret meeting of the Ku Klux Klan's Klavalier Klub whipping squad held at the klavern No. I, 198½ Whitehall Street, *Atlanta, Georgia,*

"Chief Ass-Tearer" Cliff Vittur warned the Klavaliers to be more careful, criticizing them for using the cab of a Negro cab driver they had killed a short time before, and for not wiping their fingerprints from the steering wheel. Had he not called a "brother Klansman" on the police force to wipe the wheel, the Klavaliers involved would be in "hot water," Vittur said. Atlanta newspapers the day following the lynching reported merely that the body of a Negro man had been found on Pryor Road, "apparently the victim of an auto accident." Inside reports on this Klavalier meeting were turned over to the Georgia Department of Law and the Federal Bureau of Investigation by Stetson Kennedy, of the Georgia Bureau of Investigation, but no prosecution was forthcoming.

May 18.—WILLIAM ARTHUR was killed in *Baltimore, Maryland,* while allegedly resisting arrest by police officers. The following day, May 19, WILBUR BUNDLEY was killed by an officer. Nine witnesses stated that he was shot in the back while running. A few days later, ISAAC JACKSON was shot and killed by a policeman. A number of organizations began a protest against consistent police brutality in Baltimore.

June.—ELLIOTT BROOKS of *Gretna, Louisiana,* was killed by the Gretna chief of police because he "knew too much" concerning the disappearance of another Negro who was a prisoner, according to affidavits filed with the Gretna branch of the NAACP.

July.—SUTTER MATTHEWS was killed in *Moultrie, Georgia* some time in July, 1946, according to a county coroner's report made on July 31, 1946. The killers had laid the corpse across the tracks of the Georgia Northern Railroad, but Matthews was already dead, killed with a blunt instrument.

July 17.—PVT. SAMUEL HICKS was discovered dying of a fractured skull on a road near Geiger Army Field near *Spokane, Washington.* A white soldier stated that he had seen Hicks slugged by two whites and left on the road. There had been feeling against Negro soldiers at the field for some time. When Hicks' death was discovered on July 17, 1946, Negroes started a search for the killers. Then a force of white MPs, armed with guns, clubs, and tear gas, invaded the area. One MP carefully aimed and fired at a fleeing Negro soldier. Two tear gas bombs were tossed into the Negro soldiers' quarters.

July 20.—One of the comparatively few Negroes who voted in the 1946 *Georgia* elections was a veteran, MACIO SNIPES. Snipes voted in Rupert's district of Taylor County. On July 20, 1946 he was dragged from his home and killed by four white men. He died of pistol wounds. The killers were freed. The killing of Snipes was one of the first fruits of the election compaign waged by Eugene Talmadge. Talmadge had warned Negroes to keep away from the polls. One of the methods used to intimidate the Negro community was the posting of signs on Negro churches which read: "The first Negro to vote will never vote again."

July 24.—The body of Leon McTatie was found in a Sunflower County bayou near *Lexington, Mississippi.* The condition of the body showed that McTatie had been lynched. Six white men were charged with whipping him to death for stealing a saddle. They were acquitted by a jury after ten minutes deliberation.

July 25.—MR. AND MRS. ROGER MALCOLM AND MR. AND MRS. GEORGE DORSEY were lynched near *Monroe, Georgia.* Dorsey was a World II veteran. A group of 20 to 30 white men beat the two women, then lined the four against trees and shot them dead with a sixty-shot broadside from rifles, pistols and shotguns. Roger Malcolm, a sharecropper, had quarreled with his landlord about the disposition of the crop. Malcolm had also objected to advances made to his wife by a member of the landlord's family. After the quarrel, a lynch mob gathered on July 14. It dispersed, but gathered again on July 25. Eugene Talmadge, white supremacy candidate for governor of Georgia made an official visit to the landlord's family. The Federal Government investigated, but took no action against anyone. Walter White, secretary of the NAACP, revealed on August 6, 1946, that Atty. Gen. Tom Clark had the names of the six men charged with the lynching in his possession. On October 28, 1946, Clark told the *Herald Tribune* forum in regard to the Monroe lynchings that "the jurisdiction of the federal government depends upon a thin thread of law. The Federal statutes give me the power to prosecute only when a person has been deprived of a federally secured right. The right of life, liberty and property, the Supreme Court has repeatedly held, is not a federally secured right." The federal jury reported in December that it was unable to find anyone "guilty of violating the civil rights statute."

July 29.—HARRISON JOHNSON, sharecropper, was shot to death near *Eatonton, Georgia.* His body was perforated with six revolver bullets and he was beaten with a gun butt. The slaying took place on the highway and the killer was given his freedom at once by the sheriff.

August.—JAMES WALKER was shot dead by a hail of bullets as he sat on his father's porch at *Elko, South Carolina.* The shots were fired by a white filling station owner and his brother who had quarrelled with Walker.

August 3.—JOHN J. GILBERT, chalk mill worker, was found shot to death by the roadside near his home at *Gordon, Georgia.* Investigation showed that he had been active in the work of union organization and was killed on his way to work by whites who hated unions.

August 3.—BUDDY WOLF was murdered by a deputy sheriff in *Hattiesburg, Mississippi.*

August 3.—While his mother stood 100 yards away, J.C. FARMER, a veteran, was shot dead near *Bailey, North Carolina,* by a posse of twenty to twenty-five men who swooped down on him in eight cars. Farmer had been waiting for a bus when he was attacked by a policeman, and a scuffle started. Farmer was lynched one hour later.

August 8.—JOHN C. JONES, a veteran, was lynched on August 8, 1946, near *Minden, Louisiana,* shortly after his release from jail when a charge against him collapsed. On August 15 his lash-welted body was found in a lake two miles from Minden, indicating the floggers had operated on Jones before he was dumped in the lake. The deputy coroner reported "multiple bruises and contusions apparently made by a wide leather belt or a thick strap." At the same time and in the same place, ALBERT HARRIS, JR., 17 years old, was shot at by the lynchers. He feigned death until they had quit the scene and then he fled the state. Young Harris' father, ALBERT HARRIS, SR., was beaten by Minden mobsters in an attempt to force him to tell of his son's whereabouts. Investigation showed that when Jones returned from the army, he began suit to recover the rights to oil-producing land owned by his grandfather and leased to an oil syndicate. The land was producing thousands of barrels of oil per month for which Jones' family received less than $1 monthly. In February 1947, six white men including the Minden chief of police were identified as Jones' lynchers by Albert Harris, Jr. Two of the six, deputy sheriffs, went on trial in Shreveport before a federal jury. Young Harris told the jury how he saw the lynchers beat and burn Jones with a blow torch. He saw Jones' wrists chopped off with a cleaver; he saw Jones' eyes pop out of his head from the white-hot flame of the torch. Young Harris also told how he and Jones had been released from the Minden jail into the arms of a waiting mob. Both Harris, Jr. and Harris, Sr. had to be closely guarded by a number of U.S. marshals during the trip to Shreveport and during the trial, because of KKK violence let loose in the area. All of the accused lynchers were freed.

September 27.—WALTER LEE JOHNSON, a veteran, was fatally wounded in *Atlanta, Georgia,* by a street car motorman. Johnson was standing on an Atlanta street when the street car drew to a stop. Johnson recognized one of the passengers inside and called out to him jokingly. The motorman thought the joke was meant for him, he left the car, stepped to the sidewalk, and shot Johnson dead. The motorman was freed.

October.—BERRY BRANCH, elderly Negro citizen of *Houston, Texas,* was killed by a bus driver.

November 1.—JOSE ADRANO TRUJILLO SEIJAS, a veteran, and the adopted son of the brother of President Rafael Trujillo of the Dominican Republic, was shot to death by a deputy sheriff in *Bunnell, Florida.* Young Seijas had protested Jim Crow practices in a local cafe. The deputy sheriff had been called to the cafe by phone. He went up to Seijas who was seated in his own car outside the cafe and shot him through the chest.

November 2.—CHARLES W. SCOTT died in the prison infirmary in *Washington, D.C.* Injured in the crash of an allegedly stolen car, Scott was taken to the hospital where he received twenty minutes of treatment. When he appeared in court, the judge ordered that he be returned to the hospital as he was too ill to remain in court. He was brought back to court on that same day, but the judge again ordered him taken away for treatment. He died within twenty-four hours. The National Negro Congress and other organizations demanded a full investigation of why Scott had not been kept in the hospital and whether Scott was beaten in jail after a policeman involved in the crash had died.

November 15.—A seventy-five-man sheriff's posse hunted down and killed GEORGE HILL, a sharecropper, at *Toomsboro, Georgia.*

December.—WILLIAM DANIELS, a veteran, was shot to death in *Westfield, Alabama,* a small mining town outside Birmingham. It was near Christmas and Daniels was doing some shopping in the Tennessee Coal, Iron and Railroad commissary store. A white woman employee complained that Daniels had jostled her. In response to her complaint, a guard called Daniels outside the store and shot him dead.

December.—Nine white farmers charged with the lynching of JAMES EDWARD PERSON in *Danville, Illinois,* in October, 1942, entered a plea of *nolo contendere* and were ordered to pay a fine of $200 each and court costs.

1947

February 17.—WILLIE EARLE was removed from the county jail at *Pickens, South Carolina,* by an armed mob and lynched between Pickens and Greenville, South Carolina. Earle was being held in jail on a charge of robbing and wounding a Greenville cab driver. The mob had received Earle from the hands of the jailer and when the lynching was over, they dumped his knife-ripped, shot-sieved body near a rural slaughterhouse. The head was gaping with shotgun wounds on both sides and the torso had been mutilated by knives. A telephone call to the Greenville mortuary told where Earle's remains could be found. Thirty-one white men, twenty-nine of them taxi drivers, were arrested, and full confessions obtained from twenty-six. At the trial in Greenville, most of the members of the lynch party admitted their share in the deed. They said they had gone to Pickens in eight or nine cabs and abducted Earle, that en route to the lynching several of them had beaten Earle in the car. He was then knifed five times and blasted to death with a shotgun. All the mob was freed, although twenty-six signed confessions describing their plan to do the deed and its actual commission.

May.—*Sardis, Georgia.* JOE NATHAN ROBERTS, 23-year-old veteran, was shot to death when he failed to say "yes sir" to a white man. A student at Temple University in Philadelphia on the G.I. Bill of Rights, Roberts was visiting relatives. No one was tried for the killing.

May.—HENRY GILBERT was beaten to death in the county jail near *La Grange, Georgia.* No one was tried.

May 4.—*Camp Hill, Alabama.* MRS. MAY NOYES, 22-year-old pregnant mother of three children was shot to death by Albert Huey. Mrs. Noyes was only one victim of Huey's one-man reign of terror in the Negro community after he had an argument with a Negro veteran, AUSTRALIA FARROW. Huey shot up the Negro community, beat and slapped several Negro men and women, and when Mrs. Noyes ran away from him, he shot her in the hip. She slumped to the street and Huey kicked her, shouting "get up." She got up and as she began to run, Huey shot her again in the back. She crawled on to the porch of a white woman, Mrs. Emory Reeves, and died there. Huey was arrested, but was later released on $1000 bail and no charges were ever placed against him. Instead Farrow was charged with attempted murder and the testimony of Huey was used to jail and frame him.

May 5.—The United States Supreme Court denied the appeal of the two Negro children, JAMES LEWIS, JR., 14, and CHARLES TRUDELL, 15, of *Natchez, Mississippi.* The boys had been convicted of killing a white farmer in 1946. They were electrocuted after the denial by the Supreme Court.

May 9.—Eighteen-year-old WILLIE FRANCIS of *St. Martinsville, Louisiana,* went to the electric chair for the second time. The first attempt at his execution had been on May 3, 1946 but the electric switch had failed to operate. Many organizations tried to save him on the ground that a second attempt at electrocution would be "cruel and inhuman treatment." No court would grant the plea and Francis died in the chair.

May 24.—ERNEST GILBERT, 68-year-old farmer, was shot to death at his home in *Gretna, Virginia.* Three unmasked white men entered Gilbert's home and demanded the right to look into his safe. When he refused permission, they attacked him. When he defended himself, they riddled him with bullets, killing him with five pistol wounds.

May 27.—The body of WILLIAM PITTMAN, taxi driver, was found, horribly mutilated on the side of a country road near *Rocky Mount, North Carolina.* He had been dead for some time. The story was hushed up, but a report was given to officials of the National Negro Congress on May 27, 1947. Pittman was believed to have been the victim of lynchers. His head was bashed in, the legs and arms were severed and the body split open. His taxi was discovered in the nearby woods.

June 7.—WILLIE G. ANDREWS was shot and killed in *Warrenton, North Carolina,* by Police Chief Will Carter of Norlina, who claimed Andrews tried to seize his gun.

June 30.—*Louisiana.* WESLEY THOMAS, 31, Negro woodchopper, was shot in the back and killed by W. D. Thompson, 21-year-old white. Thomas had engaged in an argument that morning with a white farmer for whom he worked and from whom he was asking back pay. A posse was looking for him when Thompson found him and shot him as he was running toward his house. "He tried to run into the house and I let him have it," Thompson said. He was exonerated on the grounds that there were weapons in the house towards which Thomas was running.

July.—ELIJAH MYLES, 21, was shot in the back by Ferdinand J. Mohr, foreman of the *Orleans Parish, Louisiana,* Agricultural Dump. Dr. George Fasting, pathologist at the Charity Hospital of New Orleans declared the fatal bullet had entered Myles' back though Mohr claimed the dead man threatened him. In spite of this evidence, a no-true bill was returned in the case.

July 11.—Eight Negro prisoners in the Anguilla Stockade, *Brunswick, Georgia,* were mowed down by pistol and rifle fire. The men were part of a group of twenty-seven that had refused to work in a snake-infested swamp land without boots. Back at the camp Warden W. G. Worthy became enraged with the men, opened fire and was joined in the massacre by four other guards. Two other Negroes were wounded.

July 17.—WILLIAM BROWN, 83, was slain by Charles Ventril, game warden of *Point Coupee Parish, Louisiana.* Brown was hunting at the time, as was his daily custom for many years. Ventril, white game warden, came along and engaged Brown in an argument concerning the contents of his hunting bag, took him to the edge of the woods, and shot him in the back of the head. The warden is alleged to have walked to a nearby white sharecropper and told him, "I just shot a nigger. Let his folks know." This slaying was uncovered by a white labor union official. According to him the official coroner's report stated: "The Negro's gun was cocked; the killing was justifiable because the warden shot in self-defense."

August.—VERSIE JOHNSON, 35-year-old saw mill worker of *Prentiss, Mississippi,* was shot to death by a posse after he had been accused of raping a white woman. Three white law officers were arrested and charged with manslaughter. They were exonerated.

August 11.—JAMES WALKER, JR. was shot by a white man, Bill Craig, after an altercation with a group of Craig's friends. Craig was later exonerated by a Coroner's jury, which ruled justifiable homicide.

October 12.—BEVERLY LEE, 13-year-old youth, was shot by Policeman Louis Begin of *Detroit, Michigan.* Mrs. Francis Vonbatten of 1839 Pine testified that she saw the dead youth and another walking down the street, saw the squad car approach. She heard, "Stop, you little so-and-so" and then a shot. The officer was subsequently cleared by Coronor Lloyd K. Babcock.

November 6.—ROLAND T. PRICE, 20-year-old veteran, was shot to death in *Rochester, New York,* by six patrolmen who fired a total of twenty-five bullets into his body. Price had just come from seeing the "Freedom Train" and was short-changed in the Royal Palm Restaurant. He argued with the bartender who called Policeman William Hamill. Hamill rushed into the restaurant, drew his gun, forced Price into the street, where he and the other officers began shooting. All were cleared.

November 15.—WALTER PALMER of *Edwards, Mississippi,* a Negro veteran, was shot dead after being arrested at a party. Palmer was shot in the back and the officer claimed he tried to escape. Case was reported to Atty. Gen. Clark.

November 16.—RAYMOND COUSER was walking down Montrose Street in *Philadelphia* when eye witnesses saw Patrolman Frank Cacurro stalking him with a drawn revolver. Cacurro fired, Couser staggered, wounded. The patrolman fired three more shots and Couser dropped dead. The patrolman claimed he had been dispatched to the Couser home after being notified of a quarrel and that he shot Couser because he thought Couser was armed.

November 16.—CHARLES FLETCHER of *Philadelphia* was slain by Patrolman Manus McGettingan who claimed he shot after receiving a call about a prowler. Fletcher worked at the Exide Battery Co. for ten years and had no police record.

November 23.—CHARLES SMITH was slain by Marvin Matthews and Wyatt Adams in *Lillington, North Carolina,* while they engaged in a reign of terror in the Negro community. At the same time, the terrorists shot DANIEL LEE BRASFORD. They shot from a car and attempted to run other Negroes down. Eugene Williams, William Talton, A. E. Woods, Robert Perry and several other Negroes likewise testified that the terrorists had attacked them previously. A Harnett County jury freed the men after deliberating 27 minutes.

December.—ELMORE BOLLING, 30, was found riddled with shot gun and pistol shots in *Lowndesboro, Alabama.* Clark Luckie, a white man who claimed the

Negro had insulted his wife over the telephone, was arrested for the killing, but was later released.

December 17.—CHARLES CURRY, 23, was slain by Nolan O. Ray, *Dallas, Texas* policeman, during an altercation on a trolley bus. Ray, in civilian clothes at the time, had ordered a Negro who had sat down beside him to move. The Negro passengers became incensed and Ray jumped to his feet, drew his revolver, and ordered all Negroes to "take your hands out of your pockets." When Curry did not comply fast enough, Ray shot him dead. He claimed he thought he saw Curry drawing a knife from his pocket. There was no weapon found on the dead man, however. According to witnesses, Curry had neither moved nor spoken during the entire incident. Two days after the slaying, Police Chief Carl Hansen dismissed Ray from the force. He was subsequently indicted for murder.

1948

January 28.—JAMES HARMON, *Camden, New Jersey,* 30-year-old construction worker, was arrested and held incommunicado for twenty-five days. He then died under mysterious circumstances at Lakeland General Hospital. Harmon was arrested by Patrolmen William Yeager and Joseph Hooven and booked as drunk and disorderly. But relatives and friends declared Harmon was a teetotaller. When he died his eye was swollen and the cause of death was admitted to be blood poisoning, after officials first claimed he died of heart disease. A severe beating was suspected at the hands of police.

February 2.—GEORGE THOMAS, Negro youth, was shot dead by a *Kosciusko, Mississippi* policeman who claimed he tried to escape after being arrested. Case was reported to Atty. Gen. Clark.

February 27.—ROY CYRIL BROOKS, member of Local 309, Food, Tobacco and Agricultural Workers, was shot down in cold blood in the crowded bright sunlit public square of *Gretna, Louisiana.* Brooks' murderer was a uniformed policeman, Alvin Bladsacker. Brooks had become involved in a minor altercation with the driver of a bus. Bladsacker, a traffic cop in the square, heard the driver's raised voice, entered the bus, and immediately slugged Brooks across the back of the head. Blood spurted from the base of Brooks' skull, and Bladsacker then prodded him out of the bus, announcing that he was going to take him to the police station. As they walked down the square, Bladsacker hauled out a .38 revolver and held it against Brooks' back. Brooks half turned and attempted to tell the policeman that he had done nothing wrong. Bladsacker shot him twice. Brooks fell on his back in the street and forty minutes later he was dead. The original incident with the bus driver had been this: a Negro woman passenger, after paying her nickel fare, discovered she was on the wrong bus and asked for her nickel back. When the driver refused, Brooks gave her a nickel, she left, and Brooks asked to ride on the woman's already paid fare. It was while the driver was loudly refusing Brooks that Bladsacker heard him. A Committee for Justice in the Brooks case protested and under pressure, Bladsacker was indicted for manslaughter. He was later released and put back on his job.

Week of February 28.—JAMES TOLLIVER, 40, of *Little Rock, Arkansas*, was beaten to death by Policeman Blaylock. Tolliver was trying to help a drunken woman when Blaylock came up behind him and struck him in the head. He died almost instantly.

March 7.—RAYFIELD DAVIS, 35, was slain by Horace Miller during a "civil rights squabble." A *Mobile County (Alabama)* Grand Jury freed the killer.

Week of March 21.—ELLIS HUDSON of *Nacogdoches, Texas*, 50, was shot to death by a Texas constable, one Heppenstead. Hudson had come to court to arrange bail for his son, Ellis, Jr., who had been beaten by the same officer when the boy did not address him as "sir."

Week of March 21.—SAMUEL BACON, 55, was shot to death in a *Fayette, Mississippi* jail by Town Marshal S. D. Coleman. Bacon, an employee of the Firestone Rubber Co. of Akron, Ohio, had been arrested and taken from a bus while on his way to Natchez, Miss., to visit relatives.

March 27.—IKE MADDEN, 27, was slain by *Birmingham, Alabama* police who claimed he was "resisting arrest."

March 29.—JOHN JOHNSON, 50, was slain by *Birmingham, Alabama* police who claimed he was "resisting arrest."

Week of April 4.—OTIS NEWSOM, of *Wilson, North Carolina*, 25-year-old war veteran and father of three children, was shot and killed by N. C. Strickland, gas station operator. Strickland killed Newsom after the Negro demanded that he properly service his car with brake fluid he had just purchased.

April 19.—ALMAS SHAW, of *Birmingham, Alabama*, was killed during a fight with police. Police claimed he ran and that when they caught him, he hit his head on the base of stone building. Killing was third in three weeks by police, as terrorist group Black Raiders resumed operations.

April 27.—MARION FRANKLIN NOBLE, 19, was slain by *Birmingham, Alabama* policeman C. L. Borders who claimed the youth attacked him when he was arresting him.

April 30.—EUGENE WARD, 1910 13th Avenue, *Bessemer, Alabama*, was shot to death by Patrolmen Lawton Grimes and Sam Montgomery. The cops claimed Ward "resisted arrest and reached for a knife."

May 2.—HOSEA CARTER, of *Sandy Hook, Mississippi*, a Negro, was found dead of a shotgun blast in the chest. Deputy Sheriff T. W. White reported that a white man "whose name I don't remember" killed Carter. White claimed that Carter and his brother Willie and a third Negro, William Harris, tried to enter a home and that a "neighbor" accosted them and shot Carter. "He did what any decent white man would have done," White said of the unnamed murderer. The other two Negroes were jailed.

May 5.—HENRY ROGERS of *Harlem, New York City*, was killed by 32nd Precinct Patrolman Thomas Hollinsworth. The policeman was called to settle an argument between Rogers and Clifton Smith, superintendent of a building at 301 West 151st Street. Police claim Rogers attacked Hollinsworth, and he shot in self-defense.

May 23.—Augusta, Georgia. Prison guard ordered unidentified Negro prisoner into snake infested ditch. Prisoner refused, was severely beaten and died.

June 5.—IKE CRAWFORD, 29-year-old prisoner in the *Richmond County, Georgia* stockade, died after he was beaten to a pulp by guards David L. Turner, Horace Wingard, and Alvin Jones. The men were indicted for "prison brutality." A coroner's jury, however, reported that Crawford died of a liver disease.

June 12.—JESSE JEFFERSON of *Jackson, Georgia*, was slain on his farm, after two white men drove up behind his wagon and accused him of not giving them room to pass by.

July 12.—JAMES BURTS, 23, was slain by policemen R. C.Wooddall and S. C. Kelly in *Greenville, South Carolina.* Burts was beaten to death with a blackjack and a night stick and died in General Hospital. Dr. J. R. Bryson, Jr. said Burts was "in a pretty bad condition when he arrived." A General Sessions Court jury freed the policeman in November.

July 14.—WILLIE MILTON, of *Brooklyn, New York*, was shot in the back by Patrolman Kilcommons. Milton, a tenant leader in his community, had an altercation with a local bartender who assaulted him and two friends and abused them with racist epithets. JOE MILTON, the dead man's brother, was beaten by police in the Bedford Ave. station, who tried to make him admit he started a fracas in the bar.

August.—JOE W. PERKINS, 26, was killed by *Birmingham, Alabama* police who said he was trying to escape. He was the ninth Negro slain by police in the past four months.

August 21.—HERMAN BURNS, Negro war veteran was beaten to death by *Los Angeles* police outside the La Veda Ballroom. At the same time, his brothers Julius and John were attacked by several police. Mrs. Virginia Burns, the widow of the slain man sued the city for $200,000 naming Mayor Bowron, Police Chief Clement Horrall, and Asst. Chief Joseph Reed as being derelict in their duty for failing to suspend or discharge the killer cops.

September 6.—ISAIAH NIXON, 28-year-old veteran, was killed in *Montgomery County, Ga.* in the presence of his wife and children after he had voted in the September 6 primary. A jury freed M. L. Johnson, the killer.

September 26.—HOSEA W. ALLEN of *Tampa, Florida*, was shot to death by Victor Pinella, proprietor of a beer tavern, when Allen asked to be served a bottle of beer. Justice of the Peace Spicola freed Pinella.

Week of October 16.—DANNY BRYANT, 37, of *Covington, Louisiana*, was shot to death by policeman Kinsie Jenkins after Bryant refused to remove his hat in the presence of whites.

November 20.—In *Lyons, Georgia*, ROBERT MALLARD, riding with his wife and two teen-age relatives was ambushed and slain by a gang of over twenty robed terrorists. Mallard was shot several times before his wife's eyes. Mrs. Mallard identified two of the killers as Roderick L. Clifton and William L. Howell, farmers. They were later acquitted. (Mrs. Mallard is a signer of this petition.)

1949

Posse hunting down suspects in assault case in *Groveland, Florida,* shot and killed ERNEST THOMAS in pine woods. Posse was made up of deputies. They claimed Thomas was armed. Several teams of dogs were used to find Thomas.

MALCOLM WRIGHT, 45, tenant farmer of *Houston, Mississippi* was beaten to death for allegedly not moving his wagon off the road fast enough to let white men in car pass.

Week of January 2.—HERMAN GLASPER, 30, was shot and killed in *Bryan County, Georgia,* by State Trooper Corporal Dee E. Watson. Glasper had been arrested on suspicion of being a hog thief. Sheriff E. W. Miles claimed that the shooting was an accident, that Watson shot when he stumbled over some bushes.

January 10.—JOHN FERRELL, young Negro father of 25 Mulberry Street, *Albany, New York,* arrested on a misdemeanor charge, was found dead in the First Police Precinct 10 minutes after being jailed. Police claimed Ferrell hanged himself. Ferrell, father of two children, had been arrested at his home, and police began beating him when they took him away according to his wife, Mrs. Marguerite Ferrell.

January 16.—CHARLES PHIFER was shot in the back and killed in the home of his stepmother, Mrs. Anne Phifer, of the *Bronx, New York.* Patrolman Eugene Stusiuk had been called to settle an argument and claimed Phifer attacked him. He failed to explain how he shot him in the back.

February 18.—GEORGE WADDELL was shot in the back and slain in his home by *Brooklyn, New York,* policemen who invaded it without warrant, with no charges against him. The police claimed they were looking for a gambling game when they forced their way into Waddell's home.

February 26.—An unidentified Negro prisoner was shot to death by a policeman. The prisoner, who was locked in a room with several officers in *Manchester, Georgia,* was shot three times in the back.

April 2.—JIM MITCHELL, 65, and IRV LEE PARKER, 18, were lynched near *Macon, Georgia,* according to the confession made April 2nd by John McKinney, who implicated Louis DuBose. After dragging the Okmulgee River, Mitchell's body was found with his throat slashed and his stomach ripped open.

Week of April 10.—HAYES KENNEDY, 45, died in a *Birmingham, Alabama* hospital after he had been beaten in jail. Sheriff Lacey Alexander claimed Kennedy fought with officers in the jail.

May 3.—WILLIE JOHNSON was shot to death by two *Brunswick, Georgia,* policemen who claimed that "he was looking suspiciously at a house." Johnson, 58, had been a resident of Brunswick for fourteen years, was a county employee, and a deacon of St. Paul's Baptist Church. The case was reported to the Civil Rights Section of the Justice Department by Mrs. Constance Baker Motley of the NAACP Legal Department.

May 30.—CALEB HILL, 28-year-old farm hand of *Irwinton, Georgia,* was taken from the County jail by an armed mob and several hours later, his body was found hanging near a creek. He had been shot through the heart several times. Hill was in the custody of Sheriff George Hatcher, charged with creating a disturbance and resisting arrest.

June 12.—RICHARD BROWN, and his cousin, JAMES TAYLOR, were shot and killed in *Harlem, New York City,* by plainclothes no-badge Patrolman Abraham Yudenfreund. No prosecution.

July 2.—MALCOLM WRIGHT, 45-year-old tenant farmer was slain near *Houston, Mississippi,* before his wife and four small children. Subsequently three men, James Moore, James Kelum, and Eunice Gore were arrested and indicted in the killing.

July 4.—CHRISPIN CHARLES, a Navy veteran, was slain in *New Orleans, La.* by Patrolman E. Landry and E. Sahuc after they had arrested him during a family quarrel. The veteran was slain with six bullets after he protested, "I haven't done anything."

July 18.—FRANK BATES was "found" dead in a *New Orleans* jail cell. His body was battered, his ribs crushed and broken, his eyes swollen. Bates had been arrested after being picked up in the vicinity of the killing of a Catholic priest. No proof was ever produced that he knew anything of the killing, though a confession was third-degreed out of him. The coroner's verdict on his death was "malnutrition."

July 29.—WALTER DANDRIDGE, 32, was killed by *Birmingham, Alabama* police. His mother, MRS. SUSIE DANDRIDGE, 60, and his brothers JOHN, 44, and JAMES, 26, were wounded.

August.—JAMES SCOTT, 56, of *Peoria, Illinois,* was shot dead by Fred Lang, a bartender in the Century Club. Scott had been assured by the proprietor that he could be served, but the bartender took matters in his own hands. He ordered the Negro not to come into the club again and in the ensuing argument pulled a gun and shot Scott. The killer was sentenced to from six to 14 years.

August 10.—GEORGE WESTRAY, 31, was shot and killed in the Lincoln Hospital, Bronx, New York, by Patrolman Daniel McEnery. Westray had been previously beaten unmercifully.

August 11.—JAMES PERRY, 41-year-old Negro unemployed war veteran, died in Homer G. Phillips Hospital, in *St. Louis, Missouri,* after being beaten by four police officers. Cause of death was listed as intracranial hemorrhage. Perry had been picked up by the four police on complaint of a park watchman, who tried to evict Perry from a small park in a Negro section, at 4:00 p.m. that afternoon. His companion, a Miss G. Burns, told Civil Rights Congress representatives that police beat Perry about the head. She had been threatened, she said, and was forced to leave the park. The inquest said cause of death was unknown, and evidence presented there proved the police charge of larceny against Perry to be false. (Police claimed he had stolen soda from a soda wagon but the vendor testified it had been stolen by children.)

September 1.—A 17-year-old youth, DAVID HANLEY, was shot to death in *Lexington, Kentucky* by Patrolmen William B. Foster and William Lewis. The police claimed he tried to escape them. A Fayette Circuit Court jury found them not guilty of murder.

Week of September 8.—HOLIS RILES, 53, prosperous owner of a 200-acre farm was slain on his land at *Bainbridge, Georgia* by a group of white men. Riles was slain after he ordered the men from his land when they trespassed to go fishing. Jesse Gordon, a Negro eyewitness said the murderers drove away in two cars. Previously Riles had trouble from white men trespassing on his land. He had been warned to leave the district, but refused. Sheriff A. E. White called the murder premeditated. The Georgia Bureau of Investigation studied the case.

October 2.—LINWOOD MATTHEWS, 19-year-old Negro was stabbed to death by a gang of white mobsters who attacked him and six others of his athletic club as they sought to play football in Carroll Park of *Baltimore, Maryland.* The youths were attacked and chased from the park. They then went to another section of the park but were attacked again. This time Matthews was slain. The mobsters fled before police arrived.

November 4.— Police of *New Orleans and Jefferson Parish* beat to death 42-year-old EUGENE JONES. His wife Martha, 25, told how police, identified as Earl Rolling, Dick Massa, and a third unidentified officer, came to their home in the dead of night and seized Jones. He was beaten before her eyes. Jones was taken away. Then the officers returned and asked Mrs. Jones for more clothes. She ran to the car and saw her husband on the floor covered with blood. The next day she was told he died of "natural causes."

November 12.—MICHAEL RICE, 69-year-old Negro farmer was shot and killed by Leroy Parker and Roy Lawing in *Walhalla, South Carolina.* The men then robbed Rice of from $400 to $500 and forced a terror-stricken 14-year-old Negro boy, HENRY DAVIS, to remain with the corpse on pain of death. Parker confessed that they shot the farmer when he refused to tell them where his cotton money was.

Week of November 19.—EUGENE JONES, an ex-Marine, was beaten to death by two *Jefferson Parish, Louisiana* Deputy Sheriffs in the Gretna jail. Jones' wife testified that he had been spirited away by four officers, and that when she called the jail a day later, she was told her husband was dead.

November 20.—SAMUEL LEE WILLIAMS, 34 (who died Nov. 28), and two other Negroes were shot by a *Birmingham, Alabama* street car conductor, M. A. Weeks. Williams and the other Negroes argued with Weeks about being ordered to move into the car's jim crow section, whereupon the conductor pulled his gun and fired. Police refused to arrest or place any charges against the conductor. The wounded Negroes were AMOS CRISBY, 24, and JOHN CARLINGTON III, 21.

December 31.—SAMUEL TAYLOR, 38, *Baldsville, Virginia* farmer was mutilated to death by a group of whites. Frank Clayton, a white farmer was arrested. Local reports charged that all the killers were known and that they included a woman.

1950

January 1.—GEORGE WEST was shot and killed by James W. Beaman, a *Harlem, New York* policeman. Beaman was subsequently discharged by the Police Department for "unsatisfactory conduct."

January 8.—Three Negro children, RUBY NELL HARRIS, 4, MARY BURNSIDE, 8, and FRANKIE THURMAN, 12, of *Kosciusko, Mississippi,* were slain by three white men, Leon Turner, Malcolm Whitt and Windol Whitt, who also raped PAULINE THURMAN, 17, and shot THOMAS HARRIS, father and stepfather of the children. Harris died later of his wounds, on April 12. Turner and Windol Whitt got life, while Malcolm Whitt got 10 years.

MRS. MATTIE DEBARDELEBEN, of *Birmingham, Alabama,* refused to sell some chickens to three Federal revenue agents and a deputy sheriff. They beat her and she died "of a heart attack" on way to jail.

Jauary 9.—NATHANIEL GRACE, 28-year-old citizen of *Brooklyn, New York,* died in the City Hospital of injuries following a forcible arrest by police. Essex County Medical Examiner Martland said that Grace did not suffer any skull fracture or apparent brain injury.

February 28.—*Fernandina, Florida.* Victim and another Negro, JAMES WILLIAMS, 18, picked up by Deputy Sheriff Dave Stokes who intended to arrest them for vagrancy. They told him they worked on a nearby farm. While driving around with the prisoners in his car, Stokes stopped at service station to get friend, Reginald Johnson. Stokes claimed that unidentified man grabbed his gun and began shooting, whereupon Johnson killed Negro with shotgun.

March 2.—Seventy-six-year-old JAMES TURNER, Negro Baptist minister, of *Cairo, Georgia,* was found slain in his bed and his three young children were also found dead—all their heads smashed in with an axe. His wife said that someone dressed in a white garment that looked like a gown ran after her. She escaped and went to the police.

May 8.—THURMOND TOWNS, 19-year-old garment worker of the *Bronx, New York* was killed in *New York City,* by police of the 32nd Precinct. Towns was shot in the St. Nicholas Park after police claimed he ran when they sought to question him about a purse snatched from a woman passerby. TOWNS, however, was found to have a large sum of money in the bank, and was known as a model citizen and unionist.

June 5.—An unidentified Negro man was beaten to death in the *Washington, D.C.* penitentiary. Attested to by fellow prisoners. No mention of incident in press.

June 19.—LORENZO BEST, 32, of *Anniston, Alabama,* was killed with four bullets by Police Sgt. J. D. Thomas. A coroner called it "justifiable homicide."

August.—LEROY FOLEY died in Breckinridge County Hospital, *Hardinsburg, Kentucky,* after he and two other Negroes lay on the floor three hours and were refused medical attention for automobile injuries. The other Negroes were JESSIE WALLACE and JOHN H. SMITH. According to Nurse Betty Graves, they were put on the floor "because we don't have facilities for colored people." Foley died an hour after his arrival. To get the men out of the hospital a Negro ambulance service was called from a distance of seventy miles, and arrived after three hours. Jesse Lawrence, the driver of the ambulance, charged: "The blood had not even been wiped from their faces. Their shoes had not been removed, and their belts had not been loosened." The hospital sent the injured men bills for $11.50 and $1.50 for the telephone call to get the ambulance.

Week of October 7.—MORRIS SCOTT was slain in *Linden, Alabama* by William R. Welch and George Baker. Welch admitted firing the shotgun blast that killed Scott in his home. County Sheriff T. Wilmer Shields declined to disclose a motive for the killing.

October 20.—SAMUEL ELLIS, Navy veteran of *Philadelphia* was slain by a rookie cop on a subway. Ellis died an hour after being admitted to Hahneman Hospital.

October 20.—HARVEY WILSON of *Vanndale, Arkansas* was shot and killed by W. M. Stokes during an argument over the purchase of a small amount of coal oil. Stokes was arrested and charged with first degree murder.

November 1.—JAMES R. CLARK, 28-year-old former policeman, received ten months in an *Opelika, Alabama,* Federal Court on the charges of violating the civil rights of a Negro he and another policeman, Doyle Mitchum, had beaten to death while holding him under arrest. Both were acquitted of the murder of WILLIE B. CARLISLE, 19, of Lafayette. They beat him to death with a rubber hose. Mitchum got six months.

December.—SAM JONES, 35, *San Pedro, California,* construction worker and member of AFL Laborers' Local 802 was beaten to death by Policemen James R. Graham and Richard W. Clare. At the same time, they severely beat Jones' companion, NATHANIEL RAY, 46, shipbuilder and member of CIO Shipyard Workers Local 9. Ray is the father of eight children. The policemen claimed the men drew knives after being arrested for drunkenness.

December 7.—JOHN DERRICK, veteran just discharged from Fort Dix, N.J., was shot down in *Harlem, New York City,* at 119th Street and Eighth Avenue, by Patrolmen Louis Palumbo and Basil Minakotis attached to the 28th Precinct. Derrick was slain with his hands in the air. The policemen were subsequently cleared by the New York County Grand Jury.

December 8.—MATTHEW AVERY, 24, student at the North Carolina A. and T. College, died after an auto accident and being refused admittance to Duke Hospital at *Durham, North Carolina.* Duke doctors said there was no space for Avery and he died an hour later, while being transferred to another hospital.

December 12.—ROBERT J. EVANS, 86, was shot by *Norfolk, Virginia* Patrolman E. M. Morgan who claimed the old man pulled a knife on him. Evans was shot when Morgan accosted him during an alleged search for a man involved in a knifing.

Week of December 23.—KELLY GIST of *Wake County, North Carolina* was slain near Raleigh, by a former convict and parolee, N. G. Williams, who shot him point blank in the chest with a 20-gauge shotgun. Williams claimed Gist cursed at him. Williams was arrested and held without bond.

December 29.—FRED PRETTYMAN, 28, of *Birmingham, Alabama,* was slain by police, who claimed he tried to escape. Coroner Joe Hildebrand immediately called it "justifiable homicide." Prettyman was the fifth Negro slain by police since Feb. 9, 1950, and the eleventh slain in the state since January 22.

1951

January 13.—ANDREW JOHNSON, 19, was killed by *Chicago* police in the Central Station. The young worker was arrested and charged with the murder of Coleman Hairston, a barber, during a holdup, but Sonny Porter, a porter in the shop, said Johnson did not look like the holdup man. Porter's testimony was barred by Coroner A. L. Brodie. Johnson was picked up by Edward Cagney and Joseph Corcoran, policemen, who gave him the third degree in the station. He was dead by 3:30 p.m. after being arrested that morning. He died of internal injuries including a lacerated liver. Police said, "he just keeled over and died."

January 19.—BOBBY LEE JOYNER, 17-year-old high school student was slain by Police Chief J. A. Wheeler and Policeman W. E. Williford who pumped seven bullets into the youth's body, claiming he tried to attack them with a knife, in *La Grange, North Carolina. The Greensboro Record* and the *Raleigh News and Observer* demanded that the officer be prosecuted. They were cleared by a Grand Jury.

February 2 and 5.—The *Martinsville Seven Negroes* were electrocuted in Richmond, Virginia for a crime they could not have committed, according to the evidence. The alleged crime was rape of a white woman who had since disappeared. They were *Clabon Taylor, Frank Hairston, Jr., Joe Henry Hampton, James Hairston, Booker T. Millner, Francis Grayson, J. L. Hairston.* (Mrs. Josephine Grayson, widow of the executed Francis Grayson and the mother of five children, is one of the present petitioners.)

February 6.—DR. M. A. SANTA CRUZ, prominent dentist, was beaten to death in *Pulaski, Virginia* by two hoodlums when he sought to protect two Negro girls they were molesting. Police arrested Charles Simmons, 20, and E. Buford Owen, 18, and charged them with murder. A taxi driver, Hubert Matthews Costigan, is charged with "aiding and abetting" since he carried them from the scene of the crime. The girls, Evelyn Bland, 17, and Marie French, 14, were accosted by the hoodlums and manhandled. When Dr. Santa Cruz intervened and went to a police call box, the youths attacked him from behind. He later died in an ambulance.

February 7.—The bodies of four Negroes slain under mysterious circumstances were found in *Edgecomb* and *Nash Counties, North Carolina.* The body of JOHN MELVIN, 50, was found on a farm in Edgecomb. WILLIAM BATTLE, 29, was found on his door steps. Both were nude and partially burned. The body of G. W. BATCHELOR, 80, was found in a corn crib. The one-year-old son of TOM GEORGE BATTLE was found dead in bed and Battle himself was shot in the arm.

May 8.—The state of *Mississippi* electrocuted WILLIE McGEE, World War II veteran and father of four children for the framed "rape" charge made against him by a white woman, Mrs. Willametta Hawkins. The cause of freedom for Willie McGee had been taken up around the world during the five years that elapsed between his arrest on November 3, 1945 and his death on May 8, 1951. Because of the protests that continued to mount on behalf of McGee's innocence and the lynch atmosphere in which he was first tried and convicted, McGee was tried four times. As the evidence revealed, Mrs. Hawkins had forced McGee into a relationship with her, which he later tried to sever. It was in these circumstances that the white woman charged "rape." It was because the relationship between McGee and the woman had become known that the state of Mississippi ordered his death. The relationship between a Negro man and a white woman "violated" all the white supremacy patterns of oppression against the Negro people in the South. For this McGee was killed. (Mrs. Rosalee McGee, widow of the murdered defendant, and the mother of his four fatherless children, is a signer of this petition.)

June 9.—EDWARD HONEYCUTT was put to death by the state of *Louisiana* on a framed "rape" charge. At the time he was charged with rape, Honeycutt was kidnapped from the St. Landry parish prison in Opalousa, La. by a lynch mob. He was dumped on the low level of the Atchafalaya River as three members of the mob started matching coins to see which would shoot him. As they argued, Honeycutt dove into the river. He was dragged out and rearrested. None of the mob was convicted for kidnapping or attempted homicide. During Honeycutt's trial, guards patrolled the courtroom armed with pistols. Honeycutt said he had never seen the white woman who cried rape until he saw her in court. On May 28, 1950 an all-white jury found him guilty in 24 minutes.

William L. Patterson, ed., *We Charge Genocide: The Crime of Government Against the Negro People. A Petition to the United Nations* (Civil Rights Congress, 1951, N.Y.). See Patterson's autobiography *The Man Who Cried Genocide* (International Publishers, 1958, N.Y.). Information also from the editor's recollections and a typed document given him by Oakley C. Johnson, being the text of a speech Johnson gave in Austin, Texas, July 20, 1952.

6

COLOR AND DEMOCRACY: COLONIES AND PEACE (1945)

by W. E. B. Du Bois

Du Bois completed *Color and Democracy: Colonies and Peace* in January 1945 expressing his views now that he was director of special research for the NAACP. The book was published in May 1945; its reviews were abundant and very favorable. Indicative of the new quality then prevalent in official circles was that in June 1945 the U.S. Navy purchased twenty-four hundred copies of the book for distribution among its leading personnel. Neither Du Bois's position nor the new quality in official circles lasted more than two years.

The present war has made it clear that we can no longer regard Western Europe and North America as the world for which civilization exists; nor can we look upon European culture as the norm for all peoples. Henceforth the majority of the inhabitants of earth, who happen for the most part to be colored, must be regarded as having the right and the capacity to share in human progress and to become copartners in that democracy which alone can ensure peace among men, by the abolition of poverty, the education of the masses, protection from disease, and the scientific treatment of crime.

From these premises I have written this book, to examine our current efforts to ensure peace through the united action of men of goodwill. I have sought to say that insofar as such efforts leave practically untouched the present imperial ownership of disfranchised colonies, and in this and other ways proceed as if the majority of men can be regarded mainly as sources of profit for Europe and North America, in just so far we are planning not peace but war, not democracy but the continued oligarchical control of civilization by the white race.

I am aware that such a thesis needs to be backed by a far wider collection of facts, scientifically arranged, than are at present available. But I am convinced from long study and wide travel that the truth of what I say is fairly well attested, and at least the dangers which I seek to point out are sufficiently evident to call for action.

What is needed today is a new Mandates Commission calling upon the United Nations to recognize the fact that the first Mandates Commission established by the statute which organized the League of Nations has a place in international law, and that the United Nations have no right in law or justice to ignore this statute and hand over the former colonies of Germany to France, Britain, the Union of South Africa, or Japan; that a new Mandates Commission should immediately be organized to take charge of the mandated colonies and to go farther, as was suggested in the original Covenant, and lay down new procedures for the treatment of all colonial peoples.

The General Assembly of the United Nations should begin by insisting that there sit in the Assembly not simply representatives of the free nations, but with them representatives of all colonial peoples over whom they claim control. The matter of the number of such colonial delgates can well wait on time and experience. The method of their choice and the fair representation of all angles of opinion can be gradually adjusted as the Economic and Social Council gains power to investigate. But it is absolutely essential that, at the beginning, the voices of all peoples that on earth do dwell be raised fearlessly and openly in the parliament of man, to seek justice, complain of oppression, and demand equality. Difficult as this program will doubtless prove, it will not be nearly so difficult, horrible, and utterly devastating as two world wars in a single generation.

Evidently there is indicated here the necessity of earnest effort to avoid the nondemocratic and race-inferiority philosophy involved. There should be consultation among colonial peoples and their friends as to just what measures ought to be taken. This consultation should look toward asking for the following successive steps:

One, representation of the colonial peoples alongside the master peoples in the Assembly.

Two, the organization of a Mandates Commission under the Economic and Social Council, with definite power to investigate complaints and conditions in colonies and make public their findings and to hear oral petitions.

Three, a clear statement of the intentions of each imperial power to take, gradually but definitely, all measures designed to raise the peoples of colonies to a condition of complete political and economic equality with the peoples of the master nations, and eventually either to incorporate them into the polity of the master nations or to allow them to become independent free peoples.

W. E. B. Du Bois, *Color and Democracy, Colonies and Peace* (N.Y.: Harcourt Brace, 1945), preface and pp. 139–41. For an account of the creation and impact of this book, see my introduction to the edition published by Kraus-Thomson (Millwood, N.Y., 1975).

7

A RISING WIND (1945)

by Walter White

Walter White, executive secretary of the NAACP, toured the European theater of the war during its final year. In 1945 his book *A Rising Wind* appeared. The title was taken from a speech by Eleanor Roosevelt affirming a rising wind "throughout the world," heralding a new sense of freedom for all. The volume's clear anticolonialist and anti-imperialist character helps explain why the NAACP was prepared to invite Dr. Du Bois in 1944 to serve as its director of special research. Here is the book's essence:

World War II has given to the Negro a sense of kinship with other colored—and also oppressed—peoples of the world. Where he has not thought through or informed himself on the racial angles of colonial policy and master-race theories, he senses that the struggle of the Negro in the United States is part and parcel of the struggle against imperialism and exploitation in India, China, Burma, Africa, the Philippines, Malaya, the West Indies, and South America. The Negro soldier is convinced that as time proceeds that identification of interests will spread even among some brown and yellow peoples who today refuse to see the connection between their exploitation by white nations and discrimination against the Negro in the United States.

The evil effect of misbehavior by a minority and the timorousness of the American Government in meeting such misbehavior will cost America and other white nations dearly so far as colored peoples, constituting two thirds of the earth's population, are concerned. Winston Churchill's recent statement that, as the war nears its end, ideology is being forgotten increasingly means to colored peoples that idealism is being conveniently shelved. Colored peoples, particularly in the Pacific, believed, whether correctly or not, that in its later stages the war was being fought to restore empire to Great Britain, France, Holland, and Portugal. The immediate resumption of control of Hollandia and other sections of Dutch New Guinea by the Dutch, and similar action by the British in Guadalcanal and Tarawa as soon as the Japanese had been driven out, the preparations being made by France to take over again control of Indo-China the minute the Nipponese are ejected, created increasing skepticism of the Allies throughout the Pacific.

Any person of normal intelligence could have foreseen this. With considerable effectiveness, the Japanese by radio and other means have industriously spread in the Pacific stories of lynchings, of segregation and discrimination against the Negro in the American Army, and of race riots in Detroit, Philadelphia, and other American cities. To each of these recitals has been appended the statement that such treatment of a colored minority in the United States is certain to be that given to brown and yellow peoples in the Pacific if the Allies, instead of the Japanese, win the war. No one can accurately estimate at this time the effectiveness of such propaganda. But it is certain that it has had wide circulation and has been believed by many. Particularly damaging has been the circulation of reports of clashes between white and Negro soldiers in the European and other theaters of operation.

Indissolubly tied in with the carrying overseas of prejudice against the Negro is the racial and imperialist question in the Pacific of Great Britain's and our intentions toward India and China. Publication of Ambassador William Phillips' blunt warning to President Roosevelt in May 1944 that India is a problem of the United States as well as of England despite British opposition to American intervention is of the highest significance. It reaffirmed warnings to the Western world by Wendell Willkie, Sumner Welles, Pearl Buck, and Henry Wallace, among others, that grave peril which might bring disaster to the entire world was involved in continued refusal to recognize the just claims for justice and equality by the colored people, particularly in the Orient. These people are not as powerless as some naive Americans believe them to be. In the first place they have the strength of numbers, unified by resentment against the condescension and exploitation by white nations which Pearl Buck calls "the suppression of human rights to a degree which has not been matched in its ruthlessness outside of fascist-owned Europe," which can and possibly will grow into open revolt. The trend of such awakening and revolution is clearly to be seen in the demand which was made by China at the Dumbarton Oaks Conference of August 1944 that the Allied nations unequivocally declare themselves for complete racial equality. It is to be seen in Ambassador Phillips' warning that though there are four million Indians under arms they are wholly a mercenary army whose allegiance to the Allies will last only as long as they are paid; and in his further revelation that all of these as well as African troops must be used to police other Indians instead of fighting Japan.

Permit me to cite a few solemn warnings of the inevitability of world-wide racial conflict unless the white nations of the earth do an about-face on the issue of race. "Moreover, during the years between 1920 and 1940 a period in the history of the Asiatic and Pacific peoples was in any event drawing to its close," says Sumner Welles, former Undersecretary of State, in his epochal book, *The Time for Decision.*

The startling development of Japan as a world power, and the slower but nevertheless steady emergence of China as a full member of the family of nations, together with the growth of popular institutions among many other peoples of Asia, notably India, all combined to erase very swiftly indeed the fetish of white supremacy cultivated by the big colonial powers during the nineteenth century. The thesis of white supremacy could only exist so long as the white race actually proved to be supreme. The nature of the defeats suffered by the Western nations in 1942 dealt the final blow to any concept of white supremacy which still remained.

While there are British and Dutch colonial administrators who show a "spirit of devotion, of decency and of self-abnegation," Mr. Welles remarks, there also are "yet only too many British representatives in the Far East [who] have demonstrated that type of thinking which is so well exemplified in the words of a high British official in India at the outset of the present century when he expressed a conviction which he asserted 'was shared by every Englishman in India, from the highest to the lowest... the conviction in every man that he belongs to a race whom God has destined to govern and subdue.'"

The distinguished former Undersecretary might well have gone on to point out that had not the Russians and Chinese performed miracles of military offense and defense in World War II, or had not the black Governor-General of French Equatorial Africa, Félix Eboué, retained faith in the democratic process when white Frenchmen lost theirs, the so-called Anglo-Saxon nations and peoples would surely have lost this war. And Mr. Welles could have reminded his readers that brown and yellow peoples in Asia and the Pacific and black peoples in Africa and the West Indies and the United States are not ignorant of the truth that the war was won by men and women—white, yellow, black, and brown. Resumption of white arrogance and domination in the face of such facts may be disastrous to the peace of the world.

The distinguished novelist, Pearl Buck, hits hard on the same issue in her *American Unity and Asia* in the chapter ominously captioned, "Tinder for Tomorrow."

The Japanese weapon of racial propaganda in Asia is beginning to show signs of effectiveness [she declares]. This is not because of peculiar skill in the way it is being used, but because it is being presented to persons who have had unfortunate experiences with English and American people.... It will be better for us if we acknowledge the danger in this Japanese propaganda. The truth is that the white man in the Far East has too often behaved without wisdom or justice to his fellow man. It is worse than folly—it is dangerous today—not to recognize the truth, for in it lies the tinder for tomorrow. Who of us can doubt it who has seen a white policeman beat a Chinese coolie in Shanghai, a white sailor kick a Japanese in Kobe, an English captain lash out with his whip at an Indian vendor—who of us, having seen such oriental sights or heard the common contemptuous talk of the white man in any colored country, can forget the fearful bitter hatred in the colored face and the blaze in the dark eyes?

Miss Buck tells how such stupid cruelty is put to use by the Japanese among the one billion colored people of the Pacific.

Race prejudice continues unabated among white people today, the Japanese are saying. Tokyo radio programs daily send their broadcasts over Asia in their campaign to drive out the white man. They dwell upon white exploitation of colored troops and cite mistreatment of Indian troops by the English.... "The colored peoples," Japanese propaganda says over and over again in a thousand forms, "have no hope of justice and equality from the white peoples because of their unalterable race prejudice against us."...The effect therefore of this Japanese propaganda cannot be lightly dismissed. It lies uneasy in the minds and memories of many at this moment who are loyally allied with Britain and the United States, in the minds and memories of colored peoples of Asia. Yes, and it lies uneasy, too, in the minds and memories of many colored citizens of the United States, who cannot deny the charge and must remain loyal in spite of it. For such minds realize that, though Nazism may give them nothing but death, yet the United States and Britain have given them too little for life in the past and not even promises for the future. Our colored allies proceed to war against the Axis not deceived or in ignorance. They know that it may not be the end of the war for them even when Hitler has gone down and Nazism is crushed and Japan returned to her isles again. The colored peoples know that for them the war for freedom may have to go on against the very white men at whose side they are now fighting.

These are grim words not pleasant to the ears of white America and Britain, who believe that the last shot fired in this war will mean the complete restoration of the way of life which preceded it. But the consequences of denying or ignoring them are solemnly voiced by an Englishman, Harold J. Laski, who bluntly warns that "Englishmen who put imperial power before social justice, Americans who think the color of a man's skin determines his rights—these are only some of the elements in our midst who might easily pervert the great victory into an epoch barren and ugly."

Will the United States after the war perpetuate its racial-discrimination policies and beliefs at home and abroad as it did during the war? Will it continue to follow blindly the dangerous and vicious philosophy voiced in Kipling's poem, *The White Man's Burden,* which Paul Hutchinson characterized in *World Revolution and Religion* as "the most significant cultural expression of the nineteenth century: even more significant than Nietzsche's discovery of the *"Ubermensch"?* Will decent and intelligent America continue to permit itself to be led by the nose by demogogues and professional race-hate mongers—to have its thinking and action determined on this global and explosive issue by the lowest common denominator of public opinion?

Or will the United States, having found that prejudice is an expensive luxury, slough off the mistakes of the past and chart a new course both at home and in its relations with the rest of the world? Miss Buck supplies one answer:

This also the Far Eastern Allies are asking. Japan is busily declaring that we cannot. She is declaring in the Philippines, in China, in India, Malaya, and even Russia that there is no basis for hope that colored peoples can expect any justice from the people who rule in the United States, namely, the white people. For specific proof the Japanese point to our treatment of our own colored people, citizens of generations in the United States. Every lynching, every race riot, gives joy to Japan. The discriminations of the American army and navy and air forces against colored soldiers and sailors, the exclusion of colored labor in our defense industries and trade unions, all our social discriminations, are of the greatest aid today to our enemy in Asia, Japan. "Look at America," Japan is saying to millions of listening ears. "Will white Americans give you equality?"

Who can reply with a clear affirmative? The persistent refusal of Americans to see the connection between the colored American and the colored peoples abroad, the continued, and it seems even willful, ignorance which will not investigate the connection, are agony to those loyal and anxious Americans who know all too well the dangerous possibilities.

Is Japan right in what she says to Asia and the Pacific? And whether right or not, what effect is her propaganda—unhappily based largely on truth—having upon hundreds of millions of people in what were once far places but today are but a few hours away from New York or Washington or San Francisco? Upon people whose good will and faith in our integrity are vital to our own national security?

During the middle stages of the war I made a study of Japanese radio and other propaganda among the people of the Orient and of German propaganda, almost invariably identical in language and content to the Japanese, in Latin America and Africa. Every lynching, every race riot like the one in Detroit in 1943 and the one in Philadelphia in 1944 against employment of qualified Negroes on streetcars, every killing or other mistreatment of a Negro soldier in a Southern training camp or city, every anti-Negro diatribe on the floor of Congress, every refusal to abolish racial segregation in the armed services of the United States was played up over and over again. Significantly enough, there was little embellishment of the details, probably because little was needed. In one form or another this moral was driven home: See what the United States does to its own colored people; this is the way you colored people of the world will be treated if the Allied nations win the war! Be smart and cast your lot with another colored people, the Japanese, who will never mistreat fellow colored people!

What will America's answer be? If already planned race riots and lynchings of returning Negro soldiers "to teach them their place" are consummated, if Negro war workers are first fired, if India remains enslaved, if Eboué's people go back to disease and poverty to provide luxury and ease for Parisian boulevardiers, World War III will be in the making before the last gun is fired in World War II. In *One World,* Wendell Willkie reported that "everywhere I found polite but skeptical people, who met my questions about their problems and difficulties with polite but ironic questions about our own. The maladjustments of races in America came up frequently." Such skepticism is but beginning. The question is posed bluntly: Can the United States, Britain, and other "white" nations any longer afford, in enlightened self-interest, racial superiority?

What to do?

The United States, Great Britain, France, and other Allied nations must choose without delay one of two courses—to revolutionize their racial concepts and practices, to abolish imperialism and grant full equality to all of its people, or else prepare for World War III. Another Versailles Treaty providing for "mandates," "protectorates," and other devices for white domination will make such a war inevitable. One of the chief deterrents will be Russia. Distrustful of Anglo-American control of Europe, many and perhaps all of the Balkan states may through choice or necessity ally themselves with Russia. If Anglo-Saxon practices in China and India are not drastically and immediately revised, it is probable and perhaps certain that the people of India, China, Burma, Malaya, and other parts of the Pacific may also move into the Russian orbit as the lesser of two dangers.

As for the United States, the storm signals are unmistakable. She can choose between a policy of appeasement of bigots—which course she gives every indication now of following—and thus court disaster. Or she can live up to her ideals and thereby both save herself and help to avert an early and more disastrous resumption of war.

A wind *is* rising—a wind of determination by the have-nots of the world to share the benefits of freedom and prosperity which the haves of the earth have tried to keep exclusively for themselves. That wind blows all over the world. Whether that wind develops into a hurricane is a decision which we must make now and in the days when we form the peace.

Walter White, *A Rising Wind* (1945), pp. 144–55.

8

APPEAL TO THE UNITED NATIONS CONFERENCE ON INTERNATIONAL ORGANIZATION ON BEHALF OF THE CARIBBEAN PEOPLES (1945)

by Richard B. Moore

This appeal, of immigrants from the Caribbean living in Harlem, was written by Richard Benjamin Moore (1893–1978) and presented on May 25, 1945, to Alger Hiss, the conference's secretary general. The latter refused to submit it to the conference, since, he said, the purpose of the San Francisco meeting was to prepare "the best possible charter...to maintain peace...and it is not intended that the matter you mention will be the subject of action here." However that may be, the appeal, offering views of some African-American people in the second half of the twentieth century, does belong in this volume.

To this historic Assembly of Delegates of the United Nations met to lay the foundations of World Security and Peace, the Caribbean Peoples which are still held as colonial dependencies now look with eager hope and confident expectation. In this Conference these peoples see the great opportunity never before afforded by history for the adoption at last of those democratic principles and the establishment of effective means of enforcement which will enable them to realize their long sought goal and inalienable human rights to freedom, security, and self-government along with all the liberty-loving nations of the world.

Events preceding and during this war have shown that security and peace depend upon organization which will ensure justice, equal rights and protection to all peoples, to small and weak nations as well as to great and strong, and which will provide guarantees for the effective exercise of genuine democratic rights by all people who cherish and defend democracy.

It is therefore essential that the voice of dominated peoples, seeking justice and the exercise of those democratic rights for which they fought and bled, should be heard and accorded due consideration by this World Conference upon which the solemn responsibility rests to rescue mankind from the ravages of war, insecurity, and slavery.

Colonial Status Renders Appeal Necessary

Because the very status of colonial dependency imposes onerous restrictions which render it extremely difficult if not impossible for these peoples to make direct representation, it is necessary for the West Indies National Council to present this Appeal on behalf of the peoples of the British, French, and Dutch West Indies, the Guianas and British Honduras. This Council, organized by natives of these areas, and supported by liberty-loving individuals and organizations irrespective of nationality, creed, or race, reflects the fundamental aspirations of these peoples based upon original ties, constant contact and knowledge, and the statements of responsible democratic representatives of the peoples of these areas.

This Appeal is therefore respectfully and earnestly presented together with seven proposals, adopted by this Council and endorsed by a public meeting assembled on April 16, 1945, at the Renaissance Casino in New York City and further endorsed by the Paragon Progressive Community Association, Inc., the Congress of Dominated Nations, and other organizations and prominent individuals. The Council requests that this Appeal be duly considered and urges this World Conference to adopt its recommendations and proposals in the form appropriate to secure their enforcement. The Council further desires to assure this World Conference that the peoples of these Caribbean areas may be depended upon wholeheartedly to support every measure necessary to the establishment of security, peace, and democracy, as their record amply demonstrates, and also to assume and discharge all duties and responsibilities in furtherance thereof.

Declaration of Rights—Act of Havana

The Declaration of Rights of the Caribbean Peoples to Self-Determination and Self-Government was presented by the West Indies National Emergency Committee to the Pan-American Foreign Ministers' Conference at Havana in July 1940. As a result, the Act of Havana while providing for concerted action by American Powers, recognized certain democratic rights of the Caribbean peoples.

Nevertheless, the Act of Havana was never invoked, though the French and Dutch Empires failed to provide protection and ceased in fact to exist as effective governing heads for these colonies. For a period indeed the people of the French West Indies and Guiana found themselves subject to the control of the fascist Vichy regime against their will and profound democratic conviction.

Vital Support Rendered by Caribbean Peoples

Despite the debilitating hindrances and galling yoke of colonial domination, the Caribbean peoples have loyally and unstintingly supported the United Nations in the present war against Nazi barbarism and fascist domination. In proportion to their size and numbers and the meager actual resources left to them after centuries of colonial retardation and impoverishment, they have made notable contributions to the armed forces and in labor power, finance, and essential materials such as oil, bauxite, etc.

Situated around the approaches to the Panama Canal, which was built mainly by their labor, at the strategic center of the defenses of the Americas, the peoples of the West Indies have suffered and withstood savage attacks by German submarines. Sites for vital bases and labor for their construction have been willingly furnished for the defense of the Americas and the United Nations, even though the rights of these peoples to consultation were not considered.

The Anglo-American Caribbean Commission has conducted broadcasts, made studies, and held conferences, but has done nothing practically to implement the rights of these peoples to self-government and self-determination. These fundamental rights are contravened by the very composition of this Commission which does not include a single direct representative of the Caribbean peoples or any one allied with them by ties of origin, feeling, and contact, in spite of repeated requests for such representation.

Colonial Conditions Menace World Security

The economic and social conditions prevailing in these areas are inhuman, tragic, and unbearable. The overwhelming majority of the population must labor when employment is available at wages far below the level of human subsistence. Housing and health conditions are among the worst in the world; illegitimacy, illiteracy, and the death rates are appallingly high. These dire conditions, resulting directly from centuries of slavery and colonial rule, have been intensified by the war to the point of "almost famine conditions in some places," as acknowledged in a recent bulletin of the British Information Services. Yet the Secretary of State for the Colonies of Great Britain in a recent statement publicly laments that the British taxpayer will be called upon to contribute to a small proposed fund for social development in the colonies.

The West Indies National Council respectfully but firmly submits to the United Nations' Conference that such colonial conditions constitute a major menace to World Security and Peace. The resolute liquidation of these menacing economic conditions should therefore be begun immediately. For this is imperative to raise the level of living standards and purchasing power of the Caribbean peoples, as of all peoples still subjected to colonial rule, in order to transform them into free and valuable participants in that increased production and exchange of goods and services which is no less essential to the security and peace of the people of the industrial advanced nations than it is to the welfare and progress of these now retarded colonial peoples.

Abolition of Imperialism Essential to World Peace

The Council also submits that such economic rehabilitation and progress, so essential to World Security and Peace, can be achieved only by breaking the fetters of imperialist domination and colonial dependency. For in no other way can the free political relations of mutually cooperating, self-governing peoples, fully respecting the democratic rights of each and all, be realized as the indispensable condition for social development and for the full release and stimulation of the energies of all in that increased production and exchange so vital to the security and peace of all mankind.

The Council further submits that the abolition of imperialist domination and colonial dependency will at the same time eliminate those conflicts over colonies which constitute the major source of war in the modern world. The logic of history now demands that imperialist control and colonial subjugation must cease that men may live and attain security and peace. A definite time in the immediate future should therefore be set in agreement with these peoples for the realization of full self-government and democratic rights for the Caribbean peoples and for all other colonial peoples.

Recommendations for Economic Rehabilitation

In accordance with the foregoing, the West Indies National Council earnestly recommends that a Fund adequate for the economic rehabilitation and social development of the Caribbean areas should be established under international supervision through the proposed International Bank for Reconstruction and Development or some similar agency. This Fund should be open to private and government subscription and substantial contributions to this Fund should be made by the British, French, and Dutch Empires. Since a large share of the vast fortunes and immense wealth of these Empires has been derived from the forced labor of the Caribbean peoples, these contributions would not only be in accord with justice but would also materially spur the increase in production and exchange which is recognized to be necessary to world prosperity, security, and peace.

Oppose Any Change Without Self-determination

In respect to their readiness for self-government, it is undeniable that the Caribbean peoples possess all the characteristics of nationality and have many times proclaimed their demand for self-government. To settle this question it is necessary only to point to the numerous West Indians who have occupied and now hold administrative posts in every branch of government and to the late Governor General of Free French Africa, Félix Eboué, a native of West Indies, whose administrative genius and timely action saved the greater part of Africa, and perhaps all Africa, from falling into the barbarous hands of the Vichy regime and the Nazi hordes in the darkest hours of the present war for the United Nations.

Present discussion and renewed proposals affecting the sovereignty of the West Indian peoples render it our duty to call attention to the following statements affirmed in the Declaration of Rights presented to the Havana Conference and to the supporting evidence adduced therein.

Reflecting and expressing the profound sentiments of the peoples of the Caribbean areas, this Committee declares that it is firmly opposed to any sale, transfer, mandate, trusteeship, or change of sovereignty of these peoples without the exercise of their inalienable human and democratic right of self-determination.

Trusteeship Thoroughly Discredited

In view of the urgency with which various proposals for mandates and trusteeships are being pressed upon this World Security Conference, it is imperative to affirm with renewed emphasis the following protest contained in the Statement of the West Indies National Emergency Committee on the Address delivered by Secretary Hull at the Havana Conference:

For, however well intentioned such a proposed trusteeship might appear, it cannot be forgotten that this device of trusteeship of mandate has been used and is now being used by imperial governments of the Old World as a means of maintaining control over various peoples and subjecting them to tyrannous oppression and unbridled exploitation.

It cannot be conceded for a moment that this discredited formula of trusteeship could be successfully employed in connection with the Caribbean peoples, when it is well known that it has signally failed either to ensure the democratic rights or to preserve the vital interests and welfare of the many down-trodden peoples to whom it has been applied.

International Commission Acceptable

In the opinion of this Council however, no truly representative objection might be expected from the Caribbean peoples to an International Commission specifically established to supervise the transition from colonial dependency to full self-government, provided their rights to self-government and self-determination were unequivocally recognized and a definite time mutually agreed upon for the realization of such complete self-government, and provided also that adequate and effective representation on such an International Commission were accorded to bona fide natives of these areas truly representative of the majority of these peoples.

Action Requisite Against Prejudice and Terror

This Council would fail in its sacred duty if it did not urge this World Security Conference to give serious consideration to the grave menace to world security and peace which stems from racial, national, and religious prejudices. This venomous ideology was developed to its monstrous height in the "master race" mania with which the Nazi imperialist butchers, the Italian fascist slaughterers, and the Japanese military war mongers incited their followers to plunge the world into the present holocaust of slaughter and terror. Full cognizance must therefore be taken of the existence of racial, national, and religious prejudices and of the fact that such poisonous prejudices have already reached alarming proportions within most of the democratic nations themselves, with dire results to minorities therein and to colonial peoples controlled by these states.

Moreover, it is imperative to be aware of the fact that these vicious prejudices are inherent in the system of imperialism in which they are rooted and from which they inevitably develop. It is likewise salutary to mark that the horrible atrocities perpetrated at Belsen, Buchenwald, Dachau and elsewhere, at which mankind is now properly aghast, differ only in detail and degree from similar atrocities perpetrated upon colonial and semi-colonial peoples. The security and peace of mankind require that the lesson of history be now practically drawn that terror and torture developed first in colonial areas inevitably reach back to the dominating peoples and menace all mankind.

The resolution adopted at the Chapultepec Conference, recognizing the existence of racial, national, and religious prejudices within the frontiers of any country to be a matter of international concern, is an important step forward. This Council earnestly recommends that this World Conference adopt such a resolution, as a vital principle for the organization of world security and peace, requiring that all nations shall enact and enforce laws with adequate penalties against any and all overt manifestations of such racial, national, and religious prejudices, and shall undertake a vigorous campaign of education for the extirpation of such prejudices and animosities.

Urges Adoption of Seven Point Proposals

The West Indies National Council earnestly and finally urges this World Security Conference to consider and to adopt the following seven proposals in the interests of the Caribbean peoples and of World Security and Peace.

1. Forthright recognition of the inalienable right of the Caribbean peoples to self-government and self-determination.
2. Practical recognition of the age-long objective of the West Indian peoples for voluntary federation.
3. Integration, on the basis of equality, of the Caribbean peoples into the regional organization of the American nations and for their representation in

the making of all plans for the political, military, economic and social security of all the peoples of the Americas.

4. Specific inclusion of the Caribbean peoples in the plans of the Conference for post-war rehabilitation and social security in view of the dire economic conditions of these peoples, resulting from colonial rule, which have been intensified by the war and which have reached almost famine conditions.

5. Recognition of the right of the Caribbean peoples to representation at the United Nations' Conference by delegates of their own choosing, as a matter of democracy and justice and by virtue of the vital contribution which the Caribbean peoples have made to the war effort and to democracy in this hemisphere and to the world.

6. Guarantees for the abolition of all discriminatory laws and practices based on race, religion, color or previous condition of servitude or oppression, and for the assurance of full protection of life and liberty for the Caribbean peoples, for the African peoples, and for all peoples without regard to race, creed, or color.

7. Genuine equality of rights both in fact and in law for all peoples everywhere and full democratic citizenship rights, including universal adult suffrage, for all people.

The West Indies National Council sincerely hopes for the success of this World Security Council and for the adoption of these measures which will enable the Caribbean peoples to take their rightful place among the nations of the world in a new era of freedom, security, peace and prosperity.

WEST INDIES NATIONAL COUNCIL
RICHARD B. MOORE
Vice-President and Chairman Conference Committee
LEONARD LOWE
Secretary
CHARLES A. PETIONI, M.D.
President

This was issued as an oversized four-page pamphlet; the original is here used. It contains an appendix detailing the total number of inhabitants in each of the English, French, and Dutch colonies, which came to about three and a half million. It is published, minus the appendix, in W. Burghardt Turner and Joyce Moore Turner, eds., *Richard B. Moore, Caribbean Militant in Harlem: Collected Writings, 1920–1972* (Bloomington: Indiana University Press, 1988), pp. 270–76. The information on Hiss is on p. 80.

9

A PSYCHOLOGICAL APPROACH TO RACE RELATIONS (1945)

by Horace Cayton

Horace Cayton, a graduate of the University of Washington, worked as a longshoreman, a porter, and a waiter. In the 1930s he held Rosenwald Fellowships and was a research assistant in sociology at the University of Chicago. He was coauthor, with St. Clair Drake, of *Black Metropolis* (1945). In the fall of 1945 he delivered a lecture at Reed College in Portland. He was then director of the Parkway Community House in Chicago. The lecture was published by Reed College as a *Bulletin* in November 1946. Extracts follow.

Within the past twenty-five years the Negro problem has changed from a sectional to a national, and finally, to a world problem. The migration northward following World War One initiated the stream of migrants which continued to flow throughout the depression years and grew into a mighty river during the period of World War Two. Now there is hardly a city in the United States which does not have some acquaintance with the problems involved in having a racially mixed population. This, then, was the first step which raised the Negro question to one of national status. It was not until the Second World War, however, that the American Negro became of world importance, became a part of the world problem of color and democracy. In the process of fighting a war against facism, the hopes for liberation and freedom of all subject people came to include the American Negro; the American Negro's fight was just one concrete manifestation of that global struggle. Our concern at the moment is with his change of status to one of national importance, and what it means to America.

One could enumerate the many concrete forms in which Negro life in America has been degraded. One could describe at length the share-cropping and semi-peonage system of the Deep South, the lack of educational and health facilities, which are reflected in a phenomenally high death rate, or the system of political disfranchisement of the poll tax states which has corrupted our national body politic as well as that of the South. Further, one could dwell at length upon the particular injustices which exist in our Northern urban communities and are manifested in a job ceiling which prevents Negroes from competing fairly and with equality in the field of employment, the vicious system of residential segregation which creates sprawling black ghettos, only slightly different in character from those of pre-war Poland.

I assume, however, that most readers are more or less familiar with this type of data. Further, I do not believe that the continual recitations of these disabilities which have been placed on our Negro population satisfy either our desire for a deeper analysis of motivation, or prepare us for a more aggressive type of social action. Without under-evaluating the necessity to know and be familiar with the system of race relations and its objective manifestations in our culture, I believe that it is time to devote some of our attention to the deeper, more elusive and irrational elements which make the perpetration of these phenomena possible and make it so difficult even for men of good will to effect a change.

Any discussion of the Negro question which will be fruitful must be one in which this problem is analyzed in the context of our entire American culture so that we can realize the contradictions and paradoxes existent in that culture. Glib references to the American way of life, our democratic institutions, and emotional statements expounding the belief in the equality of American citizens confuse the question unless we realize the conflicts which exist in our culture and find reflection in the division within our individual personalities. We must now know how these injustices came about, the social sanctions which allow them to be maintained, and the deep subterranean areas of conflict, frustration, hate, hope and fear in the mentality of Negroes and whites alike which result from this schism. Failure to do this will prevent our understanding of the behavior of our people and our own reactions to this confused, contradictory, and paradoxical society.

First we must consider the American culture which allows, permits, even encourages, the injustices which I have mentioned. Second, we must consider our individual internal conflicts which confuse our will and paralyze our action. Third, we must note the result this has on individual personalities—white and black—who live under our system of racial super- and sub-ordination. Fourth, we must consider the devastating effect this has in confounding our attempts to arrive at a more mature culture. . . .

The Negro in the United States is an oppressed minority. This oppression, based in some sections of the country on law, is further reinforced by tradition and custom. It finds its final sanction in the application of force and violence. It is a little difficult for us to think of the Negro as an oppressed people. Such terms as minority group, caste, second class citizens, etc., are more to our liking. But the hard fact is that the Negro is oppressed and his oppression finds its ultimate sanction in force....

I recall a trip I made in the Deep South with a famous sociologist and his wife. We rode on that trip as conspirators in an enemy country. Each meal presented itself as a challenge, a battle to be fought, and each success was greeted by us as a victory over the enemy. As lunch time grew near we were all silent with a tension which descended over the entire car. Would we, under some pretext, be able to eat together? If not, could I find a Negro restaurant? If there were no Negro restaurants, should I go to the kitchen of the white hotel and pretend to be their chauffeur or should I remain in the car and have them bring sandwiches to me? At night came the question of finding a place to sleep. Should I again pretend to be their servant and attempt to get servant quarters at the hotel? Could I find a Negro family who might have a clean guest room? Should I sleep in the car or should we all travel on, in spite of fatigue, until we could find a city where I could obtain lodging?

Even normal body functions presented a problem. They could be performed only with considerable opposition, delay, annoyance and irritation. Could I drink from the water fountain at the filling station? Would there be provisions for washing my hands or face? If a toilet was not marked "white" or "colored," dare I use it?

Every mile of the road we encountered difficulties, hindrances, and frictions which bothered, annoyed, and infuriated. All of these impeded our progress and upon all we expended energy which detracted from our pleasure and exhausted us physically and emotionally. Added to this friction was of course the fear which arose out of both the real danger and the irrational over-evaluation of possible danger in the environment. As a Negro, in performing the simple act of living, I found myself irritated by the frictions set up against me, endangered by real possibilities of harm, and the target of all of those barbs, indignities, heartaches, and the thousand shocks that black flesh is heir to.

10

"NEGROES! JEWS! CATHOLICS!" (1945)

by Roy Wilkins

Roy Wilkins, Walter White's assistant at the NAACP, contributed an article to the *Crisis*, June 1945 (pp. 217–19, 237–38), devoted largely to quoting from a filibuster conducted by Mississippi's senators, Theodore G. Bilbo and James O. Eastland. The filibuster was directed against a bill, introduced by Sen. Dennis Chavez of New Mexico, providing funds to continue the work of the Fair Employment Practices Committee (FEPC) for the ensuing year. In introducing the remarks of the filibusters, Roy Wilkins wrote:

The appropriation for the Fair Employment Practices Committee (FEPC) to continue its work through June 30, 1946 was supposed to be included in the War Agencies Bill, required to be passed by June 30. The amount originally requested for the FEPC was $599,000, but had been cut to $446,200. When the House finished with the War Agencies Bill, it omitted FEPC altogether. The Senate was disposed to restore the $446,200 item, but Senator Theodore G. Bilbo of Mississippi announced he would fight "to the death" against any money for the agency. He talked for two days (June 27–28) against the measure, and his colleague, Senator James O. Eastland of Mississippi, joined him on the last day (June 29) with a speech distinguished chiefly for its sweeping slander on Negro soldiers in World War II.

The principal ammunition of the two Senators was ranting against Negroes, Jews and Catholics. There were slurs on other racial groups including Mexicans (Senator Dennis Chavez of New Mexico, Senate sponsor of FEPC, is both a Spanish-American and a Catholic).

As shocking as the Senate speeches were, they become relatively insignificant in comparison to the revelation that it is possible for the representatives of the people in Congress to be denied an opportunity to express themselves on pending legislation. This bodes no good for democracy and suggests something of the stormy time ahead.

11

ERASING THE COLOR LINE

by A. Philip Randolph

The above was the title of a booklet published in September 1945 by Fellowship Publications in New York City. Also represented in producing this work was the then newly formed Congress of Racial Equality (CORE), with headquarters in Cleveland, Ohio. The booklet described instances of nonviolent direct-action campaigns, in the North and West, during the war, that succeeded in ending racist discrimination in several public establishments. The foreword by A. Philip Randolph heralds the efforts of the postwar era culminating in the crusade of which Dr. King became the symbol.

This little book discusses the principle of non-violent, good-will direct action as an instrumentality for achieving ethnic democracy in the United States. It is applied Christianity. It is applied democracy. It is Christianity and democracy brought out of gilded churches and solemn legislative halls and made to work as a dynamic force in our day-to-day life.

Since two-thirds of all the peoples of the world are colored, if racial democracy is not realized there is not much hope of creating permanently much of any other kind of democracy in the world. And racial democracy must consist in unequivocal recognition of equality among human beings regardless of race, color, religion, national origin, or ancestry, in our social relations, government, industry, labor, law, and education. People do not have to be all of the same color, religion, height or weight, or with long, round, or square heads, in order that their personalities may be considered of equal human worth and dignity.

Principles and modes of human behavior have been set forth in this booklet to help men and women respect each other as rational people so that they will be willing not only to die for democracy and peace on the far-flung battlefields and seven seas of the world, but will also work, study, play, worship God, and live together in creative co-operation here at home. For how can we love God whom we have not seen, if we hate our brothers—whatever their color, race, religion, national origin, or ances-try—whom we have seen? By the same token, how can we hope to win democracy by fighting abroad, if we are not willing to practice it at home?

Non-violent, good-will direct action is based upon the acceptance of the following assumptions as being valid and workable: First, the organic unity of the human family, without regard to race, color, religion, national origin, or ancestry. Second, the inevitable corollary of this principle, namely, that no human being is the natural enemy of another, but that human antagonisms of all kinds are the product of ignorance, fear, or anti-social selfishness, and that all hostile attitudes between persons and groups are subject to influence and change by some form of non-violent direct action for good-will. Third, human beings are not born with prejudices of race, color, religion, national origin, or ancestry, but they acquire them in the homes, schools, churches, press, movies, radio, books—that is, from our environment. Fourth, violence has not settled and cannot permanently and constructively settle any basic social prob-lem. Violence begets violence. He who draws the sword will perish by the sword. From these fundamental truths will flow the varied techniques: investigations, negotiations, and direct action with non-retaliation, the disciplined absorption of violence, non-violence in speech and action, refusal to engage in legal action for damage because of physical injury, and repetitive, non-violent, good-will direct action to make token victo-ries real, for repeated action makes for the development of group cause-consciousness.

I have great faith in the efficacy of non-violent, good-will direct action as one of the sound methods of avoiding violence and devastating racial wars and building a creative, co-operative ethnic democracy. In this booklet, Mr. George Houser has presented this philosophy with force and conviction. The cases of the principle in action are simple but graphic.

Thus, I wish to commend this treatise to all lovers of democracy who are courageous enough to stand up and be counted in the interest of a better world.

12

ADULT EDUCATION PROGRAMS IN HOUSING PROJECTS WITH NEGRO TENANTS

by Frank Horne and Corienne K. Robinson

Frank S. Horne and Corienne K. Robinson, of the Federal Public Housing Authority, offered a description of one phase of a war-born program affecting tens of thousands of African-American men and women. The optimism conveyed reflects the general atmosphere appropriate to a war against fascism. An elaborate table and numerous footnotes have been omitted. This was in the *Journal of Negro Education,* published by Howard University [Summer 1945], 14, 353–62.

The Federal Public Housing Authority, one of the three constituents of the National Housing Agency, is responsible for publicly financed war housing and low-rent slum clearance programs. Low-rent housing projects are initiated, owned, and operated by local housing authorities with specifically limited financial, technical, and advisory aid received through FPHA. War housing projects, however, are programmed by the Administrator's Office of the National Housing Agency, and remain in Government ownership. Although there are basic differences in responsibility as between the two programs, all low-rent housing and more than half of the FPHA war housing is actually managed by local agencies.

Both programs provide communities which dynamically affect the lives of the tenants during the period of residence. The pre-war slum clearance program was definitely aimed at wiping out the physical blight of a neighborhood and eliminating slum living and slum thinking. Not only shelter but a way of living was provided. The war program, however, is to provide shelter to newly arrived war workers. The associated amenities were designed to facilitate personal adjustment to a new environment under the stresses and tensions of wartime living.

War housing and low-rent housing represent tremendous expenditures of public funds or of funds secured by Federal credit. Almost $2,500,000,000 was announced in late 1944 as the total cost of these developments, representing the biggest real estate operation under a single agency in history. Some $680,000,000 of this amount is invested in low-rent housing. These large sums have been spent upon planning, site selection and acquisition, and building construction to eradicate the degenerating filth of the slum and provide a clean shell within which a new way of life may evolve. This is no mean dividend itself, but the major pay-off on the investment depends upon what goes on within the physical walls of the project, in its rooms and on its walks, streets, and playgrounds. Herein lies the major function of management and especially that phase known as "Project Services."

The most vital management function involves a complex range of responsibilities as between public housing and other agencies. Public housing provides shelter and facilities, management standards and guidance, and what might be called a unifying center for community organization in its broadest sense. The fact that large groupings of tenants are brought together under an organizational structure affording central contact and channels through to every tenant is an invaluable asset to program promotion of all kinds. The actual operation of project services activities, including adult education, however, is primarily regarded as the responsibility of those agencies which are responsible for these activities in the larger community. One of the underlying principles of public housing is that the project be an integral part of the community and its residents be members of the neighborhood.

The project management staff, however, plays a vital role in establishing contacts with cooperating agencies, stimulating tenants' interest, and otherwise offering guidance necessary in any given situation. As one manager states in his report, program development is not brought about by waving a magic wand.

Successful operations of these activities depend essentially upon tenant organizations. These associations, made up of a majority of the tenants or in the form of representative councils elected by a majority of the residents, serve as advisory groups to work with management in planning and promoting tenant activities and services and in making and carrying out regulations. Successful adult education activities, like all other tenant programs, almost invariably grow out of tenant groups. This is recognized in the majority of reports and is typified by the following statement:

> The purpose of this organization is to assist the management in every way in making our project one of the finest in the city.... To encourage and help in every way possible any endeavor that will tend to upgrade the thinking and habits of the folk of our community...making this city a better place in which to live.

Scope of the Program

According to a statistical summary of the participation by Negroes in the public housing program up to September 30, 1944, over 128,000 or 18 percent of the total 710,000 dwelling units under the Federal Public Housing Authority, were available to Negroes, in projects either totally or partially occupied by them throughout the United States. These units consisted of 46,000 in 190 low-rent projects and over 82,000 in 482 war housing projects....

By a conservative estimate, about 230,000 of the approximate 410,000 Negroes living in public housing projects are adults, and 90,000 of these adults are occupants of slum-clearance, low-rent housing developments.

While admission to war housing projects is determined by employment in essential war occupations, and not by previous residency in substandard housing or by low-income status, as is the case for low-rent housing, it is unquestionably true that the vast majority of Negro tenants in war housing projects differ from the Negro tenants in low-rent housing far less in these respects than is true of white tenants. Accordingly, it would follow that all of the 90,000 Negro adults now living in low-rent housing projects and the vast majority of 140,000 in war housing, have come from sub-standard living conditions.

Fundamental Needs to Be Met

Although many of the fundamental needs which should be met by the adult education program in the project community are identical for all racial groups, the intensity of these needs is generally greater for the Negro tenant, and there are several distinctive features related to the prevailing social mores. These needs which are typical of all low-income families require no introductory emphasis, but those which distinguish the Negro family either in terms of degree or character, should be kept in mind in evaluating the adult education activities.

The Negro war housing occupant, like the white tenant, is usually a newcomer in the locality. As such he frequently becomes the "goat" for the community's antagonism against the "intruding outsiders," and suffers extremely from the cultural and class conflicts inevitable in this situation. In too many cases, the Negro in-migrant is no more welcome to the resident Negro community than he is to the dominant group in the community.

Like all families who have come from slum neighborhoods and substandard housing, Negro families suffer all of the economic and social disadvantages that result from their low-income status. The Negro tenant, may, therefore, be said to need all that the comparable tenant of the white race might need, but he needs it more intensely and has fewer opportunities for satisfaction.

The Negro generally, to say nothing of the slum dweller, and especially the Negro in areas where racial separation is practiced, is isolated from the mainstream of civic, social, economic, and political life. This separation from the flow of American culture distorts his entire outlook, gives him a sense of "not belonging," and is indicative of the gap that still remains between present practices and the democratic ideal.

The reports, accordingly, are replete with statements to the effect that the public housing project in many communities has provided the first or only facilities available to Negroes for community improvement and civic activity and has effected channels for linking the Negro community with the larger group either by bringing services into the project or by the relationships established between the project and the total resources of the community.

One manager reports that the community in which the project is now located suffered from a disease known as "LACKS"—it lacked everything.

How Negroes Participate

In terms of racial patterns, which are primarily local determinations, there are, roughly, three significant conditions influencing the participation of Negroes in adult educational activities. *First,* where there is no arbitrary concentration or separation by racial groups, Negroes are likewise integrated in the activities. In addition to all other by-products of specific activities, here, obviously intercultural education takes place. One manager asserts that "the very fact that a number of racial and cultural groups live side by side on a democratic basis and learn to gain a measure of respect and appreciation, one for the other, has within itself been of the highest educational value."

Second, there are border line situations particularly in projects jointly occupied by the two racial groups, but with various degrees of racial separation, either physical location or by activities. In these developments, there are, likewise, various patterns of participation by Negroes. They may take part in many of the tenant activities, for example, resident councils or tenant organizations and certain officially sponsored programs in association with all other tenants. Other operations tend to be dual in every respect.

Third and *finally,* complete separation upon the basis of race, resulting either in projects or sections totally tenanted by Negroes, effect comparable separation in the activities. There are projects, however, where residential separation by race is supplemented by joint participation of all groups in project activities.

Numerical participation cannot, of course, be accurately demonstrated in the absence of surveys including racial breakdowns. Through observation and experience, however, it is revealed that Negroes, by and large, utilize project service facilities and take part in adult educational opportunities afforded by the project to an even higher degree, proportionately, than do their white prototypes. This, obviously, is due to the fact, previously indicated, that the project frequently offers the only facility or activity in the community to which the Negro has free access. As a matter of fact, an operation in the Northwest reports that efforts to achieve joint tenant activities have, to some extent, been handicapped by the disproportionately high percentage of Negroes using the facilities. It was found that they were not welcomed in the larger community to which tenants of other racial groups were attracted and had full access.

The Core of Adult Education

Although the adult education programs conducted within the facilities provided by public housing are unquestionably important and have made a significant contribution to the lives of the project tenants, these activities are not generally considered as direct responsibilities of the public housing program. Furthermore, in character they do not essentially differ from these programs as conducted outside of a project community.

That part of adult education which is truly unique and extensive in the program of public housing is related to and inherent in the process of *living in a public housing project.* This is the real core of adult education in public housing. Further significance is attached to this in light of the fact that every tenant, though in varying degrees and with diverse results, is affected by tenancy in the project; whereas, only a part of any project population takes part in the activity and group programs.

From the moment a public housing project is initiated in a given locality, adult education, in its broadest sense, is introduced. The first direct line to the potential tenants of the project begins at that point where the community learns that a project is being developed. In many cases, however, the impact of the program is most direct when site acquisition is begun and the occupants of substandard housing on the chosen site are moved from the dwelling to be demolished. In this situation, the occupants of a slum neighborhood frequently find themselves for the first time involved in a position of active concern with the policies and procedures of a municipal agency, drastically affecting their living habits. In the course of this entire process of displacement and relocation, explanation and adjustment, the site occupants are introduced to (a) the purpose of the program and its justification in terms of the "public interest," (b) their rights and privileges, and (c) their future stake in the project under development.

At the tenant selection stage, those who make application for admission to the project are introduced, and usually for the first time, to a concept of *new housing*, to which they have access, as well as to standard occupancy practices. They learn about the composition of families eligible for the project, the number of rooms suitable for each given family size, the age and sex of persons who may occupy the same sleeping quarters, and other similar standards of privacy, health, and decency. In addition to this, they are given an interpretation of many other conditions of life in a large-scale standard development, generally outlining the privileges and responsibilities of each tenant in relationship to a project community. One report describes this as follows:

> Since it is a new experience for Negroes to live in a housing project, the manager adopted his own policy of visiting with prospective tenants to acquaint them with the apartments. All rules and regulations were explained and all advantages and accommodations of the Courts were extended to them.

If the applicant is eligible and secures a dwelling unit, this process goes even further. The head of the family signs a lease establishing on a formal and business-like basis, a tenant-management relationship and outlining the mutual responsibilities involved in this relationship.

For example, one manager reports as "business education" the process of regular rental payments. At this stage, also, tenant maintenance methods and benefits are indicated, and management resources and services explained.

The actual "move-in" marks another serious modification of the tenants' lives. Personal effects and appearances are usually "dressed up." Several managers observe that living in a project is training for future home-ownership and property protection. Then the educational processes which are a function of space, design, equipment, environment, and facility begin to operate. It is in this milieu that the family absorbs an alternative to slum-living. And it is in relationship to these factors that those, who are not impervious to the influence—as is occasionally true—reorient family life, personal interests, as well as general outlook and attitude. In the sense of belonging, community pride, and awakened responsibility, the project tenant becomes a part of those activities identifiable as programs.

Tenant Associations

Among the "programs," one most distinctively or uniquely developing as a direct result of public housing projects is the tenant association or resident council. "We consider our Tenants Association our greatest adult education program," witnesses the manager of an outstanding project located in Georgia. The objectives of this association, he states, are to establish a pattern of organization, to familiarize the tenants with the national and local governmental structure, to develop community consciousness of social problems, and to acquaint the tenants with proper organizational procedures. The organization consists of president, vice-president, senate, house of representatives, and an impressive secretariat including one each for community welfare, labor, health, education, and recreation. The editor of the project newspaper also has "cabinet" status.

Citizenship education is promoted through annual election of officers. At the last election the Association was divided into "Republican" and "Democratic" campaigns.

. . . Outstanding citizens of the city were presented in behalf of the candidates [to association offices] of each party. The project was divided into precincts with strategically located voting booths. . . . Already we know that many of our tenants have become registered voters as a result of their interest in the political life of the project. . . .

Another project, located in Tennessee, reports that through the

tenant's associations, a considerable number of tenants have been trained in the art of conducting meetings, keeping records, handling budgets and spending other people's money. Through this medium a number of individuals have learned how to serve on committees and how to think and express themselves while before an audience. An understanding of parliamentary procedure and the technique of balloting has been a useful by-product.

Intercultural Education

With the exception of organizations devoted to race relations, like the National Association for Advancement of Colored People, relatively little adult education, effective upon attitudes of either the Negro or white people, is found in projects totally occupied by Negroes. It is noteworthy, nevertheless, that frequent references to the impact of projects upon race relations, even with respect to these projects, are included in the reports. For example, a report from a Texas development states that in the locality, which is described as "a place of strong racial feelings" the project has "brought about a spirit of good relationship between the races." The limitations of this are, nonetheless, self-evident.

Interracial and intercultural education, however, frequently takes place in jointly occupied projects. The range of these programs is extensive: A tenant sponsored newspaper of one project community published serially the Public Affairs pamphlet, "Races of Mankind" and, on the same development, an exhibit was shown with photographs and narratives on the contributions Negroes have made to American culture. Others report classes in the history of Negroes in the United States, forums and religious services focusing discussion on cultural, nationality, and racial questions. But outstanding among the educational activities along this line is the experience of resident councils and tenant associations, clubs and other organizations, in which officers and members generally reflect the racial composition of the project occupants. As one report states, "this sustained, day-by-day collaboration of races in solving community problems has been of benefit to all participants." Another report asserts that "the existence and activity of a resident's council, made up of seven Mexican-Americans, seven Jews, seven Negroes and seven Anglo-Americans, not only has contributed materially to the successful operation of the project, but represents a real step toward inter-racial and inter-national cooperation." And from two areas where racial tensions have resulted in rioting, reports indicate that the communities of jointly occupied projects have not been affected.

These kinds of experiences have been most significant in war housing projects where the tenants, both white and Negro, have migrated in large numbers from all sections of the country.

Tenant's Newspapers

Also, relatively distinctive in the project community is the tenants' newspaper, published in a large number of developments. One manager states that "selling advertising space, dealing with printers, and writing articles has developed talent among least likely individuals," and another observes that the tenant participants learn about "propaganda and circulation." This is also believed to have stimulated interest in advanced English classes.

Forums

The tenant sponsored forums have been of unusual interest. Discussions on such subjects as the poll tax, registration requirements, G.I. Bill of Rights, housing, and citizenship are reported. Sponsorship of a discussion of veteran's interest by a war wives and mothers club is observed.

Homemaking and Maintenance

There have been two major approaches to homemaking or housekeeping and property maintenance. One, which has affected all tenants, has grown out of the requirement for tenant maintenance on low-rent housing projects. Tenants learn the best practices in care of equipment, interiors, furniture, lawns, etc. Training in fire prevention, safety, and heating is also conducted universally by management. The other approach is through homemaking and housekeeping programs in which tenants voluntarily participate and to which a large number of them have been attracted.

These programs have benefited from extensive professional assistance. In some cases, particularly in several projects located in Texas, trained home counselors have conducted these programs. Cooperation has frequently been received from the municipal public school systems and, of course, such agencies as the Office of Price Administration have made important contributions.

These programs are highly diversified and certain phases, for example, furniture make-over workshops, are of interest to men. The general pattern covers conservation and preparation of food, nutrition, canning, gardening, sewing, and needlework, home decorating, rug making, and pest-control. Clubs, clinics, demonstrations, exhibits, and even formal classes are utilized to conduct these programs.

Buying clubs and cooperative stores are becoming increasingly popular in project communities, and the emphasis, as is usually taken, upon "buying by the pound instead of by the teaspoon" is of unquestionable importance for low-income families.

A formal class in home management is reported, and it has stressed thrift, savings accounts, and War Bonds. In another case, the War Bond club, featuring stamp purchase, is so organized as to commit the tenants to hold their bonds at least one year unless the club gives permission for them to be cashed.

Vocational Training

Many programs directly related to developing job skills have been conducted especially in areas of wartime industrial activity. In these, the project facilities have been utilized by groups sponsoring the programs, and the activity has been the responsibility of the cooperating agency. Management has also, in some reported instances, encouraged project tenants employed in unskilled labor, to take advantage of training offered elsewhere for semi-skilled and skilled jobs, and has in effect, offered recruiting services for these courses.

The most extensive program in vocational education was that conducted by the Works Progress Administration, and substitute sponsorship since that program was abandoned has not been found on large-scale.

One of the most interesting examples, however, of successful training is a class in ceramics taught by an instructor from the University of Southern California. After public demonstrations, "three members of the class had progressed far enough to open shops for the sale of their products.... Some have built small electric kilns for ceramic jewelry. The goal of most of the students is to learn enough to start a home industry in ceramics, providing dignified employment in a satisfying profession." Classes in leather and metal work and other hand-crafts are conducted on a few projects.

Incident to the Victory Garden programs, training in agriculture, use of tools, pest control and horticulture have gained considerable stimulus. Cooperative buying is another by-product of this program.

Cultural Education and the Arts

Adult reading classes, originally sponsored by WPA, have been continued in many cases through cooperation with municipal Boards of Education and, in one case, the Council of Social Agencies. Advanced English classes, languages, and many other miscellaneous courses are reported.

Another phase of this approach has been focused around the many libraries, several of which are formally established branches of city systems, located in projects and operated by volunteer librarians who are project residents. Tenants' book review clubs, and reading societies are associated with these.

Dramatic groups, art classes, and folk and block dancing have also been introduced. Numerous music clubs have been organized—and the activities include music appreciation, concerts, recitals, community singing, choral work, orchestras, and bands. These are especially important links to the larger community.

Health

Health programs report a high proportion of tenant participation, and cover such phases as physical culture, prenatal and well baby clinics and conferences, first aid and safety courses, communicable disease control, immunization, sex education, and personal hygiene. These are, however, all conducted within the project facilities by cooperating agencies such as public health services and the American Red Cross.

Community Resources and Agencies

While many low-income families, who have lived through the era of economic depression, are acquainted with public relief, the management practice of referring tenants to various service agencies has served to educate them extensively in fuller use of community resources. Thus, tenants have often learned through their project experience about old age pensions, aid to dependent children, health and family resources outside of those within the project community.

Cooperative working relationships by formal agreements are also established with many public and private agencies through which their services are made available to project occupants. Among these are the

National Urban League, Travelers Aid, the Family Welfare Association of America, American Women's Voluntary Services, Library Division of the U.S. Office of Education, Office of Civilian Defense, National Federation of Settlements, the National Recreation Association, and the National YWCA and YMCA.

The Future of Adult Education

Despite many influences tending to establish standard approaches, management practices vary extensively from community to community and from project to project. The experiences upon which this article are primarily based are admittedly selected because they serve to illustrate not only the actual performance in many projects, but also the potential of every public housing development. It is further true that many project activities, during the war, have been handicapped by shortages of personnel, lack of leisure time, curtailment of many customary activities, and other demands upon time, energy, and resources in the interest of the war effort. But most important of all is recognition of the fact that all management is not equally competent or inclined to develop the fullest possibilities of the project services activities, a factor significant both to the success of these operations in general and to the pattern of Negro participation.

It may be safely estimated that the lives of more than 2,000,000 people are directly affected through their occupancy in public housing developments, and, to the extent that they are a part of the total community and crystallize patterns of sound, democratic living in such communities, their indirect influence is immeasurable.

Both in the protection of this huge investment and in the ultimate effect of the operation upon thousands of human lives, the Federal Government and the municipal agencies concerned with the management of these developments share a tremendous responsibility. And the sound results of the programs, in terms of eradicating slums and their degenerating effects and in achieving high standards of property maintenance, to say nothing of the social considerations, are determined by the quality of management.

Inept and irresponsible managements will not only prevent all the people from realizing the potential dividends of their tax funds, but may allow these projects to fix, under government auspices, patterns of living which may be subversive of the ideals of the Constitution and its Bill of Rights.

Under sound, skillful and imaginative management, these projects and their associated services may become veritable arsenals of democracy, fashioning day by day in the routine of living the tools and the attitudes to strengthen and extend our "way of life" to embrace all races, colors and creeds.

13

JIM CROW CHALLENGED (1946)

Two editorial paragraphs in the January 1946 issue of the organ of the NAACP reflected a sense of optimism that marked the Allied victory. The headings are from the magazine:

New Year, New Ideas

As 1945 drew to a close, the North Carolina Student Legislative Assembly voted to invite Negro colleges in the state to send delegates to the session next year. Not content with this, the students also proposed the abolition of the Jim Crow law on street cars and buses in North Carolina.

Congratulations to the young men and women in the white colleges of North Carolina! They see clearly that the old must give place to the new, that in race relations, as in everything else, in order to make progress, we must have action, not merely talk. Some of the elders in the state are more than a little disturbed by the action of the young people. Outspoken was Thad Eure, Secretary of State, who fears that the students are going "too fast." Mr. Eure belongs to the school that believes "the time isn't ripe."

In education for Negroes, North Carolina more than a decade ago broke away from the traditions of the region and became the most advanced state in the entire South. It has always boasted (with considerable justification) that relations between the races generally in North Carolina are better than elsewhere in the South.

This step that its college young people have taken is the natural next move for a leader. The recommendation on Jim Crow laws in transportation is understandable when considered in the light of the North Carolina (rather than the Dixie) tradition. It has been hinted that state officials may put some pressure on Negro college heads to get them to persuade the Negro students not to accept the invitation, but it is to be hoped that the elders will recognize the opportunity their state has to make history in 1946 as it did in education years ago and thus contribute immeasurably to interracial understanding and progress.

Jim Crow Home to Roost

The Preparatory Commission of the United Nations Organization has voted to locate the site of the world headquarters in the United States, but before the actual spot is selected, Americans will have to answer the question brought up by the delegate from India. He asked:

"Will the site be such that every delegate of every delegation will have the same freedom of movement and thought as everyone else?"

Sir Ramaswand Mudaliar, who asked this truly $64 question, told reporters he had been "shocked" recently in Washington, D.C., when he was told that he could not invite a Negro member of the State department staff to have dinner with him at his hotel.

Louisiana, Virginia, South Carolina and Florida are among the many states and cities seeking the UNO headquarters, but these Jim Crow localities might as well save their breaths, their cablegrams, and their delegations. A world organization containing many nations that are not white cannot be bothered with the petty prejudices of the American South. The South can have its Jim Crow and Boston, New York or San Francisco can have the UNO.

Crisis, January 1946, p. 9.

14

A CRUCIAL PROBLEM IN RACE RELATIONS: HOUSING (1946)

This study of housing conditions in five northern cities, 1940–45, was prepared by Rose Helper, research fellow, Department of Social Sciences, Fisk University. It is a detailed examination of a "crucial problem" that has marked African-American life in the second half of the twentieth century.

Negro citizens of America are the worst housed of all Americans.
From Resolutions adopted at the Cincinnati Conference, N.A.A.C.P.
Bulletin, July, 1946.

Shortage in Housing

There has been a shortage in housing for the country as a whole for
some years. The National Resources Planning Board issued the following
statement in 1940:

> It was estimated in 1937 that 800,000 nonfarm homes should be built each year
> for the next five years if we were to catch up with the deficit which has
> accumulated up to that time. But in 1937 about 300,000 were provided, in 1938
> about 350,000 and in 1939 about 450,000.

The influx of war workers into the cities of the North resulted in a
crisis in housing. To make matters worse, housing programs were reduced
on account of the shortage of building materials. The present shortage in
housing is apparent in the statement of John B. Blandford, administrator
of the National Housing Agency, that an annual average production of
1,250,000 nonfarm houses will be needed during the first ten post-war
years to take care of new families, returning veterans, families now living
doubled up and to replace half of the clearly substandard housing in the
country.

During the second World War, conditions of Negro housing in Chicago,
Detroit, Cleveland, Buffalo, St. Louis and other cities changed on the
whole from bad to worse. The shortage in housing for Negroes was even
more pronounced than it was for the white population, since racial
segregation had maintained a constant shortage in nonwhite dwelling
units apart from and beyond the general shortage in housing. When the
war began the housing available to Negroes was already crowded and
although resident Negro families showed a generosity which would be
hard to match, they simply could not absorb newcomers in the volume that
appeared.

CHICAGO

By 1944 some 70,000 Negroes had come to Chicago. The Mayor's
Committee on Race Relations in Chicago stated in its 1944 report
"Because of the volume of Negro immigration, Chicago has one of the
most pressing housing problems in the nation." Negro immigrants

continued to pour into Chicago throughout 1945. It was estimated that the total increase in the Negro population by the end of 1945 was between 80,000 and 100,000, which brings the Negro population from 280,000 in the 1940 Census up to about 375,000.

The general shortage in housing in Chicago is considered to be of "crisis proportions." At the end of 1945 there existed an *immediate* shortage of 100,000 dwelling units. Families even moved into the Mecca building, condemned as unfit for years, and were finally allowed to rent the quarters they occupied at their own risk. The need for additional homes available to Negroes has become "catastrophic."

DETROIT

Detroit's Negro population increased by 62,555 in the wartime in-migration, which represents an increase of forty-seven per cent. The extreme shortage of housing for Negroes in Detroit has been given as one of the causes of the June riot in 1943. During the war, the production of houses for white occupancy nearly kept up with the demand. Continued production is necessary but there is no serious crisis. The situation for Negroes, already serious before the war, is almost "beyond comprehension." During the war thirty per cent of the total in-migration was Negro. In March, 1945, at least 6,000 families of essential war workers were living in single rooms, usually the families were split up and the whole situation was demoralizing. Estimates of housing needs for Negroes range from 6,000 to 20,000 dwellings.

The reason for the lack of homes for Negroes in Detroit is not hard to find. The question has not been one of Negro ability to pay or disinterest on the part of the Negro in improving his housing conditions. Bankers, realtors and builders are almost unanimous today in their recognition that there are thousands of Negroes who are good mortgage risks and who are able to buy good houses. Public housing authorities have found that they make equally good tenants as compared with white tenants. The problem for both public and private developers has been entirely one of locating housing sites. Private developers as a group have themselves produced the situation by having followed the practice in the past of restricting the use of the land to whites only. Government agencies, however, are showing no more wisdom or courage, inasmuch as government has the power to sweep the restrictions aside, but the responsible officials do not have the courage to face the opposition.

CLEVELAND

In 1940, the total population of Greater Cleveland (Cuyahoga County) was 1,217,000, of which 110,000 were Negroes. During the years 1940–1945, the total population increased by 33,000 or 2.7 per cent, while the Negro population increased by 22,855 or 26.2 per cent. A housing shortage for the population as a whole and for the Negro population in particular has kept increasing. The vacancy rate went from less than one per cent in 1940 to zero at the beginning of 1946.

BUFFALO

It was estimated that the Negro population of Buffalo increased by 6,281 from 1940 to August 1, 1943, an increase of 35.5 per cent, and that the total Negro population in 1943 was 23,975. The need for additional housing for the Negro population in Buffalo was so acute by December of 1945 that "some immediate action" was believed to be imperative.

ST. LOUIS

The population of St. Louis has increased from the Census enumeration of 816,045 in 1940 to approximately 850,000 as of February 5, 1946. The percentage of Negro population of St. Louis was 13.3 as of the 1940 census. This percentage increased over the war years owing to the influx of Negro war workers, but the precise amount of increase was not established by February 5, 1946. According to a report of 1941 of the St. Louis Housing Authority, St. Louis was not a city with a housing shortage. Housing was not even scarce for low income families. Decent housing for Negroes, however, was at a premium. A study recently made by the Commerce Department of the Census Bureau revealed that in St. Louis the vacancy rate in residential property available to white people was .9 per cent while for Negroes the vacancy rate was .3 per cent. In other words, the proportion of available houses for whites was three times that for Negroes.

Overcrowding as a Result of In-migration

The influx of a large number of war workers into the cities of the North has intensified the already overcrowded condition of Negro areas both as to land density and number of persons per room.

In 1939 the main South Side Negro area in Chicago had 252,201 persons living in 4.2 square miles. The 80,000 Negroes who came into Chicago after 1939 are chiefly concentrated in the main South Side Negro Section and they have added to the pressure and overcrowding in this and other areas open to Negroes. Overcrowding in Chicago's Negro areas during the war became so great that in one district where whites were crowded to a ratio of 35,000 to 40,000 per square mile, one Negro neighborhood reached the unbelievable density of 90,000. Since 12,000 to 15,000 persons per square mile is the average residential density desirable in the city of Chicago in new areas, according to the Chicago Plan Commission, at least five square miles of vacant land are necessary to house adequately the excess population (75,000 to 100,000) now cramped in the Black Belt. In a survey of dwelling occupancy conducted by the Bureau of Census in March, 1944, which covered the major part of the South Side Negro Community (Douglas, Grand Boulevard and Washington Park areas), it was found that over a fourth (26.3 per cent) or about 15,780 dwelling units were overcrowded—that is, had more than one and one-half persons per room. Of the 15,780 dwelling units, 11,160 consisted of only one room. Over nine thousand (9,180) or 82.2 per cent of these single room units were occupied by two persons. The remaining eighteen per cent (1,980 units) had three or more persons living in one room. In six hundred one-room units, four or more persons were residing. Six hundred and sixty dwelling units of two rooms had five or six occupants. The vacancy rate in this whole area has not changed since August 1943 when it was 0.3 per cent of all dwelling units.

The Detroit Housing Commission made a special survey of 4,900 applicants and reapplicants for housing who applied during February and March of 1945. Of the 2,992 Negro applicants, over 1,900 or sixty-five per cent, were living under greatly overcrowded conditions. In most cases the overcrowded homes were also inadequate. In many of the Negro households over ten persons slept in three rooms. It was reported that as many as 16 Negro persons were found living in one room in Detroit, eight working on a day shift and eight working on a night shift.

In Cleveland in 1945 the percentage of overcrowding in dwelling units occupied by Negroes was 8.7 per cent as compared with 1.9 per cent of the white occupied dwelling units. A survey of vacancy in the Cleveland area revealed that in Area II, the eastern section of Cleveland, the gross vacancy rate in white neighborhoods was 1.3 per cent and in Negro neighborhoods was 0.7 per cent.

The General Housing Manager of the St. Louis Housing Authority wrote recently that the City is extremely crowded as the result of war in-migration and "that Negro conditions are worse because of a larger percentage of influx of Negroes and because the quarters occupied by Negroes were more greatly substandard at the beginning of the immigration." In St. Louis, in 1945, 20.2 per cent of dwelling units occupied by Negroes were crowded, as compared with 5.1 per cent of the white dwelling units.

In Cincinnati the percentages of overcrowding were whites 6.9 per cent, Negroes 15.3 per cent.

Overcrowding has not been limited to the cities of the North. In Los Angeles more than a quarter of a million people arrived after Pearl Harbor. While the total population increased twice as fast in the years 1940–1944 as in the decade before, the Negro population increased seventeen times as fast and housing for the Negro did not increase proportionately. All unrestricted districts were "packed and jammed." In the spring of 1944, almost 79,000 Negroes crowded into the old Japanese quarter, renamed Bronzville.

In Atlanta, Georgia, in 1945, 5.9 per cent of the white tenant families were overcrowded. For Negroes the percentage was 18.8. In Mobile, Alabama the percentages were whites 6.9 and Negroes 21.1.

Physical Aspects of Negro Housing Conditions

The housing of the country as a whole was found to be unsatisfactory in the real property surveys which were conducted between 1934 and 1936 in 203 urban areas and later in other cities and which included over two-fifths of the urban families in the United States. Of all the dwelling units covered in the surveys, five per cent had no private indoor flush toilets, twenty per cent were without private bathtubs or showers, over forty per cent lacked central heating equipment and sixteen per cent (exclusive of New York City) were rated as either in need of major repairs or unfit for use. The real property inventories served to substantiate the claim that one-third of the nation was ill housed in the thirties.

In 1940 one in every four urban houses occupied by whites was substandard; in the case of non-whites, two out of every three houses were substandard.

Since building materials were lacking, Negro housing conditions, which were among the worst in the country before and during 1940, could not help but grow worse during the war, even if landlords had been prevailed upon to make any improvements.

Negro housing in Chicago was described in a report of the Chicago Housing Authority in 1941 as being "the worst in the city." The report goes on to say:

> Areas available for Negro occupancy are walled in by deed restrictions so that the increase in population within the limited areas is resulting in terrific overcrowding and all the other evils that result from an intense shortage. In a sample survey made by C. H. A. of 854 dwelling units ranging in rental from $5.00 to $45, there were no families living in standard conditions.

In 1942, two-thirds of the main Black Belt was classified as "blighted" or "near-blighted" by the Chicago Plan Commission. That the quality of Negro housing has not improved over the 1920–1945 period is made clear in the following statement from the report of the Chicago Conference on Home Front Unity:

> In 1920, the Governor's Commission on Race Relations appointed to study the causes of Chicago's 1919 riots concluded:
> We recommend better enforcement of health and sanitary laws and regulations in the care, repair and upkeep of streets and alleys and the collection and disposal of rubbish and garbage in areas of Negro residence, where the commission has found those matters to be shamefully neglected. Our inquiry has shown that insufficiency in amount and quality of housing is an all-important factor in Chicago's race problem.
> In 1945, the members of this subcommittee can find no improvement in the quality of housing which might temper its damage to race relations.

According to the census of 1940, thirty-four per cent of the dwelling units occupied by Negroes in Detroit were substandard. Substandard housing here includes basement, garage and store front quarters, housing lacking bath facilities and cooking facilities, infested with rats and vermin, and having no inside toilet and no running water. In 1940 one out of every three Negro families was living under these conditions. The situation in 1944 was much worse. It was estimated that at least two out of every three Negro families were living in substandard homes.

The housing picture in Cleveland has become progressively worse during the war years. The situation as it relates to Negroes was more serious in 1940 than it was for the whites and is even worse at this time.

In April of 1943 a survey was made by the Buffalo Municipal Housing Authority to determine the amount of Negro in-migration. The sample area was chosen within Census Tract No. 14, a tract almost entirely occupied by Negroes and known to be heavily populated and overcrowded in normal times. This area, which in 1940 had contained 1,603 nonwhite dwelling units, contained 2,003 nonwhite dwelling units in October, 1943. This increase in dwelling units was due largely to makeshift accommodations not fit for habitation.

In the North area of St. Louis, before Carr Square Village was built in 1941, 88.5 per cent of the dwelling units were substandard. More than ninety-three per cent of the families of the North area were Negro in 1941.

Private and Public Housing

The serious overcrowding in Negro areas in the five cities of the North as a result of in-migration has been alleviated by private and public housing to a very slight degree.

In Chicago the in-migrant war workers were housed in a variety of ways. The Homes Use Service found homes for some. About ten per cent of the priorities issued to private contractors were for houses intended to go to the Negro Market, but only slightly over two per cent of this housing was made available to Negroes. The Chicago Housing Authority with federal funds put up six war housing developments. Of these the Robert H. Brooks Homes, with 834 dwelling units, the West Chesterfield Homes, with 250 dwelling units, and the Altgeld Gardens, with 1,500 dwelling units, were entirely occupied by Negro war workers, with in-migrants given preference. Of the Frances Cabrini Homes forty per cent of the total 586 dwelling units were made available to Negro families. Of the 4,076 apartments in the Ida B. Wells Homes, 1,707 units were to be occupied by Negroes. The Negro Housing situation was not greatly relieved, however, because about 10,000 more units were necessary.

The 1943 report of the Detroit Housing Commission states in part:

Despite the extent of Negro migration, there has been no building or expansion for this group. Their housing problem goes back to the twenties and thirties when the Negro population increased and restrictive covenants prevented their residential expansion. Today the same fear of residential encroachment exists.

It is evident from the above statement that restrictive covenants have been hindering the expansion of the Negro areas in Detroit ever since the twenties and have intensified the additional overcrowding resulting from war in-migration.

Between 1940 and 1944 public housing provided 2,177 units for Negroes in Detroit, but conversions, lodging houses and doubling up in substandard homes constituted the main part of the other accommodations. Approximately 10,000 dwellings were converted from white to Negro occupancy while additional housing facilities were created from chicken shacks, attic and basement apartments and store fronts. Because the increase in Detroit's Negro population since 1940 was 62,555, it is clear that a critical need exists for construction of postwar housing for the Negro group and a lifting of restrictive covenants.

In Cleveland, practically no housing which a Negro could purchase or rent was constructed by private enterprise. Approximately 120 units were made available for Negro occupancy by private housing. In addition to these units approximately 2,600 dwelling units were made available for Negro occupancy during the years 1940–1945 under public auspices. During the same period, Negroes purchased two to three thousand houses in geographical areas of Cleveland in which few Negroes resided in 1940. These houses are fairly old but in a state of excellent repair, "which means that the new neighborhoods offer the potentialities for well conserved residential areas." These neighborhoods are still populated predominantly by white families.

Despite the increase in Negro population in Buffalo after 1940, no new or additional housing was made available to Negroes, except through public housing for the low income families. The Buffalo Municipal Housing Authority produced 588 units for colored occupancy (about two hundred of which were still under construction in October 1943) which "does not begin to meet the need."

The experience of the Buffalo Municipal Housing Authority with the Willert Park Courts, a project of 172 units, built in 1939, completely "refutes the time-worn impression that the colored tenant is not a good risk." This project showed a total rent collection from its opening in July of 1939 through July of 1943 of $178,379.18 with a collection loss over the entire four years of $172.03. This splendid record reflects the integrity of the tenant as much as good management. There was little or no damage to property and the individual units were found to be kept in a clean and orderly fashion. In the spring and early summer of 1943 the B.M.H.A. converted two factory type buildings into 115 apartments. These units, on completion, were filled quickly and entirely by colored families. These families displayed an amazing ability to adapt themselves to a new environment, new equipment and new responsibilities in their relationship to the landlord.

In St. Louis, up to November, 1944, aside from the establishment of housing units at Neighborhood Gardens, F. H. A. Clinton-Peabody and Carr Square Village, Federal Funds had financed, on a twenty-six-year-basis, over 5,000 individual homes. Over 3,000 additional homes built by real estate promoters had been taken over with Federal funds. These homes were all, however, for white people. Not a single home was a Negro able to finance with government money. This was not the fault of the Negroes, but was due to the conditions set by the Federal Housing Authority for obtaining the money which it had to loan. These conditions required the approval of administrative officials of the town or city and the approval of neighboring home-owners, who consistently prevented Negroes from obtaining Federal funds. Carr Square, St. Louis' only Negro Housing Project with 658 family units, has also disproved many fallacies about Negro housing. Prompt payment of rent is the rule.

Private capital has been showing some interest in building for Negroes in Chicago, Detroit, Cleveland, St. Louis, Milwaukee, Indianapolis and Los Angeles. In Chicago nearly five hundred new Negro dwellings have been built by private capital and several large projects are under way. Detroit has 550 new privately financed Negro homes which sell for from $5,000 to $6,000. In Milwaukee there is the ten-family Sherman Hill Project. Private capital has become interested in Negro housing but "has not gone overboard."

High Rentals

The relatively high rentals which Negroes had to pay in the twenties and thirties remained at their high level due to the continuing housing shortage and the freezing of rents. In Chicago, about 1937, when a few of the larger real estate companies finally broke the restrictive covenants surrounding the Washington Park District and allowed Negroes to move into one or two apartment buildings, they immediately raised the rents from twenty to fifty per cent. In 1940 there were many cases of whites and Negroes living in the same building, the latter paying for equivalent accommodation rentals higher than those paid by the whites. The realtors would then urge the whites to move so that their apartments could be rented to Negroes at a higher rate. It has been maintained that the speculative value of the land on which the residential property of the Black Belt stands is so high that it, even more than the restriction on supply, has a tendency to drive rents up. The Chicago Housing Authority in the 1940 report blamed the intense shortage for the exploitation of the Negro and stated that "like accommodations are nearly always rented to Negroes at a higher rate than to white families."

In Philadelphia, despite rent ceilings, flagrant cases were reported of rent increase to Negro tenants in both South Philadelphia and the city of Chester. In the latter case, the tenants of substandard houses were told that their rents would be raised for each boarder or lodger taken in.

Result of Overcrowding and Slum Conditions

The effects of unsafe, insanitary and overcrowded housing on the life of the people in Negro inhabited slum areas are extremely harmful. The Mayor's Conference in Chicago in 1944 listed among the "ghetto conditions" high sickness and death rates; a heavy relief load during the depression; inadequate recreational facilities; lack of building repairs; neglect of garbage disposal and street-cleaning; overcrowded schools; high rates of crime and juvenile delinquency; high incidence of insanity; high illegitimacy rates; and rough treatment by the police. There are other factors than housing, to be sure, which enter into the making of these "ghetto conditions," but poor housing, congestion and neglect as results of restriction and discrimination are among the basic factors.

Overcrowding as a result not only of poverty but of segregation causes resentment and bitterness in those who are compelled to endure it. The resultant feelings of resentment have been recognized as a serious threat to peaceful race relations. The Chicago Conference on Home Front Unity has summed up the situation in trenchant terms:

So long as the housing offered to the Niseis (sic) the Filipinos, the Negroes, the Mexicans is hazardous to life and limb, overcrowded and underserviced, such housing will remain the number one breeding ground for racial disunity, tensions and even violence. This has been demonstrated in Detroit, in Los Angeles and in New York. When at the same time such housing yields exorbitant rents to absentee owners, it nurtures long-run interracial bitterness, further jeopardizing the health of the community body.

A Monthly Summary of Events and Trends in Race Relations, under direction of Charles S. Johnson, Fisk University, November 1946, pp. 117–22; footnotes omitted. Hereafter cited as *Summary*.

15

A CONSERVATIVE'S OUTLOOK (1946)

by Spencer Logan

Politically conservative African-Americans have not been numerous, but even in the era of slavery, there were some. Generally, the rewards have been ample. An example is the book *A Negro's Faith in America*, published by Macmillan in 1946 and awarded the Macmillan Centenary Prize. Extracts will convey the argument.

Have the Negro people developed a man or group of men who can lead them and speak for them in the postwar era which lies just ahead?

The mere development of creative talent, no matter how great, does not, it seems to me, necessarily fit an individual for leadership. Many of the Negroes who are prominent because of their creative talents or their success as interpretive artists are not in the real sense leaders of the Negro people.

These men and women, including some of the most eminent and distinguished members of the Negro race, are obviously moved by the artist's desire to give of himself to humanity. But I wonder if it is not also from a sense of social frustration—which even with their gifts they cannot shake off—that some of them have attempted a leadership for which they are not emotionally fitted. Between these individuals and the Negro masses which they represent, there is a spiritual gulf. These gifted men and women are not of the people. Their policy of stressing social equality rather than the building of a strong Negro society is indicative of their desire to get away from being Negroes. Any kind of leadership that arises from such frustration is not of the Negro people as I know them. . . .

The ideal of democracy demanded by many Negro leaders is in harmony with the theory of democracy for all; but it ignores reality. The reality of the situation is that many Negro and white people are not ready to assume the responsibility of citizenship in a progressive modern state. One of the first needs of the mass Negro is a better understanding of the present-day crisis in American life and a recognition of his own responsibility in relation to it.

The extent to which Negro leadership has drifted from a program in harmony with the needs of the Negro in this crisis is indicated by certain aspects of the Negro press. Negro editors, aware of the inconsistency between the ideal of democracy as advocated by the Negro leaders and the discrimination and injustice endured by the average Negro, have attempted to emphasize the discrepancy by resorting to a type of headline which stresses the basic defects of Negro-white relationship: "White Policeman Shoots Negro Boy"—"White Man Slays Negro Sweetheart"—"Negro Youth Denied Entrance to White College."

These editors will say that, by political agitation, social and economic equality can be gained. Yet the feeling lingers in the hearts of many responsible Negroes that the problem presented has bread-and-butter roots, and that agitation yields at best only a few jobs....

Dr. George Washington Carver was a leader of quite a different sort. He avoided the many pitfalls of the Negro publicists. He developed his talent to the utmost, then gave freely of his wizardry to all people. He earned the gratitude and respect of white people. Dr. Carver set the highest possible standard for good race relationship, for he, as a Negro, achieved and practiced a concept of democracy which was in harmony with its greatest social and spiritual possibilities. Dr. Carver often said that he gave so freely of his talent because it was given to him by God. He subordinated his racial instincts to the good of democracy, and he believed that by dedicating his energies to the well-being of all mankind he would best serve his race. Dr. Carver more than any other Negro has set an example for Negro leadership of the future.

There are many Negro organizations which are dedicated to the task of obtaining social equality and a fuller share in democracy for the Negro by means of political pressure and court decisions. Such groups operate on the theory that the ideals upon which a government is founded can be enforced through the legal code of that country by test cases which establish definite precedents. They fight segregation by proving that it is legally wrong. They would wipe out lynchings by fining the county involved, or by making prison sentences mandatory for anyone involved in them. They would loosen the economic noose about the neck of the Negro by the passage of more laws designed to make job discrimination illegal.

Negro leaders ruled by this thought pattern are in my opinion guilty, along with their white counterparts, of the gravest injustice to their cause if they attempt to gain by force of law alone the advantages of social equality from people who are not spiritually or morally prepared to grant it. They should realize that those who live by political agitation are by this very fact often handicapped as leaders; for a man who fights for the legal recognition of a principle may in the process lose sight of the human values involved....

If the people of America are to get along with one another, regardless of racial and religious differences, they must become more aware of the need of making their democratic principles a part of their everyday lives. No citizen should be allowed to fail in the realization of his own responsibility for the welfare of the whole, with stress upon mutual respect among all. America has learned the technique of selling the public almost anything. We have been taught lessons of health and cleanliness, have been influenced to spend or save money, and have been united for the purpose of waging war against a common enemy. Why cannot similar educational techniques be used against those attitudes on the part of many of our citizens which may well prove to be as destructive as any foreign foe could have been?

Cited work pp. 12, 15, 16, 18–19, 86. The author was identified as a staff sergeant in the U.S. Army.

16

FILIBUSTERING FAIR EMPLOYMENT (1946)

The outstanding and most far-reaching event of the month [January] was without doubt the defeat of the bill to prevent discrimination in employment on account of race, color, or religion. The device employed to defeat this proposed legislation was the filibuster conducted by seventeen Southern Senators. After holding the floor of the Senate for twenty-four days with such obvious and unseemly parliamentary tricks as correcting the record, debating the position of commas and semicolons in the hitherto respected prayer of the Senate Chaplain, and expressing directly and indirectly their determination to block any legislation designed to promote equal opportunity for American citizens, the issue was ended in the failure of the Senate by a vote of 48–36 to get the two-thirds necessary to invoke cloture. The real sufferers were not alone the minorities who could not defend themselves in this unrestricted and unbridled marathon attack. The demonstration was in itself a dark warning for the nation, not so much on the status and fate of minorities, but on the status and fate of the American democratic process. It was admitted that if the issue had been permitted to come to a vote it would have passed the Senate with a margin to spare. The men who blocked it represented less than one-fourth of the Senate. The eleven Southern states represented by the filibusterers had theoretically only eighteen of the eighty-three million potential voters. Being poll tax states, the filibustering senators represented only a fraction of the potential voters of their states.

Senator Eastland was elected by only 4 per cent of the potential voters of Mississippi (that is to say, by only 2 per cent of the total population); Senator Russell of Georgia, by 8 per cent of the voters and 2 per cent of the population; Senator Maybank of South Carolina, by 2 per cent of the voters and 1 per cent of the population. Senator McKellar of Tennessee, President Pro Tem of the Senate and a filibuster collaborator, and Senator Bilbo of Mississippi, well-known race baiter, represent not much larger proportions of their states' population. The spectacle of the obstruction of legislation in the chief lawmaking body of the world's greatest nation has been more effective in calling the attention of the world to American fascism than years of exhortation on brotherhood and social justice. Now it is perfectly clear what the minorities are up against, and how easy it is for a small wilful group, however wrong and un-American, to thwart the will of the majority, and to make or break legislation as personal or regional interest dictates.

Summary, February 1946, vol. 3, p. 198.

17

VIOLENCE AND TERROR (1946)

From the authoritative Fisk University publication *A Monthly Summary of Events* and from an issue of *The Crisis* come accounts of the systematized violence and terror practiced against the African-American population as soon as the war against fascism ended:

FREEPORT, LONG ISLAND, NEW YORK

The "Ferguson affair" involving the recent killing of two brothers, the wounding of a third, and the sentence of a fourth to one hundred days in jail on a charge of disorderly conduct has caused considerable comment. The four Ferguson brothers, celebrating the fact that they were all together for the first time in several years, went out on the evening of February 4. They had been drinking beer, but decided that they would like some coffee. With this in mind they went into a tea room across from the Freeport bus terminal and ordered coffee. When the proprietor said he had no coffee, one of the young men suspected that he was being refused service because of racial discrimination. He began an argument but was quickly taken out of the place by his brothers. After a brief walk the four men decided to take the bus home, and started back to the terminal to board the bus. As they approached the terminal, a city policeman, Joseph Romeika, accosted them and lined them up against a wall at the point of a gun.

The brothers had been drinking, but all were unarmed. According to persons who witnessed the scene, one of them argued but none made a move to attack the patrolman. Romeika maintains that Charles Ferguson reached toward his back pocket, saying that he had "a forty-five," and that Joseph Ferguson tried to attack him. In any case, Romeika fired, fatally wounding Charles and Alfonso and wounding Joseph. Joseph, a cook in the Navy, was turned over to Naval authorities. The other brother was tried a few hours later and sentenced for disorderly conduct. Immediately after the shooting, according to the Freeport *Newsday,* Chief of Police, Peter Elar, ordered a cordon of police, armed with tommy guns, to surround the terminal "to await a possible uprising of local Negroes."

Despite the suspicious circumstances of the killings, Romeika was exonerated immediately by the local police—before there had been time for a thorough investigation. The Nassau County Grand Jury has also cleared the policeman.

Through the efforts of about forty organizations Richard Ferguson has been released on bail pending an appeal. These same organizations have petitioned Governor Dewey and Attorney General Tom Clark to intervene. . . .

MEMPHIS, TENNESSEE

Frank Allen, twenty-six-year-old Negro taxi driver, was slain by Memphis police under suspicious circumstances. According to police reports, Officers Johnson and Phillips shot Allen after the latter had fired at them. Another version of the story is that the police officers took Allen out of his cab and accompanied him into a vacant field. Here they are alleged to have shot the victim who was unarmed and completely at their mercy. This is the third police killing of a Negro in Memphis during

1946. The first was perpetrated by Inspector A. O. Clark who is remembered as the killer of George Brooks, a Negro postman, in 1938. Back of the brutalities lie a sordid and credible set of rumors of police brutality, espionage (stool pigeons), intimidation, and petty "shake down" rackets involving the police and Negro operators of such small enterprises as taxis, juke boxes, and lunch stands.

Summary, March 1946, pp. 236–37.

BALTIMORE, MARYLAND

Various civic organizations are protesting strongly against what they consider unwarranted police brutality in Baltimore. The matter was brought to public attention when three Negroes were killed recently by police officers within a period of less than two weeks.

William Arthur, 22, was killed on May 18 while allegedly resisting arrest. Wilbur Bundley, 54, was fatally shot on May 19 when, according to the officer involved, Bundley threatened him with an open knife. Nine witnesses claim that Bundley was shot in the back while fleeing. A new autopsy was ordered at the insistence of the NAACP and other organizations. Dr. Robert S. Jason of the Pathology Department of Howard University School of Medicine performed a post mortem, and his report filed with the State's attorney and jury foreman substantiates the claim that Bundley was shot in the back.

The third victim, Isaac Jackson, 24, was shot by Patrolman Russell Lambdin who was accompanied by a police sergeant at the time of the shooting. Mystery was added to Jackson's shooting by the fact that the officers first had claimed that they were cruising along in Carroll Park when they saw Jackson running, observed him fall, then called an ambulance which took him to a hospital. He was pronounced dead on arrival. The officers later claimed that the victim was running through the Park and was shot by Lambdin when Jackson ignored the officer's order to halt. Patrolman Lambdin is charged with the killing, but is free without bail....

WINONA, MISSISSIPPI

Two senior medical students at Meharry Medical College, one of them a native Mississippian, report that on June 23, while driving on Highway 51, near Winona, Mississippi, they were stopped by two policemen in a State Highway Patrol car. Without accusing them of any offense, the officers addressed them in abusive language, searched their car, beat and kicked the student from Mississippi, brandished a gun at him and threatened his life. The officers then forced the two victims to thank them for "kindness and generosity" in not arresting them. (Special Report)

GRETNA, LOUISIANA

Affidavits filed with the Gretna Branch of the NAACP charge that Chief of Police Beuregard Miller killed Elliott Brooks, Gretna Negro, because Brooks knew "too much" about the disappearance of a Negro prisoner. Chief Miller is said to have killed seven Negroes during his law-enforcement career.

Summary, July 1946, 368–69.

Lynchings

The months of July and August witnessed the heaviest lynching outbreak in recent years. During this period there were six confirmed reports of lynchings and at least three unconfirmed allegations of lynching. The latter reports came from Wilson, North Carolina; Elko, South Carolina; and Marshall, Texas. Moreover, there were attempted lynchings in New York (of a Negro charged with rape) and near Savannah, Georgia (of a white man accused of rape and murder)....

MONROE, GEORGIA

The first large-scale lynching to be reported in many years occurred on July 25 when a mob estimated at twenty to thirty unmasked white men took four Negroes—two men and two women—from an automobile driven by a plantation owner and lynched them. The victims were Mr. and Mrs. George Dorsey and Mr. and Mrs. Roger Malcolm. Dorsey was a veteran of World War II. Mrs. Dorsey was Malcolm's sister. All four were sharecroppers.

The mass murder was reported by Loy Harrison, the man on whose "place" the Dorseys lived. According to Harrison, he had just made bail for Malcolm, who was charged with stabbing Barney Hester, a white farmer, and was on his way home. Arriving at a wooden bridge on a back road, he found the way ahead blocked, stopped, and found his car surrounded by a mob. The two men victims were taken from the car, bound by their wrists, and told that they were to be lynched. One of the women called to a mobster by name, asking him not to kill her husband (Harrison claims that he did not hear the name clearly). Realizing that one or more members of the lynching party had been recognized, the leader ordered his followers to bring the women on to join their husbands. The lynchings occurred in the afternoon. Harrison reported the crime a couple of hours later. By twilight, Tom Brown, the semi-literate coroner of the county, had found that the Malcolms and Dorseys had come to their deaths "at the hands of a party or parties unknown." When investigators from the Georgia Bureau of Investigation arrived the following day, it is reported that nearly all material clues to the crime had been removed.

Roger Malcolm, the man who had been in jail, is alleged to have cut Barney Hester on July 14. According to the official story, Hester was the innocent victim when he sought to make peace in a fight between Malcolm and his wife. Another story is that Malcolm stabbed Hester in resentment against the white man's advances to Mrs. Malcolm. At the time of Malcolm's arrest a near-lynching was averted by the intervention of a white woman who had known him for many years.

The report of the lynching brought a feeling of revulsion to the entire country. Governor Ellis Arnall immediately dispatched the Georgia Bureau of Investigation (GBI) to the scene and invited the cooperation of the FBI. Moreover, the Governor offered rewards up to $10,000 for information leading to the arrest and conviction of the culprits. Organizations have added to the reward until the amount now offered totals over $64,000. Clergymen from Monroe itself—and other small neighboring towns—deplored the sin of lynching. Newspapers were unanimous in condemning the atrocity. Even Governor-designate Talmadge, vacationing from his campaign, called the mass murder "a regrettable incident."

Despite the size of the rewards offered and the proficiency of the state and federal bureaus of investigation, progress in solving the crime and building a case has been reported as "slow." The NAACP, the Workers Defense League, the Civil Rights Congress, and other private agencies which have investigators in the field, on the other hand, report that there is much evidence and that there are people who will "talk"—though not necessarily for the record. The following facts seem important in the case:

1. The names of several persons alleged to have been members of the mob have been turned over to the GBI and FBI.

2. The innocence of Loy Harrison is seriously questioned because:

   (a) the back road down which he traveled was not his accustomed route home from town and was longer than the hard-surfaced road usually traveled;

(b) George Dorsey, the returned veteran who farmed on Harrison's place, is known to have been beaten by his landlord on July 4 and ordered off the plantation—Dorsey elected to remain, accusing Harrison of using this method of gaining possession of the tenant's crop;

(c) Though it is certain that the mob was composed largely of his neighbors, Harrison, admitting that the men were unmasked, claims that he recognized none of the twenty or thirty;

(d) Investigators claim that they found no official record of the $600 bail said to have been posted by Harrison and further pointed out that the deputy who released Malcolm is a relative of Hester.

3. The relationship of the white-supremacy campaign waged by Talmadge, which ended only a week before the lynching appears to have had more than a tenuous relationship to the affair—it is known that the Sage of Sugar Creek was in Monroe on July 15 or 16 and that he conversed with Barney Hester's father.

LEXINGTON, MISSISSIPPI

During the week of the Monroe atrocity, news of a fifth lynching was broken by a Greenwood, Mississippi paper when it was reported that seven white men, including a deputy sheriff, were being held in connection with the lynching of Leon McTatie, a thirty-six-year-old Negro farm hand. According to Sheriff Murtagh who made the arrests, the men flogged the victim and then threw him into a river. The accused men are reported to have admitted flogging McTatie, but claim that they did not know that he had been seriously injured. The farm hand was being "punished" for allegedly stealing a saddle. He denied the accusation, and after he had been lynched two other men confessed that they had committed the theft.

MINDEN, LOUISIANA

The lynching of John C. Jones had been known to Webster Parish officials for several days before the lynching was made public. Like George Dorsey in Walton County, Georgia, John Jones was a veteran of World War II who had seen overseas service. On returning to his home at Cotton Valley, near Minden, it is reported that he raised embarrassing questions concerning the low rents being paid for oil lands owned by his unschooled grandfather. He soon earned a reputation for being "uppity" and a "smart nigger." A foreign pistol, a German Luger, which he brought back as a souvenir was the envy of some of his white contemporaries.

Jones, along with seventeen-year-old Albert Harris, Jr., was finally arrested for entering a white woman's yard. Whether or not the youths were guilty is not known, but the woman failed to prosecute and Jones and Harris were released and started back to Cotton Valley. A group of white men forced the two Negroes into automobiles, blind-folded them and drove them into the woods. Here Harris was brutally beaten and left to die. For Jones, the "smart nigger," were reserved the blow torch and meat cleaver. Harris recovered consciousness after the mob had left the scene and in time to bring Jones a shoe-full of water and to hold his head while he died.

Harris managed to find his way home. Mr. Harris, Sr. took him and fled. The NAACP heard of their flight and notified each of its branches to be on the look-out for the father and son, to give them asylum if they appeared, and to notify the national office. The pair were finally discovered in a midwestern town. An NAACP official was dispatched to the scene and brought the Harrises to New York where young Harris' testimony has been made available to the FBI. According to reports from the NAACP, the youth knows and has given to the FBI the identity of thirteen members of the mob that flogged him and lynched the returned veteran. Mr. White has described Albert Harris as one of the most important witnesses ever discovered by the National Association in its long fight against lynching....

Manhunt

MAGEE, MISSISSIPPI

A full-scale manhunt with bloodhounds, a family feud over sharecropper labor, and mystery concerning relationships described in various ways are involved in recent happenings in and around Sullivan's Hollow, near MaGee. The first story to reach the press was to the effect that some of the Craft boys (Negroes) had fired an unprovoked shot into an automobile occupied by white men. According to this version, a deputy sheriff, along with a few civilians deputized for the purpose, then went to the Craft home in Sullivan's Hollow in search of the person or persons who had fired the shot. As the officers approached, a member of the Craft family is alleged to have fired a shot-gun, wounding Deputy Sheriff Glenn Hester. The Crafts and their neighbors, the Coopers, then took to the woods; an armed posse of about two hundred white men and boys was deputized to look for them.

Garfield, Alford (age (eleven), W.O., T.J., and Bill Craft, along with nine other Negroes, were apprehended by the posse. Johnny Craft, twenty-one-year-old marine veteran, considered the real prize of the chase, was not captured; but eluded the searching party and eventually presented himself at the "mob-proof" Hinds County jail in Jackson. According to the former leatherneck's own story, he attempted at one point to surrender to the posse, but was met by a rain of gunfire. Using the skills which he learned jungle-fighting Japanese on Pacific islands, young Craft slipped through swamps and woods, headed toward Jackson sixty miles away.

The Crafts and other Negroes from the area of Sullivan's Hollow had hardly been placed under arrest when the Jackson, Mississippi *Clarion-Ledger* came out with the story that there was serious doubt that they had been implicated in the wounding of the deputy. According to this story, the Negroes were caught in the machinations of a feud between the Sullivans in the Hollow and the Sullivans who live on Merry Hell Ridge. Weight was given to this interpretation a few days later when H. J. Sullivan, the planter for whom the Crafts worked, was arrested and charged with shooting Hester. Sullivan is reported to have admitted being at the scene of the shooting at the time of the "raid" on the Craft household.

There is also a non-official version of the first incident, which relates that someone from a truck carrying members of the Craft family fired upon the white men who threatened the Negroes with violence and attempted to block the road down which the group was returning home.

At this writing Sullivan and his nephew are out on bail bond of $1,000 and $500 respectively. Ten of the Negroes are out on bond and three were released without bond. Johnny Craft is being held, pending the posting of $11,000 bond. He, along with his brothers Garfield and W.O., is charged on eight counts of assault with intent to kill.

As soon as the news of the manhunt became known, Walter White, executive secretary of the NAACP, telegraphed Governor Bailey asking that he intervene to see that there be no mob violence. Lieutenant Governor Fielding Wright, as acting governor, replied to the wire saying, in part, "Organizations such as yours should acquire the true facts of incidents before beating the drums of racial propaganda." After visiting MaGee and vicinity the Governor reported that there are "no elements of racial tension in Smith County."

Isaac Woodard

NEW YORK CITY, NEW YORK

The story of Isaac Woodard first came to the attention of the public on July 17, when persons interested in Mr. Woodard, a veteran of four years in the United States army (fifteen months in the South Pacific), made public an affidavit which the ex-serviceman had sworn out on April 23, stating that he had been attacked and permanently blinded by police in South Carolina. The reported attack occurred on February 12, a few hours after Woodard had been discharged from the army and while he was on his way to Winnsboro, North Carolina to meet his wife, who was to accompany him to his father's home in New York City.

According to the ex-sergeant's statement, he was traveling by bus and was about an hour out of Atlanta when the vehicle stopped at a small drug store. Woodard stated that he inquired of the bus driver whether there was time for him to go to a rest room. The bus driver is reported to have sworn at the veteran and to have answered in the negative, but when Woodard swore in response, he was told to go but "hurry back." The incident seemed to have been closed; however, when the bus arrived in a larger town, the driver summoned two policemen, pointed Woodard out, and charged him with creating a disturbance. As the ex-soldier sought to deny the operator's charges, the officers struck him, subsequently beating him into unconsciousness. When Woodard began to revive, he was taken to a jail and given a cot. On awakening the following morning the vet found that he was blind.

According to his story, he was taken to a veterans hospital in Columbia, South Carolina by the officers. On leaving the jail, he inquired what town he was in and the officers told him he was in Aiken. It was this incident that gave Woodard the idea that the attack had occurred in Aiken. It later developed—through the affidavit of an eye-witness to the incident and through the admission of Police Chief M.L. Shull of Batesburg—that the scene of the attack had been Batesburg, South Carolina. After two months in the veterans hospital in Columbia, Woodard was returned to Bronx, New York, where he resides.

Chief Shull insists that Woodard was drunk and disorderly when taken from the bus and that the severe beating which resulted in his blindness had to be administered in order to bring him under control. Negroes who live in Batesburg and in nearby Leesville, according to an early

September dispatch of the Associated Negro Press, insist that Chief Shull and his fellow-officers are noted for their brutality toward Negroes. They cite the Chief's participation in a general "head-beating" and wholesale arrest on Christmas night, 1944, and also mention several unprovoked beatings of Negroes, including the unexplained beating of a local veteran who was chatting peacefully with friends when attacked by Shull and another officer.

The National Association for the Advancement of Colored People and other organizations have demanded a thorough investigation by the Veterans Administration and by the Department of Justice. Inasmuch as the attack occurred before the end of the man's final day in the army, the War Department was asked to intervene. The Assistant Secretary of War has stated that Woodard was "no longer under military control" at the time of the incident. It is reported that several thousand dollars have been raised on Woodard's behalf. He has also been inducted into the Blinded Veterans Association which limits membership to persons who lose their sight "in the service of their country."

The Ku Klux Klan

During the past few months the sentiments of the Klan apparently have made considerably more headway than have its various organizational drives. There has been alarming progress of the racial suppression and overt acts of violence which are synonymous with the Klan; yet from scattered sections of the country it is reported that there is much hesitancy, even on the part of persons who believe wholeheartedly in its tenets, to join the Klan—hesitancy not unrelated to the "Empire's" growing reputation as an unmitigated racket for the enrichment of a few officers. There have been several developments worthy of mention.

Klan Activities

The very frank and open admission by Senator Bilbo, during an interview over the Mutual Network (Meet the Press, August 9), that he is a member in good standing of Bilbo Post of the Klan and his observation, "Once a Ku Kluxer, always a Ku Kluxer," did not surprise persons who know Mississippi's Senior Senator. The admission, however, is being used as added ammunition by forces seeking to deprive Bilbo of his Senate seat. Attorney Charles H. Houston pointed out in a broadcast in reply to Bilbo over the same network that a senator is sworn to uphold the constitution and that the oath of the Klan is contradictory to this oath.

Klan activities are reported to have been noted frequently in Eastern Tennessee, in and around Chattanooga and Knoxville. Governor McCord has denied that the Klan is active in Tennessee, but Stetson Kennedy pointed out last spring that there had already been five cross-burnings in the Chattanooga area, that much progress had been made in organizing policemen and firemen, and that J.B. Stoner serves as a fulltime organizer....

Summary, August–September 1946, pp. 13–17.

Southern Schrecklichkeit

THE ISAAC WOODARD CASE: Southern police contempt for human decency and dignity where Negroes are concerned is made clear in the case of the brutal blinding of Isaac Woodard, a twenty-seven-year-old Negro veteran, by Batesburg, S.C., police. The wholly unnecessary and unbelievably fiendish beating and blinding of Woodard took place hardly more than three hours after the veteran's discharge from a mobilization center.

Woodard, who spent fifteen months in the Philippines and New Guinea with the 429th Port Battalion, served in the Army from October 13, 1942, to February 12, 1946, when he received an honorable discharge from Camp Gordon, Ga.

After his discharge from Camp Gordon, Woodard took a Greyhound bus in Atlanta, Ga., for Winnesboro, S.C., where he was to pick up his wife for a trip to New York to visit his parents. Somewhere between Atlanta and Aiken, S.C., Woodard got into an altercation with the driver over a "comfort stop." When the bus reached Batesburg, the driver had Woodard arrested for creating a disturbance. Neither the driver nor the police gave him a chance to explain, and when they got him to the jail the police pummelled and beat Woodard until he was unconscious, crunching out his eyes with the end of a billy.

Next morning Woodard was taken before the local judge and offered the choice of a $50 fine or thirty days on the road. But having only $40 cash and his mustering out check of $694.73, which he refused to sign,

Woodard was taken back to the jail where the cops made clumsy attempts to treat his now sightless eyes. The police later took him to the veterans' hospital at Columbia, S.C., where he stayed from February 13 to April 13, 1946, until he was released in custody of his sisters.

The Association has demanded that the Department of Justice investigate the beating and blinding of Woodard and that the guilty parties be prosecuted to the full extent of the law. On July 15, Howard C. Peterson, assistant secretary of war, notified the NAACP that Woodard's case is "now under study by the governor of South Carolina, the Veteran's Administration and the Department of Justice."

Mr. Peterson adds that "by reason of the fact that Woodard was a civilian at the time of this unfortunate incident and no longer a member of the Army or under military contract, the case does not come within jurisdiction of the War Department."

On July 24, at an Association sponsored meeting of veterans' organizations in the Wendell Willkie Memorial building, a reward of $1,000 was posted for any person or persons supplying information that will lead to the apprehension and conviction of the policemen responsible for the outrageous attack upon Woodard. On August 10 Woodard was admitted to membership in the Blinded Veterans Association at organization headquarters, 80 Warren Street, New York City. The NAACP has already had the American Red Cross file an application for full compensation for Woodard with the Veterans Administration.

In the meantime funds are pouring into the national office to aid Woodard. Ethel S. Epstein, former labor secretary under LaGuardia, enclosed a check for $250. Employees of the Dell Publishing company in New York have also contributed funds for the blinded veteran. Joe Louis, heavyweight boxing champion, sponsored a benefit for Woodard at the Lewisohn Stadium on August 16. Contributions to date total $2,118.89.

Crisis, September 1946, vol. 53, p. 276.

BATESBURG, SOUTH CAROLINA

Chief of Police Lynwood L. Schull, accused of gouging out the eyes of Isaac Woodard . . . was acquitted in fifteen minutes by a federal jury. The police official was charged with depriving a citizen of his civil rights and if convicted would have been subject to one year's imprisonment. During his arguments, Schull's attorney warned the jury against allowing the

Federal government to "interfere" with the administration of justice in South Carolina. At one point he went so far as to suggest that if Schull were convicted South Carolina should again secede from the Union.

Summary, November 1946, vol. 4, p. 108.

ALTON, ILLINOIS

Three deputy sheriffs took five hours to transport a Negro prisoner (suspected of rape) twelve and one-half miles from Alton to Edwardsville, Illinois. Enroute the officers are said to have administered repeated beatings to the man and to have encouraged him to run "so we can shoot you." Moreover, the guardians of the law visited several taverns where white customers were invited to assist in the beatings. The deputies have been suspended pending hearings on the affair....

SAINT LOUIS, MISSOURI

A white patrolman in Saint Louis is charged with shooting and killing a Negro pedestrian who did not move out of the way fast enough as the officer drove through an alley. The policeman claims that the victim "lunged" at him with a penknife. Five eyewitnesses to the incident declare that the shooting was entirely without provocation. The NAACP and the National Negro Congress are pressing for dismissal of the officer and criminal action against him....

Summary, August–September 1946, p. 16.

ATLANTA, GEORGIA

An Atlanta streetcar motorman has been exonerated in the slaying of a Negro veteran. W. D. Lee, the motorman, fatally wounded Walter Lee Johnson, a twenty-two-year-old honorably discharged Negro veteran of three years' overseas service, on September 27. According to eyewitnesses, Johnson was standing on a corner when the streetcar stopped to discharge a passenger. The veteran had not been on the car and was not attempting to enter it, but, seeing an acquaintance aboard called to him, "Straighten up and fly right." The motorman, apparently thinking that the jibe had been addressed to him, is reported to have stopped his car, debarked, and shot the man. Lee then reported to the police that Johnson had cursed him and had put his hands in his pockets "as if to draw a knife or gun." The police charged Lee with "disorderly conduct and shooting another" and released him on his own recognizance.

By the time the motorman's case was heard in Recorder's (Police) Court, Johnson had succumbed to his wounds. Attorney A. T. Walden, retained by the NAACP to represent the victim's family, asked that the defendant be bound over to the grand jury, inasmuch as there was considerable contradiction in the evidence given by witnesses—most of it to the effect that the slaying was unprovoked. Recorder A. W. Calloway, who had just returned from the State Democratic Convention which had made Talmadge's nomination official and had voted to circumvent Negro enfranchisement, stated, "No jury on earth would convict him, so I am going to dismiss the case."

Johnson is the third Negro veteran to be shot by an Atlanta streetcar motorman this year, and is the second to die....

HOUSTON, TEXAS

Following the slaying of Berry Branch, sixty-five-year-old Negro barber and prominent citizen, by a bus driver, Houston Utilities Director Clinton Owsley urged that bus drivers be made bonded police and permitted to carry guns. A committee from the City Council conferred with the Transit Company on the matter and discovered that the Company did not think it wise to arm its operators legally....

Summary, November 4, 1946, vol. 4, pp. 107–8.

18

THE POGROM AT COLUMBIA, TENNESSEE (1946)

The most sensational instance in 1946 of violence against African-American people—and their resistance thereto—came in February in the town of Columbia, Tennessee. It aroused nationwide interest; in it lives were lost, and Thurgood Marshall was very nearly lynched. Accounts from the *Monthly Summary* of Fisk University and the *Crisis* follow. First there is the report in the *Summary* (March 1946, pp. 233–36); and second that in the *Crisis* (April 1946, pp. 110–11, 125). This is concluded by two accounts of the trial that followed (c and d).

An excellent account is in Herbert Shapiro, *White Violence and Black Response* (Amherst: University of Massachusetts Press, 1988), pp. 362–65. See also Linda Reed, *Simple Decency and Common Sense: The Southern Conference Movement* (Bloomington: Indiana University Press, 1991), pp. 108–11.

[a]

A fight between a white and a Negro World War II veteran, after the former had allegedly assaulted the Negro's mother, precipitated the first major interracial violence since V-Day. The woman, Mrs. Gladys Stephenson, went into the Castner-Knott Shop on the Public Square in Columbia to inquire about a radio which she had left for repair. With her was her nineteen-year-old son, James, recently discharged after three years in the United States Navy.[1] The radio repairman was William Fleming, twenty-eight-year-old veteran and brother of the Democratic nominee for sheriff of Maury County. There was a disagreement between Mrs. Stephenson and Fleming concerning the repair job. Fleming apparently resented the fact that a Negro woman would take issue with him, and according to the most reliable reports available, followed her and her son downstairs and out of the store, finally slapping and kicking her.[2] At this point, young Stephenson intervened, struck Fleming, and knocked him back through a plate glass window. According to persons who were standing nearby, three or four other white men, including a town policeman, came to Fleming's aid. The policeman struck at Stephenson with his nightstick, whereupon Mrs. Stephenson is quoted as saying, "You shouldn't hit my boy before you find out." In response, the peace officer struck the woman over the eye. Mrs. Stephenson and her son James were arrested and placed in jail on charges of assault. Fleming was not arrested. He was only slightly injured.

Tension created by the fight and arrest mounted throughout the late afternoon. Crowds of white persons began to mill about the Public Square. There were open and jeering threats of lynching. Negroes began withdrawing to the two-block section of Negro-operated businesses on East Eighth Street.[3] Hearing rumors of an imminent lynching, the more affluent Negroes hastened to supply bond for the Stephensons. Their fears were heightened when the magistrate repeatedly raised the price of bail bond and attempted to persuade the Negro bondsmen to let the Stephensons remain in jail. Finally, however, they were released on a bond of $3,500.

[1]He had "raised" his age to enlist.
[2]Another version is that Fleming struck Stephenson when the latter objected to the fact that his mother was being sworn at and that the Negro veteran fought back.
[3]Known to whites as "Mink Slide," a name opprobrious to Columbia Negroes.

Within two hours of James Stephenson's release, approximately seventy-five white men approached the jail and kicked on the door. Sheriff J. J. Underwood reportedly came to the jail door, and leveling a submachine gun at the mob, ordered them to disperse.[4] The men withdrew; but two members were in such a state of inebriation that they could not leave under their own power. They were arrested on charges of disorderly conduct.

Meanwhile, three county police officers had come into the East Eighth Street area. Two of these had reported on sentiment among whites, urging that James Stephenson be sent out of town. This was done. The third officer, Sheriff Underwood, is said to have requested that the Negroes who had gathered in the area disperse. When some of the men made the counter-suggestion that the white crowd be dispersed, the Sheriff is quoted as saying, "I'll see what I can do."

As darkness fell, business houses in the Eighth Street area closed in an effort to prevent "trouble." All lights were turned off in the area. By this time Negroes in Columbia were completely convinced that there would be an attempted lynching or—in view of Stephenson's having been spirited away—an indiscriminate attack on the Negro community. According to persons in the Eighth Street area, there was no disposition to "take it lying down." Having little faith in the ability or willingness of the city police to avert mob action, the Negroes settled down and prepared to defend themselves. Those living outside, who had to cross "white" territory in order to reach home, were afraid to leave. Other Negroes passing through streets inhabited by whites told of being fired upon and otherwise molested. Furthermore, frequent gunfire was heard coming from East Ninth and South Main—"white" streets close to the Negro business area. This gunfire was accompanied by wild yells which were interpreted as signs of drunkenness and frenzied excitement.

Sometime shortly after nightfall (accounts vary as to the exact time) city policemen started into Eighth Street, allegedly to investigate reports of shooting. The street was dark, and it is uncertain that their identity as officers was known. There was shooting. Whether initial shots came from the police or from the people is not clear. Given the state of apprehension among Columbia Negroes at the time—growing out of knowledge of lynching threats, mob activity, and gunfire in adjacent streets—it is not surprising that the entrance of these white men into the area was

---

[4]Sheriff Underwood is respected among Maury County Negroes as a man who "tries to be fair."

interpreted as the beginning of attack. In the exchange of fire, four policemen, including Chief of Police Griffin, were wounded, one seriously.

Immediately after this incident Mayor Eldridge Denham called upon Governor Jim McCord for assistance from the State Highway Patrol and State Guard. One hundred patrolmen and four hundred members of the State Guard were ordered into Columbia. They threw a tight cordon around the East Eighth Street business area and set up a close watch of the entire Negro community. At dawn on February 26, members of the Highway Patrol moved into the street in force. At one place Lynn Bomar, State Safety Director, claims there was resistance. This was met with machine gun fire. Elsewhere the citizens came peaceably. About seventy Negroes were arrested in the early morning. Although it is not yet clear whether formal charges have been preferred against anyone, persons were told that they were being arrested for assault with intent to murder.

It was with these early morning arrests that police action in a situation of violence involving Negroes and whites became clearly directed toward the suppression of what was apparently construed to be an "uprising" of the Negro community. The Highway Patrol and State Guard were transformed from preservers of civil law and order into an army of occupation. It is likely that the mobilization of outside police and guards saved bloodshed in a situation that was plainly beyond the power of local city and county police to control. Moreover, Chief Bomar and State Guard Adjutant Butler are quoted as having admonished their men that theirs was the role of impartial protectors of life and property, though there is little in the actual performance of their subordinates to indicate that this was taken seriously.

Evidence of this is seen in the irresponsible vandalism and looting that took place in East Eighth Street. In the search for weapons in this area there was wanton destruction of property. A physician's office was a shamble after small instruments had been stolen, furniture damaged, and decorations mutilated. The office of an insurance company was ransacked; files containing valuable records were overturned and their contents scattered.

Much has been made in the general press of the number of guns, rifles, and pistols taken from Negro homes. This has been cited as "proof" of a conspiracy by Negroes. It should be remembered, however, that game hunting is a favorite sport around Columbia and that most of the weapons—aside from war souvenirs—were hunting guns and such pistols as many, if not most, American families in the South keep in their homes. It should be noted that almost no white persons were disarmed and that the homes of white residents were not searched. A State Guard Colonel, credited with persuading a crowd of whites not to enter the Negro section on Tuesday morning, is quoted as saying to them, "Boys *take those guns home*. We'll take care of any situation that needs them." Newspaper photographs show white civilians, armed with sawed-off shot guns, walking the streets unmolested. The press has reported only four white persons arrested.

Despite the absence of a proclamation of martial law, there was *de facto* military government in Columbia during the week of February 25 to March 3. The writ of habeas corpus was virtually suspended. Negroes were arrested without charges, held incommunicado, questioned without benefit of counsel, and detained on excessive bail. Telephone wires were tapped and persons required special passes in order to move freely about. The home of virtually every Negro in Columbia and its immediate environs was searched and all firearms taken. These are facts of which public officials have spoken and boasted in conversation and the press.

United States District Attorney Horace Frierson, a resident of Columbia, has stated in a report to the Department of Justice that there were no violations of civil liberties. (Attorney General Tom Clark has announced that the FBI, "in force," is investigating the entire incident.)

On Thursday, February 28, while in jail, two of the Negro prisoners were mortally wounded and a third injured. William Gordon and James Johnson were killed by officers who claim that the prisoners shot first. They were being "questioned" in a jail office in which confiscated firearms were stacked. Several officers and a newspaper reporter were present and the jail was surrounded by guardsmen and members of the Highway patrol. Only the official version of the story is known, but the National Lawyers Guild, after a brief investigation, has characterized the killings as "murder."

Meanwhile, of the more than one hundred Negroes arrested—apparently at random—all but eighteen are out on appearance bonds ranging up to $5,000. Attorney General Bumpus has announced that he will present evidence at the current session of the Maury County Grand Jury.

As an historical and psychological background for the events in Columbia, the following facts should be remembered:

1. There have been two lynchings of Negroes in Maury County within the last two decades. The more recent of these was that of Cordie Cheek, a fourteen-year-old boy, after a grand jury had returned a no bill, on a charge of molesting a white girl. (An old resident spoke of four lynchings within his memory.)
2. Thanks to some industrial employment and good soil, Negroes in Maury County have relative economic security.
3. Negro employees of the Monsanto and Victor Chemical Companies in nearby Mt. Pleasant, along with white workers, are members of the Mine, Mill and Smelter Workers Union (CIO) and have been working recently for abolition of a wage differential based on race.
4. Politically, Negroes have been active and an important factor in Maury County.
5. A measure of economic security and political importance has produced a Negro citizenry not disposed to be "pushed around." The presence of more than 150 Negro veterans has served to strengthen this attitude.
6. The lack of real communication between Negroes and whites in Columbia has resulted in much latent mutual suspicion. There are many otherwise rational white persons in Columbia, including some public officials, who believe that Columbia Negroes have been "conspiring for an uprising." The fact that persons from Nashville, Chicago, and Chattanooga telephoned Negroes in Columbia when news of the trouble became known has been construed as proof that Negroes all over the country instigated the recent violence. Apparently these people are unimpressed by the facts that all shootings, except those in the jail, took place in the Negro area and that Negroes did not go out of this area to attack.
7. Finally, the way in which the violence in Columbia will be resolved is of importance, for it may well set a precedent for the South and for the country as a whole. . . .

[b]

On Monday, February 25, 1946, at or about 10:00 the Stephensons, Mrs. Stephenson and her son, James Stephenson, went into the Castner-Knott Electric Appliance Store in Columbia, Tennessee. Mrs. Stephenson believing that the faulty repair work done on her radio was not what she had paid for declared to the radio repairman that he was taking her money without giving her full value. The radio repairman being the brother of the sheriff-elect of Maury County was indignant and slapped and kicked Mrs. Stephenson. Whereupon her son reacted by hitting the man who had assaulted his mother. At that time the Stephensons were assaulted by people on the street and attacked by police officer Frazier, who hit at the young man, James Stephenson, and when Mrs. Stephenson declared that the police officer should investigate the facts, she was struck over the eye by the officer. Various people witnessed the incident from across the street and will testify to the above facts. They are Negro people in part and presently are afraid and in great fear for their lives and ask that they not be named as witnesses in this matter.

The sheriff being the chief law enforcement agent for Maury County is hereafter quoted. Due to the fact that he is charged with this responsibility as a most responsible person in the County, the sheriff made the following statement to Maurice Weaver of Chattanooga regarding the developments after the assault on the Stephensons.

The Sheriff Explains

After the incident of the attacks on the Stephensons, the sheriff declared voluntarily that he was in court at the time the incident occurred and that reports reached him in the court that a Negro and a white man were involved in an affray but that they had been placed under arrest and were in custody. The sheriff declared that he remained in court and continued about the court business until the court adjoined at or about 2:00 o'clock. During that time, however, he heard rumors and reports of the development of mass public opinion against Negroes in the community. After he was out of court he went back to the jail and thereafter was about town and the ominous threat of mob violence against the Stephensons, so he declared, came so forcibly to his attention that he called Mr. Saul Blair and other Negro citizens and asked them to cooperate with him to the end that they might be able to take the Stephensons out of town to avert possible and probable mob action.

At 6:00 o'clock, according to the sheriff, there was a mob of white men congregating on the public square at the courthouse numbering approximately seventy-five (75). The sheriff declares that he asked the mob of white men to disband and to go to their homes and thereafter went into the Negro section and talked to Mr. James Morton giving him assurance that he and all of the Negro people would be protected against the mob that was congregated on the public square. The sheriff declares that after he talked to Mr. Morton he came back by the public square; the mob was still formed and assembled, and after the sheriff returned to the jail a mob of white men came down to the jail at about 6:30 or 7:00 o'clock at night on

Monday, February 25, and kicked on the door of the jail. The sheriff reports that he responded by throwing open the door and levelling a tommy-gun on them; whereupon they demanded the release of the Stephensons to them. The sheriff told them, he declares, that he would not permit mob violence to be committed against the Stephensons if they were in jail, but that they had already been released (mother and son are now reported to be in Chicago) and thereupon told the mob to disband. Two white men were so drunk that they were unable to get away and were placed under arrest for being drunk. No charges as far as we were able to determine were placed against them for inciting to riot or mob action.

Lynch Action Threatened

After the arrest and after the mob action for the declared lynch purposes, there continued to be mob and lynch action on the public square less than one block from the Negro section. There is definite and concrete evidence that members of the mob had purchased rope and declared they were doing so for the purpose of hanging the two Negroes.

The Negroes were so afraid lest their section be invaded they turned out all the lights in the principal Negro business sections of town. The only illumination was at the center of the block on East Eighth Street and Chaffin Alley. During this time the city police went into a dark street with no illumination to show that they were policemen. The Negroes were afraid lest the mob was moving in on them. A cry was set up that "Here they come," and then there was firing. No one knows who fired the shots but the policemen were shot.

Thereafter the police retired from the business section and following it the sheriff reports a cordon of State Patrolmen and Guards were thrown around one block of the Negro section so that no one would be permitted to enter that section. After the official control of the Negro business section had been established, and at about dawn on Tuesday morning, members of the State Patrol and the State Guard entered the section, firing into various buildings and invading these business establishments, committing officially the following vandalism.

Gestapo-Like Vandalism

They shot out windows, broke up the show-cases, tore up the cash register taking about $60.00 in money, broke and robbed the piccolo, tore up the radio, threw the pool table balls away, cut the cloth off, broke up all tables, chairs, tore the top off the frigidaire, knocked the clock off the wall.

In Dr. Hawthorne's place they threw out all the instruments and generally destroyed his office. In the Atlanta Life Insurance Company office they destroyed all files and records and at the Morton Funeral Home they likewise destroyed all records, broke chandeliers, lights, venetian blinds, cut up draperies, broke floor lamps, file cabinets and sprinkled white powder on a navy blue casket and marked on the casket "KKK." They soiled all caskets. The barber shop was shot into and completely wrecked after the State Patrol had entered and had the situation under control. The four barber chairs were completely cut up and destroyed, the big mirror shot up, all electric clippers were taken out, and the premises completely destroyed.

It is significant that the entire section, after it was under control and in the hands of the State Guard and the State Highway Patrol, was invaded and wanton destruction of property occurred. Thereafter the sheriff declares the State Highway Patrol and State Guard, it is assumed, were acting under his orders went to all the Negro homes removing from them all arms. In the jail were many shot guns and rifles people would normally have for hunting purposes. The sheriff declares that they had been taken uniformly from Negroes and whites for the purpose of disarming completely and totally the town. He also declared that they had been taken without search warrants.

Police Terror

All of the Negroes had retired to their homes for their own protection. The State Guard and State Highway Patrol terrorized the entire Negro residential as well as the business section. They fired into the homes, searched them and lined up all the Negroes, men, women and children, with their hands in the air, and arrested most of the Negroes in the area. All were held in jail and not permitted to get in touch with their families, friends or lawyers. All were held without bail and without formal charges.

One of the leaders arrested who was said to be a leader of the armed rebellion of Negroes for the past three years has been assistant chairman of the Red Cross drive. His business was the center for the meeting of the Red Cross drive—all monies were collected and turned over to the white chairman by him. He was chairman of the Sixth War Loan Drive and Seventh War Loan Drive. His wife is co-chairman. He represents the third generation of colored undertakers in Columbia and has been in business himself for the past twenty-three years.

Two men were killed at the jail waiting to appear before the Board of Investigation. The declared official position is that one of these men endeavored to take a rifle or gun that had been confiscated from some citizens in the town, which was in the sheriff's office, and endeavored to load this gun with ammunition from the confiscated ammunition in the sheriff's office. It is charged officially that this Negro man shot a white officer in the arm with a Japanese rifle or gun.

The entire pattern in Maury county appears to be an attempt to develop and support the idea that there has been an endeavor on the part of the Negro citizens to establish and bring about an armed insurrection; that some six or more Negroes in Maury county were endeavoring to set up a dictatorship of Negro citizens. It is further declared that there would be no peace until white and "good" Negro citizens organize to surmount the bad relations existing.

The entire investigation has been carried on by the State with the greatest intimidation and coercion with milling mobs of authority, so that Negro citizens held in jail have been alarmed and disturbed for their future safety and have been forced to make completely involuntary statements that may probably in the future be held or used against them.

At the request of the victims of the unlawful action of the officials in Columbia, Tennessee, the NAACP has agreed to defend the Negroes wrongfully charged with crimes and to take all necessary action to punish the local and state peace officers guilty of disregarding the constitutional rights of these people. The entire resources of the NAACP are pledged to this end, and a series of nationwide mass meetings to collect defense funds and to publicize the facts will be held.

The authors were two attorneys—Maurice Weaver, of Chattanooga, and Z. Alexander Looby, of Nashville.

[c]

LAWRENCEBURG, TENNESSEE

Twenty-three of the twenty-five Negro defendants in the Columbia, Tennessee affair were acquitted on October 4 by an all-white jury of Lawrence Countians. Two of the men, Robert Gentry and John McKivens, were found guilty of first degree attempted murder. Attorneys for the

NAACP, Z. A. Looby, Negro Attorney of Nashville, Leon Ransom, former acting dean of the Howard University Law School, and Maurice Weaver, a white lawyer of Chattanooga, Tennessee have entered a motion for a new trial in the cases of the convicted men, and have indicated their determination to carry the fight to the U.S. Supreme Court, if necessary. Attorney General Paul Bumpus and his staff were openly hostile toward Attorneys for the defense during the course of the trial. When Attorney Weaver charged that the prosecution had used intimidation in order to secure Negro witnesses for the state, the Attorney General "dared" him to make the statement "outside of the courtroom." At another time Bumpus told Weaver in conversation that he, Bumpus, would "wrap a chair around" Ransom's head if the latter continued to contradict him. However, the spectators in the unsegregated courtroom were remarkably calm throughout the trial.

There are no public facilities for eating or sleeping in the town that are open to Negroes.[1] This fact made it necessary for the defendants to travel sixty-eight miles each of the nearly sixty days that the court was in session. The attorney for the defense had to travel 166 miles per day back and forth between Lawrenceburg and Nashville.[2]

Specifically, some of the accused men had been charged with the attempted murder of Will Willsford, Columbia police officer. Others had been charged with being accessories before the fact; while a few had been indicted on both charges. During the trial the prosecution sought to show that Willsford and his three fellow-officers who were injured on the night of February 25 were clearly recognizable as police officers when they entered the Negro business section (East Eighth Street) to investigate shots that they had heard coming from the area. Attorney General Paul Bumpus and his staff presented witnesses, including the injured officers, who testified that the lighting conditions at the time were such that the uniforms of the officers were clearly visible.

Several of the officers testified that they had made a previous visit to

---

[1] It was known to the Negro people in and around Columbia that food could be left for the defendants at certain specified places. For each of the nearly sixty days of the Lawrenceburg phase of the trial the defendants and any of their friends among the spectators were amply supplied with food.

[2] On one occasion Judge Ingram assessed fines of fifty dollars each upon defense attorneys Maurice Weaver and Leon Ransom because automobile trouble had caused them to be ten minutes late for the beginning of the court day.

Summary, October 1946, vol. 4, pp. 68–69.

East Eighth Street during the evening of the shooting at which time they had seen several of the defendants; but did not recall any of them as being armed at the time. None of the prosecution witnesses identified any of the persons who fired shots.

Chief defense counsel Z.A. Looby and his colleagues tried to show that the shots that injured Willsford and his fellows were fired in self-defense, inasmuch as the Negroes in East Eighth Street were fearful of a white mob which they knew was present a block away on the Public Square. In support of this argument they attempted to introduce accounts of the two lynchings that have occurred in and around Columbia during the past twenty years. Judge Joe Ingram, who presided at the trial, disallowed evidence concerning the two lynchings as immaterial to the case on trial. However, defense attorneys were successful in getting an opportunity to read into the record—while the jury was excused—a statement to the effect that Squire C.H. Denton, the magistrate who fixed bond for James Stevenson and his mother, was known in the Negro community of Columbia as a leader and instigator in the lynching of seventeen-year-old Cordie Cheek in 1932.

Several witnesses for the prosecution testified as to the good reputation and character of Julius Blair (seventy-five-year-old business man), his son, Julius Blair, James Morton (local undertaker) and several other defendants. Moreover, the defense introduced witnesses, including the principal of the Negro high school and the county supervisor of Negro schools, who testified that Messers Blair and Morton were attending a meeting of community leaders, seeking to raise money for a new school building, at the time police officers claim to have conversed with them during their earlier visit to East Eighth Street.

The conviction of Gentry and McKivens was based upon the testimony of a young Negro woman who said that she had been in the presence of the two men on the night of the shooting and that someone had said, "We just shot some officers." On cross-examination, the young woman could not remember whether the person speaking—never definitely identified by her—had said *we* or *they*. It was also brought out on cross-examination that she had been arrested on the night of the shooting (Monday) and held in jail until the following Sunday. She also claimed that the attorneys for the prosecution had threatened to see that she received a prison sentence if she failed to testify as she did.

The verdict of the jury has generally been hailed as a victory for democracy. The fact that twenty-three out of twenty-five Negroes charged with the attempted murder of a white peace officer should be acquitted was surprising to all of the defendants and to their attorneys as well. Lawrenceburg, the county seat of Lawrence County, is a town of 3,486 white persons and 321 Negroes. (There are 28,025 whites and 701 Negroes in the entire county.) It is located in an unprosperous farming area eighty-three miles southwest of Nashville and thirty-four miles southwest of Columbia. . . .

[d]

Although 23 of the 25 Negro defendants were acquitted October 4, by an all-white jury in Lawrenceburg, Tenn., the shouts of rejoicing were premature.

The sobering facts are: (a) two more defendants, separated from the 25 on a technicality, are still to be tried on the same charge of attempted murder; (b) they are also under indictment on a charge of assault with intent to kill; (c) all defendants are also under indictment on lesser charges; (d) the two men convicted and sentenced to not more than 21 years in prison must have their cases appealed to higher courts.

Thus the only rejoicing must be over the fact that the *first* hurdle has been taken. There is still a long, weary way to go.

Said Dr. Leon A. Ransom, one of the three NAACP attorneys in the case: "I am a bit concerned over expressions of jubilation over the Lawrenceburg verdict. I am afraid that many people are of the opinion that this case is finished. Nothing could be farther from the truth."

Defendants Partially Free

For the defendants acquitted it was a great day, but outwardly no different from the other days. Each day of the long trial they had been coming to the courtroom from their homes in Columbia, 34 miles distant. Each night they returned to their homes, being free on bail. On the day of acquittal they followed their same routine. They now go about their business in Columbia awaiting the next legal moves in the case.

Columbia is quiet. There is no more racial tension than usual. The trial is not discussed. The colored people of Columbia are confident that in the long pull they will win. They have this confidence in spite of (or, perhaps, because of) the fact that the trial just completed in Lawrenceburg was one of the most fantastic ever held in an American courtroom.

Trial Unwelcome

The town of Lawrenceburg did not want the trial in the first place. It was thrust upon the community by a change of venue granted in Columbia where the trouble occurred last February. Lawrenceburg business men and citizens generally held that they did not want to "wash Columbia's dirty linen." Lawrenceburg said it had "solved" its Negro problem by excluding Negroes from the town; now Columbia had had an interracial scrap and wanted to dump it in the lap of Lawrenceburg to be settled.

In this atmosphere the first legal skirmishes were held, with the defense lawyers, two colored and one white, being overruled and insulted on every point. In this atmosphere the selection of the jury began. It took five weeks. White veniremen paraded to the witness stand and asserted they were prejudiced, that they would take the word of a white man over that of a Negro, that they would not give a Negro a fair trial in a dispute with a white man. Defense counsel became so searching with their questions (searching, that is, to the locality, but in reality asking only the routine questions anyone would ask) that Judge Joe Ingram finally astounded the court and the public by announcing that he would take over the questioning of jurors.

The Battle for a Jury

Typical of the examination of prospective jurors was that of Albert Patterson, former boss of a chain gang. Patterson testified that he would believe a white man before he would a colored man. Ransom asked Judge Ingram to excuse Patterson for cause. Ingram turned to Bumpus who declared Patterson was qualified. The judge upheld Bumpus. Under further questioning Patterson said:

"I worked a lot of colored men on the chain gang six years ago when I was a guard.

"The only colored people I ever dealt with were either criminals or criminally inclined."

"Do you think all Negroes are criminally inclined?" asked Ransom.

"Yes," replied Patterson.

Ransom again moved to challenge Patterson for cause, but was overruled by Judge Ingram. The defense was compelled to eliminate Patterson with a peremptory challenge.

The court also forbade defense attorneys to ask questions of prospective jurors on their membership in the Ku Klux Klan.

Judge vs. Defendants

From this point on the defense attorneys had to battle in a courtroom hostile to them personally as well as to the defendants. Maurice Weaver, the white NAACP attorney whose home is in Chattanooga, was the chief target of District Attorney Paul F. Bumpus, and his assistant prosecutor. Weaver to them was a traitor to the white race. Z. Alexander Looby, with his kindly voice, his sharp logic, his sarcasm and dry wit, and his fascinating West Indian accent drew many heated attacks from the red-faced prosecutors. As for Dr. Leon A. Ransom, his clear superiority as a lawyer, a strategist, and student of law, infuriated the opposition.

Bumpus used outrageous language in the courtroom. He threatened to "wrap a chair around his head"—meaning Ransom. He challenged Weaver to come outside the courtroom and fight. He called one defense attorney a sonofabitch in open court. Toward the end of the trial he turned purple language on Vincent Sheean who sat at the press table, whose syndicated articles on the trial enraged both Bumpus and Lynn Bomar, head of the state police. When Weaver asked Judge Ingram if he was going to permit such an attack in his court without rebuke, Ingram replied that it was a matter between Bumpus and Sheean!

A high point, illustrating not only the atmosphere in the courtroom, but the manner in which these defendants had been arrested, occurred during the testimony of Lynn Bomar, head of the state highway patrol. Bomar admitted on the stand that he had led state troopers into the homes of Columbia Negro citizens without a search warrant.

Q. Did you get Morton's permission to enter and search?
A. I just went right in.
Q. (By the court) Was the door open when you entered the house? Did you turn the knob?
A. I turned the knob and walked right in.
Q. Did anybody object?
A. I didn't wait to see. I knew a felony had been committed and I went in to get the guilty parties.

Bomar roared a denial when asked whether his men had ransacked and wrecked Negro property. Later he said he would enter Negro property again without a warrant if he wanted to do so.

Gloom Before Victory

In this atmosphere the trial dragged on. No defendant was identified as having fired a shot at the policemen who were wounded. In no manner whatsoever were any of the defendants connected with the crime except that one witness said she had walked with one of the defendants who had told her he was in Columbia on the night of the trouble. Mere presence in the town where the shooting had occurred thus became "proof" of guilt!

The defendants told their stories, and then came the summing up to the jury. District Attorney Bumpus and his assistant performed as was expected. The Vincent Sheean articles syndicated in daily papers throughout the country had roused the ire of Bumpus. He ranted at outsiders and newspaper writers. He raved about white supremacy. He called for the conviction of all 25 defendants.

On the speeches of the three defense lawyers to the jury, Sheean offers this description:

The three lawyers were excellent, each in a different way. Andy Ransom made the argument of reason and courtesy and common sense—deliberately appealing to those qualities in the jury, I mean. His was the first argument for the defense and had the effect (I believe) of reasonableness, the evocation of reasonableness. Then Weaver made his rather fiery speech, which could *not* have been made under the conditions by any Negro; he established the analogies to Nazi practise and made the appeal to historical conscience ("You are making history in this courtroom"). Then Looby made his searching appeal to their religious instincts. He had varicose veins badly and had to speak from a seated position with his right leg upon a cushion arrangement in front of him. His voice was better than it had been before, his manner and language simple, his argument less studded with legal authority than I had expected. His essential argument was of a purely religious nature and it was my impression that it reached home with that jury.

Victory—Why?

Why was the surprising verdict rendered? No one will know unless the jurors themselves tell their reasons. Was this the way Lawrenceburg had of showing Columbia how distasteful the trial was—if you want these Negroes convicted you will have to do it yourself?

Did Bumpus and Judge Ingram overplay their hands? Did the judge muzzle the defense lawyers so obviously and so continuously and so unfairly that even those Tennessee jurymen thought the Negroes were not getting a fair shake? Did Paul Bumpus stress the white supremacy argument too much even for rural Tennessee?

Did the defense lawyers by their courage, their brilliance, and their persistence under handicaps and discouragements capture the sporting fancy of the jury? Did the jury really mean to indicate that the South was ready to change its attitude and that hereafter Negroes could expect a fair deal?

The Optimists have seen a "new day" in the verdict, a sign that democracy is here for the Negro in the rural South. The cynics say the jury was just trying to wash its hands quickly of the Columbia "dirt." But the truth would seem to be somewhere in between. The first round has been won. It may be that its winning will cause the state to drop all charges and close the book on the shameful chapter of the Columbia disturbance of last winter. Or, angered by the acquittal, the District Attorney Bumpus may continue his fight. The defendants, their lawyers, and the thousands of Americans who contributed to the defense fund, await the next move.

> The two convicted defendants, John McKivens and Robert Gentry, were granted a new trial on October 26 by Circuit Judge Joe M. Ingram, who declared he was not satisfied with the evidence presented against them. The motion for a new trial was granted by Judge Ingram only ten minutes after it was presented by NAACP attorneys.*

*They were released—ed.

Crisis, November 1946, pp. 329–30; Roy Wilkins was author of this report.

19

PROTESTING TERROR AT HOME AND ABROAD (1946)

In 1946, protests against racist terror and brutality, at home and abroad, were frequent. Four illustrations, two dealing with the situation in the United States, and two with the question overseas, follow. The first three are from Fisk

University's *Monthly Summary*, August–September 1946, pp. 17, 39–40; the last is from an advertisement in the *New York Times*, June 3, 1946.

[a]

Mayor's Group Fights Police Brutality

CINCINNATI, OHIO

The Mayor's Friendly Relations Committee of Cincinnati and the local branch of the National Association for the Advancement of Colored People are making extensive efforts to curb evidence of police brutality in the city.

At a recent executive board meeting of the Mayor's committee, a special subcommittee was appointed to investigate the need for further in-service training of police in race relations techniques and to consider ways in which the Race Relations Detail might be permanently established.

Following an interview with Joseph T. Kluchesky, former chief of the Milwaukee police and now consultant to the American Council on Race Relations in police training, the sub-committee made the following recommendations:

1. That at least two hours of in-service training be devoted to good race relations practices techniques, the subject to be presented by men competent in this specialty;
2. That similar training be given all new police recruits;
3. That a series of conferences of key officers be held under the direction of some such expert as Chief Kluchesky;
4. That a permanent Committee on Law and Order be established in the Mayor's Committee to carry on the study made by the sub-committee.

The American Jewish Committee is also making efforts to eliminate police brutality in certain areas. The community service department of the Committee is circulating a memorandum throughout the nation which urges local police departments to adopt measures forbidding their membership to join organizations fostering racial and religious prejudice. The Committee points out that the success of the KKK in Indiana and other states during the 1920's was due in part to the fact that its members included a large number of police, magistrates and others with civil authority....

[b]

Action Taken on Monroe, Georgia Lynching

Among the significant developments in connection with the Monroe, Georgia lynching are the following: (1) sentiment has increased for passage of a Federal Anti-Lynch Bill (Attorney General Tom Clark has announced his intention to ask the 80th Congress, when it reconvenes, to pass a Federal Anti-Lynch Law; a group of senators led by James M. Mead and Robert F. Wagner of New York have declared their support of the proposed measure); (2) rewards totalling approximately $64,000[1] at the time of writing have been offered by civic-minded groups in an effort to bring the lynchers to justice; (3) climaxing numerous protest rallies and conferences, a group of prominent citizens, headed by Paul Robeson, have formed an "American Crusade to End Lynchings," and have issued a call for a National Protest Pilgrimage to Washington, D.C., on September 23.

Throughout the entire country, citizens were aroused by news of the lynching. The American Council on Race Relations issued a memorandum urging the hundreds of mayors' and governors' commissions and other community organizations to use "every means at your disposal to help bring these undemocratic acts to a halt". The United Packinghouse Workers of America (CIO) sent a letter to President Truman demanding action on the lynching. The National Association for the Advancement of Colored People called an emergency conference of more than fifty national organizations to plan unified action to halt terrorism against minorities. With all forty-eight states represented, members of the National Association of Colored Women, meeting in annual convention in Washington, D.C., and an interracial delegation from eastern chapters of

---

[1]The figure $64,000 was reported by the American Council on Race Relations and the Pittsburgh *Courier*. The MONTHLY SUMMARY has received notice of the following rewards already posted: (1) Governor Arnall, $10,000; (2) NAACP, $10,000; (3) Citizens Defense League of Atlanta, $10,000; (4) National Baptist Convention, $5,000; (5) J. Finley Wilson, Grand Exalted Ruler of IBPOEW, $5,000; (6) Hollywood Independent Citizens Committee of the Arts, Sciences and Professions, $1,000; (7) Southern Regional Council, $1,000; (8) Los Angeles County Democratic Committee, $1,000; (9) Sports fans attending the fourth annual East-West baseball game in Chicago, $758; (10) Most Worshipful Prince Hall Grand Lodge, Masonic Order of Indiana, $200. In addition, a number of organizations have announced money-raising drives for this reward fund.

the National Negro Congress picketed the White House to protest the lynchings.

Local action was also taken. In San Francisco, more than 3,000 persons representing labor and civic groups participated in a "silent parade" of protest, under the sponsorship of the local NAACP and the Northern California Executive Committee of the California Council for Civic Unity. In Philadelphia, a day of mourning for the four Monroe victims was observed by church, civic and labor organizations. In New York, theatrical people staged a midnight rally on Broadway and raised funds to assist the victims' families. In Chicago, the National Negro Congress and the local branch of the NAACP co-sponsored a rally, attended by 15,000 persons, which raised more than $1,500 to send a delegation of fifty to Washington. In Atlanta, the Citizens' Defense League sponsored two mass rallies and raised $10,000 for rewards. A drive is now under way in Atlanta to raise $100,000 to fight future outbreaks of southern terrorism. In Fairburn, Georgia, the City Council passed an ordinance forbidding persons to congregate within the city limits for the purpose of violating the civil rights of others. Violation calls for $100 fine and thirty days in prison. In Tampa, Florida, a mass meeting, initiated by the Joint Advisory Board of the Cigar Makers International Union (AFL) and sponsored by civic, labor and religious organizations, formed a city-wide committee to fight outbreaks of terror.

[c]

The governing council of the World Federation of Democratic Youth meeting in Paris unanimously voted to call on Secretary of State Byrnes to protest the "lynch atrocities and rising tide of fascist terror which are presently being perpetrated against the Negro people in Georgia, Mississippi and the Southern part of the United States." The action was taken at the suggestion of Dorothy Burnham, Educational Director of the Southern Negro Youth Congress, who represented the Congress at the Paris meeting. From Cuba a protest came from the National Federation of Cuban Negro Organizations, urging the United States government to capture and try the "gangsters of Georgia." . . .

[d]

AN APPEAL FOR AFRICAN FREEDOM

A Message to America and the United Nations, signed by
Paul Robeson, Chairman, and Max Yergan, Executive Director,
Council on African Affairs

One hundred fifty million Africans and 93 percent of the continent of Africa are still in colonial subjection.

Thousands of Africans fought, labored, died to defeat fascism. Are these allies now forgotten?

The colonial peoples of Africa are barred from the United Nations. They ask not for promises of a remote freedom, but for ACTION NOW to end their enslavement and oppression.

Will the Union of South Africa's legalized fascist-like practice of racial oppression be outlawed, and that state's mandate control be revoked?

Will the peoples of the Italian colonies and the mandate territories cease to be mere pawns in the game of imperialist politics?

Will the European rulers of Africa be called upon to declare WHEN they will yield to the demand of Africans for freedom?

AND WILL AMERICA HELP FREE AFRICA? OR WILL IT SEEK INSTEAD A LARGER SHARE OF THE PROFITS SQUEEZED OUT OF AFRICA'S OPPRESSED PEOPLE?

AMERICA MUST ANSWER!

Published in P. S. Foner, ed., *Paul Robeson Speaks* (Secaucus, NJ: Citadel Press, 1978), p. 164.

20

FIRST PETITION TO UNITED NATIONS FROM THE AFRICAN-AMERICAN PEOPLE (1946)

This petition from the National Negro Congress was presented in June 1946. Its origin and purpose are elucidated in the first seven pages of the sixteen-page pamphlet issued by the Congress. The concluding pages (8–15) contain an essay on "The Facts" written by the editor of this volume. About 100,000 copies of this pamphlet (priced at five cents) were distributed in the United States. Objection from the U.S. delegation, mainly, accounted for its failure to be considered by the United Nations. The African-American press gave it good coverage, as did much of the media elsewhere in the world.

Foreword

For more than three centuries the Negro people have worked to build America into a great nation. We have fought to preserve the unity of our country within, and to defend it from enemies without. And when the fascist enemies of all mankind recently threatened to over-run the whole world, we joined hands with our countrymen and with freedom-loving peoples of other lands to crush the fascist monster and to lay the basis for a genuine "Parliament of Man," the United Nations.

Ironic, indeed, is our "reward." Barred from most industrial and business employment on the spurious grounds of "race," bound to the soil in semi-feudal serfdom on the cotton plantations of the Deep South, forced to live in overcrowded slum ghettos in our great cities, denied any substantial education for millions of our children, lynched and terrorized, kept from effective use of the ballot in many states, segregated like pariahs, the more than 13,000,000 Negro Americans still suffer an oppression which is revolting to all the canons of the civilized society.

It is with genuine anger and disgust that the Negro people, like all other friends of freedom, view the hypocrisy of our Government's professions to leadership in the promotion of "freedom and democracy" throughout the world. We are enraged at the knowledge that our American Secretary of State, Mr. James F. Byrnes of South Carolina, subscribes to the same policies of anti-Negro oppression as did the late Herr Adolph Hitler, and as does the present Senator Theodore Bilbo of Mississippi.

We have petitioned our own Government, time and again, for redress of grievance. This we will continue to do, for the main responsibility lies with the rulers of America.

We also call upon the United Nations, as we have every legal and moral right to do, to mobilize the influence of all organized mankind toward fulfillment, here in the United States, of the stated purpose of the United Nations to *promote and encourage "respect for human rights and for fundamental freedoms for all without distinction as to race, sex, language or religion."*

Thus it is that the Tenth Anniversary Convention of the National Negro Congress voted to address to the UN this "Petition to the Economic and Social Council of the United Nations," and to append thereto the accompanying digest of "The Facts" on "The Oppression of the American Negro."

The formal presentation of these documents was made at Hunter College, New York City, on June 6, 1946, to representatives of the United Nations. Now it is up to the progressive citizens of our country, of all races and creeds, quickly to endorse and actively to support this "Petition."

MAX YERGAN

Letters of Transmittal

I

Mr. Trygve Lie, Secretary-General   June 6, 1946
United Nations
Hunter College
Bronx, New York

Dear Mr. Lie:

It is with an expression of profound regret that we, a section of the Negro people, having failed to find relief from oppression through constitutional appeal, find ourselves forced to bring this vital issue—which we have sought for almost a century since emancipation to solve within the boundary of our country—to the attention of this historic body—and to request that you, as Director-General, place it for consideration before the Economic and Social Council, or that body which, in your understanding, it may belong.

(s)   Max Yergan, President
National Negro Congress
Revels Cayton, Executive Sec'y
National Negro Congress

II

Honorable Harry S. Truman   June 6, 1946
The White House
Washington, D.C.

Dear Mr. President:

This is an historic movement in the life of the nation. Vast internal economic and social upheavals confront us. Added to those, the traditional pre-war policy of racial oppression carried out by powerful forces in this country is now being inhumanly reflected more than ever before.

The Negro people had hoped that out of the war there would come an extension of democratic rights and liberties so heroically fought for by all oppressed peoples.

Your administration, however, has reversed the democratic program of the Roosevelt government, both internally and in relation to foreign policy. Great burdens have been forced upon the shoulders of the Negro people.

Negro citizens find the present conditions intolerable, and are therefore, presenting their appeal to the highest court of mankind— the United Nations.

The National Negro Congress in Convention assembled feels impelled to send you the information which motivates this historic petition.

(s)   Max Yergan, President
Revels Cayton, Executive Secretary

PETITION

To the Economic and Social Council
of the United Nations

A petition on behalf of the Negro people of America by the National Negro Congress of the United States of America at its Tenth Anniversary Convention, held in the City of Detroit from May 30 to June 2, 1946, for the elimination of political, economic and social discrimination against Negroes in the United States of America.

I. The Subject Matter of the Petition

The National Negro Congress, the petitioner herein, is a national organization in the United States of America, within the definition set forth in Article 71, of the Charter of the United Nations.

The subject matter of this petition is concerned with the "protection of minorities" and the "prevention of discrimination on grounds of race," within the purview of the Report of the Preparatory Commission and the Report of the Committee on the Organization of the Economic and Social Council both cited hereinafter.

II. The Jurisdiction of the Economic and Social Council of the United Nations

The basis and scope of the relation of the United Nations to the problem of racial oppression and the protection of minorities has been definitively stated in various official declarations and reports of the United Nations.

1. Reference: Preamble to Charter of the United Nations.
   "We the people of the United Nations determined to reaffirm faith in fundamental rights, in the dignity and worth of the human person, in the equal rights of men and women and of nations large and small...."
2. Reference: Article I, Sec. 3, Charter of the United Nations.
   "The purposes of the United Nations are: To achieve international cooperation in solving international problems of an economic, social, cultural, or humanitarian character, and in promoting and encouraging respect for human rights and for fundamental freedoms for all without distinction as to race, sex, language, or religion."
3. Reference: Article 13, Sec. 1 (b), Charter of the United Nations.
   "The General Assembly shall initiate studies and make recommendations for the purpose of: promoting international cooperation in the economic, social, cultural, educational and health fields, and assisting in the realization of human rights and fundamental freedoms for all without distinction as to race, sex, language, or religion."
4. Reference: Article 55, Sec. 1 (c), Charter of the United Nations.
   "With a view to the creation of conditions of stability and well-being which are necessary for peaceful and friendly relations among nations based on respect for the principle of equal rights and self-determination of peoples, the United Nations shall promote: Universal respect for, and observance of, human rights and fundamental freedoms for all without distinction as to race, sex, language or religion."
5. Reference: Article 62, Sec. 2, Charter of the United Nations.
   "It (The Economic and Social Council) may make recommendations for the purpose of promoting respect for, and observance of, human rights and fundamental freedoms for all."

The medium through which the United Nations approaches the specific problem of racial oppression and protection of minorities is the Economic and Social Council. In turn, it is through the Commission on Human Rights, a specialized Commission of the Economic and Social Council, that the functions of the United Nations upon this subject are to be exercised. The basis for this delegation of function is provided in Article 68, in the Charter of the United Nations, which states:

The Economic and Social Council shall set up commissions in economic and social fields and for the promotion of human rights, and such other commissions as may be required for the performance of its functions.

Reference is further made to the Report of the Preparatory Commission of the United Nations, Chapter III, Sec. 4:

Considerations and Recommendations Concerning the Organization of the Economic and Social Council:

15. Commission on Human Rights

In general the functions of the Commission would be to assist the Council to carry out its responsibility under the Charter to promote human rights. The studies and recommendations of the Commission would encourage the acceptance of higher standards in this field and help to check and eliminate discrimination and other abuses.

16. In particular the work of the Commission might be directed towards the following objects:

    a) formulation of an international bill of rights.

    b) formulation of recommendations for an international declaration or convention on such matters as civil liberties, status of women, freedom of information.

    c) protection of minorities.

    d) prevention of discrimination on grounds of race, sex, language or religion; and

    e) any matters within the field of human rights considered likely to impair the general welfare or friendly relations among nations.

17. Studies and recommendations would be made and information and other services provided at the request of the General Assembly, or of the Economic and Social Council, whether on its own initiative or at the request of the Security Council or of the Trusteeship Council."

Reference is further made to the Report of the Committee on the Organization of the Economic and Social Council which met in London during February 1946, and proposed the following resolution:

"Sec. A. The Economic and Social Council, being charged under the Charter with the responsibility of promoting universal respect for, and observance of, human rights and fundamental freedoms for all without distinction as to race, sex, language or religion, and requiring advice and assistance to enable it to discharge this responsibility; establishes a Commission on Human Rights.

2. The work of the Commission shall be directed towards submitting proposals, recommendations and reports to the Council regarding:

    a) formulation of an international bill of rights.

    b) formulation of recommendations for an international declaration or convention on such matters as civil liberties, status of women, freedom of information.

    c) protection of minorities.

    d) prevention of discrimination on grounds of race, sex, language or religion.

3. The Commission shall make studies and recommendations and provide information and other services at the request of the Economic and Social Council.

The Charter of the United Nations further makes provision for direct consultation between the Economic and Social Council and non-governmental organizations in connection with its functions. Reference is made to Article 71, Charter of the United Nations:

The Economic and Social Council may make suitable arrangements for consultation with non-governmental organizations which are concerned with matters within its competence. Such arrangements may be made with international organizations and, where appropriate, *with national organizations after consultation with the Member of the United Nations concerned.*

III. Proof in Support of the Petition

The evidence in support of this petition is set forth in full in the Document attached hereto and made a part hereof entitled, "The Oppression of the American Negro: The Facts," which conclusively establishes that a condition has existed throughout the United States of America during its entire history and prevails at this time, of the political, economic, and social discrimination against Negroes because of their race and color; resulting in the denial of equal democratic rights to 13,000,000 Negro citizens and requiring the consideration of the Economic and Social Council of the United Nations.

Wherefore, your petitioner respectfully prays that the Economic and Social Council through its Commission on Human Rights or otherwise:

1. Make such studies as it may deem necessary of the conditions herein described as they exist in the United States of America, pertaining to political, economic and social discrimination against Negroes because of their race and color.
2. Make such recommendations and take such other actions as it may deem proper with respect to the facts herein stated, to the end that "higher standards" in the field of human rights may be achieved in the United States of America and "discrimination and other abuses" on the grounds of race and color, may be "checked and eliminated."
3. Take such other and further steps as may seem just and proper to the end that the oppression of the American Negro be brought to an end.

Respectfully submitted,

NATIONAL NEGRO CONGRESS
by
DR. MAX YERGAN
President

REVELS CAYTON
*Executive Secretary for
the National Board*

21

THE AMERICAN CRUSADE AGAINST LYNCHING (1946)

This crusade—with considerable impact in its day—has been neglected in historical accounts, probably because its leader was Paul Robeson. Descriptions of its work in 1946 came from the African-American press; three examples follow:

[a]

WASHINGTON—Paul Robeson, Negro baritone, spearhead of the American Crusade to End Lynching, said yesterday after a White House visit that he had told the President that if the Government did not do something to curb lynching, "the Negroes would."

To this statement, Robeson said, the President took sharp exception. The President, he said, remarked that it sounded like a threat. Robeson told newspaper men he assured the President it was not a threat, merely a statement of fact about the temper of the Negro people, who comprise about 10 percent of the population.

At the head of a mixed delegation, Robeson asked the President to make a formal declaration of disapproval of lynching within the next hundred days. Robeson explained the next hundred days would be an appropriate time for the President to act, because it was on Sept. 22, 1862, that Lincoln issued the proclamation freeing the slaves and it was on Jan. 1 that it became effective.

The President, Robeson said, told the delegation that Government action against lynching was necessarily a political matter, and that timing was important. The President said, Robeson reported, that this was not the time for him to act.

Robeson also asked the President to send a message when Congress reconvenes urging immediate enactment of an anti-lynching bill.

The singer said he also pointed out what he considered misdirections in American foreign policy. He said it was hard to see the distinction between current lynchings and the Nuremberg war crimes trials. He explained that he meant by this that the United States could not logically take the lead in punishing Nazis for the oppression of groups in Germany while the Government here permitted Negroes to be lynched and shot.

To this he said the President objected that loyal Americans should not mix domestic problems like lynching with foreign policy. Robeson said he told the President he did not see how the two could be separated. When he was asked whether he was a Communist, Robeson described himself as "violently anti-Fascist." He said he had opposed Fascism in other countries and saw no reason why he should not oppose Fascism in the United States.

Philadelphia Tribune, September 24, 1946.

[b]

WASHINGTON—In terms which left no doubt in the minds of the delegation from the American Crusade to End Lynching, President Truman today emphatically refused to take the initiative to end mob violence and the spread of terrorism in America.

The delegation, led by Paul Robeson, chairman, and Mrs. Harper Sibley, president of the United Council of Church Women and wife of the former president of the United States Chamber of Commerce, asked the President to make a public statement expressing his views on lynching and to recommend a definite legislative and educational program to end the disgrace of mob violence.

Despite strong urgings from several members of the delegation, President Truman insisted that the moment was not propitious for a forthright statement from the Chief Executive, and that further, the whole question of lynching and mob violence was one to be dealt with in political terms and strategy. He stated that such a strategy must be worked out by responsible political leadership and patience must attend the final solution.

When Mrs. Sibley made a comparison between fascism as it manifested itself against the Jews in Europe and fascism in America as levied against Negroes, the President showed impatience and a flare of temper.

Aubrey Williams, publisher of the Southern Farmer and former administrator of the National Youth Administration, a member of the delegation, speaking from first hand knowledge told Truman a veritable reign of terror exists in the South. He warned unless the President takes action now, the whole situation is likely to become a tragedy on a scale unknown in America. He marshaled all the facts and logic at his command to coax the President into making a definite statement that would allay the fears and apprehension of the people.

Robeson tried to show the President that the mood of the Negro had changed. He said returning veterans are showing signs of restiveness and indicated that they are determined to get the justice here they have fought for abroad. Robeson warned that this restiveness might produce an emergency situation which would require Federal intervention. The President, shaking his fist, stated this sounded like a threat.

Dr. Metz T.P. Lochard, editor-in-chief of the Chicago Defender, who joined the delegation representing John H. Sengstacke, who was unable to attend, told Mr. Truman that the Defender policy was unalterably opposed to lynching and mob terror, and that he felt the moment was ripe for the President to make his position properly known.

Other members of the delegation were Dr. Charlotte Hawkins Brown, president of Palmer Memorial Institute; Dr. W. N. Jernigan, president, Federated Council of Churches; Dr. Joseph L. Johnson, president of the Washington Committee of the Southern Conference of Human Welfare; Rabbi Irving Miller, American Jewish Congress; Max Yergan, president, National Negro Congress, and H. Murphy of Chicago.

Outside, David Niles, presidential assistant and unofficial adviser to the President on Negro affairs, sought to soften the President's harsh position to waiting white newsmen. He said, "The President feels that this is a political matter and that the element of timing is important."

Niles said, "This is not the time for the Chief Executive to make a pronouncement of any new course." He added, "The President conveyed to the delegation that his general position was a matter of record." Robeson, who was listening, replied, "This is an issue that cannot be ducked."

Chicago Defender, September 28, 1946.

[c]

WASHINGTON—Standing at the feet of Abraham Lincoln's statue here Monday night, Paul Robeson, chairman of the American Crusade to End Lynching, climaxed a day-long rally high-lighted by a visit with the President, by reading a new Emancipation Proclamation to thousands of assembled Negro and white citizens.

Citing the abolition of slavery nearly 100 years ago as the end of the slaveholding heritage only, Robeson stated that oppression of the Negro never ended in fact. The proclamation pointed up the resurgence of violence which has taken the lives of a score of men and women since the war against fascism. It called mob violence a threat to the democratic freedom of the country.

"We, more than 1,500 citizens assembled in our nation's capitol to inaugurate the continuing American Crusade to End Lynching, are determined that the duly elected government of the U.S. shall fulfill its sacred trust by using the country's every resource to end now the growing reign of mob violence in America," the proclamation stated.

The proclamation, delivered after the President told Crusade members that lynching is not a moral issue, ended with a call to all Americans, regardless of race, creed or color, to demand that the 80th Congress pass laws to put an end to the national disgrace of mob murder.

Chicago Defender, September 28, 1946. These press reports are in Foner, ed., *op. cit.,* pp. 174–78.

22

POLITICAL DEVELOPMENTS IN THE SOUTH (1946)

In 1946 signs of the political revolution that would reach a climax in the 1960s appeared in several southern areas. Here are accounts involving Mississippi, Georgia, and Missouri.

VOTING

JACKSON, MISSISSIPPI

For the first time since the days of Reconstruction the actual participation of Negroes as voters in political elections is an issue in Mississippi. Recent decisions of the Supreme Court and other Federal courts have given Mississippi's million colored citizens some hope that they might participate in politics. There have been several significant developments—

1. Negro citizens from all over the state met in a two-day session of the Mississippi Progressive Voters League in which strategy for achieving the ballot was discussed and plans laid for raising $20,000 for civic education and court action where necessary.

2. The Jackson chapter of the NAACP addressed a letter to Herbert Holmes, chairman of the State Democratic Executive Committee saying, "The Negro

citizens of Mississippi who have qualified as electors desire to be informed by your Committee as to your intentions regarding the participation of those qualified electors in the forthcoming Democratic Primary elections." Mr. Holmes replied that the Executive Committee would consider the matter at its early May meeting. However, the May meeting was held as an "executive session," considering "matters of great importance to democracy in Mississippi." Following the meeting it was announced that no action was taken on the matter of Negro voting.

3. The Jackson *Daily News* has devoted much editorial space to efforts of Negroes to become enfranchised. On May 19, commenting on a statement by President T.W. Wilson of the Progressive Voters League ("We challenge the right of anyone to prevent us from voting."), the *Daily News* said, "In spite of all this big talk our first-best piece of advice to negroes, given in the friendliest spirit, is this: Don't attempt to participate in the Democratic primary anywhere in Mississippi on July 2nd. Staying away from the polls on that date will be the best way to prevent unhealthy and unhappy results."

On May 22 the same paper editorialized: "In the Republic of Liberia there is a constitutional provision that no white man shall take part in Liberian elections. Liberia is a negro nation. Down here in the Deep South this happens to be a white man's country." (Slightly less than fifty percent of Mississippi's population is Negro.)

4. Senator Bilbo, speaking in Okolona, Mississippi, in his campaign for re-election against what he termed "four peckerwoods," stated, "The leader or leaders of the Mississippi Progressive Voters League, composed of a number of politically ambitious Negroes who have challenged the right of anyone to prevent them from voting, should be atomically bombed and exterminated from the face of the earth." Earlier in the day Bilbo had suggested that anyone who "coddles, encourages, or otherwise tends to influence the Negro to vote in the white primary" should be "horse-whipped, tarred and feathered and chased out of the state."

ATLANTA, GEORGIA

Atlanta Negro voters came very close to their goal of 25,000 registered voters by the time registration for the coming primary ended in Atlanta on May 4. Of the 124,776 voters registered in Atlanta by the deadline 24,671 were Negroes. Evidence of the power of the poll tax is seen in the fact that the new total registration in Atlanta is nearly 250 percent greater than that for the last election.

In order to assure the fullest and wisest exercise of the newly-gained ballot in Atlanta the local NAACP has set up about a dozen citizenship schools. The initial sessions of these schools were attended by a total of more than 600 persons who learned such rudimentary but important details as the operation of a voting machine. The citizenship schools are under the general direction of a professor of political science in a local Negro university.

Summary, June 1946, pp. 331–32.

NON-VIOLENT ACTION

SAINT LOUIS, MISSOURI

A demonstration of direct and non-violent action by Negro residents of a southside neighborhood in Saint Louis proved successful recently when a playground formerly for white children was turned over to Negro children. For several months members of the Saint Louis Civic Improvement Association, in which Negro pastors of the south side settlement are very prominent, have contended that Negro children in the area had no playground facilities within a reasonable distance from their homes.

Early in June members of the Civic Association took approximately 200 Negro children over to Buder Playground, led them in, and waited while the youngsters played. A playground sign read, "Everybody Welcome!" At the close of the day, the group informed the playground attendants that they planned to return the next day. Upon arrival next morning, the Negro children encountered policemen as well as the playground attendants. The swings had been taken down, the wading pool drained, and no topsoil had been placed on the tennis court. Orders are said to have come down from the Commissioner that the children were not to be denied admission but that all portable equipment was to be kept under lock and key. The children remained and played the games they generally played on the streets.

Commissioner Palmer Baumes—who for years is said to have promised delegations from the district that he would "look into" the matter of recreational facilities for Negro children—immediately ordered a survey made. The survey showed that the number of Negro children in the immediate area of Buder Playground exceeded the number of white children and that there are other playgrounds available to the latter. The Commissioner then ordered the Buder playground turned over to Negro children. The community center and swimming pool directly across the street from the playground, part of the same plant, is still reserved for whites.

Summary, July 1946, p. 369. On post-war developments, see Robert Korstad and Nelson Sichtenstein, "Opportunities Found and Lost: Labor, Radicals and the Early Civil Rights Movement," *Journal of American History,* December 1988; 75:786–811.

EXPANDING VISIONS AND MEANS

NAACP Convention

CINCINNATI, OHIO

With approximately 2,000 persons in attendance and nationally-prominent figures on the speakers' platform, the National Association for the Advancement of Colored People held its thirty-seventh annual convention in Cincinnati from June 26th to the 30th.

A move to extend the activities of the association was expressed in the national statement of policy which proposes to expand the field of the association from a defense of civil rights for Negroes to an attack on the political, economic, and labor fronts.

Chief opposition to a resolution calling for political action on the part of the NAACP was that "the association would become too political." The measure finally adopted calls for "political action by the association and its branches, including the rating and publicizing of candidates for office," and the studying of ways and means to accomplish such action under proper safeguards. A committee of six, three appointed by the national board and three elected by the convention, will consider the type of political action the NAACP will take and report back to the national board at its meeting in September.

Other resolutions adopted called for extension of the OPA, a non-discriminatory policy in the Veterans' Administration, economic freedom of colonial peoples, adequate housing and full employment for all peoples, and continued support of the FEPC. A boycott by Negroes against consumer goods, until Congress acts to establish price control, was urged by Walter White, NAACP Executive Secretary. The new, liberalized constitution of the NAACP, granting the convention the power "to establish policies and programs of action" for the ensuing year, and allowing smaller NAACP branches more representation at conventions, was cited during the course of the meetings.

Three leading issues which affect the Negro's struggle for greater freedom were stressed on the convention's agenda. Mr. White summarized these issues as follows:

1. The need for constructive community, employer, and labor union approach to employment of Negro ex-servicemen and former war workers.
2. Nation-wide support of the political revolution now under way in the southern United States where Negroes are registering by the thousands for the summer primaries. The convention will signal the opening of the NAACP's own political action program.
3. Necessity for American Negroes to broaden their vision by turning their attention to the problems of minority people throughout the world.

Some of the speakers included on the program were: Chester Bowles, former Economic Stabilization Director; Gov. William H. Hastie, the Virgin Islands; Walter P. Reuther, President, UAW-CIO; Charles H. Houston, Attorney and former member of the President's Fair Employment Practice Commission; Attorney General Robert Kenny, of California; Thurgood Marshall, Special Counsel of the NAACP and 1946 recipient of the Spingarn Medal; the Rev. Archibald J. Carey, Jr., of Chicago, and Joe Louis, world heavyweight boxing champion....

CORE *Holds Convention*

CLEVELAND, OHIO

Delegates to the fourth annual convention of the Congress of Racial Equality, meeting in Cleveland in June, participated in action projects under the leadership of Cleveland CORE members as a regular part of the convention proceedings. Managements of department stores were interviewed in a campaign of the Congress to have Negroes used as salesclerks, and otherwise up-graded in the stores. Also, three groups of the delegates went to various Cleveland and suburban orphanages to inquire into reasons for their refusal to accept Negro children.

In reports from various local Committees of Racial Equality, it was revealed during the convention that Congress affiliates, in the past year, have broken down discriminatory practices in YMCA's, restaurants, and theaters; and have conducted campaigns against restrictive covenants and disciplinary housing projects. George M. Houser, Executive Secretary, indicated that CORE groups are now being formed in various states and that within the past few months, new groups have been organized in Los

Angeles and Berkeley, California; Portland, Oregon; Minneapolis, Minnesota; Cincinnati, Ohio, and Philadelphia, Pennsylvania.

Resolutions passed by the delegates supported the CIO in its Southern organizing campaign; censured the DAR for its undemocratic policy regarding the use of Constitution Hall and backed Clare Booth Luce's campaign to end discrimination in the organization; urged federal action against the Ku Klux Klan; promised CORE action against discriminatory practices of the YMCA and YWCA organizations in local areas where such practices still persist; opposed the poll tax, and urged support for the Fair Employment Practice Commission.

Attorney Frank Shearer, president of the Vanguard League of Columbus, Ohio, was re-elected chairman of CORE, and George Houser was re-elected executive secretary. Other officers elected were: Irene Osborne, vice-chairman, of Chicago; Marie Klein, secretary, of Chicago; and Eugene Stanley, treasurer, of Columbus. . . .

National Urban League Reports on Race Relations

NEW YORK, NEW YORK

A new Community Relations Project for interracial social planning is discussed in the 1945 annual report of the National Urban League.[1]

The project, now in its second year and made possible by a three-year grant from the General Education Board, represents a new technique in combining professional social work procedures with direct action in race relations. In each city where the project has been inaugurated, the local Council of Social Agencies works with the National Urban League in organizing an advisory and sponsoring committee of white and Negro citizens. Research workers provided by the League, with the assistance of this committee, then begin the survey and study of local conditions affecting race relations and Negro welfare. Following the completion of the study, programs of action are recommended and carried out. The report describes as "the most dramatic result" of the project's achieve-

[1]The National Urban League is an interracial social work agency which seeks equality of economic opportunity for Negroes and works in the fields of employment, health and housing, education, and research. The League has autonomously operated local affiliates in fifty-four cities in twenty-seven states and the District of Columbia, serving directly forty-five percent of the urban Negro population of the country. *Summary*, July 1946, pp. 372–73.

ments its work in establishing an Urban League in Gary, Indiana, which aided in eliminating racial tensions in the schools.

During a large part of 1945, the organization's chief concern was post-war employment for Negroes. From conferences with managements of fifty-eight multi-plant corporations, the League was able to gauge, shortly after V-J Day, post-war employment possibilities for some 150,000 Negroes employed by these firms. Consultative activity was carried on with major international unions....

23

LET THE VOICES THUNDER FORTH WITH POWER (1946)

by Mary McLeod Bethune

Mary McLeod Bethune (1875–1955) was one of the most honored and distinguished women of her time. Soon after World War II she offered her services as a speaker to help the cause of the Southern Conference for Human Welfare (SCHW). At its fourth biennial conference, held in New Orleans, November 28–30, 1946, Mrs. Bethune (and Sen. Claude Pepper of Florida) were the opening key speakers; they addressed twelve hundred black and white people in Carpenters Hall (having been banned from the Municipal Auditorium).

Let the voices of the Peppers, the Grahams, the Arnalls, the Raineys, the Blacks and the Foremans thunder forth with power and conviction. Let us give volume and vital significance to the philosophy which they utter and practice. Let them speak for full and fair employment. Let us realize that full and fair employment are altogether desirable and that we cannot rest until all have the equal opportunity to work at the fullest capacity of their skills.

Educational, economic and health conditions must be equalized for all peoples. The share-croppers, the common neglected and oppressed people of the South, white and black alike, appeal through the Southern Conference for Human Welfare for the elimination of hate and the stimulation of love, for the annihilation of segregation and discrimination, for the abolition of the poll tax and mob violence.

Today the cry is for freedom to be, to do and to have, regardless of race, color or creed. For this freedom the Southern Conference for Human Welfare is willing to fight. We are willing to inform ourselves of the needs. We are willing to dedicate ourselves to meeting those needs courageously and consistently. We are determined to promote the general welfare of all mankind and preserve to ourselves and to our posterity the security which is the abundant life. May God give us the wisdom and the discipline and the creative energy to continue our fight.

Southern Patriot, December 1946, vol. 4, p. 4. Ellis Arnall had just defeated Talmadge as governor of Georgia; Homer P. Rainey was a former president of the SCHW and was president of the University of Texas; Frank P. Graham, also one of SCHW's presidents, was president of the University of North Carolina and a U.S. senator; Clark Foreman was, at this time, president of the SCHW.

24

UNSHEATHING THE CONSUMER SWORD (1946)

by James Farmer

The idea of consumer cooperation as a way out of economic bondage and impoverishment is fairly old in African-American history. It attracted the attention, for example, of Dr. Du Bois long before World War II. An early essay by James Farmer—destined to be a major figure in the later Civil Rights movement—comments on this form of struggle in the early postwar period, apparently unaware of its history.

The dragon of segregation in the South has a soft under-belly, for it must perpetuate a fiction and conceal a fact in order to exist.

To begin with, Negroes can be kept groveling in the southern dust only as long as, and to the extent, that they believe the fiction that their ability to consume rests of necessity upon the white man. The oppressors can remain masters only so long as dark folk can be duped into thinking, when they look upon the white man: "We thank you for our daily bread; by your sufferance must we be fed."

Couple that fiction with the fact that the Negro in the South, like all consumers, has a tremendous weapon—that of consumer power. Upon the Negro as consumer the South has a great and real dependence. That is the fact which Dixie must hide from the Negro himself in order to maintain its vertical caste system.

The first is an outright and practical prevarication; the second, being a concealment of the truth, is just as much a lie. Any system based upon a lie at its heart, or, as in this case, a twin-lie, is vulnerable at that very point. Once the dual myth is exploded, not so much in theory as through demonstration, the mortality of the segregation dragon is at least in sight.

On a recent tour of the South, I observed some indications that steps are being taken to forge such a sword to destroy the lumbering beast. As yet there is no sword; there are only pinpricks besieging the under-belly of segregation. The dragon is not disturbed at present. It is not even aware of what is happening, so slight is the annoyance. Nevertheless, if sufficient pins are developed, they can be, and, I am confident, will be fused into a sword adequate for the task.

But let us probe a bit more into the nature of the vulnerability of the South's vertical caste.

The greatest compulsive force in Negro life in the South is *fear*. But the deepest fear is not one of bodily harm. Much deeper, more enervating, is the fear that the bare necessities of life will be snatched from them if they do not respect the southern code of behavior. In a word, what is feared most is economic rejection. Bodily harm, or even violent death is bad; but seeing one's family starve is a living torture worse than death. That is the greatest intimidation used to keep the masses of southern Negroes "in their place," and it is the severest punishment meted out to brave "violators" of the code.

School teachers might lose their jobs; domestics and laborers might be fired; professional men might find their "trade" frightened away by an unseen hand; preachers might lose their flocks in a like manner, and furthermore might miss numerous material gifts from white churches; farm owners might suddenly be unable to market their goods.

Holding the purse-strings of all are the white bosses. That is true. It has been true throughout the history of the Negro in America. There can be no doubt about it. The fiction, however, lies in the conclusion which is drawn from that obvious truth, and which Negroes are made to believe. Because it *is* and always *has been,* the logic runs, so it inevitably *must be.* That conclusion is the premise from which most thought and action in the South springs, with which it begins and ends. And nothing could be farther from the truth.

It is to be hoped—more, it is to be expected that the CIO, in its current "invasion" of the South, will allay some of those fears, and remove some of their sources. But the complete solution to this problem lies in the realization that the ability to consume, the ability to secure life's necessities, rests not with the white South necessarily, but with *production* and *distribution*. In the past, "white" and "production and distribution" have been synonymous—hence the present confusion. But the distinction is of utmost importance.

Generally speaking, whoever can consume can produce. If it is the southern rulers who overlord production, it is the black workers, together with the white workers, who actually produce. CIO unionization in Dixie should enable both black and white workers to obtain a more equitable share of the rewards of production. That will be a valuable help. But there are problems, despite neo-Marxist theory, which are peculiar to Negroes. Darker workers are not only workers; they are also black. Thus they are twice enslaved. However much one may wish to ignore that, it cannot be forgotten in America. The greatest liberation of the Negro consumer is to be found in the development of production and distribution by southern Negroes. In the past, this has been thought to mean exclusively the creation of individual Negro businesses. But individual Negroes in the South, or anywhere else for that matter, who have sufficient means to engage in production and distribution of any significance are few in number. Further, there is little to be gained by substituting black masters for white ones. Collectively, though, they possess the means, through co-operative enterprise, to produce and distribute in a volume that would stagger the imagination. Therein, I am persuaded, lies one of the brightest rays of hope in the Southland.

Farm Commodities

The most fruitful field for co-operative production, it appears, is that of farm commodities—the lifeline of southern communities, the backbone of the nation. The South is still overwhelmingly agricultural. There are many Negro small farm-owners in the South. Those could maintain individual ownership of their farms, and still join co-operatively in securing necessary farm and processing implements, and in providing adequate distribution of produce. Others, non-farm owners, could purchase land co-operatively.

This co-operative production of common commodities like grain and cotton, livestock and poultry, milk and eggs, could generate a solidarity unequalled in our history. Likewise it could provide a certain independence, a freedom from the tyrannical clutches of the ruling South upon the Negro's purse-strings. With the exercise of a little imagination, producible commodities which are rarer, like silk, could be added to the above. City folk could aid in production by spinning and weaving, producing fabric, clothing and other utilitarian and craft objects. Also, they would obviously be of invaluable aid in distribution. Within a relatively short time, factories could be built, owned by the people.

I submit that if such a program were developed on a wide scale, the timorousness which has so gripped large numbers of Negro people in the South would progressively evaporate. Creative solidarity is the assassin of fear, the parent of courage.

The South's reliance upon colored folk is not only as a "servant reservoir" and a "source of cheap labor." Because of the huge percentage of Negroes in towns, counties, and states below the Mason-Dixon Line, the reliance upon them as consumers is perhaps greatest of all. Yet, while filching them, the South behaves as though the mere allowance to purchase goods is the granting of a privilege! The village general store, the town market square, and the city department store would be empty skeletons without Negro trade. Of that fact the merchants are fully aware. Witness their loud cries of "bloody murder" whenever sizable numbers of Negroes sporadically desert any southern community. But when the Negro knows it, and demonstrates that knowledge through the development of consumers co-operatives to parallel and augment those of production, then they can compel respect and gain the greater freedom which comes from supplying many of one's own needs more cheaply. And here, again, the lesson of solidarity can be learned.

This is not mere theory. Practical beginnings are already underway. Within the past several years, consumers "co-op" grocery stores have sprung up among Negroes in southern towns and cities from Texas to Georgia, in college communities and in metropolitan centers.

Of even more basic significance is the recent development of a farm producers and consumers "co-op" in a rural southern community. A scant two years ago, a young Negro college graduate, whose name for obvious reasons I do not divulge, principal of a small high school in the deep South, planted a dream in red soil and sweat. Unlike most college graduates who go to work in the country, especially in the South, this young man did not hold himself aloof from the simple, unsophisticated folk with whom he worked. He became a part of the community— literally, and visited the farmers, listened to their problems, counselled them and attended their gatherings—not to satisfy curiosity or to smirk, but for the precise reason that their life was his life and their gatherings his. He laughed with their joys, shed tears with their pains. So unmistakable was his sincerity that whatever skepticism and suspicions they might have had soon evaporated. They welcomed him into their confidence, sought his advice, and because of his superior training, looked to him for leadership. And in his program they found new hope and new unity.

This school principal, a lonely man like all social pioneers, found that the farm owners, rather than the tenant farmers, were, by the very nature of the case, the most dependable persons to start the work with. In many of them he discovered a homely wisdom, a stoic loyalty, rare "horse sense" and geniality. But they had their troubles. The town boasted but one grist mill, and if its owner "got up on the wrong side of the bed" any morning, the Negro farmers could not get their grain ground. And in the marketing scramble, it was they who took the beating.

By the toil of their new found leader, sixty-one of the colored farm families were organized into a co-operative. They purchased a grist mill, rented a two-compartment store, equipped one half with a soda fountain and luncheon tables, and the other half with facilities for processing and selling their farm products. It is *their* store. They supply it with goods, and they, among others, are its patrons. They are doing thousands of dollars worth of trade. As in all genuine co-operatives, the "profit" is theirs. At the end of the year it goes to them, or into expansion of the store and the expansion of their lives.

Black cynics have shouted that black folk would not or could not co-operate, that they are hopelessly individualistic. This project in darkest Dixie eloquently brands their cynicism a cruel lie. Rarely found is an *espirit de corps* to equal this. And to the mind of the principal-leader, this is the merest kind of a beginning. They are going to buy a tractor for use on their farms, a truck for their store, and in the yard back of the store they are scattering tables to provide the town's only place for Negro farmers to congregate and "chew the rag" over a soft drink on the sultry days when they come to town. All of this for the Negro farmers, in a county in which they are numerically predominant, is tantamount to a rebirth, a new life.

The school principal has gotten in touch with a group of Negroes in a neighboring metropolitan center in the same state who plan to start a "co-op" grocery store, and has worked out a tentative arrangement whereby the farm group will supply the city group with farm goods such as corn, meal and flour, chicken and eggs.

A *Southland Dream*

This unpretentious pioneer, void of any messianic complex, envisions the establishment of a co-operative dairy farm in the same community, with pasteurizing and other modern equipment. He dreams of the building of projects similar to his own throughout the Southland, joined together as the links of a chain. And his dream is not fantastic.

In this there is a much greater significance than the mere making and saving of money for Negroes in the South. It can mean a widespread shedding of the fear which is nourished by consumer slavery. It can force more civilized treatment of the Negro by the South through the wielding of consumer power as a weapon.

More, it could be an important opening wedge toward the elimination of segregation. By the very nature of the present southern situation, the development of consumer power, as here discussed, would begin with groups predominantly, if not completely, Negro. That should be a matter of strategy and of unavoidable procedure in most southern communities, rather than a matter of principle. It should be hoped and aggressively sought that when the projects become going concerns, what genuinely sympathetic whites there are in the communities will join in. That is not too much to expect. The sight of successful production, combined with self interest, generates sympathy. History has shown that this psychological fact is even more primary than racial prejudices in the South. Southern whites are victims of the same consumer slavery, pawns of the same masters, as Negroes. The only advantage they have is their white skins. Of this they must be convinced. And demonstration of success is the most convincing agent in the world.

Workers in the South are beginning to see this. It is not too much to expect that what is beginning to happen to men as laborers can also happen to them as producers and consumers? The basis of any economy is production, distribution, and consumption. If a cooperative, raceless system of production, distribution, and consumption is developed in the South, parallel to the prevailing racist one, and designed to undercut it, a sword will have been forged capable of setting the dragon to rout.

Success is not guaranteed. It never is. Victory will go to the economy possessing the greater vitality and providing the greater satisfaction for the basic needs of men. Therein lies the impoverished South's soft underbelly.

Crisis, December 1946, vol. 53, pp. 362–64.

25

CASES AGAINST PUBLIC CARRIERS (1945–47)

The accounts below of cases arising immediately after World War II may throw some light on the unity of the African-American people during the Montgomery bus boycott a decade later.

INTRODUCTION

More than fifty legal suits protesting segregation in travel have been filed in courts throughout the country following the United States Supreme Court's decision in the Irene Morgan interstate bus case on June 3, 1946 (see below).

Although many suits of this sort had been filed previously, court actions by Negroes were accelerated following the ruling in this case.

Progress has been made in this direction, but, so far, courts have not outlawed segregation of Negroes in travel on railroads nor in intrastate travel on buses. The Supreme Court's decision in the interstate bus case did not mention railroad travel.

IRENE MORGAN INTERSTATE BUS CASE

In October 1944, Mrs. Irene Morgan was convicted on a charge of disorderly conduct in the circuit court of Middlesex County in Virginia, and fined $10 and costs of court for refusal to move to a rear seat of a Greyhound Company bus at the request of the driver, while she was traveling from Virginia to Baltimore, Md.

The National Association for the Advancement of Colored People interceded and appealed the decision. The Virginia Supreme Court of Appeals upheld the lower court's decision on the grounds that the assignment of Negroes to certain seats in a bus does not constitute inequality of treatment.

On June 3, 1946, the United States Supreme Court held that the separation of passengers by race in interstate bus travel cannot be accomplished by state statute.

Six Justices concurred in the majority opinion, with Justice Harold H. Burton dissenting. The decision was based on the conclusion that the Virginia law requiring the separation of passengers by race is an "undue burden" on interstate commerce, where "uniformity" is necessary for the smooth and unimpeded operation of interstate bus travel. The question of racial equality, the Justices held, was not before the court.

LOTTIE E. TAYLOR CASE

In an effort to get around the United States Supreme Court's decision in the Irene Morgan case some bus companies operating in Virginia tried a new procedure of attempting to enforce segregation in interstate bus travel by adopting their own regulations of seating passengers, which, they contended were not a part of state law.

The Virginia Assembly cooperated in this action by amending a state statute in 1946 making it a misdemeanor for any persons to cause any unnecessary disturbance in a public conveyance by "running through it, climbing through windows or upon seats," or by "failing to move to another seat when lawfully requested to do so by the operator."

A test of the validity of the amended state code was made in several cases in Virginia, including this case.

Mrs. Taylor was arrested in Fairfax County, Va., in September 1946, for refusing to move to a rear seat on orders of a driver of a Virginia Stage Line bus. She was convicted of disorderly conduct and fined $5 and costs of court. The National Association for the Advancement of Colored People entered the case and filed an appeal.

In January 1947, the circuit court upheld the lower court's ruling, upholding the bus company's contention that Mrs. Taylor was asked to move under a company regulation, and convicted under the state's new statute—Section 4533a.

On March 1, 1948, the Virginia Supreme Court of Appeals reversed the lower courts. In a unanimous opinion the court held that the state's disorderly conduct law could not be used to maintain the separation of races in interstate bus travel, in violation of the United Supreme Court's decision.

In delivering the opinion, Justice C. Vernon Spratley said, in part:

The refusal of the defendant to obey such a request constituted at most a breach of the rules and regulations of the carrier...as such a breach it related only to the dealings and acts of private persons—the defendant and the carrier.

The General Assembly alone has power to define crimes against this Commonwealth. This power cannot be delegated to the courts, or to individuals, or to corporations. Code Section 4533a does not purport to delegate any such authority to a common carrier.

While common carriers may adopt and enforce reasonable rules and regulations, independent of statutory authority, for the conduct and management of their business, they are wholly without authority to provide that a violation thereof shall constitute an offense punishable by fine or imprisonment.

The rules and regulations of the Virginia Stage Lines...do not undertake to make the failure of a passenger to occupy a seat in conformity therewith a criminal offense. They provide simply that upon such failure or refusal the passenger shall be subject to removal.

SAMUEL TUCKER CASE

In November 1946, Samuel W. Tucker was convicted by a police court in Richmond, Va., and fined $5 on a disorderly conduct charge. The court held that he had created a disturbance when he refused to move to a rear seat on a bus operated by the Trailways Bus Company, while en route to Emporia, Va., from Washington. The court based its ruling on Section 4533a of the Virginia Code, as amended in 1946. (See Lottie Taylor case, above.)

Mr. Tucker appealed, and in January 1947, Judge John L. Ingram of the Hustings Court in Richmond reversed the lower court's decision. In doing so he explained that the Virginia statute in question, which empowers drivers to arbitrarily assign persons to certain seats in a bus, is unconstitutional.

ETHEL NEW CASE

A suit for $10,000 in damages was filed in June 1946 against the Atlantic Greyhound Bus Company in Richmond, Va., by Mrs. Ethel New who complained that she was forcibly ejected from a bus in Lynchburg, Va., when she refused to move to a rear seat. Mrs. New was traveling at the time from Blackstone to Appalachia, Va.

She stated that she boarded the bus at Blackstone and soon thereafter was transferred to another bus in which all seats were taken. At Lynchburg a number of passengers got off, leaving some seats vacant, and she took one immediately in front of the rear seat. The driver ordered her to move to the rear seat and she refused. She was arrested and convicted of violating the state's segregation law.

At the first trial the jury decided against Mrs. New and in October 1946 Judge Willis D. Miller of the Law and Equity Court in Richmond upheld the verdict. The decision was based on the grounds that the plaintiff was traveling intrastate and not interstate. The Virginia Supreme Court of Appeals upheld the lower courts.

ELMER W. HENDERSON CASE

In May 1942, Elmer W. Henderson filed a complaint against the Southern Railroad with the Interstate Commerce Commission, charging that his rights had been violated in the refusal of dining car officials to serve him in the diner on two occasions during an interstate trip.

The ICC held that the failure of the railroad to serve him subjected him to "undue and unreasonable prejudice and disadvantage," but that there was no basis for the awarding of damages and that the diner's regulations setting aside certain tables for Negroes did not result in any substantial inequality of treatment between Negro and white passengers.

Mr. Henderson complained that when he appeared for service in the diner, some of the seats allocated to Negroes were occupied by white persons, the others occupied by Negroes, with a curtain drawn between the two racial groups, and that he was told that there was no seat available for him.

Appealing the decision of the ICC, Mr. Henderson filed suit in the federal district court of Maryland in Baltimore. This court held, in 1945, that the company's regulations did not provide equality of treatment inasmuch as provision had not been made to take care of all Negro passengers when they wanted service. The court remanded the case for further trial.

In February 1946, the ICC reopened the case. Again, in April 1947, it ruled that the company was within its rights to make certain regulations concerning its passengers and that it had corrected the inadequacies pointed out by the district court.

The company had, meanwhile, changed its regulations, providing (1) that one table in each dining car would be reserved exclusively for Negroes, (2) that a curtain would be drawn about that table, and (3) that a "reserved" card would be placed on the table whenever it was not occupied by Negroes. Mr. Henderson again appealed the ICC's decision.

In September 1948 the U.S. District Court in Baltimore again ruled in favor of the railroad, declaring that racial segregation of interstate passengers is not forbidden by the Federal Constitution.

JERNAGIN ET AL, CASE

In February 1944, the Rev. William H. Jernagin, Ralph Matthews, and William J. Scott sued the Southern Railroad, seeking damages of $15,000 each for being forced to give up reserved seats for which they had purchased tickets in Philadelphia for a trip to Greensboro, N.C., and being ejected from the train at Lynchburg, Va., because of their refusal to change their seats for some in the Jim Crow coach.

The plaintiffs contended that they were denied the first-class passage for which their tickets called. A jury in the United States District Court in Washington, D.C. ruled against the Negroes in April 1945, on the grounds that the police, and not the railroad, were guilty of ejecting them from the train.

In September 1946, an appellate court reversed the lower court's ruling, deciding that the police were called at the instance of railroad officials and acted as their agents, and remanded the case for another trial on its merits.

In November 1947, before the case came up for another trial, the railroad compromised and paid the plaintiffs damages totaling $992, and the case was dropped.

STAMPS AND POWELL CASE

In March 1946, James E. Stamps and Ennis Powell filed a complaint with the Interstate Commerce Commission against the Louisville and Nashville Railroad for refusing to serve them in a dining car when they were en route from Cincinnati, Ohio, to Nashville, Tenn. In addition, they filed suit in the Kentucky courts asking $25,000 damages, inasmuch as the incident occurred in Kentucky.

At the trial, agents for the railroad testified that ordinarily six seats are reserved on each diner for Negro passengers and that when the two men appeared for service, four of the seats were occupied by white persons and the other two by Negroes, with a curtain drawn between the two racial groups.

An all-white jury in Louisville, in April 1947, ruled in favor of the plaintiffs and awarded them damages of $400 each. The railroad appealed the verdict and in June, the judge of the Jefferson County Circuit Court refused to grant a new trial.

The state court of appeals upheld the verdict in November 1948.

In July 1947, the ICC held that the company was within its rights to adopt regulations concerning the seating of passengers, but that it should advise the public of all regulations and all circumstances affecting its regulations. This right was given the railroads in the absence of a federal act in regard to separation of the races, the ICC declared, as stated in the Irene Morgan interstate bus case, so long as its actions did not bring an undue burden on interstate travel.

An appeal against this ruling was entered by Messrs. Stamps and Powell, whose petition stated that the "presumption that the railroad company is not violating the law and the conclusion that there is no inequality of accommodations are erroneous, and was based on testimony that is incompetent and inadmissible." In March 1948 the ICC upheld its former decision.

JOHN H. RAIGNS CASE

In October 1947, John H. Raigns was arrested in Richmond, Va., on a charge of disorderly conduct for refusal to move to a rear seat while traveling from Washington, D.C., to North Carolina on a bus of the Carolina Coach Company. He was fined $5 in the police court. He appealed the verdict and filed a civil suit against the bus company asking $10,000 damages for violation of his civil rights.

In February 1947, the Law and Equity Court in Richmond reversed the lower court's decision and ruled in favor of Mr. Raigns in the civil rights suits, awarding him damages of $250.

WILLIAM J. SIMMONS CASE

In October 1946, the Rev. William J. Simmons was ordered off a bus of the Greyhound Lines in Roanoke, Virginia, for refusing to take a rear seat. He had boarded the bus to make an interstate trip, and when told that he would have to take a rear seat or get off, he got off.

He filed suit against the company, asking $20,000 damages for humiliation and violation of his civil rights. When his case was first tried in the United States District Court in Roanoke, the jury ruled against him, but Judge John Paul refused to accept its decision and ordered the jury to return a verdict fixing nominal damages. The jury then changed its verdict and awarded the minister $25.

NINA BELTRAM CASE

In August 1945, Mrs. Nina Beltram boarded a train of the Pennsylvania Railroad in New York to go to Columbia, S.C. She changed trains in Washington, D.C., and boarded one of the Seaboard Air Line. When this train reached Raleigh, N.C., she was ordered from the reserved-seat coach, in which she had been sitting with white persons, into the Jim Crow coach.

Loaded with baggage and leading her five-year-old son, Mrs. Beltram made her way to the segregated coach. Finding no seats available she returned to her former seat. At Hamlet, N.C., the conductor called a policeman, who, Mrs. Beltram charged, "punched" her and forced her from the coach to the segregated coach.

When she returned to New York, she sued the Seaboard railroad, asking $75,000 damages. In December 1946, the railroad compromised the case, paying her $3,000.

CHARLES HAUSER CASE

Charles B. Hauser of Winston-Salem, N.C., was arrested in Mt. Airy, N.C., in October 1947, at the instigation of a bus operator on the Atlantic Greyhound Lines, for refusing to move to a rear seat during an interstate trip. Following a trial in the Recorder's Court, Judge Harry Llewellyn dismissed charges against Mr. Hauser, on the grounds that he was within his rights as an interstate passenger.

Mr. Hauser filed suit against the bus company, and in an out-of-court settlement was awarded $2,000.

LEONA PARKER CASE

Mrs. Leona Parker was arrested in Greensboro, N.C., in March 1947, for refusing to move to a rear seat in a bus operated by the Greyhound Lines. She was on her way from Washington, D.C., to her home in Winston-Salem, N.C.

In April Judge E. Earle Rives of the municipal court dismissed charges against Mrs. Parker. She sued the bus company asking $20,000 damages for false arrest and the company later compromised with a payment of $200, which she accepted.

Florence Murray, ed., *The Negro Handbook, 1949* (NY: Macmillan), 1949, pp. 64, 67–70.

26

THE FIRST "FREEDOM RIDE" (1947)

A momentous result of the Morgan case and the numerous other cases against discrimination aboard buses was the first of what later became known as "freedom rides."

Journey of Reconciliation

In the spring of 1947 the Committee on Racial Equality and the Racial-Industrial Committee of the Fellowship of Reconciliation sponsored a "Journey of Reconciliation"—a trip through the Upper South to determine to how great an extent bus and train companies were recognizing the decision of the United States Supreme Court, handed down on June 3, 1946, in the interstate bus case involving Irene Morgan.

The trip was begun on April 9 and lasted for two weeks, during which time fifteen cities in Virginia, North Carolina, Tennessee and Kentucky were visited. Sixteen Negro and white men participated in the journey.

The Negroes were Bayard Rustin of the staff of the Fellowship of Reconciliation, New York; Wallace Nelson, lecturer, New York; Conrad Lynn, attorney, New York; Andrew Johnson, Cincinnati student; Dennis Banks, Chicago musician; William Worthy, of the New York Council of the Committee for a Permanent Fair Employment Practice Committee; Eugene Stanley, teacher at A. and T. College, Greensboro, N.C.; Nathan Wright, social worker, Cincinnati.

The white persons were George Houser of the Fellowship of Reconciliation, New York; Ernest Bromley, minister from North Carolina; James Peck, editor of the Workers Defense League *News Bulletin;* Igal Roodenko, horticulturist, New York; Worth Randle, botanist, Cincinnati; Joseph Felmet, of the Southern Workers Defense League; Homer Jack, of the Chicago Council against Racial and Religious Discrimination; Louis Adams, minister from North Carolina.

During the trip, twenty-six tests of company policies were made, and there were twelve arrests.

INCIDENTS REPORTED

No incidents occurred on the Trailways and Greyhound bus lines from Washington into Virginia, although the Negroes in the group sat in front seats and white persons sat in the rear. Little attention was paid to the group by other passengers.

From Richmond to Petersburg, Va., there were no incidents, although some white persons glanced apprehensively at the interracial group from time to time. But in Petersburg, on April 10, Conrad Lynn was arrested at the instigation of a Trailways bus operator when he refused to move from a front to a rear seat at the order of the driver. The driver was courteous, but insistent, saying that he had to comply with the bus company's orders. The policeman who arrested Mr. Lynn was restrained and used no abusive language. Lynn was found guilty of disorderly conduct in a police court and was released on a bond of $25, pending an appeal.

On a Greyhound bus en route to Durham, N.C., on April 11, there were no arrests made, although two were threatened with arrest by the driver, who, after consulting with other drivers at a station, changed his mind.

At Durham, Andrew Johnson and Bayard Rustin (both Negroes) were arrested, but immediately released without having charges lodged against them.

On April 13, en route to Greensboro, N.C., Mr. Johnson and Joseph Felmet (white) were arrested and the latter was handled roughly by police at Chapel Hill, N.C., where they were removed from the bus for refusing to move from a front seat. Mr. Rustin and Igal Roodenko (white) took the seat that the first two had occupied, and they too were arrested. All were charged with disorderly conduct and released under bonds of $50 each, pending appeals.

Here the bus was delayed for two hours. After placing bond, the four got into a car of the Rev. Charles Jones, white local minister, and were driven to his home. A group of white men, who had been threatening to cause trouble when the men were arrested, followed them to the minister's home. They were about to stone the house, but were persuaded not to do so by other white persons. The interracial group left Chapel Hill before nightfall in a private car.

No incidents occurred between Greensboro and Winston-Salem, N.C. En route from the latter city to Asheville via a Greyhound bus, they changed to a Trailways bus at Statesville, N.C. About ten miles out of Statesville, the driver asked Wallace Nelson to move to a rear seat, but when the group explained the Supreme Court decision to him, he drove on. During this trip several white passengers protested the driver's failure to make Mr. Nelson move to the rear, but the driver told them that he was following the Supreme Court's decision.

At Asheville, N.C., a Trailways bus driver asked Dennis Banks to move from a front seat and called police. Mr. Banks was arrested and Mr. Peck (white), who was sitting with him, asked police to arrest him also; but when the police refused, he moved to a rear seat, and was promptly arrested. The two were convicted of violating the state law calling for separation of white and Negro passengers, and were sentenced to 30 days each in jail. They were released, pending appeal of their cases, under bonds of $250 each.

Traveling from Knoxville, to Nashville, Tenn., via a Greyhound bus, at the instigation of a white passenger, the driver approached Nathan Wright, who was sitting in a front seat and asked him politely whether he would move to the rear. When Mr. Wright explained his rights under the Supreme Court decision and refused to move, the driver continued the trip without interfering further.

When Mr. Wright and Mr. Jack (white), were traveling by train from Nashville, Tenn., to Louisville, Ky., in an all-coach reserved-seat train, the conductor asked the former to move to a Jim Crow coach, but he refused. Some words passed between the two, but nothing more was done.

From Bristol to Roanoke, Va., on a Greyhound bus, the driver approached Mr. Banks and Mr. Peck (white), who were sitting together in a front seat, and appeared to be about to say something to them on two occasions, but each time he seemingly changed his mind and said nothing.

From Roanoke to Lynchburg on a Greyhound bus, no incidents occurred. But on a Trailways bus at Amherst, Va., Mr. Nelson was arrested for sitting in a front seat with George Houser (white). The driver was apologetic for taking the action. Nelson was charged with disorderly conduct and released on a bond of $50.

En route from Charlottesville, Va., on a Trailways bus, Mr. Banks was asked to move to a rear seat by the driver, but no attention was paid to Mr. Peck (white) and Worth Randle, who were sitting together in a rear seat. When the bus reached Culpeper, Banks was arrested and released on bond of $25.

AFTERMATHS OF PREVIOUS ARRESTS

In May 1947, at a trial in Chapel Hill, N.C., Rustin was fined $8 and costs of court, and Roodenko, white, was sentenced to thirty days in jail. At the trial in Asheville, N.C., Banks was sentenced to thirty days. All were charged with violating the state's segregation law. The judge declared that although their tickets were for interstate passage, they provided for stop-overs in the state.

Later, Johnson and Felmet were convicted in the same court. Conrad Lynn's conviction, in Petersburg, Va., on April 10, was reversed in May by the Hustings Court there.

In March 1948, the Orange County Superior Court in Hillsboro, N.C. upheld the conviction of four of the men convicted earlier in Chapel Hill. They were released pending appeals.

Florence Murray, ed. *op.cit.,* pp. 65–67.

27

MISCELLANEOUS CIVIL RIGHTS CASES AND CONTROVERSIES

Places of Amusement and Recreation

LISNER AUDITORIUM, WASHINGTON, D.C.

In October 1946, an interracial group of thirty World War II veterans and their guests were denied admission to the Lisner Auditorium in Washington, D.C., owned by George Washington University, when they attempted to attend the play, "Blythe Spirit." The play was being presented by a student dramatic group of the university.

Leading the group were Don Rothenberg (white), chairman of the American Veterans Committee chapter at the university, and Wendell Freeland, chairman of the Howard University chapter (Negro).

A campaign was launched immediately to break down the auditorium's color bar. The Committee for Racial Democracy, an interracial organization, took the lead, aiming its first actions at the forthcoming performance of "Joan of Lorraine" which was to be given by the Playwrights Company of New York, a union of playwrights, for the benefit of the American Veterans Committee.

Maxwell Anderson, author of the latter play, and Ingrid Bergman, its star, both white, joined with other members of the all-white cast in censuring the university for its policy of discrimination. When the cast reached Washington, it adopted a resolution asking that the Actors' Equity Association, with headquarters in New York, issue a ruling forbidding its members to participate in future plays in Washington theaters which discriminate because of color. (Actors' Equity is a national union of stage actors, which includes actors performing in practically all commercial legitimate theaters.)

The cast performed the drama, after having explained that it did not know until it had reached Washington that Negroes were barred from the auditorium and that it had to live up to its contract. But the group pledged to work for the elimination of discrimination in legitimate theaters in Washington, because it is the capital of the nation. Meanwhile, other organizations joined the fight, both Negro and interracial.

Early in November, thirty-three members of the Dramatists' Guild, among whom were the nation's leading playwrights and producers, pledged to boycott Washington theaters until they lifted their discriminatory ban.

Following this action, George Washington University officials, in February 1947, announced that henceforth Negroes would be allowed to attend "public" performances at the Lisner, and that commercial shows would be banned. They left the way open for private groups renting the auditorium to set their own racial policy.

NATIONAL THEATER, WASHINGTON

Coupled with the fight against the Lisner Auditorium a campaign was launched to break down the color bar of the National Theater, Washington's only commercial legitimate playhouse. This theater permitted Negroes to act in performances on the stage, but refused to admit them to the audiences. For many years Negroes had periodically protested against its racial policy.

It was decided by the Committee for Racial Democracy, a local group which led this fight, that the method of attack would be the purchasing of blocks of tickets by white persons previous to the performances of the plays, these tickets to be used by interracial groups.

When the first interracial group, for whom tickets had been purchased in advance, appeared at the theater, the Negroes were denied entrance. Whites in the group then refused to enter and the money for the tickets was refunded.

After this was done for several performances, the manager of the theater, Edmund Plohn, tiring of the procedure which caused financial losses, posted a notice in the lobby stating that thereafter the money expended for tickets by these groups would not be refunded. When he attempted to carry out his new regulations and denied to the purchasers the return of their money, several suits were filed against the theater.

Another, filed by Edwin B. Henderson, Negro, charged that the theater violated the civil rights act of 1875. This suit sought to test again the constitutionality of the act, which the Supreme Court had declared unconstitutional in 1913. The other suits were filed in the Small Claims Court in an effort to have the costs of the tickets refunded to the purchasers.

During the hearing of the first suit in the Small Claims Court, the manager of the National urged that the case be dismissed on the grounds of "deceit and fraud." But the judge refused to dismiss the suit and set a date for trial.

When the trial came up, counsel for the theater confessed judgment, admitting that the theater had erred in refusing to refund the ticket money and offered to negotiate settlements with the plaintiffs. Thus, these suits ended in victories for the committee.

In the case of the civil rights suit filed by Mr. Henderson Judge Nathan Margold of the Municipal Court, after hearing the case, took it under advisement.

Meanwhile, in New York, Actors' Equity Association, during the latter part of April 1947, voted overwhelmingly to adopt a regulation forbidding its members to perform at the National Theater under its present racial policy, and set May 31, 1948, as the date for the theater to change its policy and admit Negroes on an equal basis with whites.

By early 1947 more than one hundred prominent white actors had signed the Playwrights Company pledge not to permit their plays to be produced at the National Theater as long as it maintained its color bar.

In Washington, the theater manager's reply to the actors and producers was that the theater would not rescind its racial policy unless and until the general segregation pattern of the District of Columbia was changed by law, or other business and civic groups in the city revoked their racial restrictive policies. Rather than change the policy of the theater, he said, he would discontinue stage plays and show only movies in the theater.

Judge Margold died before he had an opportunity to hand down his decision in the civil rights case filed by Mr. Henderson. On June second, 1948, Judge Frank H. Myers, after a new hearing, dismissed the suit on the grounds that it was based on a law that had been declared unconstitutional, saying that he was bound by the statutory construction of the act made by the Supreme Court in 1913. He denied the contention of Mr. Henderson's counsel that the Supreme Court had erred in its 1913 decision, or that the decision did not rule specifically on the question of civil rights as it affected the District of Columbia. (The municipal court of appeals in Washington upheld the lower court's ruling in November 1948.)

On June 3, 1948, the manager of the National Theater announced that the theater would inaugurate a policy of showing moving pictures only, beginning in September, 1948. He took the step in view of the action taken by Actors' Equity, forbidding members to participate in shows in Washington theaters which barred Negroes. The theater actors' union's policy went into effect on June 1, 1948.

One of the results of the National Theater fight was the opening of an interracial movie house in Washington, the Dupont Theater, in the spring of 1948. No "legitimate" theater exists in Washington at this writing, but a number of plans have been offered to provide one.

UTE THEATER CASE, COLORADO SPRINGS

In 1946, Mrs. Juanita Hairston filed suit against the Ute Theater in Colorado Springs, Colo., asking for $10,000 in damages for having been ejected from a seat in the orchestra and arrested for refusing to move to the balcony, at the order of the theater management.

During the melee she lost her purse, which she valued, with its contents, at $120. She contended that the action was in violation of the state's civil rights act. District Judge G. Russell Miner, in April 1947, awarded her damages totaling $617.25—$117.25 for the loss of her purse, and $500 for violation of her civil rights. The $500 penalty was awarded as the maximum penalty under the state's civil rights act.

CONSTITUTION HALL CONTROVERSY, WASHINGTON, D.C.

The fight waged periodically since 1939 against the Daughters of the American Revolution for refusing to permit certain Negro artists to appear in recital at Constitution Hall in Washington, D.C., flared again in 1946. The hall is owned and operated by the DAR under tax-exempt and other privileges granted by Congress. The cause of the 1939 protest was the refusal of the DAR to grant to Marian Anderson, noted Negro contralto, use of the hall for a recital.

The racial policy of the DAR in connection with Constitution Hall has been an inconsistent one. Some Negro artists have been permitted to appear on its stage at various times, while others have been refused. Also, there appears to be no regulation against Negroes attending the various affairs at the hall without being segregated.

The next *cause célèbre* concerning Constitution Hall was the refusal of its management to permit Hazel Scott, noted pianist and wife of Congressman Adam Clayton Powell, Jr., of New York, to appear there in concert during 1945. At this time the DAR announced that it was abiding by a regulation adopted by the national board in 1932, granting rental of the hall to white artists only.

When, in April 1946, it was announced that Tuskegee Institute would present its choir in Constitution Hall, a nation-wide protest went up from Negroes against the acceptance of its use by Dr. Frederick D. Patterson, president of Tuskegee. It was disclosed at that time that the Tuskegee Institute Choir would give a concert in the hall, the use of which was granted without cost. Proceeds from the concert were to go to the United Negro College Fund.

Mrs. Julius Y. Talmadge, white, of Atlanta, Ga., president of the DAR, said that the granting of the hall to Tuskegee was not in violation of the organization's "white-artists clause," because it was not being rented, but given free of charge. She also expressed the interest of her organization in the United Negro College Fund.

Many Negroes condemned Dr. Patterson for asking for the hall in view of its discriminatory policy, and urged that he cancel the engagement. They pointed out further that the reason behind the liberality of the DAR in this instance was the maintenance of separate colleges for Negroes. Dr. Patterson took issue with those protesting and refused to cancel the engagement. Then the Washington branch of the United Negro College Fund refused to accept the money raised by the concert and the funds were sent directly to the national headquarters in New York.

SWIMMING POOL CASE, MONTGOMERY, W. VA.

In September 1947, Paul Lawrence filed suit against the city authorities of Montgomery, W. Va., on behalf of himself and other Negroes in the city because of being denied admission to the municipal swimming pool.

The city park association had leased the pool to a private concern which discriminated against Negroes, according to Mr. Lawrence's complaint. He charged further that construction of the pool was financed by a general revenue bond. It had not been used from its completion in 1942 to the beginning of 1946, the plaintiff stated, because of the question of permitting Negroes to use it.

In February 1948, Judge Ben Moore of the federal court in Charleston ruled that all citizens must be permitted to use the pool regardless of race or color.

ROLLERDROME CASE, CINCINNATI, OHIO.

William Sefferino, manager of the Sefferino Rollerdrome in Cincinnati, was sued in May 1946 by Andrew Merryweather because he was refused permission to use the skating rink, in violation of the state's civil rights law.

In September, Judge Daniel C. Hanley, Jr., ruled that Mr. Sefferino had not violated the state laws. During the trial the defendant had contended that on the day that the Negro sought to enter the rink, a private club had chartered it for the evening.

SWIMMING POOL CASE, WARREN, OHIO

Sometime in 1946 some white persons objected to using the municipal swimming pool in Warren, Ohio, while Negroes were in it. Following their complaints city officials leased the pool to a private club, which permitted Negroes to use it on one day each week, which was set aside for them exclusively.

In July 1947 James Culver and a group of Negroes filed suit against the municipal officers, seeking use of the pool at any time that it was in use. The Trumbull County Common Pleas Court ruled against the Negroes, but in July 1948, Judge Joy Seth Hurd of the appellate court reversed the ruling of the lower court, ordering the lessees to permit Negroes to use the pool at any time that it was open for use.

WHITE CITY SKATING RINK CASE, CHICAGO, ILL.

In December 1945, the White City skating rink in Chicago, Ill, was sued by the Committee for Racial Equality for its refusal to admit Negroes. While the case was pending the committee kept a picket line outside the rink. Management of the rink filed an injunction suit to prevent the group from picketing the place, but the court held that the pickets were within their rights. Meanwhile attendance at the rink had dropped so low that the management decided to lift its color bar, and the case was dropped.

PALISADES PARK CASE, NEW JERSEY

In early 1947 the Committee for Racial Equality and Modern Trend in New York launched a campaign against the Palisades Park swimming pool in New Jersey, across the Hudson River from New York City, in an effort to break down its color bar. Interracial groups were sent to the pool at various times seeking entrance, and each time the parties were refused admittance on the grounds that the pool was operated by a private club and only club members were admitted. During the campaign several members of the committee were arrested on charges of disorderly conduct.

Nine Negroes and one white man filed suits against the pool authorities seeking $260,000 for damages, charging unlawful arrest and violation of the state civil rights act. In February 1948, Judge William F. Smith of the federal court in Newark dismissed the suits on the grounds that swimming pools were not included in the state's civil rights act. Meanwhile a new constitution was adopted by the state which expands the civil rights act to include all public places, schools, and the state militia.

In December 1948, the appellate division of the New Jersey Superior Court overruled the lower court's ruling in the suit of one plaintiff on the grounds that the court's interpretation of the civil rights act was too narrow.

BALTIMORE GOLF COURSE CASE

In December 1947, Charles R. Law sued the Baltimore (Md.) Park Board because of its refusal to let him play golf on the Mt. Pleasant golf course owned by the city, because of his color. He contended that since the municipal park was supported by taxes paid by residents of the city, the board deprived him of his civil rights in refusing to permit him to use that court, as well as the Carroll Park course which had been assigned to Negroes.

On June 18, 1948, Federal Judge W. Calvin Chesnut ruled that so long as the city furnished golfing facilities, the quality must be substantially equivalent for both races. He decided that the Carroll Park golf course, hitherto allotted to Negroes, was not on a par with the Mt. Pleasant Park course, or with the other two courses allotted to whites.

He held that Mr. Law was entitled to use of the courses hitherto restricted to whites, but added that he would not direct how the city officials should meet the situation. He suggested, however, that among other things, since the number of Negro golf players was comparatively small, certain hours or days could be set aside for them. Latest reports were that Negroes were admitted to the courses on certain days.

Hotel Cases

BENJAMIN FRANKLIN CASE, PHILADELPHIA

Six members of the New York University track team entered suit against the Benjamin Franklin Hotel in Philadelphia, in May 1946, for having been refused rooms after their reservations had been accepted through the mail. The men were Frank Dixon, Maurice and Stanton Callender, Alex Jordan, Homer Gillis, and Milford Parker.

The manager of the hotel apologized to the plaintiffs before Magistrate Joseph H. Rainey, and the case was dropped. In his apology, the manager had stated that the desk clerk who refused to register the Negroes had not been authorized to do so.

TUDOR TOWER CASE, NEW YORK

In March 1947 Claude Marchant, a dancer, was refused permission to ride in a passenger elevator at the Tudor Tower, a hotel apartment house, at 25 Tudor City Place, in New York City. He subsequently filed suit for damages under the state's civil rights law.

On May 25, 1948, a city court jury found the manager of the apartment guilty on two counts of violation of the civil rights law, and awarded Mr. Marchant $500 damages on each count.

At the trial, the manager of the building contended that he had issued orders to employees not to act in a discriminatory manner against anyone because of race, creed, or color, but that the two elevator operators who had refused to permit the plaintiff to ride in their cars had mistaken him for a delivery man because he was carrying packages, and had directed him to the service elevators. Marchant testified that he carried only a brief case at the time.

Justice Francis E. Rivers, a Negro, presided at the trial.

Cases Against Eating Places and Bars

PIONEER CAFE, LOS ANGELES, CALIF.

In August 1946, Clarence Hill and Eugene Loughridge filed suit against the Pioneer Cafe in Los Angeles, Calif., for refusing to serve them. Superior Court Judge Carl M. Sheldon ruled against the cafe and awarded damages of $200 and costs. During the hearing Julian Cangelosi, proprietor, denied that he had refused to serve the Negroes, saying that he was too busy at the time and that they would not wait.

DOUGHERTY'S BAR, MINNEAPOLIS, MINN.

In September 1947, Joseph Jacob, bartender at Dougherty's Bar in Minneapolis, was convicted of violating the state civil rights act. He had charged two Negroes $5 for a thirty-cent drink, and had spit in the glasses, according to the plaintiffs, who were John Williams and James T. Wardlow.

The bartender was sentenced to thirty days in the workhouse, or a fine of $100. He paid the fine.

GEORGE'S CAFE, LOS ANGELES, CALIF.

Sometime in 1947 three residents of Los Angeles were refused service in George's Cafe and filed suit against the restaurant for violation of the state's civil rights act. They were Mrs. Estelle W. Wilson, Mrs. Mauvolyene Carpenter, and Ulysses Thompson.

In April 1948, Judge Leo Freund of the municipal court decided against the restaurant and ordered civil damages of $250 paid to each of the plaintiffs.

LAS FLORES CASE, MALIBU BEACH, CALIF.

In July 1947 five Negroes were refused service by the Las Flores Inn-by-the-Sea at Malibu Beach, near Los Angeles. They entered suit against the restaurant, and in September 1948 Judge Ralph McGee of the Los Angeles Superior Court awarded them individual and collective damages.

The plaintiffs were Mr. and Mrs. Dooley Wilson, Mr. and Mrs. Alfred Logan, and Mrs. Katie Logan.

CONCLUSION

An unestimated number of cases against eating places and bars, similar to those recounted above, were filed by Negroes in northern states during the past several years. In many cases, results were not learned, but it is safe to presume, on the basis of the facts known, that the majority of them were won by the Negro plaintiffs.

Marriage Cases

HARRISBURG (PA.) CASE

Sgt. Percell McKamey was refused a marriage license to wed Ingeborg Franke, a German woman, by a clerk at the marriage bureau in

Harrisburg, Pa., in January 1948. The War Department had brought Miss Franke from Germany to Harrisburg at the sergeant's request so that the couple could marry. The clerk was reported to have told the soldier that it was against the policy of his office to grant marriage licenses to interracial couples and advised him to go to Reading to get married. The sergeant took the matter to court and Judge Carl Richards of the Orphans Court ordered the marriage license bureau to grant a license to the couple. When they returned for the license and made out the marriage application, the clerk, incensed, tossed the pen they used into the waste basket.

The clerk's action in refusing the license had been upheld by the registrar of wills who stated that it was not the practice of his bureau to issue marriage licenses to Negro-white couples.

MCALESTER (OKLA.) CASE

Ted Sesney, white farmer, married Miss Josie Douglas in Nowata County in the northwestern part of Oklahoma in 1945. He was later sentenced to a year in prison in McAlester, Okla., for having violated the state law which makes it a felony for Negroes to marry white persons in the state. After completing his prison term he and his wife were banished from the state.

YUMA (ARIZ.) CASE

Mr. and Mrs. Allen Bradford Monks were married in Yuma, Arizona, in 1930. Mr. Monks, white, died in 1937 while living in San Diego, Calif., and his widow sued to establish rights to a share in his estate in Arizona.

An Arizona court decided that she was one-eighth Negro and therefore could not claim shares in the estate as his widow, since a state law forbids interracial marriages.

Mrs. Monks took the case to the United States Supreme Court in an effort to have the Arizona law declared unconstitutional. The Supreme Court, in January 1946, refused to review the lower court's decision on the grounds of lack of jurisdiction.

NEW ORLEANS (LA.) CASE

About 1920, Azealia Barthelmy was married to Tony Rice (of Italian descent) in New Orleans. She bore him seven children. Mr. Rice reputedly deserted her in 1931. In October 1946, Mrs. Helen Ryan, white, purchased from Mr. Rice the house in which Mrs. Rice and her children lived, and ordered the family dispossessed.

Mrs. Rice filed suit in an effort to void the sale on the grounds that the property had been recorded in her name along with that of her husband, and she had not signed any papers conveying it to Mrs. Ryan.

Mrs. Ryan's reply to the suit was that Mrs. Rice was not the legal wife of Tony because interracial marriages are not permitted by state law. During the trial, Mr. Rice testified that he had married the Negro woman, not knowing at the time that he was violating a state law.

The 24th Judicial District Court in New Orleans declared, in March 1947, that the marriage was null and void under Louisiana law, and ordered Mrs. Rice to vacate the property. Throughout the trial the judge referred to Mrs. Rice by her maiden name, refusing to recognize the marriage.

The verdict was appealed, and the appellate court upheld the lower court's decision.

LOS ANGELES (CALIF.) CASE

In August 1947, Sylvester S. Davis, Jr., classified as a Negro, and Miss Andrea D. Perez of Mexican descent, classified as white, filed a petition for a writ of mandamus against Los Angeles County authorities in an effort to compel the latter to issue to them a marriage license. The license had been refused in keeping with the California law barring the marriage of white persons to other than Caucasians. The petitioners contended that the law interfered with their religious and civil rights.

They are both Catholics, and church authorities supported their right to marry.

The case was carried directly to the state's supreme court in an effort to test the legality of the statute, which was passed in 1872. (Mexicans were formerly classified as Latin Americans belonging to the colored races, but the United States Census in 1940 changed their classification to "white.")

Replying to the couple's petition, counsel for the county, Deputy Counsel Charles C. Stanley, contended that the state has the right to prevent any relationship which it deems inimical to the peace, good order and morals of society.

He branded "pure" Negroes as inferior mentally and physically to whites, and "mulattoes" as moral and physical degenerates afflicted with some of the most repulsive diseases, according to "certain authorities."

In his reply to the county, Daniel G. Marshall, counsel for the plaintiffs, refuted the charges of Mr. Stanley as being without authority and opposed to the findings of the world's most noted anthropologists. He termed the law banning interracial marriages as a violation of the religious and civil rights guaranteed by both the federal and state constitutions.

Arguments were heard before the state's supreme court in October 1947. On October 1, 1948, the court held that the law was unconstitutional, and directed the Los Angeles County clerk to issue a marriage license to the couple. The court split 4 to 3 on the issue.

In handing down its opinion, the court said that "marriage is something more than a civil contract subject to regulation by the state," that "it is a fundamental right of free men."

MALLORY CASE, CHICAGO

In November 1945, Detective John Gaca, white, arrested Mr. and Mrs. Edward Mallory as they left a theatre in Chicago and began to walk down Garfield Boulevard. The couple was held for fourteen hours, fingerprinted and placed in the line-up. They were then dismissed without having a charge lodged against them.

The couple sued the detective for false arrest and asked monetary damages. In the testimony at the trial the plaintiffs asserted that the detective called Mrs. Mallory a prostitute and her husband a pimp. They presumed, they said, that the detective believed Mrs. Mallory to be white.

Florence Murray ed., *op. cit.*, pp. 70–77.

28

LEGAL PROSECUTIONS OF LYNCHERS (1946–47)

Rarely were lynchers brought to trial; convictions were almost unknown. Indeed, according to Tuskegee Institute, at least forty-four persons were implicated in lynchings or lynching attempts in 1947; all were exonerated by all-white juries. Here is a record of prosecutions of lynchers in the first two postwar years.

Monroe, Ga., Case

The most sensational lynching reported during 1946 and 1947 was the one at Monroe, Ga., on July 25, 1946, when two married couples were slain near the Walton County-Oconee County line. According to local authorities, the four were taken from the car of J. Loy Harrison, white farmer, by an armed mob consisting of approximately twenty white men, and killed by shooting. The victims were Mr. and Mrs. Roger Malcolm and Mr. and Mrs. George Dorsey, farm hands, all in their twenties.

Malcolm had been released from the Walton County jail under bond of $600 a few hours before the crime was committed. He had been arrested on a charge of stabbing a white farmer, Barney Hester, over the attention of the latter to his wife. Dorsey and his wife worked on Harrison's farm and the Malcolms worked for Hester.

After Malcolm's release from jail on bail allegedly supplied by Harrison, the latter decided to drive him to his farm. Harrison said that he picked up Malcolm, his wife and the Dorsey couple, and was en route to his farm when his car was halted at a bridge by the armed mob which ordered the two Negro men to get out. The white men then proceeded down a side road with the two Negro men, and one of the band returned to the car and demanded that the two women follow them because one of the women had recognized some members of the group.

When the group was lost from his view, a volley of shots was heard, Harrison said. Soon thereafter, the four bodies were found on the roadside. The coroner estimated that at least sixty shots had been fired into them.

Ellis Arnall, then governor of Georgia, offered a reward of $10,000 for evidence leading to the identification of the lynchers; $500 was to be paid for each person identified. Agents of the Federal Bureau of Investigation were called into the case, following a nation-wide clamor for apprehension of the killers.

Immediately other rewards were offered. The American Civil Liberties Union and the Civil Rights Congress, interracial organizations, offered $1,000 each. The Southern Regional Council offered $500; the National Association for the Advancement of Colored People added $10,000; the Baptist Ministers Conference of Chicago, $15,000; the Atlanta Defense Group, organized to work for prosecution of the lynchers, $10,000; the Ohio Negro Chamber of Commerce, $3,000; the Elks, $5,000; and other groups and individuals various sums. The rewards offered totaled at least $64,000.

The White House and the Department of Justice were flooded by telegrams and letters of protest and were besieged by delegations, urging that the guilty be prosecuted and that the Congress pass antilynching legislation, which they contended had been overdue for many years. On July 30, Attorney General Tom Clark expressed "horror" over the crime and promised that his department would investigate the case "with all its resources."

Meanwhile, both the NAACP and the Civil Rights Congress had sent its agents to the vicinity to investigate the lynching. Both turned over to the Department of Justice evidence they had gathered, which, they contended, should "crack the case open."

After a three-month investigation by the FBI, a federal grand jury was convened in Athens. The farmer, Loy Harrison, was questioned, along with Farmer Hester, who was a pistol dealer in the vicinity, and about one hundred other witnesses. Two Negroes were on the jury. No witness questioned during the three-week hearing of the grand jury revealed the identity of any of the lynchers and no one was indicted. A year after the crime had been committed, the Justice Department announced that it had closed its investigations of the case.

Corporal Jones Case

Another death classified as a lynching by both Tuskegee Institute and the NAACP was that of Corporal John C. Jones, 28, whose battered body was found near Minden, La., on August 9, 1946. He had been arrested and placed in jail on a charge of breaking into the house of a white woman. He was released when the woman failed to press formal charges and was killed on the day that he was released from jail.

Jones' cousin, a 17-year-old youth, was with him when two car-loads of white men accosted the two Negroes behind the jail immediately after their release. According to the youth, Jones was forced into one automobile and he into the other. The boy reported to local police that he did not know what had happened to Jones, for he was beaten into unconsciousness by the men and left on the roadside, thought to be dead.

The body of Jones, a veteran of World War II, was found horribly defaced, burned, and partially castrated. The coroner reported that he had probably been beaten by a wide leather belt or a thick plank, and that a blow torch had been applied to his body.

The 17-year-old youth was later identified as Albert (Sunny Boy)

Harris. His spectacular escape from death and subsequent return to Georgia became the subject of headlines to the press stories concerning the crime and its aftermath.

After Harris was discovered alive, he was hidden by members of the local branch of the NAACP who later spirited him out of Louisiana to a near-by town in Texas. They called the New York office of the organization, which immediately made plans to bring him North by plane, which was successfully accomplished.

Among the men allegedly participating in the crime, according to Harris, was the sheriff of the county.

On October 18, a federal grand jury meeting in Minden indicted six white men named by the boy, who had been taken back to Minden to testify under guard of FBI agents. His father, who had also been removed from the vicinity by the NAACP, accompanied him.

The grand jury indictment charged that Chief of Police B. Geary Gantt, Deputy Sheriffs Charles Edwards and O.H. Haynes, Jr., had deprived the Negroes of their constitutional rights by "causing them to be released from jail and handed over to a mob which inflicted the beatings," resulting in the death of Jones. The others indicted for complicity in the crime were Samuel Madden, Sr., H.E. Perry and W.D. Perkins.

Before the trial was held, Police Chief Gantt was exonerated by the federal court on recommendation of United States Attorney La Farge. The other five were tried in a federal court in Shreveport, La., and all were exonerated. The trial jury was composed entirely of white persons.

Leon McTatie Lynching

Another lynching, so classified by the NAACP, which received nation-wide attention was that of Leon McTatie, 35, whose body was found in a bayou near Lexington, Miss., in July 1946. He was reported to have been beaten by white men and forced into the bayou where he drowned, on July 22. He had been accused of stealing a saddle, which was later proved to be untrue.

Six white men were arrested for the crime. They were Dixie Roberts, Jeff Dodd, Sr., Jeff Dodd, Jr., Spencer Ellis, James E. Roberts, and Vernon Vale. They were charged with manslaughter. In October, the men were tried and acquitted by a jury in the Holmes County Court after ten minutes' deliberation. They had confessed to beating McTatie, but denied forcing him into the bayou.

Willie Earle Lynching

One of the most widely publicized lynchings of the two-year period, and the only one reported in 1947, was that of Willie Earle, whose mutilated body, riddled with bullets, was found on a road near Pickens, S.C., on February 17. The young man had been arrested, charged with the fatal stabbing of a taxicab driver.

According to local police reports, he was taken from the Pickens County jail by an armed mob of approximately thirty white men, all unmasked taxi drivers. Ed Gilstrap, the jailer, said that he had been forced to give up Earle to the mob.

On February 21, it was announced by Sheriff R. Homer Bearden of Greenville that 23 of the men had signed confessions of having participated in the crime, all taxicab drivers. Later a warrant was issued for 31 men. Thirty of them were apprehended and arrested, and their bails set at $2,500 each.

On March 12, the thirty men were indicted by a grand jury in General Sessions Court. At the coroner's inquest, held previously, one, Roosevelt Carlos Hurd, Sr., was named by 26 of the suspects as the man who fired the fatal bullets into Earle's body.

Hurd was later charged with murder on two counts and the others were named accessories before and after the fact, and charged with conspiracy to commit murder. Hurd was also reported to have been the ring leader in the rounding up of the mob and to have emptied his shotgun into Earle after he had been severely beaten, and to have asked for more shells to fire.

The trial got under way on May 12 in a crowded and tense courtroom, filled with newspapermen and photographers from many parts of the country, and with residents of the vicinity, both Negro and white. Police were on guard against interracial violence. Judge J. Robert Martin presided at the trial.

Jailer Gilstrap described how he had been forced to open the jail and deliver Earle to the mob, and he made partial identifications of some of the accused men. Four other witnesses presented written statements of the affair, two of the statements naming Hurd as the "trigger man."

Three other witnesses also identified Hurd as the one who had fired the fatal shots. Other witnesses testified to having heard some of the taxi drivers plotting to "get" Earle. The defense attorneys called no witnesses to the stand throughout the trial, but gave arguments.

On May 21, Judge Martin instructed the all-white jury to ignore the racial issues which defense lawyers had injected into the trial. He also instructed the jury not to be swayed by arguments concerning the guilt of the victim in fatally stabbing the taxi driver, the accusation for which he had been arrested.

After deliberating five hours, the jury returned a verdict of not guilty. Immediately after the foreman announced the verdict, Judge Martin, without thanking the jurors, as is the usual court custom, turned his back upon them and walked out of the court room.

Following the trial, federal officials were flooded with protests from outraged citizens throughout the country, and a number of newspapers in the South joined in condemning the verdict. Attorney General Tom Clark described the verdict as an "outrage."

Florence Murray, ed., *op. cit.*, pp. 93–95.

29

"A POSITIVE CONSTRUCTIVE PROGRAM"

by W. E. B. Du Bois

On request from Walter White, Du Bois submitted to the NAACP the following memorandum, which was wanted in order—quoting White—to "appraise the situation ahead of us during the next few months and years both with relation to the objectives and methods of the Association and also in relation to the national and world picture."

The views expressed here were basic to Du Bois's second dismissal from the association, at the end of 1947. Let the reader contemplate the relevance of this memorandum now that half a century has passed.

MEMORANDUM TO THE SECRETARY FOR THE NAACP STAFF CONFERENCE (TO OCTOBER 1946)

When the flow of progress in a land or age is strong, steady and unchallenged, a suppressed group has one clear objective: the abolition of discrimination, equality of opportunity to share in the national effort and its results. This was true of the American Negro at the end of the nineteenth century and the beginning of the twentieth.

But when, as in the first half of the twentieth century, progress fails and civilization is near collapse, then the suppressed group, especially if it has begun successfully to reduce discrimination and gain some integration into the national culture of America, must adopt something beyond the negative program of resistance to discrimination, and unite with the best elements of the nation in a positive constructive program for rebuilding civilization and reorienting progress.

This revised program in the case of the American Negroes must give attention to:

1. Economic illiteracy
2. The colonial peoples, and more especially, Africans
3. Education
4. Health
5. Democracy
6. Politics

Economic Illiteracy

The present breakdown of civilization is fundamentally Economic: the failure of human labor and sacrifice to bring happiness to the mass of men as rapidly as it increases the efficiency of labor. The leaders of two centuries have called attention to this threat to our industrial and economic organization; but the mass of people, even those of training, have not usually understood the increasingly complicated industrial structure of current society, and consequently have been in no condition radically to improve and rebuild it. Current education has permitted the man in the street to see industry as primarily a method of making individuals rich, and to regard freedom of individual initiative in business enterprise as the foundation for all progress. Again and again great thinkers have warned the world that this anarchy in industry would retain poverty, ignorance, disease and crime beyond possible reduction and culminate eventually in the suicide of war and destruction. This is what we see about us today.

To counteract this, prophets have demanded reform in industry based on curbing by government action the freedom of individual profit-making in the interest of social well-being. Such efforts have varied from palliatives like the New Deal to economic planning like T.V.A., to the

O.P.A. and F.E.P.C., to English socialism and Russian Communism. Even Fascism recognized this necessity but placed the power to carry it out in the hands of irresponsible dictators and the object of its benefits was an oligarchy and not the working masses. The whole trend of the forward thinking world, before and since the war, is toward economic planning to abolish poverty, curb monopoly and the rule of wealth, spread education, insure health and practice democracy.

Here then the N.A.A.C.P. must take a stand. To do this intelligently, we must encourage study of economic organization by lectures and forums and lead the masses of Negroes and their children to clear comprehension of the problems of industry; we must not be diverted by witch-hunting for Communists, or by fear of the wealthy, or by the temptation ourselves to exploit labor, white and black, through business, gambling, or by industrial fascism.

Colonies

We must look beyond the facade of luxurious cities, behind which modern civilization masquerades, and see and realize the poverty, squalor, slavery, ignorance, disease and despair under which the mass of men labor even today in our own slums, on our farms, and especially among the 200,000,000 colonial and semi-colonial peoples. Above all, we American Negroes should know that the center of the colonial problem is today in Africa; that until Africa is free, the descendants of Africa the world over cannot escape chains. We must believe Africans worthy of freedom, fit for survival and capable of civilization.

The N.A.A.C.P. should therefore put in the forefront of its program, the freedom of Africa in work and wage, education and health, the complete abolition of the colonial system. A world which is One industrially and politically cannot be narrowly national in social reform.

Education

From its founding in 1910, the N.A.A.C.P. has been curiously reticent on the matter of education. This was because, assuming that education of American Negroes was progressing satisfactorily, we saw at first our main duty in the task of fighting discrimination and segregation in the schools. Meantime education, especially the crucial elementary training in the three R's, has widely broken down in the world and particularly among

Negroes in Africa and America. It is safe to say that today the average Negro child in the United States does not have a chance to learn to read, write and count accurately and correctly; of the army recruits, from 18 to 25, one-third of our young American Negroes could not read and write. This is simply appalling. Beyond this, higher education is deprived of adequately trained students and deterred from the facts and reform of industry. Knowing that Democracy and social reform depend on intelligence, the N.A.A.C.P. should start a crusade for Negro education, and while not for a moment relaxing their fight on race segregation in schools, insist that segregation or no segregation, American Negro youth must be educated.

Health

The health of the American Negroes, of the Negroes of Africa and of the descendants of Africans throughout the world is seriously impaired and we lack physicians, nurses and hospitals to cope with this situation; we need too, teaching among the youth to curb excessive indulgence in alcohol, loss of sleep and gambling. Here again the N.A.A.C.P. has confined its activities hitherto mostly to fighting discrimination in medical schools, hospitals and public services and has accomplished much in this line. But we cannot be content to stop here. While continuing to contend for admission of Negro students to all medical schools and Negro patients to all hospitals, we ought to make redoubled effort to guard the health and cure the disease of Negroes the world over, by any method practical. Such planned effort should have immediate place on our national program.

Democracy

We, with the world, talk democracy and make small effort to practice it. We run our organizations from the top down, and do not believe any other method is practical. We have built in the N.A.A.C.P. a magnificent organization of several hundred thousand persons, but it is not yet a democratic organization, and in our hearts many of us do not believe it can be. We believe in a concentration of power and authority in the hands of a small tight group which issues directives to the mass of members who are expected to be glad to obey.

This is no new theory; it is as old as government. Always the leader wants to direct and command; but the difficulty is that he does not know enough; he cannot be experienced enough; he cannot possibly find time enough to master the details of a large group widely distributed. This has been the history of government, until men realized that the source of wisdom lies down among the masses because there alone is the endless experience which is complete Wisdom.

The problem—the always difficult and sometimes well-nigh insoluble problem—is how to tap this reservoir of wisdom and then find leadership to implement it.

This the N.A.A.C.P. has not adequately tried. It has regarded the demand of regions and branches for increased autonomy as revolt against the New York headquarters while in truth it has been a more or less crude attempt to teach New York the things New York must know in order to cooperate with Texas or California or New Jersey in the Advancement of Colored People.

The N.A.A.C.P. should set out to democratize the organization; to hand down and distribute authority to regions and branches and not to concentrate authority in one office or one officer; and then to assure progress by searching out intelligent, unselfish, resourceful local leaders of high character and honesty, instead of being content with the prominent and rich who are too often willing to let well-enough alone.

This securing of mass leadership of character and authority among young colored people of training and high ability can only be accomplished if we offer them not only adequate salaries, but even more, power, authority and a chance for initiative. This should begin right in the central office; the staff heads should be chosen not only to obey orders but to bear responsibility; the chief executive should be relieved of infinite details by distribution of real authority among his subordinates, reserving only broad matters of policy for himself and avoiding the paralysis of the whole office when he has no time personally to settle details. No one man can possibly attend to all details of an office like this and no assistant can work without power.

From such a top organism, power could flow down to the branches through chosen men armed with responsibility and power until it touches the mass of people themselves. All this is far easier said than done, but it is the essence of democracy and if it fails, Democracy fails.

Very soon a committee should be appointed to consider the reorganization of the New York office, with this in view. Such a committee, composed possibly of both office personnel and experts, should seek to consolidate and streamline the staff, reassign duties and powers, fix authority and responsibility and do away with overlapping. The office needs at least twice the space it now occupies to prevent unsanitary overcrowding and lack of privacy for work and consultation. Possibly the publishing, filing and more purely business functions might be physically separated from executive and research functions, or such a committee might seriously consider the removal of our head offices to the suburbs, to a building especially designed for this work with offices, archives, reference library, printing-plant and bindery, museum and art center, cafeteria, transient lodgings, large and small auditoriums and radio broadcasting facilities.

Politics

Finally, in our political program we should adopt two objectives—an immediate and a long term objective.

At present, realizing that party government in this nation has de.initely and disastrously broken down, we should in future elections ignore entirely all party labels and vote for candidates solely on their records and categorical promises. Each state, each county, each election precinct, should find out for itself carefully and as completely as possible the record of each candidate and strive to elect or defeat him whether he be Democrat, Republican, Labor Party or Communist. This should be a continuous job and not merely a pre-election activity; and it cannot be done on a national scale; it is a local job.

But this is only preliminary; efficient democracy depends on parties; that is on groups united on programs for progress. We must in this land make such party government possible. Today it is impossible because of the premium put on disfranchisement by making population instead of actual voters the basis of representation in legislatures and Congress, and by failure to function of that separation between the Executive and the Legislature, which the Constitution tried to make. We must work for a constitutional amendment, concentrating both power and immediate popular responsibility on a Congress elected by popular vote, with membership based on the voting electors.

Today Congress is owned and directed by the great aggregations of Business—the Steel Trust, the Copper Syndicate, the Aluminum Monopoly, the Textile Industry, the Farming Capitalists and a dozen others, while the Consumers and mass of workers are only partially articulate and can enforce their demands only by votes which are largely ineffective; the great interests can compel action by offering legislators financial security, profitable employment and direct bribes.

The N.A.A.C.P. should lead in such political reform, all the more because no other American group has yet had the foresight or courage to advocate it.

W. E. B. Du Bois, *Against Racism: Unpublished Essays,* ed. H. Aptheker (Amherst: University of Massachusetts Press, 1988), pp. 256–60.

30

CRIME AND PREVENTION
A HARLEM POINT OF VIEW (1946)
by Channing K. Tobias

Less global in outlook than Du Bois's memorandum and less radical but still retaining remarkable relevance,is this address delivered at a Cooper Union forum in New York City, November 19, 1946. Dr. Tobias (1882–1961), at the time of this address, chaired the Phelps-Stokes Fund. He had served in various U.S. government commissions and posts; he was chairman of the board of the NAACP in the late 1950s. Relevant to his views in the late 1940s is that in 1948 he supported Henry A. Wallace's presidential effort.

Crime curves move rapidly upward after every war. War time dislocations and pressures partially explain the current crime wave in the City of New York. But if we really want to get down to the bottom of the problem we must examine the deeper causes that are rooted back into community and family life. In my discussion of crime and prevention in New York City tonight, I shall approach the question by giving a picture of the one community in the City that I know best, namely, Harlem. Let me begin by admitting that the crime situation in the Harlem Area is alarmingly bad. It is a matter of deep concern to the people of the community themselves, most of whom are hard-working, law-abiding citizens. Especially shocking in recent weeks have been the killings resulting from battles fought by rival teen-age gangs, an expression of lawlessness that neither police authorities nor community leaders seem to be able to cope with successfully. The people outside of Harlem read the newspaper accounts and too often come to the superficial conclusion that because the population of the community is made up predominantly of one racial group, the crimes committed in the area are peculiar to that group. I cannot, therefore, say too emphatically that crimes committed in Harlem, like crimes committed everywhere else, grow out of the conditions under which the people live. Given the same conditions in any other part of the City, the record would be the same.

Now let us take a look at Harlem geographically. For the purposes of this discussion it is that part of Manhattan Island that is bounded on the South by Central Park, on the West by the Cathedral of St. John the Divine and the campuses of Columbia University and the College of the City of New York, on the East by the Harlem River featuring the entrance to the Triborough Bridge, and on the North by the Harlem River with the Polo Grounds on one bank and the Yankee Stadium on the other. Seventh and Lenox Avenues, the main arteries, are next to Park Avenue the longest and widest streets in Manhattan. But despite the fact that Harlem is so well laid out and so attractively environed, it has become an area that most people from other sections of the City either shun altogether, or visit infrequently, or drive through hurriedly.

Business seems to have written off the area as a bad risk. Such chain concerns as Woolworth's, McCrorey's, Kress' and Grant's have been gradually withdrawing from the community, some of them claiming that petty thievery is so prevalent as to make it unprofitable to operate. Horn and Hardart, which in other parts of the City caters to people on an economic level with the people of Harlem, does not operate a single store or restaurant in the area. Childs, which had one restaurant on West 125th Street, closed it up when the Southward movement of Negroes reached 125th Street about twelve years ago. Such branch stores as continue to operate in Harlem often sell at standard prices shop-worn stocks brought up from down-town stores.

Housing is so generally bad, especially in the side streets where the masses live, as to constitute a continuing menace to health and life. It is a common thing for little children to compete with rats for bunks on which to try to rest at night, while seldom a week passes that some person is not burned to death in an old-law tenement that continues in commission in spite of law and such public sentiment as there is on the subject. The only important multiple dwelling houses erected in Harlem since it became a Negro community are the Dunbar Apartments built by Mr. Rockefeller over twenty years ago, and the Harlem River Houses erected by the New York Housing Authority about twelve years ago. At present three major projects are under construction but after they will have been completed the surface of the housing need in that community will barely have been scratched.

Schools in Harlem are poorly housed with few exceptions, and on account of crowded conditions there is little opportunity for even those teachers who are genuinely conscientious in their work to give the kind of personal attention to the children that their needs call for.

The home life of Harlem is affected by a combination of circumstances that cannot be left out of account in considering the causes of crime, especially among children. First, it should be noted that because of job limitations and low pay, mothers as well as fathers must work. Under pressure of time in the mornings, hasty and inadequate breakfasts are fed to the children and they are hustled off to school for five hours. When they return home there are no parents waiting to greet them, so in many cases they go out into the streets where they meet up with other children similarly neglected. It is during this period from three to six in the afternoon that the contacts are made that lead to the organization of gangs of boys. Also it is during this period that many girls become victims of curbstone loafers. A second condition exerting a bad influence on home life is the unchallenged prevalence of houses of vice all over Harlem. Even the best neighborhoods are cursed with dens of iniquity that operate brazenly and openly and apparently with the connivance of police authorities. I know of one house in my own neighborhood that has a police record of at least ten years, during which time there have been killings, suicides, brawls, and gross immorality of every kind, all known to the police, and nothing has been done about it in spite of repeated complaints to police headquarters and to the district attorney's office. If children of the better homes are constantly having to stumble over drunks and assignation house habitues every time they walk down the street, you do not have to work arithmetic to conclude what is happening to the children in the crowded and unsanitary side streets. A third factor affecting home life adversely in the Harlem area is the lack of social-mindedness on the part of owners and managers of property. Too often income is the sole interest of these groups. Almost to a man they oppose housing projects whether they are administered by government or private owners, yet they do nothing to make their own properties livable, to say nothing of wholesome and attractive. Therefore, many houses in Harlem that were once attractive and beautiful have fallen into disrepair, and in some instances disintegration. The excuse that the owners and managers give is that the people are so destructive of property that there is no need to try to keep it up. The facts are against the owners and managers, however, for all over the country there are housing projects that replaced slum areas and that have as their tenants the very people who formerly occupied the slum houses, and who under competent and sympathetic supervision are keeping their homes in good repair.

In my discussion of home life so far I have dealt with problems that grow out of situations where there is some kind of family tie. But still more serious then these problems are those that grow out of the total or partial absence of home ties. Consider the illegitimate child who does not know who his parents are; or the child of the broken home who lives sometimes with one relative and sometimes with another. Then take a look at the inadequacies of our foster care services, and of our out-worn machinery for dealing with the delinquencies of youth before they become hardened criminals. And bear in mind how often we permit civil and ecclesiastical politics to make a travesty of child care in this the greatest and richest city of the world.

One further observation I would make before moving on to constructive suggestions, and that is that recreation facilities are woefully inadequate in the Harlem area for adults and children alike. Credit must be given to former Mayor La Guardia, Commissioner Moses and our present Mayor for major improvements of parks and the building of several modern playgrounds. I realize that in this respect Harlem is little different from other Manhattan neighborhoods, but the congestion is greater—therefore the risks are greater.

Now in the time that remains to me let me turn from this background picture to some things that can be done to remedy the situation.

1. We must do away with complete residential segregation in the City of New York whether it is based upon race, nationality, or economic status; for nothing so tends to create double standards of personality as the segregation of groups of people on account of such accidents as color and creed. As long as Negro citizens of New York are fenced in as they are in Harlem without opportunity for living along side of other people their personalities will be rated below par.

2. We must support housing programs of the government and private groups and individuals that are based on sound democratic principles to the end that the major housing needs of the community may be met.

3. We must give encouragement to management associations that are indi-genous to the community, such as the Urban Housing Management Association

that is applying intelligence and social-mindedness to management operations, and at the same time making reasonable profits for its investors.

4. We must call upon the city and state authorities to rid the community of houses of prostitution and restrict the licensing of saloons and liquor stores.

5. We must call upon the city and state governments for increased appropriations for education so that antiquated school buildings may be replaced by modern structures and an instruction budget to meet minimum requirements provided.

6. We must insist upon more adequate facilities and personnel for combating physical and mental ill health in the community. Public and private hospital services must be greatly expanded, and the almost totally neglected field of psychological and psychiatric examinations and treatment must be presented to the authorities as an indispensable part of any effective program of crime prevention.

7. We must call for a greater volume and higher quality of child care services by child welfare organizations. Where such organizations, either through inability or unwillingness, fail to meet minimum needs, we must impress upon the city and state governments their responsibility for rendering these services.

8. We must call upon all social agencies, private and governmental, operating within the area, to find resources for strengthening and expanding their programs. Such well known and well established organizations as the churches, the Urban League, the Children's Aid Society, the Community Service Society, the Young Men's Christian Association, the Young Women's Christian Association, the Citizens Committee on Children of New York City, the City-Wide Citizens' Committee on Harlem, the Police Athletic League, the National Association for the Advancement of Colored People, and many others that could be mentioned, are prevented by budget limitations from carrying on character education programs that would go a long way toward properly directing the energies of the youth during their leisure hours.

9. We must support the proposal made by the Mayor's Committee for a market for the Northwest Harlem area that would make it possible for people of small means to buy decent food at prices within their reach. At present they have no choice but to accept the generally poor quality of food made available to them by neighborhood stores at much higher than market prices.

10. We must call upon chain restaurants and stores to make a thorough and sympathetic study of Harlem as a field for investment and service, so that the approach to the community may be on the basis of the sales desires and needs of the people, rather than upon the basis of a pattern superimposed from without.

11. We must call upon down-town business men to become acquainted with Harlem as a potential market that can best be developed through intelligent and sympathetic cooperation with business men of the Harlem community.

12. Finally, we must call upon the people of Harlem, themselves, to accept their share of responsibility for the improvement of the community. This will

involve, among other things, the full utilization of the boundless resources of the churches for social service rather than the devotion of a disproportionate amount of time to purely emotional exercises. It will also call for loyal support of and cooperation with civil authorities and social and religious workers in the community in the interest of the maintenance of law and order.

Now in conclusion, let me sum up in a single sentence all that I have been trying to say, namely, that it is possible to prevent crime in Harlem and every where else in New York City, but it can only be done by creating an atmosphere in which crime cannot live and grow. Such a program as I have outlined will be costly, but crime is more costly than prevention.

Taken from mimeographed copy in possession of the editor.

31

NEW YORK'S LEGITIMATE THEATRE, 1946–48

by Mabel Roane

The last years of World War II and the two following saw notable developments in the participation of African-American people in the theater. A brief account of this was given by Mabel Roane, secretary of the Negro Actors Guild of America.

Apparently two-thought opinion still prevails among critics and theater-minded people as to how the theater should handle Negro actors and roles. In recent years there has been increasing agitation by many Negroes for more dignified roles for their actors, and the elimination of the so-called stereotype roles customarily assigned to Negro performers. . . .

The agitation in this connection has also had as its aim the integration of Negro actors into plays simply as actors—denoting no particular race.

Because of protests of Negroes against "stereotype" roles, some Negro actors claim that many roles formerly assigned to them, have been "written out" by producers and directors over the past few years, thereby lessening the opportunities for Negro performers at good-paying jobs. This is especially true in the movie industry, they contend.

A small group of Negro actors in New York initiated a movement within the past two years to organize a committee which would work toward offsetting what they consider the deleterious effects of the better-roles campaign, but nothing definite has been announced in this connection.

Racially mixed shows have continued to become popular on Broadway and have yielded favorable results, both financial and cultural. The exception to the smooth sailing of such an arrangement is the embarrassment and segregation encountered by an interracial cast below the Mason and Dixon Line.

In one instance, a white star refused to perform in a southern city, until the Negro members of the cast were permitted to perform in their roles; and in another instance a white dancer refused to perform when he was told that his Negro accompanist could not play for him. The Negro pianist was permitted to play as an "exceptional" case, with the theater manager specifying that such action on his part was not to set a precedent.

While these actions by white performers were hailed as progressive steps by Negroes, it was pointed out that there are few white actors courageous enough or with enough "influence" to take similar stands. In the two cases mentioned above, the southern audiences reacted normally and were receptive to the Negro performers.

Some Negro actors have asserted that they have found it easy, when assigned a role they feel to be offensive to Negroes, to make suggestions for its improvement and have their suggestions well taken by the directors and producers.

Supporting the opinion that the theater should offer better roles to Negro actors, it is interesting to note the following excerpt from an editorial in the *Philadelphia Record* (a daily paper published by white persons) of January 23, 1947, which stated in part:

"In theaters the country over—and this includes some cities below the Mason and Dixon Line—the audiences are accepting Negro actors, not because they are quaint, but because they are actors. One reason for the success of "Anna Lucasta'... is that the Negro actors play it straight, without appeal to race.... Canada Lee played Caliban in 'Midsummer Night's Dream' without any recognition of the fact that he happens to be a Negro. [He was whitened up for the role.]

"Todd Duncan, the original Porgy of 'Porgy and Bess,' acquitted himself admirably, singing Pagliacci in an otherwise white cast in New York's municipal opera company. This is coming a long way from the 'hot' Negro musical comedies of the 1920's. It is progress by white play-goers, as well as Negro performers. Both races are improving."

Some other Negro performers who sang in formerly all-white opera companies during the past two years were Camilla Williams, who sang the principal role in "Madame Butterfly," and Muriel Smith, who was Carmen in the original opera by that name, both staged by the New York City Grand Opera Company.

Some good examples of interracial dramas and musical shows on Broadway which met with success during the past two years are "Finian's Rainbow," "Cyrano de Bergerac," "The Iceman Cometh," and "Annie Get Your Gun."

An example of a show without racial identification is "Anna Lucasta," which opened on Broadway in 1944 with an all-Negro cast and met with immediate success. It marked the first time that an all-Negro cast had performed in a drama without any racial identification. It is still a popular show; was on the road with three companies (one in rehearsal) during 1946 and 1947 and was to return to Broadway the next season. Before its return to Broadway, it played in England, where it met with success.

During the past two years employment has been scarce in the professional theater, both for Negro and white actors. This has resulted in many "experimental" and "show-case" companies, including professional and non-professional actors. (Show-case companies are those which stage their shows first on a non-profit basis, with a view to having them taken over by a commercial producer.)

AMERICAN THEATER WING

The American Theater Wing of World War II fame admitted qualified Negro servicemen and, later, veterans, in its GI Theatrical School. Negroes were also admitted to other schools of theater training, marking a new departure in race relations in dramatic training.

USO CAMP SHOWS

The USO Camp Shows, which originated during the war to entertain servicemen in United States posts and on foreign fields, continued to send out units during the postwar period. The shows, called Veterans Hospital Camp Shows, Inc. sent "package" shows and variety entertainment to veterans hospitals. Several Negro units were included in the project, and Nobel Sissle, president of the Negro Actors Guild, served on its board of directors, the other members of which were white.

NEGROES ON BROADWAY

The list of shows which played on Broadway during the theater seasons of 1946, 1947 and 1948 (through March) is given below. . . . The shows listed are dramas and musical plays, serious and comical. The only show with an all-Negro cast which had a comparatively good run was "St. Louis Woman," the script for which was written by the late Countee Cullen, poet, and Arna Bontemps, novelist and short-story writer, both Negroes. The other all-Negro shows had short runs, from four days to a week or two.

BROADWAY SHOWS WITH ALL-NEGRO OR RACIALLY MIXED CASTS
1946—March 1948

Opening Date	Play and Theater	Names of Negro Actors
March 30, 1946	St. Louis Woman, Martin Beck	All-Negro cast, including Ruby Hill, Rex Ingram, Harold and Fayard Nicholas, Pearl Bailey, June Hawkins, Juanita Hall, and others
May 16, 1946	*Annie Get Your Gun, Imperial	John Garth, Leon Bibb, Clyde Turner
Oct. 21, 1946	Lysistrata, Belasco	All-Negro cast, including Etta Moten, Fredi Washington, Rex Ingram, Leigh Whipper, Mercedes Gilbert, Mildred Smith, Emmett (Babe) Wallace, Emory Richardson, and others.
Oct. 31, 1946	*Happy Birthday, Broadhurst	Musa Williams, Evelyn Davis
April 18, 1946	*Call Me Mister, National	Lawrence Winters, Bruce Howard, James Young
May 8, 1946	On Whitman Avenue, Cort	Canada Lee, Augustus Smith, Vivienne Baber, Abbie Mitchell, Richard Williams
April 30, 1946	Are You With It? Shubert	June Richmond, Bunny Briggs
July 8, 1946	Tidbits of 1946, Plymouth	Muriel Gaines
Oct. 8, 1946	Cyrano de Bergerac, Alvin	George Oliver
Oct. 15, 1946	Duchess of Malfi, Barrymore	Canada Lee
Oct. 9, 1946	The Iceman Cometh, Martin Beck	John Marriott
Oct. 10, 1946	Mr. Peeble and Mr. Hooker, Music Box	Ken Renard
Nov. 7, 1946	Bal Negre, Belasco	All-Negro dance show, with Katherine Dunham and her dance group
Nov. 20, 1946	*Another Part of the Forest, Fulton	Beatrice Thompson, Wilhelmina Williams

Dec. 26, 1946	Beggar's Holiday, Broadway (Produced by Perry Watkings, Negro, and John R. Sheppard, white. Music by Duke Ellington)	Archie Savage, Albert Popwell, Marie Bryant, Tommie More, Royce Wallace, Claire Hald, Enid Williams, Bill Dillard, Lewis Charles, Avon Long, Rollin Smith, Muriel Smith
Jan. 9, 1947	Street Scene, Adelphi (Lyrics by Langston Hughes.)	Creighton Thompson, Juanita Hall, Wilson Woodbeck, Helen Ferguson (juvenile)
Jan. 10, 1946	*Finian's Rainbow, 46th Street	Maude Simmons, William Greaves, and a group of Negro dancers
Jan., 1947	Our Land, Mansfield (Theodore Ward, Negro, author)	All-Negro show, including William Vesey, Muriel Smith, Valarie Black and others
March 19, 1947	*Eagle Has Two Heads, Plymouth	Cherokee Thornton
Dec. 3, 1947	*A Streetcar Named Desire, Barrymore	Edna Thomas, Gee Gee James
Dec. 26, 1947	The Cradle Will Rock, Broadway	Muriel Smith, Napoleon Reed
Feb. 9, 1948	*The Respectful Prostitute, New Stages	John Marriott, Ken Renard

*Plays having long runs

Florence Murray, Handbook (1949), pp. 325–27.

32

SEGREGATION: A SYMPOSIUM (1947)

The *Survey Graphic*, a publication of influence in the 1930s and 1940s, included as the twelfth number of its series "Calling America" one entitled "Segregation." The editor was Thomas Sancton, born in New Orleans and formerly on the staff of newspapers in Louisiana and Mississippi. He was educated at Tulane and Harvard. In 1942–43 he had been managing editor of the *New Republic*. At the time of the appearance of this *Survey Graphic* he was living in Mississippi.

This issue was underwritten by the Rosenwald Fund, the Carnegie Corporation, and the Phelps-Stokes Fund. The State Department ordered five hundred copies for some of its personnel and undertook its translation and circulation in Germany, Austria, and Japan. The director of the State Department's Office of International Affairs told the regular editor, Paul Kellogg: "Congratulations! It is a first rate job in every respect."

All this and the treatment of Du Bois's 1945 book, mentioned earlier, show the impact of Walter White's *Rising Wind*, which, alas, soon blew itself away.

From this special issue are printed essays by (a) Ira De A. Reid; (b) Robert C. Weaver; (c) Loren Miller; (d) Alain Locke; and (e) E. Franklin Frazier.

[a]

SOUTHERN WAYS

Ira De A. Reid (1901–68)

Dr. Reid, a professor at Atlanta University, was a visiting professor at Haverford College and at New York University—highly unusual appointments at this time and indicative of the impact of the euphoria following the defeat of fascism.

The chief device of racial segregation in the South is law. In all southern states the law defines one's racial identification and then proceeds to define status and rights, all in relation to race. A formidable example of "the southern way" is to be found in the statutes of Georgia, the state having the largest Negro population in the United States.

Under Georgia law the term "white person" includes "only persons of White or Caucasian race, who have no ascertainable trace of either Negro, African, West Indian, Mongolian, Japanese, or Chinese blood in their veins. No person, any one of whose ancestors has been duly registered with the State Bureau of Vital Statistics as a colored person or person of color, shall be deemed to be a white person." (*Georgia Code, 1932 Annotated; Chapter 34, Section 312.*)

Georgia also declares "All Negroes, Mulattoes, Mestizos, and their descendants, having any ascertainable trace of either Negro or African, West Indian, or Asiatic Indian blood in their veins, and all descendants of any person having either Negro or African, West Indian, or Asiatic Indian blood in his or her veins, shall be known in this State as persons of color." (*Georgia Code, 1932, Annotated; Chapter 79, Section 103.*)

Under the Law

There the southern color-caste system begins. Every aspect of life is regulated by the laws on race and color. From birth through education and marriage to death and burial there are rules and regulations saying that you are born "white" or "colored"; that you may be educated, if colored, in a school system separated on the basis of race and "as nearly uniform as possible" with that available for whites; that you may marry a person of your choice only if that person is colored, this being the only celebration of marriage a colored minister of the gospel may perform; and that when you die (in Atlanta, at least) you may not be buried in a cemetery where whites are interred.

But that isn't all. Between birth and death colored persons find that the law decrees that they shall be separated from white persons on all forms of transportation, in hotels or inns, eating places, at places of recreation or amusement, on the tax books, as voters, in their homes, and in many occupations.

To be specific, it is a punishable offense in Georgia for a barber shop to serve both white and colored persons, or for Negro barbers to serve white women or girls; to bury a colored person in a cemetery in which white people are buried; to serve both white and colored persons in the same restaurants within the same room, or anywhere under the same license. Restaurants are required to display signs reading *Licensed to serve white people only,* or *Licensed to serve colored people only.* The law also declares that wine and beer may not be served to white and colored persons "within the same room at any time." Taxis must be marked *For White Passengers Only,* or *For Colored Passengers Only.* There must be white drivers for carrying white passengers and colored drivers for carrying colored passengers.

Furthermore, in Atlanta, it is an offense against the public order, peace, and morals for any amateur white baseball team to play baseball on any vacant lot or baseball diamond within two blocks of a playground surrounding a Negro public school and set apart by the city for athletic purposes during the summer. It is unlawful for white and colored persons to use or frequent the same public park. The only exception to this rule is that Negroes may visit "so much of Grant Park as is occupied by the zoo."

Finally, state laws regulating the seating of colored persons on all public carriers are enforceable in Atlanta by the local police, as well as by the operators of the vehicles, who have police power.

Local Mores

There the law ends and custom and usage begin to function. Thus, a Negro in Atlanta may be born in the municipal hospital at which no Negro doctor is allowed to serve. The mother may remain there for twenty-four hours after delivery, while a white mother may remain seventy-two hours for post-delivery care.

Though Atlanta has a colored school population of approximately 30,000, until 1945 there was only one public kindergarten for Negro children in the whole city—so overcrowded that only a small proportion of the applicants could be admitted. If he goes to the public schools, the Negro child may find the school day divided into two or three "staggered" sessions because of overcrowding. There is only one high school for colored boys and girls, and that runs on double and triple shifts in some grades.

If a colored student wishes vocational training, the public schools provide for him only a fraction of the opportunity offered a white student.

If the student wishes to do "outside reading," he finds the segregated public library for Negroes as poorly equipped, in comparison with the main library for whites, as is his school library in comparison with that for white pupils.

If he wishes to pursue his higher education at one of the state colleges for colored persons, the inferiority and discrimination persist. He may decide to attend one of the many private colleges in Georgia. There is no law to prevent his doing so, but if any private educational institution should accept both white and colored students, its endowment would become subject to tax—a formidable device.

Jim Crow Enroute

When this colored Georgian travels, he gets on the front end of the street car, sits at the rear, and gets off at the rear. White persons get on at the front, choose seats from the front toward the rear, and get off at the front. The Negro finds that the system seldom works when cars are crowded—white passengers take all the seats, front and rear.

If the colored person plans to leave the city by bus, he may eventually be able to buy a ticket at the terminal. Colored travelers are served at the convenience of the white clerks. Then he may or may not get a seat, for usually colored persons are permitted to enter the bus only after white passengers have been seated. If the bus is a "de luxe" express, he may be told "All Negroes take the second bus." The second bus will make all stops, and probably be old and dirty.

If a colored person leaves the city by train, he will purchase his ticket at the city ticket office because the clerks are less discriminatory there than at the railroad station. It is easy to get a ticket for the "Jim Crow" coach on any train save on such crack trains as "The Southerner" to Washington and New York, and "The Flagler" to Chicago. Only twenty-one seats are available to Negroes on these "all reserved" trains.

If he wishes Pullman accommodations, he telephones the city ticket office and makes the reservation, hoping that he will not be asked whether he is "white or colored." If he says "colored," the chances are that he will not get a lower on the best train; he may get "lower 13"—a berth in a drawing room or a compartment—on a later train.

If the traveler goes to the station for his ticket, he enters the side entrance where the "colored waiting room" is located. He purchases his coach ticket, not when his turn in a line comes, but when the attendant decides to serve him. If he wishes a Pullman ticket he goes out of the colored waiting room into the "general" or "white" waiting room where the Pullman windows are located. If he is obviously colored, he has, perhaps a 50-50 chance of getting space "1" or "12" or "13"—depending upon who wants what is available.

Service on the trains is determined to a great extent by the individual conductors, stewards, porters, and waiters. Pullman conductors and porters usually are accommodating and reassuring. Train conductors may be bothersome since they have police power. Dining car stewards may "pull the book" on serving colored persons and seat them behind a green curtain separating the two rear tables from the remainder of the car. On a coach train the colored passenger may be called for breakfast at "first call"—5:30 A.M.—so that Negroes will be "out of the way" by the time the white travelers want breakfast.

If he travels by air, the Negro will find the devices of segregation either absent or in the making. It saves trouble if he goes to the airport in his own car or that of a friend. He is barred from the company limousines, but he may ride the omnibus. The established taxi rate printed on the airline's folders does not apply to the colored passenger unless he rides this omnibus.

If he wishes to eat at the airport he probably will be served in the kitchen—no other provision being available for him. There are makeshift toilet facilities for colored persons. As he boards his plane on one of the southern lines, the hostess will suggest—with a quick smile—that she has saved the front single seat for him. He can see only one reason for it. At meals he is the last to be served.

When he alights at another southern field, he may find the same taxi problem. If he wishes to use a car-for-hire, he finds it is not available to colored persons. And if you wonder why this Negro American has endured all of these nuisances, remember that in Georgia conductors, motormen, and bus drivers have police power—*and use it.*

Citizen of Atlanta

Upon his return to the city he may wish to see a first-run motion picture. The only seat available to him as a person of color is in the gallery, which may be reached by climbing a long flight of steps on the outside of the theater. Perhaps the film is at a theater which has the "colored entrance" through a side alley, or even at one that does not admit colored persons at all.

If he has an appointment with a real estate agent in a downtown office building, he is likely to find that there is only one elevator a Negro may ride—and that one labeled "Colored" or "Freight" or "Service." The agent, verifying the client's address in the city directory, may find a "(c)" after his name.

When this colored man goes to a bank, he probably will have to transact his business at a window marked *For Our Colored Patrons.* As a customer at a downtown store, he may find that there is no washroom he can use, that the restaurant is barred to him, that the clerks—even in a store of a nationwide chain—call him or his wife by their first names. He knows that there is an arbitrary credit limit on all "colored accounts."

The house he purchases will be located in a Negro neighborhood, or in one that is changing from white to Negro. If the latter, he arms himself for protection against hoodlums. Near his home may be a sign—"The dividing line between white and colored which was mutually agreed to by both."

In short, he is a citizen of Atlanta, who recently voted in the first Georgia primary in fifty years which was open to Negroes. Yet his vote was labeled "colored" and if he or any other colored person decided to run for public office he would become the victim of all of the region's devices of discrimination—some subtle, some violent in their cruelty.

These are the things a colored person must know—the things he may or may not do in one southern city.

But to learn the segregation devices of one city in a single state does not mean that one is equipped to operate on either side of the great wall of race anywhere else in the South. The segregation pattern varies from city to city, county to county, state to state. To know and keep one's place as a colored or a white person involves knowing its every quirk. All these details and variations are quite beyond the ken of the average man.

Up and Down the Liberty Pole

Of four things you can be certain everywhere in the Deep South:

—*white and colored persons may not travel together in the same compartments, cars, or sections of the same cars, on trains or buses;*
—*white and colored persons may not intermarry;*
—*white and colored persons may not attend the same publicly supported educational institutions;*
—*white and colored persons may not utilize the same facilities in any public agency or building.*

Beyond these four major taboos certainty becomes uncertainty, for custom and usage determine the existing practice. A Negro is not permitted to enter a moving picture theater patronized by whites in Jacksonville, Fla.; he may attend some of them in Atlanta, if he sits in the "Jim Crow" section; in some cities of the border and upper South, he may attend any theater but he must occupy seats in special sections.

A white taxi driver may not transport a colored person in most southern cities, but he will carry him in Nashville, Tenn.

There is no racial discrimination against Negro patrons in the waiting room of the airlines terminal in New Orleans, but a special seat is reserved "for our colored patrons" in Nashville and in Birmingham.

The salaries paid Negro teachers are likely to be on a lower scale than those paid white teachers in Birmingham, Ala., Jackson, Miss., Nashville, Tenn., Charleston, S.C.; but the same salaries are paid both groups in San Antonio and Houston, Texas, and New Orleans, La.

News of the Negro community may be printed on a special page in one city, in a special edition in another, printed in a special column in a third, or omitted from other newspapers—unless it deals with crime.

A colored person may be expected to enter the front end of a street car in one city, and the rear end in another.

He may be expected to take off his hat in an elevator in one building, and regarded as silly if he removes it in another.

He may not deposit his savings in a bank in one city, yet be the largest depositor in another.

He may be admitted to a private hospital in one community, but find it impossible to get either ambulance service or hospitalization—even for surgery—in another.

He may own and occupy real property in any section of some southern cities—if he dares; in others he may own and not occupy; in still others he may neither own nor occupy in certain "restricted" areas.

He may be kept off trains in Columbia or Charleston, S.C., because there is no space in the colored coach; leaving Atlanta, he may be herded into a baggage car and compelled to stand or to sit on trunks.

He may sit where he wishes in the concourse of Atlanta's Terminal Station and enter the train approach with other passengers, but in Birmingham he is shunted in and out of the station through a special walk on which he can have no contact with a white person save over an iron fence.

He may ride into Louisville, Ky., from the deeper South in a "Jim Crow" car and leave that city from a "colored" waiting room in a coach carrying white and colored passengers.

The kinds of segregation devices used in southern cities vary widely. They are limited in inconvenience and humiliation only by the ingenuity of the designers and their enforceability, as determined by political and economic pressures, and population mobility.

Change—and Resistance to Change

Political pressures—that is, the acquisition of voting strength and political power—have done much toward equalizing opportunities for colored persons in areas where the law requires "separate but equal" facilities. So far, these pressures have operated most successfully in the fields of education and public conveniences. In many instances, political action in the South has served to maintain the separation while removing some of the inequalities.

Thus, to equalize colored teachers' salaries is to reinforce the dual school system. No technical or professional higher education is provided for colored teachers in some states, but separate colleges may be established for them or special out-of-state scholarships provided.

In Tennessee or Texas, for example, Negro students are not admitted to the state universities but both states make seven-figure appropriations to "equalize" the education offered by segregated state colleges.

Each new step taken tends to increase the devices of segregation in the region. The new patterns acquire special significance when one considers them in the light of the comment of Charles H. Thompson, editor of *The Journal of Negro Education*, who estimates that at the present rate of equalization it will take two hundred years to bring education for Negroes in the South up to the white level. Meantime, will those two centuries add many new twists and turns to the South's educational pattern and bolster the "separate but equal" system while thwarting efforts toward full democratic participation?

It almost goes without saying that in the South, the question of biracial housing is never even raised. Many northern cities have apartment houses occupied by both Negro and white families. There are none in the South. White and Negro individuals and families do not enter the homes of members of the other race as guests. In all parts of the South this is a matter of custom; in some it is a matter of law. Thus, in Alabama, it is a punishable offense for a Negro and a white man to eat in the same room; or to spend the night under the same roof, except, of course in the case of servants in the homes of "masters."

Federally financed or federally stimulated housing projects in the New Deal years improved the housing available to Negroes in many communities, through slum clearance and the building of modern apartments and homes. But these projects conform meticulously to local patterns of residential segregation, as did new housing for war industry workers.

Negroes are not being overlooked in postwar public housing plans in the South. Memphis, Tenn., for example, which has set itself a goal of 8,500 new units of residential construction under the Veterans Emergency Housing Plan, has earmarked 3,500 of these for Negro occupancy. In Meridan, Miss., of 2,000 new units contemplated, 800 will be available to Negroes. Jackson, Miss., expects to have 3,000 new units, one third of them for Negroes.

All these undertakings serve to perpetuate the South's "Jim Crow" pattern, just as "better" Negro schools in the end help maintain segregated education.

Pressures and Inertias

Economic pressures, however, are causing some rearrangement of the South's discriminatory pattern. For example, discrimination in travel conveniences has been challenged in the courts in various test cases.

Recent efforts of state legislators in Mississippi, Alabama, and Georgia to introduce separate bus laws were defeated by the bus company representatives or their lobbyists. It was too expensive an undertaking. When the Alabama Public Service Commission sought to revise its infamous "Rule T18" to provide more stringent methods of segregating colored travelers, the carriers themselves (aided by a committee of Negro and white citizens) effected an adjustment that left things as they were....

[b]

NORTHERN WAYS

Robert C. Weaver

At this time Dr. Weaver was director of community service, American Council on Race Relations; he had served on various city and federal agencies. Weaver was the author of several books, including *Negro Labor* (1946). In 1966 he became the first African-American to achieve cabinet rank.

Separation of the races has no legal basis above the Mason-Dixon Line, as it has in the South. Rather it rests upon habit, extra-legal maneuvers, acts of hostility, and expressions of aversion. Each technique of segregation, once it becomes established, reinforces the color-caste system and serves to strengthen the artificial barriers dividing ethnic groups.

Despite relaxations in job discrimination in war industry, the occupational color line remains inflexible in the retail trades, in some public utilities, and in many service industries. Management says that white workers, white women in particular, refuse to use the same washrooms as Negro workers. Therefore, to take on Negroes would mean costly separate arrangements for them.

In a few instances northern employes, encouraged by management in this sort of squeamishness, have supported this assertion. But wartime experience in industry suggests that often the point is exaggerated. Certainly, where management above the Mason-Dixon Line has taken a firm stand, the problem has not been serious.

To inject this problem into the economic issue of equal job opportunities serves to emphasize segregation and gives management's blessing to the institution.

On the Job

That the public in general is more than casually concerned with the color of the hand that serves it over the counter remains to be established. Most people in the North probably have given the matter little thought. It seems safe to assume that the majority would accept a new racial pattern in this type of employment, just as they accepted Negro streetcar conductors and bus drivers when they first appeared in northern cities.

Public resentment is often cited as the reason for job discrimination in stores and service industries. The real reason for the discrimination is that such employment departs from the color-caste system accepted by many businessmen and insecure white collar workers. And once the issue is raised, the unthinking acceptance of a "place" for darker Americans fills the discussion with emotion.

Advocates of separate facilities of all types often argue that minorities prefer to be together, or that control of their own institutions gives special opportunities to minorities.

The first assertion, to the limited extent that it is true, is a most damning indictment of segregation. It illustrates the fact that people who live in ghettos become ghetto-minded; chauvinism grows among them, becoming a serious impediment to national unity and often expressing itself in anti-white attitudes.

The second assertion has historical roots. It reflects the attitude of some missionaries sent to work with "backward peoples" in all parts of the world. In most instances, the white man was doing something "*for* those people" (not *with* them), and often held himself apart from them.

Barriers in School

Public schools, because they are tax supported and subject to the state laws barring segregation in some parts of the North, have less racial segregation than Christian churches which are dedicated to the brotherhood of man but exempt from legislative restrictions. Most separate schools outside the South are the result of residential segregation. Even in those northern cities where there is not complete residential segregation, separate schools often exist.

This pattern is being challenged. Trenton, N.J., has abolished segregated schools, and Gary, Ind., is doing likewise, and will initiate the change by the beginning of the 1947 school year. Philadelphia is also attempting to modify the segregated patterns that have developed in its public schools.

Dayton, Ohio, reflects the growth of segregated schools in an area where there is no legal basis for them. First, a colored high school, named after Dayton's native son, Paul Laurence Dunbar, was set up. The separate school was proposed in order to afford employment for trained Negroes who were denied white collar and professional jobs in the community. That is, the cure for the color-caste system was to draw it tighter and extend its application.

Soon after Dunbar High School was established, two elementary schools for Negroes appeared, and last winter a third elementary school was added to the list. The perpetuation and spread of segregation in the schools and elsewhere in Dayton has been encouraged by the selection of a Negro, an avowed proponent of segregation, as the principal of Dunbar. Gradually, he has come to function as the "recognized" Negro leader in the city. The circle is closed.

The spread of segregation in the schools is tied in with the expansion of employment opportunities for colored youth; the principal center of training for colored youth is guided by a champion of racial segregation, and that champion has been given status and prestige by Dayton's white leadership.

How heavily the pattern of segregation, of "not belonging," bears on young minds and spirits is shown by current figures on juvenile delinquency. Of course both physical and psychological factors are at work. But along with bad housing, inferior schools, limited job opportunities, meager facilities for recreation, must be reckoned the unhappiness and frustration of segregated living, of being set apart and made to feel "different." Figures as to the numbers of young delinquents in court, and as to the incidence of delinquency in segregated Negro neighborhoods, unfailingly serve to drive home this point—from city to city and state to state, in the North as well as in the South.

The bright side of this somber picture is the proof that "something can be done about it." For example, the development of a housing project which includes Negro families always produces an improvement in juvenile delinquency figures in the community, and particularly Negro delinquency.

Even more striking, perhaps, are the encouraging results that follow when a neighborhood house—for example Fellowship Center, St. Louis—

carries out a successful interracial program of clubs, classes, canteens, and so on, in which Negro and white youth meet and mingle on an equal footing. Here there is no change in the make-up of the population, such as sometimes follows with slum clearance and new building, but only a change in community attitudes and opportunities.

Jim Crow Meals

Anyone familiar with the literature on American race relations knows of the various methods employed by managers of theaters, restaurants, and hotels to deny service to colored people and discourage their patronage.

Cincinnati has seen most of the old methods and many of the newer ones used in efforts to defeat a recent campaign to open restaurants to colored citizens. The story of that campaign throws light on this whole question of racial barriers in eating places. It begins with the arrangements made with the restaurant owners' association to serve Negroes during the 1946 National Convention of the NAACP in the city. Instantly, many restaurants closed "for repairs." In one of the hotels, waiters and waitresses refused to serve colored patrons. This seemed to be a good device until the cooks and waiters union of the AFL reprimanded its members and threatened them with union charges.

The next efforts to break down segregation in the city's restaurants were centered upon cafeterias. Five of the first six selected capitulated. But the sixth held out, and its owner then took the lead in finally defeating the movement to wipe out racial segregation in these eating places. He persuaded the restaurant owners' association to make things uncomfortable for the one cafeteria owner who had hired competent Negro personnel and had voluntarily stated her willingness to serve colored people.

Then this leader of the opposition devised a series of complicated steps to discourage Negro patronage. When a colored person entered the line to be served, the manager asked in a loud voice, "Are you looking for employment? If so, come around to the back door."

When the customer assured him that he was seeking food, not work, the manager stated, in an even louder voice, that the cafeteria would not be responsible for bodily harm done Negro patrons and predicted a race riot.

When a Negro approached the serving table, a bell was rung, and the manager came to the steam tables to "alert" the employes. The colored patron received portions smaller than the usual service.

When Negroes were served, the manager passed out cards quoting the Ohio Civil Rights law and stated he was serving Negroes only because the law required him to do so. If a white customer sat at a table where there was a Negro, the manager insisted that the white patron move.

Needless to say, half the ingenuity and time all this involved, if otherwise directed, would have made a success of the drive to open cafeterias to Negro patronage.

But the most telling force in defeating the efforts to open downtown eating places to Cincinnati Negroes, was the apathy of the Negro community. This was a direct result of living in a segregated society and another expression of the minority group's accommodation to racial separation. This conditioning colors all phases of living and often appears in the disinclination of many colored people to associate with whites or to frequent places where a large number of white persons are present. It will continue to harass labor unions and liberal organizations when they attempt to secure widespread participation of members of segregated minority groups.

This is not only important in recreation and entertainment because the Negro who goes out for a meal or to the theater wants food or relaxation under pleasant conditions; he does not want to solve the race problem. As a matter of fact, he wants to forget the race problem; consequently, he avoids situations which may lead to embarrassment. But this disinclination of Negroes to patronize certain restaurants, theaters, night clubs, and so on, makes the occasional presence of a dark face seem peculiar. Many of the white patrons, who think in terms of white places and Negro places, see in the unusual presence of a Negro a threat to "the color line."

Swimming Pools—a Test

It is difficult for a Negro to find a meal or a hotel room in the downtown area of most northern cities; it is an achievement if he can swim in a public pool in most of the same cities. Until recently, this was so well understood in many northern cities that few colored people even tried to gain admittance. But recently the matter has been pressed in a score or more communities, and local officials have perfected devices to exclude Negroes.

In 1945 and 1946, city officials closed swimming pools in Cincinnati, Warren, and Lima, Ohio, rather than admit Negroes to them. In 1943, the pool in the Froebel High School in Gary, Ind., (where there was a "hate strike" of the pupils in 1945) was closed for four months; after that it was open on certain days for Negroes and on other days for whites. This is a fairly typical formula, in northern cities, for segregation in swimming. But public authorities have used other means to enforce segregation in this recreation. When municipal authorities are advised that they can not exclude Negroes legally, they lease swimming pools to private operators, and the latter exclude colored persons. Often guards and police resort to intimidation to keep Negroes out, the most common practice being to deny them protection from hostile whites or to discount gang fights between Negro and white youths, lightly, as the "normal activities of growing boys."

When a Warren, Ohio, swimming pool opened, Negro citizens attempted to use it. After much negotiation, the pool was operated two days of the week for the exclusive use of colored swimmers, but in 1945, Negroes began to disregard the racial schedule. The mayor then closed the pool. Later, the city solicitor advised the city administration that the pool, as a tax supported facility, could not operate on a segregated schedule. In accordance with this ruling, it was opened in June, 1946, and Negroes admitted. When there was trouble, the city negotiated a lease with a private operator, and now the pool is again closed to Negroes. This time the exclusion is absolute.

When the local Negro children attempted to use the swimming pool in the Cook County Forest Preserve, just outside Chicago, they were warned that, while colored swimmers would be admitted, there might be fights. In that event, the management of the preserve refused to guarantee protection and declared that Negroes would have to use the pool at their own risk. This failure to use the preserve's own police force to maintain law and order was usually enough to keep colored people away from the pool. When an occasional Negro braved the situation, he was rejected on the basis of a cursory physical examination or because of the type of bathing suit he wore. These devices have been effective in discouraging Negro participation, since in addition to their invitation to violence, they convinced the colored community that to try to use the pool would mean unpleasantness and humiliation.

In Lima, Ohio, where the Negro population has little political or economic power, methods of enforcing segregation and exclusion were less subtle. When Negroes arrived at the municipal pool, they were told that there was to be no swimming that day and that all were expected to leave. In a city where colored people had few rights and little consideration, the hint and the veiled threat were enough. Negroes knew that if they insisted, they would be shown in no gentle fashion that they were unwelcome.

American Ghettos

Devices used to establish and perpetuate segregation in the North can be divided into two broad categories: legal and extra-legal acts which exclude or restrict participation; psychological factors that discourage Negroes' entering places where they know they are not wanted. Closely associated with the second are the conditioning of whites to expect Negroes to keep out and the adjustment of colored people to the pattern— two features of northern life largely a result of residential segregation.

This same concentration of colored people in well defined, restricted areas leads to separate public facilities within the ghetto. As a result, the education and the recreation of most northern Negroes go on in a closed, isolated community.

Color minorities in northern urban centers are relegated to inadequate, neglected districts by extra-legal devices (called race-restrictive covenants), social pressures, municipal action (through planning boards and housing authorities), "gentlemen's agreements" among real estate operators, and violence to person and property. Of these, the most important is the restrictive covenant, defined thus by Gunnar Myrdal in "The American Dilemma": "The restrictive covenant is an agreement by property owners in a neighborhood not to sell or rent their property to colored people for a definite period."

Restrictive covenants have become all but universal in many cities. For example, it has been estimated that as high as 80 percent of the residential area of Chicago is covered already by these restrictions. Fully as serious as their extent is the fact that covenants are becoming habitual and automatic in property transfers in many communities, so that once established in a land title, they cling to the title and are passed on automatically whether or not the new owners especially desire them.

This Jim Crow formula is becoming so universal that even government policies have served as devices to strengthen residential segregation. The Federal Housing Administration has actually adopted the policy of the private financing institutions by advocating restricted covenants—on the assumption that such agreements are necessary to safeguard the value of mortgages insured by FHA.

The Underwriters Manual of FHA warns valuators to consider the importance of the prevention of the infiltration of "...lower class occupancy and inharmonious racial groups," and advises "effective restrictive covenants...recorded against the entire tract, since these provide the surest protection against undesirable encroachments and inharmonious use. To be most effective," the manual continues, "deed restrictions should be imposed upon all land in the immediate environs of the subject location," and finally refers to the "prohibition of occupancy of properties except by the race for which they are intended."

For the record, it must be said that this manual has been in the process of revision for several years, and FHA Commissioner Raymond M. Foley, soon after he took office a year ago, publicly stated that for some time the manual has had no official status. He indicated further that in the new manual (to appear early this year) all references to race and covenants in this connection will be eliminated.

Many of the segregated Negro neighborhoods in northern cities are slum areas because ethnic islands are overcrowded and under-serviced, and because their inhabitants are, as a rule, people of limited and uncertain earnings. Crime and disease breed in such surroundings, regardless of the color of the occupants. But ghetto conditions become convenient justifications for the perpetuation of residential segregation and its spread into other aspects of community life.

Segregation North and West

The rise of segregation in the North and West during and after World War I followed the entrance of colored labor into new areas of employment. In that period, the black worker was resented by established wage earners as a new addition to the "labor pool." Management and the craft unions were quick to champion segregation.

The rise of industrial unions, and the new recognition of organized labor together with the manpower shortage have forced a wider acceptance of colored labor. At the same time, the insistence of management and unions on the spread of segregation has lessened. Today, the chief advocates of racial separation are small businessmen, neighborhood merchants, and most important, real estate operators.

The West Coast, often called the new frontier in race relations, offers some of the most striking examples of the new trend. In the San Bernardino area, for example, businessmen in a township defeated the amalgamation of an Anglo American school with a Latin American and Negro school. The basis for this opposition, frankly expressed, was the fear that if colored and white students attended the same schools, there would be an immediate influx of Negroes and Mexican-Americans into the neighborhood of the consolidated school and these groups would "take over the property and ruin business."

In a nearby town, real estate operators and the former president of the local Chamber of Commerce led a movement—fortunately unsuccessful—to have a Negro teacher who had been appointed to a school with only one colored pupil transferred to a school that served minorities almost exclusively. Again, the reason was fear lest the presence of the colored teacher would bring more Negroes and Mexicans into the community.

Some years ago, similar attempts to transfer all colored teachers to schools with large Negro enrollments were made in several midwestern cities including Cleveland and Chicago. In Chicago, the move followed the rise of neighborhood protective associations and the spread of restrictive covenants.

Gary, Ind., in the summer of 1945, offered an extreme expression of the same attitude. When war industry spread over the section of the lake front where Negroes had bathed, efforts were made to open another section—separate, of course—to colored swimmers. It failed because influential white residents objected to having Negroes pass their homes or share public transportation with them on the way to the beach.

Housing for War Workers

World War II brought a tide of war workers—white and colored—to northern industrial centers. Few cities provided additional living space for Negroes, and this intensified all the hardships of residential segregation. The establishment of "Negro districts" automatically fixes a pattern of white and black housing. Given this attitude, strong community forces opposed any shelter for colored people outside the prescribed areas, and in a period of large-scale migration, there was no room for the newcomers in the already overcrowded sections where whites insisted Negroes must live.

In Chicago, for instance, a public housing project open to Negroes in an outlying area surrounded by factories and vacant land was fought as a threat to property values in residential areas miles away from the proposed project. In other northern cities, attempts were made to pass municipal legislation which would block the expansion of Negro occupancy.

In Toledo, Ohio, priorities were allocated for the construction of 150 new homes for Negroes. But, priorities or no priorities, the scheme hung fire. Not a single home was built for colored war workers. Every site proposed proved undesirable for residential use, or the choice met with violent neighborhood opposition. The controversy almost exploded in violence, in August 1944, when hearings on a suggested site were held in the City Hall. A large number of white residents had signed a petition to the City Council to pass an ordinance prohibiting the use of a desirable site for the housing project. Colored citizens appeared to oppose the ordinance. Although the white petition was defeated, no houses were built.

A similar situation developed in Milwaukee. At the beginning of the war, eighteen Negroes bought lots near the outskirts of the city, a long way from the Sixth Ward where practically all the city's 16,000 colored citizens are involuntarily concentrated. Since the lots had been purchased from the city, white people living nearby appealed to the City Council to "do something." One of the councilmen thereupon introduced an ordinance rescinding the sale and reserving the land for the development of parks and playgrounds. The ordinance passed. This precipitated a stormy meeting at which the council restored title to the lots to the eighteen Negro purchasers, but no other sales were made in the area.

In May 1944, a local contractor announced his plan to build 108 dwellings for Negroes in another district outside the Sixth Ward. There was a wave of indignation from whites in many sections of the city, and a petition of protest was filed with local officials. Immediately, the municipal planning body discovered that the land in question was needed for construction of a viaduct, and the housing project was abandoned.

Detroit and Pittsburgh

Detroit today has as acute a housing problem as any city in the nation and the most urgent aspect of it is the need for more space for colored residents. All authorities admit that the sections where Negroes now live are dangerously overcrowded. All recognize the need for more housing for

Negroes. The mayor, whose handling of the 1943 race riot was so widely criticized, recently stated again his fixed belief that the racial composition of neighborhoods should be preserved.

The local housing authority, after comprehensive study of the matter, recommended that 1,000 public housing units available to Negroes be constructed in the southwest area of the city. This aroused protests which culminated in a public hearing in the city hall on March 9, 1945. The opposition was carefully organized, and thousands of letters supporting its position poured into the councilmen's office.

Typical of the level of the discussion was a letter written by the leader of the opposition:

Please don't cry discrimination—it is a very badly misused term. We firmly believe in the God-given equality of man. He did not give us the right to choose our brothers, but, with reservations, He did give us the right to choose the people we sleep with.

After a stormy hearing, the common council by a five to four vote rejected the housing commission's recommendation. Two councilmen urged that *no* housing be built for Negroes within the city of Detroit.

Pittsburgh and Los Angeles have followed relatively progressive interracial housing policies. Public housing projects in Los Angeles observe a general rule that every development shall be open to all groups in the urban population. The interracial character exists to some degree in every housing project in the city. The racial minorities present are sometimes Negroes, sometimes Americans of Japanese or Mexican descent.

The Pittsburgh practice of establishing a separate building or group of buildings for Negro families in each public project is a less democratic policy than that followed by Los Angeles, but is more advanced than the practices of most other northern cities. . . .

[c]

THE POWER OF RESTRICTIVE COVENANTS

Loren Miller

Although race restrictive covenants are most often used to effect segregation of Negroes in urban areas, they are essentially a device to limit land ownership or use by any unwanted or unpopular ethnic or religious group.

The first reported case involving such agreements concerns an attempt to forbid use of a laundry by a Chinese in San Diego, Calif., in 1892, and Californians have shown a great deal of ingenuity in their use of such devices since that time.

Convenants in that state proscribe land use by Armenians, by Chinese, by Japanese, by Hindus, by Mexicans, and by "persons who are descendants of former residents of the Turkish Empire." The latter agreement was obviously an attempt to prevent Armenian use and occupancy, without naming the group directly.

That same kind of delicacy is displayed in latter day covenants in Virginia, where an agreement obviously directed against Jews proscribed land use by "persons who customarily observe the seventh day of the week as the Sabbath." Ironically enough, the first person to get entangled in it was a Seventh Day Adventist.

Earlier covenants used specific racial definitions such as "Negro," "Chinese," or "Japanese" but of late years those terms have been abandoned in favor of the sweeping generalization "non-Caucasian." That change has bred its own problems, with the courts being called upon to define the term.

In a recent California case, a witness for the defendants was a distinguished anthropologist who testified that the terms "Caucasian" and "non-Caucasian" are almost meaningless and that, contrary to popular belief, neither skin color nor hair texture are infallible guides to racial identity. That particular judge resolved the conflict by holding that the terms are used in their ordinary, rather than in their technical, sense and are sufficient to bar land use by persons customarily called Negroes.

The next complication arose when an attempt was made to oust an American Indian couple who had occupied a home covered by a race restrictive agreement forbidding use by "non-Caucasians." The trial court held summarily that American Indians are non-Caucasians and ordered the couple to vacate. On the other hand, courts, following census classifications, are apt to rule that Mexicans, no matter how large their degree of Indian blood, are "Caucasians" and are not proscribed by covenants barring non-Caucasians.

In fact, the attempts to prevent use of land by Mexicans have not been very successful in California where most such attempts have been made. The courts have rested their decisions on the good neighbor policy in those cases and have resisted most attempts to oust Mexicans even where agreements specifically forbid their residence.

Occupancy, by mixed couples, of covenanted land has also vexed the courts. A Michigan judge forbade a Negro husband to visit his white wife, but of course could not disturb her occupancy under a covenant forbidding Negro use. The judge stated, however, that in his estimation about the only circumstance that could relieve the husband of contempt of court if he were found on the premises would be his presence there to rescue his spouse in case of fire.

Even the term "non-Caucasian" has undergone some refinement, and up-to-the-minute covenants often forbid use of the land by "any person whose blood is not entirely that of the white race." There again, anthropological difficulties have intruded. It's indeed a wise litigant who knows all his ancestors; and stubborn defendants have pressed the courts to make the ostensibly white plaintiffs prove that their own blood is "entirely that of the white race."

An increasing number of covenants in midwestern cities have directly proscribed Jews, and still others have been drawn up with what look like attempts to bar Jehovah's Witnesses and other dissident religious sects. Proscriptions against non-Caucasian use of land are on the increase everywhere.

There are numerous sizable suburban cities in which it is boasted that no "non-Caucasian" may live except as the employe of a white occupant, and Chambers of Commerce in those cities will gladly furnish maps showing complete covenanting of all land. If the courts continue to uphold these exclusionary agreements there is no sound reason why landholders may not bar any group against whom there is dislike or prejudice. Then each city might become a chain of isolated little islands of ethnic or religious groups.

[d]

MORE THAN BLASTING BRICK AND MORTAR

Alain Locke (1885–1954)

Alain Locke, a father of the Harlem Renaissance, had edited two earlier special numbers of the *Survey Graphic:* "Harlem," (March 1925) and "Color: Unfinished Business of Democracy," (November 1942). He was chairman of the philosophy department at Howard University; in 1946 he was elected president of the American Association for Adult Education. A later document, by Du Bois, evaluates his life.

That World War II sprang from fascist and racialist aggression has brought two marked and invigorating changes in the climate of American opinion with respect to race relations.

First came the wartime realization that minority issues here at home were hampering the United States as a standard bearer for democracy. This global dimension of what had hitherto been regarded merely as matters for domestic reference was explored, four years ago, in COLOR—seventh "Calling America" number of *Survey Graphic*.

The other change, recent enough to be regarded as the postwar transformation of the minority question, is the equally momentous shift by which a war-enlightened society has taken on the removal of minority handicaps and disabilities as a positive task of general social reconstruction. Thus, this twelfth special issue on the pattern of SEGREGATION interprets prejudice and discriminatory practices not merely as ills and burdens borne by Negro citizens, but as shortcomings of democracy at large which involve at once the fate of such minorities, the social health of the majority, and the common welfare of both.

A mere twenty years back, liberal opinion was with some difficulty making the rudimentary shift from philanthropic concern for the Negro in terms of need—to recognition on the score of merit. With the depression in the Thirties came awareness of the common denominators of all our minority situations, with accompanying gains in both depth and breadth of social understanding. Then, with World War II, followed a rude but sobering discovery that any minority's disability was also the majority's defect, default, and danger. With the unexpected spotlight of world opinion, these things became matters of world reputation and responsibility.

Intelligent circles accordingly manifested a new sense of majority concern and, today, if I read the social pulse correctly, progressive opinion has passed to a sounder pragmatic attitude. On political, industrial, social, and cultural levels, social action groups are bestirring themselves, increasingly aware that their efforts are converging toward a present-generation crusade to round out American democracy.

Social Education

In the field of education, we have too long expected to underpin political democracy simply by establishing free schools and equipping an ever widening number of children to get on in life as individuals. Our wartime experience has driven home the need to augment this function with training both for citizenship and for effective participation in a democratic society. Education, in both its formal and informal aspects, is awakening to this new task of social education, particularly that most vital phase of it based on the situations and interests of minority groups, which has come to be known as intercultural education.

Old as is the tradition of a connection between schooling and self-government, we may just have discovered the most vital link of all in these comparatively new objectives deliberately to communicate our democratic ideals and traditions—thereby implementing their actual practice. We have come to realize that the more complex and diversified our society, the greater the need for common denominators of strong but uncoerced solidarity.

We have also begun to understand how, in spite of a democratic corporate structure, a nation without education of this type may lose both its democratic vitality and its soul. Educators today are convinced as to the need for bringing up such timely and important reinforcements to our American way of life.

A New Pedagogy of Democracy

In addressing themselves in increasing numbers to this challenge, American teachers have fortunately worked out new approaches and a new emphasis. Old and unfruitful didactic teaching of commonplaces and of platitudes has all but been abandoned, and in its place more realistic methods and objectives have been defined. Relevant study materials bearing on intergroup relations have been gathered by collaborating educators, stemming from a general recognition that achievements and shortcomings in minority situations are the acid tests of democracy in action.

On the higher levels of instruction, this calls for critical appraisal of community behavior and the concrete comparison of various programs of remedy, and it is to the credit of the new social realism that such controversial issues are no longer evaded. Also, the limited social experiences of students are now supplemented by educative contacts designed to yield deeper human insight, wider social understanding.

Yet no matter how sanguine one may be about this new pedagogy of democracy, its adoption, especially in the lower grades, confronts hurdles ranging from adult conservatism and community custom to head-on opposition by counter forces of reaction.

Early hopes of practical success center in simultaneous spread of kindred programs of adult education. It is indeed on this front that we must mobilize whatever forces are available, now that headway in teaching democracy has been made in our schools.

In a recent article in *The Journal of Adult Education*, Willard S. Townsend calls upon the adult education movement itself to "break through the maze of many inconsequential activities" to "render a great service to the democratic aspirations of the common people." His challenge is timely and pertinent:

If mass social intelligence and responsible citizenship are of an inferior quality today, the fault lies in our refusal to use adult education as a means of making the democratic process effective, and of giving the people the full use of their mass intelligence in determining their own destiny.

Some Salients in Adult Education

The organizers of the well known Springfield Plan soon found that it was imperative to enlist mothers and fathers no less than children. Harder to do, this was found neither impossible nor unprofitable, although now that war enthusiasms have flagged, it may not prove as easy to muster adults today. Indeed, some wartime gains have been lost, with others lapsing—but all the more, a challenge.

We shall never be able to reckon the tragic loss to this generation of servicemen that, in the main, they lost the democratizing experience of an unsegregated army and navy. However, much casual enlightenment did come to individuals, as the militant social democracy of wide segments of the veterans organizations indicates.

More fortunately, many war workers came within the orbit of that wartime mechanism for democracy in industrial relations—the Fair Employment Practice Committee. Wherever put to work, it proved a potent force for the democratic education both of employers and employes. Shelved for the time being at the federal level, but taken up by several of the states, FEPC laid the ghost of the old academic debate over whether antisocial attitudes can be modified by legislation. It is good news that they can.

Next in constructive importance (and second only because as yet confined to the more progressive sections of the labor movement) comes workers' education. Along with a main goal of labor solidarity, these programs offer one of the greatest of all potentials for training large sections of the adult population in the practices of social democracy. They reach segments not readily accessible to more formalized education, and hold them by a commonsense working bond that has realistic and durable appeal.

Labor union pressures and techniques, moreover, have demonstrated singular ability to break down long established prejudice and segregation in the South. Similarly, came such common cause movements as the Southern Congress of Human Welfare, the Society for the Abolition of the Poll Tax, and the Farm Tenants' Union. Based on constructive democratic action, they are consistently interracial in commitment and practice. To the Negro minority, they stand out as newly won bases of vital and self-respecting liaison.

It is often forgotten that many minorities, especially the Negro, need the discipline and enlargement of the common cause type of movement to become broadly democratic themselves in viewpoint and action. Obviously, such movements serve as touchstones of genuine and convinced liberalism for those of the majority who take part in them. From either side they weld a democratic front that is as new as it is progressive. It is these integrated movements that in the near future will give segregation itself strongest and perhaps final opposition.

In the Church

Current signs of ferment among both Protestants and Catholics indicate renewed efforts to overcome segregation in its most paradoxical precinct—the Church. Recent liberal pronouncements, such as those of the Federal Council of Churches, the Catholic Committee for Social Action and the Council of Catholic Bishops, the United Council of Church Women, the Conference of Christians and Jews, the Malvern and the Delaware Conferences are heartening. Any large scale development of interracial churches depends, however, on a lay educational campaign that would make common cause with other moves to liquidate segregation.

As Buell Gallagher puts it in "Color and Conscience":

If we want integrated churches, the most effective way is to draw the membership from integrated communities. Once segregation in residential matters is eliminated, each church, [each school, we might add] then normally serves the people of its neighborhood, becoming inclusive because it is in a neighborhood that is no longer exclusive.... Such churches are springing up in different parts of the nation: they are not mere experiments, they are a prophecy.

The New Outlook

These trends toward greater democracy in race relations breach segregation and discrimination at many points, but they do not sweep over them. For this, they lack what is most necessary—concerted attack. Social reason not just commonsense expediency, militant democratic convictions not just piecemeal reforms, must be marshalled to the assault. Only by an encompassing and well organized siege of the ancient and stubborn Jericho walls of prejudice will these, as in the old symbolic story, really come tumbling down.

But for our immediate encouragement in combating segregation, recent experiences prove that large groups of adults, even in the South, can learn to overcome racial feelings in furthering mutual interests. Such fragmentary gains can and must be welded into a common front.

It is at this point that we can see the role and the long run prospects of the newly inaugurated program in American education for implementing thoroughgoing democracy in human relations. If carried through, this will bring to the fore a younger generation, who will add to the pragmatic forces of special interest and expediency the force of new doctrinal imperatives of democratic conviction and insight.

Our historic evolution in the United States has moved forward in three successive phases: first, in the struggle for political rights and liberties; then, for economic and social justice; and now, for social democracy in human relationships. The French founders of democratic thought foresaw the vital unity of this sequence when they made liberty and equality culminate in fraternity.

[e]

HUMAN, ALL TOO HUMAN

E. Franklin Frazier (1894–1962)

Frazier had been director of the Atlanta School of Social Work and a professor of sociology at Fisk University. At the time of the publication of this essay he was head of the sociology department at Howard University.

Behind the walls of segregation that prevent the Negro from participating fully in American life, an organized life has grown up similar to that in the larger white community. There are institutions, such as the church and fraternal societies, which are deeply rooted in the culture and traditions of the Negro. There are the more consciously planned business enterprises and professional associations.

Then there are institutions and organizations, notably the schools, which embody both cultural and material interests. Some of these agencies have grown out of the long history of the race, while others represent changing adjustments to the pattern of segregation. The various institutions and organizations reflect the economic and social stratification of the Negro community which owes its character largely to economic discrimination and to the isolation of its members from their fellow Americans.

All these various bodies—even the class structure itself—have become vested interests, of a sort, for some elements in the Negro group. They have become vested interests in the sense that Negroes feel that they have a right to the exclusive enjoyment of the social and material rewards they derive from the system of segregation. As the system is under attack today, it is necessary to take into account these special interests behind its walls.

Separate Churches

The various independent Negro churches represent the vested interests associated with institutions and organizations rooted in Negro traditions and history. These religious bodies came into existence because the Negro was denied an opportunity for self-expression and equal status with whites within the church.

When Richard Allen and his colored associates withdrew from St. George's Church in Philadelphia in 1787, he expressed the opinion that Methodism was better suited to the needs of Negroes than the Episcopal form of worship. Although Allen did not attribute the peculiar religious needs of Negroes to racial factors, both racial and cultural influences have been used since as justification for separate Negro churches.

For example, in a recent article in *The Quarterly Review*, published by the Sunday School Board of the Southern Baptist Convention, E. P. Alldredge states that because of the Negro's religious endowment he should have separate church organizations. While Mr. Alldredge is obviously attempting to justify his racial prejudices, Mr. Allen had referred to something that had nothing to do with race. Sixty years ago, George W. Cable pointed out in his book "The Silent South" that the failure of the white Methodists to incorporate Negroes in their churches after the Civil War was not due to racial differences but to the fact that the Protestant churches had never been able "to get high and low life to worship together."

It is generally recognized today that the form of worship preferred by Negroes is due to their level of culture rather than to some peculiar racial endowment or African background. Both illiterate poor whites and Negroes of like condition always have enjoyed the same type of emotional religious expression. So, separate churches turn out to be factors in the attempt to keep the Negro in the position of a lower class.

Because of the exclusion of Negroes from full participation in American life, the segregated church has provided a field in which leaders could obtain social and economic security. Moreover, the separation of the races has placed the Negro minister in a very special relationship to the members of his church.

To many Negroes there is something incongruous in having a representative of the dominant white race preach brotherly love and Christian humility and offer them the solace of religion in sickness or bereavement. A white doctor may enjoy prestige among Negroes because he may possess special professional skill; but for the things of the spirit, they feel that only a black minister who has the same peculiar relation to God as have they themselves can give help and comfort.

The Shepherd and His Flock

Many Negro pastors, for their part, feel they have a vested interest in ministering to the spiritual needs of Negroes. Of course this involves certain social and material advantages. Moreover, in the Methodist church organizations, there is the coveted office of bishop, which not only provides a good living but confers considerable authority over large numbers of people. This concentration of power within a segregated Negro institution also places the Negro minister in a strategic position in relation to the white community.

Thus, recently it was suggested in a midwestern city that as a means of breaking down segregation in churches, a white church might take on an assistant Negro minister. The suggestion was immediately opposed by the

Negro ministers in the city. Seemingly, they feared that if the plan were carried out members of the segregated Negro churches would be drawn away, into the white church.

In view of the shortage of trained Negro ministers and the difficulty of attracting young Negroes to the theological seminaries, it might be assumed that the vested interest of Negro pastors in the separate churches would be easy to overcome. Because of the historic background of the Negro church and its place in the life of the Negro, this is not the case. The elimination of segregated Negro churches, in all probability, will follow rather than precede the breakdown of the secular color line.

This is also true of fraternal and similar organizations that have provided the chief means by which Negroes have accumulated capital. Consequently, their leaders wield power and enjoy financial rewards.

Job Rights and Segregation

Vested interests in separate Negro schools, libraries, hospitals, and welfare organizations (some, but by no means all of them, rooted in historic tradition) offer resistance to the removal of the color line. In the separate schools, as in the separate churches, many Negroes have found a field for leadership. Some of the separate schools in the South have enabled their heads to accumulate means; more often they have been the source of authority in interracial relations. In border states and even in northern cities, some Negroes have regarded separate schools as an opportunity to acquire an exclusive right to employment.

Some Negro social workers have favored separate agencies to handle the problems of colored people. The Negro's professional interest in segregated schools, hospitals, and welfare agencies is generally accompanied by rationalizations about the peculiar needs of the race; or the exclusion, real or potential, of trained Negroes from employment in nonsegregated institutions.

Thus, Negro physicians may advocate separate hospitals on the grounds that in them they would have more opportunities to develop their skill and to serve their "own people." But this, too, is only a rationalization because there is abundant evidence that the standard of medical care in segregated hospitals, where Negro physicians are supposed to have every professional opportunity, is lower than in unsegregated institutions. It is scarcely necessary to point out that to abolish segregation would create technological unemployment for Negroes who secure a living from the existence of segregation.

Clearly, only certain elements in the Negro community have a vested interest in segregation. Since this fact is often overlooked, its implications should be made clear. It is the Negro professional, the business man, and to a less extent, the white collar worker who profit from segregation. These groups in the Negro population enjoy certain advantages because they do not have to compete with whites.

For example, the writer heard a Negro college president excuse the inefficiency of his administration on the grounds that the Negro was a "child race" and only seventy years out of slavery. In thus flattering his white listeners, he was fortifying his own position in the segregated Negro world. Imagine, on the other hand, a Negro steel worker or shipyard riveter excusing his inefficiency thus.

The Negro doctor who favors separate hospitals is in a position similar to that of the Negro college president. In fact, in one northern city, Negro doctors, instead of fighting the exclusion of Negro patients from municipal hospitals, have opened their own hospitals to which only Negroes are admitted, with the city paying a daily stipend for each patient. Very seldom, however, is the vested interest of the Negro professional man in segregation so patently opposed to the interests of his racial group.

Negro Enterprises

The institutions and organizations embodying the more material interests of the Negro have never acquired great importance because they have had to compete with similar institutions in the larger white community. This is shown especially in regard to business establishments. Negro enterprises are no more significant today as a source of income for Negroes than they were fifty years ago when the Negro began to place so much faith in them as a means of economic salvation. Nevertheless, these organizations represent vested interests, and since every such interest by its very nature is opposed to competition, it is in this field that the Negro's vested interest in segregation finds its clearest expression.

But as a rule, Negro businesses are not willing to compete with businesses generally; they expect the Negro public to support them because of "race pride." Colored people are told that Negro enterprises are rendering a service to the "race." In fact, however, the majority of Negro businesses are operated by the owners themselves, and therefore provide few, if any, jobs for Negro workers. Moreover, patrons of these enterprises usually have to pay high prices for inferior goods and services.

Negro restaurants in the black ghettos of our cities are a striking example of this fact. Not only are Negro patrons forced to pay higher prices than are charged in comparable white restaurants but they must often tolerate poor service and outright incivility on the part of the employes. The chief benefits of Negro enterprises are enjoyed by the operators who have a monopoly on services which Negroes cannot get elsewhere.

If segregation were eliminated, the social justification for the existence of Negro business would vanish and Negro businessmen would have to compete with other businessmen. Undoubtedly, many Negro enterprises would disappear, along with the sentimental justification which helps support them.

Negro insurance companies and newspapers are the largest and most successful business undertakings among Negroes. Both provide employment for Negro white collar workers, both have enabled a few Negroes to acquire enough wealth to maintain the standards of the moderately well-to-do.

If segregation were abolished, the efficient white collar workers would probably be absorbed in the business enterprises of the community—but the Negro entrepreneurs would no longer enjoy the vested interest which segregation provides. Despite all the talk about discrimination on the part of white insurance companies, their rates are lower than those of insurance companies which are compelled to use actuarial tables based solely upon the life expectancy of Negroes.

Segregation and discrimination provide prime reasons for the existence of Negro newspapers. In fact, they thrive upon the injustice under which Negroes suffer. The integration of the Negro into American life offers a threat to their very existence.

During the war, there was a growing disposition on the part of white papers to handle news about Negroes just as they handled similar items concerning white people. On one occasion when white papers were about to carry a story of a distinguished achievement of Negroes in the military forces, they were requested to withhold the story until Negro newspapers had carried it.

The Question of Status

The class structure which has grown up in segregated Negro communities is due partly to discrimination in employment and partly to the social isolation of the Negro. Consequently, occupations and incomes of the Negro community do not have the same relation to the social status as they do in the white community. Persons whose jobs and resources would place them in the middle class, or perhaps lower middle class, in the white community are at the top of the social pyramid in the Negro community. Further, a fair complexion often plays an important role in social distinctions and preeminence among Negroes.

The extent to which certain occupations, a fairly secure income, or a light complexion cause some colored people to attempt a leisured, upper class style of living depends upon the degree of isolation of the Negro community. In northern cities where the Negro professional and white collar workers often associate freely with whites of similar occupations, they are more likely to conform to middle class standards. But where the Negro community is completely segregated, as in border and southern cities, the professional and white collar workers are more likely to assume an upper class style of life.

As members of the "aristocracy" of the Negro community, professional and business men and women acquire certain vested interests in segregation. For example, a Negro doctor who has acquired a certain skill has been known to keep it within an upper class clique of doctors.

Usually, however, the status of a Negro doctor or college professor in the Negro community bears little or no relation to his professional achievements. In fact, he is relieved of competing with white men in the same profession.

He enjoys certain rewards and advantages solely because of his social position in the Negro world. Like other members of the upper class, he is treated with a certain deference by the general Negro public and the attention of the Negro world is focused upon him through reports of his activities in the Negro press. If the walls of segregation were broken down, the Negro doctor or college professor would be thrown into competition with whites in his profession and, in most instances, he would suffer a deflation of his social status. In addition to the organized phases of their life, many Negroes as individuals have vested interests in the pattern of segregation. Although these include certain pecuniary rewards, material interests are not always as important as other elements in such vested interests—the psychological and social.

Because of segregation, the dominant white group has been forced to select certain Negroes to act as mediators between the two races. These Negro go-betweens have acquired an eminence unrelated to intellectual ability or moral character. Oftentimes Negroes have been chosen for this role because they lacked these very qualities. But as long as they played the role assigned them by white individuals and organizations, they have been "built up" as great "interracial statesmen" or great "intellectual leaders" or great "spiritual leaders." Simply because of their strategic position in the pattern of segregation, they have enjoyed prestige and power among Negroes and whites as well. If there had not been a pattern of racial segregation, many of these mediators would have become faithful servants, successful traveling salesmen or small town revivalists.

Double Standards of Achievement

The pattern of segregation has created generally an attitude of tender condescension on the part of many whites toward the Negro. This is shown especially in the exaggerated evaluation of the Negro's intellectual and artistic achievements. In fact, it is difficult to obtain an objective appraisal of the work of Negro students and artists. A foreign visitor once said to the writer that he was tired of being told that a certain Negro was a great scholar when it was obvious that he had a mediocre mind and had not produced any outstanding work. Such designations as "Negro psychologist" or "Negro artist" reveal the double standard implicit in the criticism of the work of Negroes by whites.

The achievements of Negroes in scholarship and the arts are most likely to be overvalued when they conform to what whites think Negroes should study, write, or paint. These warped estimates of the work of Negroes form a part of the folklore of race relations which has grown out of segregation. The road to distinction and to more concrete rewards in the segregated Negro world is not as rough as whites who invest the Negro with pathos think it is.

The segregated Negro community, which is essentially a pathological phenomenon in American life, has given certain Negroes a vested interest in segregation—involving more than dollars-and-cents consideration. As the walls of segregation "come tumbling down," the Negro will lose all these petty advantages. If this results in the social and psychological deflation of some, it will nevertheless cause Negroes generally to acquire a saner conception of themselves and of their role in American society. Through the same process, white people will come to regard Negroes as human beings like themselves and to make a more realistic appraisal of their personalities and of their work.

Survey Graphic, January 1947, vol. 26, pp. 39–43.

33

BLACK WOMEN WORKERS SPEAK (1947)

by Estelle Flowers and Moranda Smith

In the 1930s serious organizing efforts of rural and urban workers in the South were undertaken by Left—socialist and Communist—forces. The war placed such efforts in abeyance, but immediately after its conclusion union movements again appeared in the South. Strikes against giant tobacco companies occurred, beginning in 1946 in South Carolina and North Carolina. Those in Winston-Salem in 1947–49 were very hard fought and produced significant labor and political consciousness, especially among African-American women and men. Testimony from two of these women workers follows:

[a]

WHY I NEED A PAY RAISE

by Estelle Flowers

Sister Estelle Flowers works at the Piedmont Leaf Tobacco Company in North Carolina and makes $21 a week. Mrs. Flowers has four children and is their sole support. "Food takes about all of my wages," she says. "What do we eat? Beans, collards, cornbread. I can't afford milk for the children. My six months old baby has to have milk—one can of evaporated milk—15¢ a can a day. It takes $2 a week for coal and that doesn't keep the home warm. What would I do with more wages? Buy the clothes the children need—more food and I could give more to the church."

FTA News, January 15, 1947.

[b]

Moranda Smith

Moranda Smith (1915–50), the now legendary figure in southern labor history, when educational director of the Food and Tobacco Workers Union (CIO) in North Carolina, spoke at the October 1947 Convention of the CIO:

I work for the R. J. Reynolds Tobacco Company in Winston-Salem, North Carolina. I want to say a few words on this resolution for the reason that I come from the South and I live in the South. I live where men are lynched, and the people that lynch them are still free.

The Taft-Hartley Bill to Local 22 in Winston-Salem is an old, old story. The Taft-Hartley Bill was put before the workers in Winston-Salem about four years ago when the CIO came to Winston-Salem to organize the unorganized workers in the R. J. Reynolds Tobacco plant. We were faced at that time with a lot of court actions. They tried to put fear into the hearts of the workingmen in Winston-Salem.

One of the things in the Constitution of the United States is a guarantee to a human being, regardless of his race, creed or color, of freedom from fear. I say the Taft-Hartley Bill is nothing new to us. When men are lynched, and when men try to strike and walk the picket line, the only weapons that the workers in America, especially in the South, have to protect themselves is action. When they are put in jail, they must protect themselves. If that is the protection of democracy in the United States of America I say it is not enough.

I want to emphasize a few of the things that you have in this resolution. Too long have the Negro people of the South and other workers in America heard a lot of words read to them. It is time for action, and I am now wondering if the CIO is going to stop and do some of the things by action. You talk about political action and you talk about politics. How can there be any action when the Negroes in the South are not allowed to vote? Too long have the workers in the South stopped and looked to Congress for protection. We no longer look to the government in Washington for protection. It has failed. Today we are looking for an organization that says they are organized to fight for the freedom of all men regardless of race, creed or color, and that is the CIO.

I will tell you this and perhaps it will interest you. To the Negro workers in Winston-Salem it means a great deal. They told us, "You cannot vote for this and you cannot vote for that." But last May in the city of Winston-Salem the Negro and white workers, based on a program of unity, were able to put in their city government two labor men. I am proud to say one of those was a Negro. The other was a white labor leader. (Applause.) Yes. We are faced today with this word that they call "democracy." I want to say to this convention let us stop playing around. Each and every one of you here today represents thousands and thousands of the rank and file workers in the plants who today are looking for you to come back to them and give them something to look forward to: not words, but action.

We want to stop lynching in the South. We want people to walk the picket lines free and unafraid and know that they are working for their freedom and their liberty. When you speak about this protection of democracy, it is more than just words. If you have got to go back to your home town and call a meeting of the rank and file workers and say, "This is what we adopted in the convention, now we want to put it into action," if you don't know how to put it into action, ask the rank and file workers. Ask the people who are suffering, and together you will come out with a good program where civil rights will be something to be proud of. When you say "protection of democracy" in your last convention, along with it you can say we have done this or that. The people that lynch Negroes in the South, the people that burn crosses in the South, the people who put men in jail because they wanted 15 or 20 cents an hour wage increase will learn that the workers can walk as free men, because we have done something in action.

One thing more. I have looked over this delegation, and I wonder if you cherish the word "democracy." I say to you it means something to be free. It means a great deal. I do not think you have ever read or have ever heard of a Negro man or a Negro woman that has ever been a traitor to the United States of America. . . .

They can lynch us. They can beat us. They can do anything they want to, but the Negroes of America who have always been true to the American flag, will always march forward. We are just asking your help. We are not asking for charity. We do not want charity. We belong to America.

Our forefathers fought and bled and died for this country and we are proud to be a part of it just as you are. When the civil liberties of Negroes in the South are interfered with [and] you do nothing about it, I say to you you are untrue to the traditions of America. You have got to get up and do something in action, as I have said before and not by mere words. So we are looking forward to your help and we call on you, because we have called on you before and you have given us aid. We will call on you again, and we ask you not to fail us.

Gerda Lerner, ed., *Black Women in White America: A Documentary History* (New York: Pantheon, 1972), pp. 267–71.

34

RACIAL DISCRIMINATION IN GOVERNMENT AGENCIES (1947)

by Thomas Richardson

President Truman, by Executive Order 9808, issued December 5, 1946, established the President's Committee on Civil Rights. He ordered that "the Committee shall make a report of its studies to the President in writing, and shall in particular make recommendations with respect to the adoption or establishment, by legislation or otherwise, of more adequate and effective means and procedures for the protection of the civil rights of the people of the United States."

On the committee were fifteen people; its chairman was Charles E. Wilson, chief officer of General Motors. Two black people were on the committee: Sadie T. Alexander and Channing Tobias.

The committee met ten times from January to September 1947 and heard about twenty witnesses. In November 1947, its report, "To Secure These Rights"—a book of 178 pages—was issued by the Government Printing Office. It remains pertinent today.

One of the witnesses who testified was Thomas Richardson, then international vice-president of the United Public Workers, CIO. His testimony is published below from a mimeographed copy in the editor's possession.

Job discrimination by Government against minority groups, particularly Negroes, has reached serious and alarming levels. The subtlety with which this discrimination is being practiced does not reduce in the least its wide-spread effectiveness and makes it all the more sinister. The inclinations of the Civil Service Commission and other authorities to deny the existence of racial discrimination permits those prejudiced persons who conduct such practices to work with additional freedom.

As a result, thousands of Negroes are suffering serious economic hardships. Bitterness and disillusionment on the part of Negroes concerning Government's protestations that every citizen has a right to a Government job according to his ability is growing. And the great feeling of unity between Negro and White which was achieved during the war is being rapidly erased.

I. *Sharp discrimination against employment of Negroes in Government in the pre-war period.*

Until the beginning of the war, the right of minority groups, particularly Negroes, to Government jobs according to their ability, was in large measure simply an academic one. The major sections of Government employment were lily-white, with the exception of the custodial workers, many of whom were Negroes with Bachelor, Master and PHD degrees. This condition arose because of the Government's unwillingness to make the right to a Government job according to ability more than just an academic right. Moreover, the Civil Service Commission regulations and procedures were so constructed as to make it possible for prejudiced hiring officers to give full vent to their desire to keep Negroes out of Government jobs.

The July 1945 report of the President's FEPC shows that in 1938 only 10% of all Negroes employed in Government held jobs other than custodial. The well-known fact that large numbers of Negro college graduates had taken and passed Civil Service examinations for clerical and professional jobs in the '30's and the significant number of Negroes with college training in the custodial force indicates that it was not a lack of qualifications which kept these people in jobs below their abilities.

II. *Negro job gains in Government during the war years.*

With the tremendous job of conversion from peacetime to wartime operations, Government agencies encountered a serious manpower problem. Many of the government agencies which heretofore had not employed Negroes in clerical and professional categories were forced to do so because of manpower pressures, the activities of President Roosevelt's FEPC, the activities of the CIO and a strong public sentiment. In addition, the creation of many war agencies which operated under a more liberal personnel policy than the old-line agencies, brought about the hiring of additional Negroes in jobs other than custodial.

The total number of Negroes employed in Government during the war rose to an unprecedented total of 300,000 as compared to approximately 40,000 before the war. (These figures include industrial as well as white-collar workers). It is universally acknowledged that these employees performed their duties capably and efficiently.

The fact that the size of Negro employment in the white-collar grades increased so considerably, indicates not only that Negroes were ready and willing to serve their country during its period of crisis, but also that they had always been available and that the only reason their skills and abilities had not been used by the

Government service before on such a scale was the unprincipled and prejudiced discrimination against them as a minority group.

Never before in the history of this country had its Government service come so close to reflecting the basic principles and rights set down in our Nation's constitution. The unprecedented job gains made by Negro citizens in Government employment was an achievement of which Government and the nation should well be proud. For here in concrete terms were made real the rights of "life, liberty and the pursuit of happiness" regardless of race, color or religion.

III. *Wiping out of Negro job gains in Government in the post-war period.*

However, the major portion of the job gains made by Negroes in Government employment during the war came in the "War Service" category; that is, the major portion of the clerical and professional workers were hired for the duration and six months. Moreover, in the main, they were hired by the War Agencies which, on the whole, operated under more liberal personnel policies than did the old-line Agencies. Since V-E Day, these Agencies have been rapidly liquidating, thus cutting Negro employment by large numbers.

For the Negro War Service government workers who wished to make a career out of Government work, it was necessary to secure a job in another Government agency which was hiring. The major Agencies doing the hiring during this period were the permanent, old-line Agencies which, before the war, had exhibited such reluctance to hire Negro clerical and professional workers.

Consequently, when the Negro clerical or professional worker, laid off from a War Agency, attempted to secure employment in an old-line Agency, he began to run into the subtle but effective Negro discrimination which had been a characteristic of Government hiring before the war.

So, then, we have two factors which serve to reduce sharply Negro job gains in Government employment.

IV. *Evidence of discrimination against Negroes in post-war Government hiring.*

The United Public Workers, CIO, has called the attention of the Government to case after case of such discrimination and, to this date, the basic problem has not been corrected. Instead, we have seen on the part of the Civil Service Commission and various Government officials a concerted effort to excuse the actions of prejudiced hiring personnel and a general unwillingness to apply firmly the President's policy against discrimination.

I wish to present now evidence which has been brought to the attention of the United Public Workers of America, indicating conclusively that discrimination is being practiced by Agencies of the Federal Government. (See appendix)

A. *The Case of the Ten Agencies.*

The case of discriminatory policies of these ten agencies arose when the Wage Stabilization Board, a wartime Government Agency, was liquidating. The personnel office of this Agency sought to place its employees in comparable jobs with other Agencies. The discrimination against Negroes which was encountered during this situation is clearly outlined in the photostat.

I would also like to introduce some facts with regard to Government Agencies which are not included in the photostat just submitted.

B. *Post Office Department.*

In Birmingham, Alabama only two Negroes were included among the scores of temporary workers added for the Christmas rush.

C. *Veterans Administration.*

Regional offices of the Veterans Administration use virtually no Negroes in jobs other than custodial or the lowest clerical grades. Individual Negro job seekers have faced delay, evasion and ultimate failure in their search for jobs in the Veterans Administration in Washington.

I introduce for the record the report of the Civil Service Commission Ninth Region in the case of James H. Miles, a returned war veteran employed by the VA at Jefferson Barracks. Despite this report which states that "a wide atmosphere of prejudice and racial discrimination exists in this facility," the Civil Service Commission in Washington, under its regulations, permitted the VA to appeal the Ninth Region's decision that Mr. Miles should be returned to his job. As a result of this appeal for which the VA spent considerable money—bringing in some of its highest-salaried personnel to Washington—the Civil Service Commission in Washington has concurred with the VA in the decision that Mr. Miles should be fired.

However, even in its decision, the Civil Service Commission notes that "...Charge No. 1, 'Inefficiency in the operation of the dishwashing machine' be disregarded as resulting from the prejudice of his supervisor, Mrs. Heilmann...." This statement, together with the findings of the Regional CSC with regard to the density of racial prejudice and discrimination in this situation, certainly indicates that whatever Mr. Miles' actions were, he was driven to them by the determination of his supervisor to drive him from his job because he was a returned Negro veteran who did not propose to tolerate the contemptuous treatment accorded him and other Negroes at this facility. Moreover, it is apparent that the Civil Service Commission ignored the findings of its Regional Office and cooperated with the Veterans Administration in this discrimination.

D. *State Department.*

This Department has had one of the worst pre-war records on discrimination. Ironically enough, it applied to the FEPC itself during the last days of that Agency, for an employee qualified for fiscal work and specified "White only." Upon inquiry, this specification was expanded in the following words: "Just didn't think of a colored person as being able to do that kind of work any more than you would think of asking for a white janitor." This quotation is entirely typical of the atmosphere in the State Department for years.

In addition to being included in the list of 10 Agencies which I have submitted, I introduce for evidence this copy of a State Department inter-Agency application form. You will note the space calling for race. Moreover, it is common knowledge in Washington, D.C. that a high State Department personnel officer who had taken a forthright stand against Negro discrimination has now become extremely unpopular with his fellow officials because of his position on this question.

E. *Treasury Department*

The Bureau of Internal Revenue is one of the 10 Agencies listed as having discriminatory hiring policies. Reports to UPW from individual job seekers in the Treasury Department indicate delay and ultimate failure to obtain clerical positions.

The Bureau of Internal Revenue in Washington witnessed several weeks ago an illegal and most shameful expression of racial prejudice, when over 50 white employees engaged in a work stoppage because a Negro was placed in their section. The Agency has so far failed to create the kind of atmosphere which would eliminate this sort of friction. By atmosphere, I mean the complete abolition of segregated sections, segregated payrolls, and segregated lunchrooms. The Agency has demonstrated no insistence whatsoever that President Truman's policy on this question must be observed by *all* government workers. As of this date, the situation which gave birth to a race-hatred work stoppage still prevails in that Agency.

The Bronx Office of the Bureau of Internal Revenue, Processing Division, has recently come in for considerable public criticism because of the anti-Negro actions and statements of the Chief of the Processing Division, E. H. Campbell. Here in this Division can be seen the very essence of discrimination against Negroes. Over 80% of the approximately 3,000 employees in this Division are Negroes. In fact, it is suspected that such a high proportion of Negroes are employed here because during the war this was the most unattractive Agency from the point of view of working conditions in the New York region.

Workers are being hired for a six-month period only at the lowest clerical grade in the Federal Service, a grade practically non-existent in other Government Agencies in the New York area and elsewhere. At the end of six months, a large number of the workers are fired instead of being promoted to the next grade for which they are eligible. In this way the Head of the Division continues to exercise his preference for not having Negroes employed in classifications higher than CAF-2. Some of the employees are rehired a few months later, together with many new employees, all at the same low grade—CAF-1.

Many veterans are included in this unfair hiring and firing practice. Veterans who have 10% or over disability are entitled to permanent status. Many veterans have not been given permanent status.

Now that the Government is returning to a peacetime status and examinations have already been given in that region, the Negro employees in that Agency are being intimidated and demoralized by Mr. Campbell's statements that very few of them will be able to pass the exams and that they have no rights to the job which they have filled and performed adequately; and that as far as he is concerned, since the ratio of Negro to White is 1 to 15 in that area, he is discharging his responsibility with regard to carrying out anti-discrimination policies, by employing Negroes in that same ratio. This, of course, is an admission on his part that workers are chosen not according to their ability and experience, but, on a discriminatory basis, according to color. Moreover, since more than 80% of his employees are now Negroes, it is clear that his policy of one of every 15 would mean serious job losses for the Negroes presently employed in this Agency, with a corresponding slash in the purchasing power of that group of citizens, representing millions of dollars.

Imagine the uneconomic results of this policy of discrimination! Not only is the low morale a real hindrance to maximum efficiency, but the program of constant hiring and rehiring necessitates repeated training of new employees.

F. *Interior Department*

The administration in this Department was one of the few old-line Agencies which made a definite effort to overcome the discriminatory pattern. Nevertheless, discrimination persists there. I would like to cite the instance of a Negro veteran who travelled 2,000 miles with his wife to take a job in the Indian Service but on arrival was rejected on the grounds that Indians are prejudiced against Negroes. A displaced employee qualified for a CAF-3 job reported to the UPW his repeated visits to the Bureau of Mines and to the Interior Department personnel office after having been told of definite vacancies. After various delays he was informed in both instances that the vacancies did not exist.

G. *Labor Department*

UPW was informed in the latter part of 1945 that the Labor Department personnel office, after indicating interest in laid-off CAF-3 employees, reversed itself and said there were no jobs after being informed that the individuals involved were Negroes.

To this must of course be added the segregated procedures of the District of Columbia United States Employment Service which persisted through the first year of postwar readjustment and helped to restrict Negro opportunity during the period when a number of old-line Agencies were bringing staff up to normal strength after having been restricted by the wartime manpower shortage. This practice of segregation in the District USES has now been eliminated.

H. *Federal Trade Commission*

UPW recently handled a grievance of a whole group of employees being transferred from OPA to FTC. Sixty percent of the employees were Negroes and it was the intention of FTC to retain none of these. UPW-NAACP action brought some satisfaction in this matter.

The usual experiences of Negro job seekers in these agencies, as well as in such places as General Accounting Office, Library of Congress, Department of Agriculture, National Archives, which have not increased their total employment since the war but nevertheless have been doing some hiring, follows a definite pattern. The job seeker is informed of vacancies in his grade either through the Civil Service Commission, personnel office of his former agency, or USES. He visits the personnel office or individual supervisor concerned and is immediately put off by statements that there are no vacancies yet, that there may be vacancies in lower grades, etc., etc. He is told to leave his application and will be notified, or else to return in a few days or a few weeks. He may be sent to various individual officials who give varying reasons why he cannot be hired immediately. But the ultimate result is the same. Somehow the exactly suitable vacancy is never found for him.

I. *Agriculture Department.*

As an example of how this works I submit the case which arose some weeks ago in the United States Department of Agriculture.

The Personnel Office of the Wage Stabilization Board, still seeking to place its laid-off employees, referred four Negro clerical workers to the Agriculture Department. The employees were interviewed by the Agriculture Department, were told to leave their applications and that they would be contacted. Several days later one of them received an official, postage-free envelope from the Agriculture Department a batch of four applications, including her own, of Negro applicants. I submit now the photostats of the memorandum which was attached to the application forms, along with photostats of the applications and one of the envelope. These applicants have not yet been hired by the Agriculture Department and we have been informed that, although the personnel office of Agriculture knows the identity of the writer of this memorandum, no disciplinary action is contemplated. In other words, discrimination is clear, but the Agency shows no intention of carrying out the President's policy on this matter.

For every case which has come to the attenion of the Union, we realize that there are at least 15 or 20 undiscovered cases which occur, working hardship on members of minority groups, with the perpetrator going free to continue his sinister activities.

The Civil Service Commission has demonstrated only half-hearted willingness to clear up the discrimination against Negroes in Government. Between October, 1941 and March, 1946 the Civil Service Commission handled 1,871 complaints of discrimination based on race, creed, color or national origin. Of this number, it made a finding of discrimination in only 58 cases.

Not only have those more recent cases been presented to the Civil Service Commission, but they have also been carried to the White House by the Union. Our charges have been substantiated by various Government officials. This problem has received wide-spread discussion in the national press and radio. Yet, no apparent change has been observed. Negroes are still being discriminated against by the Federal Agencies.

There is serious doubt as to whether or not the Civil Service Commission is interested in carrying out the President's policy on this matter if it means a conflict with the individual Government Agencies.

V. *The UPW proposes the establishment of a central hiring register for the discharge of Civil Service responsibilities in regard to temporary jobs.*

It is clear that the responsibility for the maintenance of the principle of equality of opportunity rests squarely upon the shoulders of the Civil Service Commission and the Government. It is ridiculous to argue that such pedestrian problems as lack of funds and the principle of decentralization in Government personnel operations prevent the Civil Service Commission and Government from acting to correct this problem. The UPW-CIO maintains that the problem of discrimination against Negroes and other minority groups in Government hiring is so basic as to warrant any corrective steps which may be found necessary. We have consistently advanced that position without any favorable response from the Civil Service Commission. In fact, despite serious warnings that practices of discrimination by the various Agencies were imminent, the Civil Service Commission prepared an Executive Order for the President's signature which gave the Agencies the right to hire temporary workers without prior Civil Service approval. This order is now known as Executive Order 9691. The warnings our Union gave are substantiated by the body of evidence just submitted.

The Union had advocated that the Civil Service Commission create a central hiring register which would serve to reduce the violations of the rights of Negro job applicants. Such a central hiring register would have centralized applicants and centralized job referrals, so that Agencies would not be able to pick and choose according to the prejudices of the individual hiring officers.

Our Union contends that a central hiring register could well be utilized during the period of hiring for temporary jobs, which will go on for at least another year and a half, for a sum of approximately $100,000, a small cost for the solution of such an important problem. The failure of Government to institute such a central hiring register is partly responsible for the fact that there is an unofficial but well-known policy of discrimination on the part of the ten Agencies listed above, despite the efforts of the Civil Service Commission Inspection Division.

VI. UPW proposes that laid-off Government workers who pass Civil Service exams be given preference in the filling of permanent jobs.

The waste of trained manpower brought about by the policy of discrimination represents a most uneconomic approach to the question of Government administration.

The Civil Service Commission states that it is holding as rapidly as possible examinations for permanent jobs in Government. The United Public Workers of America contends that the experience and training of laid-off War Service workers should be utilized by Government by granting them some preference in the setting up of lists for permanent jobs. In Executive Order 9691, a laid-off War Service worker, if he has taken and passed the examination, may be given preference of five points if the Agency so desires. The Union contends that, like other provisions regarding the rights of people who worked for the Government during the war, this should not be an optional provision but that the Government should guarantee such a provision by making it compulsory.

The waste resulting from the failure to apply this policy can be seen by the example of the Processing Division of the Bronx Bureau of Internal Revenue.

VII. *UPW proposes the establishment of an FEPC in Government.*

The looseness of Executive Order 9691 which permits discrimination in hiring for temporary jobs and the general lack of concern and sensitivity on the part of the Civil Service Commission and other Government authorities to the problem of discrimination, presents the country with a situation which will mean the almost complete elimination of Negroes from Government jobs if allowed to continue.

For example, with the return of the "Rule of Three," an Agency will have certified to it three job applicants who are at the top of the current list for a particular job. The Agency can choose any of the three for the job. If a Negro is Number 1 on the list, and the Agency is so disposed, it can pass over his name and pick Number 2. If the first and the second names are both Negroes, the Agency can pass over these names and pick Number 3. Thus, even within the framework of Civil Service regulations, discrimination is completely possible. UPW proposes that the Agency be compelled, when passing over the first and/or second names, to give its reasons for doing so in writing and to make these reasons available to the Civil Service Commission, the job applicant or his representatives.

The Civil Service Commission states that its Inspection Division will prevent discrimination in both temporary and permanent jobs. The Inspection Division is totally inadequate to deal with this problem. It is responsible for the handling of veterans' problems. It is responsible for the policing of examinations. It is responsible for the general application of Civil Service rules and regulations. The staff of this Division is small. It has so far failed to handle satisfactorily the problem of racial discrimination.

The statement of the Civil Service Commission that its Inspection Division can adequately handle this problem is merely another indication of the Commission's refusal to address itself directly to this problem.

In order to narrow as much as possible the areas which permit discrimination, the United Public Workers proposes that the President create by Executive Order a Committee to guarantee adherence to his fair employment practices policy in Government, a Committee which would have the authority to adjust problems of discrimination brought before it. Such a body need not be an elaborate one, but would consist of 3 Commissioners and a staff of seven, which could operate under a minimum budget of $85,000. Such an action by President Truman would serve as a warning to all that he intends to see his statement against discrimination in Government brought to life firmly and with determination. Such an action by the President would come as a ray of light to those hundreds of Negroes who today are facing a dark picture of disillusionment with regard to achievement of their basic rights as American citizens.

VIII. *Summary.*

It is our contention that Government as an employer has the responsibility of setting an example for all other employers in carrying out those basic citizenship rights which are set forth in our Constitution. The existence of discrimination against Negroes which has been described above, is a clear indication of Government's failure in this field. Government cannot convincingly attack the problem of civil rights for the nation as a whole unless it, first of all, grants full civil rights in the operation of the Government service. By civil rights in this case, I mean the right to a job. Otherwise, the great body of discrimination which has arisen in this country in the state, county and municipal governments and in private industry will continue to grow and the American nation as a whole will continue to be guilty of repudiating those principles for which the last war was fought.

I, therefore, reiterate the recommendations which my Union makes to correct this cancerous situation:

A. That a central hiring register be established immediately for the recruiting of temporary workers on the basis of service and experience.

B. That War Service workers, laid off from Government jobs, who take and pass the coming Civil Service examinations for permanent jobs, be given preference over all applicants from the outside, except for veterans.

C. That there be created immediately by Executive Order a Fair Employment Practices Committee for Government hiring.

D. That the "Rule of Three" be corrected to require the Agency to submit in writing reasons for passing over names of applicants and to make available these reasons to the job applicant or his representatives.

E. That agencies be penalized for violations of rules and regulations governing anti-discrimination policies.

APPENDIX

1. Following are the names of the Agencies having clerical vacancies for Whites but not for Negroes:

   Bureau of Standards and the Patent Office in the Dep't of Commerce
   Bureau of Internal Revenue in the Treasury Department
   Public Health Service in the Federal Security Agency
   Public Buildings Administration in the Federal Works Agency
   Alien Property Custodian in the Justice Department
   Navy Department
   Government Printing Office
   Office of Army Security in the War Department
   State Department

   The Bureau of the Budget maintains a "quota" system.

   The photostat submitted as evidence to the Subcommittee of the President's Committee on Civil Rights indicated the names of the placement officers carrying out the discriminatory policies of the Agencies named.

2. The photostat of the State Department inter-agency form submitted as evidence is a "Request for Personnel Action" form. In addition to spaces for information on present and proposed job status, name, date of birth, sex, etc., it has a space for indicating the race of the applicant.

3. The photostatic material on the Agriculture case comprised the following:

   a. A postage-free, *official envelope* from the United States Department of Agriculture, addressed to one of the four applicants involved.

   b. *A written Office Memorandum,* which was attached to the applications. Standard Form No. 64
   Office Memorandum UNITED STATES GOVERNMENT

   Date: 1/27

   To:
   From: John
   Subject: Attached are the applications I talked to you about. *Except for* COLOR—they look like good girls.

   (Signature illegible)

35

LYNCHING: AN ANALYSIS (1947)

by Oliver C. Cox

Lynching may be defined as an act of homicidal aggression committed by one people against another through mob action for the purpose of suppressing either some tendency in the latter to rise from an accommodated position of subordination or for subjugating them further to some lower social status. It is a special form of mobbing—mobbing directed against a whole people or political class. We may distinguish lynching from race rioting by the fact that the lynching mob is unopposed by other mobs, while it tends to be actuated by a belief that it has a constituted right to punish some more or less identified individual or individuals of the other race or nationality.

Lynching is an exemplary and symbolic act. In the United States it is an attack principally against all Negroes in some community rather than against some individual Negro. Ordinarily, therefore, when a lynching is indicated, the destruction of almost any Negro will serve the purpose as well as that of some particular one. Lynchings occur mostly in those areas where the laws discriminate against Negroes; sometimes, in these areas, the administrative judicial machinery may even facilitate the act. However, the lynching attitude is to be found everywhere among whites in the United States.

A lynching, as the definition given above suggests, is not primarily a spontaneous act of mob violence against a criminal. Where the interracial situation is not agitated, it will not occur. There seems to be a recognizable lynching cycle, which may be described as follows:

(a) A growing belief among whites in the community that Negroes are getting out of hand—in wealth, in racial independence, in attitudes of self-assertion, especially as workers, or in reliance upon the law. An economic depression causing some whites to retrograde faster than some Negroes may seem a relative advancement of Negroes in some of the latter respects.

(b) Development, by continual critical discussion about Negroes among whites, of a summatory attitude of racial antagonism and tension.

(c) The rumored or actual occurrence of some outrage committed by a Negro upon some white person or persons. The ideal act is the rape of a white girl. But if the tension is very high, whites will purposely seek an incident with the Negroes.

(d) The incident having occurred, the white mob comes into action, lays hands upon the Negro, and lynches him. He is burned, hanged, or shot in some public place, preferably before the courthouse, and his remains dragged about the Negro section of the community. Ordinarily, in the heat of mob action, other Negroes are killed or flogged, and more or less Negro property is destroyed—houses are burned, places of business pillaged, and so on. There is usually a scramble among the mob for toes, fingers, bits of clothing, and the like, which are kept as souvenirs of the lynching occasion.

(e) During a lynching all Negroes are driven under cover. They are terrified and intimidated. Many put themselves completely at the mercy of their non-militant "white friends" by cowering in the latter's homes and pleading for protection from the enraged mob. Sometimes they leave the community altogether.

(f) Within about two or three days the mob achieves its emotional catharsis. There is a movement for judicial investigation, and some of the "best white people" speak out against lynching. On the following Sunday a few ministers of great courage declare that lynching is barbarous and un-Christian; and in time the grand jury returns its findings that "the deceased came to his death by hanging and gunshot wounds at the hands of parties unknown."

(g) There is a new interracial adjustment. Negroes become exceedingly circumspect in their dealing with whites, for they are now thoroughly frightened. Many are obligated to their "white friends" for having saved their lives, and few will dare even to disagree with white persons on any count whatever. The man who does so is not considered a hero by the majority of Negroes; rather he earns their censure.

(h) In a more or less short period of time Negroes begin to smile broadly and ingratiatingly over the merest whim of white men. They are eager to show that they bear no malice for the horrible past. The lynching has accomplished its purpose, social euphoria is restored, and the cycle is again on its way.

Some lynchings may appear to have a high degree of spontaneity. It should be remembered, however, that in the South the threat of lynching is continually impending, and this threat is a coercive force available to white people as such. Says Arthur F. Raper, "Lynching is resorted to only when the implied threat of it appears to be losing its efficacy." Both the overt threat of lynching and prevented lynchings function to maintain white dominance. They provide, in fine, the socio-psychological matrix of the power relationship between the races.

Lynching in the South is not a crime, and this notwithstanding the fact that a few state statutes apparently proscribe it. It is quite obvious that the constitutions of the Southern states and their supporting black codes, the system of discriminatory laws intended to keep Negroes in their place, intentionally put the Negro beyond the full protection of the law, and that the former take precedence over any contravening statute. Furthermore, it is clear that the political power of the area aims at class exclusiveness. Consider, for example, the following not uncommon public threat to Negroes of South Carolina by a United States senator—the normal attitude of the Southern politician [Cole Blease]:

> Whenever the Constitution comes between me and the virtue of the white women of South Carolina, I say, "To hell with the Constitution"...
>
> When I was governor of South Carolina you did not hear me calling out the militia of the State to protect Negro assaulters.
>
> In my South Carolina campaigns you heard me say, "When you catch the brute that assaults a white woman, wait until the next morning to notify me."

It is certainly true that all white people in the South will not thus express themselves, and some are decidedly opposed to this view. But where a leading politician could hold himself up for election on the grounds that he is a potential lyncher, the presumption is inevitable that lynching is not a crime.

The dominant opinion of the community exalts the leaders of the mob as "men of courage and action." Raper reports an incident in point:

> Women figured prominently in a number of outbreaks. After a woman at Sherman had found the men unwilling to go into the courtroom and get the accused, she got a group of boys to tear an American flag from the wall of the courthouse corridor and parade through the courthouse and grounds, to incite the men to do their "manly duty."

To be a crime lynching must be an offense against the local state, but the propagandized sentiment of the community registered by votes determines what offenses shall be. "Mobs do not come out of the nowhere; they are the logical outgrowths of dominant assumptions and prevalent thinking. Lynchings are not the work of men suddenly possessed of a strange madness; they are the logical issues of prejudice and lack of respect for law and personality." To be sure, the law loses respect naturally when it seems to contravene the powerful interests which lynching protects.

Moreover, the sense of penal immunity which pervades the mob, amounting frequently to elation in performance of a social service, tends to belie the theory that lynching is criminal. A story of crime does not read like the following [from Arthur Raper]:

> Shortly before midnight, with an acetylene torch and high explosives, a second story vault window was blown open and the Negro's body was thrown to the crowd below. It was greeted by loud applause from the thousands who jammed the courthouse square. Police directed traffic while the corpse was dragged through the streets to a cottonwood tree in the Negro business section. There it was burned.

A person or group of persons committing a crime might be expected to go to great pains in relieving themselves of any trace of the act. Lynchers, however, expect to be glorified in identifying themselves. In reviewing one case Ray Stannard Baker writes: "They scrambled for the chains before they were cold, and the precious links were divided among the populace. Pieces of the stump were hacked off, and finally one young man... gathered up a few charred remnants of bone, carried them uptown, and actually tried to give them to the judge."

The mob, then, is seldom, if ever, apprehensive of punishment. The law stands in a peculiar relationship to lynching. Nowhere is lynching advocated on the statute books; yet there is a prepotent sanction in the South that whites may use force against any Negro who becomes overbearing. According to Raper, "The manhunt tradition rests on the assumption of the unlimited rights of white men and the absence of any rights on the part of the accused Negro." Negroes can ordinarily be taken from police custody because there is a controlling assumption that the formal law is not available to Negroes. The mob is composed of people who have been carefully indoctrinated in the primary social institutions of the region to conceive of Negroes as extralegal, extrademocratic objects, without rights which white men are bound to respect. Therefore, most Southern official criticism of mob action against Negroes must necessarily be taken largely as pretense. The jury and courts could hardly be expected to convict, since their "hands are even as dirty." Mrs. Jessie Daniel Ames puts it in this way:

Newspapers and Southern society accept lynching as justifiable homicide in defense of society. When defenders of society sometimes go too far in their enthusiasm, as in the Winona, Mississippi, torch lynchings of 1937, public opinion regrets their acts, deplores them, condemns, but recognizes that too much blame must not be attached to lynchers because their provocation is great and their ultimate motives are laudable.

Such functionaries as the sheriff, mayor, or prosecuting attorney have not only been known to take part in lynchings, but also the court sitting formally has answered the purpose of the mob. "Mobs do not loiter around courtrooms solely out of curiosity; they stand there, armed with guns and threats, to see that the courts grant their demands—death sentences and prompt executions. Such executions are correctly termed 'legal lynchings,' or 'judicial murders.'"

We should make the distinction between that which is socially pathological and that which is criminal. Although these two phenomena may converge, they are nevertheless capable of separate existence. All criminal acts indicate some form of social maladjustment, but not vice versa. In illustration, certain types of speculation on the stock and commodity exchanges may be socially pathological and yet not crimes. If the economic system and supporting laws are such that unwholesome speculation cannot be but inevitable, then clearly it will not be criminal. In like manner, although the lynching of a Negro involves some social wrong against Negroes besides some increment of degeneracy among the lynchers, statutory impotency or even implied encouragement may necessarily exclude it from the category of crime.

Lynching is socially pathological only in the sense that it is incompatible with the democratic Christian spirit of the Western world. The spirit of the age is antipathetic to both the Southern system of social values and its stabilizer, lynching; but lynching happens to be the more obtrusive. Like a society of head-hunters or cannibals where the individual hunter is never inculpated in terms of the values of his society, the Southern lyncher can be considered criminal and degenerate only in the judgment of an out-group.

Lynching is crucial in the continuance of the racial system of the South. From this point of view lynching may be thought of as a necessity. This is not to say, however, that lynching is "in the mores"; it is rather in the whip hand of the ruling class. It is the most powerful and convincing form of racial repression operating in the interest of the status quo. Lynchings serve the indispensable social function of providing the ruling class with the means of periodically reaffirming its collective sentiment of white dominance. During a lynching the dominant whites of the community assume an explicit organization for interracial conflict. By overt acts of aggression they give emotional palpability to their perennial preoccupation with racial segregation and discrimination. Their belligerency tends to compel the conformity of possible indifferent whites in the community, and it defines opposing whites as unpatriotic and traitorous to the cause of white dominance.

Oliver C. Cox, *Caste, Class and Race* (Garden City, N.Y.: Doubleday, 1948), pp. 549–55. Footnotes omitted. The book's preface is dated July 18, 1947. Mr. Cox was professor of sociology at Lincoln University in Missouri.

36

PEOPLE VERSUS PROPERTY (1947)

by Herman H. Long and Charles S. Johnson

This study was prepared for the Department of Race Relations of Fisk University. Charles S. Johnson (1893–1956), one of the leading sociologists in the nation, became president of Fisk in 1946. Herman H. Long was associate director of the Race Relations Department.

Community Stake in Home Life

A poet once complained that the world was too much with us, that "getting and spending," we ended up by having few real possessions and allowed the sustaining values of life to escape. In spite of this idealism, the stark reality of life today is that we must get and spend in order to satisfy the most elementary and demanding human needs, and that whenever any community neglects these, the sustaining human values have a way of disintegrating. Indeed, the unpoetic truth of the matter is that the world has not been with us enough. There has not been enough of its food and clothing, which agriculture, science and technology can supply amply, and untold millions of people either do not have shelter or are crowded into rotted, unhealthful dwellings which stunt the development of body, mind and spirit.

The dispossessed people of Europe and Japan have neither houses nor homes, family nor community. Housing in the United States, unsullied by bomb and cannon-fire, has failed to supply the conditions necessary for decent home and community life. Crime, disease and family disorganization, spawned in the crowded ghettoes, give telling evidence of the tremendous loss of human values and resources. The regrettable tragedy of our plight is that, although it has been convincingly demonstrated that good housing produces sound, healthful community life and that it reclaims and rehabilitates wasted physical and human resources, the full measure of planning, technology and promotion required to meet present housing needs has been immobilized. Efforts of private enterprise have been limited, selective and restrictive, while large sections of the population with the most serious housing needs—the war veteran, the Negro, and low income groups of every color and nationality—have been neglected.

There is perhaps no aspect of housing which contains more important implications for community welfare than the problem of Negro housing. Not only do Negroes possess some of the most extreme housing needs of any section of the population, but they are generally prevented from improving their housing status by pressures and practices which limit and regiment their living space and housing opportunity. The practice of racial segregation is at the heart of the Negro housing problem. The fears and suspicions which it engenders not only feed the slums and augment the ghettoes, but they also present a grave challenge to the democratic ideal itself.

PROBLEMS OF NEGRO RESIDENCE AREAS

In every major American city, the pattern of population distribution provides residence areas that are either predominantly or exclusively Negro. Whatever the character of the general population, even in the cities of the North and West where there are many different cultural and national groups, the Negro district stands out boldly and few Negroes may live outside of it.

There are certain characteristics almost invariably associated with these Negro residence areas:

1. They tend to be located in the oldest part of the city, where the first housing was erected, and thus they contain the oldest and most obsolete dwellings. This has also been generally true of the areas of concentration of other newly arrived

in-migrant groups, such as the Little Italys and Little Bohemias of many northern cities, now tending to disappear because of restrictions on foreign immigration. The difference has been that with improved economic standing and "Americaniz- ation" a significant number of the members of European nationality groups have been able to move into areas of better housing and greater dispersion. Negroes whose economic status and adjustment to new ways of living have similarly progressed have been unable to move out in the same way.

2. The Negro areas tend to exhibit the greatest municipal neglect, not only because the dwellings and surrounding facilities are hardest to keep in repair but because the residents themselves have the least to say about the services provided by the city. The result is that these areas afford least protection from fire hazards, least enforcement of health and sanitary codes, and smallest attention to the collection of rubbish and garbage and to the repair and upkeep of streets and alleys. Also, as a result of municipal neglect, these areas become the dumping ground for vice, poor quality merchandise, and inferior city officials.

3. Most of the unsightly and uncomfortable structures in these areas are owned by persons other than the occupants and are kept for rental purposes. Because the properties lack modern conveniences and have been rejected by successive economic levels of white residents with freedom to move to more desirable areas, the over-all rent levels tend to be low. But compared with similar accommodations available to white tenants the rents are generally high. The situation permits extremes of rent exploitation. Investigation following a recent fire in a Chicago tenement occupied by Negroes disclosed that the tenants were paying more rent for a two-room flat in this run-down and rat-infested building, sharing a toilet with several other families, than was being charged for an up-to-date two-room apartment with every modern convenience in one of the finest lake-front apartment buildings in the city.

4. There is exploitation not only in rentals but also in other living costs, such as food prices. The Commissioner of Public Welfare in Chicago testified before a General Conference called by the Mayor's Committee on Human Relations, that food prices in the Negro residence areas were the highest in the city.

5. Most of the structures in these areas are not only old and in disrepair but are being used for purposes other than those for which they were originally designed. Residences designed for a single family have been cut up into apartments or are used as rooming houses; three-family apartment buildings have been made over into kitchenettes. To the tenants, these "improvements" mean lack of facilities, small airless rooms, and awkward sleeping, living, cooking and washing arrangements. To the landlords, they often bring a disproportionately high return on a relatively small investment.

6. The high rents, the pressure of population, and the low income of most of the families in the area are all factors in the large number of lodgers and boarders. These supplement income but have a disorganizing effect upon family life.

7. The intense congestion has its effects not only upon family privacy and family organization but also upon the schools and other public institutions. The evil of overcrowding produces the further evil of a fatalistic attitude toward the possibility of maintaining high standards of upkeep and service.

8. In these areas are to be found the highest mortality, disease and crime rates because of the unregulated and frequently unsupervised group living on a low and depressing economic level.

RACIAL ISLANDS AND ATTITUDES

The ill-kept and unsightly outward aspect of these areas, with their teeming population, becomes associated in the minds of other city residents with the current occupants themselves, who merely inherited the area in the last stages of usefulness as a dwelling place. The significant result is that the condition of this housing actually becomes the reason for public insistence that Negroes continue to live in it. Whatever the economic or cultural level of the Negro family, the forces of law, custom, real estate, economics, and the very process of urban expansion itself conspire to keep the boundaries of the area fixed and to exact the most serious penalties for the crime of seeking better physical or social or moral or aesthetic surroundings.

Increases in the Negro population, whether through migration or through the excess of births over deaths, merely intensify the settlement in these few racial islands and contributes to the land crowding that is noted in every such area in every city of the country. If a new island or a new extension of the old is at length established as a result of the sheer weight of physical and economic pressure, all the same factors which contributed to the progressive deterioration of the old areas continue in unabated pressure on the new ones. Ironically, this becomes an argument against further expansion. The Negroes themselves, rather than the unplanned, exploitative and conflict-ridden conditions under which expansion takes place, are blamed for subsequent deterioration of the area. For the mass of white citizens, if they give the matter any thought at all, the unsightly appearance of the overcrowded Negro areas is sufficient evidence of carelessness, neglect and a disregard for the upkeep of property; and these are cited as racial traits.

No consideration is given to the fact that the segregation itself, by producing overcrowding and disproportionately high rents, is chiefly responsible for the situation. Yet there is no reliable evidence that, given a normal distribution, Negro occupancy results in any greater deterioration than would result from occupation of similar properties by any group of similar income levels. In fact, a study conducted by the National Association of Real Estate Boards and referred to elsewhere in this volume indicates that experienced real estate men themselves do not actually believe in these conventional arguments which support residential segregation. Asked whether the Negro takes good care of his property if it is in good repair when he obtains it, real estate men in thirteen cities answered "yes," while only five said "no." With only one exception, the real estate men replied "yes" to the question "Does the Negro make a good home buyer and does he carry through his purchases to completion?"

Akin to the argument that Negroes do not take good care of property, and even more compelling in its effects, is the argument that the presence or threatened presence of Negroes in a neighborhood depresses property values. There is considerable evidence that makes this theory questionable. Over and again, urban neighborhoods become blighted and the property values depreciate in response to conditions which have nothing to do with the racial character of the occupants. The same factors can be found to be operating in blighted areas where no Negroes live as in Negro occupied areas. The age of buildings, municipal neglect, encroachment of industrial property, and such intangibles as changes in fashion may bring a decline of values of residential property. Almost always, Negroes have been able to find a place to live only in areas which were already subject to many of these factors. Instead of being responsible for the lower property values, the Negroes are brought into the area as a means of rescuing the property owner from the economic consequences of deterioration. Because of their need for housing and their lack of effective means of self-protection, they can be the means of extracting increased income from old and inconvenient structures.

Where the factor of decline in property values can be directly linked to Negro occupancy or threatened "invasion," it is evident that the phenomenon is a psychological one existing in the minds of white people rather than attributable to the Negroes themselves. The whole situation was summed up in the arguments presented by a group of white property owners who took the unusual step of appearing in court to support the right of a Negro purchaser to retain his property in a contested area, the Washington Park District of Chicago. A revealing statement was made in a brief filed by the lawyer for this group:

> Your plaintiffs further allege that in view of the large Negro occupancy in said area...there are only a certain class of the poorer white people that desire to

remain there; that they are poor rent payers; careless with the upkeep and care of the property; and will pay only very low rentals, and that said property cannot be operated at a profit.

Your plaintiffs further allege that the Negro tenants pay substantially larger rentals and permit the buildings to be maintained from the income of said property; that the buildings now classed as white properties are not maintaining themselves and will result in ultimate financial ruin and loss of property.

In brief, the disposition of white owners to sell at any price in fear of a Negro "invasion" is the most important factor in depressing market values. Once Negro occupancy is accomplished, the value of the property may actually be considerably enhanced, in terms of the income derived from it or the purchase price which may be exacted from a Negro buyer.

The problem of congestion in Negro areas has been accentuated by the vast migration of southern Negroes to northern industrial centers in the wake of two world wars. Although these workers were critically needed for industrial production in these cities, especially in the crisis of war, the industrial necessity for their productive power as workers has seldom been related in the thought of the community to the social necessity of finding them a home as people. Even during the war period, some otherwise patriotic persons worked to prevent the location of public housing projects for Negro war workers or of privately financed war housing for Negro families in neighborhoods which they considered too close to themselves. Each community group defended what it considered its own sphere of interest. The total result was to block the location of housing for Negroes in every possible residential area in the entire city. Still the migration continued in undirected but positive response to the need for workers, until in some of these cities there is a population in the Negro area unsurpassed by that of any urban areas in the world.

SOCIAL COSTS OF SEGREGATION

Such a condition might be expected to call forth the active concern of the whole community. The social dangers involved cannot be restricted by legal and extra legal devices as is the area which produces them. The disease, the crime, and the family disorganization noted in such areas take their toll of the whole community, not only in the dollars and cents cost of police, fire, and health protection, but in the waste of human resources and the disfigurement of personalities. The community's stake in a wholesome life for its citizens has often been expressed, but seldom related in a constructive program to the restrictions which perpetuate areas of this kind.

A further danger lies in the isolation of one part of the community from another. There is an increasing recognition in present-day thought of the dangerous consequences of isolation, both in national and international living. We are spending millions of dollars to effect the exchange of students between countries, so that understanding may develop from the process of living together. But we are continuing to maintain, in our local communities, practices which determine that one racial group shall be separated from another not only in living but in going to school, to church, and in the give and take of daily living which promotes understanding. Here and there are exceptions which prove the rule— public housing projects in which Negroes and whites are living side by side in harmony, neighborhoods in which workers of both races live without friction. It has been shown that racial violence rarely spreads to such neighborhoods. It has been shown, on the other hand, that isolation breeds misunderstanding and antagonism which at times have flared into destructive violence, as in the Detroit race riots [of 1943], where damage, violence and looting were concentrated in segregated areas, both white and Negro, but were almost non-existent in areas where both races lived together.

The very process of establishing restrictions which keep one group separate from the other fans the flame of racial antagonism and mistrust. On the one hand, organized groups have made it their business to produce and encourage in the individual white city-dweller deep-seated fears concerning the value of his property, the safety of his family, and the sanctity of his home. On the other, there are the demoralizing effects upon Negroes of a policy which accepts race as the final criterion of acceptability as a neighbor and fellow-citizen, and which interprets every effort to escape from intolerable conditions as a shameful desire to "live with white people."

In the face of all this, there have as yet been only sporadic and ineffective evidences of community concern to change a pattern so expensive and destructive. Here and there a few courageous organizations and civic leaders have spoken out against racial restrictive covenants and the conditions which they help to produce. Here and there some lawyers have advanced and some judges have accepted the principle that residential restrictions have an unwholesome effect upon community living and should not receive the support of enforcement by the courts. But the most vocal and most effective expressions of concern and programs of action have come from those who would maintain these restrictions. Real estate agents, merchants, bankers, workers, housewives and church congregations have drawn around the thick and squirming Negro ghettoes a cordon of formal and informal restrictions designed to make it forever impossible for any Negro family to escape this blight and depression. The policy is so conscientiously justified on the grounds of protection of property rights and values that the most gentle and God-fearing Christian can support it without moral restraint and leave to time and fate the solution of the family problems of the Negroes within this invisible wall.

Among the types of control which make up this wall, the race restrictive covenant is really the most pernicious, because the assumption that it has legal and constitutional support provides a rationalization for all the other types of restrictive practices, and forms the basis for efforts to extend them. If the restrictive covenant were deprived of its character of official sanction, it would be difficult to maintain the restrictive practices which now are given the designation of "ethical" real estate practices. Nor are the acts of violence which are denounced by the Improvement Associations unrelated to the active promotion of restrictive covenants by these associations themselves.

In these times it is important to analyze more closely the nature and effects of these agreements, the forces which have brought them into existence and keep them in operation, and the social and legal principles involving public policy....

Real Estate Organizations and Controls

The real estate agency and its associated financial institutions, at a somewhat higher level of control, exert an influence which is equally powerful as that of the neighborhood association in restricting areas against Negro residence. The individual firm and the organized body of real estate agencies constitute another instrumentality of racial segregation. The practices of real estate firms in regard to selling and renting housing to racial minorities, together with the policies which these practices either implement or aid in formulating, provide a direct and often final determination of the accessibility of the existing housing supply. The bulk of housing supply is adjusted to the demand of those needing housing largely through the system of real estate brokerage. In this system of marketing, therefore, the application of a racial exclusion policy can and does have far-reaching effects in determining where Negroes and other minorities shall be housed.

The effect of racial policies and practices governing the distribution of housing has been the creation of a separate Negro housing market as distinguished from the general housing market. For the most part, Negroes can compete with other Negroes only within the Negro market, but they are restrained from competition with whites for housing within the general market. Evidence indicates that the Negro market, especially in large urban centers with large Negro population increases resulting from immigration during the war, is one of high scarcity and heavy demand. It is accordingly, a market of facile manipulation and control.

The role of the real estate broker and financier in blocking areas of expansion for additional housing for Negroes and other minorities is finely drawn and enacted at a level of sophistication and professional respectability. It is a role which frequently is not discharged with race as a controlling, central objective. The function of the broker, operator, developer and financier, however, is none the less real and effective in supporting housing segregation whether or not conscious intent were [sic] present. There are at least four aspects of housing where racial policies and practices in the organized real estate field play a significant and determining role:

1. The sale and rental of property to minorities;
2. The financing of property which Negroes and other minorities wish to purchase;
3. The relationship between professional real estate groups—boards, exchanges, councils—and the activities of neighborhood improvement associations;
4. The influence of real estate practice upon a public racial policy in housing.

SALE AND RENTAL OF PROPERTY

The major control of real estate practice on selling and renting property to Negroes is negative. Individual brokers and firms follow the simple expedient of not handling any transaction with Negroes involving housing in white neighborhoods. Some firms even adopt the extreme policy of not handling Negro business at all. The former practice is so commonly acknowledged and widely-known that it hardly needs special documentation here. In American urban centers with large Negro populations both North and South, the practice is almost universal, with variations depending upon the housing market and opportunities for profit open to individual agents and firms. The very fact that such practice is generally known and that it is a much more elusive target than a zoning ordinance or restrictive covenant makes it all the more important as a form of control on Negro living space. There are some examples of this form of real estate practice which reveal its general importance and applicability.

The National Association of Real Estate Boards, composed of more than 460 member boards and 15,000 individual members, is the central body of control in the nation at large in the professional real estate field. It has responsibility for establishing real estate policy, maintaining high standards of business conduct in the field, and regulating practices of agents and firms. Its influence extends directly to its affiliated members, called Realtors, and indirectly to all persons in the field. With respect to racial practice in the sale and rental of property, the National Association has established a formal, codified policy which is complied with in local practice.

In substance, the policy of the National Association deters realtors from making transactions of property with Negroes and other racial and national minorities in neighborhoods which are predominantly white. The policy is written into the *Realtor's Code of Ethics* and thus is given the highest professional sanction. The wording of the code is not always specific in this connection, but its implications are clear and serve as an actual basis of determining practice. In one instance the realtor is bound to respect "public policies" which affect the interest of his client; and in another he is specifically enjoined to prevent the "infiltration of inharmonious elements" into the neighborhood. Article 34 of the code is unmistakably clear as to the policy of excluding Negroes from white neighborhoods. It reads:

A Realtor should never be instrumental in introducing into a neighborhood a character of property or occupancy, members of any race or nationality, or any individuals whose presence will clearly be detrimental to property values in that neighborhood.

Another statement of the National Association, appearing in a 1943 brochure entitled "Fundamentals of Real Estate Practice," specifically warns the broker and property manager against "objectionable" use of property and classes Negroes along with gangsters, bootleggers and prostitutes as undesirable types of occupants. The Association alerts the broker to these possibilities:

The prospective buyer might be a bootlegger who would cause considerable annoyance to his neighbors, a madam who had a number of Call Girls on her string, a gangster who wants a screen for his activities by living in a better neighborhood, a colored man of means who was giving his children a college education and thought they were entitled to live among whites.......No matter what the motive or character of the would-be purchaser, if the deal would instigate a form of blight, then certainly the well-meaning broker must work against its consummation.

Although local real estate boards disclaim action on their part in preventing agents from making sales and rentals to Negroes in white neighborhoods, the evidence indicates that the position of the Board is clearly understood and felt by the individual broker or salesman. In Atlanta, Georgia, Mayor Hartsfield made overtures to the Atlanta Real Estate Board in the Spring of 1946, asking that something be done to reduce the number of sales that were being made to Negroes in white districts. In response to the Mayor's expression of concern over this "dangerous tendency," the chairman of the Atlanta Board indicated that the Board was in complete agreement. He explained that realtors were already under obligation to the Board not to sell to Negroes in predominantly white areas, and that this tendency to sell to Negroes in these areas was due to efforts by Negro real estate men, white property owners themselves, and brokers unaffiliated with the Board.

In Cleveland, Ohio, interviews with realtors revealed that the Board had taken no preliminary action to prevent realtors from doing business with Negroes outside the established areas. However, the individual agents themselves were already adequately disciplined in the matter, and it was believed that the Board would take action to dissuade brokers against such transaction if a decided trend in that direction should develop.

An official of the Chicago Board of Realtors reported that his Board insisted that member realtors observe the *Realtor's Code of Ethics* in transactions with Negroes and that all deed restrictions be complied with in the course of any transfer of property....

The policies of another federal agency engaged in housing enterprise, the Federal Housing Administration, have been clearly segregatory. Insofar as they have, at its very inception, restricted new housing against Negro use, the practices derived from F.H.A. policy have been discriminatory in effect. F.H.A. has insisted upon the use of restrictive covenants in new developments as a basis of using federal funds to insure mortgage investments on these properties. The F.H.A. *Underwriting Manual* is rather specific in this connection. The Manual says, in part:

If a neighborhood is to retain stability, it is necessary that properties shall continue to be occupied by the same social and racial classes.

This has meant that F.H.A. will insure mortgages in segregated Negro and white neighborhoods, but that it will not accept mortgages in "buffer" or changing neighborhoods. The *Manual* further advises valuators that deeds should include:

Prohibition of the occupancy of properties except by the race for which they are intended.

This is, of course, a definite instruction for the use of racial deed restrictions. In another instance the *Manual* further elaborates:

Where little or no protection is provided from adverse influences, the Valuator must not hesitate to make a reject rating of this feature.

Adverse influences include prevention of the infiltration of business and industrial uses, lower class occupancy, and inharmonious racial groups.

The N.A.A.C.P. has fought for the deletion of these features from the F.H.A. Manual, and in 1946, race relations advisers with the National Housing Agency reported that the F.H.A. had agreed to a revision. To date, however, there is little evidence to suggest that F.H.A. has substantially altered its procedures and policies.

Herman H. Long and Charles S. Johnson, *People Versus Property; Race Restrictive Covenants in Housing*, (Nashville: Fisk University Press, 1947), pp. 1–9; 56–59. Footnotes omitted.

37

MEDICAL CARE AND THE PLIGHT OF THE NEGRO (1947)

by W. Montague Cobb

About 30 per cent of persons aged 65 and over today owe their survival to progress in medicine, public health and general welfare since the year of their birth. The benefits of this progress and the chance it affords for increased longevity have not, however, been uniformly available to all elements of the American population. We have tended to operate on the principle that one is entitled to only such medical care as he can pay for, with the result that the best medical personnel and facilities have become concentrated in our urban centers with greatest wealth. This leaves rural areas and people in the lower economic brackets, who need medical care most, receiving least.

The appalling number of physically unfit revealed by the Selective Service examinations, and the loss of war work hours from sickness, rudely awakened us to the importance of health as a national asset and made us receptive to corrective measures. We began to see clearly, rather than take for granted, that health care, even more than education, has to be readily available to *all* in a successful democracy, without regard to status or pocketbook.

Although the Negro has shared in the benefits of modern medical advances, he has never done so as fully or as rapidly as the rest of the population and he brings up the rear of backward regions. The average American life expectation has been increased from 35.5 years in 1789 to about 64 years today, but Negro life expectancy has shown a constant lag of about 10 years behind the white. In 1940 the life expectation of Negroes at birth was 52.26 years for males and 55.56 years for females; that of whites 62.81 years for males and 67.29 years for females.

The Negro mortality rate has declined from 24.1 in 1910 to 14.0 in 1940, but the latter figure was 71 percent higher than the rate of 8.2 for whites. Nearly all diseases which show excess mortality in the Negro are classed as preventable. Conditions like tuberculosis, maternal and infant mortality and venereal disease, regularly show high incidence in any group of low economic status where there is ignorance, overcrowding, poor nutrition, bad sanitation and lack of medical care.

Negro professional personnel today comprises about 4000 physicians, 1600 dentists, 9000 nurses and 1400 pharmacists, a grossly inadequate number by any standard. It is accepted as a minimal standard of safety that there should be 1 physician to 1500 of population. The national average is about 1 to 750. In 1942 the proportion of Negro physicians to Negro population was 1 to 3377. The range by states was from 1 to 1002 in Missouri to 1 to 18,527 in Mississippi. But two cities in the country, Washington, D.C. and St. Louis, Mo., have a proportion approximating the national average of 1 to 750.

Negro Medical Ghetto

The Negro medical man has had to work out his problems in a nationally dispersed professional "ghetto." Many have become so conditioned to the arrangement that too often they think it the only one possible and believe, as is frequently asserted, that one is being "unrealistic" if he thinks otherwise.

The heart of this medical ghetto is the Howard and Meharry Medical Schools. The field centers are about 10 Negro hospitals and about 10 additional hospitals in the North and West, where most of the graduates serve their internships and obtain advanced training in residencies and specialties. These few institutions, determine to a large extent, the type of medical service the public can receive.

None, second, third, or fourth rate hospitals have largely been the portion of the Negro people. This lack of adequate hospital facilities has been the greatest material handicap to the receipt of adequate medical care by the patient and adequate postgraduate training by the profession.

The two Negro schools, Howard University Medical School in Washington, D.C. and Meharry Medical College in Nashville, Tenn., graduate and from their inception have trained the large majority of Negro physicians, (about 85 per cent).

The first American Negro to receive a medical degree was James McCune Smith of New York, who had to go to Europe for his training and was graduated a Doctor of Medicine from the University of Glasgow in 1837, one hundred ten years ago.

Before the Civil War there was objection to medical education for Negroes if they intended to practice in the United States, but it was permissible if they proposed to go to Liberia, which was then being colonized. In this way, Dr. William Taylor and Dr. Fleet of Washington, D.C., Dr. John V. de Grasse of New York and Dr. Thomas White of Brooklyn received their training. The two latter received their M.D. degrees from Bowdoin College, Maine, in 1849. It was not until the Howard University Medical School was established in 1868 and the Meharry Medical College in 1876 that there was training of Negro physicians in any significant numbers.

At present about 145 Negro doctors are graduated annually. Howard and Meharry produce nearly 70 each and about a dozen are graduated annually from various medical schools in the North. The total is about 3 per cent of doctors graduated annually in the United States. The Negro forms 10 per cent of the population and is expected to constitute 11.1 per cent in 1960. Surgeon General Parran of the U.S. Public Health Service has estimated that the nation would need 95,000 more doctors by 1960. This would mean significant stepping-up of our annual production of doctors. Obviously, the present production of Negro doctors cannot keep pace even with the growth of the Negro population, much less contribute to the general need.

Howard and Meharry

It has been a common mistake, even among Negroes, to regard Howard and Meharry as justifying their existence only by being responsible for training nearly all physicians needed by the Negro group. Medical education is an expensive and exacting enterprise. There are 77 medical schools in the United States. Their only ethical justification is the training of first class physicians, a priority of competence, not race. Fifty years ago Howard and Meharry might still have been the only solution to a difficult problem, but this is no longer the case. The present indication is for Howard and Meharry to open their doors to more white students and for the other 75 medical schools to admit such qualified Negro applicants as might appear. It is only through a program of intelligent integration that the health needs of the Negro, which are inseparable from those of the general population, can be met. Over the years, the two Negro schools, isolated and struggling alone, have done a remarkable job. They have worked with too many poorly prepared, often ill-chosen students; with facilities in large measure over-worked, undermanned, poorly paid and frequently inadequately trained; and with hospital and preclinical facilities which have been such as, at critical times in the life of each institution, to have jeopardized the standing of the schools.

A distinguished white medical friend recently remarked that he knew of about 25 openings for Negro students in leading medical schools, the result of special efforts, for which qualified applicants had failed to appear. This is understandable, providing even that the openings had become well known.

Howard Medical School has over 1300 applicants for over 70 places in its next class and Meharry a list similarly large, yet from this enormous number of medically ambitious, neither school will be able to fill its class with first-line applicants. The professional aptitude test ratings of applicants for our two Negro medical schools have regularly averaged below the national mean.

This infers an inadequate preparation going back through college, secondary, and primary school levels. The disparities between educational expenditures for whites and Negroes where there are separate systems is well known. A recent survey of 17 states and the District of Columbia showed that an average of twelve times more is spent on white as on Negro education, the range being from 3 to 1 in the District of Columbia, to 42 to 1 in the state of Kentucky.

These facts bring into bold relief the truth that supplying additional medical personnel is much more than a matter of new openings in professional schools. The recent testimony of President Conant of Harvard in behalf of the bill for a National Science Foundation is decidedly to the point. He said,

The bottleneck of our scientific advance is essentially a man power shortage, and unless something is done about it, the bottleneck will be more constricted a decade hence. Now let no one imagine that, like some of the man power shortages in the war, this can be cured by mobilizing and training for a short time the first people who came to hand. Scientific and technical advances depend on quality as well as on quantity or, to put it another way, on the quantity of exceptional men. These men have to be located when they are young and then given a long and expensive scientific education.

The more advanced the field of endeavor the more wasteful and futile becomes the attempt to justify a segregated system.

State Board Records

The history of the Negro professional schools reveals an incessant struggle for quality. The accompanying table shows the state board examination records of Howard and Meharry graduates for the 44 years, 1903–1946, the entire period of record. For a convenient frame of reference, the same data are presented for three representative schools in the North, South and Middle West. We find Howard and Meharry to have all-time failure percentages of 16.7 and 28.9, respectively, as compared with Harvard's 3.1 (Boston, Mass.), Emory's 6.2 (Atlanta, Ga.), and Washington's 3.1 (St. Louis, Mo.). Not until 1930 and 1935 did Meharry and Howard graduates, respectively, show consistently lower than 10 per cent failures. It is an ironic compliment to the late Dean Numa P. G. Adams of Howard, who was unflinchingly insistent upon quality in the practitioner, as opposed to quantity, that the last four classes admitted under him graduated after his death and had no state board failures. This crudest of criteria, success in the examination for certification for competence to practice, indicates that the caliber of Negro graduates as a whole has not been what is to be desired and indicates further need for continuous, self-espoused, post-graduate study and training.

Internship and Residencies

The first level of post-graduate training is the one year internship. As this came increasingly to be a requirement for admission to practice, there was a struggle to find enough approved hospitals to accommodate the annual crop of Negro medical graduates. As late as the middle twenties, this was an acute problem. Today, fortunately, the number of available approved internships slightly exceeds the average annual number of graduates. A recent tabulation showed 158 such openings, of which 109 were in Negro institutions.

The swift, unceasing advance of medical science has in more recent years made requisite additional approved training in hospitals for two or more years beyond the internship. During this period a physician specializes in one particular field of medicine.

Again special, and even more arduous, efforts to secure openings of the proper type for Negro physicians have been necessary. At present there are 116 such opportunities available covering the fields of internal medicine; surgery; obstetrics and gynecology; eye; ear, nose and throat; bone and joint surgery; pathology; pediatrics; psychiatry; X-ray; tuberculosis; urology; and anaesthesiology.

Eighty-five of these residencies are located in 8 Negro hospitals, of which the four institutions, Freedman's in Washington (27), Homer Phillips in St. Louis (30), Provident in Chicago (9), and Hubbard in Nashville (9), together provide 74. Freedman's with 17 internships and 27 residencies; Homer Phillips with 36 internships and 30 residencies; and Harlem in New York, a mixed institution, with 35 internships and 13 residencies, are carrying the heaviest training loads and their teaching programs conform to excellent standards.

Specialists and "Colleges"

Another recent development in medicine has been the remarkable growth of specialization. To become a specialist today a physician must comply with rigorous requirements of a specialty board. Here, even greater difficulties faced the Negro practioner in obtaining opportunities for the training necessary for qualification.

The late Dr. W. Harry Barnes of Philadelphia was the first certified Negro specialist. He became a diplomate of the American Board of Otolaryngology in 1927. Since, and including Dr. Barnes, a total of 93 Negro specialists have been certified by various boards. Five of these men have died and one, Dr. Chester Chinn of New York, is a diplomate in both otolaryngology and ophthalmology, making a total of 87 living Negro specialists.

Of these 26 are in Washington, 22 in Chicago, 10 in New York, 8 in St. Louis, 5 in Philadelphia, 5 in Nashville, 3 each in Detroit and Tuskegee, 2 in Cleveland and 1 each in Jersey City, New Orleans and Miami.

Forty-three of the specialists are from Negro schools (Howard, 28; Meharry, 15; and Shaw, 1), 48 graduated from 20 northern schools, and 2 from European institutions. They have been about evenly divided between the medical (49) and surgical (44) specialties.

Certification for specialties was extremely slow at first, but the greatly increased opportunities for residencies in recent years have permitted the very creditable acceleration of the past decade. No topical review of this nature could give justice to the multilateral efforts responsible for these still modest advances.

In addition to the speciality boards, which are available to all applicants, there are various "colleges" of specialists of a more exclusive nature, to which the admission of Negro physicians has been more difficult.

The late Dr. Daniel Hale Williams of Chicago was inducted into the American College of Surgeons at its organization in 1913. Dr. Louis T. Wright was admitted in 1934, but the color bars were definitely up and have been relaxed only in the last two years when 15 additional surgeons have been made "Fellows."

The late Dr. Algernon B. Jackson of Philadelphia is the only Negro to have been admitted to the American College of Physicians. Dr. William E. Allen of St. Louis and Dr. J. Edmond of Chicago have just been admitted to the American College of Chest Physicians.

Old Clothes to Sam

In denying adequate hospital facilities to Negro patients and physicians, our segregated social system has achieved some of its most vicious effects. All over the country the secondhand hospital stands as a symbol of what the system means. Let us see how it operates.

"I'm getting a new suit, but this old one is too good and cost too much to throw away. I'll turn it over to Sam. He needs a suit. This one isn't new, but it's better than anything he has or can get now. With a few alterations this will be just right for him. He ought to appreciate it, even be grateful enough to pay as much as he can afford for it. Maybe he'll pay more than it's worth, prices being what they are. After all, for him this will mean progress.

"Sam is getting a little sensitive though. Time was when he would thankfully accept whatever was offered. Now he talks about not wanting 'castoffs.' I'll have to find a way to give this an 'anointing with oil.' After all, this suit was designed and made by one of the world's leading tailors. How could he get one like it—and it's practically as good as new. I'll just tell him frankly that his needs have been recognized and received a great deal of thought for a long time. In his economic position, he will understand that he can't have everything at once and something as good as this is ten times better than nothing. Don't we all have to be realists? Sam will be realistic and not be mislead by any of his dreamer friends."

Rationalizations of this type accompany the transfer of many sec-ondhand products of modern American culture to Negro hands as the brown population increases in an urban community. When the whites vacate a neighborhood or section, they generally move to a newer and better one, leaving behind not only their dwellings usually sold at a profit or retained at higher rentals, but also their institutions—schools, churches and hospitals.

The transfer of residence ownership or rental involves no great problems, being a series of simple real estate transactions (covenants permitting). Schools and churches follow in natural order. The children of the newcomers either supplant those of their predecessors in the schools, or where there are separate systems, the building is "turned over" to colored when the numbers of the newcomers require it. Schools are public institutions, and as little private interest is concerned, this transfer occasions no excitement. Churches, particularly large ones, represent considerable private investments and are too expensive for the Negro newcomers to purchase outright; consequently the "turning over" of these is ordinarily delayed until brown encirclement is complete or so far advanced that the less pigmented Christians consider its relinquishment to their fellow worshippers of darker hue an absolute necessity. After the change, the fate of the Lord's temple, which may have cost enormous sums to build, is of no further concern to its original owners.

Hospitals

With hospitals, however, the situation is more complex. The white community faces two pressures. First, the necessity of disposing of the hospital they propose to vacate, either because a new one is being obtained or because a change in neighborhood, from their point of view, dictates a new one. Secondly, they are faced with providing a solution for the pressing health facility problems of Negroes, while at the same time maintaining the established segregation practices in white hospitals.

To turn over the relinquished hospital to Negroes kills both these birds and several others with the same stone. (1) It disposes of the real estate problem. (2) It provides Negroes with what appears to be better than they have. (3) It appeases the white conscience with the "do-good" activity involved. (4) From the white point of view, although the problem is not settled by this procedure, it is quieted for a while, and may be stalemated for the present generation, leaving the annoyance of further solution to descendants. (5) The cooperation of outstanding Negroes in promoting the deal may be drafted and all Negroes who oppose the arrangement may be vilified as being unrealistic, not having common sense, and foes of the progress of their own people. (6) Any deficiencies in the subsequent development of the hospital may be attributed to the inability of Negroes to conduct such institutions.

This transfer technique, often with the consent of Negroes, who are conditioned to it, is not new. As early as 1931 the Manhattan Medical Society described it. Its extension in recent years into major metropolitan centers has made it into what threatens to become a national pattern worthy of comment here. The guise under which the plan is introduced varies from place to place but the basic factors are always the same.

We shall cite five examples in various phases of development to illustrate the stop-gap, short term, sometimes desperate nature of this approach to the problem of providing adequate hospital and training facilities for Negroes. Our five examples will be Provident Hospital in Chicago, Sydenham Hospital in New York, the Carver Memorial Hospital in Chattanooga, the proposed Forest City Hospital in Cleveland, and the proposed housing of a Douglass-Mercy Hospital merger in the old Women's Hospital in Philadelphia.

PROVIDENT HOSPITAL, CHICAGO

In 1891 Provident Hospital was established at 34th and Dearborn Streets by the late Dr. Daniel Hale Williams, and others, with a mixed staff. Among its chief objectives was the provision of a nursing school where Negro nurses might be trained. The first building was at 36th and Dearborn. Here the great obstetrician, Joseph B. De Lee, became permanent friend to the institution. Out on Washington Park, De Lee "built" and made internationally famous, the Chicago Lying-In-Hospital. With the years Negroes surrounded Lying-In, except for the part on which it fronted. The University of Chicago, on the other side of the park, built its new ultra-modern hospital into which De Lee moved. Old Lying-In was thus a well-designed, well-built and almost as modern a facility as the University of Chicago's building, but it was now left vacant in a Negro neighborhood. What could be more natural than its formal transfer to Negroes? The proper respectable auspices were obtained, $3,000,000 was raised by whites and Negroes together, and in 1930 the change was made with nearly universal acclaim.

Unlike houses and churches, however, hospitals cannot be transferred and forgotten. Maintenance and standards must be continuously and meticulously preserved. Difficulties set in. Affiliations with the University of Chicago became attenuated, philanthropic funds diverted and the status of the institution declined. It became in fact, a Negro hospital. A "shot in the arm" had to come in the form of the newly organized Provident Medical Associates. When will another be needed? Can staff and endowment for a special institution of this kind ever be obtained under the present social set-up which will give it the status and security a first-class hospital should have? Chicago was the first major city to acquire a "realistic" institution, which was not frankly jim crow. The plan in operation has now a seventeen year history. He who runs may read.

SYDENHAM HOSPITAL, NEW YORK

Harlem population expansion enveloped Sydenham Hospital at 565 Manhattan Avenue, which formerly served a Jewish neighborhood. Hospital space being at a premium in crowded New York, vacating was not practicable, but in the face of rising financial liabilities, something had to be done. A plan was devised whereby in December 1943 a certain number of Negroes were added to the directorate and staff of the institution and the reorganization skillfully portrayed as the first "interracial" voluntary hospital.

Our concern is not with the fact that admission of 24 Negro physicians to a staff of over 200, all but one of whom were in the less privileged grades, cannot be considered a solution to the problem of admitting Negroes to the staffs of voluntary hospitals in New York. A mixed staff has been functioning effectively at the city-owned Harlem Hospital since 1919. The danger is that now the public conscience will regard Sydenham as enough for the present and that the energy used by white friends in the fund-raising campaign just closed to write-off the inherited debt will make them feel they have done their share for the Negro health problem, because indeed great energy was so used, without the basic issue of frank integration being broached.

Undoubtedly, the controversy aroused by the Sydenham development has, with salutary effect, alerted many of its more influential proponents to criticism and the potential dangers to which they might otherwise have not been properly sensitive. The stated policy of the administration to make appointments of internes and residents primarily on merit, and as far as possible, in equal ratio as to race, is above reproach. As long as hospital space is acutely needed in New York, Sydenham may be able, even in the face of continued expansion of the encircling Negro neighborhood, to resist the forces which gradually convert it into a uniracial institution.

CARVER MEMORIAL HOSPITAL, CHATTANOOGA

Over a period of thirty years the Negro physicians of this historic Tennessee city have clamored for hospital facilities and grown old with waiting for promise after promise and understanding after understanding with the local authorities to be translated into concrete expression.

At long last an old white private hospital of 50 bed capacity has been renovated and in large measure reequipped, at an expense of some $81,000, to be opened as a hospital where Negro physicians may treat private patients. The Carver Hospital will be under the supervision and control of the local white general hospital. The cost of modernization is expected to be recovered by means yet undetermined.

FOREST CITY HOSPITAL ASSOCIATION, CLEVELAND

In Cleveland, Ohio, normal integration of Negro physicians into existing hospital staffs has proceeded further than anywhere else in the country. Thirty internes have served in the City Hospital, one or more completing residencies in medicine, surgery, psychiatry and tuberculosis. A Howard graduate is now deputy superintendent of the hospital. Six physicians are on the teaching staff of Western Reserve Medical School and of these two have advanced as far as any physician might in the same time.

For some years, however, some physicians and citizens have felt a Negro hospital was needed and formed the Forest City Hospital Association to obtain one. The idea found acceptance in certain influential quarters and a plan for funds was promulgated. At a meeting of the Cleveland Hospital Council, July 9, 1946, the NAACP offered objections to the proposal and assumed that the construction of a new hospital in the brown belt was contemplated. It suddenly slipped out from an elder statesman present that although the site had not been discussed, he and other responsible citizens felt that the old Glenville Hospital would be the ideal place for the proposed Forest City institution. Glenville is a section of Cleveland recently "turned" colored. It developed that under the Cleveland master plan the Glenville Hospital would receive a new building in a fine outlying location. Here was the old, old story again. What to do with the old building? Dress the proposition up fine and turn it over to Negroes.

DOUGLASS-MERCY, PHILADELPHIA

For years it has been apparent that the financial structure of the Douglass and Mercy Hospitals, in the city of the Cradle of Liberty, was not adequate for maintenance of first-class institutions. Various surveys and remedies have been made and suggested. The most recent, the Carr report, recommended the merger of Douglass and Mercy into a single institution which would be housed in the Women's Hospital. The latter is in a section which has become colored, and has new quarters in view. It was pointed out that the housing of the merged Negro Hospital is the best practicable measure in a bad situation.

Well-known additional examples of the pattern are the Provident Hospital in Baltimore, which the Union Memorial Hospital vacated when the neighborhood changed, to new luxurious quarters across town, and the Wheatley-Provident Hospital in Kansas City which was a Catholic school, abandoned when the area "turned colored." The theme with a local variation is in process of recurring in Los Angeles, California.

There you have it. Send 'em to the cleaners first, but give the old clothes to Sam.

Reflection: The System

This review of one phase of hospital developments in respect to the Negro cannot afford basis for comprehensive conclusions. Some things are obvious, however.

1. Under the present plan of privately owned duplicating hospital set-ups, new institutions are beyond the financial reach of Negroes and they must, therefore, accept "cast-offs" under protest, embrace them opportunistically, or refuse them.
2. No matter how auspiciously launched it remains to be proved that the financial burdens and requisite professional standards can be maintained at these transferred institutions over any considerable period of time.
3. Under existing arrangements private financing cannot ever meet the needs of Negroes; hence the question of public funds is raised. We are catapulted at once into the bizarre present-day situation where, for purposes of hospitalization, all citizens are either indigent or able to pay. If indigent a Negro can often go to a tax-supported hospital. If not, for much of the country, he is out of luck.
4. In the light of this single problem our whole philosophy of hospitalization may be questioned. The Hospital Construction Act, as passed, provides no remedy. The matter of Federal support for a broadly conceived and comprehensive plan for health care does offer possibilities of solutions.

Here and there differing factors have contrived to erect brand new hospitals for Negroes. Such cases in the desert of cast-offs are the Lincoln Hospital in Durham, N.C.; the Flint-Goodrich Hospital in New Orleans, La.; the Community Hospital in Norfolk, Va.; and the best and most recent, the Kate Bittings Reynolds Hospital in Winston-Salem, N.C. The largest tax-supported institutions which have been built new are the Homer G. Phillips Hospital in St. Louis and General Hospital No. 2 in Kansas City.

The awkward, illogical, but firmly established hospital system which obtains in the United States classifies all citizens into two categories, the indigent and those who can pay.

For the indigent, public institutions are erected; and if one may be officially declared indigent, he may enter such a hospital and receive the full treatment required for his ailment *free,* at the hands of a staff routinely assigned.

For those who have demonstrable income, what are called private, non-profit voluntary and private institutions for private profit exist. At present rates an ordinary citizen can have many years savings completely wiped out by a relatively short stay in a hospital. He does have the choice of his own physician. Consultants are extra, however.

In the municipal tax-supported institutions, facilities and quality of service range from excellent to damnable. The best of the type are good training institutions with high caliber internes and residents, supervised by attending staffs which include leaders of the profession from outstanding medical schools. The worst are as bad as material inadequacy, incompetence, and political corruption can produce.

The character of the voluntary hospitals is in general closely related to the wealth of the communities in which they are located. Richer urban centers tend to have first-class facilities; poorer districts, inferior or none.

Where good voluntary hospitals are not available, strictly private institutions of limited capacity and type of service tend to come into being as a business proposition. Since quality of professional service must always compete with the profit motive in these places, their possibilities for public service are always restricted.

Service to the Negro

What kind of service does the Negro obtain under this system? In most of the North and West where his legal rights are recognized, those who qualify as indigent will generally be admitted as patients to tax-supported hospitals. Yet usually few if any Negro physicians have been able to obtain staff positions on these institutions.

In the same area, Negroes may or may not be admitted as paying patients in the voluntary hospitals, but only in isolated instances are Negro physicians on such staffs. The Negro physician most often surrenders his patient by sending him into a voluntary hospital.

To prevent this loss, strictly private institutions of limited capacity where rigid professional standards cannot be enforced, have tended to appear, without significantly meeting the hospital needs of the Negro. . . .

Harlem Hospital is in the world's largest concentration of Negro population. Most of the patients are colored. The staff is co-racial. One major department, surgery, has a Negro director, Dr. Louis T. Wright. This service has been the most productive source to date of clinical research from any auspices under Negro direction. The surgical service has become well recognized for its work in traumatic surgery and lymphogranuloma inguinale. It is the only clinical division in an instituion predominantly Negro which has come to have recongition of this kind in any field. This fact is particularly significant because the lament is widely and loudly sounded that research is impossible, where ample funds, facilities and leisure are not available. Harlem is tax-supported, has no endowment and all its work has been done by busy men.

The keen competitive environment of a big municipal hospital without racial bars or preserves is no place for the sluggard. Negro physicians have acquitted themselves well in Harlem.

At Cook county in Chicago competition again is keen. For many years Negroes have been able to win interneships and more recently residencies. Staff appointments had not been obtained, however, until Dr. Leonidas H. Berry's recent placement as a gastroenterologist.

Separate but Equal

The two metropoles, St. Louis and Kansas City, flanking the great state of Missouri on east and west, show the best and the worst that can come of the "separate but equal" scheme.

Despite conditions which had become intolerable in hospital accommodations for Negroes in the 20's and early 30's, Kansas City and St. Louis would not abandon the segregation principle. New separate municipal hospitals were built in Kansas City in 1931 and in St. Louis in 1937. The effort which led to these is history in itself. Both institutions have seen much travail.

Homer Phillips has had the advantage of size, location, larger available professional personnel, utility as a training institution and two local white medical schools with which benefits could be exchanged. The local profession is currently alive and active and contains many ambitious members, eight of whom are certified specialists. The dangers of isolation and consequent retrogression are ever present, however. As a local medical leader states, "many of our men, although desirous of equal facilities and opportunities, do not take advantage of what we have. Nor are they willing to make the sacrifices necessary to achieve these ends."

During the War, three Homer Phillips residents conducted research on burns on government contract through Washington University, both at the University and in the hospital. Beginning July 1, 1947, three senior resident physicians have been chosen to do investigative work in pediatrics, internal medicine and general surgery under the direct supervision of the heads of those departments in Washington University. This is significant progress.

General No. 2, in Kansas City, has had the major disadvantage of being suddenly thrust into the hands of a Negro profession that was not prepared to take over. Subsequent difficulties have prevented the development of a long term program that would give the institution a properly qualified staff throughout. Reorganization has just been effected which should produce substantial improvements. The local profession is predominately an older-age group with essentially an unprogressive outlook.

For voluntary hospital facilities, the St. Louis profession is limited to the 83 beds at Peoples Hospital and the 150 beds of the St. Mary's Infirmary, a Catholic institution which affords recognized training to five Negro physicians; that of Kansas City to the 67 beds of the Wheatley-Provident Hospital, an obsolete plant, supplemented by the newly re-modeled Douglass Hospital in Kansas City, Kansas.

In its totality the "separate but equal" plan is always an illusion. At best it is on shaky and never secure ground. In hospitals the idea is young, but have we not seen what it means in Washington's 80-year old "separate but equal" school system?

Benighted Regions

In the great area south of the Mason and Dixon line, in which Negro physicians are excluded from membership in their county medical societies and hence from membership in the American Medical Association, the effects of the segregated pattern are more keenly felt even than in northern cities where, denied hospital appointments, these physicians are damned for not having the competence good hospital experience develops.

Bereft of clinical facilities and isolated, the Negro doctor tends to retrogress. This becomes known to the patient, who does not develop confidence in him; therefore areas are legion where the majority of Negro patients will seek medical attention from white physicians, whom they believe better, no matter how badly they are treated or even exploited.

The basement "colored ward" is notorious. Here no attempt at an acceptable hospital set-up is made. Negro patients are admitted for what attention the white physicians will give them, often with a single untrained attendant as the nursing staff.

One sees white institutions which admit Negro patients long enough to permit them to be operated upon, but a few hours afterward shunt them over to a nearby Negro institution without staff, equipment, or technical knowledge to supply the requisites for the modern post-operative care responsible for saving countless lives.

Seeing himself unable to compete even against this kind of service, the Negro physican develops embittered frustration complexes. Younger, better trained men will not come into these areas where their training cannot be applied; for this reason the tragic picture may be frequently encountered of an older-age group of physicians, the sole resource of a community, who realize they are back numbers, that their community knows it, and that there is nothing they can do about it.

Postgraduate Training Needs

In such areas the responsibility to lift by one's own bootstraps is heavily on the physician. Where his pre-medical background and professional training have been deficient he owes it to himself and his patients to fill out, in the course of his practice, the gaps which only he can best know.

While it is true that in many places the physician is barred from membership in his county society and regular attendance upon meetings for professional improvement, from hospital facilities and from medical libraries, he can still buy books and subscribe to journals. The difference in the monthly payment on a Cadillac and a more modest but equally efficient and attractive, if less pretentious, means of transportation would build an excellent private medical library. However, we find physicians who change their cars almost as soon as the models change, but who have scarcely bought a new book or subscribed to a medical journal since their graduation. Further, there is no bar to two or three meeting seriously for mutual improvement through the discussion of medical problems.

In our northern cities one may meet the same attitudes and habits on the part of the physician as in the rural South. An outstanding young Negro medical leader has written, "I agree wholeheartedly that our goal should be total integration. However, until such time as our men are afforded more opportunities in white hospitals, Negro hospitals that provide recognized training must prove beyond the shadow of a doubt, to individuals in our respective communities, that we are interested in graduate medical education, investigative work, and are willing to maintain standards equal to or above those of the other group. These have been the problems facing those who are interested in postgraduate medical education."

In a survey of formal opportunities for postgraduate study for Negro practitioners in the South, [P.B.] Cornely found in twelve of seventeen southern states, and the District of Columbia, some programs for postgraduate study, held with some degree of regularity. Of the 26 specific opportunities in these 12 states and the District of Columbia, 9 were sponsored by 7 Negro organizations and 17 by 15 white groups. The courses varied in length from three days to a year, but more than half were under a week's duration. Approximately 30 to 40 per cent of the physicians practicing in the South availed themselves of these limited educational opportunities in 1939–40.

It is needless to comment that much more needs to be done and a more determined interest on the part of the Negro physician will be required for substantial improvements.

The NMA

"Conceived in no spirit of racial exclusiveness, fostering no ethnic antagonisms, but born of the exigencies of American environment, the National Medical Association has for its object the binding together for mutual cooperation and helpfulness, the men and women of African descent who are legally and honorably engaged in the practice of the cognate professions of medicine, surgery, pharmacy and dentistry." In these words, now classic, Dr. C. V. Roman, late Canadian-reared patriarch of Meharry Medical College, stated the purpose and *raison d'etre* of the National Medical Association. The organization was formed in 1895 and is now in its fifty-second year. It instituted its *Journal* in 1909, and was incorporated in 1924. Its 44 annual meetings have been held in 23 leading cities of the North, South and Middle West. This year it goes to the Pacific Coast. A record of registration of over 1,200 physicians in attendance at its Louisville, Kentucky, meeting in 1946 indicates that the Association is very much alive today.

The Journal of the National Medical Association is its most concrete and outstanding achievement. This has been from the beginning under the editorial guidance of one of its founders, Dr. John A. Kenney, of Newark, N.J. The publisher, Mr. Charles C. Morchand, of New York, has made it a first-class product in respect to format, appearance and printing, and a recognized medical advertising medium.

The general plan of organization of the NMA is patterned after that of the American Medical Association. The scientific programs of its annual meetings have been of representative quality for a long time.

The most significant stand on public policy which the NMA has taken was its endorsement of the National Health Bill of the 79th Congress, in which it followed the lead of its constituent body, the Medico-Chirurgical Society of the District of Columbia, and opposed the position of the American Medical Association against the bill.

There is vital need for the NMA to make itself felt today on a national level in such matters as public health programs, medical insurance, housing and education. There is a strong feeling in some quarters that such subjects receive inadequate attention at the annual meetings of the Association because of the political mechinations centering around who shall next stand first in the kingdom.

The striking evidence of need for better prepared medical applicants indicates that the NMA may well bestir itself in the interest of greater funds for all educational levels.

The low economic status of Negroes, with the associated problems in slum clearance, sanitation, housing, and other public health matters, all demand that the NMA take a vital interest in medical insurance, public health programs, and housing.

There is no need for the NMA to govern its thinking by the positions of the AMA. Rather it needs to develop thoroughly its own thinking and programs. In such measure as these become clear and effective, in that measure will the NMA become recognized and respected as it should be.

Veterans' Hospitals

A sphere in which the National Medical Association may especially exert itself is in the elimination of the scheme of segregated hospitals for veterans, a plan which it supported after World War I. The Manhattan Medical Society alone then condemned the proposal in an open letter to the American Legion which fostered it. The letter demanded identical care and treatment by the Federal government as the right of all veterans. A right obviously impossible of attainment under a segregated plan.

Fortunately, however, one separate veterans hospital was enough, and in a memorable conference with Gen. Paul R. Hawley, medical director of the Veterans' Administration, in October 1945, the National Medical Association was in united front with the National Association for the

Advancement of Colored People, the National Association of Colored Graduate Nurses, the Medico-Chirurgical Society of the District of Columbia and the Negro press, in showing cause for abandonment of the segregated system and adoption of a program for complete integration in the Veterans' Administration hospital system both as to patients and professional personnel of all categories.

Herculean and persistent effort will be necessary to secure this simple justice from the arm of the Federal government, which should be foremost in showing all veterans they really fought for democracy in an atomic world.

Legislative Remedies

Facilities and money have been the great obstacles to the poor and the remote in obtaining the medical care they needed. In the 79th Congress, two major pieces of legislation were introduced to overcome those obstacles. One, the Hill-Burton Bill, was designed to plan and construct hospital and health facilities of modern type all over the country, placed according to need, so that the best would be at hand to everyone. This measure received universal support and, considerably modified and reduced in scope, became law, as the Hospital Survey and Construction Act in August, 1946.

The other measure, the National Health Bill (Wagner-Murray-Dingell), was prepared to provide a means of financing complete health care for our whole population. It proposed to do this by increased appropriations for existing public health programs and by wage deductions for a health insurance fund. This bill did not pass. Major opposition was from the American Medical Association. Labor and welfare organizations generally, the Physicians Forum, which includes many eminent members of the profession, the NAACP, and the National Medical and Dental Associations, representing Negro physicians and dentists, supported the bill. These groups did not regard this omnibus legislation as perfect, but they viewed it as the best solution so far evolved for bridging the economic gap between medical care and those who need it most.

Although the National Health Bill did not pass, it has been re-introduced, with revisions, in the present 80th Congress and President Truman has made an even more urgent plea for its adoption than for the previous measure. The opposition has sensed public demand great enough to require it to produce a counter-measure, S.545, commonly known as the Taft Health Bill, which is essentially the proposal of the American

Medical Association. This bill has many major objectionable features, such as organizational arrangements which would permit AMA control of the plan, and non-discrimination clauses which would be nullified by the prescription for administration of the program by the states, and so on, but bad as it is, S.545 makes unanimous the acknowledgment that "something must be done."

Finale

The health plight of the Negro will be solved as the health plight of the nation is solved. The Negro can no more view himself as a creature apart than he can permit others to do so. In solving the total health problem both Negro physicians and community must assume a much heavier share of responsibility. To do this is strictly up to them. They have come far, they have yet far to go.

From this brief review it is completely obvious how badly the segregated social system has retarded improvement of health in the Negro. It is also only too clear, from the patterns which his medical advances, no matter how commendable, have had to take, that there is no real intention on the part of the majority to uproot the confines of the ghetto. Silent penetration with quiet demonstration of merit and need has certain limited values, but the Negro has nothing to hide in aims or objectives. The situation demands that America be informed and that she take notice and remove the entrenched and discriminatory practices in education, professional training and hospital customs which so blatantly indict us before the world, and impair the prestige of our leadership in the health organization of the United Nations.

Dr. Cobb was professor of anatomy at the Medical School of Howard University and a leading member of the NAACP. This essay appeared in the *Crisis*, July 1947, vol. 54, pp. 201–11. Table and references omitted.

38

FROM MASSACRE TO INTEGRATING THE AIR FORCE
(1947)

Several editorial paragraphs succinctly comment on significant events and developments in the summer of 1947.

Massacre

On July 11 eight Negro convicts at the Anguilla, Ga., prison camp near Brunswick were slaughtered by guards and by Warden W. G. Worthy, who gave the command to fire, and who led off by firing his pistol into the group.

The men claim they had been ordered to work in a snake-infested swamp without proper boots. They refused to go. At a coroner's inquest there was testimony that the warden was under the influence of liquor, but this was vigorously denied by Worthy. It was also testified that Worthy ordered one Willie "Pee Wee" Bell to step forth from the group of convicts because "I want to kill you." Also that Worthy had sent for a man with an automatic shotgun and that this weapon was trained on the men. With the threat to Bell, the convicts, certain that they were to be shot down in cold blood, broke for cover. On this excuse (that they were fleeing) Worthy ordered the shooting. The fact that only eight were killed was due, apparently, to the jamming of the automatic shotgun.

A grand jury quickly exonerated Warden Worthy and his guards. A letter smuggled out to the NAACP by one of the convicts says Worthy is back on the job making death threats, and acting in such a manner that the men fear they will be shot "if they even stoop over."

When two Negro men and their wives were lined up and shot to death by a white mob of twenty men last summer near Monroe, Ga., it was hard to imagine how even Georgia could match that crime. In the Anguilla camp massacre Georgia has more than matched the Monroe lynchings. The convicts were unarmed and were in a sort of enclosure. It was like shooting fish in a barrel.

The latest word comes from Governor M.E. Thompson to the effect that since the grand jury exonerated the killers, the state does not intend to proceed further.

And America gagged at Nazi concentration camp cruelties!

Speed—When Desired

The Republicans in the House passed the anti-poll tax bill July 21, five days before adjournment of Congress, by a vote of 290–112. They denied they were acting for political revenge against southern Democrats who had opposed the tax cut bill, but the suspicion remains, since the measure was literally dragged out of the hat a few scant weeks before adjournment and acted upon with the greatest haste. As late as mid-June it definitely was not on the House program of bills to be passed.

The most significant aspect of this decisive action was the demonstration of what the House leadership can do when it makes up its mind. The story is that the anti–poll tax bill was reported out of committee to the House in a session lasting *three minutes*. When the bill reached the floor under suspension of the rules Speaker Joseph W. Martin choked off all attempts at parliamentary filibustering by the Dixie Democrats, invoking rules that are seldom used. Speaker Martin rode roughshod over the opposition and drove the bill to passage.

In sharp contrast to this procedure is the House inaction on the Case anti-lynching bill, H.R. 3488. This bill has been buried in the House judiciary committee whose chairman, Rep. Earl C. Michener (R. Mich) has flatly refused to do anything to get it moving. Rep. Michener has been quoted as saying that he did not need the votes of the supporters of anit-lynching legislation. Perhaps not, but the GOP may need them.

From Congress: Nothing

Negro voters got little or nothing from the first session of the 80th Congress which adjourned July 26.

Nothing was done on the FEPC bill except to hold it for "further study."

Nothing was done about lynching.

Nothing was done about federal aid to education.

Nothing was done about low-cost housing and slum clearance.

Nothing was done about runaway prices.

But—the Taft-Hartley bill to weaken labor unions was passed, along with a bill permitting rent increases of 15%.

Voters should take this record and have a talk with their Congressmen and Senators at home between now and January.

A Good Beginning

Announcement has been made that six Negro air force trainees are at Randolph Field, Texas, receiving their instructions without segregation. This is long overdue. The Army should have started all Negroes in the air force in 1941 on a non-segregated basis since it had a special atmosphere in which to work, an atmosphere with only traces of other Army hidebound traditions, and since it was working mostly with pliable youngsters of 25 and under. But, better late than never.

Britain has just announced the end of the color bar in the Royal Air Force and the Royal Navy. The Army color bar is already discarded. America should do likewise. The so-called Gillem plan is not abolishing segregation in the Army, even gradually, but is perpetuating it. Let the Randolph Field training become the pattern for our entire armed forces.

Crisis, August 1947, vol. 54, pp. 233.

39

"FREEDOM TRAIN" (1947)

by Florence Murray

The euphoria from the victory over fascism lingered until the close of 1947; thereafter the Cold War and the harbingers of McCarthyism ended that interlude. One manifestation of the hopes engendered by the Allies' victory was a project called the "Freedom Train." Since it rode the rails of the United States, this train had some jolting moments.

The "Freedom Train" began its year's journey on September 17, 1947, at which time it was announced that the train would cover at least 23,000 miles of United States territory, going into every state and stopping in the larger cities for a day or two so that the public could view its historic exhibit.

The train was specially equipped, and carried reproductions of or original historical documents on the history and development of the country. Among the documents it carried were: the manuscript of the Declaration of Independence, the Treaty of Paris recognizing the independence of the United States, a printed draft of the Constitution with annotations by George Washington, the original manuscript of the Bill of Rights, the Emancipation Proclamation, and the Declaration of the United Nations.

The idea of the train, attributed to Attorney General Tom Clark, was worked out in May 1947, in a conference at the White House, which two Negroes attended—Lester B. Granger, executive secretary of the National Urban League, and Walter White, executive secretary of the National Association for the Advancement of Colored People.

In connection with the tour of the train, it was proposed that each community which it visited proclaim a "Community Rededication Week," to be climaxed by the visit of the train. During this week, exercises were to be held. A committee set up to conduct the project was called The American Heritage Foundation.

Immediately upon announcement of the project, Negroes began to question federal authorities and the Heritage Foundation as to the racial policy that would be carried out in the celebrations and in the visits to the train by the public, pointing out how farcical segregation and discrimination would be in connection with the train, which proclaimed freedom for all Americans. They questioned officials as to whether "White" and "Colored" signs would be posted at entrances to the train, as is the custom in public places in the South, and whether policies of segregation practiced in this area would be tolerated.

As one of the sponsors of the train, Mr. Granger issued a press release, stating that he had been "assured" by the Heritage Foundation that there would be no segregation of visitors to the train, nor discrimination against Negroes in the community celebrations; and urged the local Urban Leagues to be on the look-out for violations of the announced policy.

"Freedom Train" became a subject for song and story. The official dedication song was written by Irving Berlin (white) composer of popular music. But Langston Hughes, Negro poet, wrote an unofficial ballad, which gained wider popularity, especially among Negroes and white left-wing groups. The music was composed by Sammy Heyward, composer and singer of folk songs.

The "Ballad of the Freedom Train," as the song was commonly called, was sung at various rallies and on other occasions throughout the country. The music is in Negro folk rhythm, similar to that of Negro spirituals and the lyrics point up the methods and pattern of segregation and discrimination, especially in the South. It ends, however, on a hopeful note.

Reception of the Train

Just before Freedom Train started on its southern tour, the American Heritage Foundation announced that it would not visit any community that enforced segregation upon the visitors to the train. "All of the communities are aware of this policy," said Louis A. Novins, vice-president of the foundation. "If any of them insists officially on segregated visiting hours, then we simply won't participate."

The scheduled visits of the train to Memphis, Tenn., and Hattiesburg, Miss., were withdrawn when city officials announced that they would not adhere to the no-segregation policy. Later Hattiesburg officials announced the withdrawal of their proposed plans to have separate hours for whites and Negroes to visit the train, but proposed instead that they stand in separate lines.

The train stopped in Hattiesburg under these conditions, but it was re-routed around Memphis, because Mayor James J. Pleasants, Jr., was adamant in his stand to have separate visiting hours. The train was also re-routed around Birmingham, Ala., for the same reason.

At Oklahoma City, Okla., where the train stopped, a Negro group of one hundred singers refused to participate in the celebration because they were not integrated into the program. Officials of the train announced later that if they had known of the situation beforehand, they would not have permitted the Freedom Train to stop there.

Reports from other cities, as reported in the Negro press, were that in Roanoke, Lynchburg, Norfolk, and Charlottesville, Va., Negroes were made to enter the train from separate lines and/or at separate times; in Augusta, Ga., they entered from separate lines, as they did in Columbus, Ga., and other southern areas.

The practice involving separate lines, which was carried out in Columbus, it was reported, was to permit a few white persons to enter the train and after they had gone a "safe" distance, to permit a few Negroes to enter, keeping a certain distance between the two groups. This practice, was, no doubt, followed in other southern cities where separate lines were maintained.

In Augusta, Ga., however, it was reported that there was no separation of Negroes and whites, and no racial conflicts occurred.

Florence Murray cited work, pp. 346–47.

40

AN APPEAL TO THE WORLD! (1947)

edited by W. E. B. Du Bois

In 1945, Dr. Du Bois began assembling a volume for presentation to the United Nations, documenting the systematic oppression of African-American people.

The result was a ninety-four page booklet, edited by him and presented to the United Nations in 1947. Its introduction was written by Du Bois.

The Du Bois effort contained chapters by leading scholars (black and white) on various aspects of the oppression. It took months of letter writing before the completed petition could be presented on October 23, 1947, to an assistant of the UN general secretary; this was done by Walter White and Dr. Du Bois. It received worldwide publicity and friendly support from some UN nations—especially India and the USSR—but was never presented to the General Assembly. The battles for this petition—and, especially, to get it before the UN—were consequential in Du Bois's departure from the NAACP.

There were in the United States of America, 1940, 12,865,518 citizens and residents, something less than a tenth of the nation, who form largely a segregated caste, with restricted legal rights, and many illegal disabilities. They are descendants of the Africans brought to America during the sixteenth, seventeenth, eighteenth and nineteenth centuries and reduced to slave labor. This group has no complete biological unity, but varies in color from white to black, and comprises a great variety of physical characteristics, since many are the offspring of white European-Americans as well as of Africans and American Indians. There are a large number of white Americans who also descend from Negroes but who are not counted in the colored group nor subjected to caste restrictions because the preponderance of white blood conceals their descent.

The so-called American Negro group, therefore, while it is in no sense absolutely set off physically from its fellow American, has nevertheless a strong, hereditary cultural unity, born of slavery, of common suffering, prolonged proscription and curtailment of political and civil rights; and especially because of economic and social disabilities. Largely from this fact, have arisen their cultural gifts to America—their rhythm, music and folk-song; their religious faith and customs; their contribution to American art and literature; their defense of their country in every war, on land, sea and in the air; and especially the hard, continuous toil upon which the prosperity and wealth of this continent has largely been built.

The group has long been internally divided by dilemma as to whether its striving upward should be aimed at strengthening its inner cultural and group bonds, both for intrinsic progress and for offensive power against caste; or whether it should seek escape wherever and however possible into the surrounding American culture. Decision in this matter has been largely determined by outer compulsion rather than inner plan; for prolonged policies of segregation and discrimination have involuntarily welded the mass almost into a nation within a nation with its own schools, churches, hospitals, newspapers and many business enterprises.

The result has been to make American Negroes to a wide extent provincial, introvertive, self-conscious and narrowly race-loyal; but it has also inspired them to frantic and often successful effort to achieve, to deserve, to show the world their capacity to share modern civilization. As a result there is almost no area of American civilization in which the Negro has not made creditable showing in the face of all his handicaps.

If, however, the effect of the color caste system on the North American Negro has been both good and bad, its effect on white America has been disastrous. It has repeatedly led the greatest modern attempt at democratic government to deny its political ideals, to falsify its philanthropic assertions and to make its religion to a great extent hypocritical. A nation which boldly declared "That all men are created equal," proceeded to build its economy on chattel slavery; masters who declared race-mixture impossible, sold their own children into slavery and left a mulatto progeny which neither law nor science can today disentangle; churches which excused slavery as calling the heathen to God, refused to recognize the freedom of converts or admit them to equal communion. Sectional strife over the profits of slave labor and conscientious revolt against making human beings real estate led to bloody civil war, and to a partial emancipation of slaves which nevertheless even to this day is not complete. Poverty, ignorance, disease and crime have been forced on these unfortunate victims of greed to an extent far beyond any social necessity; and a great nation, which today ought to be in the forefront of the march toward peace and democracy, finds itself continuously making common cause with race-hate, prejudiced exploitation and oppression of the common man. Its high and noble words are turned against it, because they are contradicted in every syllable by the treatment of the American Negro for three hundred and twenty-eight years.

Slavery in America is a strange and contradictory story. It cannot be regarded as mainly either a theoretical problem of morals or a scientific problem of race. From either of these points of view, the rise of slavery in America is simply inexplicable. Looking at the facts frankly, slavery evidently was a matter of economics, a question of income and labor, rather than a problem of right and wrong, or of the physical differences in men. Once slavery began to be the source of vast income for men and nations, there followed frantic search for moral and racial justifications.

Such excuses were found and men did not inquire too carefully into either their logic or truth.

The twenty Negroes brought to Virginia in 1619, were not the first who had landed on this continent. For a century small numbers of Negroes had been arriving as servants, as laborers, as free adventurers. The southwestern part of the present United States was first traversed by four explorers of whom one was an African Negro. Negroes accompanied early explorer like D'Ayllon and Menendez in the southeastern United States. But just as the earlier black visitors to the West Indies were servants and adventurers and then later began to appear as laborers on the sugar plantations, so in Virginia, these imported black laborers in 1619 and after, came to be wanted for the raising of tobacco which was the money crop.

In the minds of the early planters, there was no distinction as to labor whether it was white or black; in law there was at first no discrimination. But as imported white labor became scarcer and more protected by law, it became less profitable than Negro labor which flooded the markets because of European slave traders, internal strife in Africa; and because in America the Negroes were increasingly stripped of legal defense. For these reasons America became a land of black slavery, and there arose first, the fabulously rich sugar empire; then the cotton kingdom, and finally colonial imperialism.

Then came the inevitable fight between free labor and democracy on the one hand, and slave labor with its huge profits on the other. Black slaves were the spear-head of this fight. They were the first in America to stage the "sit-down" strike, to slow up and sabotage the work of the plantation. They revolted time after time and no matter what recorded history may say, the enacted laws against slave revolt are unanswerable testimony as to what these revolts meant all over America.

The slaves themselves especially imperiled the whole slave system by escape from slavery. It was the fugitive slave more than the slave revolt, which finally threatened investment and income; and the organization for helping fugitive slaves through Free Northern Negroes and their white friends, in the guise of an underground movement, was of tremendous influence.

Finally it was the Negro soldier as a co-fighter with the whites for independence from the British economic empire which began emancipation. The British bid for his help and the colonials against their first impulse had to bid in return and virtually to promise the Negro soldier freedom after the Revolutionary War. It was for the protection of American Negro sailors as well as white that the War of 1812 was precipitated and, after independence from England was accomplished, freedom for the black laboring class, and enfranchisement for whites and blacks was in sight.

In the meantime, however, white labor had continued to regard the United States as a place of refuge; as a place for free land; for continuous employment and high wage; for freedom of thought and faith. It was here, however, that employers intervened; not because of any moral obliquity but because the Industrial Revolution, based upon the crops raised by slave labor in the Caribbean and in the southern United States, was made possible by world trade and a new and astonishing technique; and finally was made triumphant by a vast transportation of slave labor through the British slave-trade in the eighteenth and early nineteenth centuries.

This new mass of slaves became competitors of white labor and drove white labor for refuge into the arms of employers, whose interests were founded on slave labor. The doctrine of race inferiority was used to convince white labor that they had the right to be free and to vote, while the Negroes must be slaves or depress the wage of whites; western free soil became additional lure and compensation, if it could be restricted to free labor.

On the other hand, the fight of the slave-holders against democracy increased with the spread of the wealth and power of the Cotton Kingdom. Through political power based on slaves they became the dominant political force in the United States; they were successful in expanding into Mexico and tried to penetrate the Caribbean. Finally they demanded for slavery a part of the free soil of the West, and because of this last excessive, and in fact impossible effort, a Civil War to preserve and extend slavery ensued.

This fight for slave labor was echoed in the law. The free Negro was systematically discouraged, disfranchised and reduced to serfdom. He became by law the easy victim of the kidnapper and liable to treatment as a fugitive slave. The Church, influenced by wealth and respectability, was predominately on the side of the slave owner and effort was made to make the degradation of the Negro, as a race, final by Supreme Court decision.

But from the beginning, the outcome of the Civil War was inevitable and this not mainly on account of the predominant wealth and power of the North; it was because of the clear fact that the Southern slave economy was built on black labor. If at any time the slaves or any large part of them, as workers, ceased to support the South; and if even more decisively as fighters, they joined the North, there was no way in the world for the South to win. Just as soon then as slaves became spies for the invading Northern armies; laborers for their camps and fortifications, and finally produced 200,000 trained and efficient soldiers with arms in their hands, and with the possibility of a million more, the fate of the slave South was sealed.

Victory, however, brought dilemma; if victory meant full economic freedom for labor in the South, white and black; if it meant land and education, and eventually votes, then the slave empire was doomed, and the profits of Northern industry built on the Southern slave foundation would also be seriously curtailed. Northern industry had a stake in the Cotton Kingdom and in the cheap slave labor that supported it. It had expanded for war industries during the fighting, encouraged by government subsidy and eventually protected by a huge tariff rampart. When war profits declined there was still prospect of tremendous postwar profits on cotton and other products of Southern agriculture. Therefore, what the North wanted was not freedom and higher wages for black labor, but its control under such forms of law as would keep it cheap; and also stop its open competition with Northern labor. The moral protest of abolitionists must be appeased but profitable industry was determined to control wages and government.

The result was an attempt at Reconstruction in which black labor established schools; tried to divide up the land and put a new social legislation in force. On the other hand, the power of Southern land owners soon joined with Northern industry to disfranchise the Negro; keep him from access to free land or to capital, and to build up the present caste system for blacks founded on color discrimination, peonage, intimidation and mob-violence.

It is this fact that underlies many of the contradictions in the social and political development of the United States since the Civil War. Despite our resources and our miraculous technique; despite a comparatively high wage paid many of our workers and their consequent high standard of living, we are nevertheless ruled by wealth, monopoly and big business organization to an astounding degree. Our railway transportation is built upon monumental economic injustice both to passengers, shippers and to different sections of the land. The monopoly of land and natural resources throughout the United States, both in cities and in farming districts, is a disgraceful aftermath to the vast land heritage with which this nation started.

In 1876 the democratic process of government was crippled throughout the whole nation. This came about not simply through the disfranchisement of Negroes but through the fact that the political power of the disfranchised Negroes and of a large number of equally disfranchised whites was preserved as the basis of political power, but the wielding of that power was left in the hands and under the control of the successors to the planter dynasty in the South.

Let us examine these facts more carefully. The United States has always professed to be a Democracy. She has never wholly attained her ideal, but slowly she has approached it. The privilege of voting has in time been widened by abolishing limitations of birth, religion and lack of property. After the Civil War, which abolished slavery, the nation in gratitude to the black soldiers and laborers who helped win that war, sought to admit to the suffrage all persons without distinction of "race, color or previous condition of servitude." They were warned by the great leaders of abolition, like Sumner, Stevens and Douglass, that this could only be effective, if the Freedmen were given schools, land and some minimum of capital. A Freedmen's Bureau to furnish these prerequisites to effective citizenship was planned and put into partial operation. But Congress and the nation, weary of the costs of war and eager to get back to profitable industry, refused the necessary funds. The effort died, but in order to restore friendly civil government in the South the enfranchised Freedmen, seventy-five percent illiterate, without land or tolls, were thrown into competitive industry with a ballot in their hands. By herculean effort, helped by philanthropy and their own hard work, Negroes built a school system, bought land and cooperated in starting a new economic order in the South. In a generation they had reduced their illiteracy by half and had become wage-earning laborers and sharecroppers. They still were handicapped by poverty, disease and crime, but nevertheless the rise of American Negroes from slavery in 1860 to freedom in 1880, has few parallels in modern history.

However, opposition to any democracy which included the Negro race on any terms was so strong in the former slave-holding South, and found so much sympathy in large parts of the rest of the nation, that despite notable improvement in the condition of the Negro by every standard of social measurement, the effort to deprive him of the right to vote succeeded. At first he was driven from the polls in the South by mobs and violence; and then he was openly cheated; finally by a "Gentlemen's agreement" with the North, the Negro was disfranchised in the South by a series of laws, methods of administration, court decisions and general public policy, so that today three-fourths of the Negro population of the nation is deprived of the right to vote by open and declared policy.

Most persons seem to regard this as simply unfortunate for Negroes, as depriving a modern working class of the minimum rights for self-protection and opportunity for progress. This is true as has been shown in poor educational opportunities, discrimination in work, health and protection and in the courts. But the situation is far more serious than this: the disfranchisement of the American Negro makes the functioning of all democracy in the nation difficult; and as democracy fails to function in the leading democracy in the world, it fails in the world.

Let us face the facts: the representation of the people in the Congress of the United States is based on population; members of the House of Representatives are elected by groups of approximately 275,000 to 300,000 persons living in 435 Congressional Districts. Naturally difficulties of division within state boundaries, unequal growth of population, migration from year to year, and slow adjustment to these and other changes, make equal population of these districts only approximate; but unless by and large, and in the long run, essential equality is maintained, the whole basis of democratic representation is marred and as in the celebrated "rotten borough" cases in England in the nineteenth century, representation must be eventually equalized or democracy relapses into oligarchy or even fascism.

This is exactly what threatens the United States today because of the unjust disfranchisement of the Negro and the use of his numerical presence to increase the political power of his enemies and of the enemies of democracy. The nation has not the courage to eliminate from citizenship all persons of Negro descent and thus try to restore slavery. It therefore makes its democracy unworkable by paradox and contradiction.

Let us see what effect the disfranchisement of Negroes has upon democracy in the United States. In 1944, five hundred and thirty-one electoral votes were cast for the president of the United States. Of these, one hundred and twenty-nine came from Alabama, Arkansas, Georgia,

Louisiana, Oklahoma, North and South Carolina, Texas, Virginia, Florida and Mississippi. The number of these votes and the party for which they were cast, depended principally upon the disfranchisement of the Negro and were not subject to public opinion or democratic control. They represented nearly a fourth of the power of the electoral college and yet they represented only a tenth of the actual voters.

If we take the voting population according to the census of 1940, and the vote actually cast in 1946 for members of Congress, we have a fair picture of how democracy is working in the United States. The picture is not accurate because the census figures are six years earlier than the vote; but this fact reduces rather than exaggerates the discrepancies. The following are the figures concerning the election of 1946.

UNITED STATES

Total Population, 21 and over, 1940	79,863,451	
Total Voters, 1946	34,410,099	43%
Non-Voters: (Disfranchised, Incompetent, Careless)	45,453,442	57%

SOUTH ATLANTIC STATES

Total Population, 21 and over, 1940	10,402,423	
Negroes, 21 and over, 1940	2,542,366	
Actual Voters, 1946		22.2%
Non-Voters: (Disfranchised, Incompetent, Careless)		77.8%

EAST SOUTH CENTRAL STATES

Total Population, 21 and over, 1940	6,100,838	
Negroes, 21 and over	1,532,291	25%
Actual Voters		16.5%
Non-Voters: (Disfranchised, Incompetent, Careless)		83.5%

WEST SOUTH CENTRAL STATES

Total Population, 21 and over, 1940	7,707,724	
Negroes, 21 and over	1,382,482	17.9%
Actual Voters		14.2%
Non-Voters: (Disfranchised, Incompetent, Careless)		85.8%

The number of persons of voting age who do not vote in the United States is large. This is due partly to indifference; women particularly are not yet used to exercising the right to vote in large numbers. In addition to this, there is a dangerously large number of American citizens who have lost faith in voting as a means of social reform. To these must be added the incompetent and those who for various reasons cannot reach the polls. This explains why only 43% of the population of voting age actually voted in 1946. Rivalry and economic competition between city and country districts has led to deliberate curtailment of the power of the city vote. Notwithstanding all this, in New England, the Middles Atlantic States and the Middle and Far West, about 100,000 persons cast their votes in a congressional election. In the sparsely settled mountain states this falls to 90,000. But where the Negro lives, in the Border states, less than 50,000 elect a congressman; while in the Deep South, where the Negro forms a large proportion of the population, men are sent to Congress by 22,000 votes; and in South Carolina by 4,000.

When we compare with this the record of the South, we see something more than indifference, carelessness and incompetence and discouragement. We see here the result of deliberate efforts not only to disfranchise the Negro but to discourage large numbers of whites from voting. In the South as a whole, eighty-two percent of the persons of voting age did not vote, and in the West South Central States this percentage reached nearly eighty-six per cent.

Two tables follow which show the respective votes in three pairs of states where the same number of members of Congress were elected but the difference in number of votes cast is enormous. In the second table the number of votes cast for a single Congressman is contrasted for a series of states, showing a hundred and thirty-eight thousand votes to elect a Congressman from Illinois and four thousand votes to elect a Congressman in South Carolina.

ELECTION OF 1946

VOTE FOR 8 MEMBERS OF CONGRESS

Louisiana	106,009
Iowa	593,076

VOTE FOR 9 MEMBERS OF CONGRESS

Alabama	179,488
Minnesota	875,005

VOTE FOR 10 MEMBERS OF CONGRESS

Georgia	161,578
Wisconsin	983,918

NEGRO CONGRESSMEN

Powell, New York .... 32,573 in total of 53,087
Dawson, Illinois .... 38,040 in total of 66,885

SOUTHERN WHITE CONGRESSMEN

Dorn, South Carolina .... 3,527 in total of 3,530
Rankin, Mississippi .... 5,429 in total of 5,429

HOW MANY VOTERS DOES IT TAKE TO ELECT A REPRESENTATIVE IN CONGRESS?

IN

Illinois	137,877	voters	
Rhode Island	136,197	"	
New York	104,720	"	NORTH AND WEST
California	101,533	"	
Iowa	74,135	"	
Kentucky	64,811	"	
North Carolina	37,685	"	
Virginia	28,207	"	UPPER SOUTH
Arkansas	21,619	"	
Tennessee	19,345	"	
Alabama	19,943	"	
Texas	16,542	"	
Georgia	16,158	"	
Louisiana	13,251	"	LOWER SOUTH
Mississippi	7,148	"	
South Carolina	4,393	"	

In other words while this nation is trying to carry on the government of the United States by democratic methods, it is not succeeding because of the premium which we put on the disfranchisement of the voters of the South. Moreover, by the political power based on this disfranchised vote the rulers of this nation are chosen and policies of the country determined. The number of congressmen is determined by the population of a state. The larger the number of that population which is disfranchised means greater power for the few who cast the vote. As one national Republican committeeman from Illinois declared, "The Southern states can block any amendment to the United States Constitution and nullify the desires of double their total of Northern and Western states."

According to the political power which each actual voter exercised in 1946, the Southern South rated as 6.6, the Border States as 2.3 and the rest of the country as about 1.

When the two main political parties in the United States become unacceptable to the mass of voters, it is practically impossible to replace either of them by a third party movement because of the rotten borough system based on disfranchised voters.

Not only this but who is interested in this disfranchisement and who gains power by it? It must be remembered that the South has the largest percentage of ignorance, of poverty, of disease in the nation. At the same time, and partly on account of this, it is the place where the labor movement has made the least progress; there are fewer unions and the unions are less effectively organized than in the North. Besides this, the fiercest and most successful fight against democracy in industry is centering in the South, in just that region where medieval caste conditions based mainly on color, and partly on poverty and ignorance, are more prevalent and most successful. And just because labor is so completely deprived of political and industrial power, investors and monopolists are today being attracted there in greater number and with more intensive organization than anywhere else in the United States.

Southern climate has made labor cheaper in the past. Slavery influenced and still influences the conditions under which Southern labor works. There is in the South a reservoir of labor, more laborers than jobs, and competing groups eager for the jobs. Industry encourages the culture patterns which make these groups hate and fear each other. Company towns with control over education and religion are common. Machines displace many workers and increase the demand for jobs at any wage. The United States government economists declare that the dominant characteristics of the Southern labor force are: (1) greater potential labor growth in the nation; (2) relatively larger number of non-white workers (which means cheaper workers); (3) predominance of rural workers (which means predominance of ignorant labor); (4) greater working year span, (which means child labor and the labor of old people); (5) relatively fewer women in industrial employment. Whole industries are moving South toward this cheaper labor. The recent concentration of investment and monopoly in the South is tremendous.

If concentrated wealth wished to control congressmen or senators, it is far easier to influence voters in South Carolina, Mississippi or Georgia where it takes only from four thousand to sixteen thousand votes to elect a congressman, than to try this in Illinois, New York or Minnesota, where one hundred to one hundred and fifty thousand votes must be persuaded. This spells danger: danger to the American way of life, and danger not simply to the Negro, but to white folk all over the nation, and to the nations of the world.

The federal government has for these reasons continually cast its influence with imperial aggression throughout the world and withdrawn its sympathy from the colored peoples and from the small nations. It has become through private investment a part of the imperialistic bloc which is controlling the colonies of the world. When we tried to join the allies in the First World War, our efforts were seriously interfered with by the assumed necessity of extending caste legislation into our armed forces. It was often alleged that American troops in France showed more animosity against Negro troops than against the Germans. During the Second World War, there was, in the Orient, in Great Britain, and on the battlefields of France and Italy, the same interference with military efficiency by the necessity of segregating and wherever possible subordinating the Negro personnel of the American army.

Now and then a strong political leader has been able to force back the power of monopoly and waste, and make some start toward preservation of natural resources and their restoration to the mass of the people. But such effort has never been able to last long. Threatened collapse and disaster gave the late President Roosevelt a chance to develop a New Deal of socialist planning for more just distribution of income under scientific guidance. But reaction intervened, and it was a reaction based on a South aptly called our "Number One Economic Problem": a region of poor, ignorant and diseased people, black and white, with exaggerated political power in the hands of a few resting on disfranchisement of voters, control of wealth and income, not simply by the South but by the investing North.

This paradox and contradiction enters into our actions, thoughts and plans. After the First World War, we were alienated from the proposed League of Nations because of sympathy for imperialism and because of race antipathy to Japan, and because we objected to the compulsory protection of minorities in Europe, which might lead to similar demands upon the United States. We joined Great Britain in determined refusal to recognize equality of races and nations; our tendency was toward isolation until we saw a chance to make inflated profits from the want that came upon the world. This effort of America to make profit out of the disaster in Europe was one of the causes of the depression of the thirties.

As the Second World War loomed the federal government, despite the feelings of the mass of people, followed the captains of industry into attitudes of sympathy toward both fascism in Italy and nazism in Germany. When the utter unreasonableness of fascist demands forced the United States in self-defense to enter the war, then at last the real feelings of the people were loosed and we again found ourselves in the forefront of democratic progress.

But today the paradox again looms after the Second World War. We have recrudescence of race hate and caste restrictions in the United States and of these dangerous tendencies not simply for the United States itself but for all nations. When will nations learn that their enemies are quite as often within their own country as without? It is not Russia that threatens the United States so much as Mississippi; not Stalin and Molotov but Bilbo and Rankin; internal injustice done to one's brothers is far more dangerous than the aggression of strangers from abroad.

Finally it must be stressed that the discrimination of which we complain is not simply discrimination against poverty and ignorance which the world by long custom is used to see: the discrimination practiced in the United States is practiced against American Negroes in spite of wealth, training and character. One of the contributors of this statement happens to be a white man, but the other three and the editor himself are subject to "Jim Crow" laws, and to denial of the right to vote, of an equal chance to earn a living, of the right to enter many places of public entertainment supported by their taxes. In other words, our complaint is mainly against a discrimination based mainly on color of skin, and it is that that we denounce as not only indefensible but barbaric.

It may be quite properly asked at this point, to whom a petition and statement such as this should be addressed? Many persons say that this represents a domestic question which is purely a matter of internal concern; and that therefore it should be addressed to the people and government of the United States and the various states.

It must not be thought that this procedure has not already been taken. From the very beginning of this nation, in the late eighteenth century, and even before, in the colonies, decade by decade and indeed year by year, the Negroes of the United States have appealed for redress of grievances, and have given facts and figures to support their contention.

It must also be admitted that this continuous hammering upon the gates of opportunity in the United States has had effect, and that because of this, and with the help of his white fellow-citizens, the American Negro has emerged from slavery and attained emancipation from chattel slavery, considerable economic independence, social security and advance in culture.

But manifestly this is not enough; no large group of a nation can lag behind the average culture of that nation, as the American Negro still does, without suffering not only itself but becoming a menace to the nation.

In addition to this, in its international relations, the United States owes something to the world; to the United Nations of which it is a part, and to the ideals which it professes to advocate. Especially is this true since the United Nations has made its headquarters in New York. The United States is in honor bound not only to protect its own people and its own interests, but to guard and respect the various peoples of the world who are its guests and allies. Because of caste custom and legislation along the color line, the United States is today in danger of encroaching upon the rights and privileges of its fellow nations. Most people of the world are more or less colored in skin; their presence at the meetings of the United Nations as participants and as visitors, renders them always liable to insult and to discrimination; because they may be mistaken for Americans of Negro descent.

Not very long ago the nephew of the ruler of a neighboring American state, was killed by policemen in Florida, because he was mistaken for a Negro and thought to be demanding rights which a Negro in Florida is not legally permitted to demand. Again and more recently in Illinois, the personal physician of Mahatma Gandhi, one of the great men of the world and an ardent supporter of the United Nations, was with his friends refused food in a restaurant, again because they were mistaken for Negroes. In a third case, a great insurance society in the United States in its development of a residential area, which would serve for housing the employees of the United Nations, is insisting and reserving the right to discriminate against the persons received as residents for reasons of race and color.

All these are but passing incidents; but they show clearly that a discrimination practiced in the United States against her own citizens and to a large extent a contravention of her own laws, cannot be persisted in, without infringing upon the rights of the peoples of the world and especially upon the ideals and the work of the United Nations.

This question then, which is without doubt primarily an internal and national question, becomes inevitably an international question and will in the future become more and more international, as the nations draw together. In this great attempt to find common ground and to maintain peace, it is therefore, fitting and proper that the thirteen million American citizens of Negro descent should appeal to the United Nations and ask that organization in the proper way to take cognizance of a situation which deprives this group of their rights as men and citizens, and by so doing makes the functioning of the United Nations more difficult, if not in many cases impossible.

The United Nations surely will not forget that the population of this group makes it in size one of the considerable nations of the world. We number as many as the inhabitants of the Argentine or Czechoslovakia, or the whole of Scandinavia including Sweden, Norway and Denmark. We are very nearly the size of Egypt, Rumania and Yugoslavia. We are larger than Canada, Saudi Arabia, Ethiopia, Hungary or the Netherlands. We have twice as many persons as Australia or Switzerland, and more than the whole Union of South Africa. We have more people than Portugal or Peru; twice as many as Greece and nearly as many as Turkey. We have more people by far than Belgium and half as many as Spain. In sheer numbers then we are a group which has a right to be heard; and while we rejoice that other smaller nations can stand and make their wants known in the United Nations, we maintain equally that our voice should not be suppressed or ignored.

We are not to be regarded as completely ignorant, poverty-stricken, criminal or diseased people. In education our illiteracy is less than most of the peoples of Asia and South America, and less than many of the peoples of Europe. We are property holders, our health is improving rapidly and our crime rate is less than our social history and present disadvantages would justify. The census of 1940 showed that of American Negroes 25 years or over, one-fifth have had 7 to eight years of training in grade schools; 4 per cent have finished a 4 year high school course and nearly 2 per cent are college graduates.

It is for this reason that American Negroes are appealing to the United Nations, and for the purposes of this appeal they have naturally turned toward the National Association for the Advancement of Colored People. This Association is not the only organization of American Negroes; there are other and worthy organizations. Some of these have already made similar appeal and others doubtless will in the future. But probably no organization has a better right to express the wishes of this vast group of people than the National Association for the Advancement of Colored People.

The National Association for the Advancement of Colored People, incorporated in 1910, is the oldest and largest organization among American Negroes designed to fight for their political, civil and social rights. It has grown from a small body of interested persons into an organization which had enrolled at the close of 1946, four hundred fifty-two thousand two hundred eighty-nine members, in one thousand four hundred seventeen branches. At present it has over a half million members throughout the United States. The Board of Directors of this organization, composed of leading colored and white citizens of the United States, has ordered this statement to be made and presented to the Commission on Human Rights of the Economic and Social Council of the United Nations, and to the General Assembly of the United Nations.

41

"TO SECURE THESE RIGHTS" (1947)

by P. B. Young, Sr.

The post-war rise in opposition to racism, nationally and internationally, led President Truman to appoint, in December 1946, a Committee on Civil Rights. The committee submitted a notably powerful indictment of racism and proposals for significant change.

Commentary on that report was extensive. Illustrative was the editorial devoted to it by P.B. Young, Sr. (1884–1962). His newspaper had the largest circulation of any weekly, white or African-American, south of Maryland.

What is the historic civil rights goal of the American people?

In what ways does our present record fall short of the goal?

What is government's responsibility for the achievement of the goal?

What further steps does the nation now need to take to reach the goal?

It was to these questions that the President's Committee on Civil Rights sought answers during its investigations and studies authorized by Mr. Truman on December 5, 1946. The answers are provided in the committee's report, entitled "To Secure These Rights," submitted to the President on October 29, 1947. In evaluating its assignment from the Chief Executive, the committee points out, it took cognizance of the fact that "we were not asked to evaluate the extent to which civil rights have been achieved in our country. We did not, therefore, devote ourselves to the construction of a balance sheet...Instead, we have almost exclusively focused our attention on the bad side of our record—on what might be called the civil rights frontier."

It took occasion to acknowledge the progress that had been made, however erratic it might have been, but it reiterates that "our purpose is not to praise our country's progress." Therefore, its report stresses, "our decisions reflect what we consider to be the nation's most immediate needs." This viewpoint should not be lost sight of in any consideration of the report.

Another fundamental principal is given emphasis by the committee—and it cannot have too much emphasis, defenders of "state's rights" to the contrary notwithstanding. That principle, in the words of the committee's report, is

The protection of civil rights is a NATIONAL problem which affects everyone. We need to guarantee the SAME rights to every person regardless of who he is, where he lives, or what his racial, religious, or national origins are.

A Reaffirmation of Faith

It was to be expected that any forthright report on civil rights, any documentation of the shortcomings in the equal application of civil rights, would meet with a mixed reaction and be the source of controversial discussion and comment. Any sanely thinking person cannot but realize, however, that the declarations of the committee are in truth but a *reaffirmation of faith* in all of those things we call "the American way" of life. They are, in addition, an indictment of the nation's failure to achieve anything like uniform realization of the democratic principles laid down in the Declaration of Independence and particularly in the Bill of Rights of the U.S. Constitution.

If this country now rejects and repudiates such a reaffirmation of faith in democratic living, after fighting two wars in one generation to preserve and spread democracy, it will make itself morally defenseless against the criticism and propaganda of other nations and peoples, thus weakening its useful influence in the world at a time when that influence is critically needed if the world, and itself, are not to be engulfed by chaos.

The committee deserves the gratitude of the American public and of the government for not minimizing our shortcomings and not evading the responsibility it had for recommending remedial action.

Equally, the President has earned the nation's gratitude for creating the committee. Many politicians, even many statesmen, have recognized as did Mr. Truman that "all parts of our population are not equally free from fear" and that the "federal government (has) the duty to act when state or local authorities abridge or fail to protect...constitutional rights." But few of them have had the moral courage to take the lead in seeking remedies. Mr. Truman has such moral courage.

Change Gradually, or Now?

The committee states pointedly that "we believe that the time for action is *now*" if this nation is to "move forward toward a nobler social order in which there will be equal opportunity for all."

That declaration will serve to highlight two principal views on the solution of our interracial maladjustments. It sharpens the line between the gradualists, who believe evolutionary and educational processes will achieve the goal, and those who are less patient and share the committee's viewpoint.

The *laissez-faire* school believes in the inevitability of gradualness, to appropriate a phrase from certain British philosophers. Much of the critical comment on the committee's report, voiced understandably by the press and other spokesmen in the South, takes issue with the committee chiefly on this point. They plead for time and object to extending federal authority into the jurisdiction of the states.

The issue is certainly sharpened by the committee's report. Shall it be gradualism or a strict adherence now to principles long ago fought for and made integral to our way of life?

Many Negro people have patiently and sincerely accepted the technique of gradual improvement of their lot; have accepted in good faith the pledges of the gradualists that first-class citizenship "will come in time." Looking with a clear eye at the results they have begun to wonder.

It is only logical to expect suffering, rights-cheated millions to ask "What time, when?" They begin to want to know the deadline. Do the gradualists have such a time in mind? Do they want full equality of civil rights at any time? Or do they delude themselves and mislead others?

If this report had been made a quarter-century ago, it would have been met with the same critique "the time is not ripe now." If it were to be made a quarter-century hence, no doubt, the charge would again be that the recommendations are ill-timed. When, then, *is* this more *appropriate* time? Has anybody any idea?

For those who think that postponement, instead of facing up to conditions, is the only way out, history offers many disconcerting facts. Has postponement helped prevent a bloody and distressing situation in Palestine? Did appeasement and postponement prevent World War II and, among other things, the extermination by the Nazis of seven million noncombatant Jews? Did procrastination save would-be refugees to other countries? Has it solved the pressing problem of displaced persons? Did such a policy prevent Japan, Italy, and Germany from becoming aggressors?

These are questions that patient, long suffering people are asking with more frequency. They want to know, Is or isn't it time to face up to conditions? Do pleas for more time mean only more time to fix and freeze the pattern of inferior status?

Views of Report's Critics

Some sincere folks who would approach the problem differently than the President's committee speak of the progress being made now, of the reduction in lynchings, of the harm done by "confusing the issue," of the danger of the imposition of laws by Congress on the South, and of "the state of mind" that accounts for America's democratic shortcomings. There is possibly some merit in all of these points. However, those who come forward with them owe the public answers to other points, among them these:

(1) How valid is relative progress against the continuance of different degrees of democracy for different strata of the citizenship?

(2) If the total number of lynchings *is* declining, what of the number of horrible ones which *still* take place with the guilty going free because of legal technicalities, inept or cowardly enforcement, and (in the President's words) because of "weak and inadequate statutes" or the failure to "provide the Department of Justice with the tools to do the job." What of the travesties of justice that took place after the lynchings at Monroe, Ga., and Greenville, S.C., and the near-lynching at Jackson, N.C.

(3) Wherein lies the confusion of issues? If our way of life entitles every man to freedom and equality but some are short-changed, the answer is to correct

the situation. There can be no "confusion" about that, nor in advocating such correction.

(4) If any laws are imposed on any of our states, it will be by the will of a majority of the people's elected representatives in Congress. That surely is the democratic way. Are a minority of the states or a minority of the whole people to impose the dictatorship of its recalcitrant will upon the nation?

(5) As to the present inequalities and proscriptions resulting from a state of mind among some of the people who wish to arrogate to themselves rights they would deny others, what of the state of mind of Hitler, who would have dominated the world with his "master race?" What of the state of the British mind that would have continued to subjugate the 13 original American colonies, but which did not prevail because great men in this land, both North and South, wanted freedom and created the Declaration of Independence and our Constitution?

A Blueprint for Democracy

The Committee has proposed a *joint* federal-state program to strengthen the machinery for the protection of civil rights; it has not proposed reliance solely in the national government. In some cases it recognizes that only the uniformity of federal law can hold any promise of effectiveness. In other instances it recommends that states initiate action. In still others it recommends remedial legislation by both federal and state legislatures.

It has not equivocated. It has urged action at every major point where our practices, be they the consequence of federal or state action or inaction, are at variance with our vaunted democratic principles. It has provided the blueprint for putting democracy into practice. The extent to which its recommendations are adopted will test the sincerity of this nation's people.

"As the committee concludes this report we would remind ourselves that the future of our nation rests upon the character, the vision, the high principles of our people. Democracy, brotherhood, human rights—these are practical expressions of the eternal worth of every child of God. With His guidance and help we can move forward toward a nobler social order in which there will be equal opportunity for all."

Norfolk (Va.) *Journal and Guide*, November 8, 1947.

42

FOR ABOLISHING JIM CROW IN THE MILITARY (1947)

In the fall of 1947 a movement was begun, under the leadership of Grant Reynolds and A. Philip Randolph, to eliminate racist discrimination in military service and training. A statement conveying the views of the founders was mailed to Dr. Du Bois, in a letter dated November 17, 1947, asking for his support. In addition to Reynolds and Randolph, several distinguished people joined this effort, including Raymond Pace Alexander, Sadie T.M. Alexander, Charles Houston, Charlotte Hawkins Brown, L.D. Reddick, and Charles H. Wesley. Dr. Du Bois, in a letter dated December 18, 1947, conveyed his "sympathy" for this effort and offered full support.

Later documents will convey the subsequent history of this effort. The original proposal, marked "Not for Publication," follows:

NEGROES THREATENED BY U.M.T. SEGREGATION

At a meeting on October 10, 1947, in the New York office of A. Philip Randolph, International President of the Brotherhood of Sleeping Car Porters, AFL, the Committee Against Jimcrow in Military Service and Training was organized. Captain Grant Reynolds, New York State Commissioner of Correction and former Army Chaplain, was elected Chairman. Mr. Randolph, at the time attending the AFL Convention in San Francisco, was elected Treasurer. The following statement represents the point of view of the Committee which will fight to the limit against any form of jimcrow military service:

On June 1, 1947, the President's Commission on Universal Training recommended a plan for peacetime conscription which provides for the segregation of Negroes. Although paying lip service to racial equality by recommending that there be no *discrimination*, the Commission nevertheless outlines a plan in which *segregation* is clearly accepted. The compulsory military training bill, H.R. 4278, designed to implement the Commission's report, would, if adopted, fasten jimcrow on American youth at their most impressionable age. This bill, now before Congress, does not even *mention* racial discrimination or segregation.

Under the plan every boy would have to spend six months in a jimcrow U.M.T. training camp. At the end of this time he could "choose" to enter the Regular Army, where there is segregation, or a college R.O.T.C. unit, most of which discriminate, or the National Guard, or the Reserve Component of the Army. In regard to the National Guard, the appendix of the Commission's report says: "Regulations concerning enlistment of Negroes and formation of Negro units are determined by local authorities of the state, since the primary responsibility of organizing these units rests on the states by law. According to an inquiry made by the War Department of the adjutants general of all states, most of them do *not* plan to have Negro units in the National Guard. Of those that do, all but three *require* segregation by regulation." (Emphasis ours.) The commission further states that the Air National Guard will follow "AAF policy in respect to Negro units. *No mixed units* will be established." (Emphasis ours.)

Aside from the humiliation to young Negroes involved in this segregated program, there would be additional handicaps. A large percentage of Negroes cannot afford to attend college. With the National Guard completely closed to them in at least 22 states, most Negroes would be forced into the jimcrow regular army or would have to remain an additional six months in jimcrow U.M.T. camps.

Promises of equal treatment in the future are not enough. Section 4-A of the Selective Service and Training Act of 1940 forbade racial discrimination. Yet the clause was willfully violated by the Army as a matter of policy and the violations were upheld by the courts. It is significant that Southern Democrats who wholeheartedly believe in jimcrow are almost unanimous in support of the U.M.T.

One should note that in the War Department's experimental U.M.T. Camp at Fort Knox, Kentucky, no Negroes were included among the 600 trainees. The unit has been widely advertised as the "model" for a nationwide U.M.T. program. A clergyman member of the Fort Knox Advisory Committee in a *New York Post* dispatch of April 16, 1947, regretted it but said that "the South might oppose U.M.T. if Negroes were included." Brig. Gen. John M. Devine, in charge of the camp, indicated that in such a small unit it would not be practical to bring in enough Negroes *to form a separate platoon*! In other words, Negroes would definitely be segregated into special units if Congress passes U.M.T.

One of the principal benefits claimed by the Commission for its program of Universal Military Training is that it would "contribute to the development of national unity" by "bringing together young men from all parts of the country to share a common experience." Can national unity be promoted by subjecting a million young men each year to federally sponsored jimcrow? Boys who have grown up in communities where racial segregation is not practiced would be forced to accept the jimcrow pattern which would prevail under the proposed program. For many white boys, this would mean learning to regard segregation as the normal way of life; for the Negro, it would mean permanently, as in World War II, the degrading experience of being treated as an inferior citizen by a government which conscripts him in the name of democracy. So long as the American government attempts to sponsor any program of jimcrow, its aspiration to moral leadership in the world will be seriously impaired.

The original was sent to the library of the University of Massachusetts by the editor for inclusion with its Du Bois papers.

43

COORDINATING THE ANTI-RACISM STRUGGLE (1947)

This document calls attention to a development among significant sections of the African-American people, which has been missed in secondary literature. It is of some consequence in helping explain the development of various forms of repression that soon emerged, culminating in McCarthyism.

The document was in the form of a mimeographed letter dated December 15, 1947, addressed to Dr. Du Bois. The Reverend John H. Johnson chaired the committee involved; Dorothy Height was its secretary. A copy now is in the Du Bois Papers at the University of Massachusetts in Amherst.

This is a report of progress on an idea in which you have shown genuine interest.

On November 8th, 18 people met in the auditorium of the New York Public Library in response to a letter of invitation sponsored by, Dr. W. E. B. DuBois, Judge Hubert Delaney, Mr. Roscoe Dungee, Mrs. Beulah Whitby, Dr. Benjamin Mays, Dr. Joseph Johnson, Mrs. Rosa Bragg, Rev. Marshall Shepard, Mr. and Mrs. Paul Robeson and Rev. John H. Johnson. Those who came represented a variety of interests. Others who were unable to be present sent letters indicating their desire to participate.

Everyone realized that now is the time for those who are concerned with the rights of Negroes to unite efforts on a program on which all are agreed. It was felt that issuance of the report of the President's Committee on Civil Rights, the presentation by the N.A.A.C.P. of the petition for Negro Rights to the United Nations, have served to create a moment in which positive action can be most effective.

Throughout the country, Negroes organized and unorganized are anxious to see some action taken. Wherever they are, whatever their walk in life, there are certain things upon which Negroes can get together. In fact, we are together on these three points: All of us want legislation to outlaw the Poll Tax, legislation out-lawing Discrimination in Employment and a Federal Anti-Lynch Law. There was the consensus of the group that what we needed was not another organization, but rather a loose temporary committee to unify our efforts so that together we can exert mass pressure on the 80th Congress for the specific legislation all of us want.

It is felt that this can be done best if all organizations already working on these issues, and as many others as can come together, will coordinate their efforts. In this way, we shall have coordinated effort, but not another organization. To assure maximum results, we shall have to stimulate the masses of Negroes through such projects as can capture their imagination. So that we could have a nucleus with which to begin, those present consented to serve as a temporary central group to work to interest other individuals and organizations in joining in the project.

It was agreed to call that nucleus the Provisional Coordinating Committee because there cannot be a truly representative coordinating committee until the idea is shared and accepted by individuals and groups all over the country, who were unable to be present.

Of course, we had to have some people take on temporary responsibilities and the following were chosen: Rev. John H. Johnson, Chairman, Dorothy Height, Secretary-Treasurer; Steering Committee: Eunice H. Carter, Ada B. Jackson, Dr. W. E. B. Du Bois, Magistrate Joseph Rainey, Dr. Joseph Johnson, Paul Robeson and Belford Lawson. The Steering Committee was instructed to meet and crystallize the essence of the discussion at the meeting into a "Statement of Purpose and Program."

On November 22nd, several members of the Steering Committee, with the Chairman and Secretary, met together and discussed the purpose and program and the enclosed Statement is an out-growth of the discussion and the intensive work of a small sub-committee. When the Steering Committee analyzed the many suggestions which had been made, they realized that several things were needed:

a/ Those who indicated interest in the idea of united efforts among Negroes should be given an opportunity to indicate suggestions and changes in the "Statement of Purpose." Therefore, it is hoped that you will give immediate attention to this Statement and send into us your suggestions or revisions.

b/ We can test the idea and gain support by asking key people throughout the country to call together small groups to talk it over to see whether they are willing to work together to get this three-point program accomplished during the 80th Congress. Through such regional meetings, it will be possible to broaden representatives for a national conference to be called at the earliest possible moment.

c/ All of us are busy people; if we are to do an effective job, we shall have to have skilled employed leadership to help use our time most effectively, therefore the Steering Committee felt that a staff was essential. Such a staff should include an Executive Director and adequate stenographic assistance.

d/ To do a national job competently, our leadership needs suitable headquarters. A sub-committee was introduced to find such space in downtown New York and to find qualified personnel.

e/ Anything so significant as this task requires money, but all of us together will have to decide how we can finance our efforts.

On December 11th, the sub-committee found desirable office space at 59 Park Avenue, New York, and as of December 12th began its work from that headquarters.

Every person who wants to achieve the objectives of the three-point program is called upon to think through the steps taken so far and make whatever suggestions deemed wise to help us make sure that every move is in the right direction of developing sustained and effective action in behalf of our three-point program.

PROVISIONAL COORDINATING COMMITTEE
59 Park Avenue
New York 16, New York

Statement of Purpose

Realizing that now, if ever in our life time, legislation which will give to the Negroes of America their full political and economic rights as American citizens must be enacted, the PROVISIONAL COORDINAT-

ING COMMITTEE has been formed to give impetus to an all out effort to have the forthcoming session of Congress enact:

1. Legislation removing discriminatory voting qualifications in Federal, state and primary elections, such as poll tax laws and other similar devices.
2. Legislation outlawing discrimination in employment because of RACE, CREED, COLOR, or NATIONAL origin.
3. A federal anti-lynch law.
4. Legislation making restrictive covenants illegal.*

This Committee, representing a broad cross-section of Negro life, has been formed solely for the purpose of serving as a rallying point for all those many groups who are eager to work for and see the passage of this legislation.

Your united effort can help make a reality this program to which many organizations have for so long devoted so much time and labor and which the report of the President's Civil Rights Committee has recently brought into sharper focus.

*The inclusion of this point depends on the decision of the Supreme Court on cases of restrictive covenants now on the docket. (The reference is to *Shelley v. Kraemer* (1948) in which the Supreme Court held that the state judicial enforcement of restrictive covenants violated the Fourteenth Amendment. See, on this, the essay by Loren Miller in the *Nation*, May 29, 1948, hereafter—ed.)

44

RACISM IN THE PANAMA CANAL ZONE (1948)

by Thomas Richardson

In March 1948, Thomas Richardson, vice-president of the United Public Workers of America, CIO, testified before the Sub-Committee of the Senate Committee on Appropriations relative to appropriations being considered for the operation of the Panama Canal Zone. The closing section of this testimony follows:

The term "silver" employees is used to distinguish non-citizen United States Federal workers from "gold" employees who are citizens of the United States. These two terms cloak a *system of discrimination against thousands of human beings. The entire world is aware of the formal, official pattern of Jim-Crow and discrimination which has been carried on by the United States Government for the past 43 years on the Canal Zone.* You no doubt have noticed that the construction of 99 apartments for "gold" workers would cost $1,613,700 or approximately $16,000 per unit, whereas the 184 apartments for the "silver" workers would cost $754,000 or approximately $4,000 per unit. This type of disparity is another form of racial discrimination and the sum to be spent, if approved, will only expend money for additional slums. When Congressman Engel pointed out this wide difference in cost per unit in the House Committee Hearings, General Mehaffey stated that the apartments are smaller. I would like to show you two pictures of one of the "silver" units known as "Titanic," since it is the largest housing unit for "silver" employees in the Canal Zone. It contains 48 families for a total of 288 persons. There are 24 toilets (mostly without seats) and 24 crude shower stalls. There are no wash basins except the crude iron sinks in the kitchens. These are supposed to serve the cooking and washing needs of the six and seven member families in the building.

The "Titanic" was constructed in 1906 and served as a hospital. It literally crawls with rats, vermin, and cockroaches. The timbers and supports are termite infested. Rat droppings and filth have accumulated in the walls and ceilings for decades. A sudden jolt in the room overhead is sufficient to send a spray of filth raining down on the apartment beneath. Persons frequently awake in the mornings to find themselves and their beds littered with debris from the ceilings. The rooms are small and cramped, barely large enough to permit the comfortable seating of three persons. Note the one exit in the picture and imagine the panic resulting from fire in this fire-trap. One of the occupants recently asked the District Quartermaster what he should do with his family if the place caught fire and the front exit was blocked. He was told to jump the 32 feet from the second floor to the ground.

The interior view graphically illustrates the General's statement that "silver" quarters are smaller than those of the "gold" workers. This corridor view shows that two persons could not pass each other. It shows the flimsy wall separations and lack of ceilings.

Like a cancer, the "silver-gold" system has eaten its way into all phases of the life of its people. It can be cited as the single, most important factor for the great wave of bitterness and disdain now being directed at the

United States in that section of the World. In the face of this most inhuman practice, our statements on democracy and freedom are received with jeers.

The above condition is further strengthened when it is revealed that without the "silver" workers the Panama Canal could not have been dug or maintained. The record of sacrifice, loyalty and service of the "silver" employees in aiding the United States to create and maintain one of the great wonders of the World reads like a saga. There is a saying in Panama that one "silver" worker's life was lost for every railroad tie in the 50-mile long Panama Railroad which spans the Isthmus. These non-citizen workers have an outstanding history of loyalty to the United States Government. During the entire period of World War II, there was not a single act of sabotage. Their contribution to the war effort was of the utmost and their loyalty has been repeatedly attested to by the Governor of the Canal Zone and the other Zone officials. This record indicates that there is a reservoir of good-will that the United States Government cannot discard or ignore.

In this connection, I would like to call attention to section 2 of the Bill which provides for a form of discrimination that would limit the holding of skilled, technical, clerical, administrative, executive or supervisory positions to citizens of the United States or Republic of Panama. Many thousands of the present employees of the Panama Canal are not citizens of either country. Yet, they have clearly demonstrated their loyalty, their competence and their skill in various jobs of trust connected with the operation of the Panama Canal. In order to erase this discrimination which is produced by this section of the legislation, we recommend that the entire section be eliminated from the Bill. . . .

In fact, we suggest that the recommendations of the President's Committee on Civil Rights be established on the Canal Zone. This recommendation calls for the abolition of the "silver-gold" system. A system should be established which would permit the following:

1. Equal pay for equal work.
2. Equal opportunity for jobs and promotions.
3. Adequate and equal housing, health, recreational and educational facilities.

Unfortunately, the United States Government stands now indicted in the eyes of decent people as an ungrateful miser and as a perpetrator of the Hitlerian theory of race supremacy because of its shocking treatment of its "silver" employees on the Canal Zone. The present formal, government-sponsored system of racial segregation and discrimination is completely at variance with the official position of the United States Government in its treatment of racial minorities.

Refusal to solve this problem can only continue to hurt the prestige and dignity of the United States in that section of the World. This Committee has the opportunity to alleviate an extremely embarrassing and shameful situation. Favorable action on the recommendations we made earlier will go far towards convincing the "silver" workers, the peoples of Latin America and decent people everywhere that the United States does mean what it says in its official statements on the rights of racial minorities. We are confident that the average American will look with disfavor upon the continuance of the present situation. We are convinced that the average American is in favor of fair play and democratic treatment on the part of our Government towards all of its employees, wherever they may be in the World.

This is from a mimeographed copy of the testimony in the editor's possession. Italics in original.

45

CALL TO SOUTHERN YOUTH LEGISLATURE (1948)

Long before "Snick" (SNCC) of the 1960s, there was what some of us in the movement of the late 1930s and 1940s remember as "Snick," meaning Southern Negro Youth Congress. In the spring of 1948, SNYC held in Birmingham its eighth biennial all-Southern conference. The hall originally secured for this conference withdrew permission, at the urging of government officials, especially police commissioner Eugene ("Bull") Connor. One day late, on May Day, the conference was opened in a small black church, the Alliance Gospel Tabernacle.

The meeting was invaded by Connor's police; the church's minister, Claude Herbert Oliver; James Dombrowski, executive Secretary of the Southern Christian Human Welfare organization; Doris Senk, a white visitor from New York; Edward Forrey, representing the International Maritime Union, CIO, were arrested for participating in a nonsegregated meeting. Also arrested was the senator from Idaho, Glenn Taylor, vice presidential candidate of the Progressive party. Taylor was, in fact, physically assaulted by the police. Senator Taylor was fined fifty dollars and given a 180-day suspended jail sentence. It was Taylor's threat to contest the segregation law through the federal courts that led to the release of the other four defendants and his own freedom. Of course, this event created a national and international scandal of major proportions. The call to this Southern Youth Legislature follows:

THERE IS A VOICE IN THE SOUTHLAND

The Voice Calls:
Young Southerner oppressed and beaten...
Young Southerner burned and hung...
Young Southerner suffering daily the injustices of the Klansman's law...

Arise
Throw off the chains of sharecroppers slavery
Break the bonds of poverty and ignorance...
Tear away the mantle of shame placed over you by the greed of men...

Fight
Fight for your land, and for freedom...
Fight for your home and your American heritage...
Fight for the rights for which your brothers died across the sea...

Vote
Cast your vote for freedom and democracy...
Cast your vote for peace and security...
Cast your vote for a new world of brotherhood...

Youth of the South—*you* must answer this Call. Let it rise from the hilltops and resound in the valleys of the Mississippi. Let it rush like the mountain streams in Kentucky and beat upon the land like the fresh spring rains.

Young Southerner, tell your brother, tell your neighbor to join hands with you and march to Birmingham. There together, black and white, we shall raise our united voice as one great chorus, singing our demands for justice, freedom, peace, and the American way of life.

This year of the great election is our year of decision. We look back down the path just traveled and remember the words of our song: "Stoney the road we trod, bitter the chastening rod...Felt in the days when hope unborn had died." Today our hope is not dead; it is a living reality. We see the future ahead and it is bright, but we must struggle to make it ours.

The aims of our struggle are clear. We call for:

—The abolition of the poll tax and all barriers to voting;
—The enactment of an F.E.P.C. law;

—The passage of a federal anti-lynching bill;

—Equality in education through the elimination of segregation;

—Adequate health, housing, recreational and cultural facilities;

—An end of the degrading practices of "white supremacy" which violate our dignity as human beings and impede the progress of the masses of white Southerners;

—The defeat of Universal Military Training and all attempts to militarize American youth and provoke a third world war.

The issues are sharply joined. The future direction of the Southern people, the nation, and the world, will depend on what *you say and do* between now and November.

WILL YOU JOIN US?

You are welcome and you are needed. From the mountains and hills, from the beaches and bayous, from the farms and universities, from churches, labor unions and community clubs, we will congregate at the Southern Youth Legislature.

Will you join us?

When we sing the songs of solidarity and truth, will your voice be heard?

Will you stand in the square and speak for freedom? Will you march under the Stars and Stripes and demand your Bill of Rights? Will you sit with us to draw the plans for the battles that lie ahead? Will you be a partisan in the resistance against Southern fascism?

The time is now. The hour of advance is here. Youth of the South, hope of the future, guardians of our sacred traditions, select your spokesmen without delay. Let every organization and institution be represented. Let every individual come. Raise funds. Hold meetings. Instruct your delegates. Stand up and be counted in the SOUTHERN YOUTH LEGISLATURE, the 8th all-Southern conference of the Southern Negro Youth Congress.

On to Birmingham, April 30, May 1 and 2, 1948! Let us build the SOUTHERN YOUTH LEGISLATURE into a dynamic congress of the peoples of the South!

The "Call" is in the editor's possession. On the Senator Taylor confrontation, see Linda Reed, cited work, pp. 152–53. The "Call" itself was the first page of a publication, *Young South* (vol. 1, no. 2, March 1948), issued in Birmingham and edited by Edward K. Weaver, the SNYC president. Louis Burnham was its executive secretary; Maenetta Steel, its Treasurer. Of its five vice presidents, two were women (Esther Cooper Jackson and Rose Mae Catchings); Junius Scales, white, of North Carolina, also was a vice president. SNYC's advisory board contained some of the greatest names in the freedom movement, including Dr. Du Bois, Mary McLeod Bethune, Dr. Horace Mann Bond, Dr. Benjamin A. Mays, Charles C. Gomillion, and Modjeska Simkins.

46

THE AFRICAN-AMERICAN ELECTORATE (1948)

by Henry Lee Moon

Henry Lee Moon, who had been Sidney Hillman's assistant in the CIO-PAC, at this writing was public relations head of the NAACP. His book-length examination of African-American and U.S. politics had a preface dated March 1948. From that book come the following extracts:

The ballot, while no longer conceived of as a magic key, is recognized as the indispensable weapon in a persistent fight for full citizenship, equal economic opportunity, unrestricted enjoyment of civil rights, freedom of residence, access to equal and unsegregated educational, health, and recreational facilities. In short, a tool to be used in the ultimate demolition of the whole outmoded structure of Jim Crow.

Already recognized as an important and sometimes decisive factor in a dozen northern states and in at least seventy-five non-southern congressional districts, the Negro is beginning to exert increasing political influence in the nation, although still not accorded the recognition his voting strength warrants. Meanwhile, he is again emerging as a positive political factor in the South, where for nearly two generations his suffrage rights have for all practical purposes been nullified.

The area of his political activities and influence, once confined largely to the great industrial cities in the East and North, has been expanded and extended by wartime migration into the Pacific coast states and into many of the smaller midwest and northeastern cities. The war stimulus, too, has generated a resurgence of political activity in the South following the invalidation of the "white primary" by the Supreme Court decision of April 3, 1944.

The maximum Negro voting strength is about seven and a quarter millions, which represents the total number of colored citizens over twenty-one years of age, according to the 1940 census. For the nation as a whole there are 91,600,000 citizens of voting age. These figures are, of course, far in excess of the total vote which under present conditions can be turned out. In 1940, the year of the greatest vote, there was a total turnout of only 49,815,000. In 1942, an off year, this figure dropped to 29,441,000, rising in 1944 to 48,025,000, and dropping again in 1946 to 35,000,000.

Two thirds of these potential Negro voters still reside in the South. Most of these, living as they do in inaccessible rural areas and small towns, probably will not become politically activized for a number of years, despite the truly significant increase in Negro voting strength in many southern cities.

By the end of 1946 there were 750,000 qualified Negro voters in the southern states, a significant increase over the 250,000 Ralph Bunche estimated in 1940.[1] Meanwhile, this number has steadily increased despite efforts of some southern legislatures to circumvent the Constitution and Supreme Court decisions. Despite, also, intimidation and fraud. By November 1948, more than a million southern Negroes may well be qualified to vote. A total of 3,500,000 Negro voters in the 1948 elections is not only possible but likely.

Politicians of both major parties have long been aware of the strength of the Negro vote in the cities of such states as New York, Pennsylvania, New Jersey, Ohio, Indiana, Michigan, Illinois, and Missouri. And no one today seriously contemplates launching a third party without considering this vital vote along with other potentialities necessary for the success of such an undertaking. Southern and western politicians have now joined their eastern and northern colleagues in bidding for this vote.

The size, strategic distribution, and flexibility of the Negro vote lend it an importance which can no longer be overlooked. As significant as was this vote in the 1944 elections—and without it Franklin D. Roosevelt could hardly have been reelected—it can, with wise and independent leadership, be even more important in the 1948 elections.

The importance of this vote is now generally conceded. What is not usually recognized, and even less acknowledged, is that this vote is more

---

[1] Ralph J. Bunche, *The Political Status of the Negro*. Unpublished MSS. quoted by Gunnar Myrdal, *An American Dilemma* (New York: Harper Bros., 1944), pp. 487–88.

decisive in presidential elections than that of the Solid South. In sixteen states with a total of 278 votes in the electoral college, the Negro, in a close election, may hold the balance of power; that is, in an election in which the non-Negro vote is about evenly divided. The eleven states of the old Confederacy comprising the Solid South have a total of 127 votes in the electoral college. And these votes, except on rare occasions, are pre-committed to any candidate the Democratic party may nominate on whatever platform. Unlike the southern vote, the Negro vote today is tied to no political party. It cannot be counted in advance.

This development is of prime importance not only to the political future of the Negro, but also to that of the South and the nation. If the white politicians are unwilling to face the full implications of this historic shift of political power, the Negro leaders are fully aware of its significance and are prepared to press for fuller recognition of the race's just demands for first-class citizenship.

An alert, independent, and aggressive Negro electorate in collaboration with organized labor and other progressive forces may be an important factor in determining the political complexion of Congress. The growing Negro vote in the South, allied with white progressives, can bring about changes of far-reaching importance in that region. Indeed, the resurgence of Negro voting in Dixie presages the return of the two-party system. The passing of the "white primary," the imminent demise of the poll tax in the seven states which still retain it, the progressive militancy of Negro citizens, all tend toward broadening the base of suffrage in the South among both blacks and whites. This new electorate of both races threatens the continued domination of the courthouse gangs which have been the controlling factors in the Democratic party in the southern states. The success of such a coalition is limited only by the degree to which the white working class in the South can be liberated from the specious doctrine of "white supremacy" as preached by the Bilbos, the Rankins, and the Talmadges.

The Negro's political potential is not merely positive through the exercise of the franchise. The negative aspect of his political existence has permeated the political thinking of this nation from colonial times down to the present. Indeed, the struggle to negate the positive political influence of the Negro remains the dominant factor in southern politics to which all other considerations have been ruinously subordinated. A great body of crippling, discriminatory legislation in the South attests the negative influence of the Negro citizenry. As a result of this preoccupation with the political status of the Negro, the South remains, culturally and economically, the most backward region in the nation.

All our noble expressions of political idealism, from the Declaration of Independence down to the enunciation of the Truman Doctrine, have been confronted with the grim specter of the disfranchised Negro mocking our democratic pretensions. Our national schizophrenia has not only retarded the development of democracy at home but has also been a continuing source of embarrassment in our international relations. It has earned for us the scorn of Communist and Fascist alike, of colonial and imperialist, as well as of true democrats everywhere. It effectively thwarted Secretary Byrnes in his demand for democratic elections in the Balkans. Again and again it has exposed our vulnerability. Even the passionate and all-inclusive humanitarianism of Franklin D. Roosevelt was unable to surmount completely this needless handicap.

The campaign of 1948 promises to be one of the most vitriolic in the history of the nation. The Democratic coalition which has been in power since 1933 has been split into at least three well-defined groups: the left-wing followers of Henry A. Wallace who have launched a new party; the center which continues to follow the leadership of the party's chief, Harry S Truman; and the political zombies who comprise the anachronistic right wing. Within the ranks of the major divisions there is further fragmentation. What with Universal Military Training and the Marshall plan dividing their ranks, the Republicans have little enough to crow about on the score of party unity. In this fluid and confused political milieu it would take a rash prophet to say in March for whom the Negro voters will cast their ballots in November. This much it is safe to predict: they will not vote for any candidate satisfactory to the political zombies who infest the sub-Potomac region....

Recognizing the Negro's growing political potential, both major parties will undoubtedly intensify their efforts to win his support in 1948. Certainly any progressive third-party movement will seek to integrate the Negro into its basic structure. Which way will Negro voters turn? Who will be their favorite candidate? To whose blandishments will they respond? It does not now appear that either party will get the overwhelming support that went to President Roosevelt, who in 1944 carried Negro districts in Detroit, Pittsburgh, and New York approximately four to one. While Roosevelt won wide personal following among Negro citizens, he did not win them to the Democratic party. He could not so long as Bilbo, Rankin, and Talmadge sailed under that party's banner. He did, however, cut them loose from their traditional Republican moorings and launched them on a career of political independence. The professional Negro politicians, just as the politicians of any other race, have already taken sides, but the independent Negro leaders and the Negro masses will have some very definite demands to make before they give support to either side. They will want to know how the candidates and the parties stand on such vital issues as fair employment practices, abolition of the poll tax, the protection of the right to vote, elimination of Jim Crow in all government agencies, the suppression of mob violence, the outlawing of segregation in public life, the extension of civil rights, particularly in the vulnerable District of Columbia. In short, they will want to know what practical steps the candidates and the parties will be able and willing to take to implement the proposals submitted by the President's Committee on Civil Rights.

The universal and enthusiastic response of colored citizens to the committee's memorable, and indeed revolutionary, report gave early indication that this historic document would play an important role in the 1948 campaign. While it is not generally anticipated that adoption of the thirty-five recommendations for legislative, executive, and educational action will mean the immediate eradication of discrimination from all phases of American life, there is wide concurrence with the committee's conclusion that government "must assume greater leadership" and "that the time for action is now." The committee, appointed by President Harry S. Truman and composed of fifteen distinguished and representative Americans, called for an end of all forms of discrimination and segregation in public life. "The protection of civil rights," the committee report said, "is a national problem which affects everyone. We need to guarantee the same rights to every person regardless of who he is, where he lives, or what his racial, religious or national origin."

Walter White, the executive secretary of the National Association for the Advancement of Colored People, hailed the report as "the most uncompromising and specific pronouncement by a governmental agency on the explosive issue of racial and religious bigotry.... The report puts Congress, and particularly the conservative Republican-Southern Democratic bloc, squarely on trial. But the job is not one for Congress alone, as the report points out. State legislatures, private organizations and each individual American have been told by the President's committee what needs to be done."[2] The Negro press, which has grown cynical about

[2]New York *Herald Tribune*, November 9, 1947.

governmental pronouncements, joined in the chorus of praise for the work of the committee. "In a short time," the Pittsburgh *Courier* asserted, "the United States can become a perfect democracy if there is only the will to implement the recommendations of the President's Committee on Civil Rights *now*." To the Chicago *Defender* it was "a call to the American people to accept the challenge of ruthless racism which has so long crippled our democracy...It is a call to freedom which must be heeded." The committee, the *Journal and Guide* of Norfolk, Virginia, said, "has provided the blueprint for putting democracy into practice." The Baltimore *Afro-American* valued the report as "one of the most significant documents of all time."

The ink on the report was hardly dry before it was projected into the political arena. Lem Graves, the *Courier's* Washington correspondent, exclaimed: "For Negroes of America, their 1948 political issue has been found! It will be on the basis of the committee report and recommendations that candidates will be weighed, Democratic or Republican...and his record through the years will be an indication of his sincerity....He will be faced with the inevitable question: Will you support with your vote the legislation recommended by President Truman's Committee on Civil Rights? And on the answer may well hinge the direction of the Negro vote next year."

The report on civil rights was followed by the equally forthright report of the President's Commission on Higher Education which, with only four white Southerners dissenting, reached the conclusion, "that there will be no fundamental correction of the total condition [inequalities in educational opportunities] until segregation legislation is repealed." The nonconforming Southerners expressed the belief "that pronouncements such as those of the Commission on the question of segregation...impede progress, and threaten tragedy to the people of the South, both white and Negro."

Certainly the reports embody all the basic long-standing issues with which the Negro minority is vitally concerned. And only as their recommendations are implemented will the race move toward its goal of equality of citizenship. The dynamic political content of the reports will become even more apparent as the 1948 campaigns get under way. Neither party, nor any candidate for the presidency, can afford to dismiss it. The extent and kind of reservations that may be expressed will depend upon many factors—the prospective closeness among prejudiced white voters, the amount of support that can be rallied among progressive whites, the stability of international relations, and the skill and intelligence of Negro leadership, political and non-political alike, in pressing for positive action on the national level. It has become increasingly evident that the country can no longer maintain the status quo in race relations. . . .

The colored citizen is an American as well as a member of a disadvantaged minority. Because of the inclement climate of the culture in which he lives, he is compelled to divert a great portion of his time, energy, and thinking to defensive and protective measures. Nevertheless, as an American and as a citizen of the New World of the Atomic Age he is vitally concerned with the larger issues of war or peace, of scarcity or plenty, of depression or prosperity. But he rightly sees that the problem of the color line is an integral phase of these major international and domestic issues. For generations the South has maintained that the race problem is her own peculiar area to be handled in her own provincial manner. The problem has long since ceased to be regional or even national. It is, as W. E. B. Du Bois prophetically warned half a century ago, one of the major problems of the twentieth century. Neither time nor science nor humanity will permit this nation to continue in the outmoded racial practices of the nineteenth century. Both President Truman and Mrs. Franklin D. Roosevelt expressed recognition of this inescapable development in their addresses before the Lincoln Memorial at the Washington conference of the NAACP in July 1947. Mrs. Roosevelt told of the embarrassments she suffered at sessions of the United Nations when some foreign representative called her attention to newspaper accounts of discriminations against Negroes in this country. And Mr. Truman unequivocally called for national leadership in the fight against discrimination. We can no longer wait until the most backward areas catch up with the main movement of liberalism, he said.

After the NAACP had presented its petition to the United Nations, praying for relief from the discriminations suffered by the Negroes in the United States, Attorney General Tom Clark, a Texan, expressed dismay that any citizens of this country should feel compelled to go over the heads of their government in seeking redress of grievances and further stated that he intended to remedy such evils in so far as the law and the Constitution permitted. Shortly thereafter Soviet delegates to the United Nations Subcommission on Minorities and Discrimination, meeting in Geneva, proposed making a crime of the "advocacy of national, racial and religious hostility or of national exclusiveness or hatred and contempt as well as of any action establishing privilege or discrimination based on distinctions of race, nationality or religion." The hapless American delegates were again caught out on a limb. Not only in areas under Soviet domination but elsewhere throughout the world the denial of basic rights to Negro citizens in America is bringing the nation into ill repute, alienating potential allies in any future conflict.

Not only in the international field but also on the domestic front discrimination is proving costly. Certainly a more wholesome distribution of the national wealth through fair employment practices would help stave off another depression through the spreading of mass purchasing power. The low wages paid to Negro workers in the South is an important factor in depressing the standard of living for both whites and blacks in that region. Unemployment and underemployment of any considerable segment of the population reduces the market for the producers of consumer goods throughout the nation. This is a factor seldom considered by those... number of political liberals within the race. The Negro vote today is in the vest pocket of no party. It is certainly as independent as the vote of any other considerable segment of the American electorate.

The Ultimate Objective

What the Negro wants in this post-war world is simple and obvious. His hopes may be summed up in a phrase—full equality and the elimination of Jim Crow. In this, Negroes are united as never before. Indeed, the attainment of that goal is today more than a mere hope. It is now the grim determination of practically all elements within the race.

It would be a mistake to assume, as many white persons appear to do, that this demand is something artificial—something cooked up and stimulated by the Negro press and other race spokesmen for demagogic purposes. Rather it is a demand which wells up from the masses and is merely articulated by the militant Negro press and the responsible Negro leaders. Indeed, it is not uncommon to find among the masses a more insistent demand for equal rights than that voiced by the leaders. This determination to achieve equality has been reinforced by the return of nearly a million veterans disillusioned and embittered by the discriminations they have encountered in the armed service—senseless discriminations with which many of them had had no previous experience.

What does the Negro mean when he says that he hopes for equality? Simply this: that he is entitled to and must have every right, privilege, and opportunity accorded to any other citizen group. Negroes must have equal opportunity for the development of individual personality, the attainment of a fair and adequate share of the world's economic goods, and the enjoyment of life. This is little enough to hope for. This need is not alone for Negroes; America needs it to become a truly democratic nation. There are certain basic equalities without which that objective cannot be gained. They are economic, political, civil, and educational.

The Negro must have the right to work, to be upgraded, to occupy any position for which he may be individually qualified by training, experience, and skill. He must have the opportunity to demonstrate his abilities in the industrial field. Discriminations, both by employers and certain unenlightened labor unions, have restricted the opportunities of colored workers for employment and promotion to skilled jobs and responsible positions. To halt such discrimination is the Negro's first objective.

In the field of politics the Negro demands the unrestricted exercise of those political rights guaranteed to every American by the Constitution. The right to participate freely in the selection of local, state, and federal officials. The right to be elected to any office for which the candidate may obtain the necessary votes. The right to hold appointive office in accordance with individual merit, including appointments to the judiciary, to administrative positions—to the Cabinet itself. The right to vote has been restricted by the poll tax, the "white primary," complicated registration and educational requirements, and by intimidation and lynch terror. The right to hold responsible office has been limited by the selfishness, timidity, and lack of understanding of politicians. Denial of political rights imposes a status of second-class citizenship, which the Negro is no longer willing to accept. Elimination of all discriminatory restrictions is demanded.

Civil equality is basic to any democratic society. The civil rights of the citizen must be protected, irrespective of race, color, creed, national origin, economic status, or political affiliation. Every citizen has the right to expect protection of the law and even-handed justice in the courts of the nation. It is only a matter of time before we get rid of Jim Crow in transportation, hotel accommodations, restaurants, recreation and entertainment, and in all other public facilities. It has long since been demonstrated that so-called equal but separate accommodations mean inferior facilities for Negroes.

Finally, and urgently, the Negro must have equal educational opportunity. His children must have facilities and instruction equal to those offered to other children of the nation. Educational opportunities must be equalized at all levels, from the nursery school through professional and graduate training offered at the university level. Equalization will inevitably bring an end to segregation in education. The sheer cost of maintaining an adequate dual system will lead to its collapse. Meanwhile it is necessary to resort to legal tests and mobilize for political action in the drive to push back the frontiers of segregation in education as well as in all other fields.

While Negroes are insistent in the demand for equality, there is realization, among the advance guard at least, that equality in the status quo is not enough. What is it to be equal to the undernourished white sharecropper in South Carolina? What is it to be equal in the disease-infested slums of Detroit? Were the status of Negroes in Mississippi miraculously elevated overnight to that of the white population, they would still be in a sad plight. Their social, economic, and cultural levels would still be far below standard. Equality is not enough.

The struggle must be for equality with meaning. Such equality requires the raising of the social, economic, and cultural levels of the common people throughout this country. In a word, that means we must have a new society in which poverty can be abolished and racial prejudices eradicated—a society in which equality is possible.

To end job discrimination, we must first achieve full, stable employment. Then there need be no mad scramble for jobs; no need to exclude or restrict large bodies of workers because of race, sex, creed, or national origin; no fear of insecurity. With jobs for all, we can work hopefully and consistently toward economic equality—an equality with significance, a status from which stems all other equalities.

Were there decent homes enough for all the people of America, it would be impossible to crowd Negroes or other racial minorities into the back alleys and filthy slums of our great industrial cities. Our slums and blighted areas could be cleared. With planning, the ghetto and all the evil it spawns could be erased from the map of America. Likewise there must be food and clothing enough to meet the needs of the nation and at prices within reach of the masses. Only in an economy of abundance can we hope for full equality.

Equality the Negro must have. And that equality can have meaning only in terms of the level of our total society. And even after meaningful equality shall have been attained, as eventually it must be, there remains the objective of a society in which equality will be not only possible but also normal and effortless. Once this is achieved, the white "liberal" who now derives great satisfaction out of "doing good for the poor colored people" will be stripped of his cloak of self-righteousness. Such a society will free the individual Negro of any hindering sense of personal obligation for any advantages he may receive as a special favor. No longer will he need to depend upon the patronage of his "good white folks." Not, however, until the people of America are able to view racial differences in proper perspective may we expect a society in which equality is normal.

Now, whenever the Negro raises this demand, he is confronted with those who say: "Be patient—you can't go too fast—let's take this easy. Remember, you've made wonderful progress in three generations—don't upset the applecart." Those millions who have been penalized in America because of their color never like that kind of talk from white persons, whether or not they claim to be friends. They ask: "Who is to determine when progress is too fast or too slow?" To reactionaries living in a dead past, to those who reap unclean profits out of race hate, *any* progress in racial relations is too fast. Among those striving to make democracy a living reality, the present pace is all too slow. The doctrine of gradualism finds scant acceptance among the Negro people today. While it is recognized that all the barriers against the race cannot be eradicated overnight by executive fiat, court decree, or legislative action, the Negro people of America believe that it is the obligation of government, of the labor movement, and of all true progressives to take a clear, consistent, and unequivocal line against racial discrimination and segregation. They believe that the objective of national policy should be full equality for all citizens. And they have been encouraged in this conviction by the report of the President's Committee on Civil Rights.

Recognizing that the attainment of this goal depends upon the social progress of the nation as a whole, Negroes are coming to realize the necessity for co-operating with and supporting those organizations, agencies, and individuals who are committed to the task of improving the lot of the common man. It is among these that the Negro should find his natural allies in the struggle for equal rights. It is not by accident that some of our worst labor baiters also hate Negroes, Jews, Latin Americans, and other minority groups. These elements are intent upon obstructing every step in the direction of a better world of decent human relations. Not until we are able to eliminate them from positions of power can we hope to improve the conditions of the common man and create a society in which equality is possible and acceptable.

Despite the bitter opposition of entrenched reaction, President Roosevelt's program of social legislation contributed immeasurably to the advancement of the common people in this country. The New Deal not only recognized the need for raising the economic, social, and cultural levels of the masses of the American people; it was also aware of the special disabilities under which the Negro minority lives. Accordingly, the administration took certain positive steps to assist the Negro in overcoming these disadvantages. It is only through such combined efforts, improving the lot of the common man and exerting special effort to overcoming the Negro's underprivileged position, can we move forward to our goal of full equality. Many Negroes believe that the steps taken have been inadequate and far too cautious. Nevertheless, it is generally realized that a sound beginning has been made. And further, those who have studied the voting record of Congress know that much of the New Deal social-reform program was sabotaged by reactionary members of Congress, Tory-minded northern Republicans in "unholy alliance" with Negro-baiting southern Democrats. Intelligent political action on the part of Negro voters, in collaboration with other progressives, can assure and accelerate the fight for full, significant, and normal equality.

Clearly this goal can be reached only through federal action of a strong and representative central government. The states have repeatedly demonstrated their inability or unwillingness to provide a broad program to improve the status of the common man. Those states where the need is greatest are commonly the ones least able and least willing to undertake such a program. Certainly such a program cannot be implemented under the discredited and tattered banner of "State's Rights" which certain Republican elements have lately espoused. So long as any states are permitted to exclude large segments of the population from active participation in politics, the phrase "State's Rights" will remain, as it originated, an anti-democratic slogan to further the interest of the ruling oligarchy. The banishment of this doctrine should be accompanied by the abolition of the outworn electoral college in order that every citizen's vote may count directly in determining who shall be President.

The universal demand among Negroes is for full equality. In order to attain that objective and invest it with significance, we must have an economy of abundance—a society with jobs for all, decent housing available to the masses, plenty of food, and adequate educational, health, and recreational facilities. Under the New Deal, government recognized its responsibility to develop such a society. The initial steps have already been taken. The adoption of Roosevelt's eight-point Bill of Economic Rights as a national objective would give additional evidence of the government's recognition of its responsibility to create a new and healthier society.

Henry Lee Moon, *Balance of Power: The Negro Vote* (Garden City, N.Y.: Doubleday, 1949) pp. 9–12; 199–201, 202–214, 215–219. For another examination of the African-American growing impact on postwar U.S. politics, see Walter White, "Will the Negro Elect Our Next President?," in *Colliers*, November 22, 1947.

47

A. PHILIP RANDOLPH'S CALL FOR DRAFT RESISTANCE (1948)

In March 1948, A. Philip Randolph testified before the Armed Services Committee of the U.S. Senate; his questioner was Senator Wayne Morse (R.: Ore.).

Senator MORSE. Mr. Randolph, I want to question you a bit on your proposal for civil disobedience. Up until now refusal to serve in the military forces of this country in time of national emergency has been limited as far as one's psychological attitudes are concerned, to conscientious objections to war, the participating in war.

It is based upon the legal theory of freedom of religion in this country, that if one's religious scruples are such that in good conscience he cannot bring himself to participate in war, which involves the taking of human life, our Government has protected him in that religious belief, and we have our so-called exemption on the ground of conscientious objection.

Now, this proposal of yours—I am not one to minimize your testimony—your proposal is not based upon conscientious objection in the sense that the American law has recognized it to date; am I not right about that?

Mr. RANDOLPH. That is correct.

Senator MORSE. But your proposal, and put me straight on this, your proposal is really based upon conviction that because your Government has not given you certain social, and economic rights and protection from discrimination because of race, color, or creed, you feel that even in a time of national emergency, when your Government and the country itself may be at stake, you are justified in saying to any segment of our populace—whether it is the colored group or, as you say in your statement, the white group with like sympathies—that under those circumstances you would be justified then in saying, "Do not shoulder arms in protection of your country in this national emergency?"

Mr. RANDOLPH. That is a correct statement, Mr. Senator.

I may add that it is my deep conviction that in taking such a position we are doing our country a great service. Our country has come out before the world as the moral leader of democracy, and it is preparing its defense forces and aggressive forces upon the theory that it must do this to protect democracy in the world.

Well, now, I consider that if this country does not develop the democratic process at home and make the democratic process work by giving the very people whom they propose to draft in the Army to fight for their democracy, then that democracy is not the type of democracy that ought to be fought for, and, as a matter of fact, the policy of segregation in the armed forces and in other avenues of our life is the greatest single propaganda and political weapon in the hands of Russia and international communism today.

Senator MORSE. I understand your position, Mr. Randolph, but for the record I want to direct your attention to certain basic legal principles which I want to say, most kindly are being overlooked in your position. I want to discuss your position from the standpoint of a couple of hypotheticals and relate them to certain legal principles which I think you ought to give very careful consideration to before you follow the course of action which you have indicated.

Let us assume this hypothetical. A country proceeds to attack the United States or commits acts which make it perfectly clear that our choice is only the choice of war. Would you take the position then that unless our Government granted the demands which are set out in your testimony, that you would recommend a course of civil disobedience to our Government?

Mr. RANDOLPH. In answer to that question, the Government now has time to change its policy on segregation and discrimination and if the Government does not change its policy on segregation and discrimination in the interests of the very democracy it is fighting for, I would advocate that Negroes take no part in the Army.

Senator MORSE. My hypothetical assumes that up to the time of the emergency set forth in my hypothetical, our Government does not follow in any degree whatsoever the course of action that you recommend.

Mr. RANDOLPH. Yes.

Senator MORSE. So the facts of the hypothetical then are thrust upon us and I understand your answer to be that under those circumstances even though it was perfectly clear that we would have to fight then to exist as a country, you would still recommend the program of civil disobedience?

Mr. RANDOLPH. Because I would believe that that is in the interest of the soul of our country and I unhesitatingly and very adamantly hold that that is the only way by which we are going to be able to make America wake up and realize that we do not have democracy here as long as one black man is denied all of the rights enjoyed by all the white men in this country.

Senator MORSE. Now, facing realistically that hypothetical situation and the assumption that it has come to pass, do you have any doubt then that this Government as presently constituted under the Constitution that governs us would necessarily follow a legal course of action of applying the legal doctrine of treason to that conduct? Would you question with me that that is the doctrine that undoubtedly will be applied at that time under the circumstances of my hypothetical?

Mr. RANDOLPH. I would anticipate Nation-wide terrorism against Negroes who refused to participate in the armed forces, but I believe that that is the price we have to pay for democracy that we want. In other words, if there are sacrifices and sufferings, terrorism, concentration camps, whatever they may be, if that is the only way by which Negroes can get their democratic rights, I unhesitatingly say that we have to face it.

Senator MORSE. But on the basis of the law as it now exists, going back to my premise that you and I know of no legal exemption from participation in military service in the defense of our country other than that of conscientious objection on religious grounds, not on the grounds in which you place your civil disobedience, that then the doctrine of treason would be applied to those people participating in that disobedience?

Mr. RANDOLPH. Exactly. I would be willing to face that doctrine on the theory and on the grounds that we are serving a higher law than the law which applied the act of treason to us when we are attempting to win democracy in this country and to make the soul of America democratic.

I would contend that we are serving a higher law than that law with its legal technicalities, which would include the group which fights for democracy even in the face of a crisis you would portray. I would contend that they are serving a higher law than that law.

Senator MORSE. But you would fully expect that because the law of treason in this country relates to certain specific overt acts on the part of the individual irrespective of what he considers to be his spiritual or moral motivation in justification, there would not be any other course of action for our Government to follow but indictments for treason?

Mr. RANDOLPH. May I add something there, Mr. Senator?

Senator MORSE. First, do you agree with me that that would be certain to follow?

Mr. RANDOLPH. Let me add here in connection with that that we would participate in no overt acts against our Government, no overt acts of any kind. In other words, ours would be one of nonresistance. Ours would be one of noncooperation; ours would be one of nonparticipation in the military forces of the country.

I want you to know that we would be willing to absorb the violence, to absorb the terrorism, to face the music and to take whatever comes and we, as a matter of fact, consider that we are more loyal to our country than the people who perpetrate segregation and discrimination upon Negroes because of color or race.

I want it thoroughly understood that we would certainly not be guilty of any kind of overt act against the country but we would not participate in any military operation as segregation and Jim Crow slaves in the Army.

Senator MORSE. I think you will agree with me that this is not the time and place for you and me to argue the legal meaning of aiding and abetting the enemy but if you refresh your memory of treason cases, as I have been doing, sitting here this morning, I would only point out to you most kindly that the legal concepts of aiding and abetting are flexible concepts that can be applied to the behavior of individuals which in effect serve the enemy in time of war to the endangerment of the rest of the people of our country.

Furthermore, and I know you are aware of the fact, any such program as you outline would not be a passive program but would be one that would be bound to result in all sorts of overt actions you could not possibly control, but for which you who sponsored it would, as a matter of law, be fixed with the proximate cause of the conduct and, therefore, would be legally responsible for it.

Mr. RANDOLPH. I recognize that fact just as for instance a union may call a strike. The union does not promote the violence but the forces that are opposed to the union may create the violence.

Well now, in this instance we are definitely opposed to violence of any kind; we are definitely opposed to any overt acts that would be construed in the form of violence but, nevertheless, we would relentlessly wage a warfare against the Jim Crow, armed-forces program and against the Negroes and others participating in that program. That is our position.

Now I do not believe the law up to the present time has been faced with such conditions as to enable it to envisage these principles. In other words, American jurisprudence has never been faced with this kind of a condition and consequently its definition of treason could not possibly take in the type and nature of action which we propose in civil disobedience. But however the law may be construed we would be willing to face it on the grounds that our actions would be in obedience and in conformity with the higher law of righteousness than that set forth in the so-called law of treason.

Senator MORSE. I appreciate that the case would go to the United States Supreme Court for final decision as to the application of the legal principles I have discussed here this morning. I would say most kindly and most sincerely that I have no doubt in my mind that under the circumstances of my hypothetical there is only one decision that could be handed down and that is that the law of treason would be applicable.

Now, Mr. Chairman, I am through with this line of questioning. I felt it necessary to raise these questions. I know Mr. Randolph and I know the fight he has put up for social justice in support of the principles that he believes to be right. I think he knows me, at least I think he knows that I sincerely believe in fighting for putting into effect in America the civil-rights guaranties of the Constitution which for too long have not been put into effect in their full meaning. I agree that both parties too frequently have been guilty of political professings rather than political action in support of the principles of Constitutional Rights.

I do want to say with all the sincerity that I possess that I do not think the proposal you offer is the way to establish full civil rights in America.

Congressional Record, Senate, April 12, 1948, pp. 4312–13.

48

WALTER WHITE ON THE RANDOLPH PROPOSAL

Walter White sent a telegram to Senator Morse on April 1, 1948, relative to the Randolph testimony. It reads:

You have been a good friend of minority groups and a supporter of civil rights legislation, but it apparently is not possible for you to realize how bitterly Negro Americans feel about Jim Crow in the armed services. The treatment of Negroes in uniform seems to be beyond the understanding of United States Senators, even those as sympathetic as yourself. The National Association for the Advancement of Colored People will never cease its fight for the abolition of the vicious and undemocratic discrimination and segregation in the armed services. We would have valiant allies if you and some of your colleagues in the Senate could darken their faces and don a uniform for 6 weeks. Our association is not advising Negroes to refuse to defend their country if it is in danger. But those who expect them to be enthusiastic fighters should remember that their memories of mistreatment in the last war are bitter green. Negro veterans returned home to be terrorized in Columbia, Tenn., lynched in Walton County, Ga., denied the ballot in most Southern States, barred from taking GI courses in many schools, and slandered on the floor of the United States Congress. Consequently there is sympathy in many hearts for the Randolph point of view. The remedy is not to threaten treason trials, but to give these loyal citizens the democracy they are expected and asked to defend.

WALTER WHITE

Congressional Record, Senate, April 12, 1948, p. 4318.

49

A. CLAYTON POWELL SUPPORTS RANDOLPH (1948)

Representative Powell told the Senate committee early in April that he supported Randolph's position. Here is how a leading African-American newspaper reported that fact:

WASHINGTON.—Representative ADAM C. POWELL, JR. (Democrat, New York), testifying last Friday before the Senate's Armed Services Committee, fully supported A. Philip Randolph's civil disobedience threat to keep colored youth out of a Jim Crow army, and called on 60,000 fellow ministers to preach that doctrine. He declared:

"I want to assure you that the testimony given you by Mr. A. Philip Randolph on March 3 did most emphatically state the mood of the vast majority of the 15,000,000 colored Americans. He did not overestimate it."

Tired of Hypocrisy

"They are sick and tired of the hypocritical pretense at democracy now being evidenced by our Congress. . . .

Can't Be Frightened

"We are not going to be frightened by the cry of 'Treason.' We, the colored people, for over 400 years have been the most loyal element of this democracy.

"If the finger of treason can be pointed at anyone, it must be pointed at those of you who are traitors to our Constitution and to our Bill of Rights."

Not Enough Jails

"There aren't enough jails in America to hold the colored people who will refuse to bear arms in a Jim Crow army.

"If you threaten our leaders, then the 60,000 pulpits of the colored church will thunder through their ministers, against the immoral hypocrisy of you, the leaders.

"I dare you to arrest the 60,000 ministers of God in order to whitewash your un-Americanism."

Congress Scored

"Step by step, this Congress is pushing the colored people's backs against the wall. Last March you refused to accept my amendment and you set up a permanent Nurse Corps for the Armed Services which rigidly excluded colored women. You are now planning to present a bill authorizing a permanent Women's Auxiliary to the Armed Services.

"The bill again rigidly excludes colored people, despite the fact that I appeared before the House Armed Services Committee and presented my amendments, but they were overwhelmingly defeated."

Will Seek Amendment

"And now you think you can ram Universal Military Training down the throats of the colored people.

"Well you can't. We won't take it. We refuse to bear arms in un-

American Jim-Crow armed services. That choice is forced upon us by our God, our conscience, our Constitution, and the Bill of Rights.

"When UMT comes before the House, I promise you that I will fight vigorously and militantly to amend it so that there will be complete nonsegregation in every phase of our armed services."

Washington Afro-American, April 6, 1948.

50

EARL BROWN ON RANDOLPH'S VIEWS (1948)

A leading African-American columnist of the postwar period was Earl Brown. His column in the *New York Amsterdam News*, April 19, 1948, entitled "Once Over Lightly" read:

A. Philip Randolph is no demagog. Therefore, when he recently told the Senate Armed Services Committee that millions of Negroes will refuse to register or serve under the draft or universal military training system, unless racial segregation and discrimination are ended in the Army, it was more than the statement of a publicity-seeking sensationalist.

Randolph is also no Communist. Neither is Commissioner of Corrections Grant Reynolds, who, as president of the Committee Against Jim Crow in Military Service and Training, also spoke before the Senate committee. Randolph is an old-time Socialist, and as such, a bitter enemy of communism. Reynolds is a Republican, who is being supported to run for Congress from the Twenty-second District by Governor Dewey.

It is important to know that Randolph and Reynolds are neither Communists nor crackpots. Randolph's word particularly carries a great deal of weight among the colored people. He is known as a courageous and honest fighter. He, more than any other man, forced the Pullman Co. to recognize the Sleeping Car Porters Union. Reynolds was a captain-chaplain in World War II. Like all other Negroes who were in the armed forces, he saw and no doubt was subjected to the rankest kinds of segregation and discrimination. Naturally, he will remember them until the day he dies.

Even more important than Randolph's and Reynolds' attitude about the draft and UMT, is that of millions of other Negroes. Many of them feel even more bitter about the raw undemocratic deal they got and are still getting in the armed services than Reynolds and Randolph. They may not be as articulate as these two men, but in their souls they hate the Army, the Navy, and the entire military set-up of the United States. They hate it, because they are made to feel inferior to white soldiers; they are treated like colonials instead of citizens.

The important point for the Senators who serve on the Armed Services Committee to remember about what Randolph and Reynolds said is this: a man, white or black, cannot fight for his country with any heart or courage unless he knows he has the respect of his country. This, the Negroes know they do not have, in spite of some protestations to the contrary by those who want to use the Negro for whatever they can get out of him.

The fact that Randolph and Reynolds voiced the attitude of millions of Negroes about the armed forces should sober the people of this country more than ever before. For the United States is faced with a worldwide revolution with communism and socialism sweeping everything before them. In order to stop the march of the former and in order to get along with the socialistic countries in Europe and elsewhere, America must practice democracy not only in her armed forces but also in her civilian life.

For it is possible that American democracy will lose in the battle against communism because of racial and religious discrimination and segregation.

If colored Americans refuse to shoulder a rifle for their country, they would be guilty of treason under the law. They would also give the native Fascists an excuse to lynch and otherwise terrorize more of them than they are now. But this would not help the United States win in its world-wide fight against communism. On the other hand, it would aid the Communists from Manchuria to England in their determination to gain control of the world.

The challenge is clearly up to the Government and the generals and admirals. The challenge was not made by Randolph and Reynolds, but by democracy itself. For Reynolds and Randolph, though they spoke boldly, did not cause millions of Negroes to hate the Army and the Navy. The Army and Navy did that themselves. The only way they can win the respect and support of the colored citizens is by demonstrating their ability to practice democracy by abolishing Jim Crow and discrimination.

In the meantime, Randolph, in championing civil disobedience or passive resistance relative to the draft and UMT is taking a leaf out of the late Gandhi's book. Randolph, however, is going a step farther. The Indians were not citizens during Britain's control of India. On the other hand, American Negroes are legally citizens of the United States, and therefore are in a different position than colonials. Indeed, Negroes have a greater responsibility to their country than the Indians had to Britain. By the same token, their country has a greater responsibility to the Negroes. It is time that the United States stopped making a farce out of the citizenship of 15,000,000 colored Americans.

51

ON RACIAL SEGREGATION IN ARMED FORCES

by Council for Civic Unity, San Francisco

Reflective of the wide impact of A. Philip Randolph's call for nonviolent resistance to a Jim Crow defense force was a letter from the above council signed by its president, Ralph A. Randolph, M.D., and its executive director, Edward Howden.

General press criticism of A. Philip Randolph's dramatic stand of 31 March against "Jim Crow" in the armed forces failed, in our opinion, to focus on the main issues involved.

Randolph told a Senate committee that large numbers of Negro Americans would refuse to enter another racially segregated Army. He urged provision in any draft or UMT legislation for nonsegregation and for civil rights of trainees. This, he pointed out, can be done now, in peacetime; if it is not done, he said he would lead a civil disobedience campaign against the draft.

We agree with editorialists who write that civil disobedience is not to be taken lightly. It is a serious, even dangerous matter. This very fact, we suggest, should prompt us not to moralize from a loftier plane, but to probe dispassionately into why Mr. Randolph took his avowedly drastic position.

The real issues here are twofold. First, the immediate question of nondiscrimination in the Army and protection of the civil rights of

trainees. Second—the deeper ground from which this question springs—
the harsh fact of the color line which divides America, relegating
"minority" Americans to lifelong second-class status.

Mr. Randolph is not attacking the arms program. He does not *want*
civil disobedience. He is simply appealing to all Americans to take a
small step now toward a more democratic and effective armed force.

Editorial comment seems to indicate agreement with Randolph's
objectives, yet editorial fire is concentrated upon his promised last-ditch
tactics. Such criticism, we respectfully suggest, would be more impressive if the press would begin to fight with equal vigor both for these
immediate objectives and for other civil rights measures which do reflect
the desired "calm, cooperative, painstaking application of reason over the
years."

Cries of "treason" directed at the ultimate civil disobedience tactic
presuppose a state of war. But we are now at peace. And, as Randolph
reminded the Senate committee, "The government *now* has time to
change its program on segregation and discrimination." This is fundamental. The opportunity is ours now to take these reasonable steps ahead.

We would of course oppose any treasonable act. We do recognize,
however, the ugly facts of racial discrimination and how they may
occasionally drive men to the tactics of showdown. It would seem that the
times call for less complacency in human relations and more positive
action.

Let us inquire whether nonsegregation in the armed forces is (1)
desirable; (2) necessary; (3) workable.

1—*Is it desirable?* Most Americans outside the deep South—and an increasing
number inside—would agree that soldiers training or fighting under the American flag should suffer no discrimination by reason of color, creed, or ancestry. In
the interest of justice and efficiency, segregation for any of these reasons should be
prohibited.

2—*Is it necessary?* Here is the heart of Randolph's argument: that many Negro
Americans are so fed up with Jim Crow in most phases of their lives that they will
now draw the line at compulsory segregation in uniform. In the war just ended,
segregation, with its attendant humiliation, frustration, personal danger, and even
death within the United States, was a bitter experience for thousands of colored
soldiers. The scars left by that experience deserve better than casual con-
templation by white Americans.

Even prior to the Randolph testimony we have perceived a growing feeling among Negro veterans and others against serving again on one side of a compulsory military color line. . . .

The whole situation is sharp with irony. Note that on the same day when Randolph appeared, and before the same Senate committee, Senator Lodge stated that he had Army approval for his proposal for enlistment of 50,000 overseas aliens. These aliens, he said, would be "sprinkled" throughout the ranks (i.e. nonsegregated) and given, after a certain term of service, US citizenship (i.e., voting and other rights). During the last war colored American soldiers were refused entrance to some restaurants which were serving meals to German prisoners of war.

3—*Is it workable?* Nonsegregation is a fact in some areas of American life, and is workable whenever it is initiated with a genuine desire to make it work. This is particularly true when the policy can be made clear and firm—one matter in which, as every veteran knows, the Army is thoroughly experienced. The argument is not theoretical. World War II records contain significant accounts of interracial amity and nonsegregated operations, both in combat and in the supply lines.

The special commission which called for UMT also recommended nonsegregation; the Navy announced abandonment of its segregation policy at the peak of hostilities, and recently issued a favorable report on the results; two months ago Army Secretary Royall, at the insistence of the Governor of New Jersey, permitted that State to observe nonsegregation in its National Guard; the Army's own Gillem Report (March, 1946) admitted the desirability of ending military segregation eventually. The question was not whether, but when. *Why not now?* Later may be too late.

We are well aware that the *Chronicle* has always stood for civil rights. We suggest that it is now time to: (1) Demand enactment of the recommendation of the President's Committee on Civil Rights that America end "the injustice of calling men to fight for freedom while subjecting them to humiliating discrimination within the fighting forces." (2) Place renewed and militant support squarely behind the other major civil rights measures.

Given such action, the unity, strength, and world prestige of American democracy will be tremendously enhanced.

San Francisco Chronicle, May 4, 1948. A mimeographed copy of the original letter is in the editor's possession. This shows some cutting in the text as published, but the cuts were not substantive. The original letter was dated April 8, 1948. The first quotation above is from an editorial in the *Chronicle*, April 2, 1948.

52

CIVIL DISOBEDIENCE ACCOMPLISHED MISSION (1948)

by A. Philip Randolph and Grant Reynolds

A statement issued by Randolph and Reynolds on October 11, 1948, contains significant material. The editor has italicized the comment herein that both men had "hopes of utilizing it [nonviolent civil disobedience] again in other fields." While the main content of the statement was critical of Bayard Rustin and A.J. Muste, their vital role in subsequent nonviolent disobedience efforts makes that comment noteworthy.

Considerable confusion arose in the public mind when on August 18 we announced our belief that civil disobedience was no longer required to force the ending of racial segregation in the armed services.

We take this opportunity to acknowledge our responsibility, in part, for the confusion. During July and early August, both of us were traveling considerably, and several press statements which appeared to contradict our final announcement of August 18 were issued by our administrative staff in the League for Civil Disobedience without our having first seen them. Because we felt *at the time* that the statements had been released in good faith—although they did not express our views—we did not embarrass the staff by publicly repudiating them. In brief, these statements blasted President Truman's executive order even after he had announced that under it he contemplated the eventual abolition of segregation and after Senator J. Howard McGrath, chief spokesman for the President, had personally re-affirmed to us this interpretation of the executive order. Not believing in civil disobedience for its own sake but only as a drastic last resort, we had publicly stated that the campaign would be called off if Congress passed an anti-segregation amendment to the draft bill or the President issued an executive order banning segregation.

It subsequently became apparent that a religious pacifist nucleus within the League was intent on using the movement to resist military segregation as a front for ulterior purposes. We had originally welcomed into the League such known pacifists as Bayard Rustin and A. J. Muste whose experience, we felt, would help keep a potentially violent movement nonviolent in spirit and action.

However, the unauthorized letters and statements to leaders of both political parties sent by Mr. Rustin revealed finally the basic split in philosophy and also the internal weakness of the League. On several occasions Mr. Rustin violated our specific injunction to clear all press statements in advance with half a dozen key persons during our absence from New York. While Mr. Randolph personally shares a firm opposition to conscription whether segregated or not, he believes that good faith demands above-board dealings with draft-age youth and a separation of pacifist aims as such from the anti-jim crow campaign. The common denominator uniting League supporters was resistance to a jim crow draft, not opposition to conscription per se. We became very much disillusioned with unethical tactics within the pacifist nucleus.

Although unrelated to our commitment to end civil disobedience in the event of an executive order, other facts deserve publication. The League was financially weak. Out of his own pocket Mr. Randolph had advanced, since passage of the draft bill on June 19, over $800.00. This sum constituted almost the entire amount the administrative staff had raised for civil disobedience. We faced the launching of a revolutionary movement with a deficit in excess of a thousand dollars. To proceed in the face of no resources would have been reckless and fatuous. The civil disobedience technique would have been discredited at the beginning, *and our hopes of utilizing it again in other fields* would have been in vain. Gandhi in India and South Africa never engaged in mock heroics and from time to time called off civil disobedience campaigns when circumstances warranted.

It has been broadly hinted that we were personally unwilling to face imprisonment, despite our testimony before Congressional committees. We can only cite Mr. Randolph's violation of the draft act on July 17th— nine days prior to issuance of the President's executive order—when, at a Harlem street meeting, he singled out a youth of draft age and "advised and counseled" him not to register. Despite the presence of FBI agents, he was not arrested nor indicted—a decision of the government hardly attributable to us.

We have also been criticized for publicly revealing that the League had no mass following. Years of organizational experience, however, have proved to us the futility of attempting to build movements without complete candor and integrity. It was not the fault of the civil disobedience technique nor basically the fault of the handful of salaried persons who sought to organize the movement. We simply did not have time, between March 31st and August 30th, to build a mass revolutionary movement. But the fact remains that we obtained the executive order because our program was morally unassailable.

In addition to the executive order, we point with pride to the other achievements which must be credited to our resistance campaign: Mr. Truman's anti-segregation interpretation of his order, the anti-poll tax amendment to the draft bill and our raising of military jim crow to the stature of a top national issue which neither major party in 1948 could evade in its platform. The unprecedented refusal of 16 Negro leaders in April to form a defense advisory group within the framework of segregation can also be attributed to the uncompromising position we took.

We intend to push vigorously the legal and constitutional work of the Committee Against Jim Crow in Military Service and Training. If sufficient funds are forthcoming, we shall continue in other cities, North and South, the Commission of Inquiry hearings which were launched last May in Washington to investigate the wartime treatment of Negro GIs. We shall monitor and "police" the executive order by keeping public attention focused on the newly appointed committee of seven civilians. It will be remembered that President Roosevelt's FEPC executive order in 1941 required constant policing.

Finally, we have asked Mr. William Worthy, Jr., to serve as executive secretary of the Committee Against Jim Crow in Military Service and Training. Mr. Worthy brilliantly, tirelessly and almost single-handedly managed the publicity and administrative work in the intense campaign for anti-segregation amendments to the draft bill and a presidential executive order. We have utmost confidence in his integrity and his ability to arouse the nation to constant vigilance on this issue.

Mimeographed copy of the statement in the editor's possession.

53

A RIGHT SECURED (1948)

by Loren Miller

Loren Miller, a Los Angeles lawyer, was an official of the National Bar Association and a member of the legal committee of the NAACP. He helped prepare and argue this case before the Supreme Court.

When the United States Supreme Court, on May 3, held that judicial enforcement of agreements barring the sale of land to, or its occupancy by, Negroes violated the equal-protection clause of the Fourteenth Amendment, it knocked the last legal props from under residential segregation. The decision put the finishing touches on a job begun in 1917 when the court decided that segregation laws or ordinances violated the due-process clause of the same amendment. However, Chief Justice Vinson, who wrote the opinion, was careful to point out that "so long as the purposes of those agreements are effectuated by voluntary adherence to their terms it would appear that... the provisions of the amendment have not been violated." Proponents of segregation are already engaging in vigorous campaigns to induce property owners to abide by the terms of existing restrictive covenants and, indeed, to enter into new agreements of like character with provisions for damages against violators.

At present the major metropolitan areas in the North and West, particularly suburban developments, are pretty thoroughly covered by race-restrictive covenants. State trial courts, backed by appellate-court decisions in sixteen states and the District of Columbia, have been enforcing them since 1915, and the Supreme Court itself, in a 1926 decision that was "distinguished away"—that is, differentiated from the present case—by Chief Justice Vinson on technical grounds, at least said, without making this the crux of its decision, that judicial enforcement did not run afoul of constitutional guaranties. Moreover, the federal government through FHA furnished a model race-restrictive clause for builders and subdividers from 1935 to 1947, and during that period the FHA refused to guarantee home-construction loans unless race restrictions were inserted in subdivision deeds. Racial covenants became a fashion, almost a passion, in conveyancing, and were demanded by banks and lending institutions in all real-estate developments.

It would be folly to expect an overnight reversal of social attitudes implemented by court decisions and rooted in custom. The importance of the recent decision from a practical standpoint is that it admits Negroes and members of other proscribed groups to the open housing market from which they have been excluded for three decades. That exclusion was onerous because it forced the Negro buyer or renter to pay whatever price was exacted in an artificial seller's market. The Negro buyer can now drive a sharper bargain, and one of the immediate results may well be a decline in property prices in defined Negro neighborhoods.

However, real-estate speculators, by playing on existing antipathies,

will still be able to exact premium prices when Negroes seek property
outside those neighborhoods. Such premiums will undoubtedly be lower
in communities adjacent to Negro neighborhoods, and expansion will
occur there first. Well-to-do middle-class Negroes will certainly begin to
seek homes in preferred residential districts, and by overbidding the
market will just as surely find willing sellers. The present tendency of
white home owners to flee from communities when a Negro moves in will
diminish as such home owners come to understand that there are no
"safe" districts. This, combined with the natural desire of Negro workers
to find dwellings close to their places of employment, will gradually
create a pattern of integrated living. The tempo of that tendency will
depend on many factors, such as the earning power of the middle class,
the creation of job opportunities for workers, the success or failure of
damage suits against violators of agreements, and the willingness of law-
enforcement authorities to protect the venturesome Negro home buyer
from the sporadic violence that will occur here and there.

Quite apart from the practical consequences, the decision is a landmark
in constitutional law. To begin with, the court underscored the proposition, implicit in the 1917 segregation-ordinance case, that "among the
civil rights intended to be protected from discriminatory state action by
the Fourteenth Amendment are the rights to acquire, enjoy, own, and
dispose of property." Obviously no person can be secure in a private-
property economy unless that complex of rights is recognized and
protected. Proponents of race-restrictive covenants had always contended—successfully in the state courts—that judicial enforcement of
covenants was beyond the reach of the equal-protection clause of the
Fourteenth Amendment. They rested their contention on the language of
the amendment, which provides that no state shall "deny to any person
within its jurisdiction the equal protection of the laws."

Construing that and related clauses in the Civil Rights cases in 1883,
the Supreme Court held that the Fourteenth Amendment did not protect
the Negro from an "individual invasion of individual rights" and that he
could claim constitutional protection only when the state acted to deprive
him of a civil right. While proclaiming adherence to this principle, the
court neatly turned the Civil Rights cases against those seeking to uphold
covenants by pointing out that the decision exempts individual action from
constitutional inhibitions only when the individual is able to work the

discrimination without calling on the state for aid. It then went on to point out that it had long been recognized that judicial action in such matters as jury selection, maintenance of a fair trial, and the like is state action within the meaning of the amendment.

However, none of the cases had ever held or intimated that the action of a state court in construing a private contract, such as a restrictive agreement, and giving effect to its terms was *state action*. It was here that the court took its boldest step. "It is clear," it said, "that but for the active intervention of the state courts, supported by the full panoply of state power, petitioners [Negroes] would have been free to occupy the properties in question without restraint. These are not cases...in which the states have merely abstained from action, leaving private individuals free to impose such discriminations as they see fit. Rather, these are cases in which the states have made available to such individuals the full coercive power of government to deny to petitioners, on the grounds of race or color, the enjoyment of property rights."

That unequivocal language leaves no room to doubt that state courts may not, under the guise of enforcing private contracts in this or any other field, construe state laws in such a manner as to deny civil rights on the basis of race or color. The same result was reached for the District of Columbia by holding that although the Fourteenth Amendment is inapplicable, a federal statute forbids judicial enforcement of racial covenants. The court's attitude also negatives the suggestion made in some quarters that its decision does not apply to restrictive agreements of this character based on religion rather than on race.

The question of whether a damage action would lie against a signer who violated his agreement not to sell to Negroes was not involved, but the assertion that "the Constitution confers upon no individual the right to demand action by the state which results in the denial of equal protection to other individuals" would seem to prevent individuals from demanding that the courts levy a penalty on another individual who had exercised his right to sell his property to whomsoever he chose.

The successful termination of the long battle against racial covenants illustrates both the weakness and the strength of a political democracy, its weakness because the courts were so laggard in protecting a civil right that the highest court in the nation says has existed since 1868, its strength because a disadvantaged minority was finally able to vindicate that right.

The manner of that vindication deserves a word of comment. The N.A.A.C.P., which spearheaded the struggle, began its opposition thirty years ago, but the question became less acute during the depression years as Negro migration to Northern and Western cities died down. The war brought both an acute housing shortage and a flood of Negro war workers to urban centers. Coincidentally war preparations and war boosted the income of the Negro middle class. The war workers had to find living space somewhere, and the middle class began to look around for better homes. The result was wholesale violations of racial covenants and a vigorous counter-attack. A staggering number of lawsuits were brought— approximately two hundred were filed in Los Angeles in a four-year period, and other cities had much the same experience.

As a crisis neared, the N.A.A.C.P. called a meeting of its national legal committee in Chicago in 1944, and plans were made for a Supreme Court test of the issue. The success of the litigation is proof enough of the soundness of the legal strategy. It was also decided to fight a battle for public opinion on the ground that the issue was a critical test of democracy. The fact that Attorney General Tom Clark filed a brief in behalf of the Negro litigants and Solicitor General Perlman argued their case gives a prospect of success in that field. Also indicative is the fact that two dozen other briefs protesting against continued judicial enforcement of covenants were filed by such diverse groups as the A.F. of L., C.I.O., American Jewish Congress, American Jewish Committee, American Association of United Nations, Council of Protestant Churches, and various civil-liberties organizations.

This widespread public support is important, for now that the legal basis of residential segregation has been destroyed, the job of educating Americans to live together without strife and without reference to race rests on the very groups that filed supporting briefs in the Supreme Court. If they believe that the ghetto is the evil proclaimed in their briefs they should set about their educational task without delay. The legal victory will prove a hollow triumph unless the battle against residential segregation is also won in the field of public opinion.

Nation, May 29, 1948, pp. 599–600.

54

FROM NEW JERSEY TO VIRGINIA TO SOUTH AFRICA
(1948)

Negro Defies Jersey Klan

A scant six weeks after the United States Supreme Court held by unanimous vote that residential restrictive covenants are illegal, a group of kluker-minded citizens of Wall Township, N.J., have tried to intimidate a respectable Negro citizen into abandoning his recently purchased home.

Mr. Leroy Hutson, a 35-year-old radio engineer employed by the United States Signal Corps laboratory at Evans, bought his little home in Wall Township in order to be near his work and to eliminate his four hours of commuting. The entire community is small, consisting of about thirty bungalows, and the presence of Mr. Hutson could hardly be an affront to anyone except the racially prejudiced. Klan sentiment is said to be still strong in the area because about twenty years ago Wall Township was favorite Klan country. The old Marconi home, now the site of the Evans laboratory where Hutson works, was said to be their favorite meeting site.

But Klan sentiment or no Klan sentiment, Mr. Hutson did not flee. Nor did he put in his first call for assistance to the police. He called in the Negroes from the surrounding communities. Within a few hours it is reported that twenty-five Negroes from the surrounding towns showed up with shotguns, rifles, baseball bats and sticks to stand a twenty-four hour vigil until all danger was over.

This incident is one more of the multiplying indications that the present-day Negro, knowing his rights, is not to be easily intimidated by the burning of twelve-foot Kluker crosses and the threats of fanatics. He is resolved to fight for his security if necessary. And having learned from the experience of Negroes in Detroit and Columbia, Tenn., that the "protection" of the police is often worthless, he is resolved to protect himself.

New Richmond Councilman

The election of Oliver W. Hill to the Richmond, Va., city council is a signal honor for Mr. Hill and a sign of the increasing political astuteness of Richmond's Negroes. His election also shows that there are many white people in Richmond who are not afraid of the bogey of "black rule," since many whites must have voted for him.

The June 9 issue of the *Richmond Times Dispatch* comments sagaciously on Mr. Hill's election:

"Richmond is fortunate in the caliber of men who were chosen yesterday [June 8] for its first one-chamber Council, under the new City Charter which takes effect September 1. All nine of those elected are sympathetic to the city manager-unicameral form of government. It is certain, therefore, that the inauguration of the new and modern form will be in the hands of its friends.

"The Richmond Citizens Association has reason to feel proud of the outcome, since eight of the nine members of its slate were elected, and the ninth successful candidate is a long-time friend of the Charter. Only one critic of the Charter came close to success, and most of the others were badly defeated....

"Something of a milestone in Richmond's modern political history was set with the election of Oliver W. Hill, Negro attorney, to the Council. No colored citizen has been chosen to public office here since the late nineteenth century, and some white Richmonders may be inclined to view the novel phenomenon with alarm.

"Actually, however, there is no real basis for such a feeling. Mr. Hill is a valuable citizen who is well-qualified by education and background to sit on the Council. Trained in the law, he is highly regarded by the Negro community, and competent to pass upon the issues which will come before him on the municipal body.

"Since the population of Richmond is nearly one-third colored, it is altogether natural and proper that this large segment of the city's life should be represented on the new Council by a man of Mr. Hill's character and capacity. His presence on the lawmaking body should give our Negro citizens a sense of participation in municipal affairs here that they have not had during this century, and should promote better interracial relations. While the propriety of "single-slotting" by Negroes may be questioned by some, it is obvious that several thousand whites also voted for Hill."

Slowly but surely the door to political opportunity opens wider for the Negro in the South.

From Bad to Worse

In South Africa, the parliamentary elections of May 26 turned out the 78-year-old General Jan Christian Smuts and voted in the 74-year-old Negrophobic Dr. Daniel F. Malan, leader of the Nationalist party. As a racial reactionary General Smuts was bad, but the Nazi-minded Dr. Malan is worse. General Smuts did build up a reputation abroad as a liberal and a statesman, but it is largely phony and did not for a moment fool that small band of South African liberals who know their local racial situation to be intolerable. General Smuts' "statesmanship" has been largely exercised in keeping the natives in their "place." Now along comes the even more reactionary Dr. Malan who proposes to take away the few rights his predecessor has grudgingly conceded to the Colored and the Natives.

Even under Smuts South Africa was worse than Mississippi, though the lot of the Negro in Mississippi is bad enough. Negroes in Mississippi are citizens. They can own land, they have access to education, even though inferior, the professions, and the ballot, despite the restrictions. But in South Africa the Natives enjoy none of these. And Dr. Malan proposes to take away from the Colored the few privileges they now enjoy. The barbaric cruelty of his program is evident in these excerpts from the Apartheid Manifesto:

"The white race in South Africa must be protected.... We must remove all colored voters from the voters roll and place them on separate rolls.... There must be rigid separation in the church, the school, the home and in different spheres of labor.... Moreover the Colored people must be removed from where they live at present in the towns and designated to separate living areas.... Finally, the Colored people may belong only to those churches which believe in segregation."

Dr. Malan tries to turn back the hand on the clock of civilization. He is too late. He cannot win.

Editorials, *Crisis,* July, 1948, vol. 55, p. 201.

55

CONDEMNING ANTI-COMMUNIST HYSTERIA (1948)

by W. E. B. Du Bois, Roscoe C. Dunjee, Charles P. Howard, and Paul Robeson

This document reflects a fact ignored in conventional historical accounts; namely, there existed considerable opposition in the United States to what is now called McCarthyism. Not least this existed in the African-American community. This document was released for publication on August 23, 1948.

President Truman and Attorney General Clark were "strongly condemned" this week by nearly 400 Negro citizens for jeopardizing the rights of minority groups by the recent "hysteria-breeding arrests of national leaders of the Communist Party."

This condemnation is expressed in a "Statement by Negro Americans to the President and Attorney General of the United States," endorsed by 395 citizens in thirty-seven states, including 17 southern states. Additional endorsements are being sought through publication of the "Statement" this week in a number of Negro weekly newspapers under the caption "THE FIRST LINE OF DEFENSE."

The project is sponsored by Dr. W. E. B. Du Bois, New York City; Roscoe C. Dunjee, publisher of the *Black Dispatch*, Oklahoma City, Okla.; Attorney Charles P. Howard, Des Moines, Iowa, key-note speaker at the recent Founding Convention of the Progressive Party; and artist Paul Robeson.

Asserting "we raise here no defense of the principles of the Communist Party," the "Statement" declares: "Our concern is to defend the *right* of political and other minorities, especially the Negro people, to fight for the kind of society they consider democratic and just." The Negro leaders further declare: "We agree fully with... Henry A. Wallace: 'Defense of the civil rights of Communists is the first line in the defense of the liberties of a democratic people.'"

Two Negroes are among the twelve Communist leaders indicted several weeks ago for alleged "conspiracy" in reconstituting the Communist

Party in 1945. They are Benjamin J. Davis, Jr., New York City Councilman; and Henry Winston, Administrative Secretary, Communist Party, U.S.A. The entire group goes to trial in New York on August 27.

Commenting on the arrests, Paul Robeson, one of the sponsors of the "Statement by Negro Americans," pointed out that the Civil Rights Congress (205 E. 42 St., N.Y.C.) is conducting the legal defense of the Communist leaders. He expressed the "hope that liberty-loving Americans everywhere will rally to the support of CRC in this case which involves the freedom of us all."

The 395 Negro leaders endorsing the "Statement" compared these arrests to those of the Nazi Gestapo, and declared their obvious purpose to be "to frighten people away from the Wallace Movement and progressive people's organizations generally,...to strengthen the current drive to war."

The President and Attorney General are called upon "to give more than lip-service to civil rights" by taking effective steps "to defend the lives and liberties of the Negro people in the South"; to "repeal the poll tax, establish a national FEPC and outlaw lynching"; and to "abolish discrimination in Federal employment and segregation in the armed forces."

Many of the top Negro leaders in the country are among the endorsers of the "Statement." They include:

Bishop R. R. Wright, Jr. (A.M.E.), Wilberforce, Ohio; Bishop C. C. Alleyne (A.M.E.Z.), Philadelphia, Pa.; Bishop Reverdy C. Ransom (A.M.E.), Wilberforce, Ohio; Bishop J. H. Clayborn (A.M.E.), Little Rock, Ark.

Also business executives Augustine A. Austin, Antillian Holding Co., New York City; Jake J. Simmons, Jr., Simmons Royalty Co. (oil investments), Muskogee, Okla.; Attorney Willard B. Ransom, Asst. Mgr. Mme. C. J. Walker, Manufacturing Co., Indianapolis, Ind.

Progressive Party congressional candidates Ada B. Jackson, Brooklyn, NY; Magistrate Joseph H. Rainey, Philadelphia, Pa.; Dr. John E. T. Camper, Baltimore, Md.,; Dr. Ulysess Campbell, Newark, N.J.; and senatorial candidate Larkin Marshall, Macon, Ga.

Also trade union leaders Moranda Smith, FTA-CIO, Winston-Salem, N.C.; Coleman Young, Wayne County CIO, Detroit, Mich.; Hilliard Ellis, UAW-CIO, Cicero, Ill.; Charles Collins, AFL Hotel Employees, New York City; Thomas Richardson, UPW-CIO, Washington, D.C.; and Raymond Tillman, ILAW, New Orleans, La.

Also artists, actors and writers Canada Lee, New York City; Shirley Graham, New York City; Allan R. Freelon, Philadelphia; Charles Enoch Wheeler.

Also educators Dr. Oliver C. Cox and Charles G. Gomillion, Tuskegee Institute, Ala.; Rudolph Moses, Dillard University, New Orleans, La.; Dr. Helen A. Bryant, Wayne University, Detroit, Mich.; Dean Edward K. Weaver, Texas College, Tyler, Tex.

Also Mildora Payne, Denver, Colo.,; Alma V. John, New York City; Mary Church Terrell, Washington, D.C.; Mrs. Andrew W. Simkins, Columbia, S.C.; Fred Nicklewhite, Manchester, Vt.; Capt. Hugh Mulzac; and publisher Henry Graham, Newark, N.J.

Mimeographed release from "The First Line of Defense," in New York City, in the editor's possession.

56

WHY WAS DU BOIS FIRED? (1948)

by Shirley Graham

Shirley Graham, a nationally known author—her biography of Frederick Douglass was her most acclaimed book—was a close friend of Du Bois's. The decision of the NAACP to adhere to the Truman position once the Cold War commenced and Du Bois's contrary stance were basic to the process here described. The reference to the earlier action of Ella Baker is noteworthy.

We will not be satisfied to take one jot or tittle less than our full manhood rights. We claim for ourselves every single right that belongs to a free-born American, political, civil, and social; and until we get these rights we will never cease to protest and assail the ears of America. The battle we wage is not for ourselves alone, but for all true Americans. It is a fight for ideals, lest this, our common fatherland, false to its founding, become in truth the land of the thief and home of the slave—a byword and a hissing among the nations for its sounding pretensions and pitiful accomplishment.

Those words were penned over forty years ago by Dr. W. E. B. Du Bois. They formed the heart of the creed of the Niagara Movement, organized by the same man, which united those Negro leaders—most of them teachers, lawyers, ministers, editors—who opposed Booker T. Washington's policy of acquiescence and preferred instead one of militant struggle for freedom and equality.

It was this movement and these Negro leaders who joined, in 1910, with such white liberals and reformers as William English Walling, Oswald Garrison Villard, Charles Edward Russell and Mary White Ovington to found the National Association for the Advancement of Colored People. Of the five original incorporators of the organization, one was a Negro and he was Du Bois.

On September 13, 1948, the Board of Directors of the N.A.A.C.P. passed a motion, "that it will not be in the best interest of the Association to continue the employment of Dr. Du Bois...."

To understand this action and its significance for the Negro liberation movement it is necessary to review some salient features in the history of the N.A.A.C.P. In its origins the organization was largely middle-class; its approach never questioned seriously the basic pattern of the American social order. Rather it attempted to achieve reforms within that pattern by court action and by appeals for decent treatment.

Dr. Du Bois was the key force in the agitational and propagandistic work of the early Association. In the Spring of 1910 he left Atlanta University to become Director of Publications and Research of the N.A.A.C.P., and set about planning a monthly magazine. The treasurer, Mr. Villard, said frankly: "I don't know who is going to pay your salary; we have no money." One thousand copies of the first issue of the *Crisis* (November, 1910) were printed. Within a year it sold 15,000 copies, and within a decade the fearless, pungent editing of Du Bois had brought its circulation above the 100,000 mark, an unprecedented event in the history of Negro journalism.

Meanwhile, the selfless organizational work of Mary White Ovington, plus that of the poet-philosopher-statesman, James Weldon Johnson, and the Field Secretary, William Pickens, was laying the foundations for the transformation of the N.A.A.C.P. from a closely-knit, professionally-minded reform body into that of a genuine mass organization.

In 1918, James Weldon Johnson, returning from a Southern trip, remarked to Dr. Du Bois, "There's an energetic young chap in the Atlanta branch—a recent graduate from the university there—says you know him. His name's Walter White. He'd like a job with us." After a moment's thought Dr. Du Bois replied, "Oh, yes, his brother was a student of mine. I know his father and mother well. Why don't you ask for him as an assistant?"

So Walter White was brought up from Atlanta. He had taken his A.B. from Atlanta the year before, had no professional training, but he made up for his lack of knowledge and experience with a boundless energy and daring initiative. With his flair for drama and publicity, the young man began to add color to the Association's activities. His investigations of lynchings became sensational not only because he got facts but because by posing as a white man in the deep South he added suspense and amusement to grim horror.

Up to this time Dr. Du Bois was the only Negro in the National Administration of the Association. However, practically all the active members throughout the country were Negroes. Their personal contact with the Association was through the field secretaries, also Negroes, and they looked to Du Bois as their most powerful spokesman.

During the years of boom, N.A.A.C.P. dollar memberships poured in. Negroes were in earnest about supporting the organization which they believed was defending their rights and advancing their progress on all fronts. Then came the depression. The stream of dollars diminished to a trickle. A high price now had to be paid for philanthropy.

In 1931, James Weldon Johnson was replaced as Executive Secretary by his assistant, Walter White. For some time. Mr. Johnson's health had been poor. Many people thought a temporary adjustment might have been made to relieve Mr. Johnson for a period. However, Mr. White wanted the job and James Weldon Johnson left the Association.

Immediately policies expressed in the *Crisis* were called into question. Since January, 1916, the magazine had been entirely self-supporting. It had, indeed, contributed support to the National Office, and it had been completely uncensored by the organization itself. As the depression deepened and the *Crisis* ceased to be self-sustaining, the right of free expression in its pages became an issue. The executive officers and the board of the Association demanded increased control and the right of censorship. This Dr. Du Bois opposed. Indeed, he felt that instead of backtracking the Association should have pushed its thinking further along economic and political lines and shed some of its purely reformist character. He had become convinced by 1930 that "in a world where economic dislocation had become so great as ours, a mere appeal based on liberalism, a mere appeal to justice and further effort at legal decision was missing the essential need. " That essential need, he believed, was to fight for the basic economic rights of the Negro people, to expose the connection between the promotion of racism and the maintenance of "wealth and power." "We must seek," he concluded, "to increase the power and economic organization among Negroes" and he proposed to battle for this in the *Crisis*.

Du Bois was defeated. In May, 1934, the Board of Directors voted "that the *Crisis* is the organ of the Association and no salaried officer of the Association shall criticize the policy, work or officers of the Association in the pages of the *Crisis*." The editor's reply to this ruling was:

> In thirty-five years of public service my contribution to the settlement of the Negro problem has been mainly candid criticism based on a careful effort to know the facts. I have not always been right, but I have been honest. I am unwilling at this late day to be limited in the expression of my sincere opinions in the way in which the Board proposes...I am, therefore, resigning.

The editing of the *Crisis* was given to Roy Wilkins, under the very rigid control of the Secretary and Board of Directors. Power in the Association was concentrated in a few hands; the resulting bureaucracy has caused an extraordinary turnover in personnel. Yet with the growing social consciousness evidenced among the masses during the depression decade and the last war, membership in the N.A.A.C.P. reached half a million, and included not only professional and middle-class elements but more and more industrial workers and farmers. Thousands of dollars came in from Negro soldiers, frequently one soldier collecting a dollar membership from every man in his outfit.

Because the history, achievements and ideals of the N.A.A.C.P. are so deeply rooted in the consciousness of Negroes everywhere there has been real reluctance to criticize it. Yet people all over the country are asking questions. With no stated policies, no over-all program, branches attempting to function in their own communities find themselves repeatedly in hot water with the National Office. Is collecting dollars to be their sole purpose?

At the annual convention in 1946 the growing demand from the membership for democratic control of the organization rose to a new high. Committees were formed, there was talk of changes, of increased representation on the Board, of branch autonomy. In May, 1946, Ella J. Baker, for three years Director of Branches, and known throughout the

South for her devotion and courage, resigned from the Association. She told Mr. White:

My reasons for resigning are basically three—I feel that the Association is falling short of its present possibilities; that the full capacities of the staff have not been used and that there is little chance of mine being utilized in the immediate future. Neither one nor all of these reasons would induce me to resign if I felt that objective and honest discussion were possible and that remedial measures would follow. Unfortunately I find no basis for expecting this. My reactions are not sudden but accumulative, and are based upon my own experiences during the past five years and the experiences of other staff members both present and former. . . .

Meanwhile, Dr. Du Bois once more enters the picture. Following the announcement of his retirement from Atlanta University in 1944, he was invited to rejoin the N.A.A.C.P. as secretary of a committee to prepare material on the Negro for the expected World Peace Conference.

"I did not answer this invitation," Dr. Du Bois recently wrote, "until both Arthur Spingarn, President of the Association, and Louis Wright, Chairman of the Board, both old friends, strongly urged me to accept. June 23rd I wrote Messrs. Spingarn, White and Wright saying, 'You will realize that any decision I make now will have to be final for the rest of my working days. I have four offers before me—two very attractive ones from universities. I could not afford to turn them down and take a temporary job at high pressure which might leave me at the end of a year's work exhausted mentally and physically and without prospect of employment. On the other hand, the offer which you make would fit very well into my scheme for collecting authoritative data concerning Negroes of Africa and persons of Negro descent elsewhere in the world.'"

Dr. Du Bois met in conference with the Secretary, President and Chairman of the Board, and it was agreed that Du Bois join the staff of N.A.A.C.P. as Director of Special Research and that his main work would be "to collect facts and documents, arrange statements, articles and booklets concerning the peoples of Africa and their descendants and concerning other colored races so as to form a body of knowledge and literature, designed to educate the world in matters of race and cultural relations."

In the forty months since his appointment Dr. Du Bois twice crossed the continent on lecture tours, visited and spoke extensively in Haiti, presided over the Pan African Congress in Manchester, England, attended U.N.E.S.C.O. and the World Youth Congress in London, was an observer at the founding session of the United Nations in San Francisco, attended several State Department conferences in Washington, presided over conferences on the Near East, Greece and China, edited the N.A.A.C.P.'s petition to the United Nations, as well as the preparatory volume for an *Encyclopedia of the Negro,* and wrote the books, *Color and Democracy* and *The World and Africa,* in addition to numerous articles appearing in journals and newspapers throughout the world. Despite this brilliant record of achievement Dr. Du Bois has been summarily fired.

Setting aside for the moment any case which the Executive Secretary and Board might have against Dr. Du Bois, how dare they insult Negroes all over the world by treating so contemptuously the one man who has been our foremost spokesman, our most eminent statesman for half a century?

On the occasion of his eightieth birthday at a dinner tendered him in New York, *not* by the National Association for the Advancement of Colored People but by the Fisk Alumni Association, greetings came to this man from the great of all lands, and from the plain folk, too, as this from a workers' union in Johannesburg, South Africa: "We South Africans are particularly indebted to Dr. Du Bois who has contributed so greatly in the solution of race problems and the adjustments in race relations. Dr. Du Bois' example and consistency will serve as an inspiring example to all of us."

The campaign against Du Bois and his ideas began with the first days of his re-employment. It started with petty needling. Office space was "unavailable" and when he rented a place of his own the Association refused to meet the expense. When a place was finally found for him it was about the size of a powder room, without shelves and desks. When shelves for Du Bois' 2,500 books were installed, fretting followed as to their costliness. Objection was raised to Du Bois opening his own mail. When Dr. Du Bois testified before the Foreign Affairs Committee of the U.S. Senate he was reprimanded by Walter White for having appeared without consulting him—though Dr. Du Bois had made it quite clear that he was testifying as an individual.

I am told that at a board meeting which took place at the end of 1945 most of the day was consumed with argument over these details concerning Dr. Du Bois, and that finally Mr. White "threw down the gauntlet" and declared that either the Board would back him against Dr. Du Bois or he would quit. Dr. Du Bois was "reprimanded" for exceeding his authority. An oral directive was circulated to the effect that Dr. Du Bois was not to be consulted about anything.

Assured of his "backing," the Secretary now moved from petty heckling into matters of policy. In September, 1946, Paul Robeson wrote Dr. Du Bois asking him to endorse the "American Crusade to End Lynching." When Dr. Du Bois did so, Walter White wrote him that the Association had just formed the National Emergency Committee against Mob Violence and therefore he should not have signed the Robeson statement. Dr. Du Bois replied:

Your memorandum of September 19th was the first notice I have had of your Anti-Lynching movement. Had I been notified I would have gladly co-operated. On the other hand I have been fighting lynching for forty years and I have a right to let the world know I am still fighting it. I therefore gladly endorsed the Robeson movement.

The entire matter of presenting and printing the petition of the N.A.A.C.P. to the United Nations on discrimination and segregation of Negroes was a long-drawn-out battle. With no discussion, the Board appointed Dr. Du Bois to draw up such a statement. However, when Eleanor Roosevelt, who is a member of the Board, heard of it she opposed the whole idea. When the final draft was finished, Dr. Du Bois sent a copy to the Secretary and asked him about formal presentation and publicity. After Mr. White had told Dr. Du Bois to make his own arrangements, and after these had been made, Mr. White intervened, declaring some corrections had to be made. He then changed the arrangements for the petition's presentation from a public affair as had been planned to a restricted one for Association officials only. He delayed the printing for several weeks, finally recalling the proofs in order to add thirty-four pages of additional material. When Dr. Du Bois asked, "How can a corrected manuscript be added to or be changed without consultation with or at least notification to the editor?" Mr. White revealed that he had been negotiating for book publication by a firm and that as it needed more text for that purpose he proposed to write an introduction himself. To which Dr. Du Bois replied:

I strenuously and definitely object to any explanatory introduction being added to the printed Petition. The Board voted for the printing of this Petition as it now stands. I shall not consent to any addition to it.

No addition was made.

In March, 1948, Dr. Du Bois received from the Secretary a copy of a directive made by the Board four years earlier forbidding "employed executive officers of the N.A.A.C.P. from partisan activity in political campaigns." Dr. Du Bois replied that while he fully appreciated the necessity of maintaining the nonpartisan character of the organization, he assumed

that the Board could not possibly have meant to forbid any individual, in his capacity as a private citizen from casting his ballot as he pleased or of defending his convictions and candidates. To do this would be seriously to interfere with that political freedom for which this organization has fought for nearly forty years.

Dr. Du Bois continued to support with vigor the Wallace movement.

Staff members of the N.A.A.C.P. soon learned that appeal to the Board of Directors, discussion with them or suggestions to them are not easy. It is the unwritten rule of the organization that approach to the Board must be through the Secretary and largely at his discretion. The Board of Directors is a body of some forty-eight members widely scattered over the country; their monthly meetings are usually attended by a dozen persons. The meetings are more or less perfunctory, consisting of the report of the Secretary and recommendations of the Committee on Administration which are usually confirmed without debate. New business or the details of old are usually referred to this committee for examination and recommendation.

This Committee on Administration is a recent innovation. It consists of nine members of the Board and six members of the staff of the National Office. Thus the Secretary sits in this body with six votes, since the five members of the staff are virtually his appointees. Moreover, while the staff members are usually present, the other members are more or less irregular, four of them usually attending. The Secretary has large and continually increasing power. His vote with two members of the Board can over-rule the vote of a thousand members in annual meeting. The staff is appointed on his recommendation and dismissed in the same way. He controls the collection of funds and therefore has large influence in expenditures, including salaries. He is the sole medium of communication between the Board, branches and membership. The staff makes all reports to him. He decides which of these reports shall reach the committee on Administration and the Board. Dr. Du Bois writes:

When Mr. White complained of my lack of co-operation and I replied that this was often due to my ignorance of what was going on, Messrs. Spingarn and Wright suggested that I become a member of the Committee on Administration. I had not asked this, because I had not come to the N.A.A.C.P. to make its policy. But of course I did not want to be entirely ignored on plans and policy in my own department. Nevertheless, I was never asked to join or meet with this committee.

The power and responsibility assumed by the Secretary is more than any one man should have. The present form of the organization resembles that of a business with one simple objective: money. It is not conducive to such democratic control as is necessary for an organization devoted to efforts at a people's liberation.

For several months Dr. Du Bois has been fighting to bring the framework of the N.A.A.C.P. in accord with its needs as a mass organization. This is the heart of the Du-Bois-White conflict. In 1946, after the Secretary had invited members of the staff to submit suggestions which would "appraise the situation ahead of us during the next few months and years," Dr. Du Bois submitted a memorandum which, among other things, said:

> When, as in the first half of the twentieth century, progress fails and civilization is near collapse, then the suppressed group, especially if it has begun successfully to reduce discrimination and gain some integration into the national life of America, must adopt something beyond the negative program of resistance to discrimination and unite with the best elements of the nation in a positive constructive program for rebuilding civilization and reorienting progress....
>
> At present realizing that party government in this nation has definitely and disastrously broken down, we should in future elections ignore entirely all party labels and vote for candidates solely on their records and categorical promises. Each state, each county, each election precinct, should find out for itself carefully and as completely as possible the record of each candidate and strive to elect or defeat him whether he be Democrat, Republican, Labor Party or Communist. This should be a continuous job and not merely a pre-election activity; and it cannot be done on a national scale. This is a local job.

In November, 1946, Dr. Du Bois wrote the Secretary:

> The N.A.A.C.P. has taken no stand, nor laid down any program with regard to Africa. I have repeatedly urged this since my return from the Pan-African Congress.... If we are to enter into conference with regard to trusteeships and other programs we should be prepared with a policy and clear statement of position. I asked two years ago for authority to collect and publish the various demands of Africans for freedom and autonomy. Permission was never given. Such a series of documents would now be invaluable before the Assembly of the United Nations.

He received neither acknowledgement nor information as to whether this request ever reached the Board.

On August 20, 1948, Mr. White wrote Dr. Du Bois: "The Committee on Administration has recommended to the Board that I represent the N.A.A.C.P. at the U.N. General Assembly beginning September 21st in Paris. I would be grateful if you would give your recommendations of action on the issues which will arise there, particularly those dealing with human rights and trusteeship." In reply, Dr. Du Bois made four specific recommendations. He realized, however, that this was an entirely futile gesture, that no words of his would have the slightest influence on the U.S. delegation in Paris, that the N.A.A.C.P. was being "loaded on the Truman band wagon." He knew that the next meeting of the Board would take place *after* Mr. White sailed.

Nevertheless this indomitable fighter for the advancement of colored people resolved to storm the fort of reaction within his own organization. He sat down and wrote the now famous Memorandum condemning the Secretary's acceptance of membership "in this delegation without a clear, open and public declaration to the Board of our position on foreign policy"; as tying the Association "in with the reactionary, war-mongering colonial imperialism of the present Administration...."

I insist that here, if anywhere, in an organization seeking the welfare of the millions of colored people the world over is the place for careful knowledge of all facts and thoughtful consideration as to just what our plans and purposes are in this world crisis....I deny the right of any official to tie this organization to a foreign policy of an administration which stands against public discussion of our civil rights, for the despoiling of Ethiopia, for delaying the recognition of Israel, and in all matters against the best interests of colonial peoples.

I have before me Walter White's answer to Dr. Du Bois, a copy of which was sent to the Board of Directors for their meeting on September 13. From this insulting communication the Board drew the very words of its dismissal of Dr. Du Bois.

Fourteen years ago on July 9, 1934, the N.A.A.C.P. Board of Directors wrote:

It is with the deepest regret that we now accept the resignation of Dr. W. E. B. Du Bois...the ideas which he propounded...transformed the Negro world as well as a large portion of the white world, so that the whole problem of the relation of black and white races has ever since had a completely new orientation. Many who have never read a word of his writings are his spiritual disciples and descendants. Without him the Association could never have been what it was and is....He had been selected because of his independence of judgment, his fearlessness in expressing his convictions and his acute and wide-reaching intelligence. A mere yes-man could not have attracted the attention of the world, could not have stimulated the Board itself to further study of various important problems. We shall be the poorer for his loss in intellectual stimulus, and in searching analysis of the vital problems of the American Negro.

Of the Board members who passed this resolution, Joel Spingarn, then president, is dead; Mary White Ovington lies helpless in a hospital; John Haynes Holmes has withdrawn from any active part in the Association and Oswald Garrison Villard—well, two years ago they kicked him off the Board!

Is it any wonder that a rising wave of protest from the membership is now sweeping across the country? Is the present Board of Directors for the *advancement* of colored people or for their control? And is this power of control of the masses being paid for by advantage to the few? It is on record that Board-member Eleanor Roosevelt at the meeting of the Human Rights Commission in Geneva voted against placing the N.A.A.C.P. petition on the agenda, that she has since requested Dr. Du Bois not to press for its consideration by the U.N. General Assembly. It is also on record that several members of the Board are affiliated with the Truman Administration. At a time when imperialistic powers are vying with each other for control of Africa it is obviously safer in colonial matters to "consult" Walter White, who is blissfully ignorant of Africa, its peoples, its resources and its struggles, than W. E. B. Du Bois, who recently published *The World and Africa* and is in close touch with many colonial mass organizations.

People have built the N.A.A.C.P. for "organized determination and aggressive action on the part of those who believe in Negro freedom and growth."Through the years Dr. Du Bois has hewed to his credo upon which the Association was founded: *"We will not be satisfied to take one jot or tittle less than our full manhood rights."*

From Savannah, W. W. Law, chairman of the N.A.A.C.P. Youth Conference and College Chapters, has recently written Dr. Du Bois: "I am happy to join you in a fight that I trust you will not relinquish until the membership—not the Board—is fully aroused. To the youth of the Association, Dr. Du Bois has always symbolized the spirit and direction of the Association we all love."

Dr. Du Bois has yet to relinquish a fight. This one, to democratize the N.A.A.C.P., has just begun.

Masses and Mainstream, November 1948, vol. 1, no. 9, pp. 15–26.

57

WHY NEGROES ARE OPPOSED TO SEGREGATED REGIONAL SCHOOLS (1949)

by Charles H. Thompson

The editor of *The Journal of Negro Education,* published by Howard University, offers clear reasons to reject segregated education no matter how prettified.

On December 13, 1948, it was announced in the daily press that the Regional Council for Education, meeting in conjunction with the Southern Governors' Conference in Savannah, Georgia, had approved plans and allocated funds to begin regional cooperation in graduate and professional education in the South. This action, the result of a number of preparatory conferences, was taken to meet a threefold problem faced by the South. *First,* as is true in many states of the Union, as well as in adjoining states in the same region, there are a number of duplications in plant, equipment and personnel which could be greatly reduced, if not eliminated, by greater cooperation among the higher institutions in the same states or in the several states comprising the region. *Second,* in addition to this "normal" duplication there is the abnormal duplication resulting from the policy and practice of racial segregation which theoretically requires the establishment of two "separate-but-equal" systems of schools, thereby further intensifying the "normal" problem. *Third,* there has been and is inadequate provision of certain graduate and professional facilities, for both racial groups, because of the inability, in most cases, (and the inadvisability, in others) of the individual states to provide adequate educational services in certain areas such as forestry, veterinary medicine, and the like.

This recent news release is the announcement of the fact that the South through the Southern Governors' Conference has taken the first concrete step in the direction of meeting these problems on a regional basis. The Regional Council for Education, with former Governor Millard F. Caldwell of Florida, as chairman; Clyde A. Erwin, State Superintendent of Education in North Carolina, as vice-chairman; and H. C. Byrd, President of the University of Maryland, as secretary-treasurer, has been set up to work out ways and means of providing certain graduate and professional education on a regional basis.

Unfortunately, the Southern Governors' Conference and the Council itself have decided that such regional cooperation will be set up and administered on a segregated basis. Thus, regional services will be provided for Negroes and whites separately. It is this segregated aspect of the plan to which Negroes object, and with greater unanimity than I have noted in some time. In an effort to ascertain the reasons for this near unanimity of opposition against segregated regional cooperation in higher education, I have made some extensive inquiries, and have found that the bases of this opposition are not only sound but persuasive.

The first phase of this opposition appeared at the Hearings, held on March 12 and 13, 1948, by a sub-committee of the Senate Committee on the Judiciary, on S. J. Res. 191. This resolution embodied the request of the governors of 14 Southern states for "the consent of Congress to a compact entered into between the Southern States at Tallahassee, Florida, on February 8, 1948." In addition to a number of telegrams and letters, representatives of some ten or twelve organizations appeared in opposition to the granting of Congressional consent to this compact because it contemplated the setting up of segregated regional educational services. No one was opposed to the compact on any other grounds. All of the opposition was centered around the segregation aspect. It was argued that Congressional consent was not necessary to do what was contemplated under the compact, since the State of Virginia and the Meharry Medical College had had such an agreement for four years, and the State University of West Virginia and the University of Virginia had also had a similar contract for an equally long time. Thus it was insisted that the main purpose (if not purpose, certainly the effect) of this request was to obtain the implicit consent of Congress to the policy of separate schools, thereby giving aid and comfort to the proponents of segregation when that issue came before the U.S. Supreme Court.

Apparently this argument was partially persuasive with the Senate Committee because it recommended that the compact be approved with the following amendment: "*Provided,* That the consent of Congress to this compact shall not in any way be construed as an endorsement of segregation in education." However, when the Compact reached the Senate, some senators thought that the Committee's amendment did not go far enough, and thus a further amendment was proposed prohibiting the establishment of segregated schools or services under the Compact. The Senate after several hours of debate, effected a compromise between denying assent to the Compact altogether, and approving it with an amendment prohibiting segregated schools, by sending it back to the Committee—thus killing any chance of further consideration by the 80th Congress.

In addition to the organizations (the majority of which were Negro) which appeared in opposition to S. J. Res. 191, several organizations have recently reiterated their opposition in resolutions passed at their annual meetings. Just to mention a few: The Conference of Presidents of Negro Land Grant Colleges which met in Washington in October, 1948, reaffirmed its opposition to segregated regional schools and appointed a committee to study the question and recommend such action as seemed necessary. The Association of Colleges and Secondary Schools for Negroes which met in Wilmington, N.C., December 8–10, 1948, not only reaffirmed its opposition to segregated regional schools and services, but "resolved that this Association... will refuse to cooperate in this endeavor as long as the principle and practice of racial segregation are adhered to." Moreover, numerous Negro educators in the South have declined to serve on the study committees which have been set up by the Council to explore certain problems connected with the project. They have refused to stultify or prostitute themselves by cooperation in an enterprise which they feel is both unconstitutional and inconsiderate, if not unjust; and by cooperating on a level which is so far removed from policy-making as to be futile so far as affecting policy is concerned. Thus, it would appear that most of the opposition is persistent and calculated; rather than sporadic and misinformed.

In the first place, in my analysis of the opposition, I have been impressed by the fact that an overwhelming majority of Negroes and many Southern white people have come to the conclusion that you cannot have "separate but equal" educational provisions even in theory, and that least of all is it possible in the graduate and professional fields. They agree wholly with the conclusion of the President's Committee on Civil Rights, that the very act of segregation is per se an act of discrimination. Thus, they are opposed to segregated regional educational services because they are inherently discriminatory, and therefore patently unconstitutional. Moreover, it is noted that nowhere in the country can one produce a single example where "separate but equal" educational opportunity is provided by public funds. In each of the 17 states which require segregation by law, there is at least one state-supported Negro college. In no one of these instances is the Negro college equal to the comparable public higher institution for white students. Accordingly, Negroes conclude that these states are either unable or unwilling to provide "separate but equal" educational opportunity, and they do not see how separate regional schools will give them any more equality.

In the second place, it is the further contention of those who oppose segregated regional schools that not only is it impossible to provide "separate but equal" educational opportunity in principle, but what is more important, segregated regional graduate and professional programs are unnecessary in practice, and represent a backward step in the educational progress in the South. A dozen or more instances are cited where integrated education is taking place in the South, with everyone the better off for the experience. Moreover, white Southern educators and students, particularly in the graduate and professional fields, have indicated in numerous polls and in other ways that not only is there but little opposition to the admission of Negroes to the universities now attended almost exclusively by white students, but that the most economical thing to do is to provide for such integration. This is particularly true of the states in the upper South. Negroes are therefore opposed to any plan to extend inevitably inferior segregated education across state lines, because (1) it is unconstitutional; (2) it will make more difficult resort to the courts to get redress; and (3) it will impede the present trend toward integration.

In the third place, it is maintained that even if it were possible to have "separate but equal" regional graduate and professional schools in theory, they would not only be uneconomical but unattainable in actual practice. As an example of the uneconomical aspect of segregated regional schools, a recent action of the Council is instructive. It has been proposed that the Alabama Polytechnic Institute at Auburn, Alabama, and the University of Georgia at Athens, Georgia, provide training in veterinary medicine for white students in the Southeastern states; and that Tuskegee Institute, also in Alabama, provide veterinary medical training for the Negroes in the 17 Southern states. At a conference held on this question by the Council on October 6, 1948, it was reported that: "Representatives from all three schools stated that they face major problems in securing adequate staff and adequate clinical material.... An additional difficulty is the fact that API and Tuskegee must draw on the same geographic areas for clinical material." Here you not only have unnecessary duplication of facilities at API and Tuskegee, but even more important, you have direct competition for clinical material which is essential for the efficient operation of both. (In such competition it is clear that the Negro school at Tuskegee is likely to suffer more, as is usually the case.) To say the least, this is an example of uneconomical duplication which is inherent and inevitable in the practice of maintaining separate schools, and results in poorer education for both racial groups.

It is even more instructive to observe that "separate but equal" graduate work, for example, is unattainable in actual practice. While the Council has not made specific proposals concerning graduate education, any unbiased examination of the practical possibilities of segregated regional graduate work, as far as Negroes are concerned, reveals that it would be practically impossible to establish even *one* regional graduate school for Negroes which could equal any one of several in state universities for white students in the South at the present time. (And I might add parenthetically that it would be foolish to attempt it.) For example, graduate work is offered in at least one public institution for white students in each of the 17 Southern states in an average of 50 different fields; and graduate work leading to the doctorate is offered by at least one public institution for white students in each of 12 states. From the point of view of teachers alone (white and Negro), it would be impossible to staff even *one* regional university for Negroes which would be competent to give graduate work in half of the fields now offered to white students in the average Southern state, to say nothing about providing a program leading to the doctorate which could by any stretch of the imagination be equal to the work now given at the University of Texas, the University of North Carolina, the University of Missouri, or the University of Oklahoma, just to mention a few.

Other examples could be given in other fields but these two are sufficient to illustrate the point that even if it were granted (which it is not) that you could have "separate but equal" graduate and professional work in theory, it is not possible to do so in actual practice. And what is more, the Regional Council for Education being composed of intelligent people must be aware of this fact. Thus, when proposals are made which contemplate setting up segregated regional institutions or services for

Negroes, there is no other conclusion to which Negroes can validly come, except that there is no intention on the part of the proponents of this plan to provide Negroes with equal educational opportunities; that this latest move (in addition to whatever benefits which may be gained by white students) is merely another scheme to evade the constitutional mandate that Negroes be given equal educational opportunity; and that the end-effect will be to increase the disparity in the provisions which now obtains.

In view of the persistence of the Regional Council in its plans to set up segregated regional services and in view of its protestations that it is not interested in the extension of segregation, but rather in providing better education for everyone, it seems desirable to explore this point a step further. Implicit in the arguments of Governor Caldwell and others before the Senate sub-committee which held hearings on S. J. Res. 191 last spring, as well as in the subsequent expositions of the Regional Council, is the following line of reasoning: Regional schools will provide greater educational opportunity than schools supported by the individual states. Since we have separate Negro schools in the Southern states, segregated regional schools will provide greater educational opportunity than the present Negro separate schools in the individual states. Hence, Negroes would be short-sighted to oppose segregated regional schools.

Curiously enough, only a handful of Negro educators have professed to see enough merit in this argument to go along with it, and all of them, admittedly, have ulterior motives in doing so. On the other hand, the overwhelming majority of Negroes and their white friends have categorically rejected this proposition for several reasons, of which the following are the most important.

First, it is pointed out that this argument is based upon the invalid assumption that some additional makeshift graduate and professional work on a wider scale is better than none at all (as is true in some places now), or better than what is being given for Negroes in some of the states at the present time. If this proposition had been presented to Negroes ten years ago, before they had had considerable experience with inferior graduate and professional work, it might have appealed to them as being realistic. However, ten years of experience with such inferior graduate provisions as have been established has convinced them that *no* graduate and professional work for the time being would be better than what has been and can be provided. And especially is this true, since such work has been and is provided at the expense of the undergraduate program which is uniformly sub-standard. Negroes are convinced that the only way to provide graduate and professional work for Negroes equal to that provided for white students in the South is on an integrated basis. Thus, they think it would be short-sighted, indeed, to accept any compromise which would jeopardize the attainment of this objective, as well as that of developing a first class undergraduate program.

Second, it is emphasized that the above argument is based upon the half-truth that segregated schools are inevitable for a long time to come, and that integration is not possible in the near future. Negroes are well aware of the fact that the *complete* elimination of segregation in education in the South may take a long time, and they are willing to cooperate with any gradual but progressive program of elimination. However, they insist that the elimination should be started and that the most logical place to start is in the graduate and professional fields where the students involved are fewer in number and more mature in emotional development, where it is absolutely impossible to provide even the semblance of equality under segregation, and where it would be financially prohibitive even to try. Moreover, as has been pointed out, there are sufficient instances of integration on this level in the South to suggest that a well conceived and honestly administered plan for integration in the graduate and professional fields would be successful. Negroes therefore feel that any further compromise on this issue at this time would not only be shortsighted and unwise, but a distinct disservice to higher education in the South.

Third, it is noted finally that the above argument is based upon the fallacious, if not callous, assumption that the Southern Governors' Conference and the Regional Council for Education have no responsibility for the existence and extension of segregated schools in the South, and therefore all that they can or should do is try to improve the situation within the framework of the status quo. This is such an amazing assumption that it probably would be profitable to spell it out in some detail. At the Hearings on S. J. Res. 191 last spring, the Chairman permitted Dr. Martin D. Jenkins, a witness against approval of the Compact, to put a question to Governor Millard F. Caldwell of Florida, Chairman of the Regional Council for Education. Dr. Jenkins: " . . . . Is it the purpose of the Southern Governors' Conference to set up regional institutions under this compact which are segregated on the basis of race?" Governor Caldwell: "The question has never been discussed, but my guess is that the only thing that the regional compact can provide for is such types of education as are authorized by the constitutions of the several states . . . ." Moreover, subsequent to this dialogue, the Council adopted and published the following policy statement: "Regional services, whether developed at existing institutions or directed by the board are subject to applicable State and Federal laws and court decisions." Obviously, the most charitable construction which might be put upon these quotations (which are typical) is that the Southern Governors' Conference and its offspring, the Regional Council for Education, disclaim any interest in, or responsibility for, the segregated schools of the South, except to try to improve them within the framework of segregation.

It has seemed almost inconceivable that a group of the most potent politicians in the South, complemented by a group of the most intelligent white educators in the South, could or would sit around a conference table for several days at a time on more than one occasion and arrive at the conclusion that segregated education is none of their business; or come to the conclusion that even if it is their business, they are powerless to do anything about it, except to make an ineffective attempt to improve the situation within the segregated framework. Such a position is neither statesmanlike nor realistic; and is understandable only if the Southern politicians who dominate the Council have decided to take the same intransigent and unstatesmanlike attitude toward this problem that they have taken in almost every situation involving race relations since the Civil War. In every instance involving the civil rights of the Negro in the Southern states, the South has decried outside interference and vowed that it would do the just thing, if allowed to do so of its own volition. However, history records that the South has seldom, if ever, taken a statesmanlike stand on the race problem and has only acted fairly in the face of extreme pressure. Negroes and their friends had thought that the South had arrived at a point, in connection with the problem of regional cooperation, where it would face all of the issues involved and demonstrate that it has the statesmanship and the courage which are necessary to make a forward social step without undue pressure.

But in this hope Negroes have been disappointed and aggrieved. The Regional Council for Education knows that the courts have ruled that Negroes should have equal educational opportunity. It also knows that such opportunity cannot be provided under a segregated regional plan; in fact, the Council makes no claim that equal opportunity can or will be provided under its scheme of regional cooperation. Negroes not only reject the position, which is implicit in the Council's plan, but resent the "take-it-or-leave-it" attitude that goes along with it. They are pretty certain that it would be shortsighted to "take it" and they feel that there are other alternatives to that of "leave it."

Why are Negroes opposed to segregated regional graduate and professional work? The answer briefly is that they are opposed only to the segregated aspect of it. They have no objection to and see considerable advantage in regional services which are based upon a principle which looks forward to a greater educational future for the South, rather than backward to a decade or more ago. More specifically, Negroes are opposed to segregated regionalism, (1) because they are convinced that equal educational opportunity cannot be provided for Negroes under the theory of "separate but equal," and thus they refuse to cooperate in any plan which is so patently and inherently discriminatory in its very conception. (2) Negroes are convinced by recent events and the present climate of public opinion that segregated graduate and professional work in the South is unnecessary, and constitutes a backward step in the educational progress of the South. (3) Negroes have concluded that even if "separate but equal" educational opportunity were at all possible in theory, it would be definitely uneconomical and actually unattainable in practice. (4) Empirical evidence obtained during the past ten years has convinced Negroes that the old cliché—a half loaf is better than no bread—as far as segregated graduate and professional work is concerned, is fallacious. The extension of grossly inferior graduate and professional work, and particularly at the expense of the undergraduate program, is shortsighted—so much so, that *no* segregated graduate and professional work for the time being is better than what is contemplated. However, Negroes are still hoping that the Regional Council for Education will reconsider its decision and set up regional services on a sound and constructive basis.

The Journal of Negro Education 18 (Winter 1949): 1–8.

58

"ON BEHALF OF OUR CHILDREN" (1948)

by Atlanta Parents Council

On December 3, 1948, the Atlanta Parents Council for Better Public Schools, chaired by Mrs. E. L. Dixon, petitioned for equality in the education of African-American and white youngsters. This illustrates the kind of organizational activity against Jim Crow that continued for decades and—combined with other stimuli—finally vanquished *legal* segregation.

TO: The Superintendent and Board of Education of Atlanta, Georgia

FROM: *Atlanta Parents Council for Better Public Schools.*

On September 14th, parents with children enrolled in the thirteen public schools for Negro children filed with the Board of Education a petition in behalf of their children, and the thirteen thousand other Negro elementary school children similarly situated.

The Board of Education subsequently admitted in the press that "inadequate housing facilities" are a major handicap in the provision of equal educational opportunity for Negro children. . . .

Our concern however is with the difficulties experienced by our children which are caused by "inadequate housing facilities." Too few classrooms and inferior school buildings are responsible for the following conditions:

1. Of the 13,000 Negro elementary school children enrolled in Atlanta, more than 11,650 or approximately 90% attend school only 2 to 3 hours each day because of "double or triple sessions."

   The number of Negro elementary school children on double sessions this year, is greater than the total Negro elementary school enrollment last year. Although there may be "only 8% of the colored teachers with double sessions" the *number of children on double sessions increases yearly.*

   We believe that it is too great a compliment to the intelligence of Negro children, to assume that they can learn as much as other children, in one-third or one-half the time.

2. The majority of these children are required to walk long distances, to cross dangerous traffic intersections and railroad tracks, in order to attend school for even the short period of two or three hours.

3. The efforts of the Board of Education to alleviate overcrowding at the high school level are recognized, but the congestion in elementary schools steadily increases. The housing of all seventh grades in elementary school buildings to which no additional space has been added contributes to this serious over-crowding.

4. The failure to provide running water and flush toilets at the Bush Mountain and Armour Schools is a constant menace to the health of the children who attend these schools, and to a larger population.

The Board of Education finds it necessary because of rising costs, to authorize an expenditure of $1,126,409 or 26 percent more than was allocated in bond funds for the white school projects which are underway.

It would therefore seem reasonable to expect an equal percent of increase to be necessary in the authorized cost of construction of Negro school projects. It is surprising to note, however, that the authorized cost for construction of the Negro school projects is *one percent less* than was allocated for those projects in the bond program.

Citizens may legitimately be concerned that the cost of construction for school projects for one group of our city's children exceeds to such an extent the bond funds allocated, while construction for another group can be authorized at costs which permit a small saving within the bond allocation.

The Board states that "it has no policy for Negro schools separate or different from that for white schools." It is therefore reasonable to expect the same rate of progress in the authorization for construction of Negro schools designated in the bond program, as is evident in the authorization of other school projects. It is also reasonable to expect the use of additional funds to meet increased building costs in the same proportion for all schools. The failure of the Board of Education to apply in practice its "frequently announced policy of treating all school children alike," means that the existing racial differentials in unit costs for investment in school plants will steadily increase.

The considered judgment of many citizens supports the opinion that increased financial support for the improvement of all schools is necessary, but that such increased support should serve to decrease rather than to increase existing inequalities. The social consequences of prevailing inequities in the Atlanta public schools have been all too evident, too long. The development of consistency between stated administrative policy and administrative practice would tend to sustain and improve American democracy.

Mimeographed copy of petition in the editor's possession. Tables omitted.

59

THE EMBATTLED SOUTHWEST (1948)

The Southwest Region Staff of the NAACP, whose secretary was Donald Jones, issued a *Newsletter* at the close of 1948. It discerned an "important change in the circumstances surrounding our Fight for Freedom." The *Newsletter's* summary follows:

In Louisiana, in 1948, the salaries of Negro public school teachers were equalized all over the state with salaries paid white teachers amounting to more than $2,000,000 in increased income and an unlimited amount of increased self-respect and independence. Also, Louisiana Negroes have at last broken through the registration barriers and are voting in good numbers all over the state. In New Orleans alone 13,000 Negroes voted in the recent elections.

In Texas, in 1948, several important legal victories were won against public school boards, and the celebrated Sweatt Case finally cleared state courts and headed for the United States Supreme Court. Following a prearranged plan, Texas in 1948 laid the groundwork for an all-out assault on segregation in education in 1949. The sale of some $10,000 worth of unique Freedom Bonds demonstrated a refreshing ability among Texas Negroes to embrace an imaginative appreciation of their struggle and lay out hard dollars to pay for it.

In Oklahoma, in 1948, the famous Sipuel Case won a partial victory, resulting in the establishment of a Jim Crow law school which no Negroes have yet attended, before the U.S. Supreme Court, then started back through the courts to attempt gaining a greater victory before the Supreme Court. Three other cases, meanwhile, were filed against the University of Oklahoma, and the plaintiff in one of them, J. W. McLaurin, has now been admitted to classes at the University on a segregated basis. Early in 1949 Mr. McLaurin's case is expected to reach the U.S. Supreme Court, setting forth as its plea that Mr. McLaurin be admitted to his classes without segregation.

In Arkansas, in 1948, Negro students were admitted to Arkansas University's School of Law and School of Medicine without segregation. The State took this action voluntarily, although it is felt that the pressure being put on the states of Texas and Oklahoma had a lot to do with the decision. Also, suit was filed in November, 1948, against the school board of Fort Smith, Arkansas by Negro parents of the community claiming discrimination on account of race.

And then—there was the result of the national election on November 2nd, which Mr. Truman won. As pointed out before in the NEWSLETTER, millions of Southern white people gave evidence of the change taking place in their hearts and heads by marching to the polls and voting for Truman and Civil Rights.

In addition, there are thousands of other evidences of change around us, everywhere we look. By no means is the evil beast of segregation conquered; by no means can any Negro be sure from hour to hour that he won't be insulted and humiliated or beaten or killed on the slightest excuse. But no longer is our situation at a standstill—hopeless and heartrending. CHANGE is taking place—things are MOVING—the forces of prejudice and injustice are being PUSHED BACK. We are on the way to a better day, and we cannot now be stopped. . . .

AT SOWERS COMMUNITY, TEXAS, as the *Newsletter* has previously informed you, a suit was filed by the people of the community through their NAACP Branch against the school board some time ago. In all honesty, although as usual we went into it to *win*, the legal staff didn't regard the Sowers Case as one of its really big and important cases. But the School Board, spurred on by screams of pain from the *Dallas Morning News,* evidently thought that we had cocked both barrels and were ready to let them have the full load in the pit of the stomach. Because the School Board did some powerful running. It hauled truckloads of equipment over to the school. It dug a well, announcing that it had gone down so deep it had struck "the best water in the county." It bought a bus to haul the children. It returned about $350 in back bus fares to parents. And then, when the trial approached, its attorneys met with NAACP Attorneys Durham and Tate and said, in effect, "Gentlemen, we don't want to fight. All you say is true. Just write out the judgment, we'll admit that what you say is true, and we'll ask the Judge to sign it." And that's what was done. Judge H. H. Atwell signed the summary judgment on the morning of December 20th.

IN THE FORT SMITH, ARKANSAS CASE, a similar education case filed by Negro parents against the school board, matters have taken a different turn. Ten parents agreed to act as plaintiffs, but when the case was filed by NAACP Attorneys J. R. Booker of Little Rock and Tate, Regional Special Counsel, some of the parents pulled out of the case. They were scared by the big black headlines in the daily paper the morning after the filing, and maybe some white folks dropped a word or two of advice to them just in passing—you know what advice: "This thing might cause you to lose your job—"

At any rate, some of them dropped out—but for every *one* that quit, *two* took his place. When word got around that the knees of some of the plaintiffs had gotten weak, Branch Officers Rutledge, Davis and

Mitchiner were approached on the street by other Negroes who asked to be allowed to serve as plaintiffs. Let's all give a rousing cheer for these staunch brothers of ours. And let's have only pity in our hearts for those other weak brothers, whose weakness was the weakness of ignorance. They tried, but were found wanting.

And maybe, at that, they were fleeing from a shadow. Here's what happened to show that not all, at least, of the white people in Fort Smith are against Negroes having their rights:

When the suit was filed on November 10 in the Federal Court Building in Fort Smith, the Regional Secretary took the elevator for the clerk's office, the same elevator in which, a few minutes before, the attorneys and members of the branch delegation had ridden up. The elevator man, a white fellow, asked the Reg. Sec.:

"What y'all trying to do, get a new high school?"

"That's about the size of it," replied the Reg. Sec.

"Good!" said the elevator operator, slapping his leg. "That's sure fine! Y'all sure need it, and I wish you the best of luck."

Perhaps we ought to send our frail brothers around to talk with the elevator operator.

IN TEXAS, A GREAT NUMBER OF our people appear to believe that all the hopes of the NAACP to break down segregation are wrapped up in the Sweatt Case, and that if, by chance, we lose the Sweatt Case, we are sunk.

Now it's true that we do have high hopes for the Sweatt Case, and we think we have a better than even chance to win it.

But if we don't, then what? Why, then we simply start all over again, building a better and stronger case using the experience we have gained in the Sweatt Case. One thing is certain: If the state of Texas, or any other state, thinks that by whipping us in the Sweatt Case or any other case it can sit back comfortably and twiddle its thumbs, it is due for a rude awakening. Their lawyers had better make up their minds to keep their noses buried in law books until the day they decide to live up to their laws, or change them. . . .

IN ITS LAST ISSUE THE NEWSLETTER had some hard things to say about the Uncle Tom type of Negroes who are presidents of many Negro colleges. Perhaps it should be mentioned that, very fortunately, some of our schools are headed up by truly great, courageous, unselfish men, an outstanding example being Dr. Joseph J. Rhoads of Bishop College, Marshall, Texas.

Besides being a scholar, of sterling character and winning personality, Dr. Rhoads is recognized in Texas as the militant leader of that state's highly militant leaders. He is president of the Texas Council of Negro Organizations which includes in its membership 31 state-wide organizations, the leaders of which come together at intervals to decide what stand to take on issues and formulate general policy in the struggle for freedom. As president, and as willingly acknowledged leader, Dr. Rhoads wields large influence in the Council and is responsible in great measure for the fact that Texas Negroes for the most part are a well-knit, organized body, moving solidly in one direction.

Incidentally, those of you who know and love Dr. Rhoads will be happy to know that he is recovering nicely from the amputation of one leg, and is chomping at the bit to be up and about again.

Mimeographed copy of the *Newsletter*, vol. 2, no. 20, dated December 22, 1948; in the editor's possession. Published in part. The reference to the 1948 election reflects the defeat of the States Rights party's challenge to President Truman.

60

OPTIMISM IN THE NORTHWEST (1949)

by Edwin C. Berry

For its "Brotherhood Month" issue in February 1949, the *Christian Register* "searched for an outstanding success in race relations." It offered an essay by Edwin C. Berry, executive secretary of the Urban League of Portland, Oregon.

As late as 1945, Portland was known as the "Worst City in Race Relations North of the Mason Dixon Line." There were many reasons for this reference. Although I could not refute this, I used the somewhat milder description of my community—"A Northern City with a Southern Exposure."

In interpreting the Portland race relations arena in 1945, I wrote as follows:

America is a Democracy—a nation whose people fight for a chance for every individual to become what he is capable of becoming; for the right of each individual to freedom and the pursuit of happiness. But our exciting and inspiring American Creed is bluntly contradicted in Portland and elsewhere in America by the denial of the freedom of opportunity and choice—America's birthright—to fifteen million Negro Americans.

Jim Crow is the antithesis of our American Creed. Jim Crow divides Americans; causes fear, suspicion and hate to set Americans one against the other; causes our nation to become internally weak.

Jim Crow lives in Portland!

His presence is manifested by the "White Only" signs in restaurants, hotels, and places of amusement; by the symbolic "White Only" signs on jobs, and on houses for sale and for rent; by rigid segregation in our public housing communities; by slanderous utterances of bigots and demagogues that appear in print, and are passed on by word of mouth.

Jim Crow is a relic of the Feudal System. His counterpart, the ghetto, is an alien technique of compressing a group of people in a certain residential area, and degrading them to the point that one might find some credence for the stories which have been invented about them. The despicable Hitler used this technique in the process of maligning the Jews.

Jim Crow is degrading to Negro Americans who are forced to live by his dictates.

Jim Crow dooms the children of Negro Americans, even those who are as yet unborn.

Jim Crow is more vicious than all of this, because he is causing America to lose her moral leadership in world affairs. Our utterances of the American Creed and our enunciated war aims sound hollow indeed when superimposed upon the actual lives of millions of Americans.

The reasons for this dual system of citizenship—one set of rights and privileges for whites and another, and more limited set, for Negroes—are manifold. Greed, hate, and vested interests all play a part. The unfortunate history of human bondage in America cannot be overlooked. These inequalities and injustices are bred more often by misinformation than by malice. The Urban League, therefore, looks upon that phase of its work which deals with public education—the correction of this misinformation—as fundamental to any lasting progress in the arena of race relations.

Present Scene

In 1948, Portland had won for itself the distinction of "Nation's Most Improved City in Race Relations." I must caution my readers at this point that the description "most improved" should not be confused with "best." We know we are not the "best." But "best" is our goal and we are moving steadily and with dogged determination toward that goal.

Here follows a partial delineation of the reasons we have won our new title in a span of but three years:

On The Job Front: Negroes have secured employment in more than four hundred establishments which did not employ them prior to 1945. Negroes are working on all levels of civil service and are consistently securing added union status. Among the better positions which have been filled by qualified Negro workers are: public school teachers; one instructor on the college level; laboratory technicians; hospital nurses; social workers; and a public welfare supervisor. Innumerable secretaries have been placed (so many, in fact, that we have exhausted the supply, and job orders still continue), as well as the multitude of opportunities for skilled artisans and unskilled jobs.

The Housing Field: Portland has progressed in the housing field notwithstanding the "code of ethics" of the Realty Board and its attempts at rigid segregation on non-white minorities in an old, worn out section of the city. The boundary lines have been broken. Realtors have been forced to revise the limits on several occasions and the expansion continues. During the past twelve months more than one hundred families have purchased decent homes outside the area which realtors had designated for Negro occupancy. This was accomplished by purchase from *real estate dealers—not "realtors"—*or directly from owner.

Another important step toward integration in housing has been the breaking of rigid segregation by the Portland Public Housing Authority. The present enunciated policy is "first come, first served," and though this policy has not yet been completely accepted by housing staff, the first steps of integration are in evidence.

Police Brutality: Brutality on the part of police officers, due to racial bias, has practically disappeared. There has been no case reported for one year.

Public Schools: Our public schools are among the best in the nation when evaluated from a race relations point of view. Teacher appointments are being currently made on the basis of qualification and without regard to race. Nine Negro teachers were appointed at the beginning of the school year. All are assigned where their skills indicate, and several are working in schools where no Negro students are in attendance. Students are welcome, and do participate in all branches of extra curricular athletics.

Higher Education: Negro students are enrolled in all Portland colleges and at the local medical and law schools. Portland boasts two colleges, one university, and two junior colleges. Each is anxious to increase attendance of non-white students.

Social Services: At this point, we can state without equivocation, social services in Portland are freer of discrimination than in any other large city in the country. This statement is true for both public and private agencies. Public Welfare is above reproach; all group work and leisure time agencies are open to all. We do not have the traditional Jim Crow YMCA and YWCA to plague us. All thirteen summer camps serving this community are operated on an integrated basis and Negro youth were in attendance at all camps in the season past. Many Negroes are serving in responsible staff positions. An increasing number of Negroes are being elected to board and committee positions.

Health Service: All Portland hospitals are operated on a non-segregated basis. Negro physicians, nurses, nurses aides, technicians and other personnel are employed.

The Press: Portland's two daily newspapers operate in a highly enlightened manner. Both papers have discontinued the use of racial identification technique (approximately 95% of the time). Both freely carry news about Negroes and interracial affairs and treat it with objectivity. Both papers use pictures of Negroes throughout the paper (not just in the sports section) and editorial treatment on subjects of race relations has been generally fair and sympathetic to those working for improvement.

Pulpit and Pew: Portland churches have been great allies in our battle against bigotry. Many churches are making a determined effort to achieve interracial congregations. This is difficult because of established patterns of religious segregation and because of brick and mortar interests in churches which have been traditionally segregated. However, the amount of interracial teaching and encouragement for social action that has come from Portland churches has been of immeasurable assistance. The church is unquestionably the bearer of moral values in our society. Recently Portland churches have been active in developing a "conscience about race relations." The absence of this "conscience" in the past has been a moral deficiency in our national character. This deficiency has been a distinct deterrent to progress.

The How of Achievement

The actual "how" of this achievement process is so simple that it hardly seems worthwhile recording. It would not be worth recording except that to many practitioners in the field of race and group relations, the obvious and easy approach is overlooked and the elaborate and impossible used.

Improvement in race relations in Portland began with the establishment of the Urban League of Portland. Let me say parenthetically, at this point, that my own identification with the Urban League and personal modesty should not permit this revelation—but my training in social science dictates complete objectivity.

The steps in the program that have led to partial accomplishment of our goals are these:

1. Public Education.
2. Continuing efforts to broaden our circle of friends.
3. Community organization—constant cooperation with other agencies, churches and groups.
4. Demonstration.
5. Crystallization in action, codes of procedure, policy and law, gains accomplished and accepted.
6. Vigiliantly watching and constantly guarding each progressive step.

PUBLIC EDUCATION

The initiation of our program here was based on the following fundamental beliefs:

1. There is gross ignorance, misinformation and superstition accepted by otherwise intelligent people, about race.
2. Most Caucasians in the Northwest were not bigots; they were bewildered, not malicious, but misinformed.
3. Conditions under which Negroes were forced to live, work, play, and worship were not widely known to most persons whose lives were untouched by Negroes and who were, therefore, unconcerned about them.
4. Most Americans are a part of the great army of "bystanders." They are neither a part of the small forward looking citizens, nor of the reactionaries. The bystanders are overwhelmingly possessed with inertia and are likely to be governed by tradition rather than by conviction.
5. Most business men, politicians, and others in responsible positions believe all Caucasians are racists unless they have declared themselves otherwise.

6. Most decisions related to race made by persons in policy-making positions, are based on the crude premise that "you'll holler when you're hurt," and the absence of a complaint indicates consensus.

7. To most community leaders "the public" excludes Negroes and any other minorities that happen to be a part of the "out group."

8. Minority groups are equally as capable of bigotry as those of the majority.

9. No program for human decency and social justice can be achieved with apologies and defensive mechanisms.

10. Negroes are in greater need of a courageous, intelligent and forthright program of public relations than any other type of program.

We have interpreted our public relations program as one of telling and getting told, and supplying information to others who wish to tell the truth about race, race relations and interracial affairs. In prosecuting this phase of our program we have:

1. Distributed 300,000 individual pieces of educational material—both original work and the best publications available free or for a very small cost.

2. Carried on a campaign by radio and press.

3. Furnished outstanding speakers for thousands of groups and meetings.

4. Furnished material for other speakers and innumerable study groups, schools and colleges.

5. Kept libraries well supplied with the best current materials on race relations.

This part of our program has been the springboard for all other efforts, and in my opinion, is basic to any real and lasting progress in race relations. This phase of the effort in Portland has been dealt with in a more comprehensive manner than those which follow. This is true, for the reasons that this section is by far the most significant and the space allocated would not permit so detailed a discussion of each point which follows.

DEMONSTRATION

We have felt it a wise and useful technique to exploit and draw wide attention to good examples of democracy in action. We know that nothing so shakes the confidence of bigots as to be brought face to face with reality. Nothing so impresses the "bystander" as living proof that interracialism works.

I will cite two examples of the demonstration technique. Both occurred in Portland.

1. The disastrous Vanport Flood of May 30, 1948: This flood completely demolished an entire city of 22,000 persons—5,000 of them were Negroes.

The emergency housing of these persons was a problem which Portland had to face in a matter of minutes. Negroes were housed in non-segregated mass shelters. And several hundred Negro families were invited to share homes of white Portlanders. In administering the mass shelter program, we worked closely with the American Red Cross. The Red Cross carried out a completely integrated program, without a single unfavorable incident. This action on the part of the Red Cross seemed to amaze some of its own workers, equally as much as it surprised observers. One worker from Georgia or Mississippi—I seem to confuse those two States—was delighted with the program. This was especially pleasant coming from one who spoke with a decided Southern accent. She told me that in a dozen years of disaster work, in all sections of the country, she had never participated in a plan of integrated housing.

We were particularly diligent in seeing that this story was widely known. The interpretation carried proper commendation for the Red Cross job. We issued several newsletters, press and radio releases and assisted in the preparation of two full page news and picture stories. Result: information on how Portland handled the emergency was circulated throughout the State and the Nation. Commendations poured in from all sections of the country. All concerned were made to feel proud and happy. Those who stubbornly and loudly had insisted it would not work were forced into a state of silence and retreat.

2. The CIO Convention, held in Portland, November, 1948: In preparation for the Convention, CIO elicited a promise from the Restaurant and Hotel Associations that there would be no racial discrimination for the duration of the Convention. Many Negro delegates attended. They stayed in hotels and ate in restaurants that have maintained the color ban from time immemorial. Result: no harmful effects, no guests walked out of any hotels, the buildings did not disintegrate and the sun continued to shine, as often as the sun shines, in Portland.

We joined in commending local operators of public accommodations for their democratic action, even though we realized they had simply called a moratorium on discrimination for one week. However, since the moratorium, we have pointed out to the community that decency and democracy can work in the use of public accommodations. We are now able to document our assertion with the obvious proof that it did work.

Efforts to Crystallize Gains: We believe that once a group, organization, community, or State, has been enlightened on democracy in race relations, it is important that a policy relating to democratic practices be made permanent. This has an important psychological effect on those charged with the responsibility for executing the policy. It also provides positive public relations material and serves to influence other organizations to take similar action. We have used this technique successfully in Portland, with organized groups, agencies, schools, and with public bodies up to and including government of the State.

Constant Vigilance: The task of improving race relations is very difficult for a variety of reasons. One of the important reasons is that we seldom complete any phase of it in a way which permits us to forget it and move on. Once a progressive step (I believe "progressive" can be used in this context without misunderstanding) has been achieved, it has to be watched, lest undemocratic forces abolish it.

Conclusion

In Portland, we have Jim Crow down, but not quite out. We've had him out but the opposition applied artificial respiration. Right now, he's existing in an oxygen tent. This is costly. The community has to pay the bill. Our community is getting tired of it. It is our job to keep them informed about that, also.

Reprinted as a pamphlet—in the editor's possession—by the Urban League of Portland in 1949. For a strikingly contrary view of this city at this time, see W. E. B. Du Bois, *In Battle for Peace.*

61

DISCREDITING RADICAL AFRICAN-AMERICANS (1949)

With the intensification of the Cold War and its related "loyalty" investigations, African-American militants of significant fame were selected by government agencies—especially the FBI—for campaigns of slander. Leading media cooperated. Among the earliest victims was Paul Robeson, head of the Council on African Affairs, a leader in worldwide peace efforts and internationally celebrated artist. A high point of this destructive campaign came in 1949 when Paul Robeson was nearly lynched in Peekskill, New York, and when he was widely portrayed as a traitor.

Two documents illustrating these developments in 1949 follow. First (a) is a brief press release by the Council on African Affairs in New York City, dated July 20, 1949; the second (b) was entitled "My Answer," as told to a leading black reporter, Dan Bailey, later that year.

[a]

STATEMENT ON UN-AMERICAN ACTIVITIES COMMITTEE

Quite clearly America faces a crisis in race relations. The Un-American Activities Committee moves now to transform the Government's cold war policy against the Negro people into a hot war. Its action incites the Ku Klux Klan, that open terrorist organization, to a reign of mob violence against my people in Florida and elsewhere. This Committee attempts to divide the Negro people one from another in order to prevent us from winning jobs, security and justice under the banner of peace. The loyalty of the Negro people is not a subject for debate. I challenge the loyalty of the Un-American Activities Committee. This committee maintains an ominous silence in the face of the lynchings of Maceo Snipes, Robert Mallard, the two Negro veterans and their wives in Monroe, Georgia, and the violent and unpunished murders of scores of Negro veterans by white supremacists since V-J Day. It is not moved to investigate the attempted legal lynchings of Mrs. Rosa Lee Ingram, Negro mother of 12 living children and her two sons, now jailed for life in Georgia for protecting her honor; or of the Trenton Six, or the Martinsville Seven or the denial of simple justice to our people in the every day life of the nation's capitol. Every pro-war fascist-minded group in the country regards the Committee's silence as license to proceed against my people, unchecked by Government authorities and unchallenged by the courts.

Our fight for peace in America is a fight for human dignity, and an end to ghetto life. It is the fight for the constitutional liberties, the civil and human rights of every American. This struggle is the decisive struggle with which my people are today concerned. This fight is of vital concern to all progressive Americans, white as well as Negro. For victory in this struggle, Americans need peace, not war on foreign fields.

No country in the world today threatens the peace and safety of our great land. It is not the Soviet Union that threatens the life, liberty and the property and citizenship rights of Negro Americans. The threat comes from within. To destroy this threat our people need the aid of every honest American, Communist and non-Communist alike. Those who menace our lives proceed unchallenged by the Un-American Activities Committee. I shall not be drawn into any conflict dividing me from my brother victims of this terror. I am wholly committed to the struggle for peace and democratic rights of free Americans.

P. S. Foner, *Paul Robeson Speaks, op.cit., p. 218.*

[b]

MY ANSWER

I'm in the headlines and they're saying all manner of things about me such as "enemy" of the land of my birth, "traitor" to my country, "dangerous radical" and that I am an "ungrateful" cur. But they can't say that I am not 100 percent for my people. The American Press has set out on its own campaign of deliberate misquotation and distortion of the things I say and do, trying to set my people against me, but they can't win because what I say is the unadulterated truth which cannot be denied.

Everybody is trying to explain Paul Robeson. That isn't hard. I'm just an ordinary guy like anyone else, trying to do what I can to make things match, to find and tie up the loose ends. I am asked do I think the salvation of the American Negro lies in complete integration—social, political and economic, or in a highly developed Negro nationalism. Let me answer it in my way.

The whole Negro problem has its basis in the South—in the cotton belt where Negroes are in the majority. That is the only thing that explains me completely. The Negro upper class wants to know why I am out here struggling in behalf of the oppressed, exploited Negro of the South when I could isolate myself from them like they do and become wealthy by keeping quiet on such disturbing subjects. This, I have found, would not be true of me. What I earn doesn't help my people that much. I have relatives in the South still struggling to make a living. The other night in Newark, one relative of mine was in the audience. He is a mason and a carpenter. What I do personally doesn't help him. I found I have to think of the whole background of the Negro problem. Therefore I have taken my obligations to the Negro people very seriously.

I have asked myself just what Negro people am I fighting for. The big Negroes take it that I am fighting for them and since they're comfortable and living good, they don't want too much fighting or things said that might prove embarrassing to their positions. My travels abroad, however, have shown me what and whom I am fighting for. During my travels, I met native Africans, West Indians, Chinese, East Indians and other dark people who are fighting for the same thing—freedom from bondage of the imperialistic Wall St., the bankers and the plantation bosses, whether in London or in New York. The big Negro wants somebody to fight for him, but his objectives are purely selfish. If I am fighting for the Negroes on Strivers Row, I must fight for every Negro, wherever he may be.

Let's return again to the fact that the whole Negro problem has its basis in the South. Do you know that out of 15 million Negroes in the United States, nearly 10 million live and die in the South? I've got to be interested in basic problems, the people and conditions on the lower levels of life. I found that Negroes constitute 98 per cent of the population of the West Indies. Without the Negro there could be no economic South and there could be no economic West Indies to make the bankers and overlords of Wall St. fabulously wealthy. In the South, Negroes do most of the work and get nothing from it in return.

I understand these things better on my travels abroad. In England I met boys and girls from Africa working on ships, in the schools and elsewhere and I met fellows from the West Indian Islands, all trying to work out their destinies the best way they could. It became very clear to me what is happening to them. The continent of Africa belongs to them and should belong to them now. The same goes for the West Indies which the Negro built up, only to have a few people from the United States and from England move in and take it away from them and then rule them by absentee landlordism with headquarters in Wall St. and in London. These are the people who own the sugar plantations in the West Indies and in Louisiana and the tobacco plantations in North Carolina.

It is very easy to see, as in the question of India, China, Africa and the West Indies, the future of these people in the independence of their own countries. I see the Negro's struggle as demanding great concentration on the question as to where he is going and who is leading him there. We must come together as a people, unite and close ranks and with our own unity we must try and find the right allies—those whose struggles are identical to our own. We cannot escape the fact that our struggles over the last 300 years have driven us together.

Suppose that in the South, where the Negroes are in the majority in the agricultural belt, we had the vote like everyone else? What would happen? Wouldn't Negroes be in Congress, be governors, judges, mayors, sheriffs and so on? Wouldn't they be in control in the South and run things as the minority people down there are doing at this very moment?

There you have your answer to that charge that I am fomenting strife and plotting with a foreign government to establish a Black Republic in the South. What would happen—even tomorrow—if the Negro was allowed to vote? Without any nonsense, you would have a tremendous concentration of Negro power in the United States. Many people would object and oppose it on various grounds, principally racial and economic, but you have a concentration of Irish power in Boston, Italian power in New York, and so on. Nobody has made a major issue of that, have they? What is wrong with our struggle for our right to vote, for economic liberation, for civil rights? To me, from the economic point of view, we should think of spreading our strength around so as not to put all our wealth and power into the hands of a few Negroes who would exploit that power like any reactionary banker to the detriment of Negroes in the United States.

There are two groups of people who are worried stiff about the growth of the unified power of the Negro people: one group includes the Dixiecrats like Rankin of Mississippi, Wood and George of Georgia, Tom Connally of Texas and Eastland of Mississippi. The other includes the reactionary industrialists and financiers who own many of the farms and plantations in the South on which my people and your people are enslaved right now. These are the people who work to keep the Negro in bondage.

My basic point is that these are the fellows who want the Negro to be loyal to them, to die for them in war, to make a profit for them.

We Negroes must think this thing out. What America are we fighting for? Obviously we don't live alone in America, so we must choose the right allies, as I said before and these allies cannot be those Dixiecrats as named here. They cannot be those bankers and international financiers who run most of the country and own today all the resources of the South built on the labor of the Negro people. They own the sugar, the tobacco, the mineral wealth. They own the West Indies where Negroes are 98 per cent of the population.

They are the ones who helped take Africa from the African people. Our allies must be the progressive section of the American people—the honest progressives who find kinship in the common struggle for freedom, equality and unity. And who are these progressives? They are those who swell the ranks of labor, the poor white sharecropper of the South, presently being used as a tool by the rich plantation owners and bankers to pull their chestnuts out of the fire by warring on their Negro neighbors; the small business man and others of all races, colors, creeds and national origins, including the small, independent farmer—people who are passed up when the profits are handed out but who are the first thrown into the pot to cook up those profits for someone else. The Dixiecrats, like Wood of Georgia and those powerful reactionaries who hope to stamp out the militant struggle of the Negro for complete freedom, equality and civil rights, hope to keep all the wealth for themselves.

They are the ones who are behind the House Un-American Committee. They are the ones ceaselessly pushing the persecution of those unafraid to speak out and to champion the man down under, whether he be black or white.

When some of our leading Negroes select those most guilty of exploiting their people to get thick with in their social and economic affairs, they pick the wrong people no matter what excuse might be presented. Leopards don't change their spots and neither do those who think about us adversely change their thoughts overnight. This sort of thing I'd call "20th Century Uncle Tommism"—going back to the Big House to fawn at the boss' feet—and we shouldn't tolerate it one minute if we expect to get ahead.

Me? I'm out with the field hand. That's the only way I can see it. They tell us to stay in our place. Well, I'm staying in mine—out here with the field hand—the little fellow, the guy who gets pushed around, the fellow who has to do all the hard work and gets nothing from it.

I'm talking about the sharecroppers, Negro and white, on the sprawling plantations in the South.

I'm talking about the tobacco, steel and lumber workers; the men who tote the sandbags with chains about their legs to stem the Mississippi at flood time so as to save the empire of some guy in New York, London or Paris who has never seen the land which keeps him in luxury nor met and talked with the people on whose backs his kingdom rests.

Yes, that's the only way I can see it—stay with, work with, fight with and sing with the field hand, and if we stick it out long enough—we'll get the Big House!

We must solve our problem where we find it. Not by going thousands of miles away to take up something we are not familiar with.

Why should we leave the United States without first getting what is coming to us through a militant struggle to gain the profits that have come from our labor, our blood, our sweat, our tears? I'm talking now about the various schemes that would arouse false hopes in the Negro people about taking some other land as a homeland when we already have our home right here on American soil which will be ours when we make it our own.

Think what a Federation of the West Indies would mean economically. With Negroes 98 per cent of the West Indian population, why shouldn't they control the sugar, tourist trade, the banana and rum industries and the possibilities of further industrial development of the islands? Think of the amount of base metals and other natural wealth to be found there.

A Federation of the West Indies would give Negroes a completely integrated economy that would make the West Indies one of the most important places in the world—connected with the Latin and South American mainland. Think of the strategic position a native West Indian–controlled political and economic federation would command. Think of the weight such a setup would throw in United Nations circles?

Suppose Africa were free and a great nation like China? We must have to think for ourselves and also to include in intelligent thought those who are closest to us through the ties of blood, nationality, common interest and mutual aspirations. We want as many areas in this changing world of control as we can get as Negro people. Suppose we won the right to vote plus our proper share of the economic spoils of the South: think of the tremendous pressure Negroes could bring upon the United Nations to help kindred people in other parts of the world. There is no reason to change what have become very significant and historic facts. Certainly, any Negro in the world would have a deep feeling for his own people, wherever they are, whatever conditions they might be in.

As chairman of the Council on African Affairs, I can truthfully say that the African people are highly cultured and not savage and cannibalistic as the newspapers, radio, book and lecture propagandists would make them. That is the Dixiecrat program to keep us fighting one another and to lead us away from the true paths that lead to the doorway to freedom from which we have been detoured over the centuries.

I am proud of my African heritage. In fact, I'm so proud of it that I have made it my work to learn several African languages for conversation and musical purposes. Mrs. Robeson has been in South Africa, in the Uganda and in the Belgian Congo and the French Cameroons. She has written a book on Africa, *African Journey*. I expect to be in Nigeria and French West Africa next year. There is a tremendous liberation movement now under way in Nigeria of which Azikiwe is the brilliant, capable and resourceful leader. It is very possible that Nigeria will be the first African nation to win complete liberation. Understand that we over here, whether from the West Indies or from New York, should consult with the Africans about taking something from them. This is in answer to the question: What Do You Think of the Back-to-Africa movement?

At the Paris Peace Conference which brought all the reactionaries of America down on my neck, a Negro from French Africa spoke for an organization of one million Africans formed into trade unions in West Africa. In East Africa, Uganda and Kenya, there are very powerful movements for the rights of the African peoples. We must be very much aware of our allies of this time—and here we are dealing with 150 million in Africa, 40 to 60 million in the Caribbean and Latin America. All these people are to be considered, to be thought of as strengthening their own position in the areas where they live. Likewise Negroes in the South and West Indies must think of the areas in which they live as land that belongs to them. That is where they worked or were worked to build up things—to till the soil, plant and harvest; to chop down trees and milk them of turpentine and other basic products for the industrial mills of the imperialists and warmongers.

They—the Negroes of the South—must not grow to thank John Rankin for being allowed to live down there. They must realize that they are the ones who built that which has been and still is being taken from them. Maybe, they should think of someday gaining control through constitutional means of that which should have been theirs all along.

Where will the next Peekskill be? What new battle ground have the reactionary police and those behind them selected? Where will they demonstrate further the "old Southern Custom" of beating in the heads of Negroes and all those identified with the struggle to free the Negro people? I mean completely free the Negro from the shackles of the greedy exploiters of his labor and his talents. To be completely free from the chains that bind him, the Negro must be part of the progressive forces which are fighting the overall battle of the little guy—the sharecropper, the drugstore clerk, the auto mechanic, the porter and the maid, the owner of the corner diner, the truck driver, the garment, mill and steel workers. The progressive section sees no color line and views the whole problem of race and color prejudices and discrimination as a divisional tactic of those busy pitting class against class, dividing the masses into tiny, warring factions that produce nothing for them but discord and misery while a scant, privileged few takes all the wealth, holds the power and dictates the terms. This concentration of power in the hands of less than a hundred men is so strong that it can decide who shall eat and who shall not, who shall have decent homes and who shall be doomed to crowded tenements that are firetraps and rat-infested holes where children must be reared and the occupants live and die in despair.

I am well equipped now, although I have not always been so, to make the supreme fight for my people and all the other underprivileged masses wherever they may be. Here, I speak of those bereft of uncompromising, courageous leadership that cannot be bought, cannot be intimidated, and cannot be swerved from its purpose of bringing true freedom to those who follow it. God gave me the voice that people want to hear, whether in song or in speech. I shall take my voice wherever there are those who want to hear the melody of freedom or the words that might inspire hope and courage in the face of despair and fear.

I told the American Legion that I have been to Memphis, Tennessee, the stamping grounds of such Negro-haters as Ed Crump and others of the cracker breed, and I have been to the lynch belt of Florida. I told the Legion I would return to Peekskill. I did. I will go North, South, East or West, Europe, Africa, South America, Asia or Australia and fight for the freedom of the people. This thing burns in me and it is not my nature nor inclination to be scared off.

They revile me, scandalize me, and try to holler me down on all sides. That's all right. It's okay. Let them continue. My voice topped the blare of the Legion bands and the hoots of the hired hoodlums who attempted to break up my concert appearance for the Harlem Division of the Civil Rights Congress. It will be heard above the screams of the intolerant, the jeers of the ignorant pawns of the small groups of the lousy rich who would drown out the voice of a champion of the underdog. My weapons are peaceful for it is only by peace that peace can be attained. Their weapons are the nightsticks of the fascist police, the bloodhounds of the cracker sheriffs in the backwoods of the South, the trained voices of the choirs of hate. The song of freedom must prevail.

N.Y. Age, August 6, 13, 20; September 3, 17, 1949; in Foner, *op. cit.,* pp. 224–30.

62

FLORIDA'S LEGAL LYNCHING (1949)

by Ted Poston

On September 8, in the palm-surrounded Lake County courthouse in Tavares, Samuel Shepherd and Walter Irvin, twenty-two-year-old Negro war veterans, heard themselves sentenced to death for the capital crime of rape. Charles Greenlee, sixteen years old, who had never seen Shepherd and Irvin until they found themselves in a mob-threatened cell together, received life imprisonment for the same crime.

Sentence was pronounced by Circuit Court Judge T. G. Futch, who, incidentally, owed his election to the support of the Negro voters of Lake County. The state was represented during the three-day trial by County Prosecutor Jess Hunter. An all-white jury accepted without question the unsupported word of Mrs. Norma Lee Padgett, a seventeen-year-old white farm housewife, that she had been raped by four Negroes in the back seat of a 1946 Mercury sedan in the early morning hours of July 16. There was no medical testimony, no presentation of objective evidence like her clothes or the car in which the crime allegedly occurred. The word of one white girl was believed against that of three Negro youths who insisted that they had never seen her before.

Mrs. Padgett's charges set off a three-day reign of terror, beginning July 16, in which local hoodlums, aided by unmasked klansmen from adjacent Orange County and distant Georgia, burned and pillaged Negro homes in Groveland, Stuckey's Still, and neighboring communities and struck terror into the hearts of thousands of Negro citrus workers who had hesitated about harvesting the crop at the low prevailing wage rate. After the rioting was finally stopped by the National Guard, word was sent to at least a dozen fairly successful Negro farmers to "leave everything and get out now and stay out." Their prospering independence was a bad example in a community which thrives on keeping its workers in a state of semi-peonage.

The National Association for the Advancement of Colored People, which first exposed the frame-up of Shepherd, Irvin, and Greenlee—and the wanton murder of Ernest Thomas, twenty-seven, the fourth suspect, by a deputized mob ten days after the alleged rape—will fight the convictions all the way up to the United States Supreme Court if an aroused public will contribute the $20,000 estimated as the cost of the appeals.

Through the N.A.A.C.P.'s entrance into the case several precedents were established. Two Negro lawyers, Franklin H. Williams of the association's national office, and Horace E. Hill of Daytona Beach, recently admitted to the Florida bar, appeared among the defense counsel in the third-floor courtroom in Tavares. Prospective jurors were forced to concede that Negro lawyers should have the same rights in Lake County courts as white lawyers, "even to the cross-examination of all witnesses, including white ladies." (None of them relished the prospect, but in their anxiety to serve on what they jokingly called the "lynch jury" they consented.) And for the first time in the history of Florida, and probably of the whole South, an all-white jury, which had been expected to bring in its verdict in five minutes, deliberated for two hours before it decided to convict three Negroes on the unsupported word of a white woman. Rather than face the fury of their neighbors, the jurors finally "compromised," but in recommending "mercy" for Charles Greenlee they admitted that the prosecution had not proved its case.

The chief defense counsel was Alex Akerman, Jr., a successful civil lawyer in nearby Orlando, the state's Republican leader, and a native Southern liberal. By raising the question of the systematic exclusion of Negroes from grand and petit juries in Lake County, Akerman prepared the way for the United States Supreme Court to order a new trial. Jess Hunter, the wily state's attorney, anticipated this question when the N.A.A.C.P. entered the case, and for that reason he placed a Negro truck driver on the grand jury which indicted the youths. This Negro, the first ever summoned for such duty, indicated a reluctance to attend, but the sheriff sent out word that "he'll come or I'll go get him." Hunter also put the names of three Negroes—something that had never been done before—on the first two panels of 300 veniremen summoned for prospective jury duty at the trial, but he called only one, a gray-haired old handyman. The court clerk begged defense counsel to excuse this "boy," whom he called "one of the best niggers in Lake County," so that he could attend his father-in-law's funeral.

Akerman fought brilliantly but in vain for a change of venue to a less prejudiced county and for a postponement to give the defense time to investigate new evidence uncovered a few days before the trial opened. This evidence indicated strongly that Norma Lee Padgett had never been raped by anyone, and that her story was an attempt to cover up a fight she had had with her husband, Willie Padgett, from whom she was estranged.

Akerman dared the county prosecutor to introduce as evidence the oral "confessions" obtained from the two older boys after they had been beaten and tortured by "deputies" in a nearby woods and had been strung up by their arms and savagely thrashed in the basement of the combined jail and courthouse in which the trial was held. Hunter, a highly intelligent prosecutor who deliberately cultivates a backwoods manner, rejected the challenge because he knew that such confessions had been ruled inadmissible by the United States Supreme Court, and that their use would have made the court's reversal of a guilty verdict inevitable. He thus placed

Florida on a slightly higher legal level than New Jersey, where six Trenton Negroes were convicted of murder on the basis of similarly elicited "confessions."

The difficulties encountered in securing a white attorney were indicative of the feeling of terror that had been built up by the inflammatory editorials and cartoons in the Florida papers. In the first two weeks after the N.A.A.C.P. entered the case Franklin H. Williams, its assistant special counsel, traveled up and down the state trying to get a white lawyer who could not be lambasted by local newspapers as an "outsider interfering in local affairs."

A prominent Miami criminal attorney, approached indirectly through a liberal white Southerner, replied that he would not consider "studying" the case unless the N.A.A.C.P. paid him a retainer of $25,000, an impossible sum for an organization which was able to raise only $1,500 in defense funds; it actually spent more than $5,000 in the trial just concluded. A lawyer in Inverness demanded a $10,000 fee but called up before his offer could be accepted or rejected to say that his wife would not let him act in a rape case involving a white woman and Negro men.

The liberal son of a prominent Florida politician reluctantly decided that he could not take the case. "Although I disagree with many of my father's political beliefs and actions," he said, "I just can't take a step which would undoubtedly bring about his defeat in the next election." This man did act as an undercover investigator for the defense.

After a labor lawyer who has done some work for the C.I.O. refused to conduct the defense unless his partner also received a fee, Williams came back to Alex Akerman, Jr., who had been approached earlier without success. "A lawyer's first responsibility is to his existing clients," Akerman now told Williams, "and I have six clients whose interests might be prejudiced if I took this case." When Williams learned that the six clients were young Negro students in whose behalf Akerman was suing the University of Florida, he would not leave the Orlando attorney's office until he consented to undertake Florida's "little Scottsboro case." During the trial Jess Hunter intimated that Akerman had been paid by the N.A.A.C.P. to challenge the racial ban against Negroes at the University of Florida, but Akerman proved that he had instituted the suits as a private attorney, acting out of his belief in the justice of equal educational opportunities. He showed such fervor in the Tavares defense that another young white Florida lawyer, Joseph E. Price, Jr., volunteered his services without a fee.

The conviction of Shepherd and Irvin with a mandatory death sentence was almost a foregone conclusion. On their return to civil life both had refused to work in the local citrus groves for substandard wages. If either boy had had a chance, it disappeared when he walked to the witness stand, disdainful and unbroken despite the beatings he had received, and scorned the charge that he had assaulted Norma Lee Padgett.

Conviction, even with a "mercy" recommendation, must have come as a sharp surprise to the sixteen-year-old Greenlee, for from the moment he began his testimony it was evident that the unlettered but articulate youngster believed that "if you just tell the good white folks the truth and make them understand, then everything will be all right." Akerman proved conclusively that the youth was twenty miles away from the scene of the alleged rape at the time it was said to have occurred, but it was Greenlee's frank, simple story which kept the jury deliberating for two hours.

Dispassionately, and using the time-table established by state witnesses, Akerman also proved that Shepherd and Irvin could not have been near the alleged rape scene on that July morning; but neither one had Greenlee's persuasiveness on the stand.

Ironically, the life-imprisonment sentence for Greenlee almost brought further tragedy to Lake County. Incensed that even one of the defendants had escaped the chair, five carloads of white men chased the two Negro defense lawyers and two Negro reporters forty miles over the road to Orlando on the night of the verdict.

Nation, September 24, 1949, pp. 296–98. Ted Poston, of the *New York Post,* was one of the first African-Americans on the staff of a major daily newspaper. In 1951, while Samuel Shepherd and Walter Irvin were being transported to the town of Tavares, Florida, for a new trial, Shepherd was killed and Irvin gravely wounded. See H. Shapiro, *op. cit.,* pp. 418–19.

63

THE CASE OF MRS. ROSA LEE INGRAM AND SONS
(1949)

A Petition to the Human Rights Commission of the Social and Economic Council of the United Nations; and to the General Assembly of the United Nations; and to the Several

Delegations of the Member States of the United Nations (1949)

One of the more callous manifestations of racist injustice in the postwar United States involved a Black woman named Mrs. Rosa Lee Ingram. The details are stated in a petition drafted by Du Bois and signed by scores of Afro-American women. The death sentences meted out to Ingram and two of her teen-age sons were commuted to life imprisonment as a result of the worldwide campaign against this particularly flagrant instance of injustice.

The petition itself was presented to the United Nations by Mrs. Mary Church Terrell on 21 September 1949. In August 1959 Ingram and her sons were paroled; in 1964 the sentences were commuted with full restoration of rights.*

The signers of this petition wish to lay before the Assembly of the United Nations, a case of injustice done by the United States of America against its own citizens. We are bringing this case to your attention and begging you to give it your earnest thought and discussion, not because we are disloyal to this nation, but especially because we are citizens of this land and loyal to the freedom and democracy which it professes far and wide to observe.

This case of callous injustice is typical of the treatment which thousands of our fellows receive, who have slaved and toiled and fought for this country and yet are denied justice in its courts or consideration in its deeds.

In the state of Georgia alone, where this latest injustice is taking place, over 500 Negroes in the last sixty years have been publicly lynched, by mobs without trial; the latest victim being murdered this very year. Last year an election was held in the state in which the man elected governor [Herman Talmadge] publicly promised to break the laws of this land and deprive a million black citizens in his state of the right to vote. In this state a legal caste system is in vogue which condemns American citizens to unequal education, unequal treatment for disease, segregates them in living quarters and discriminates against them in the right to work at decent wage. The governor promised to maintain this "race segregation" "at all hazards."

In this same state, the following incidents occurred in 1947: a Colored mother of 14 children, 12 of whom are living, lost her husband, Jackson Ingram, a share-cropper, who died in August.

*I am indebted to Professor Herbert Shapiro of the University of Cincinnati for much of this information. See, Charles H. Martin, "Rosa Lee Ingram Case," *American Journal of Legal History,* July 1955; 29: 259-68.

With her children she tried to carry on the tilling of her farm in Schley county which was rented from C. M. Dillinger, a white man living in the town of Americus. Her neighbor was a white man named John Stratford, also a share-cropper. No fences were provided between the two farms or even between the farms and highway and often cattle strayed across the boundaries. On November 4, 1947 Stratford called the woman, cursed her and told her to drive her mules and pigs off his farm. She hurriedly left her washing and children and ran to his farm to find her stock. She found that her mules and pigs, and also stock belonging to her landlord, were on Stratford's place. As she entered his lot to drive them back, he met her, armed with a shotgun and began to pound her over the head with it. She begged him to stop and seized the gun. He kept beating her, until the blood ran. Her two little sons 13 and 12 stood by crying and pleading, until at last a third son 16, ran from the house, seized the gun, struck Stratford over the head with it and Stratford died.

Mrs. Ingram immediately reported the death to the sheriff. She and her two oldest sons were arrested and put in jail, leaving the nine little children alone in the cottage. On January 26, 1948, she and her two sons were tried by a jury on which no Negro sat, and sentenced to be hanged for murder. Her landlord, Dillinger, seized all her stock, tools and growing crops. Colored people of the state and nation rallied to her defense and finally, April 5, the same court which sentenced her to death, changed the sentence to life imprisonment. This sentence the three are now serving.

This crucifixion of Mrs. Rosa Lee Ingram is of one piece with Georgia's treatment of Colored women. In 1946, twenty-five white lynchers in Walton county, Georgia killed two untried colored men, and then wantonly shot their wives to death because the women recognized the murderers. No one has ever been indicted or punished for this outrage.

Thus it is clear that the part of this nation which boasts its reverence for womanhood is the part where the women of Africa were slaves and concubines of white Americans for two and a half centuries; where their daughters in states like Virginia became human brood mares to raise domestic slaves when the African trade stopped; and where their grand-daughters became mothers of millions of mulattoes.

Today these colored women and their children bear the chief burden of the share-cropping system, where Southern slavery still lingers. The women work the fields for endless hours and their children are driven from their poor schools into the cotton fields under labor contracts which disgrace humanity and debar them from all franchisement by poll taxes, and make the rural Negro family the most depressed in the world. It was such a family that Mrs. Rosa Lee Ingram tried to defend and for this she toils for life in a Georgia prison camp.

Schley County has 3,000 colored and 2,000 white inhabitants, all native born and rural. Only 455 votes were cast in the county in 1942 and of these only 100 were colored. The colored people are almost totally disenfranchised, hold no political offices of any kind, never serve on juries, and work mostly as share-croppers on land owned by whites. Of the 750 farms 600 are worked by tenants. The money income of Negro families is probably less than $200 a year; their schools are poor and short in term. Twenty-four dollars per child is spent for white children and four dollars for colored, white school buildings are worth $1000 each and colored $600. Four Negroes have been lynched in this county without trial since 1900. It can be affirmed that in this county no Negro "has any rights which a white man is bound to respect."

In this case, we submit, every canon of law and decency, much less of justice has been violated. A boy of 16 struck an armed white man who was attacking his mother. They, mother and two teen-age sons, were tried by a jury of hostile whites, with no representative of their race. Their meager property was seized and the children are today subsisting on charity.

The federal government has made no move; the governor of Georgia has done nothing. The President of the United States, when approached by a delegation from 8 states, would not talk to them and through his secretary said he had never heard of the case. The Chief of the Civil Rights Division of the United States Department of Justice, A. A. Rosen, said: "This sort of thing is in the papers every week. It's shocking to me personally, but it is a matter to be settled internally by the State." He pleaded lack of jurisdiction and no available funds.

The formula upon which this nation rests in the ignoring and mishandling of cases like this, is the legal fiction that a sovereign government can if it will renounce all responsibility for securing justice to its citizens and leave such matters entirely in the hands of subordinate and irresponsible local corporations, even when such bodies openly transgress the law of the land. In the face of this, the United States of America declares its practice of democracy before the world and sits in the United Nations which has promised in its fundamental Charter to promote and encourage "respect for human rights and for fundamental freedoms for all without distinction as to race, sex, language or religion."

We are painfully aware that all matters of this sort, have by vote of the General Assembly been put under the jurisdiction of the Social and Economic Council; and that this Council has established the Commission on Human Rights to consider such cases. But the world knows what the Commission on Human Rights has done or rather has not done to fulfill its functions. We are nevertheless handing this petition to the Commission which in this case as in the past will either bluntly refuse us the right of petition, or will receive the document and hide it in its files as though it represented treason or revolution.

We will not rest with this attempt to conceal injustice and deny the right of petition. We charge that the Human Rights Commission under Eleanor Roosevelt its chairman and John Humphreys, its secretary, have consistently and deliberately ignored scientific procedure and just treatment to the hurt and hounded of the world. Instead of receiving complaints and giving them careful investigation and, when facts are ascertained, world publicity, they have buried the complaints and drowned themselves in a flood of generalities by seeking to re-write in verbal platitudes of tens of thousands of words, those statements on Human Rights which the American Declaration of Independence and the French Declaration of the Rights of Man set down a century and a half ago in imperishable phrase which no man can better today.

Hiding in this forest of verbiage, the Commission on Human Rights has worse than wasted three fatal years, until no sufferer has the slightest confidence in either its ability or honest intentions. It is not so much a question of the phraseology of a universal treaty on which all nations can agree, as the much more practical matter as to how far nations are living up to their own laws and professions. Even members of the Commission are becoming disgusted at the tactics of delay. Jonathan Daniels has recently said: "That if some means of grappling with the practical problem of petitions was not found, and the sub-Commission devoted itself only to theorizing in 'textbook style,' its members might just as well quit work and go home."

The sincere and scientific way to work out a Bill of Rights would be to examine carefully and thoroughly specific instances of injustice and from such basis of proven facts to build up methods of prevention and redress; instead of reverting to the outmoded scholasticism of seeking universal truth and eternal verities.

We appeal in this case to the Social and Economic Council and ask them to insist that the fundamental right of petition be affirmed and enforced in the Human Rights Commission. And further than this, we appeal to the General Assembly itself and to every member of it, to place on the agenda of its next meeting and publicly discuss, the relation of democracy in the United States of America to its citizens of Negro descent. We affirm that if the Assembly can and should discuss at length matters affecting the fifteen million Jews of the world, the thirteen millions of Czechoslovakia, the seven and a half million people of Greece, the ten millions of Arabia, the six millions of Austria, and the four million of Finland, it might find a half hour to discuss fifteen million of Negro Americans without disrupting the Charter of the United Nations or affronting the dignity and sovereignty of the United States.

Any nation has the right by law to curtail, for the greater good of the nation, the individual liberties of its citizens; but no country has the right to break faith with itself and deny its citizens rights which its own laws guarantee and its own declarations proclaim; and when it does this, is not this action a matter of International concern? Division of powers between nation and locality may satisfy the metaphysics of practical administration but it cannot divest a nation before the world of its responsibility for elementary justice to its citizens. This was admitted years ago when Louisiana lynched Italians and arrogantly refused punishment or reparation. The nation after years of vain quibbling was compelled by International law to pay damages to their kin. The state of Georgia with its illiteracy and lawlessness is not a nation in the eyes of the United Nations, but the United States of America is a nation and as such bears sole responsibility for the miscarriage of justice in the case of Mrs. Rosa Lee Ingram.

It may seem a very little thing for 59 nations of the world to take note of the injustice done a poor colored woman in Georgia, when such vast problems confront them; and yet after all, is it in the end so small a thing to "do justly, to love mercy and walk humbly" in setting this mad world aright?

"Not by might, nor by power, but by my spirit" saith the Lord!

We Americans can send Communists to jail and drive honest citizens to suicide but can we stand before the world and defend the life imprisonment of Mrs. Rosa Lee Ingram as an example of democracy which the United Nations is teaching?

The undersigned colored women of the United States, legal citizens, voters, wives and mothers have commissioned Dr. W. E. B. Du Bois to draw up this petition, because he has devoted much of his life to the cause of Negro equality. We endorse and subscribe to his words and urge action on the part of all nations who have signed the Charter of the United Nations.

H. Aptheker, ed., *Unpublished*...261–65. Footnotes omitted. For a fine study of the Ingram case—and that of McGee—consult Charles H. Martin, "The Civil Rights Congress and Southern Black Defendants," in *Georgia Historical Quarterly* 61: 25–54 (Spring 1987).

64

LISTEN TO JESSE B. SIMPLE (1950)

EQUALITY AND DOGS

A good way to begin the 1950s is by listening to Jesse B. Simple. Here is a sample:

"Even a black dog gets along better than me," mused Simple. "I have discovered that much since I been up North with these *liberal* white folks. You take this here social equality that some of them is always bringing up. I don't understand it. White folks socialize with dogs—yet they don't want to socialize with me."

"True," I said.

"White dogs, black dogs, any kind of dogs," Simple went on. "They don't care what color a dog is in New York. Why, when I first got here I used to drive for a woman out on Long Island who were so rich she had six dogs. One of 'em, a big black dog, slept in bed with her—right in bed with his rusty back up next to her white feet. But if a Negro set down six tables away from her in a restaurant, she almost had a fit. I do not understand it."

"You see plenty of dogs walking with white ladies on Park Avenue," I said.

"But no Negroes."

"That's right."

"They walk dogs and *work* Negroes," explained Simple. "While them rich white ladies is out walking with their dogs, Negroes are working back in their kitchens. Since the days of defense workers are long gone, that's where we are again. Them rich white folks gave their big old yard dogs they didn't like much to the army during the war, you remember? The army trained 'em to fight just like a man. But the army mostly trained Negroes to work—Quartermasters, Engineers, Port Battalions, Seabees...."

"Yes."

"Um-hum-m-m! But they trained dogs to fight. Why, I saw a picture of a dog getting a medal hung on his chest for fighting so good he tore down a German machine-gun nest. It were in a Southern white paper where I never did see a picture of a Negro soldier getting a medal on his chest. Every time them Southern papers had pictures of Negroes in uniforms during the war, they was always unloading some landing barge or digging on some road. A dog got a better break in the army than a Negro."

"You sound kind of bitter," I said, "about your army."

"How do you figger it's *my* army?" asked Simple as he set his beer glass down.

"You pay taxes for it," I said.

"I do," said Simple, "but it pays me no mind. It Jim Crows me, but it don't Jim Crow dogs. White dogs and black dogs all served together in the army, didn't they? And they didn't have no separate companies for black dogs."

"You've got something there," I said.

"Come another war, I had rather be a dog in the army any time than colored—especially down South. Why, I saw in the newsreels once where they trained army dogs to leap at a man and tear him down—to leap at a *white* man, at that. But if I even as much as raise a hand at a cracker when he pushes me off the sidewalk, my head is beat and I am put in jail. But a dog in the army, they taught him not to let nobody push him off no sidewalk in Mississippi nor nowhere else. Here I am a human, and I get less of a break in the U.S. than a dog! I do not understand."

"Neither do I," I said.

"How come you ain't arguing with me tonight?" asked Simple. "You mighty near always disagree."

"How can I disagree about dogs?" I said.

"I remember in the first depression times before the war, when they had the WPA and the PWA and all those things that it was so hard to get on, and that you got so little from after you did get on 'em. I remember seeing folks come into meat markets and buy great big pieces of good red meat for their dogs, while plenty colored folks, and white, too, didn't have meat for themselves and their children. I said to myself then that it must be good to be a dog. I said, eating *fine* red meat and not having to worry about getting on WPA. Black dogs and white dogs all eating good red meat and no color line between 'em. I tell you, dogs rate better in America than colored folks."

"Anyhow, I love dogs," I said, "and I'm glad they get a break in our paradoxical society."

"I love dogs, too," said Simple, "but I love colored folks better."

"Still you want to take the meat out of a dog's mouth."

"I do not," said Simple. "I just want some meat in my own mouth, that's all! I want the same chance a dog has. Furthermore, I do not care to argue about it. Doggone if I'm going to argue about dogs!"

Ways and Means

"You see this, don't you?" said Simple, showing me his N.A.A.C.P. card. "I have just joined the National Organization for the Association of Colored Folks and it is fine."

"You mean the National Association for the Advancement of Colored People," I said.

"Um-hum!" said Simple, "but they tell me it has white people in it, too."

"That's right, it does."

"I did not see none at the meeting where me and Joyce went this evening," said Simple.

"No?"

"No! There should have been some present because that *fine* colored speaker was getting white folks told—except that there was no white folks there to be told."

"They just do not come to Negro neighborhoods to meetings," I said, "although they may belong."

"Then we ought to hold some meetings downtown so that they can learn what this Negro problem is all about," said Simple. "It does not make sense to be always talking to ourselves. We know we got troubles. But every last Italian, Jew, and Greek what owns a business all up and down Seventh Avenue and Eighth Avenue and Lenox in Harlem ought to have been there. Do you reckon they belong to anything colored?"

"I don't expect they do," I said.

"Well, next time I go to a A.A.C.P. meeting..."

"N-A-A-C-P meeting," I said.

"...N.A.A.C.P. meeting, I am going to move that everybody get a coin can," said Simple, "and go from store to store and bar to bar and hash-house to hash-house and take up collection for the N.A.A.C.P., from all these white folks making money in colored neighborhoods. If they don't give, I will figure they do not care nothing about my race. White folks are always taking up collections from *me* for the Red Cross or the Community Chest or the Cancer Drive or the March of Dimes or something or other. They are always shaking their cans in *my* face. Why shouldn't I shake my can in *their* face?"

"It would be better," I said, "if you got them all to be *members* of the N.A.A.C.P., not just to give a contribution."

"Every last white businessman in Harlem ought to belong to the N.A.A.C.P., but do you reckon they would ever come to meetings? They practically all live in the suburbans."

"They come to Harlem on business," I said, "so why shouldn't they come to the meetings?"

"That is why they go to the suburbans, to get away from the Negroes they have been selling clothes and groceries and victuals and beer all day. They do not want to be bothered with me when they close up their shops."

"Do you blame them?" I said.

"I do," said Simple. "Long as the cash register is ringing, they can be bothered with me, so why can't they come to an N.A.A.C.P. meeting?"

"Have I ever heard of you going out to the Italian or Jewish or Irish neighborhoods to any of their meetings to help them with their problems?" I asked.

"I do not have any stores in the Italian or Jewish neighborhoods," said Simple. "Neither do I own nary pool hall in an Irish neighborhood, nor nary Greek restaurant, nor nary white apartment house from which I get rent. I do not own no beer halls where Jews and Italians come to spend their money. If I did, I would join the Jewish N.A.A.C.P., and the Italian one, too! I would also join the Greek N.A.A.C.P., if I owned a hash-house where nothing but Greeks spent money all day long like I spend money in their Greasy Spoons."

"You put social co-operation on such a mercenary basis," I said.

"They would want me to have mercy on them if they was in my fix," said Simple.

"I did not say anything about mercy. I said *mercenary*—I mean a buying-and-selling basis."

"They could buy and sell me," said Simple.

"What I mean is, you should not have to have a business in a Jewish neighborhood to be interested in Jewish problems, or own a spaghetti stand to be interested in Italians, or a bar to care about the Irish. In a democracy, everybody's problems are related, and it's up to all of us to help solve them."

"If I did not have a business reason to be interested in *their* business," said Simple, "then what business would I have being interested in *their* business?"

"Just a human reason," I said. "It's all human business."

"Maybe that is why they don't join the N.A.A.C.P.," said Simple. "Because they do not think a Negro is human."

"If I were you, I would not speak so drastically unless I had some facts to go on. Have you ever asked any of the white businessmen where you trade to join the N.A.A.C.P.—the man who runs your laundry, or manages the movies where you go, or the Greek who owns the restaurant? Have you asked any of them to join?"

"No, I have not. Neither have I asked my colored landlady's white landlord."

"Well, ask them and see what they say."

"I sure will," said Simple, "then if they do not join, I will know they don't care nothing about me."

"You make it very simple," I said.

"It is simple, because everybody knew what stores to pick out the night of the riot."

"I was in Chicago that summer of '43 so I missed the riot."

"I was in it," said Simple.

"You don't say! Tell me about it. Where were you that night?"

"All up and down," said Simple.

"Grabbing hams out of broken windows?"

"No," said Simple, "I did not want no ham. I wanted Justice."

"What do you mean, Justice?"

"You know what I mean," Simple answered. "That cop had no business shooting a colored soldier!"

"You had no business breaking up stores, either," I said. "That is no way to get Justice."

"That is the way the Allies got it—breaking up Germany, breaking up Hiroshima, and everything in sight. But these white folks are more scared of Negroes in the U.S.A. than they ever was of Hitler, otherwise why would they make Jackie Robinson stop playing baseball to come to

Washington and testify how loyal we is? I remember that night after the riots they turned on all the street lights in Harlem, although it was during the war and New York had a dim-out. Wasn't no dim-out in Harlem— lights just blazing in the middle of the war. The air-raid drill was called off, likewise the blackout. Suppose them German planes had come with *all* our lights on full."

"You're so dark the cops couldn't see *you* in a dim-out so they had to turn on the lights."

"Make no remarks about my color, pal! You are the same complexion. And I'll bet if you'd been in New York when the riot started, you would have been out there in the streets with me."

"I would have emerged to see the excitement, yes, but not to break windows looking for Justice."

"Well, *I* was looking for Justice," said Simple. "I was tired."

"Tired of what?"

"Of hearing the radio talking about the Four Freedoms all day long during the war and me living in Harlem where nary one of them Freedoms worked—nor the ceiling prices neither."

"So I threw a couple of bricks through a couple of windows when the riots started, and I felt better."

"Did you pick your windows or did you just throw?"

"Man, there wasn't no time to pick windows because the si-reens was blowing and the P.D.'s coming. But I aimed my foot at one grocery and my bricks at two big windows in a shoe store that cost them white folks plenty money to put back in."

"And that made you feel better?"

"Yes."

"Why?"

"Well, I figured, let them white men spend some of the profits they make out of Harlem putting those windows back. Let 'em spend some of that money they made out of these high rents in Harlem all these years to put them windows back. Also let 'em use some of that money to put them windows back that they owe my grandmother and my great-grandmother and her mother before that for working all them years in slavery for nothing. Let 'em take *that* back pay due my race and put them windows back!"

"You have things all mixed up, old man," I said, "which is one reason why I am glad you have joined the N.A.A.C.P., so that the next time a crisis comes up, you will have a more legitimate outlet for your energies.

There are more effective ways and means of achieving justice than through violence. The N.A.A.C.P. believes in propaganda, education, political action, and legal redress. Besides, the men who owned that shoe store you threw those bricks in probably were way over in Europe when you were born. Certainly they had nothing to do with slavery, let alone your grandma's back pay."

"But they don't have nothing to do now with *Grandma's grandson* either—except to take my money over the counter, then go on downtown to Stuyvesant Town where I can't live, or out to them pretty suburbans, and leave me in Harlem holding the bag. I ain't no fool. When the riot broke out, I went looking for Justice."

"With a brick."

"No! Two bricks," said Simple.

SOMETHING TO LEAN ON

"A bar is something to lean on," said Simple.

"You lean on bars very often," I remarked.

"I do," said Simple.

"Why?"

"Because everything else I lean on falls down," said Simple, "including my peoples, my wife, my boss, and me."

"How do you mean?"

"My peoples brought me into the world," said Simple, "but they didn't have no money to put me through school. When I were knee-high to a duck I had to go to work."

"That happens to a lot of kids," I said.

"Most particularly colored," said Simple. "And my wife, I couldn't depend on her. When the depression come and I was out of a job, Isabel were no prop to me. I could not lean on her."

"So you started to leaning on bars," I said.

"No," said Simple. "I were leaning on bars before I married. I started to leaning on bars soon as I got out of short pants."

"Perhaps if you belonged to the church you would have something stronger on which to lean."

"You mean lean on the Lord? Daddy-o, too many folks are leaning on Him now. I believe the Lord helps them that helps themselves—and I am a man who tries to help himself. That is the way white folks got way up where they are in the world—while colored's been leaning on the Lord."

"And you have been leaning on bars."

"What do you think I do all day long?" Simple objected. "From eight in the morning to five at night, I do not lean on no bar. I work! Ask my boss-man out at the plant. He knows I work. He claims he likes me, too. But that raise he promised me way last winter, have I got it yet? Also that advancement? No! I have not! I see them white boys get advancements while I stay where I am. Black—so I know I ain't due to go but so far. I bet you if I was white I would be somewhere in this world."

"There you go with that old color argument as an excuse again," I said.

"I bet you I would not be poor. All the opportunities a white man's got, there ain't no sense in his being poor. He can get any kind of job, anywhere. He can be President. Can I?"

"Do you have the qualifications?"

"Answer my question," said Simple, "and don't ask me another one. Can I be President? Truman can, but can I? Is he any smarter than me?"

"I am not acquainted with Mr. Truman, so I do not know."

"Does he *look* any smarter?" asked Simple.

"I must admit he does not," I said.

"Then why can't I be President, too? Because I am colored, that's why."

"So you spend your evenings leaning on bars because you cannot be President," I said. "What kind of reasoning is that?"

"Reason enough," said Simple. "If anybody else in America can be President, I want to be President. The Constitution guarantees us equal rights, but have I got 'em? No. It's fell down on me."

"You figure the Constitution has fallen down on you?"

"I do," said Simple. "Just like it fell down on that poor Negro lynched last month. Did anybody out of that mob go to jail? Not a living soul! But just kidnap some little small white baby and take it across the street, and you will do twenty years. The F.B.I. will spread its dragnet and drag in forty suspicions before morning. And, if you are colored, don't be caught selling a half pint of bootleg licker, or writing a few numbers. They will put you in every jail there is! But Southerners can beat you, burn you, lynch you, and hang you to a tree—and every one of them will go scotfree. Gimme another beer. Tony! I can lean on this bar, but I ain't got another thing in the U.S.A. on which to lean."

SIMPLE PINS ON MEDALS

"Now, the way I understand it," said Simple one Monday evening when the bar was nearly empty and the juke box silent, "it's been written down a long time ago that men are borned equal and everybody is entitled to life and liberty while pursuing happiness. It's in the Constitution, also Declaration of Independence, so I do not see why it has to be resolved all over again."

"Who is resolving it all over?" I asked.

"Some white church convention—I read in the papers where they have resolved all that over and the Golden Rule, too, also that Negroes should be treated right. It looks like to me white folks better stop resolving and get to *doing*. They have resolved enough. *Resolving ain't solving.*"

"What do you propose that they do?"

"The white race has got a double duty to us," said Simple. "They ought to start treating us right. They also ought to make up for how bad they have treated us in the past."

"You can't blame anybody for history," I said.

"No," said Simple, "but you can blame folks if they don't do something about history! History was yesterday, times gone. Yes. But now that colored folks are willing to let bygones be bygones, this ain't no time to be Jim Crowing nobody. This is a new day."

"Maybe that is why they are resolving to do better," I said.

"I keep telling you, it has come time to stop *resolving!*" said Simple. "They have been *resolving* for two hundred years. I do not see how come they need to *resolve* any more. I say, they need to *solve.*"

"How?"

"By treating us like humans," said Simple, "that's how!"

"They don't treat each other like human beings," I said, "so how do you expect them to treat you that way?"

"White folks do not Jim Crow each other," said Simple, "neither do they have a segregated army—except for me."

"No, maybe not," I said, "but they blasted each other down with V-bombs during the war."

"To be shot down is bad for the body," said Simple, "but to be Jim Crowed is worse for the spirit. Besides, speaking of war, in the next war I want to see Negroes pinning medals on white men."

"Medals? What have medals to do with anything?"

"A lot," said Simple, "because every time I saw a picture in the colored papers of colored soldiers receiving medals in the last war, a white officer was always doing the pinning. I have not yet seen a picture in *no* papers of a *colored* officer pinning a medal on a white soldier. So you reckon I will ever see such a picture?"

"I don't know anything about the army's system of pinning on medals," I said.

"I'll bet there isn't a white soldier living who ever got a medal from a colored officer," said Simple.

"Maybe not, but I don't get your point. If a soldier is brave enough to get a medal, what does it matter who pins it on?"

"It may not matter to the soldiers," said Simple, "but it matters to *me*. I have never yet seen no *colored* general pinning a medal on a *white* private. That is what I want to see."

"Colored generals did not command white soldiers in the last war," I said, "which is no doubt why they didn't pin medals on them."

"I want to see colored generals commanding white soldiers, then," said Simple.

"You may want to see it, but how can you see it when it just does not take place?"

"In the next war it must and should take place," said Simple, "because if these white folks are gonna have another war, they better give us some generals. I know if I was in the army, I would like to command white troops. In fact, I would like to be in charge of a regiment from Mississippi."

"Are you sober?" I asked.

"I haven't had but one drink today."

"Then why on earth would you want to be in charge of a white regiment from Mississippi?"

"They had white officers from Mississippi in charge of Negroes—so why shouldn't I be in charge of whites? Huh? I would really make 'em toe the line! I know some of them Southerners had rather die than to *left face* for a colored man, buddy-o. But they would *left face* for me."

"What would you do if they wouldn't *left face?*"

"Court-martial them," said Simple. "After they had set in the stockade for six months, I would bring them Mississippi white boys out, and I would say once more, '*Left face!*' I bet they would *Left face* then! Else I'd court-martial them again."

"You have a very good imagination," I said, "also a sadistic one."

"I can see myself now in World War III," said Simple, "leading my

Mississippi troops into action. I would do like all the other generals do, and stand way back on a hill somewheres and look through my spyglasses and say, 'Charge on! Mens, charge on!' Then I would watch them Dixiecrat boys go—like true sons of the old South, mowing down the enemy.

"When my young white lieutenants from Vicksburg jeeped back to Headquarters to deliver their reports in person to me, they would say, 'General Captain, sir, we have taken two more enemy positions.'

"I would say, 'Mens, return to your companies—and tell 'em to *charge on!*'

"Next day, when I caught up to 'em, I would pin medals on their chests for bravery. Then I would have my picture taken in front of all my fine white troops—*me*—the first black American general to pin medals on white soldiers from Mississippi. It would be in every paper in the world—the great news event of World War III."

"It would certainly be news," I said.

"Doggone if it wouldn't," said Simple. "It would really be news! You see what I mean by *solving*—not just resolving. I will've done solved."

Langston Hughes, *Simple Speaks His Mind* (New York: Simon and Schuster, 1950), pp. 152–54; 162–68; 176–78; 192–95.

65

THE NEGRO PRESS (1950)

The above was the title of a special issue of *The Southern Patriot* (February 1950). This publication was a monthly (except July and August) issued by the Southern Conference Educational Fund in New Orleans. Its president was Aubrey Williams; the vice president, Benjamin E. Mays; secretary-treasurer, Alva A. Taylor; editor and director, James A. Dombrowski. A substantial part of this issue follows:

[a]

Roscoe Dunjee
Editor, *The Black Dispatch*, Oklahoma City

Personally, in all of our public addresses in this section we have attacked all of the sectional taboos, and we have also done so continuously for thirty four years in our editorial column. I have said more times than I have fingers and toes to white audiences that I believe in social equality. I am against the mob, segregation, disfranchisement and every form of demoted citizenship status. No one in the radius of my circulation misunderstands me on these questions, and despite the fact I say these things I have been more sought for by white audiences than any other Negro in Oklahoma. The individual who introduces me most invariably says "Mr. Dunjee is the type of Negro classed by many as radical, but he regards the spirit in his approach to controversial subjects in such a way as not to offend."

Residential Segregation

A most grievous fight I have had with the local community has developed with the question of residential segregation. For twenty-five years I have spearheaded this fight in Oklahoma City. In fact I financed the Sidney Hawkins habeas Corpus Court Action which ended in an opinion rendered by our State Supreme Court outlawing the right of any unit of the state to enact racial zoning statutes. It was in this case that I took the stand as an expert witness and stayed on the stand five hours, during which time the city attorneys tried to prejudice the court by questioning me about irrelevant matters, such as my views about inter-marriage, disfranchisement, separate schools and what-not.

That is one instance in my public career when I discovered the spirit of the Negro is not up to the level of white liberalism, for when I took my gloves off and put in the record my thinking on this subject, and the newspapers proceeded to run lurid headlines telling what I was saying on the stand, my Negro friends assured me of hurting the cause of liberalism and good race relations. We however won that case, outlawing in a southern state court residential segregation.

You have no idea what this sort of fighting has done to me in a financial way. Many merchants in this city have banded themselves together with the understanding they will not advertise in a paper that preaches marriage of whites and blacks and who spear-heads encroachment of the blacks in white neighborhoods.

The most acute and savage attack that was ever made upon our publication came some ten years ago when we launched a fight on the Oklahoma City School Board. Most of the members were later landed in the penitentiary. The *Black Dispatch* spearheaded that fight even before the white daily in this city realized what was going on. At that time oil had made many school properties rich with the big wells gushing right in the city limits and we had a racketeering group who were not only enriching themselves out of these lush opportunities, but in addition were peddling jobs to at least fifty per cent of the Negro teachers, many of whom had to suffer many indignities, and offer to put their virtue on the block to hold a job.

Jail for School Board

This sort of thing had been going on for perhaps seven or eight years before it broke in the open, but we made the discovery that almost every prominent person in our section had to keep his mouth shut because for one reason or another he had been drawn into the racket. His wife, his sister or his friend had bought a job. One of the school board members was a member of the retail merchant's association, and he personally got out and did a job among the merchants that almost put us out of business, but we stuck by our guns to the end. Whites entered the fight only to discover that jobs were being peddled to white teachers also.

One particular man, who sought revenge, at least once each month for more than a year, would get drunk and call me up, using the vilest and most profane language conceivable. Following spending a term in the penitentiary he died. At least six of the school board were finally landed behind prison bars.

Gratifying Response

The most gratifying response to my editorial policies have come from young white people. Early I discovered that not only older white people, but older blacks were cast in the mold of slavery and that there is not much one can do about it. I have centered my attack on the problem among young white people, through addresses in churches, colleges and every interracial gathering and through identifying myself with all youth organizations.

When the American Legion and the political boys in Oklahoma decided to get rid of the Oklahoma Youth Legislature, composed of whites, Indians and Negroes, and when a number of the adult white sponsors got cold feet and ran away, I personally for almost two years financially supported the organization with printed matter and many times cash. The most inspirational moments gleaned from this effort came when I observed white and black youth sitting down in my office preparing copy for a newspaper "Youth Frontiers" which I published for these young people for two years.

I often feel that the strong wave of liberalism existing among white youths in Oklahoma was generated in the atmosphere the *Black Dispatch* has helped to create during the past 34 years in making a frontal attack upon prejudice of every character and form. It is my position that prejudice and race hate cannot stand the light of day.

[b]

Carl Murphy
President the *Afro-American*

Independence is a principle of *Afro* political action. This newspaper has campaigned with McKinley, bullmoosed with Teddy Roosevelt, expounded the cause of the Progressives and LaFollette, and advocated the election of Al Smith, Franklin D. Roosevelt and Thomas E. Dewey.

Its first editorial for Al Smith created a sensation. It was the first Eastern paper to come out for a Democratic president in a quarter of a century.

Maryland opened its eyes when the *Afro-American* in 1919 crusaded for the election of W. Ashbie Hawkins, a colored lawyer, for U. S. Senate. He polled out 6,000 votes and was robbed of hundreds of additional ballots.

From that day, no Republican machine has been able to carry the colored voters in its vest pocket. More important still, awakening civic organizations put over 55,000 registered voters on Baltimore books alone—no estimate, no guesswork; they're colored and they vote independently.

A successful 30-year fight for the equalization of teachers' salaries in Maryland was spearheaded by the *Afro*.

A continuing fight to get colored policemen on the Baltimore City police force bore its first fruit in 1938 when two were appointed. Today there are 38 policemen and 3 policewomen on the force. One of the men is a sergeant assigned to detective headquarters.

The *Afro* financed a law suit contesting the right of the Southern Railroad to Jim Crow colored passengers on all trains leaving Washington for the South. The District of Columbia Court of Appeals handed down a verdict against the railroad and ordered it to pay nearly $1,000 in damages.

The newspaper took a leading part in the Murray case which opened the University of Maryland Law School to colored students and in the Kerr case which requires the public library system in Baltimore to employ all races.

Money for a suit filed against the Maryland Art Institute which has consistently excluded colored students, was furnished by the *Afro*, which is presently conducting a campaign to open up other graduate schools of the University of Maryland.

[c]

Thomas W. Young
President, Norfolk *Journal and Guide*

The *Journal and Guide* was started in 1900 by a fraternal order known as the Knights of Gidean and operated as an organ of that group under the name *"Lodge Journal and Guide."* In 1910 my father P. B. Young, Sr., acquired the paper, changing it to a secular organ, and dropped the word "Lodge" from the title.

Its present circulation is in excess of 60,000 copies per issue. The *Journal and Guide* is a member of the Audit Bureau of Circulations, the Negro Newspaper Publishers Association, and subscribers to both the full-day wire service of International News Service, and the press service of the NNPA News Service. Its present payroll includes 75 full-time employees in addition to about one dozen part-time workers.

Modern Plant

Our plant contains some of the most modern newspaper printing machinery and equipment. We have a Hoe 32-page web perfecting newspaper press, a Pony Autoplate page casting machine, a Sta-Hi mat former, five Linotype machines, a Ludlow machine, an Elrod material-making machine and a complete engraving plant.

Our circulation is about 75 percent distributed in Virginia and North Carolina—our area of primary concentration. We have other readers up and down the coast from New York to Georgia and scattered subscribers in almost every state in the nation.

Editorial Campaigns

The *Guide*'s editorial campaigns against residential segregation laws which (1) restricted the urban areas in which Negroes could purchase and occupy homes, and (2) having been proposed, would have if enacted, restricted ownership and location of farms in rural areas, perhaps encountered the greatest adverse pressures.

The most gratifying long-range results were realized in our editorial campaigns for educational opportunities and economic advantages.

The most disappointing of our crusades has been our continuing editorial campaign to enlarge the Negro electorate in certain areas, despite the poll tax and other proscriptions.

[d]

L. C. Bates
Editor, the *State Press* (Little Rock, Ark.)

Two months after its birth, the *State Press* called editorially for the abatement of a wave of Negro cuttings, stabbings, homicides, and other crimes through the "appointment of colored policemen." (July 4, 1941.)

Then Sergeant Thomas P. Foster, a young Negro non-com, was, as he lay helpless on the street, shot to death ruthlessly by a white patrolman. The State Press went to the street headlining the atrocity of the gun-happy patrolman and his victim, "BODY RIDDLED WHILE LYING ON THE GROUND; WHITE MILITARY POLICE LOOK ON, BRANDISHING GUNS TO HOLD CROWD BACK."

The killing was whitewashed, but out of it was born under the prodding of the *State Press,* appointment of Negro military policemen at Camp Robinson, and also Negro city police to patrol the Negro business section.

A certain amount of security was thus won for the Negro citizen. But all victories have to be paid for. Sergeant Foster paid with blood. The *State Press* paid with money. Several leading stores took their ads from the columns of the *State Press* because of its "denunciations."

One of the Little Rock unions which has a large number of Negro members staged a strike.

Negro picketers walked the line in Little Rock. But oddly enough, no clash between white men and Negroes occurred. More oddly still, and almost as though it had been engineered by those with much to gain, a clash occurred among Negroes. A Negro strikebreaker stabbed and killed a Negro picketer who was armed only with a stick.

The Grand Jury, operating behind closed doors, refused to admit a representative of the *State Press* and promptly exonerated the knife wielder and killer. There followed an indictment of Negro strikers on picket duty at the time of the killing on charges of infringement of an Arkansas so-called "Anti-Violence" Act. In a trial presenting aspects of prejudices and passion against Negro unionists and preferment for their opponents, the Negro picketers were tried, convicted, and sentenced to the penitentiary.

In a bold headline extending across the top of the front page, the *State Press* summed up its view of the trial, "FTA STRIKERS SENTENCED TO PEN BY A HAND-PICKED JURY—STATE ANTI VIOLENCE LAW USED TO INTIMIDATE NEGRO LABOR—BELIEVED BY MANY FAMILIAR WITH PROSECUTION."

If there is any doubt that race-baiters read race papers, let it be remembered that a short time after the headline appeared, deputies from the Sheriff's office descended upon the *State Press* office early one morning and calling for Mr. Bates, informed him that he was under arrest, and read to him a document charging him with contempt of court. The officers then proceeded to his house where they also arrested Mrs. Bates on a charge identical with that against her husband.

At the trial, the judge, violently pressing the charge of contempt of court and disregarding all representations of the defense, fined Mr. Bates and his wife $100.00 each and sentenced them each to ten days in the county jail. He denied an appeal and instructed that penalties be immediately enforced.

Later the State Supreme Court promptly exonerated and freed the Bateses. Freedom of the Press in the State of Arkansas had been fought for, suffered for, paid for, and won by the Negro editor of a Negro weekly.

[e]

Larkin Marshall
Editor, The *Macon* (Ga.) *World*

The *Macon World* was the only Negro paper in Georgia to come out for the ideals of the Progressive Party. In May 1948 the editor of the *World* was nominated by the Progressive State convention as their candidate for Senator. This brought a storm of protest, from friend and foe. Friends, because they believed that he would be utterly destroyed because of his political convictions and foes, because they desired to discourage Negroes from seeking major political office. At the Democratic Primary Editor Marshall was challenged and not allowed to vote. This did more to dampen the ardor of the faint-hearted than any single incident. They were made to believe that if they voted Progressive they would not be permitted to vote in any city election.

Mustered Vote

Under the leadership of Editor Marshall the Negro vote had elected all of Mayor Lewis B. Wilson Aldermanic slate and given to the city one of its best mayors. This same editor and his paper had been able to see to it that even the sheriff carried a majority of the Negro vote.

His untiring efforts caused Governor Talmadge to fail to carry Bibb County. After the election in 1948 word went down the line to destroy this Negro who had essayed to run for the Senate. The attitude of many white leaders, even those who were classed as liberal, underwent a distinct change. They felt that Editor Marshall had disobeyed the 11th commandment by attacking Jim Crow and segregation in its own grounds.

Cross Was Burned

His ringing editorials demanding Civil Rights for his people created such a wave of resentment that a cross was burned on the lawn of his home in Marshall Heights, a subdivision named for him because of his fight for decent homes for Negroes. (And although 12 beautiful homes have been built and occupied by their happy owners, the fight still goes on to destroy it and take it away.)

In order to destroy the editor of the *World* a Negro preacher was persuaded to bring a libel suit against the *World* editor and an all-white jury returned a verdict in 20 minutes.

The *World* has been temporarily suspended but plans are being made to resume publication at an early date.

66

WORDS AND WHITE CHAUVINISM

by Lloyd L. Brown

Jim Crow is a talking bird, and it was inevitable that his raucous speech should become part of the American language. Just as the system of Negro oppression required and produced an ideology—white chauvinism, so did that ideology in turn require and produce a distinctive means of expression—white chauvinist words.

But this causal relationship of system-ideology-language is not a simple one. The evil growths, flowering from the basic system, produce new seeds which help perpetuate and extend the system itself. That is why Marxists, while recognizing and insisting upon the fundamental need to *uproot* the system itself, expend great energy in combatting the ideas of white supremacy and the means by which they are expressed.

In this article I wish to discuss only one phase of the many-sided struggle—the question of words and white chauvinism. In this area we find that even among those who fully agree with the Communist position on the Negro question there exists a great deal of disagreement and confusion. At the outset I would disclaim any special authority for my views on the controversial aspects involved. I offer them merely as a beginning of the fuller discussion which is needed.

First there is a whole body of words and expressions about which there can be no debate among those who support the Negro people's fight for liberation. These terms directly express the concept of Negro inferiority. But to say that is somehow terribly inadequate. No verbal characterization of such words can fully convey the whole complex of meaning, emotion and psychology that they express. Take the word "nigger." I have heard some say that this corresponds to such epithets as "frog," "guinea," "dago," "spick," "squarehead," etc. But it doesn't; there's a qualitative difference. It is a word that expresses more than contempt, more than hatred. It burns like a branding iron; it chokes like a lynch rope; it lashes like a whip; it smells of the slave-ship. It is a word that conveys the sum total of the unparalleled oppression of a people; behind it stand 300 years of human torture, misery, poverty, pain. That such a monstrous word is commonly used, spewed forth from kindergarten to Congress, is evidence of the racist cancer which has festered and eaten into our society and which stinks before the whole world.

Such explicitly anti-Negro words can be grouped into categories which reflect each phase of white chauvinist thinking. The slave-holder who bought, sold, worked, beat and killed his slaves as if they were animals, had to insist that they *were* merely animals. Words denoting that concept were regularly used by him. Thus a strong worker was a "prime" field hand; a male slave was a "buck," etc. Today these words are still in use together with many others which designate the Negro as a brute. Let a Negro suspect be questioned: invariably he is a "burly Negro" in the capitalist press. Let a Negro be arrested (or hunted) in a "crime wave": he is an "ape-man." Many newspapers, magazines and books insist upon spelling Negro with a little "n"—a proper noun is too proper for this one nationality.

The white chauvinist insists that the Negro is not only brutish but also childish. To the Southern white ruling class every Negro male is a "boy"; no Negro is ever mature enough to be dignified with the title of Mr. or Mrs. In the North the expression of this is commonly found in the designation "girl" for Negro domestic workers regardless of age. The Bourbon insistence upon calling all Negroes by their first names is another form of this white "superiority." Negroes are not religious like other people: they always have "child-like" faith.

The brute who must be hated and feared, and the child who must be treated as such is also a very comical person who must be laughed at. His name is Sambo or Rastus. His color is inherently funny and inspires a never-ending series of humorous designations: snowball, chocolate drop, spade, shine, dinge, eight-ball, etc. These are indispensable for telling anti-Negro jokes.

The "superior" white not only exploits, cheats, segregates, beats, insults and lynches the Negro—he also insists he loves him. This strange love has given us many terms of master-class "endearment": darky, pickaninny, auntie, uncle, mammy. And many expressions of "praise": good Negro, intelligent Negro, etc. (In this peculiar system of commendation the noun modifies the adjective.)

Here I have tried to be illustrative rather than exhaustive—there are more such categories and, of course, many more such words (new ones are being coined as I write.) These are not simply "bad" words which the "well-bred" will avoid using in public. They are *criminal* words, their use is anti-social, anti-human in the most profound sense. Had we a more advanced society, socialism, all of these foul terms would be illegal as they are in the Soviet Union. One of the most vicious aspects of their widespread use is that they are usually the means whereby white children first become infected with chauvinist ideas. Usually, too, they are the first blow with which Negro children are initiated into the social order. The poignant shock of this experience has been recorded in Countee Cullen's famous little poem, "Incident."

The unceasing struggle of the Negro people in the first place and of other progressive Americans against these words has reduced their public use in comparison with former times. But the evil is still enormous and pervasive. Recently, for example, Kate Smith used the term "darky" on her network program. To say that for Marxists and progressives the reactionary character of these words is undebatable does not, of course, end the question for them. I heard of one organization that drew up a list of anti-Negro words and decided that its members will never use them. Period. But it is clearly not enough personally to refrain from using such words. It is necessary to carry on a persistent *struggle* against this deadly poison wherever and whenever it appears—on the radio, in the press, in books and magazines, films, schools, jokes, conversations.

There is, however, another kind of terminology about which a great deal of confusion exists. I refer to the wide range of words and phrases in which the concept of blackness or darkness has an invidious meaning: blackguard, black market, blacklist, blackball, black reaction, etc. It is maintained by some that such words and combinations, even though their origin may have nothing to do with the Negro question, assume a white chauvinist character in our society.

There is much to lend validity to this contention. We have already noted that many anti-Negro words focus upon the skin color of the Negro people. And in a society in which, as the Negro folk expression has it, "white is right," the use of such words and phrases mentioned above can have chauvinist overtones. In fact every effort is made by the white supremacists to associate the Negro people with the supposed evilness of their pigmentation. Thus Roget's *Thesaurus,* a standard bourgeois work, associates under the word "blackness" such words as "smut, raven, crow, negro [small "n"] blackamoor, smirch, nigger, darkie, Ethiop, dingy, murky," etc.

A typical example of this color association in social life is given in *Moby Dick,* where Melville shows a sailor taunting a Negro shipmate with these words: "Aye, harpooner, thy race is the undeniably dark side of mankind—devilish dark at that." Elsewhere in this work, in a chapter discussing the quality of whiteness, the author himself makes this same point. Referring to the traditional honored place accorded the color white, he says that "this pre-eminence in it applies to the human race itself, giving the white man ideal mastership over every dusky tribe. . . ."*

Surely there never can be any justification for the use of the invidious words and phrases relating to darkness or the purity and sublimeness

---

*This chauvinist statement of Melville's is in curious contradiction to the spirit and content of this book. *Moby Dick* would be an American classic if for no other reason than the fact that in it Melville pioneered in the portrayal of Negroes and other non-whites in truly human and heroic characters.

when discussing *peoples*. I recall an incident from schooldays. Our teacher in giving us a lecture on "tolerance" (after a playground fight caused by a chauvinist insult) assured the class that "in God's eyes *all* children are white." I don't remember the classmate's epithet hurled against me, but the teacher's words burned themselves deep.

In my opinion the question of *context* is decisive. When Africa is called the Dark Continent, the chauvinist connotation is implicit. But I cannot see anything chauvinistic about the term Dark Ages, referring to medieval Europe where clearly no association with Negroes or their character is implied. When the song-writer writes about "darktown strutters," the chauvinistic meaning is obvious (and deliberate). But when the speaker says that the "outlook is dark for capitalism," it is absurd to charge him with chauvinism (as has happened).

The seemingly innocent phrase "white hope" is indelibly stamped with anti-Negro meaning because of its origin and widespread use at the time when Jack Johnson was the first Negro heavyweight champion and the cry of the press was for a "white hope" to dethrone him. But what about a word like blacklist? There are those who insist that such words should not be used. I suppose their reasoning goes like this: blacklist is bad, Negroes are black, hence to use black in a bad sense is to say that the Negro people are bad. But the word blacklist has a specific meaning which has nothing at all to do with the Negro people any more than the phrase "caught redhanded" has anything to do with the "Reds."

There is no end to the possible confusion if the *meaning* of words and phrases is lost sight of. But because this happens, some people are found denouncing as chauvinistic words like "blackeye" and "whitewash."

I would cite the following case to further clarify the importance of context. During the war I learned that in the Post Exchange at Fort Riley, Kansas, Negro soldiers would be served standing at the soda bar together with whites. But if they wanted to consume their refreshments sitting down, they had to sit at a separate table painted black! Clearly here the table color was invidious. But what is the central fact? The paint job was but the fillip, the final hideous touch to the structure of Army Jim Crow. Had all of the tables been painted black, the enforced separation would still have existed. Had they all been white, the same fact would remain. Had the colors been switched—the same. The extra viciousness of the single black table had, you can see, nothing to do with the fact of its color but with the *meaning* expressed. Had there been no segregation enforced, no one would have been bothered by the fact that one table was differently colored.

I think it would be both a divergence from the struggle and an impossibility to attempt to change the whole sector of the language which has to do with the evil or ominous connotations of black or darkness. This conception goes back to the earliest experiences of mankind. It is a natural result of the conditions of life, the significance of the sun as the source of light, warmth and growth. Obviously if one wished to eradicate the sinister connotations of darkness, one would have to expunge the beneficent meanings of its opposite, light (dawn, brightness, etc.). In other words, not only would our speaker have to avoid reference to dark outlook, but he would also not permit himself to speak of a bright outlook. A hundred similar examples could be cited.

Not only is such an endeavor quite impossible, but altogether needless. The Negro people who have always led in the fight against white chauvinist words have not been concerned with this question. Consider this fact: there is a song, "Lift Every Voice and Sing," which is popularly known as the Negro national anthem. It is generally sung at conventions, commencements and formal occasions concerned with Negro life and struggle. It contains this line:

> *Sing a song full of the faith that the dark past*
> *has taught us....*

And not only is the oppressive past of slavery "dark," but the future of liberation is

> *Where the white gleam of our bright star is cast.*

If this conception was inherently or even inferentially white chauvinist, we would have the anomaly of a militant people adopting an anthem which vilifies itself! But obviously, here, the Negro people are merely using the traditional color symbols for their general meaning.

It is true that there have been in the past and still exist (though on a diminishing scale) efforts by sections of the Negro people to abolish the use of the term Negro. These efforts, however, have not been based upon the fact that the word is from the Spanish for black, but rather because the term historically has been associated with an enslaved people, an "inferior" race, etc. Joseph D. Bibb, a columnist on the *Pittsburgh Courier* (a leading Negro newspaper), continually campaigns on this issue. He would like to disavow all such reminders of chattel slavery as the spirituals. Though such efforts are well-intended, the Negro people generally recognize—and the establishment of Negro History Week proves it—that their past is not only not something shameful, but as proud and glorious a chapter of heroic struggle against barbaric oppression as that of any people in the world. In any case, the shame of slavery is forever branded upon the slave masters.

I would further cite as evidence of the needlessness of a struggle around general "color" words the fact that in our thoroughly chauvinist society there is no prejudice at all against those colors as such. All of the terrible meanings associated with the term black do not inhibit at all the widespread use of that color (or brown, tan, beige, etc.) in apparel or other commodities. This goes even for skin color: it is the mark of highest fashion to be deeply tanned, not only in the summer time but in the winter (perhaps more so then—the dark-tanned person has obviously just returned from an expensive vacation in Florida!). More of the faces of our greatest national heroes (including such strange "heroes" as Robert E. Lee and Jeff Davis) are cast in bronze than in white marble—and even a Rankin is not outraged at this. And has not every pulp magazine sung the glories of Tall, Dark and Handsome?

No, a dark skin is "inferior" only if its inhabitant is "non-Caucasian," and a Negro is still a Negro though his skin be as fair as any "Nordic." Only a complete charlatan like Walter White can propose that the solution to the Negro question is chemically to change the color of the Negro people.

As I see it, the problem is not to do away with the general meanings of words and phrases relating to color, *but to attack the idea that these conceptions have anything to do with the character of the Negro people.*

This thought can be illustrated by another example: according to the white supremacists, the most significant characteristic of Negroes is their "inferiority." Hence in their literature the two words, Negro and inferiority, are invariably joined together. Obviously, this practice does not make the word "inferior" evil in itself. In fact it is a useful and necessary word and the fight for equality will not be advanced by abolishing it. What must be combatted is the *concept* that the Negro people are inferior. Let the word black mean, among other things, gloomy, dismal, foreboding, shadowy, somber, or anything else that is evil—what has that got to do with the Negro people? Certainly they do not accept these terms as applying to them, else there would not be a Negro newspaper named the *Black Dispatch* or a nationally-circulated magazine called *Ebony.* Nor would we have the Negro proverb which maintains that "the blacker the berry, the sweeter the juice."

In other words, it is necessary to carry on the struggle against those who painted the Fort Riley table black—and their foul ideology and system—rather than a quixotic crusade against black tables.

Recently I was told about a progressive group in Brooklyn that held a picnic last summer. They had just had a discussion on white chauvinism and felt themselves alert to the danger. Therefore they voted down a suggestion that watermelon be served—that would be chauvinistic! Fantastic, but it shows how people can be disoriented when they forget the *content* and purpose of the struggle. The time-worn stereotype about the Negro and watermelons (vicious as all such stereotypes are) really has got nothing to do with watermelons. It could just as well be pumpkins. If that group never eats a watermelon for the rest of their lives, the struggle for Negro rights in Brooklyn will not be advanced one iota. No, while they are beating watermelons over the head, the cops will continue to club Negroes on the streets.

I will give another example of this kind of thinking. A white singer wrote that he was distressed because "even our most progressive Negro concert singers continue to sing spirituals and work songs in 'dialect'...Paul Robeson may change offensive lines in Old Man River, but he keeps on singing spirituals in the old manner, as does Marian Anderson and many others. Maybe he thinks there's nothing wrong with it; maybe he hasn't thought about it at all. Next time I see him I'm going to tell him I wouldn't do it myself and wonder why he should." Such singing, he said, "becomes an aspersion on a whole people...it perpetuates the myth that folk songs come from illiterate people."

Now there are so many things wrong in the few words quoted that a whole evening might be spent in discussing them. But here I will focus on the one pertinent angle. The fact that so-called Negro dialect has always played a big part in white chauvinist jokes and insults is here confused with the quality of Negro spirituals. Not down with white chauvinism!, but down with the spirituals as they were originally composed! The great Paul Robeson whose magnificent songs and heroic struggle against the oppressors have won the hearts of millions must be "corrected" by this arrogant critic. Surely no more glaring example could be found of where this peculiar method of "fighting" white chauvinism can lead to—to an attack, in essence, upon the Negro people and their foremost exponents! Were such a view highly exceptional, I would not discuss it here, but unfortunately it is not. I recall a white progressive telling me that the most chauvinist thing he ever saw in print was a scene from a play by Theodore Ward published in *Masses & Mainstream* (May, 1948). Why? Because Mr. Ward, the leading Negro playwright of our country, wrote in dialect. (By that token Sean O'Casey must be the worst anti-Irishman in the world instead of the most brilliant spokesperson of his people!)

The question of the use of dialect is too large a subject to be dealt with in this article, but these examples are useful in indicating the dangerous confusion which arises on the subject of words and white chauvinism.

The significance of these errors is not that they are "over-zealous." No one can ever be too energetic or too militant in the struggle against the monster that is white chauvinism. It is rather that these wrong tendencies distort and confuse the struggle itself and lead up the blind alleys of fetishism and formalism. The fight against white chauvinist ideas has nothing in common with word-play. Nor can it be conducted separately and isolated from the general political, economic and social struggle for Negro rights in every neighborhood, factory, office and school.

The interest in this subject indicates a heightened awareness of the problem of white chauvinism in speech by the labor and progressive movement. However, we must emphasize that it is necessary always to bear in mind that the Negro people are slandered and vilified *because they are an oppressed people*. The struggle, based upon the closest working unity of Negro and white, against that oppression is central and paramount.

Masses and Mainstream, February 1950, pp. 5–11.

67

THE LYNCHING OF PICKIE PIE

by L. D. Reddick

Bad news, unfortunately, comes often from Georgia these days. The first lynching of 1949 took place there.

What was the trouble that time?

Who was the victim; what was he like?

Why was he murdered? What did the papers say? What did the preachers preach about it? Who bears the shame, if shame there was? What did the Governor do?

What did *anybody* do?

Irwinton, Georgia, is a sleepy town of less than 3,000 inhabitants. It is the county seat of Wilkinson county, located in the central part of the state. Negroes there outnumber whites about 7 to 5. It is a poor and bleak rural township with few cultural and recreational advantages for whites or blacks. The round of life for Negro residents includes work, church, lodge meetings, watching the trains come in, standing about the town square on Saturday afternoons, visiting each other, hunting and fishing, listening to the radio and juke boxes.

Even while lingering about the railroad station, Negroes are not expected to stand up straight and look forward directly, rather to slouch, to slink, to droop and lean with one shoulder down; to laugh merrily or be quiet; to be helpful or get out of the way of the white folks. A crowd of blacks at the County Square will let a lone, poor white drunk reel and curse his way through them. One stout blow from a black fist would sober or silence him.

This is the kind of town in which Caleb Hill lived—at least he lived down a country road near it. He had grown up in this area. He had to quit school in the seventh grade in order to help his father make ends meet for the family of ten children. He did plowing and farm work for awhile; then went into the chalk mines where he won a reputation of being a good worker and thrifty with his earnings. He had to be: Hill's father lost his health and Caleb married. By 1949 he had nine dependents, three of whom were his own children.

His neighbors and friends say that "Pickie Pie" (as he was nicknamed) had a great spirit. They liked him. He worked hard but maintained a zest for life. He was playful, witty, and enjoyed a good time. He delighted in driving his shiny Ford around town. He would make the "cut-out" talk.

He was no "Uncle Tom." Some of the white folks didn't like this—Alec Boone, for one. Boone was publisher of the *Wilkinson County News* and a member of the state legislature. He was so ardent a Talmadgite that he, too, wore those scarlet suspenders in imitation of the Governor and the Governor's deceased father, Gene. Boone described Pickie Pie as "a bad one."

In early May of 1949, Pickie Pie had a clash with two white men. He left town, remaining in Macon for a couple of weeks to let things "blow over."

Memorial Day

Memorial Day, May 30, is not as much of a holiday in Georgia as is Confederate Day, April 26. But, anyway, it fell this time on Sunday. A group of ten or fifteen Negroes gathered at the New Harlem club for "some fun." Round about midnight, Pickie Pie and another fellow at the party, Ned Burney, quarreled and scuffled. Burney got mad and called the sheriff, George Hatcher. The sheriff came in in the usual rough and insulting manner. Immediately, he tried to put handcuffs on Pickie Pie who outsmarted him, took his gun away from him, shot at him (somehow missing; the sheriff admitted that he thought his days were numbered), then threw the gun aside and made ready to have it out with Hatcher, man to man. At this time Pickie Pie's brother, Whett, who was also at the party, jumped out of a window and fled. A friend, I. W. Weeks, picked up the gun and also hurried away. At this point, the proprietor of the New Harlem handed the sheriff another pistol. Hatcher was then able to make the arrest. He marched Pickie Pie off to jail.

Beat Weeks

The jail was on the second floor of the sheriff's house. It is a common practice in these small counties for the sheriff to rent part of his home as a jail and for the sheriff's wife to provide food for the prisoners at a fee to the county. It is a good little business.

Sheriff Hatcher locked Pickie Pie in and for some unstated reason left the jail keys on the dining room table. He then went back to the New Harlem, he says, to look for his gun. He reported that he spent two hours searching about the bushes and trees, outside the juke joint. He did *not* report that about 1:30 a.m., he, four state patrolmen, a deputy and the chief of police of McIntyre, a neighboring town, went to the home of Weeks and demanded that he produce the gun. These "officers" beat Weeks, ransacked his house and upset his wife. Weeks got the gun from the hollow stump near his home where he had hidden it and surrendered it.

Meanwhile, two "heavy-set" white men came to the sheriff's home, entered, picked up the keys from the dining room table, took Pickie Pie from his cell, and on their way out quite obligingly left the keys on the kitchen table downstairs.

She Heard Noises

The sheriff's wife said that she heard noises but assumed that they were made by the sheriff. However, when the sheriff did get home later, she did not mention the noises to him. Nor did the sheriff look for his keys or check on his prisoner—after such an exciting evening!

A few hours after daylight, about 7:30 a.m., relatives of Pickie Pie were on their way to get him out of jail, if possible. An emissary of the Mayor of Irwinton told them to get off the streets and stay off. The Negro janitor of the jail also told them that "the white folks say to go home and stay out of town today."

About 8:30 a.m. the sheriff says that he was notified that Pickie Pie's body had been found on the Dublin-Jeffersonville Highway, Number 127. His body showed evidences of abuse. There were three bullets in his head.

The news of this, the first lynching of 1949, flashed across the nation. But the reaction of shock was not shared by the white people of Irwinton. They could not understand why so much "to-do" should be made over a Negro. "It's just a Negro," said one. "It didn't upset a checker game," somebody told a *New York Times* reporter.

Governor Talmadge, when asked by the *Atlanta Daily World* (Negro publication) if he was offering a reward for the killers, answered that he had not been asked by the sheriff to do so. The sheriff, in turn, said that he had been too busy to ask the Governor. They never got together on this.

The Georgia Bureau of Investigation put two men on the case. In a few days they admitted to newsmen that they were "sure" that they had enough evidence to indict Malcolm Vivian Pierce, 27, an electrician and Dennis Lamar Purvis, 37, a grocery store and cafe operator. These suspects were arrested after the widow, Mrs. Josie Hill, swore out warrants charging them with murder (a brave woman).

A special session of the Wilkinson County Grand Jury was called. This was a 23-man body (all white, of course). It met for a day, June 14, and returned no indictment. The suspects were freed.

Tears and Sobs

What would the Negroes do? They outnumbered the whites 7 to 5. But the whites had the guns, the police, the courts, the money, the GBI, the governor, the buildings, even the houses the Negroes rented, most of the fields and farms, all of the little factories and sawmills. The whites had everything. All power to the whites! The Negroes, at least, could "turn out" for the funeral. They did. It was held in nearby Jeffersonville. Two thousand came. This was the biggest crowd ever seen at a funeral here. There were not many noisy shouts; mainly tears and sobs. Grown men cried. What else was there to do?

The press reactions to this lynching are also revealing. The *Atlanta Daily World* (Negro paper), that gave the best coverage to it, was almost cynically hopeless. It remarked editorially, "We don't think the verdict [of the Grand Jury] will occasion any great surprise to anyone, either in or out of the state. For out of a total of 25 lynchings in Georgia, since 1930, figures show that there has not been a single conviction." The *World* then went on, less grimly, to call for a federal anti-lynch law.

The *Atlanta Constitution,* edited by Ralph McGill, leading "southern liberal," deplored the fact that Georgia was again presented to the nation and to "Russian newspapers" as lawless and that such acts "move us closer to Federal laws."

The *Atlanta Journal,* in two editorials, also was apprehensive that Georgia's reputation was soiled and that such occurrences gave "invaluable ammunition to the political baiters of Georgia and the South" and "off-set to a heavy degree the powerful efforts of Senator Russell and other Southern Congressional leaders to prevent federal intrusion into the state's field of law enforcement."

The really indignant editorials and those that focused upon the victim, his nine dependents left behind and the flouting of law and human rights were mostly in the Negro press and in publications north of the Mason-Dixon line. Even Hodding Carter of Greenville, Mississippi, another famous "Southern liberal," in his weekly syndicated column for the Southern press, insisted that Pickie Pie was a "small town Negro badman" and that "the mob spirit exists elsewhere besides the South." Was he more interested that lynchings should stop or that talk up North about lynchings down South should stop?

Pickie Pie is now dead and gone. His unhappy bones are rotting in the earth, where all our bones some day must rot.

His family and dependents have scattered, doubling up with relatives and friends. His little children know what happened to their father. His ghost haunts the land: for all of the hundreds of Negroes along the dusty roads of Georgia and elsewhere, who appear drunk or dazed, stupidly insensitive to inquiry or insult, are the zombies of the Pickie Pies. It is not so much that they are afraid of others, rather they are afraid of themselves. They fear to feel their feelings; a thousand resentments would explode. Sometimes they do anyway. Then the headlines say, "Crazed Negro Goes Berserk, Runs Amok."

An Ordinary Man

Pickie Pie was not rich, well-born or educated. He was an ordinary man.

He was not attempting to vote (though, of course, everyone should have that right) or achieve social equality (though every kind of equality must be achieved). He was no crusader for democracy.

He was simply an ordinary man who wanted to be a man. He liked to work, to drive his Ford, to play with his kids, to have fun sometimes. He did not like being pushed around.

They killed him.

Sunday morning preachers will preach, as before, of manhood and brotherhood. Editors will write, from day to day, of law and democracy. The Governor still sits in his seat in the capitol.

The bones of Pickie Pie are rotting in the earth of Wilkinson County. The world moves on.

Crisis, March 1950, Vol. 57, pp. 141–43, 198. Dr. Reddick, formerly curator of the Schomburg Collection in New York, at this time was librarian of Atlanta University.

68

WHY MEN LEAVE HOME (1950)

St. Clair Drake

"If you don't believe I'm leaving, just count the days I'm gone," sings the Negro male torn from his roots in the southern plantation, living here today at a turpentine camp and gone tomorrow to a river town. Under the chapter titled, "Roving Men and Homeless Women," E. Franklin Frazier interprets with rare insight the flight of the Black Ulysses in his book, *The Negro Family in the United States*. He pictures vividly this escape from the unrewarding grind of plantation life and the censuring eyes and tongues of rural parsons, from the insistent obligations of the South's large families and low incomes. Journey's end for many was the city.

In another penetrating chapter, "Fathers on Leave," Frazier as an honest social scientist states that the Negro desertion rate is probably higher in most cities than that for whites. And why? This is no simple case of "irresponsibility" or "immorality," for Frazier very brilliantly demonstrates that the desertion rate is high primarily because of the disorganization of life within the Black Ghettoes of our American cities. Uprooted directly from the southern soil or recruited from the by-ways of small towns and labor camps, the Negro males throughout the Twenties found life in the cities unusually precarious due to uncertain and low-paid employment. They found it tragic during the depression when they were "first fired." The Negro family in the city was beaten to pieces between the hammer of economic insecurity and the anvil of "slum conditions." The iron bands of restrictive covenants had condemned the Negro masses to the worst housing, under the most overcrowded conditions.

But Frazier's careful researches also show that those Negro males who were able to gain steady employment and to escape from the most disorganized sections of the Black Belts, not only did not desert their families in any greater proportion than whites, but also maintained families every whit as stable as those of their counterparts in the white middle class. The inescapable conclusion from Frazier's work is that if Negro men are to be kept at home, the first step is to make jobs and housing available to them, so that they can maintain a stable pattern of family relations. When more Negro men have the chance to become "solid middle class," with all that the term means, desertion rates will drop.

How do economic insecurity and ghetto conditions make men leave home? The ideal picture of the American husband is that he is a "good provider." American males grow up feeling that they should "hold the purse strings." The American caste-system has turned the tables for the Negro. Among the Negro masses, it is frequently the woman who has a steady job. And there were plenty of times during the Depression years when neither one had a decent job. The Negro male's position in the family is thus weakened, and the sense of unimportance and of shame must frequently operate to make him shake the dust off his feet, to go prospecting for a job here and there, or to leave just so he won't have to hear references from the distaff side to his laziness or "lack of get up." Staying on the move becomes a habit after awhile.

Also, the overcrowded ghetto with its kitchenette living makes the worst possible situation for raising a family, and I have actually heard serious barber shop discussions in which a man has said that he was going to leave home so that the old woman wouldn't have another baby. (Mesinga diaphragms are not too well known among the Negro lower classes.)

In the final analysis, Negro men leave home not because they are Negroes, but because they are men. For almost a million years after humanity emerged from the purely animal state, people roamed around in small bands with women bearing the kids and staying close to the camp, and with men bringing home the bear or kangaroo. The tradition of the male as "he who roams by right" must be very deeply set in human culture. Man the hunter and fighter is the basic image of our kind. Stock rearing has reinforced this pattern of man on the move. Where the horse and camel are available (and now the automobile) it has given mankind a wide range in which to travel and somebody has to stay home to look after the hearth and the kids.

Every war, too, has uprooted the males and set the pattern of wandering ever more deeply. When the war is over, it's pretty hard to settle down to domesticity. Tennyson has given expression to this fact in his famous poem *Ulysses*. Taking up where Homer left off, Tennyson tells us what *Ulysses* did after he came back from the battle of Troy. Nothing could be more boring than to stay quietly at home with his faithful wife who had waited all those years for him. So, calling his old cronies together, he said:

> I cannot rest from travel...
> How dull it is to pause, to make an end...
> Come, my friends,
> 'Tis not too late to seek a newer world.
> Push off, and sitting well in order smite
> The sounding furrows; for my purpose holds
> To sail beyond the sunset and the baths
> Of all the western stars until I die.

A lot of G.I.s must feel this way today.

The more one ponders this matter of Negro lowerclass men who leave home, the more one can see that they are acting out, in a permissive economic and social atmosphere, a wish that is repressed deeply in The Unconscious of *all* American males of all social classes—white and colored. Did you ever stop to think why comic strips like Maggie and Jiggs, or Dagwood are so popular? The American male running from his wife is a constant fantasy figure in American life. Whence come such expressions as "my ball and chain" or "the old battle axe"? Why our statement when the knot is being tied, "Well, she's roped him in" or "She's got her man"? Why is "going out with the boys on Friday night" considered such a relief? I suspect that one reason is the fact that women throughout American life keep the pressure on for social mobility, for getting ahead (note Marquand's *Point of No Return*) and that men—black and white—deeply resent the pressure.

It is only at the lowerclass level where institutional controls are weak and where life is hard that men can just up and walk away. Also, the conditions of existence at this level give a man a plausible excuse to square his runaway with his conscience. He can say "I've been roving around looking for a job," or "I didn't want any woman supporting me" or "I just couldn't stay there day after day not being able to look after my family as I ought to." Since more Negroes are at the low-income level than whites, more of them leave home. Middleclass men just stay there and "take it," until their wives divorce them for "running around"—not "running away."

Negro Digest, April 1950, pp. 25–27. St. Clair Drake at this time was associate professor of sociology at Roosevelt College, Chicago.

69

SUCCESSES IN INDIANAPOLIS (1950)

by Willard Ransom

On April 17, 1950, Willard Ransom of Indianapolis reported the following to Gloster Current of the national office of the NAACP:

...direct action to open restaurants [was] succeeding in forcing compliance with the Indiana Civil Rights Law in many restaurants, hotels and theaters. Method—test groups, persuasion, affidavits, suits. The Indianapolis hotels recently opened their doors to Negro members of the National Bar Association, Veterans of Foreign Wars, CIO, etc. While much discrimination in these accommodations still exists the Association program is steadily winning on all fronts.

From NAACP papers, quoted by Emma Lou Thornbrough, in *Indiana Magazine of History,* December 1987, vol. 83, p. 320.

70

PROBLEMS AND EMOTIONAL DIFFICULTIES OF NEGRO CHILDREN DUE TO RACE (1950)

by Regina M. Goff

The Problem

An indication of social direction at a given time may be obtained through a study of what is happening to the children of a culture. An adequate concept of American culture must recognize the thinking and behavior of growing Negro children who are products of and thus reflectors of that culture. An attempt was thus made to investigate the problems, fears, annoyances, frustrations, and other emotional difficulties that befall Negro children, according to their own reports, by reason of the fact that they are Negroes. Further, in order to determine individual reactions to environmental conditions, children were questioned with reference to feelings accompanying these experiences, impulses toward the disturbing environmental elements, and the overt social responses occurring as a consequence of all these.

More specifically, the problems involved may be stated as follows:

1. What are the emotional difficulties which Negro children have because of their group identity? This problem raises an additional question: Do these difficulties vary in terms of such factors as section, socio-economic level, sex, and skin color?
2. What inner feelings are associated with these problems? This problem also raises the question as to whether these inner feelings vary in relation to factors such as section, socio-economic level and sex.

3. What impulses are directed toward the environment?
4. What types of responses are made to these difficulties?
5. According to reports of children, are the overt responses indicative of what they felt like doing?
6. What social difficulties appear to produce the greatest effect on personality development?

It would appear that the isolation of difficulties might serve as a basis for the development of survival techniques or satisfying adjustment mechanisms designed to offset their effect on personality development.

General Procedure

The interview method was used because it appeared to be the best technique available, at present, to obtain information concerning the problems posed. When this method was chosen it was with the understanding that questions carefully prepared in advance could be revised and improved through preliminary try-outs. It was also aimed to use the material both quantitatively and qualitatively. The final interview form which was used was standardized on the basis of reports obtained during a two-month preliminary, exploratory period of free discussion designed to discover the kinds of questions that best could elicit the desired information.

In the first question or series of questions, the child was asked to tell who he played or sat with at school or regarded as his friend. After he had identified such persons he was asked to say what it was he liked about them, and what they looked like.

Another series bore on the topic of quarrels, fights, and misunderstandings. Here again the term or reference to "other children" was used before any specific question was raised about bad relations with white children as distinguished from other groups.

The next series of questions was designed to cover the general theme of ridicule and being made fun of as distinguished from actual fighting and person-to-person conflict.

A general comment in relation to the teacher was designed to find out if the behavior of the white teacher reflected an attitude interpreted by the child as meaning that she had a low opinion of the child.

Another series dealt with relations to store people and other tradespeople in the community at large. Somewhat akin to the above group was a question related to activities in the wider community.

Questions involving attitudes toward stereotypes or emotional assumptions were also presented. These referred to movie and radio roles accepted by Negroes.

In order to discover any other types of experiences not involved in the above series, children were asked to speak of any experiences which they had had in white neighborhoods.

The group interviewed consisted of 75 girls and 75 boys ranging in age from ten to twelve years, and representing contrasting socio-economic levels as determined by occupational status and cultural background of parents. Ninety children lived in New York City and sixty in St. Louis.

A compilation embracing all of the responses made by all of the children to questions asked, was set down in systematic order, but without regard to a particular pattern or organization. The raw data were examined to discover common elements or similar items that might be placed in the same category. A tentative set of categories representing the difficulties the children had encountered was devised. These categories were then used in analyzing individual records. A total of 487 difficulties was reported.

General Statement of Findings

A statement of the categories under which the children's replies were classified and illustrations of these follow. The categories are arranged from those representing overt verbal and physical manifestations to those representing more subtle levels.

A. Overt verbal:

Direct ridicule, including name-calling, disparaging or belittling statements referring to unfavorable qualities alleged to be characteristics of Negroes:

"White boys cuss me and call me 'Old black nigger.' One of them called me a black bitch."

"One day the teacher told us she wouldn't take us on no trips because it would be a disgrace to be seen on the street with a bunch of monkeys and laughing hyenas. She said, 'What would my friends say?'"

These statements would seem to indicate consciously designed verbal attacks which aim to stigmatize, label or belittle, and inherent in them are attitudes which imply rejection.

B. *Physical ill-treatment,* threats of violence by white persons.

"When we left the museum, we went to the Automat to eat. I went to get a glass of water and this white woman slapped me in the face."

"I went to get on the street-car, and a white man jerked me off, and let a white woman on and then he got on."

These illustrations indicate overt actions taken by majority group members in their rejection of Negro children; pain-punishment being used as a method of reinforcing the idea of disapproval.

C. *Aggressive behavior.* Actions by white children, picking quarrels, fights, throwing stones, breaking toys, snatching belongings.

"I was going down the street and the white boy kicked me, and when I went to hit him he set his dog on me. I started running and the dog bit my ankle."

"Sometimes we go to the park and over the mountains, and the white boys on the other side throw rocks at us. I was holding my airplane one day in the park and a white boy ran by real fast and knocked it out of my hand and broke it."

The instigation of conflicts by white children without provocation, other than the presence of particular individuals who represent an "out-group," would seem to indicate that attitudes have been absorbed by these children from a source whose authority they do not question.

D. Subtle Manifestations:

Rude treatment. Discourteous, insulting behavior, ill-mannered treatment.

"One day I was swinging in the park, and a white girl stuck out her tongue at me and wouldn't use the swing I had when I got through using it. She waited for a white girl to get through."

"White children laugh and make fun of my short hair."

"One day a boy was waving his handkerchief in school and the teacher told him to put it in the waste basket. Then she put her foot on it and stomped and stomped it."

In these instances, individuals dramatized their thinking in more subtle behavior which probably preserves their sense of decency in conduct which in turn enables them to remain more at peace with their conscience. At least, more so than if their rejecting behavior was more openly hostile.

E. *Discrimination,* with respect to rights, privileges, being denied access to situations because of being a Negro. Lack of acceptance on basis of equality as another human being.

"I went out to Coney Island and bought a ticket to go in the canoe. The man wouldn't let me get in. He said colored people couldn't ride on the water."

"I was riding my bicycle and got a flat. I took it in the station to get it fixed. The man wouldn't let me have no air, and he said he couldn't fix things for colored people."

"Our class went to a broadcast over W.N.Y.C., and afterwards the teacher took us to an Automat. They wouldn't let us come in. We went to another one, and they wouldn't let us come in there either. I don't know what the man told the teacher, but she had to bring us back to a restaurant on 116th Street where we could eat. We never did feel right."

Discriminatory practice may be thought of as a form of defense devised to offset the upward mobility of a group which is seeking to end its suppression and to achieve integration.

F. More subtle level of behavior:

Indirect disparagement. Disparaging stereotypes in publications, movies and radio.

"I don't like the maid and servant parts colored people have. They are always busting suds. It makes me ashamed. I don't like the radio parts either. In a play about Harry Jones and his family there is a colored woman who just loves white people so much she can't stay at home and look after her own family. It makes me mad to hear that cause it ain't true."

"I don't like Negro characters on the radio. They make them so funny, so silly. I don't see why they take those parts. They are just making fun of themselves."

In indirect disparagement we find a subtle means of portraying supposedly distinctive traits of Negroes designed to be laughed at by others. The characteristics assigned support racial mores and these are preserved through the media of the movies, radio and publications.

Of the total number of feeling responses reported, 57 per cent were of the nature of resentment, 38 per cent inferiority, 3 per cent fear reactions and 1 per cent indifference. In the picture as a whole, resentment appears to be the dominant feeling tone experienced, having been reported by the largest number of children, and appearing as a dominant pattern in the total list of feeling responses.

Accompanying these reactions were desires to fight in 29 per cent of the instances, to argue in 28 per cent, and to accept or ignore in 37 per cent. In 5 per cent of the cases there was an inability to state what the impulse was. In the absence of quantitative analysis, the intensity of the stimuli of ridicule, aggression and physical ill-treatment is indicated by the fact that resentment is most often aroused, and the drive to fight most often incurred. The reports of kinds of responses actually made may be fairly indicative of behavior expectations. In considering the total number of responses made to specific difficulties, 10 per cent of the reports indicated that fighting had occurred, 7 per cent indicated that there was arguing, and 82 per cent withdrawal.

General Conclusions

1. In our culture there are identifiable social pressures which impinge upon the Negro child and cause difficulties. Since these experiences are reported as early as the tenth year, it appears that the Negro child enjoys a relatively short period of time in which he is consciously uninhibited. In his early life he perceives clues which enable him to attach significance to himself as different, and he early learns to limit his expectations of freedom of movement and gratification of desires in the larger world.

2. Social traditions influence Negro-white relations, and restrictive measures based on tradition mold attitudes and influence behavior. It would appear that certain cultural attitudes are widespread and have a dynamic force in determining the behavior of the masses of majority group members toward Negroes. Problems such as ridicule, aggression, discrimination, and indirect disparagement transcend selective factors such as geographical location and socio-economic level of individuals.

3. Widespread reports and negative reactions to expressions of ridicule would indicate that there are in practically all children areas of vulnerability and sensitivity to this particular social pressure. Because of the magnitude of its appearance, ridicule might be thought of as producing the greatest effect on personality development.

4. Proximity is a factor influencing the kinds of experiences children have. In highly concentrated Negro communities more attention is paid to the less direct manifestations such as rude treatment and indirect

disparagement. It was also found that in these districts consciousness of self is heightened, and "cultural isolates" are bred.

5. Sex differences are apparent in relation to the kinds of pressures reported. Girls pay relatively more attention to manifestations from which an unfavorable attitude may be inferred.

A sex difference was also noted in relation to feelings aroused. Boys reported more resentment and girls more instances of inferiority.

6. Children light in skin color may be preferred members of the group in as much as they reported fewer difficulties in relation to their number in the total group. Those medium in skin color reported the largest number. These children are probably more active and less inhibited than those of dark skin color, and therefore have a larger number of contacts.

7. The impulse over-whelmingly reported was to strike back. However, true reactions were evidently concealed by adherence to social expectancies for the most prevalent response was withdrawal. This response would seem to represent the best possible adjustment of feelings and impulses to social pressures that these children know how to make.

8. While it is recognized that each child, as an individual, develops his own security system, cultural patterns imposed on all alike tend to result in behavior more reflective of these modifying social controls than of the unique individuality of the child. This is evidenced by the fact that in 82 per cent of the difficulties encountered, children responded by withdrawing from the situation. They seem to lack adequate mechanisms to free them from the fetters of the culture. Rather, there is a submission to standards.

9. An indication was given of the psychological basis of some observable social behavior. In one group studied, children as individuals reported withdrawal in relation to aggression. The same children were later apprehended as participants in a near riot provoked by the same type of conflict from which they individually withdrew. Fear, in the individual, probably suppresses hostility which finds expression in group action.

10. It appears from these data that color caste subjects the Negro child to interferences and limitations in relation to the attainment of full human acceptance and status; that such interference with social goals results in frustration; that the Negro child is therefore faced with emotional difficulties because of caste status and social controls.

Some Educational Implications

A practical application might be made of the facts revealed by children themselves to the training and guidance of the children. The needs of the Negro child are no different, of course, from those of any other children, but their chances of their being met may be less, for rewards in the larger world of which they are a part are few. Conscientious attempts on the part of individual majority members to eliminate in their behavior those manifestations which serve as instigators of ill-feeling would be a long step in reducing the odds prevailing.

Intercultural education groups might consider these specifics pointed out by children as annoying, and use the facts revealed as a basis for a constructive, active program. Well-meaning individuals may be ignorant of factors which have negative influences.

It might be mentioned in passing that unsolicited statements threw some light on the kinds of techniques which have already been successfully used by white persons in their attempts at bettering human relationships. One boy mentioned the Youth Builders and stated, "We had forums and learned about discrimination."

A girl ventured: "I went up to Columbia University once. We went to hear a doctor speak. There were white children there. The doctor told us about different people, and she said that the color of your skin didn't make any difference. That made me feel pretty good. It is all right to marry someone not your color if you can get along with them. When she got through talking, the children talked to each other, and all of us laughed and had a good time."

A boy stated: "There was a white teacher who helped us with plays. We gave one play at the Service Center. I was the main character. A white boy was the bum."

Perhaps much help and understanding is gained from direct verbal approaches by competent adults. Experiences which include first-hand contact with white children under wise guidance would also seem to make meaningful contributions. Mere proximity, however, is not in itself an ameliorating factor.

It is apparent that the Negro child needs an enriched program of training which places more emphasis on building of attitudes toward himself, attitudes of worth of self, respect for self, and confidence.

Journal of Negro Education, Spring 1950; 19:152–58. The author is identified as "Specialist, State Department of Education, Florida."

71

THE PLACE OF CARTER G. WOODSON
IN AMERICAN HISTORIOGRAPHY

by John Hope Franklin

Carter G. Woodson (1875–1950) whose parents had been slaves, was the main architect of what was, in his day, called Negro history. He died on April 3, 1950. There follow analyses of his work and character by John Hope Franklin, forty years Woodson's junior, and by W. E. B. Du Bois, seven years his senior.

The career of Carter G. Woodson parallels the coming of age of American historiography. He grew up in the turbulent years of the post-Reconstruction era, when sectional tempers were still short and when the major forces of reconciliation fostered a policy of regarding the Negro as a problem for the South to solve. As the South assumed the responsibility for determining the Negro's fate in American society, it proceeded to take steps to create a position of permanent inequality for the Negro. Through a systematic program of disfranchisement, segregation, and discrimination, the Negro was denied the rights and privileges of citizenship that had been guaranteed in the Reconstruction amendments.

In the program to fasten upon the Negro the badge of inferiority the South enlisted the support not only of the politicians, who provided legal sanction for its designs, and the business men, who rejected the Negro as a worker in the new industrial order, but also the historian, who confirmed the South's claim that the Negro never had been and never could become a worthy citizen of the community. These students of man's past experiences proved to be willing accomplices in the conspiracy to degrade a whole race of men. In their writings they blandly asserted that the Negro had never developed a civilization of his own, vigorously argued that the Negro possessed childlike traits, and claimed with conviction that the Negro's history supported the view that the best role for him was one of subordination. They re-wrote much of the nation's history from this point of view and emphasized the barbarism of the newly arrived African, the docility of the Negro slave, and the ineptitude of the Negro politician during Reconstruction. This was effective yeoman service which the historian was performing in the program to traduce the Negro.

The performance of these historians appears strange when one recalls that in the late years of the nineteenth century and the early years of the twentieth century there was so much emphasis on scientific, objective history. American historians went to Europe to study the new methods, and American universities established new departments and courses of history designed to inject the new scientific approach into the study of history. Despite the precepts enunciated in the seminars and the rigorous subscription to truth and accuracy, the large majority of American historians were as careless with the truth when dealing with Negroes as were the Southern demagogues when they took the stump to exhort their hearers to drive the Negro out of politics. In the context of the Negro in American history these writers saw little connection between the teachings of scientific history and the history of this minority group.

The era of intersectional reconciliation discouraged any move to refute the claims of the racist historians or to reveal their disavowal of scientific history when writing about Negroes. Those few historians who did not subscribe to the claims of their colleagues who were race-baiters seemed to regard it as impolitic to challenge their fantastic claims. Few Negroes had been privileged to secure the type of specialized training that would provide the techniques needed to rectify some of the assertions of their adversaries. Others, perhaps, were so pre-occupied with the more obvious efforts to destroy every effort of the Negro to obtain first-class citizenship that they did not fully appreciate the subtle and insidious effect that the historians could have on the status of Negroes.

Among those who could speak for the Negro was George Washington Williams, whose *History of the Negro Race in America* and *History of the Negro Troops in the Rebellion* had won favorable international notice, despite the limited training of Williams in the field. But death cut short a promising career in 1891, when Williams was only forty-two. William E. B. Du Bois made a brilliant beginning with his *Suppression of the African Slave Trade* in 1896 and *The Negro* almost twenty years later. The field of history proved to be too narrow, however, for the restless, impatient energy of the crusading Du Bois, who sought satisfaction in other areas of activity. By 1915, with Williams dead and Du Bois engrossed in his work with the National Association for the Advancement of Colored People, there seemed to be no one to do the much-needed work of describing the part that Negroes had played in the history of the United States.

The need for historians of the Negro continued to be urgent despite the fact that organized efforts to improve the status of the Negro were well under way by the beginning of World War I. To be sure, the N.A.A.C.P. and the National Urban League were performing important services in their respective areas of activity. These organizations could not do the entire job of rehabilitating the position of the Negro in American life any more than the Southern demagogues alone could destroy that position. Negroes needed writers—historians, essayists, and others—who could not only inspire pride in their past but refute the claims of the historians who supported the Southern demagogues.

Carter G. Woodson was especially well-qualified to meet the urgent need for an historian of the Negro people. His formal training at Berea, The Sorbonne, the University of Chicago, and Harvard provided him with the skills he needed and the appreciation for scientific study that were to be reflected in many of his writings. His years of labor in the coal fields and of teaching in this country and abroad gave him the understanding of peoples and of the need for excellent teaching materials for effective and meaningful educative experiences. When he published his first book in 1915 he was well on his way to filling the need that, for the most part, had remained unfulfilled since emancipation. For the next thirty-five years he was to labor unceasingly in the task of reconstructing the history of a people and of rehabilitating their place in society on the basis of that history. Few men in any generation have worked so tirelessly and effectively toward their chosen goal.

The books and monographs based on his own research constitute the first major contribution of Dr. Woodson to American historiography. While the dozen or more books in this group cannot all be discussed here, several deserve specific mention. *The Education of the Negro Prior to 1861*, published in 1915, is regarded by many as his most significant contribution in the area of original research. It is a meticulous description of the Negro in the antebellum period; it opened up a new area of research in American educational history. *A Century of Negro Migration* came three years later, when the impact of the migration of Negroes during World War I was being felt in many parts of the North. In this work Dr. Woodson demonstrated the importance of using statistical materials in population movements to illuminate the economic and political vicissitudes of Negroes in the United States.

In 1921 Dr. Woodson published *The History of the Negro Church*, the first scholarly effort in this important field. It not only portrays the history of religious activities among Negroes during this period of slavery but describes in much detail the rise of the independent Negro church among Negroes before and since emancipation. In 1930, with Lorenzo Greene, he published *The Negro Wage Earner*, a comprehensive activity of Negroes as freemen since the colonial period. Although more interest has been manifested by students in this area than in some others, with significant studies coming from several persons, the contribution of this book remains substantial down to the present time.

Dr. Woodson had long been aware of the need for adequate teaching materials for a satisfactory presentation of the Negro in American history. His experiences as a teacher on the secondary school and college level strengthened his conviction. Consequently, in 1922 he brought out *The Negro in Our History*, a college textbook designed not only to provide supplementary material for courses in American history but also for use as the basic textbook in courses in Negro history. The effect on the curriculums of American colleges has been profound. Scores of institutions of higher learning have introduced courses in Negro history, while teachers have devoted considerable attention to developing a proficiency in the use of materials related to this and other courses in American history. The significance and lasting importance of *The Negro in Our History* are attested by the fact that it has remained in print for more than twenty-five years and has gone through nine editions of more than 50,000 copies. Students at lower levels have benefited by Dr. Woodson's persistent efforts to improve the teaching of history. In 1928 high school students were presented valuable information on Negro history in *The Story of the Negro Retold*, while *Negro Makers of History* was issued in the same year for students in the elementary schools.

The second major contribution of Dr. Woodson to American historiography consists of his editing source materials on which others have been able to base their own researches and writings. These materials, moreover, have served to illustrate to an incredulous public the fact that the Negro has left some record of his experiences. *Negro Orators and their Orations*, published in 1925, demonstrated that some Negroes were not only articulate but eloquent. *The Mind of the Negro as Reflected in Letters Written during the Crisis, 1800–1860* appeared the following year and brought forth a veritable mine of information on various aspects of the history of the country as well as the Negro. Here is a vast array of facts, provided by Negroes themselves, regarding their organized activities, struggles in the economic sphere, race relations, politics, war, education,

One of the most recent efforts of Dr. Woodson in this area was the four-volume edition of the *Works of Francis J. Grimke*, published in 1942. These sermons, essays, letters, and other writings from the pen of a scholarly Negro minister and leader suggest that the record of the thoughts and aspirations of Negroes must be considered in any study of the intellectual history of the United States.

The records of the federal government provided another valuable source of information in the reconstruction of the Negro's history; and Dr. Woodson did sufficient work in editing them to suggest some approaches and to stimulate others to continue the work. *Free Negro Heads of Families in the United States in 1830*, published in 1925, provided the first definitive statistical information regarding this much discussed, but much misunderstood group. The introduction to the study is still one of the best general statements on the free Negro to be found anywhere in print. In the same year *Free Negro Owners of Slaves in the United States in 1830* appeared. It was a dramatic reminder that free Negroes were resourceful and that, for a variety of reasons, they participated in the practice of holding human chattel.

Dr. Woodson's founding and editing of two periodicals in the field of Negro history gave to scholars throughout the world a medium through which they could present their worthy efforts to a public that was becoming increasingly interested in the subject. *The Journal of Negro History,* now in its thirty-fifth year, contains more material for rewriting the nation's history with ample consideration of the Negro than any other scholarly periodical. Some of the most distinguished scholars of this country have published their findings in its pages, while many younger scholars have been encouraged to continue their efforts as a result of the publication of their first articles in the *Journal*. It enjoys a favorable reputation in the world-wide community of scholars and interested laymen. Dr. Woodson could not long neglect the students on the lower levels, and, in 1937, he began publication of the NEGRO HISTORY BULLETIN. Teachers were to find in it materials for use in classes in secondary and elementary schools, while students themselves were to discover in its pages stimulating and inspirational materials that would be valuable in their studies. The BULLETIN represented, perhaps, the most vigorous extension of the work of Dr. Woodson into the lives of the persons who were soon to share the responsibility of making their communities better places in which to live.

Few scholars have been able to attain success in more than one of the categories in which Dr. Woodson worked: the writing of scholarly and popular books, the editing of important source materials, and the editing of scholarly journals. It was Dr. Woodson's good fortune to have the capacity, energy, zeal, and longevity to make possible the successful exploitation of each of these areas of activity. Any one of them would have won for him an enviable and respected place among the distinguished scholars of our time. It is much too early to make any final evaluation of the contributions of this distinguished servant of mankind. Those of us who look, with deep appreciation, at his many successful undertakings can observe the very salutary effect that they have had on the writing and study of American history and the consequent regard that many have developed for the history of the Negro. It would be presumptuous, however, to make any attempt to measure the full effect of his endeavors at a time when the respect for his scholarship and the prestige of the movement that he initiated are still increasing. One can only be certain of two things: that the contributions of Carter G. Woodson to American historiography have been significant and far-reaching and that the program for rehabilitating the place of the Negro in American history has been stimulated immeasurably by his diverse and effective efforts.

Negro History Bulletin 13 (May 1950): 174–76

72

A PORTRAIT OF CARTER G. WOODSON (1950)

by W. E. B. Du Bois

Carter Godwin Woodson, who died in Washington on April 3 at the age of seventy-one, illustrates what race prejudice can do to a human soul and also what it is powerless to prevent. Of course, race prejudice is only one particular form of the oppression which human beings have used toward each other throughout the ages. Oppression cramps thought and development, individuality and freedom. Woodson was naturally a big strong man with a good mind; not brilliant, not a genius, but steady, sound and logical in his thinking processes, and capable of great application and concentration in his work. He was a man of normal appetites, who despite extraordinary circumstances carved out a good valuable career. As it happened, he did not have the chance for normal development; he spent his childhood working in a mine and did not get education enough to enter high school until he was twenty; he never married, and one could say almost that he never played; he could laugh and joke on occasion but those occasions did not often arise.

I knew him for forty years and more, and have often wondered what he did for recreation, if anything. He had very little outdoor life, he had few close friends. He cared nothing for baseball or football and did not play cards, smoke or drink. In later years his only indulgence was over-eating so that after fifty he was considerably overweight.

All this arose, in the first place, because like most people on earth he was born poor. But his poverty was the special case of being one of nine children of poor American Negroes who had been born slaves. This meant that from the beginning he was handicapped; it was difficult for him to go regularly to the very poor country school in his neighborhood, and for six years during his youth, when he ought to have been in school, he was working in a coal mine; so that he was grown before he entered high school in Huntington, West Virginia. Once started, however, he went to college at Berea, Kentucky, then to the University of Chicago. He alternated with public school teaching, travel and study in Europe and finally taught ten years, from 1908 to 1918, in the public schools of Washington, D.C.

In 1912, Woodson took his doctorate of philosophy at Harvard in history. It is quite possible that had he been a white man he might have entered a university career, as instructor and eventually as a professor with small but adequate salary; enough for marriage, home and children. But of course, at the time he got his doctorate, there was not the slightest thought that a black man could ever be on the faculty of Harvard or of any other great school. In Washington, he got his main experience of regular teaching work. It was hard and not inspiring. The "Jim-crow" school system of the District of Columbia is perhaps the best of its kind in the United States; but it had the shortcomings of all segregated schools, with special arrangements and peculiar difficulties; they are not the kind of schools which would inspire most men to further study or to an academic career.

After that experience Woodson turned to college work. He served as dean for a year at Howard University and for four years at West Virginia College. He might have ended his career in this way as president of a small Southern colored college. His duties would have been collecting funds and superintending discipline among teachers and students; or if it had been in a state school, he would have cajoled and played up to a set of half-educated Southern whites as trustees, so as to get for Negroes a third or a half of the funds they were legally entitled to. It would have been the kind of executive job which has killed many a man, white and black, either physically or mentally or both; and it was the sort of thing that Woodson was determined not to do.

He had by this time made up his mind that he was going to devote himself to the history of the Negro people as a permanent career. In doing that he knew the difficulties which he would have to face. Study and publication, if at all successful, call for money, and money for any scientific effort for or by a Negro means abject begging; and at begging Woodson was not adept.

It was a time, moreover, when all Negro education was largely charity, not only college education, but elementary and high school training. Groups of Negro and white teachers in Southern schools made regular pilgrimages to the North to collect money from churches and philanthropists in order to support their schools. But the job which Woodson had carved out for himself was not a school; it was a matter of a periodical, with research and publication, and it was to be done in a field not only unpopular but practically unrecognized. Most people, even historians, would have doubted if there was enough of distinctly Negro history in America to call for publication. For thirteen years at Atlanta University we had tried to raise money for research and publication of studies in Negro sociology; five thousand a year, outside my salary. We had to give up the attempt in 1910. But one thing that Woodson's career had done for him was to make him stubborn and single-minded. He had no ties, family or social; he had chosen this life work and he never wavered from it after 1922.

His efforts at raising money for the work had some initial success; for ten years or more Julius Rosenwald, the Jewish philanthropist of Chicago, gave him $400 a year. Woodson organized the Association for the Study of Negro Life and History and already as early as January, 1916, while still teaching, he began publication of *The Journal of Negro History*, a quarterly which is now in its thirty-fourth year of continuous publication.

The Journal was an excellent piece of work and received commendation from high sources. The Carnegie Foundation and afterwards the Spelman Memorial Fund of the Rockefellers gave him $50,000 in installments of $5,000 a year beginning in 1921. But Woodson did not prove the ideal recipient of philanthropy.

He was not a follower of the school of Booker T. Washington and had neither the humility nor the finesse of social uplifters. His independence of thought and action was exaggerated; he went out to meet opposition before it arose, and he was fiercely determined to be master of his own enterprises and final judge of what he wanted to do and say. He pretty soon got the reputation of not being the kind of "trustworthy" Negro to whom help should be given. It was not for a moment intimated that the philanthropists wanted to curb his work or guide it, but if Woodson had anticipated their wishes and conformed to their attitudes, money would have poured in. Only those persons who followed the Washington philosophy and whose attitude toward the South was in accord with the new orientation of the North, could be sure to have encouragement and continued help. After a while it became the settled policy of philanthropic foundations and of academic circles to intimate that Carter Woodson was altogether too self-centered and self-assertive to receive any great encouragement. His work was individual with no guarantee of permanence.

There was just enough truth in this accusation to make the criticism stick. Even his colored friends and admirers encountered refusal to co-operate or take counsel. Twice, alarmed because of his meager income, and his overwork, I ventured to propose alliance and help; I offered to incorporate *The Journal* into the Department of Publications and Research of the N.A.A.C.P., with promise of as much autonomy as was allowed me. He considered, but refused, unless an entirely separate department was set up for him. This the Board refused to consider, as I knew it would. Then I suggested incorporation of his work into that of Howard University; but after trial, this also fell through, and his friends concluded that he must be left to carry on his great work without interference in any way from others. Several times he took in assistants and helpers, but never gave them authority or permanent tenure. He was always the lone pioneer and remained this until his death.

It was this very attitude, however, that brought out the iron in Woodson's soul. He was forty-four in 1922 when he began this independent career. He therefore gradually buckled up his belt, gave up most of the things which a man of his age would be looking forward to and put the whole of his energy into his work. As I have said, he never married, he never had a home, he lived in lodgings as a boarder, or ate in restaurants; he schooled himself to small and uncertain income; it is probable that he lived many years on not more than $1000 and probably never as much as $5000.

Deliberately he cut down his wants and that was not difficult in Washington. Washington had no theatre for Negroes; its music was limited; there were art galleries, but they were not particularly attractive until recent years and never catered to black folk. In many cases they refused to exhibit the work of Negro artists. Parks and public recreation had many restrictions; there was little chance at club life or opportunity to meet men of standing, either American or passing foreigners. Woodson did not have enough money to spend much time in New York or abroad. He therefore concentrated his time, his energy, and his little money in building up his enterprise, and especially in organizing a constituency among American Negroes to support his work. That was the most astonishing result of his career.

From subscriptions to his quarterly, from donations made by small groups and organizations, from sale of books, he not only continued to publish his magazine, but he also went into the publishing business and issued a score of books written by himself and by others; and then as the crowning achievement, he established Negro History Week. He literally made this country, which has only the slightest respect for people of color, recognize and celebrate each year, a week in which it studied the effect which the American Negro has upon life, thought and action in the United States. I know of no one man who in a lifetime has, unaided, built up such a national celebration.

Every year in practically every state of the United States, Negro History Week is celebrated; and its celebration was almost forced upon school authorities, on churches and other organizations by the influence of the groups of people who had banded themselves together to help Carter Woodson's Association of Negro Life and History. His chief work, *The Negro in Our History,* went through eight editions, with its nearly eight hundred pages and wealth of illustration, and was used in the Negro public schools of the nation. More lately his monthly *Bulletin* of news had wide circulation and use.

It is a unique and marvelous monument which Carter Woodson has thus left to the people of the United States. But in this and in all his life, he was, and had to be, a cramped soul. There was in him no geniality and very little humor. To him life was hard and cynically logical; his writing was mechanical and unemotional. He never had the opportunity to develop warm sympathy with other human beings; and he did develop a deep-seated dislike, if not hatred, for the white people of the United States and of the world. He never believed in their generosity or good faith. He did not attack them; he did not complain about them, he simply ignored them so far as possible and went on with his work without expected help or sympathetic cooperation from them.

He did not usually attend meetings of scientists in history; he was not often asked to read papers on such occasions; for the most part so far as the professors in history of this country were concerned he was forgotten and passed over; and yet few men have made so deep an imprint as Carter Woodson on thousands of scholars in historical study and research.

In his death he does not leave many very warm friends; there were few tears shed at his grave. But on the other hand, among American Negroes, and among those whites who knew about his work, and among those who in after years must learn about it, there will be vast respect and thankfulness for the life of this man. He was one who under the hardest conditions of environment kept himself to one great goal, worked at it stubbornly and with unwavering application and died knowing that he had accomplished much if not all that he had planned.

He left unfinished an Encyclopedia Africana; it was an idea which I had toyed with in 1909, securing as collaborators Sir Harry Johnston, Flinders-Petrie, Guiseppi Sergi, Albert Hart and Franz Boas. But my project never got beyond the name stage and was forgotten. Later Woodson took up the idea as a by-product of his *Journal;* but few knew of his project at the time. Finally in 1931, the Phelps-Stokes Fund projected an *Encyclopedia of the Negro,* but invited neither Woodson nor me to participate.

However, the group called together, including Moton of Tuskegee and

Hope of Atlanta, protested and finally we were both invited. I attended the subsequent meetings but Woodson refused. I and many others talked to him and begged him to come in; but no; there were two reasons: this was, he considered, a white enterprise forced on Negroes; and secondly, he had himself already collected enough data eventually to make an encyclopedia. We demurred, not because we were unwilling to have him work on the encyclopedia; indeed we were eager; but because we knew that one man and especially one man with a rather narrow outlook which had been forced upon him, could not write a scientific encyclopedia of sufficient breadth to satisfy the world. Eventually this Phelps-Stokes project was unable to collect sufficient funds chiefly, I am sure, because I had been named Editor-in-Chief. So this project closed its effort with the publication of only one thin preliminary volume. But Woodson left the kernel of a great work. It would be a magnificent monument to his memory, if this were to be made the basis of broad rewriting and extension and published as a memorial to his life work.

As a historian, Woodson left something to be desired. He was indefatigable in research: for instance, his collection of photographs of Negroes and abolitionists is invaluable; his *Negro in American History* deserved the wide use which it has had. Some of his works like his *Education of the Negro prior to 1861, A Century of Negro Migration, Negro Orators and their Orations, Free Negro Owners of Slaves in the United States in 1830, Free Negro Heads of Families in the United States, The Mind of the Negro as Reflected in Letters Written During the Crisis, 1800–60,* are solid works of historical research. Others of his books were not of so great value.

Indeed his service to history was not so much his books as his editorship of the *Journal,* which brought into print some of the best scholars in this branch of history. On the other hand, Woodson himself lacked background for broad historical writing; he was almost contemptuous of emotion; he had limited human contacts and sympathies; he had no conception of the place of woman in creation. His book reviews were often pedantic and opinionated. Much of his otherwise excellent research will have to be reinterpreted by scholars of wider reading and better understanding of the social sciences, especially in economics and psychology; for Woodson never read Karl Marx.

The passing of Carter Woodson leaves a vacuum hard to fill. His memory leaves a lesson of determination and sacrifice which all men, young and old, black and white, may emulate to the glory of man and the uplift of his world.

Masses and Mainstream, June 1950; vol. 3, pp. 19–25.

73

WHAT FUTURE FOR NEGRO COLLEGES? (1950)

by Various Authors

A Left publication, the *Harlem Quarterly,* appeared in 1950. Though carrying illuminating articles, it lasted only two years. In its first number, spring 1950, I (pp. 4–12), it queried outstanding African-American educators on the role of traditionally black colleges. The editor was Benjamin A. Brown. On its board were John H. Clarke, Ernest Kaiser, Walter Christmas, Alain Locke, Jean Blackwell, Shirley Graham, and Langston Hughes. One white person, Dr. John Haynes Holmes, minister emeritus of the New York Community Church, participated; he opposed any segregation and advocated an end to Negro colleges and white colleges.

Charles H. Houston
Legal Counsel, N.A.A.C.P..

Last week-end I spent part of the time debating the merits of the United Negro College Fund with a close friend of mine. I supported the Fund; he opposed it.

He is an integrationist, opposed to segregation in any form and makes no compromise. He pointed out the inconsistency of fighting segregation in city hospitals, the armed forces, government services, public accommodations, and strengthening the bonds of segregation in educational institutions.

He argued that the legal efforts to get Southern boys and girls in State universities were dissipated by building up segregated institutions to take the mass pressure off the State universities.

Finally he said that even the reactionary, Southern-infested Army brass had recognized that segregation defeated national ends and was committed to eliminating all segregation in the Army in the next national emergency. He acknowledged we can not eliminate all segregation immediately, but he maintained that this is no reason for voluntarily supporting segregated institutions.

There is no denying his arguments have a punch. Far be it from me to say he is wrong; but in the meantime I still support the United Negro College Fund for the following reasons.

I want integration just as much as he does, but I want to control the terms of integrating. I don't want integration in the sense of merge and disappear.

In my book whoever brings the most attributes and superior qualifications to the market will be able to take the pick of the crop. The world position of colored peoples is improving; politically they are rapidly moving from dependence to independence.

In the United States we are making steady progress both individually and in groups.

Individuals are being integrated today, not at a sacrifice but in recognition of their distinguished personalities and outstanding achievements. But the fact remains that the masses are not integrated; when they are we will no longer be able to speak of them as the masses.

To put integration on a solid basis we must achieve integration for the masses as well as for the favored individuals; and we can not refuse to use any tool which will lift the masses to the point where integration is both possible and desirable.

The individual does not need the colored college in the year 1950, the masses do need it. So I support the United Negro College Fund because it strengthens those colleges which are educating the masses of my people and furnishing them the knowledge and the means by which they themselves will finally blast segregation out of American life.

Finally, I support the United Negro College Fund because ultimately I expect these colleges to improve and survive, not as minority colleges, but as colleges in the over-all plan of American education, with faculty, administration and student body chosen without regard to race.

America can never have too much education, and to my mind these colleges, if they are good enough, will have a place on an entirely integrated basis in the permanent scheme of things.

Dr. Benjamin E. Mays
President, Morehouse College

It is not a question of Negro colleges being perpetuated or integration in education. I think any sound-thinking American will agree that all education should be integrated and no colleges should exist primarily for one race. The only question is how best to go about perfecting integration. I do not believe, as some seem to believe, that the way to get it is to destroy every Negro college. To advocate that is to admit that we suffer with a grave inferiority complex. It is tantamount to saying that no Negro college is worth conserving. This would be true of Negro churches, newspapers, insurance companies, banks owned by Negroes, and everything else if we follow that line to its logical conclusion.

Negro colleges should not be abolished to perfect integration any more than the white colleges. As I see it, we should oppose segregation at every point and open Negro colleges to white students and also white colleges to Negro students. In other words integration is not a one way traffic, it is a two way traffic.

Dr. Frederick D. Patterson
President, Tuskegee Institute

A justification for Negro colleges in the South is that with laws against the co-education of the races, they furnish the only opportunity which exists for the masses of Negro youth to get education above the high school level unless they are sufficiently able to migrate out of the South. It has been shown, of course, that most students attend colleges near their homes because they are unable to do otherwise. For this reason, as long as laws prevent colleges from accepting students on the basis of merit without regard to race, creed, or color, the Negro college must perform a vital and, in fact, indispensable function. I hope the day will come when Negro colleges as such will not be necessary in the sense that they must of necessity enroll only Negro students. I feel, however, that when laws now on the books requiring discrimination in admission no longer exist, our stronger so-called Negro colleges will continue to be needed as a part of the pattern of higher education for American youth.

Certainly the number of colleges and universities we have are at present inadequate to meet the needs of youth now seeking an education beyond the high school. The President's Commission on Higher Education predicted that enrollment trends would be definitely on the upgrade through 1960, if not beyond. Under these circumstances it is more than apparent that we will need all of the good colleges we can get and the elimination of segregation does not mean the abolition or destruction of the physical plants of colleges which now admit only Negro students. The job before the American people is that of strengthening these institutions so that whether segregated or not, they will give education of comparable quality to that of any other institute and thus hasten the day when education on a segregated basis is no longer required.

W. J. Trent
President, Livingstone College
Executive Director, United Negro College Fund, Inc.

At the present time there are laws on the statute books of seventeen states requiring separation of educational facilities and services based on race. As a result there are Negro colleges both public and private. Ninety percent of the seventy thousand Negroes who go to college—go to these Negro colleges in the South. It is our belief that it is tremendously important that there be private colleges in the South available to Negro Youth; it would be unfortunate if the entire field of higher education for Negroes were pre-empted by Negro state colleges which have to look to state legislatures for their appropriations.

We believe that Negro colleges, which by law are required to restrict their enrollment to Negro students, ought to be made as strong and efficient as possible for two basic reasons:

1. In order that the young Negro people who attend them can have as fine an educational opportunity as is possible under the circumstances.

2. So that in the future when laws do not separate the races, these colleges can be known as excellent, well administered colleges open to serve all who are qualified.

This last point to me is very important. There are those who see the solution of the problem of segregated education in the South as one which will require the closing up of all Negro colleges and the opening up of all now-white colleges to Negro students. This view to me is extremely dangerous in that there is implicit in it an assumption that just because an institution is manned and operated by Negroes, it is per se inferior. If we accept this view then we are accepting an inferior status for ourselves.

I rather see the solution something like this. Continuous efforts must and will be made to break down the barriers of color in education and other fields. These barriers at present exist in a more rigid form in the South—the section of the country that needs all of the good educational institutions it has—and more. When the barriers are broken, Fisk will enroll white students and Vanderbilt will enroll Negro students—they both will be interracial. I am certain that there are numerous white students who would welcome an opportunity to study under Ira De A. Reid at Atlanta, or Charles Johnson at Fisk, or to take courses in vocational education at Hampton or Veterinary Science at Tuskegee, etc. Likewise there are a large number of Negro students who would want to take training at Georgia Tech, or Tulane, or the University of North Carolina.

In other words, whether we want to admit it or not, the quality of work done at a large number of Negro colleges measures up to the quality of work done at white colleges in the South of comparable size and resources. This leaves aside the consideration of the harm done to white boys and girls and Negro boys and girls who by law are not permitted to go to school together. But the harm is in both institutions, not just in Negro institutions.

So we have a choice—either we support these Negro private schools and make them the best ever, or we don't support them and they perish with two results:

1. The higher educational burden will be carried by the state colleges for Negroes with its programs determined pretty largely by state legislatures.

2. And roughly 50 percent of the young people who seek college education will be denied the opportunity to secure one.

I'd rather try to make them as strong and as efficient as possible so that more and better trained Negroes can come along to give a hand in this incessant fight for rights, privileges and responsibilities for Negroes.

A question was raised about whether these colleges would permit their educational facilities to be used to aid in the defense of the "separate but equal" doctrine. I gather that there is some little confusion on this point.

It is not the private Negro colleges that are vulnerable on this score—it is the state Negro colleges which must do whatever is required by the legislature in order to provide professional training. But even so, the policy on this must come from the Boards of Trustees of the individual private colleges. They have complete autonomy over the programs of their own institutions. The Fund has no authority to interfere in the policy, operation or administration of the member colleges. We can concern ourselves only with the question of the integrity of the handling of funds and to that end each college files an annual certified audit with us.

I have tried to state what I conceive to be the basic policy of the Fund. I am sure that there are presidents of member colleges of the Fund that are working assiduously in the fight to erase barriers of caste and color. At the recent meeting of the American Association of Colleges in Cincinnati, presidents of three colleges in the Fund led the fight to have the Association adopt a resolution calling for legislation to do away with segregation in higher education.

Doxey A. Wilkerson
Director of Faculty and Curriculum, Jefferson School of Social Science

The segregated Negro college should, and must, be abolished. The non-segregated college of predominantly Negro personnel will, and should, continue to develop and flourish for generations to come.

Mandatory school segregation on any level serves the interests of only that small ruling class whose wealth and power rest upon the exploitation of the Negro and white masses of our country. It strengthens the whole rotten system of Jim Crow oppression, whose sordid effects are seen not only in inferior educational opportunities and other special discriminations against the Negro people, but also in the unduly low living standards and limited political democracy of practically the whole population.

Any requirement that Negroes attend one school and white people another is an abomination which must be destroyed on all educational levels. Those Negro educators whose vested interests lead them to rationalize and defend the segregated school are, thereby, retarding both the liberation of the Negro people from Jim Crow oppression and the building of a secure and democratic society for all Americans.

The ultimate destruction of school segregation will come, of course, only when the people of our country have broken away from domination by the great trusts which are the mainstay of the whole Jim Crow system, when ours is a genuine people's government, truly responsive to the needs and will of the masses of white and Negro Americans. We will yet achieve such a democratic America; and the liberation struggles of the Negro people, linked with those of the progressive working class movement as a whole, will play a decisive role in its attainment.

In this genuinely democratic America, where *all* colleges are open to all who want to attend, there will continue to be an important place for the predominantly Negro college.

The historic forces which have welded Negro Americans together as a distinct people, with strong internal bonds of unity, will continue to operate long after our country has freed itself from the domination of monopoly capitalist rulers. Negroes will, in large measure, continue to develop *as a people*—a free people in a free country—with traditions, culture, problems and organizational forms peculiarly their own. The educational center for this development will continue to be the predominantly Negro (but non-segregated) college.

The coming destruction of the whole system of Jim Crow oppression should carry with it the abolition of scores of second-rate Negro colleges, which will then have no *raison d' être*. On the other hand, many vital and important centers of Negro higher education—such as Fisk, Howard, Atlanta and others—will only then enter upon their most flourishing period of development.

74

THE KILLING OF WILLIE MC GEE (1950)

by Members of His Family

In 1945 Willie McGee was jailed on a charge of rape brought by a white woman in Laurel, Mississippi. McGee, a union-conscious furniture worker, held a part-time job at a filling station in town. The affair, begun by the woman, was terminated by McGee; she then charged rape.

By his choice, the Left-led Civil Rights Congress defended him. The Left identification kept organizations like the NAACP away. As a southern white woman wrote shortly before McGee's execution on May 8, 1951: "Are we completely ignoring our own basic principles and allowing our courts to pass judgment on the basis of race, color, lawyers employed, religious, or political affiliation? (Mary Mostert, the *Nation*, May 5, 1951, p. 421).

The editor accompanied Mrs. Rosalee McGee on her journey from New York City to pick up her dead husband; but at lunch in the railroad station in Washington, Mrs. McGee told me not to go further: "I'll pick up Willie; if you come with me, they'll kill you."

At a Civil Rights dinner, held in New York, May 22, 1950, Mrs. McGee spoke as follows; other relevant documents also are published below:

I am here tonight to make a speech. I never made a speech before. But I am speaking not for myself, but for my husband and four children.

Down in Mississippi, you never have a chance to make a speech. And my husband, Willie McGee, has been down in jail for four years and seven months.

I hardly know what to say but I am here to do and say in my own words as best as I can.

On last Wednesday, I went to see Willie. And as I went into jail the warden and others laughed and said, "What are you going to do now?"

I went back and I said to Willie, "I made up my mind to go North."

He said, "Where?"

I said, "To see what I can do."

And he said, "Rosalee, go to see what you can do."

On the way out, a white preacher said, "Did you read the paper?"

And I said, "Yes."

He said, "That's it."–like he enjoyed it.

I never said any thing to him.

He said, "Don't feel bad. Here's a quarter. Go buy yourself something."

And this quarter I want to present to Mr. George Marshall of the Civil Rights Congress, the man who started the fight to save my husband's life.

C.R.C. continued the fight—not for the life of Willie McGee, but for all Negroes of America.

The following is a letter sent to the Civil Rights Congress by the four children of Willie and Rosalee McGee.

Laurel, Miss., May 28, 1950

Is my mother there? We are worried about her.

When can my daddy come home? Mother wrote she was going to see when he could come home.

We need daddy. He been gone so long. Since my momma been gone people tell me my daddy will die on hot seat. That what a man told me at the store.

Ask my mother what is a hot seat. Bring my momma home so she could get my daddy before they sit him in that seat. Come help her please. Momma said the Civil Right Congress would help her. Please folk, folk, help my daddy. My mother have to work so hard, people don't like her, and my grandmother is old. Please help my daddy till my momma come home. We ain't got a daddy to help us. I love my daddy and we need him. We ain't seen him in so long. Don't let him die.

> Della Ree
> Grace Lee
> Willie Earl
> Mary Lee

When the U.S. Supreme Court rejected Mr. Willie McGee's appeal for a review of his death sentence, Mr. William L. Patterson, executive secretary of the Civil Rights Congress, wrote him that everything possible in the way of judicial attempts and mass action would be done to save his life. Below is the condemned man's reply:

> *Hinds County Jail*
> *Jackson, Miss.*
> *June 3, 1950*

Dear Sir:

Your letter was received and glad was I to hear from you. I am glad that my wife has been of great service and I want to say that I don't give up one bit.

My faith now in you all. And do believe that after while that things will come my way through your help which have stood by me all the way.

I want to say that I know you will do all that can be done for me. I am glad that Rosalee is able to go forward as long as it is necessary.

I have the courage and the faith. I don't give up. I hold fast and trust with all my heart that some day things will come our way.

Very glad to hear from you, sir and with best wishes hoping to some day see you.

> Yours truly,
> Willie McGee
> Hinds County Jail
> Jackson, Miss.

Masses and Mainstream, July 1950, 7: 29–32.

75

PAUL ROBESON'S PASSPORT (1950)

On July 28, 1950, two agents of the Internal Security Division of the State Department told Paul Robeson to surrender his passport. His attorneys advised him to refuse this order. On August 1, 1950, they wrote Secretary of State Acheson asking for an explanation. None was offered. On August 4, the newspapers reported that Mr. Robeson's passport had been cancelled. This was the start of an eight-year struggle, when the State Department yielded and the passport was reissued.

Robeson's complaint to the U.S. District Court for the District of Columbia was submitted by several attorneys, including James A. Cobb, George E. Hayes, George A. Parker, John J. Abt, Nathan Witt, and Gloria Agrin. It was sworn to and notarized by Paul Robeson on December 4, 1950. The full text of that complaint is published below for the first time.

Complaint

Plaintiff, Paul Robeson, respectively shows to this Honorable Court:

1. This is a suit of a civil nature for a declaratory judgment and injunction. This suit arises under the Constitution and laws of the United States, and is brought to redress and prevent the deprivation, under color of alleged authority, of rights, privileges and immunities secured under the Constitution and laws of the United States, including Articles I and III, and Amendments I, V, IX and X of the Constitution, all as hereinafter more fully appears.

The matter in controversy exceeds the value of Three Thousand Dollars ($3,000.00), exclusive of interest and costs. This Court has jurisdiction under Sections 11-301, 11-305 and 11-306 of the District of Columbia Code, 5 U.S.C., Section 1009, and 28 U.S.C., Sections 1331, 2201 and 2202. Jurisdiction is also based on Articles I and III, and Amendments I, V, IX and X of the Constitution of the United States.

2. Plaintiff is a citizen of the United States and a resident of the State of New York, and brings this suit in his own right.

3. Defendant Dean G. Acheson is Secretary of State of the United States, and is sued individually and in his representative capacity.

4. Plaintiff is by profession an artist, specializing in singing and acting, and has been such for more than twenty-five years and derives his

income entirely from the practice of his profession. Plaintiff has practiced his profession not only in the United States, but in Europe and other parts of the world, and a substantial part of his income is, has been and normally would be derived from concerts and appearances in Europe and in other parts of the world.

In connection with his trips to Europe and elsewhere outside the United States, plaintiff has continuously, since 1922 applied for and been granted passports by the Department of State of the United States. Plaintiff presently holds a passport, bearing number 58303, which was issued on May 8, 1947 for a period of two (2) years, which was thereafter renewed for a period to January 25, 1951, and which would therefore otherwise be valid except for the acts of defendant hereinafter complained of.

Plaintiff's right to engage in his profession outside of the United States as well as within the United States is a property right, and as such is protected against interference or deprivation by the Federal Government or any officer, agent, or agency thereof, without due process of law as guaranteed by the Constitution of the United States and particularly the Fifth Amendment thereof.

Plaintiff, in addition to his profession as an artist, for many years has been active as a speaker, organizer and participant in political and other activities looking toward the advancement of the welfare of the American people, particularly of the fifteen million (15,000,000) Negro Americans, other minorities, and of working men and women; the welfare and independence of colonial peoples, no matter what their race, creed or color; and the advancement and preservation of peace in the world. Plaintiff has a national and an international reputation as a spokesman for large sections of the Negro people, for other minorities, and for the working men and women of the United States; and is particularly recognized as an opponent of all forms of discrimination based on race, creed, or color.

Plaintiff is and since 1941 has been chairman of the Council on African Affairs, Inc., an organization formed in said year under the laws of the State of New York for the purpose of studying the conditions of life and work in Africa, publicizing information concerning such conditions among the American people, and promoting the welfare of the African people. Plaintiff is and since 1948 has been one of the co-chairmen of the Progressive Party, a political party formed in that year with a program reflecting principally the needs of the Negro and working people of the

United States, the elimination of discrimination, improvement of standards of living, and the preservation of peace by friendship and cooperation through the United Nations. Plaintiff is and has been outspoken in the defense and extension of the civil rights and constitutional liberties of the American people. In connection with his activities and affiliations and in connection with related activities, plaintiff has appeared as a singer, speaker and participant at meetings, conferences, and conventions in all parts of the United States and in foreign countries.

For the purpose of meeting and engaging in discussions with individuals, associations and groups both in the United States and elsewhere with interests, purposes and objectives similar to those of plaintiff herein set forth, plaintiff has exercised and does exercise his right to travel freely, and his rights of freedom of speech, thought, assembly, petition, and association. Plaintiff has regularly attended and normally would attend numerous such meetings during any given period, including public meetings, conferences, conventions and executive board and similar smaller meetings and conferences throughout the United States, Europe and other parts of the world. The activities of plaintiff as set forth herein involve the exercise by plaintiff of rights guaranteed by the First Amendment of the Constitution of the United States, and particularly the right to travel freely and the rights of freedom of speech, thought, assembly, petition and association.

Plaintiff is a loyal, native-born American citizen, and by reason of his ability and achievements has deservedly won for himself the respect and recognition throughout the world not only as one of the great living Americans, but also as one of the world's leading personalities. In all of his public activities, as hereinbefore set forth, plaintiff's objectives have been those set forth in the preamble to the Constitution of the United States, to wit, to promote the general welfare and to secure the blessings of liberty, and particularly to vindicate and effectuate the rights guaranteed by the Thirteenth, Fourteenth, and Fifteenth Amendments of the Constitution of the United States and the rights set forth in the United Nations Universal Declaration of Human Rights.

At the time of and immediately before the events hereinafter described plaintiff had made and completed arrangements for a trip to Europe to attend several meetings and to fulfill several speaking engagements at Prague, Czecho-Slovakia and Nice, France and for the purpose of making a speaking and singing tour of Scandinavia and of giving several concerts in Italy and the British Isles. While in said cities and countries plaintiff also planned to record several phonographic records for fees and royalties; planned to complete arrangements for his appearance in a motion picture to be made thereafter in Europe; and planned to arrange for his appearance in "Othello" in London and elsewhere in the British Isles during the fall of 1950 and winter of 1950–51 and to arrange for a concert tour of the British Isles, Scandanavia, France, Israel and other countries during the winter of 1950–51 and the spring of 1951. The fees, royalties, and remuneration plaintiff would have received as a result of such professional and artistic activities would have been large and remunerative, and much in excess of Three Thousand Dollars ($3,000.00).

Any interference with plaintiff's right to a passport and plaintiff's possession of a passport, and any interference with plaintiff's right to travel, interferes with plaintiff's rights as a citizen and as a person practicing a profession for remuneration, and denies plaintiff due process of law as guaranteed by the Fifth Amendment of the Constitution of the United States.

5. Plaintiff avers that the defendant, under the purported authority of the Department of State, through agents designated for that purpose, at first orally unlawfully, and in violation of plaintiff's constitutional rights, demanded of the plaintiff the surrender of the passport in his possession, giving no reason whatsoever therefor. After a verbal refusal to comply without a valid reason being given for the request, plaintiff, through counsel, sought to obtain from the defendant an explanation of the unwarranted request being made of him, as will be evidenced by reference had to a letter to the defendant dated August 1, 1950 a copy of which is attached hereto, marked Exhibit "A," and prayed to be considered as a part hereof. Thereafter, and without further information to the plaintiff and as of August 4, 1950, the defendant authorized publication in the public press and gave national circulation to the statement that the Department of State had invalidated plaintiff's passport and had requested plaintiff to surrender same. Thereupon plaintiff, through his counsel, addressed a telegram to the defendant, seeking a discussion of the matter and protesting the arbitrary cancellation of plaintiff's passport, a copy of which telegram is attached hereto, marked Exhibit "B" and prayed to be considered as a part hereof. Then, and in answer to the letter to defendant from plaintiff's counsel hereinbefore referred to, and with a purported detail of the authority under which the defendant was acting, defendant had a letter sent to plaintiff's counsel, a copy of which is attached hereto

marked Exhibit "C" and prayed to be considered as a part hereof. This letter among other things, explained the defendant's action in the following language:

The action was taken because the Department considers that Paul Robeson's travel abroad at this time would be contrary to the best interests of the United States.

Protesting against this unsatisfactory conclusion of the defendant and those acting under him, the plaintiff, through counsel, again requested a meeting to discuss the matter as is shown by reference had to a letter dated August 11, 1950, addressed to Mrs. R. B. Shipley, Chief, Passport Division, Department of State, a copy of which is attached hereto and prayed to be considered as a part hereof, marked Exhibit "D." The letter of response, dated August 17, 1950 and addressed to plaintiff's counsel, marked Exhibit "E," attached hereto and prayed to be considered as a part hereof, discounted the advantage of any conference on the matter, but suggested that a conference might be had in Washington, D.C., with some officer of the Passport Division, acting on behalf of the defendant in his representative capacity.

Pursuant to said letter plaintiff and his attorneys met with representatives of the State Department in Washington, District of Columbia, on August 23, 1950, at which time said duly authorized representative of the State Department advised plaintiff and his attorneys that the basis for the acts hereinabove set forth is that defendant disapproves of the political thoughts, opinions, and ideas theretofore expressed by plaintiff at meetings outside the United States and plaintiff's associations outside the United States with individuals, associations, and groups having similar political thoughts, opinions, and ideas; and said representative advised plaintiff and his attorneys that the Department of State had no provision for hearings or appeals of any kind, nature, or description in matters of this nature and that plaintiff had no further recourse within the Department of State.

6. Plaintiff further sets forth upon his information and belief that the defendant has taken steps pursuant to Section 53.5 of Title 22 of the Code of Federal Regulations to prevent plaintiff's departure from the United States. In view of the invalidation of plaintiff's passport, and in view of the steps taken to prevent plaintiff's departure from the United States, plaintiff's departure from the United States or any attempt to do so would subject plaintiff to the criminal sanctions provided by statute (22 U.S.C., Section 225).

7. By reason of defendant's acts as hereinabove set forth in invalidating plaintiff's passport and in taking steps to prevent plaintiff's departure from the United States, plaintiff has been compelled to cancel his plans to travel abroad, to attend meetings abroad, and to give concerts abroad, all as set forth, and has in addition been compelled to abandon future plans for other trips abroad for the purpose of attending similar meetings and giving additional concerts. As a result of such cancellation of present plans for the giving of concerts, plaintiff has suffered the loss of fees and royalties amounting much in excess of Three Thousand Dollars ($3,000.00), and will suffer the loss of fees and royalties amounting much in excess of Three Thousand Dollars ($3,000.00) annually as the result of the cancellation of future plans for the giving of concerts necessitated by the acts of defendant as hereinabove set forth.

Plaintiff states, on information and belief, that defendant's acts as hereinabove set forth were and are motivated by the facts that defendant does not approve or agree with plaintiff's political thoughts, views, and opinions, does not approve or agree with plaintiff's political activities and particularly plaintiff's activities in travelling abroad for the purpose of expressing such political thoughts, views, and opinions and for the purpose of conferring, meeting, and association with other individuals and groups with similar political thoughts, views, and opinions. Plaintiff sets forth further, upon his information and belief, that defendant's acts as hereinabove set forth were and are motivated by the facts that plaintiff is a Negro and is a generally acknowledged spokesman for large sections of the Negro people, both in the United States and elsewhere, and that plaintiff is also a spokesman for other minority groups and for the working men and women of the United States.

Plaintiff's right to a passport and plaintiff's right to travel, subject only to reasonable regulations applicable without discrimination to all citizens, are rights guaranteed by the First and Fifth Amendments of the Constitution of the United States.

Plaintiff denies that his travel abroad would be contrary to the best interest of the United States.

8. The acts of defendant hereinabove set forth are arbitrary, unreasonable, illegal and unconstitutional in that by cancelling plaintiff's passport and by depriving plaintiff of the right to travel abroad for the purpose of expressing his political thoughts, views and opinions and for the purpose of conferring, meeting, and associating with other individuals and groups

with similar political thoughts, views and opinions, defendant has deprived plaintiff of the rights of freedom of speech, thought, assembly, petition and association, and the right to travel freely without arbitrary, unreasonable and discriminatory restrictions, all in violation of the Constitution of the United States and particularly of the First Amendment thereof.

9. The acts of defendant hereinabove set forth are arbitrary, unreasonable, illegal and unconstitutional in that by cancelling plaintiff's passport and by depriving plaintiff of the right to travel, defendant has arbitrarily, unreasonably, and discriminatorily interfered with and impeded plaintiff's right to practice his profession and earn a livelihood, and has deprived plaintiff of substantive due process of law, all in violation of the Constitution of the United States and particularly of the Fifth Amendment thereof.

10. The acts of defendant hereinabove set forth are arbitrary, unreasonable, illegal and unconstitutional in that by failing and refusing to advise plaintiff of the reasons for the acts of defendant hereinabove set forth, and by failing and refusing to grant or afford plaintiff a hearing of any kind, nature or description, defendant has deprived plaintiff of procedural due process of law as guaranteed by the Constitution of the United States and particularly the Fifth Amendment thereof.

11. The acts of defendant hereinabove set forth are arbitrary, unreasonable, illegal and unconstitutional in that by cancelling plaintiff's passport and by depriving plaintiff of the right to travel because plaintiff is a Negro and is a generally recognized and acknowledged spokesman for large sections of the Negro people both in the United States and elsewhere, for other minority groups, and for the working men and women of the United States, defendant has deprived plaintiff of his rights guaranteed by the Constitution of the United States and particularly of rights guaranteed by the First Amendment thereof and of due process of law as guaranteed by the Fifth Amendment thereof.

12. The acts of defendant hereinabove set forth violate the prohibition against bills of attainder contained in Article I of the Constitution of the United States.

13. By the acts of defendant hereinabove set forth, defendant has purported to exercise judicial power in violation of Article III of the Constitution which vests the judicial power of the United States in the courts.

14. By the acts of defendant hereinabove set forth, defendant has deprived plaintiff of fundamental rights reserved to the people of the United States by the Ninth and Tenth Amendments of the Constitution.

15. By the acts of defendant hereinabove set forth, defendant has violated the Charter of the United Nations as implemented by the United Nations Universal Declaration of Human Rights which provides that: "Everyone has the right to leave any country, including his own, and to return to his country." (Article 13, paragraph 2).

16. To the extent that the illegal and unconstitutional acts of defendant were taken pursuant to and under authority of said Executive Order Number 7856 and, on information and belief, other executive orders, regulations, or statutes, said Executive Order Number 7856 and such other executive orders, regulations, or statutes as so construed and applied by defendant, are illegal and unconstitutional in the following respects:

a. Said Executive Order Number 7856 and such other executive orders and regulations are authorized neither by the Constitution of the United States nor by any Congressional enactment, nor is any such statute authorized by the Constitution.

b. The acts of defendant hereinabove set forth have deprived plaintiff of rights guaranteed by the Constitution of the United States and particularly by the First Amendment thereof, as hereinabove set forth.

c. The acts of defendant hereinabove set forth have deprived plaintiff of his rights guaranteed by the Constitution of the United States and particularly by the Fifth Amendment thereof.

d. The acts of defendant hereinabove set forth violate the prohibition against bills of attainder contained in Article I of the Constitution of the United States.

e. By the acts hereinabove set forth, defendant has purported to exercise judicial power in violation of Article III of the Constitution of the United States which vests the judicial power of the United States in the courts.

f. The acts of defendant hereinabove set forth have deprived plaintiff of fundamental rights reserved to the people of the United States by the Ninth and Tenth Amendments to the Constitution of the United States.

17. Plaintiff has no right of appeal from the acts of defendant hereinabove set forth, either within the Department of State or to any other person, agency or department in the executive branch of the

government. Plaintiff has exhausted all available administrative remedies and has no adequate remedy at law. Greater injury will be caused to plaintiff by the denial of relief here prayed for than will be caused to defendant by the granting thereof.

WHEREFORE, plaintiff prays for the following relief:

1. That the Court render a declaratory judgment—

(a) that defendant had and has no right, power or authority to cancel plaintiff's passport, to demand its surrender, or to take steps to prevent plaintiff from travelling abroad; and

(b) that plaintiff's passport is valid, that plaintiff is entitled to a renewal thereof upon its expiration subject only to reasonable restrictions applicable to all citizens, and that plaintiff has the right to travel abroad without interference by defendant subject only to non-discriminatory and reasonable restrictions applicable to all citizens.

(2) That the Court order defendant to—

(a) revoke the cancellation of plaintiff's passport, withdraw his demand on plaintiff to surrender his passport, and advise plaintiff that his passport is valid pursuant to its terms;

(b) withdraw such instructions, orders or demands as he may have given to the Federal Bureau of Investigation of the Department of Justice, the Bureau of Customs of the Department of the Treasury, or other agencies of the government to prevent plaintiff from leaving the United States;

(c) cease and desist from any acts to effect the cancellation and surrender of plaintiff's passport; and

(d) cease and desist from any acts having the object of preventing plaintiff from leaving the United States for the purpose of travelling abroad.

3. That the Court grant such other and further relief as the nature of the case may require and to this Court may seem proper.

/s/ Paul Robeson
Complainant

A copy of this complaint is in the editor's possession. On Robeson, see Thomas Cripps, "Paul Robeson and Black Identity in American Movies," *Massachusetts Review* 11 (Summer 1970): 468–85.

76

IMPORTANT LEGAL VICTORIES (1950)

From a report entitled "Along the N.A.A.C.P. Battlefront."

In three unanimous decisions handed down on June 5 [1950] the U.S. Supreme Court abolished segregation at the University of Oklahoma, ordered the admission of Heman Marion Sweatt to the University of Texas law school, and struck down segregation in southern railway dining cars. Although the *Plessy v. Ferguson* decision of 1896, which set up the "separate but equal" doctrine, was not specifically overruled, its applicability to graduate and professional education has been nullified.

The three decisions must be considered together in order to get the full realization of their effect. The *Sweatt case* and the *McLaurin case* were both financed by the NAACP and under the direct supervision of NAACP lawyers. The *Henderson case* involving the Interstate Commerce Commission was handled by the Alpha Phi Alpha fraternity.

Henderson Case

The Supreme Court in an opinion written by Mr. Justice Burton held that the rules and practices of the Southern Railway Company under which its dining cars are divided so as to allocate one table for the exclusive use of Negro passengers and the remaining space for the exclusive use of white passengers violates Section 3, subsection 1 of the Interstate Commerce Act. Under that statute it is unlawful for any railroad to subject persons "to any undue or unreasonable prejudice or disadvantage."

The Court held that no matter how fair the rules and practices under consideration might operate on the average and in proportion to the volume of traffic as between Negro and white passengers, they failed to satisfy the requirements of the Interstate Commerce Act. Each passenger with a ticket entitling him to use the dining car was "equally entitled to its facilities in accordance with reasonable regulations."

Said the Court:

We need not multiply instances in which these rules sanction unreasonable discriminations. The curtains, partitions and signs emphasize the artificiality of a difference in treatment which serves only to call attention to the racial classification of passengers holding identical tickets and using the same public dining facility.

Thus, it appears that under this decision any rules and regulations which require differences in treatment between passengers in any form of interstate travel solely because of race are unlawful. The decision would appear, therefore, to reach all facilities to which an interstate passenger is entitled in accord with the type of ticket purchased. We believe that it will be fruitless for the railroads to attempt to limit the decision to dining car facilities.

It is true that the case dealt only with commerce between the states and, therefore, it can be said that it will effect interstate travel alone. However, we believe that it will be difficult and practically impossible for an interstate carrier to attempt to enforce one set of regulations as to passengers travelling within a state and one set of regulations as to its passengers travelling between states. Further, in view of the decision of the Court in *McLaurin v. Board of Regents,* the ground has been laid for an attack upon differences in treatment as to intrastate passengers under the equal protection clause of the Fourteenth Amendment.

Sweatt Case

In the Sweatt opinion Chief Justice Fred M. Vinson, speaking for the unanimous Court, insisted that the issues in the case did not involve the entire question of the validity of segregation in all its phases. He reviewed the history of the litigation of this case beginning in 1946 and traced it through the two appeals through the state courts in Texas. In reviewing the evidence as to the two law schools in Texas, the Chief Justice gave to the state's case the most favorable interpretation of their allegations concerning the alleged equality of the two schools, and after doing this showed how it was impossible to obtain an equal education in a segregated law school regardless of the physical equality between the two institutions.

The opinion pointed out that despite the alleged equality between the two schools as to student body, library and other items, the important difference was that "the University of Texas Law School possesses to a far greater degree those qualities which are incapable of objective measurement but which make for greatness in a law school. Such qualities, to name but a few, include reputation of the faculty, experience of the administration, position and influence of the alumni, standing in the community, traditions and prestige. It is difficult to believe that one who had a free choice between these law schools would consider the question close."

Although the opinion refused to overrule the decision of *Plessy v. Ferguson,* the Court nevertheless ruled that an equal legal education "is not available to him in a separate law school as offered by the state" and that "the equal protection clause of the Fourteenth Amendment requires that petitioner be admitted to the University of Texas Law School." This opinion and its language leaves no room for doubt in anyone's mind that every state which now maintains a law school must admit qualified Negro students and cannot refuse them on the basis of race and color.

McLaurin Case

In the McLaurin case, the unanimous opinion rendered by the Chief Justice was even more specific as to the unconstitutionality of racial segregation in graduate education. The opinion reviewed the action of the State of Oklahoma in first refusing to admit Professor G. W. McLaurin to the graduate school and, after legal action was commenced, of admitting him but requiring him to be segregated from the other students. It is significant that in regard to this separation, the Supreme Court recognized that the result of such separation was to handicap the Negro student "in his pursuit of effective graduate instruction," and that "Such restrictions impair and inhibit his ability to study, to engage in discussions and exchange views with other students, and, in general, to learn his profession."

Finally, the Court decided once and for all the invalidity of racial segregation in graduate education:

We conclude that the conditions under which this appellant is required to receive his education deprive him of his personal and present right to the equal protection of the laws. We hold that under these circumstances the Fourteenth Amendment precludes differences in treatment by the state based upon race.

Appellant, having been admitted to a state-supported graduate school, must receive the same treatment at the hands of the state as students of other races. The judgment is REVERSED.

Crisis, July 1950, vol. 57, pp. 444–47.

77

NEGRO WOMEN WORKERS: UNION LEADER CHALLENGES PROGRESSIVE AMERICA (1950)

by Vicki Garvin

Freedom was the name of a monthly newspaper supported by Paul Robeson. Its first number, published by Freedom Associates in Harlem, appeared in November 1950; its editor was Louis E. Burnham. The paper continued until August 1955. On its editorial board was Victoria Garvin, vice president of the Distributive, Processing and Office Workers, CIO. Here appeared her essay urging particular attention to the needs of African-American women workers.

If it is true, as has often been stated, that a people can rise no higher than its women, then Negro people have a long way to go before reaching the ultimate goal of complete freedom and equality in the United States.

Latest figures on the job status of Negro women dramatically point up the inescapable fact that they are at the very bottom of the nation's economic ladder. A glance at the record shows that the average Negro woman in the U.S.:

- Earns only $13 per week.
- Is forced into the dirtiest, least desirable jobs.
- Puts in abnormally long hours.

By and large, Negro women today are living and working under conditions reminiscent of the plantation era, even though slavery was ostensibly abolished by constitutional amendment some 85 years ago. When it's considered that seven out of every 10 Negro women workers are chained to menial service jobs as farm hands, domestics, etc., where in addition to low pay and deplorable working conditions, human dignity is least respected, it can readily be seen that raising the level of women generally and Negro women in particular is an acid test for democracy at this crucial point in history.

Low Pay in Boom

Even during the peak period of World War II when pay envelopes were considered to be fatter than ever before, domestic workers, both Negro and white, averaged a take-home pay of only $339 per year.

In New York City, where one half of all Negro women at work are domestics, labor officials admit that the present average work day is 13 and 14 hours long. In the South, the situation is complicated by the fact that while only 50 percent of white women workers have found employment as clerks, saleswomen and factory workers, Negro women for all practical purposes are barred from these "white collar" and semi-skilled jobs. In fact, the income of the average Negro family in southern rural areas is a sub-standard $942 yearly.

The Negro woman worker, whether married, or single, faces the additional burden of feeding one or more dependents besides herself. As a member of a family, whose average income in urban centers is but $42 a week, Negro women have no choice but to find employment to help meet basic food, clothing and shelter needs.

Wife Must Work

In the case of white families, where the average income is $75 weekly, the pressure upon children to leave school and seek work is not nearly so severe as it is among Negroes. Yet, significantly, more than half of all Negro college students are women. The reverse is true of white students.

Getting a husband is not the answer for the Negro woman's search for security and release from back breaking toil, for the proportion of Negro women who enter the labor force after marriage is much higher than the one out of five rate for white women. When most Negro women think about marriage and children, it is almost a foregone conclusion that she will become a co-breadwinner.

The added income the Negro wife and mother provides is vital, for white men have a virtual monopoly on the best paying jobs available in the U.S.: ninety per cent of all skilled jobs and 80 per cent of semi-skilled jobs. Negro men are thus limited in their opportunities to provide a decent livelihood for their wives and families, being restricted to unskilled labor and menial tasks.

There is a big gap between the income of the Negro and the white man, with $3,000 and over the annual income of seven out of 10 white males, while only three out of 10 Negro men are similarly paid. Veterans who served together in World War II are also paid on the basis of color; the Negro GI's paycheck is $20 less than that of his white comrade in arms.

More Broken Homes

Broken homes are another part of the exorbitant price Negro women must pay for their oppressed status. In five southern cities recently surveyed, 85 per cent of all Negro working class women were supporting families where the man of the house was missing. Setting aside any reserves for unemployment, old age, illness and accidents is out of the question for this section of the population, burdened as they are with substandard wages, job insecurity and indebtedness.

The familiar "last hired, first fired" policy for Negroes works a double hardship on women. Their jobs are immediately curtailed when slack seasons and similar "accidents" occur in the national economy. Today, twice as many Negro women are without work, relatively, as white women. The lack of training courses and a national FEPC makes job placement even more difficult.

It is an unfortunate fact that the areas where Negro women are concentrated are as yet unorganized. Employers, therefore, are free to ride roughshod over these un-protected workers. However, in a few cities, Negro women benefit from unions in industries such as food and tobacco, meat packing, electrical, hotel and restaurant, laundry, wholesale and warehouse, and white collar offices. Negro women have participated in militant struggles to win contracts and better working conditions. It is a matter of record that where given the opportunity to enter industry and become a part of the trade union movement, Negro women have demonstrated their loyalty and ability to fight for the best interests of all workers. Despite tremendous handicaps, Negro women have fought their way to the top in many unions.

Historically, it is the burning desire of every Negro woman to be free, to live and work in dignity, on equal terms with all other workers. Negro women are eager to undertake a greater role to give substance to freedom and democracy, to help build an America of peace and abundance.

It is the responsibility of progressive trade unions and women's organizations to spearhead a militant and far-reaching program that will:

1. Maintain Negro women in industry.
2. Provide opportunities for training, up-grading and employment in all categories of work.
3. Eliminate wage differentials.
4. Extend coverage of social welfare legislation to industries and occupations now excluded.
5. Promote Negro women leadership at all levels of trade union activity.

Negro working women, with their long tradition of militancy, stand ready to be an integral part of the struggle for progress.

Let's join forces now!

78

DOES THE NEGRO WANT INTEGRATION?

by Lester B. Granger

On the face of it, the question "Does the Negro want integration?" seems a very silly one. "Of course we want integration," the answer comes back. "Isn't that what we're struggling for?"

But is it? Do we really know what we're struggling for? Are all of us really struggling? Would all of us unanimously, without hesitation, accept "integration" and all that it involves if it were suddenly offered to us tomorrow? The answers to such questions as these are not as simple as they may seem at first.

For one thing, whom do we mean by "the Negro?" Do we mean the younger-aged, the middle-aged, or the older group? Do we mean the high school graduate, the college-trained professional, or the mine, mill, or farm worker? There is no such creature as "the Negro." There are nearly fifteen million Negroes in the United States, which means fifteen million different personalities and many thousands of different kinds of reactions to similar social and economic pressures.

So, if the original question is silly, its chief error lies in trying to lump fifteen million people into one arbitrary classification merely because the skin of most of them happens to be tinged with an overdose of sun. Rather than try to answer the question as phrased, it is better to try to analyze all of the requirements of "social integration" and then hazard a guess as to which types of Negroes are most apt to continue to strive for integration, once these requirements are recognized.

The word "integration" has assumed a new meaning and importance in the American vocabulary within recent years. Its predecessor was "interracial," and before that it was "equality." Whether the term was social equality, interracial or integration, it has met with unvarying and stubborn resistance from the defenders of the status quo in race relations. Because the status quo depends upon keeping the Negro in his place and not allowing him to get too many bold ideas about changing the traditional American racial system. But while we have adopted a new term for current post–World War usage, many of us have failed to adjust our ideas correspondingly. There is a big difference between equality of Negroes with whites and integration of Negroes into the total American community.

Washington School

One school of equalitarians, previously led by Booker T. Washington, held that the road to equality lay in temporary acceptance of, and capitalization upon, racial separation, building a separate group strength until it could compete on more even terms with the strength of the dominant white majority. Thirty years of following this philosophy led even its devout supporters to realize that, while the idea had some merit and offered a certain kind of progress, that progress led up a blind alley which left the Negro still separated from his white fellow-Americans and still weak because a separated minority must always be weak.

This realization encouraged the idea of interracial association and competition. Such an association breaks down segregation at every possible point, but tolerates "voluntary congregation." In other words, the Negro group takes advantage of such group resources as it has to thrust its members into positions of better advantage, where they may learn from association with whites and bring back the fruits of such association to contribute to a stronger racial group. This philosophy, practiced with increasing earnestness during the Twentieth Century, puts primary emphasis on an abolition of racial segregation and an end to racial discrimination. But its chief concern remains with the Negro group as such. It thinks in terms of a racial strategy which often unconsciously considers the white community as an antagonist to be overcome by frontal attack or carefully calculated guile.

The chief difference between the two schools of thought lies in the emphasis which the first placed upon training for economic self-sufficiency as the foundation of racial advancement and the insistence of the second that the way had to be led by unrestricted development of the Negro race's "talented tenth." Today, in our larger social wisdom we realize that the prolonged controversy between the Booker T. Washington and DuBois schools was largely unreal; that there was no conflict between the two points of view, but that the one merged into the other.

"Integrated Society"

Today we speak grandly of the "integrated society," but even now that term holds a different connotation for different Negro groups. To the great majority, integration means an absence of racial segregation and discrimination. We describe as "integrated" an employment situation where Negro workers are hired on the basis of their skills, rather than their race. We speak of an integrated Air Force or Navy, in contrast to those branches of the armed services which formerly separated Negroes from whites in company, battalion, or regimental units. We declare that the Army refuses while its sister branches adopt racial integration.

But this is an over-statement of the case. What the Navy has done is to abolish segregation. Integration has not yet been achieved, for the latter is far more than merely the relaxing of official barriers which debar a Negro from full opportunity. Segregation is an act almost physical in nature. It is imposed upon people by force or the implied threat of force. Few of us have ever met a Negro who willingly and gladly accepts segregation as a way of life. He may learn to live with it, to become reconciled to it. If he is clever enough he may manage to profit from it, and, being human, he is apt to enjoy his profits and to resist an attempt to deprive him of a monetary or positional reward. This is why in some Negro communities we find advocates of things-as-they-are, because of their fear that a different order of affairs will leave them in a personally disadvantaged position.

Integration Spiritual

Integration, on the other hand, is not physical, but spiritual in nature. It requires, first of all, that barriers to advancement be removed, but it requires moreover that those who have previously been debarred shall move forward freely to take advantage of their new opportunities. But new opportunities are accompanied by new responsibilities. It is possible in a segregated community for Negroes of better than average ability to maintain a protected position of advantage over their fellow-Negroes—to become persons of importance, and sometimes of financial means, because they are competing in a handicap race. When they are removed from the handicap race, where they are competing against their fellows of inferior ability, and thrown into the open race where most experienced and skillful competitors are also entered, they find a different condition. While their abilities may improve in comparison with other Negroes, they lag behind the pace set by the more experienced white competitors. They end up, not first or second in a handicap race, but tenth or eleventh in an open race. And some of them cannot take with good grace this denial of the victor's prize, even though that prize previously was of the second-class variety.

Ghetto Psychology

All of the foregoing has been philosophic. Let us put it in terms of its practical application to the average Negro and especially to the average young Negro of today. First, let us accept the fact that Negro life in general, in the segregated, restricted atmosphere of the typical Negro neighborhood, has become culturally and psychologically different from life in the community-at-large. A rural people transplanted to urban living conditions within the past thirty or forty years still retain heavy traces of rural culture because they have never been given a chance to move freely in urban society and become acculturated thereby. A ghetto people have developed psychological reactions to their congested living, their social lacks and their economic deprivations. They look out upon the surrounding world with sharp hostility. Or they withdraw into themselves with defeated resignation. They become cynical, disillusioned, and sullen; or they become escapist, contradictory and unrealistic. They are somewhat in the position of the hospital patient who has remained on his bed of pain for so long that he has learned first to endure and then to accept hospital routines. When the time comes for his release, he is apt to be frightened and to seek ways of remaining in the protected environment where he has managed to exist, and in the end become moderately comfortable.

New Habits

When we break down barriers of racial segregation and discrimination, this is opening the door to, but not completely accomplishing, integration. Integrated education does not begin with the Supreme Court decision that southern universities must open their doors to colored graduate students. It only offers a chance for the Negro to apply for, acquire and use that graduate education. An integrated job situation is not automatically produced when the employer hires a number of new Negro workers and assigns them solely on the basis of their skills. Integration is a fact when the Negro worker takes advantage of his job to join his union, participate in its activities as a full-fledged member, take more training and address himself to improvement of his job status, support of his union leaders, and his own elevation to leadership if he possesses the necessary qualifications.

Social integration is not a matter merely of an open door policy by restaurants, theatres, clubs and the like. It requires a painstaking, reacculturation process by the young Negro especially. It means learning new speech habits, sometimes shedding rustic mannerisms and methods of dress. It means presenting one's self for friendly associations, as well as being accepted tolerantly by one's new associates.

If we are perfectly honest with ourselves, we will admit that throughout the country there are literally millions of Negroes who are not only unready for such integration, but are also unwilling to undergo the self-discipline and self-denial that are required as a part of the integration process. We say we want it, but we seek to avoid the steps by which we arrive at the goal of our dreams. "Everybody talk about heaven ain't going there," declares the old Negro spiritual. Similarly, everybody who talks about integration does not really want it if it requires too much of a sacrifice on his part personally.

Racial Thinking

We Americans have gotten so much in the habit during our three hundred years of bi-racial living, of thinking in terms of racial differences and coloration, that we now choose our friends, plan our careers, establish our homes, and adopt personal attitudes toward each other on the basis of our racial connection primarily. Our fatal insistence upon race as a dividing factor has produced a *disintegrated* society. Our job today—for Negro and white Americans alike—is to prevent further disintegration and promote a positive *integration*. Economic self-improvement plays its part in this process. Definition and defense of our constitutional rights plays its part also. But the whole job can be done only by the addition of the spiritual factor to this process: the building of self-confidence which is a part of developing confidence in others, the recognition of personal and group lacks which must precede the elimination of our weaknesses, and the correction of our group incapabilities.

America's Future

Does the Negro want integration? Some do—and some really don't care. But the future of the Negro race in America, and indeed the future of America as a nation, depends upon our increasing and supporting the number of those who do care, and recognizing that those who do not have no role to play in producing the democratic Negro citizen in the American democracy of tomorrow.

It is not overly unkind to say that it is the exceptionally rare colored American over forty years of age who is able to assume his full share of responsibility for "integration." This is only natural, since the greater part of his life has already been spent in being "disintegrated," and his habits of thinking and patterns of association are already firmly set. He will break out of them with extreme difficulty. This puts the future of integration up to the younger generations, and especially those of student age. The young man or woman in the early twenties whose social life is restricted to the Negro "party," whose entertainment world is bounded by the limits of the Negro neighborhood, whose "jive talk" is understood with difficulty and who insists upon the "zoot-suit" touch in dress—that young person isn't ready to begin integrative steps. And even when speech, associations and dress habits have become more urbane, a reconditioning job sometimes needs to be done emotionally. Less of the chip-on-the-shoulder attitude, more curiosity about how other people think and act (and why), less hanging back and waiting for invitations, but more freely going forward and joining the activities of others. All this is part of it.

Stroking Wounds

But even more than all this, integration of the Negro into full American living must be preceded by an understanding on his part of the nature and requirements of the total community's life. Too many of us are still fighting the Civil War, just like the most reactionary Southern Bourbon. While we are stroking old wounds, we lose opportunities that are open to us. While we are "rabble-rousing" against conditions over which we have no direct control, we ignore the development of conditions that affect us and that we might control if we try in time.

Integration demands perspective, deliberate self-discipline and a sense of proportion. Which is to say that by no means all of us (or even a majority of us) want integration at this time, but progress has always been achieved by the foresight and leadership of a few, and in the end the great mass of people will follow. The question is, are our young people ready with their leadership?

Crisis, February 1951, 58: 73–77. Lester Granger was executive director of the National Urban League.

79

CANAL ZONE DISCRIMINATION (1951)

by George W. Westerman

The greatest engineering achievement in modern history is said to be the construction of the Panama Canal which brought to reality an idea that was dreamed of for centuries by kings, heads of states, navigators and adventurers. From a commercial viewpoint the Canal has proved itself to be an excellent investment for the United States. Its military value to democratic freedom loving nations is incalculable.

One phase of this achievement frequently overlooked or deliberately minimized is the contribution of the native tropical workers—non-U. S. citizens—whose brawn proved a decisive factor in the ultimate construction of the Canal. These people, who at the peak-year of employment in 1913 numbered 44,711, were recruited mainly from the colored population of the West Indies; although there were, in addition, groups of

Spaniards, Italians, Europeans, native Panamanians and other Latin Americans that made up the laboring force of the Isthmian Canal Commission.

Work conditions of these people were intolerable. Acceptance of a job on the Canal was to risk one's life in this "black hole of Calcutta." Amidst the fearful ravages of yellow fever and plague they labored. Malaria claimed thousands of them as victims, and working hazards accounted for the lives of innumerable others. A total of 95 deaths and 235 injuries resulted from dynamite explosions, collisions, and slides during the period September, 1906, to July, 1914. Practically all of these tragic occurrences affected the tropical workers who formed the bulk of the laboring forces.

The mental and physical plight of these tropical workers was even more aggravated when one considers that most of them were earning, at that time, no more than 10 cents an hour. The American administrators heaped insult upon injury for these non-U. S. tropical workers by placing them and their families in segregated communities in barrack-type houses. Segregated and inferior educational facilities were set up for their children.

Discrimination Rampant

The alien workers were discriminated against in government-operated commissaries, dispensaries, post offices, schools and recreational centres. Lavatory and water drinking facilities on the jobs and in public places were segregated and labelled, "gold" and "silver." These patterns of social segregation were all instituted and maintained by American governmental officials despite international obligations as set out in the Treaties of 1903 and 1936 between the government of the United States and the Republic of Panama, the country from which was leased the ten-mile strip of land known as the Canal Zone.

Back in the late 80's when Ferdinand de Lesseps struggled valiantly but unsuccessfully to build the Panama Canal, his skilled workers were paid in gold, and silver was used to pay the unskilled. When the Isthmian Canal Commission of the United States took over the project in 1904, the terms were found appropriate for differentiating between U. S. citizens and native employees. North Americans received their pay in gold and native laborers in silver. It was not long before the terms "gold" and "silver" had acquired the connotation of superior and inferior standards, symbolized the difference between white and colored workers, and set the stage for the establishment of two separate and distinct social systems.

The Southern racist attitudes transplanted to the Canal Zone have created vexing problems for North American diplomats accredited to the Republic of Panama, and have represented a potential explosive that any emergency could touch off. The 1947 rejection of the Defense Sites Agreement by the unanimous vote of Panama's National Assembly, preceded by violent anti-American demonstrations, is the most recent case in point.

Local and U. S. Raters

Employees on the Zone are now designated as "U.S. raters" and "local raters." However, the application of the gold and silver standard of 1904 is as much in evidence today in the operation and maintenance of the Panama Canal-Railroad organization, except for the fact that it has assumed a new flexibility under the white heat of protest and agitation on the part of the victimized workers. Furthermore, progressive elements among Americans on the Canal Zone have been gaining ascendancy in the past decade. In part this may be attributed to the fear of Communistic infiltration of the rank of the laboring classes in the strategic Canal area; in part, to the recoil from the tremendous amount of unfavorable publicity that has been given to these un-American conditions by the local CIO union.

Some reactionary elements in the Canal Administration have been opposed to liberalizing the policies of that government. They despise non-U.S. citizens and condemn without fair study and serenity all claims made for the betterment of their working conditions. However, with the second world war has come an influx of a new type of North American who feels that a fresh sense of responsibility is necessary to enforce long overdue Canal Zone reforms. This type is working earnestly to rid the Canal Zone of its gross democratic imperfections and is doing much to create a totally new climate in the socio-economic field insofar as the interests of the non-U.S. citizens are affected.

Segregation Costly

The determination of the cost of the patterns of segregation and discrimination enforced on the Canal Zone involve not merely the costs of material things, which can be translated into dollars; but also of the more intangible, but none the less real, values of a human, social and psychic nature.

The Canal Zone dual system has encouraged the existence in the federal employment service of privileged groups in which the former look at the latter through a haze of half-truths, stereotypes, myths and racial antipathies. The system has frustrated the ambition, dwarfed the personality, and embittered the soul of many a non-U.S. Canal Zone tropical worker who is regarded as inferior, lazy, shiftless, ignorant and irresponsible.

Discrimination in all its forms has become an explosive issue in modern society. On the Isthmus of Panama the U.S. Government-sponsored system of discrimination and segregation not only threatens the safety of the vitally important Panama Canal, but it has international repercussions. The discrepancy between American ideals and the American way of life on the one hand, and the American practice on the Canal Zone, as represented by the double standard system on the other hand, causes the United States to stand compromised in the court of world opinion, and has an adverse effect upon her relations with other Latin American countries.

Crisis, April 1951, vol. 58, pp. 235–37. The author was a journalist living in Panama City and research director of its National Civic League.

Index

Free Catalog!
Books of African-American Interest
From Carol Publishing Group

Thank you for buying this book!

Carol Publishing Group proudly publishes dozens of books of African-American interest. From history to contemporary issues facing Black Americans and popular culture, these books take a compelling look at the African-American experience.

Selected titles include: • **The African Cookbook: Menus and Recipes From Eleven African Countries and the Island of Zanzibar** • **African Names: Names From the African Continent for Children and Adults** • **Afro-American History: The Modern Era** • **The Autobiography of Jack Johnson: In the Ring, and Out** • **Black Hollywood: The Black Performer in Motion Pictures, Volumes One & Two** • **Black Is the Color of My TV Tube** • **The Black 100: A Ranking of the Most Influential African-Americans, Past and Present** • **Black Robes, White Justice: Why Our Legal System Doesn't Work for Blacks** • **Break It Down: The Inside Story From the New Leaders of Rap** • **Call Her Miss Ross: The Unauthorized Biography of Diana Ross** • **Caroling Dusk: An Anthology of Verse by Black Poets** • **Clotel: Or, the President's Daughter** • **A Documentary History of the Negro People in the United States, Volumes One through Six** • **Good Morning Revolution: Selected Poetry and Prose of Langston Hughes** • **Harriet Tubman: The Moses of Her People** • **Introduction to African Civilizations** • **Langston Hughes: Before and Beyond Harlem** • **Life & Times of Frederick Douglass** • **Lyrics of Lowly Life: The Poetry of Paul Laurence Dunbar** • **Man, God and Civilization** • **Michael Jackson: The Magic and the Madness** • **Muhammad Ali: A View From the Corner** • **Negro in the South** • **The Negro Novelist: 1940-1950** • **Negrophobia: An Urban Parable** • **Negro Slave Songs in the United States** • **Paul Robeson Speaks: Writings, Speeches and Interviews 1918-1974** • **Prisoners of Our Past: A Critical Look at Self-Defeating Attitudes Within the Black Community** • **Racism and Psychiatry** • **Repeal of the Blues: How Black Entertainers Influenced Civil Rights** • **Thurgood Marshall: Warrior at the Bar, Rebel on the Bench** • **To Be Free: A Volume of Studies in Afro-American History** • **Up From Slavery** • **The Way It Was in the South: The Black Experience in Georgia** • **What Color Is Your God?: Black Consciousness and the Christian Faith** • **The Whole World in His Hands: A Pictorial Biography of Paul Robeson** • **Why Black People Tend to Shout: Cold Facts and Wry Views from a Black Man's World** • **Work, Sister, Work: How Black Women Can Get Ahead in the Workplace** • **Zulu Fireside Tales**

Ask for these African-American Interest books at your bookstore. Or for a free descriptive brochure, call 1-800-447-BOOK or send your name and address to Carol Publishing Group, 120 Enterprise Ave., Dept. 1421, Secaucus, NJ 07094.

Books subject to availability